Legal Studies in Business

Douglas Whitman University of Kansas

John William Gergacz University of Kansas

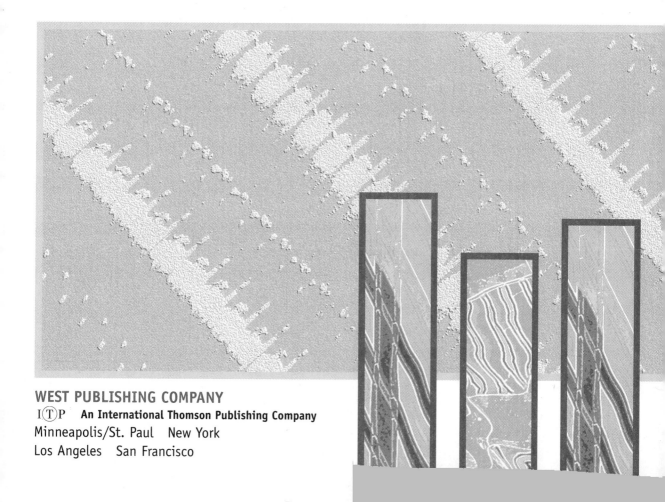

WEST PUBLISHING COMPANY
I(T)P **An International Thomson Publishing Company**
Minneapolis/St. Paul   New York
Los Angeles   San Francisco

Copyeditor: Diane L. Calvert

Artist: James W. Daggett

Design: Roslyn M. Stendahl, Dapper Design

Cover Art and Design: Roslyn M. Stendahl, Dapper Design

Compositor: Shepherd, Inc.

Indexer: Mary Burchill

WEST'S COMMITMENT TO THE ENVIRONMENT

In 1906, West Publishing Company began recycling materials left over from the production of books. This began a tradition of efficient and responsible use of resources. Today, 100% of our legal bound volumes are printed on acid-free, recycled paper consisting of 50% new fibers. West recycles nearly 27,700,000 pounds of scrap paper annually—the equivalent of 229,300 trees. Since the 1960s, West has devised ways to capture and recycle waste inks, solvents, oils, and vapors created in the printing process. We also recycle plastics of all kinds, wood, glass, corrugated cardboard, and batteries, and have eliminated the use of polystyrene book packaging. We at West are proud of the longevity and the scope of our commitment to the environment.

West packet parts and advance sheets are printed on recyclable paper and can be collected and recycled with newspapers. Staples do not have to be removed. Bound volumes can be recycled after removing the cover.

Production, Prepress, Printing and Binding by West Publishing Company.

TEXT IS PRINTED ON 10% POST CONSUMER RECYCLED PAPER

British Library Cataloguing-in-Publication Data. A catalogue record for this book is available from the British Library.

Copyright © 1997   By WEST PUBLISHING COMPANY
610 Opperman Drive
P.O. Box 64526
St. Paul, MN 55164-0526

04 03 02 01 00 99 98 97   8 7 6 5 4 3 2 1 0

Library of Congress Cataloging in Publication Data

Whitman, Douglas.
     Legal studies in business / Douglas Whitman. John William Gergacz.
        p.   cm.
     Includes index.
     ISBN: 0-314-20572-1 (alk. paper)
     1. Business law—United States.   I. Gergacz, John William.
   II. Title.
KF390.B84W47   1997   96–49178
346.7307—dc21   CIP

Contents

PART 1

INTRODUCTION TO THE
LEGAL STUDIES OF
BUSINESS 1

CHAPTER 1 *Introduction to Law and the Legal Studies of Business* 2

Even though business managers are not experts in law, every decision they make has a legal component. A precise analysis of that component is best left to legal counsel, but business executives must understand the thematic features of the law. Doing so will enable them to appreciate the legal complexities they face.

Key Features

Why was it important for business investors in reunited Germany to be certain about the ownership of the property they bought? see German Reunification and Property Ownership, *page 5.*

Should business managers be concerned about adverse legal consequences arising from their workplace policies even if the managers have not acted illegally? see Borse v. Piece Goods Shop, Inc., *page 13.*

Can business managers face a legal risk from taking steps to protect their property? see What Can Be Done to Safeguard Property?, *page 17.*

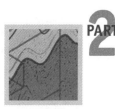

PART 2

THE AMERICAN
LEGAL SYSTEM   21

CHAPTER 2 *Introduction to the Courts*   22

Business people sometimes find themselves immersed in disputes that end up in court. State governments and the federal government operate their own court systems. Working within both the federal and state court systems, two key players may be identified— lawyers and judges.

Contents

Key Features

Can a business be forced to defend a suit brought against it in a state thousands of miles away from the headquarters of the business? see International Shoe Co. v. State of Washington, page 26.

Is it proper for a judge to criticize a businessperson prior to even hearing evidence at that person's trial? see Improper Remarks by a Judge, page 42.

If a client reveals to her attorney that she violated the antitrust laws, may her attorney reveal this violation of the law to the court? see Attorney–Client Privilege, page 44.

CHAPTER 3 *Civil Litigation and Alternative Dispute Resolution*   50

The examination of what happens to the typical business dispute from the outset of the conflict through the final resolution of the controversy by the legal system will be discussed in this chapter. Business managers need to recognize that the law permits another approach to resolving conflicts—alternative dispute resolution procedures. This approach will be specifically examined later in this chapter.

Contents

Key Features

If a business violates the rights of a person, must the injured party bring suit against the business during a certain period of time? see Statute of Limitations, page 52.

—Continued

—Continued

Why can a court not reverse the decision of an arbitrator even though the arbitrator made an error of law that caused a substantial injustice? see Moncharsh v. Heily & Blase, *page 70.*

Which type of dispute resolution proceeding affords a person the greatest control over the resolution of his or her conflict? see Degree of Control That a Party May Exercise over a Dispute, *page 72.*

CHAPTER 4 *Judicial Reasoning and Statutory Construction* 84

The legal risk of a business decision arises from the outcome of litigation imagined. The risk assessment has two components—how the legal rules would apply to the business decision, and what the influence of the legal system itself would be on the application of the rules.

Contents

Key Features

Should a business manager anticipate that different judges may disagree about similar cases? see Pretend You Are the Judge, *page 87.*

How can a seventy-year-old case influence the legal environment of professional baseball? see Flood v. Kuhn, *page 96.*

Does a business manager who follows a statute to the letter face any risk of being in violation? see Immigration Law: Purpose or Language?, *page 103.*

CHAPTER 5 *The Legislature, Executive Branch, and Administrative Agencies   110*

Business decisions are affected by legal principles that arise from a number of sources—courts, the legislature, the executive branch, and administrative agencies. Managers need to understand how each source makes law, and these managers must know how to play a role in their activities.

Contents

Key Features

Who are the beneficiaries of corporate political contributions? see Money and the Legislative Process, *page 116.*

Should a business manager expect that the role of the bureaucracy in the Japanese government works the same as that in the United States? see Japanese Ministries and a Call for Reform, *page 123.*

Are there limits to the extent in which a business manager may rely on an administrative agency employee's advice about how to comply with the agency's regulations? see Federal Crop Insurance Corp. v. Merrill, *page 126.*

CHAPTER 6 *Constitutional Law and Business   134*

The government subjects businesses to a wide range of regulations, thus impinging on a manager's freedom of action. Both the federal and state governments possess extensive power to regulate business activities. At the same time, the Constitution of the United States places limitations on governmental power.

Contents

Key Features

Is there any limit whatsoever on the power of the federal government to regulate business pursuant to the commerce clause of the United States Constitution? see United States v. Lopez, *page 139.*

—Continued

Does the federally mandated warning on cigarette packages prevent states from requiring additional warnings on cigarettes? see Cigarette Smoking, *page 141.*

Do publishers have a responsibility to prevent dangerous information from falling into the hands of people who could injure the general public? see Free Speech of Publishers, *page 149.*

CHAPTER 7 *Ethics: Its Relationship with Legal Studies and Business Decision Making   158*

Ethical (or unethical) conduct affects the legal risk of business decisions. Thus, ethics have practical implications. Making ethical business decisions is a way that legal risk may be managed.

Contents

Key Features

Does a business that acts unethically face risks in the legal environment? see Ethical Influences on Law, page 159.

PART **3**

ETHICS AND THE LEGAL ENVIRONMENT OF BUSINESS   157

—Continued

Would a business manager's high regard for ethics affect legal risk? see Tennant Company v. Advance Machine Company, *page 170.*

How could a business manager's ethics-based decision have affected a lawsuit arising from hot coffee burns? see Hot Coffee and a Concern for the Customer, *page 179.*

THE COMMON
LAW 185

CHAPTER 8 *Introduction to Contracts—*
The Essential Elements *186*

People in business enter into contracts on a regular basis. A manager needs to understand what it takes to create a binding contract. Failure to recognize the requirements of a contract may result in the inadvertent creation of a contract.

Contents

Key Features

How do Japanese business negotiations differ from the typical American business negotiation? see Japanese Negotiations, *page 193.*

Is it ethical for a person to accept a position at one firm and thereafter accept another job at another business? see Employer Offers Job, *page 199.*

Is a person who speaks only Spanish bound by a one-sided contract written in English? See Valid Contract or Unconscionable Agreement?, *page 209.*

—*Continued*

CHAPTER 9 *Contracts—Other Important Considerations* 218

Courts will not enforce a contract unless the involved parties freely and voluntarily assent to its terms. Business people also should be aware that certain types of agreements must be in writing in order to be enforceable. If a party fails to adhere to his or her obligations under the agreement, certain damages and remedies may result.

Contents

Key Features

Is it ethical to purchase a valuable baseball card for a mere fraction of its actual value? see A $1,188 Mistake, page 220.

Does a developer have an obligation to inform home buyers that it built a housing development near a hazardous waste dump? see Strawn v. Canuso, page 222.

—Continued

*Does a businessperson negotiating a
contract need to be concerned with
the physical gestures of the person
with whom the businessperson is
dealing? see* Negotiation Note: Body
Language, *page 225.*

CHAPTER 10 *Assessing External Costs of Doing Business: Tort Liability* 250

Business activity inevitably causes harm, but the law does not impose liability unless the harm was caused by a tort. A number of factors distinguish between what is or is *not* tortious conduct. Managers must understand these factors and also appreciate the costs that tort liability may impose.

Contents

Key Features

Why does a company face a greater risk of tort liability in the United States than in Europe? see Tort Risk: An International Comparison, *page 258.*

Does a company risk tort liability when it confronts a suspected shoplifter? see Great Atlantic & Pacific Tea Co. v. Paul, *page 263.*

What should a business manager consider before approving a radio station promotion? see Weirum v. RKO General, Inc., *page 265.*

CHAPTER 11 *Legal Aspects of Business Organizational Forms* 278

Selecting the legal form for a business organization involves focusing on the interests of the investors and determining which form best meets these interests. Not all forms will be equally appropriate, nor will every investor group use the same form even though the businesses may be similar.

PART 5

THE LEGAL ENVIRONMENT OF BUSINESS ORGANIZATIONS AND THEIR OPERATION 277

Contents

Key Features

If investors want to risk only the amount they invested, does it matter what legal form the business uses? see Organizational Forms and Business Interests, *page 280.*

Does it make any sense for partners to formalize their business relationship in an agreement? see Zajac v. Harris, *page 285.*

If investors use a corporate form for their business, will they automatically thereafter manage and control the company? see Compartmentalization of Business Roles, *page 293.*

CHAPTER 12 *Members of Business Organizations: Regulation of Their Activities through Agency and Fiduciary Duty Principles 304*

The personnel practices of a business are built on a foundation of agency and fiduciary duty law. These principles define the powers and duties that employer and employee owe to one another. They provide another layer of meaning to the buyer-of-labor/seller-of-labor model that would exist under pure contract law principles.

Contents

Key Features

Does a company face a liability risk when liquor is served at a company picnic? see Company Picnic Policies, *page 313.*

Under what circumstances will statements by a corporate executive be legally binding on the company? see Lind v. Schenley Industries, Inc., *page 316.*

Do members of business organizations owe fiduciary duties to each other? see The Fiduciary Relationship and Business Organizational Forms, *page 319.*

CHAPTER 13 *Legal Aspects of Capital Acquisition: Contract, Property, and Securities Regulation* 328

Capital acquisition decisions are influenced by law. Principles of contract law, property law, and the regulatory environment provide structures that managers may use to facilitate in obtaining needed capital. The structure that is chosen depends on market factors, cost, and how the law affects the decision.

Contents

Key Features

How does the international legal environment act to protect intellectual property? see The Beatles for Free?, *page 340.*

Are there different legal considerations for a business depending on which means it uses to raise capital? see Seeking Capital, *page 342.*

Does a business face the same insider trading regulation in the G-7 countries as in the United States? see Regulation of Insider Trading in G-7 Countries, *page 354.*

REGULATION OF BUSINESS 357

CHAPTER 14 *Products Liability* 358

At times, businesses may produce or sell a product that injures people. The law may impose liability on sellers for defective or unreasonably dangerous products even when they exercised reasonable care. Managers must recognize when a product they sell could result in liability.

Contents

Key Features

Is it ethical for a company to adopt a design for a vehicle when it knows that a safer design could be adopted for $11 per car? see The Ford Pinto, *page 369.*

—*Continued*

*Should a liquor manufacturer warn
people that they could die from
drinking too much alcohol? see*
Student Dies from Drinking Tequila,
page 371.

*Is peanut butter unsafe in the
absence of a warning label? see* Fraust
v. Swift and Company, *page 372.*

CHAPTER 15 *Consumer and Environmental Law* 380

At one point in the history of the United States, employers recognized the possibility of making decisions that were unfettered by concerns over consumer's needs or the environment. This is no longer the case. A large body of law exists that dictates how a business must treat consumers and what the obligations of a business are with respect to the environment.

Contents

Key Features

*Can a person be held responsible for
unauthorized credit card charges to his
or her account? see* Oclander v. First
National Bank of Louisville, *page 386.*

*How can a country clean up its
environment when it is desperately
struggling to survive? see* Bulgarian
Pollution, *page 399.*

*Does the U.S. Fish and Wildlife Service
have a right to prevent a farmer from
farming his land in order to protect
the habitat of a rat? see* The Tipton
Kangaroo Rat, *page 402.*

—Continued

CHAPTER 16 *Employee Rights in the Workplace: Discrimination and Wrongful Discharge*   *406*

Business personnel practices changed as the law redefined the traditional relationship between employer and employee. From hiring and promotion policies to downsizing, what were once employer powers became regulations by law. Creative management is needed to comply with these laws. Business managers must appreciate that "employment relationships" are quite different than the buyer-of-labor/seller-of-labor model that would exist under pure contract law principles.

Contents

Key Features

Can an employer fire a worker for discriminatory reasons without violating the law? see Discrimination, but Not Illegal, *page 408.*

Does a business manager risk a discrimination claim if a no-employee-beards policy is adopted? see Bradley v. Pizzaco of Nebraska, Inc. d/b/a Domino's Pizza, *page 413.*

—Continued

Should business managers be
concerned if the modification of
an employee healthcare plan will
affect the disabled? *see* AIDS
Health Insurance Benefits and the
ADA, *page 422.*

CHAPTER 17 *Protection of the Employee and Labor Relations* 430

In the nineteenth century, neither the federal nor state governments passed many laws
protecting workers. The government assumed that workers could look out for their own
interests. The twentieth century brought a host of laws regulating how employers must
treat their employees.

Contents

Key Features

*Should the United States permit
products to be imported that were
manufactured by children working in
other nations? see* Child Labor around
the World, *page 437.*

*Is it possible for a union to become
the bargaining representative of
employees without winning a
representation election? see* NLRB v.
Gissel Packing Co., *page 439.*

*Can an employer prohibit off-duty
employees from using the company
parking lot for the distribution of
union literature? see* Distribution of
Literature, *page 444.*

—Continued

CHAPTER 18 *Antitrust Law* 454

In business systems in the United States, managers make decisions independently. The government's role in the economic system is to preserve competition by taking action against businesses that attempt to monopolize a line of business or restrain trade.

Contents

Key Features

Was it ethical for General Motors to buy up and destroy many of America's mass transit systems? see Eliminating the Competition, *page 460.*

How was Standard Oil able to produce kerosene in the United States and sell it for a lower price than the Russians charged Europeans for kerosene? see The Standard Oil Trust, *page 462.*

Does the Japanese distribution keiretsu close the Japanese market to competition from foreign suppliers? see Keiretsu, *page 473.*

—Continued

CHAPTER 19 *International Law*   478

Multinational businesses in the United States must deal with three sets of laws—international law, United States law, and the domestic law of the foreign country in which the firm operates. Whether a business engages in the export or import of goods or services, managers need to be aware of a variety of important laws relating to this area.

INTERNATIONAL REGULATION OF BUSINESS ACTIVITY   477

Contents

Key Features

Was it lawful for the United States Drug Enforcement Agency to kidnap a citizen of Mexico? see U.S. Kidnaps Mexican Citizen, *page 481.*

Is it possible for a person who was injured in South Africa to bring suit against the South African government here in the United States? see Martin v. Republic of South Africa, *page 484.*

Is it lawful for a business to bribe a foreign official in order to obtain a contract? see Bribery to Obtain Business, *page 490.*

—Continued

Table of Cases

The principle cases are in bold type. Cases cited or discussed are in roman type.

Preface

*L*egal Studies in Business is designed to help future managers think critically about how the law affects business decisions. It is for use in a survey course—whether the name of the course is legal environment of business, business law, or some combination of the two. *Legal Studies in Business* encompasses what the legal environment approach to business was meant to provide but never did because of its focus on regulatory minutia. Furthermore, like the traditional approach, rigor and depth exists in *Legal Studies in Business*, but overwhelming detail has been replaced with context and explanation of what is truly important for the future business manager.

You will find fewer legal rules than you are accustomed to seeing in other textbooks. We hope that none of your favorites are missing. In our view, comprehensive coverage of legal rules should not be the aim of a business law course. Instead, the course must integrate and explain the key concepts that make up the legal world in which managers work.

To accomplish this, we wrote *Legal Studies in Business* with the following guideposts in mind:

- How can a business law book be made manageable, yet retain rigor?

- For each legal rule, we asked, "Is there a point to including it in a book that is to be used by future business managers?"

- Can the student be engaged critically to think about business decision making and law?

- What is the context (historical, ethical, social policy, international concerns) of the legal principle?

- How do managers respond to the legal environment that affects their business?

You can see how these questions were applied; for example, in Chapter 11 on the "Legal Aspects of Business Organizational Forms," this topic is explored by using four investor interests—limited liability, profit share, management rights, and control. These interests drive the discussion of the forms and provide a means by which students choose the form that best meets their business goals. Three investors—Jones, Thomas, and Smith—are followed throughout this chapter. Then, in the next two chapters, these investors hire employees (which emphasizes the agency and fiduciary duty principles) and seek capital for their business.

Even the Table of Contents illustrates our integrative approach. In addition to listing the topics in each chapter, we show how each chapter's coverage is geared toward the needs of the future business manager. We accomplish this in two ways. First, by highlighting the issues that capture key elements in the chapter, we draw the student's attention to important managerial concerns. For example, Chapter 16 in the Table of Contents contains the question (which is tied to a section of the chapter), "Should business managers be concerned if modifying an employee healthcare plan will affect the disabled?"

Second, we summarize why the chapter's materials are important for business. Thus, the Table of Contents connects the future business manager with the law in a compact form for each chapter in the text. Our Table of Contents is a learning tool as much as a guide to the book.

Key Features in Legal Studies in Business

INTERACTIVE MATERIAL TO ENCOURAGE CRITICAL THINKING

Legal studies should be an exciting and rewarding experience. But, this may happen only if the student is engaged by the learning process. *Legal Studies in Business* is an interactive textbook. Every chapter contains materials that require a student's participation. Thus, Thought Problems, Ethical Perspectives, International Perspectives, and Managerial Perspectives are raised throughout this textbook. The purpose of these elements is to connect the law to situations that face executives in the business world.

■ *Thought Problems:* Thought Problems are critical thinking exercises. Some of them were derived from cases, others were derived from general sources. A few of the Thought Problems are hypothetical examples. All help the student connect legal principles to managerial concerns. For example, in Chapter 10 which covers torts, one Thought Problem asks the student to make suggestions to Norfolk and Western Railway Company after one of its sleep-deprived employees caused an accident while driving home after work. This question should encourage discussions of tort principles and risk, as well as ethics and the cost to a company in changing policies. Creative suggestions may be expected from a class that is energized by the Thought Problem feature of our book.

■ *Ethical Perspectives:* Chapter 7 examines the relationship between ethical business conduct and legal risk, and then offers a model for making ethical decisions. In addition, to critically engage the student throughout the book, we provide Ethical Perspectives. Some of them illustrate ethical issues, while others ask students to apply the Chapter 7 model as if they were business managers. The students are then asked to assess its outcome on legal risk. The well publicized McDonald's hot coffee case is explored from an ethical perspective, which provides future managers insight into the relationship between legal risk and ethics-based decision making.

■ *International Perspectives:* Chapter 19 provides an overview of the international legal environment of business. However, given the importance of encouraging global thinking, we also provide International Perspectives in each chapter. For example, in Chapter 10 which covers tort liability, one such International Perspective compares Western European approaches to compensating injured people with the tort law approach used in the United States.

■ *Managerial Perspectives:* An important way that our textbook connects the future business manager to the law is through Managerial Perspectives. For example, in Chapters 8 and 9 which deal with contract law, we include contract negotiating exercises. These Managerial Perspectives not only energize the student's learning of contract principles, but they also illustrate the business manager's role in the process.

WRITTEN FOR THE FUTURE BUSINESS MANAGER

Legal Studies in Business encourages the student to approach the law as a business manager, not as an attorney. Likewise, the text has been written for this reader, not for an attorney. It is written in a clear and concise manner that is meant to provide relevant information in a challenging way, especially to the business student. In addition, we reworked the traditional cases and aimed them at the business student. Our end-of-chapter questions will also be noted and discussed later in the Preface.

■ *Cases:* We use cases to *illustrate* principles that have already been discussed in the text. They are "real life" examples of previously well explained material. We do not use cases as sources from which the students must derive the principle. Nor must the students rely on the cases to have the principle explained. These are approaches that *future attorneys* should learn—not *future business managers.*

You will find cases presented in the following three ways:

1. *Edited.* In every chapter, we edited carefully chosen, factually interesting, and pertinent judicial opinions to capture some of the issues we wanted to illustrate. Discussions of legal procedures and extraneous issues were removed, because we do not see how they would enhance the education of a business manager. Nonetheless, students will read the judge's language (and sometimes a dissenting opinion, too). This is original source material that we transformed to make useful for business students.

2. *Textualized.* These cases are still set apart from the rest of the book. However, we rewrote them so that they appear as "real life" examples. The citations are provided, however, for the curious student who wants to check the original source. For example, in Chapter 12 on *"Members of Business Organizations: Regulation of Their Activities through Agency and Fiduciary Duty Principles,"* we provide a synopsis of a case to illustrate vicarious liability arising from a company's picnic policies.

3. *Thought Problems.* Many of the textualized cases are also Thought Problems. As previously discussed, these items encourage critical thinking. In fact, the example provided in the earlier discussion on Thought Problems was a textualized case.

Every chapter ends with Review Questions. All of them are hypothetical examples designed to provide clear illustrations of the materials in the chapter. Our hypotheticals may be used for two purposes:

1. *Student Self-Testing.* The student alone (or, preferably in groups) may readily use the Review Questions to check their understanding of the materials in the chapter.

2. *In-Class Discussion.* The Review Questions may become starting points for in-class discussion, or they may be used as quick summaries of materials that the instructor has previously covered, but believes need more elaboration.

Supplements

Supplements are also available for use with *Legal Studies in Business:*

- An **Instructor's Manual** by Gary Sibeck (Loyola Marymount University) includes an overview and teaching goals, case summaries, a chapter outline with detailed teaching suggestions and discussion points, and suggested answers to the review questions.

- A **Student Study Guide** by Susan Grady (University of Massachusetts—Amherst) is available for sale to students. It offers an excellent review of key points for each chapter, as well as self-tests with answers for students to test their understanding.

- A **Test Bank** by James Hill (Central Michigan University) offers true–false, multiple choice, and essay questions. The test bank is also available in computerized form.

- **Transparency Acetates** provide key figures from the text to display during lectures.

West Publishing Company offers supplemental classroom tools to qualified adopters for use with *Legal Studies in Business.*

- Westest Computerized Testing. The test bank is available on the latest version of Westest for IBM PCs and compatibles and Macintosh. It allows you to:

  - Add or edit questions, instructions, and answers.
  - Select questions by previewing the questions on the screen.
  - Let the system select questions randomly.
  - Select questions by question number.
  - View summaries of the exam or the examination-bank chapters.
  - Set up the page layout for exams.
  - Print exams in a variety of formats.

- Videos. West's business law video library offers a variety of high-quality videos to enhance classroom instruction and interaction. Ask your sales representative for a complete listing of videos available.

- CD-ROM resources. This CD-ROM was designed to aid class preparation by providing instant and easy access to important cases, key legislation and regulation, relevant articles of the UCC, and more. This CD-ROM includes West's PREMISE© software, which allows you to search for and retrieve specific items in a matter of seconds. The CD-ROM includes material from the following sources:

  - Selected Congressional Acts
  - Selected Constitutions
  - Selected Federal Regulations
  - Selected Uniform Laws
  - Selected Business Law and Legal Environment Cases
  - The North American Free Trade Agreement (NAFTA)

- WESTLAW. WESTLAW is a computerized legal-research system that helps law professors, law students, attorneys, and paralegals do research in the law. Qualified adopters are allowed a certain number of free hours on WESTLAW. Contact your West sales representative for more details.

■ West Regional Reporter System. *The Reporter* is available free to quali-fied adopters for one year. It gives you and your students updated case decisions from your region throughout the year and helps students learn the reporting system for legal research.

We would like to thank all of the people who contributed so much to *Legal Studies in Business.* Elizabeth A. Miller did outstanding research work for portions of this textbook. Joan M. Gergacz provided exceptional editorial criticism and rewrites of parts of the book. In addition, we owe a heavy debt of gratitude to the many reviewers of *Legal Studies in Business.* The reviewers critiqued the manuscript throughout its development, and their insight inspired us to make innumerable changes that improved the book greatly. The reviewers include:

E. Elizabeth Arnold
University of San Diego
Deborah Ballam
Ohio State University
Robert Bennett
Butler University
Thomas Brucker
University of Washington
Angela Cerino
Villanova University
Lisa Druliner DeBuse
University of Nebraska—Omaha
Susan Grady
University of Massachusetts—Amherst
Nancy Hauserman
University of Iowa
James Hill
Central Michigan University
David Kent
Plymouth State College

Diane MacDonald
Pacific Lutheran University
John McGee
Southwest Texas State University
Robert McMahan
Indiana State University
Ramona Paetzold
Texas A&M University
Dinah Payne
University of New Orleans
Mark Phelps
University of Oregon
Al Roline
University of Minnesota—Duluth
Gary Sibeck
Loyola Marymount University
Joseph Solberg
Illinois State University
Susan Vance
Saint Mary's College

Lastly, we would like to thank our colleagues at West Publishing Company for their guidance and patience. Our editor, Stephanie Johnson, challenged us to aim higher and to do better. We could not imagine having a more rewarding editorial experience. Steven Yaeger and Jana Otto-Hiller provided expert production assistance. Roz Stendahl of Dapper Design designed a book that visually conveys the ideas we outlined in print. Hers was an artistic triumph.

Prologue

The Importance of Knowing the Law During the Industrial Revolution in the nineteenth century, most of the rules governing business arose from private agreements. Federal, state, and local governments tended to regulate businesses only to a minimal extent. This worked to the advantage of the nation, as it permitted the rapid industrialization of America. At the conclusion of the nineteenth century many American businesses such as Standard Oil spanned the globe.

As we no longer needed to concern ourselves with developing our industrial base, the concerns of people in America by the end of the nineteenth century began to turn to the distribution of wealth brought about by such multinational enterprises as the Standard Oil Trust and the Carnegie Steel Corporation. The perception of many people during that era was that private agreements could not bring about the social changes that many people desired in American society. For this reason, people turned to government in an attempt to change the relationship between business and society.

As the decades unfolded in the twentieth century, we began to see more and more laws created at all levels of American government. We entered a new era of supervision of business by government. Today's business manager not only needs to know the fundamentals of business—finance, marketing, and accounting—but he or she must also keep abreast of the law. In many ways the law controls what can and cannot be done in business, and how various managerial functions must be performed. Something that may seem to make sense in terms of finance or marketing may nonetheless not be possible because of the law. For this reason, before embarking on a given course of action, a wise manager needs to consider the legal environment of business.

The law is dynamic and ever changing. It responds to social forces such as public opinion. What may have been permissible in one year may no longer be legal behavior. A manager needs to consult with lawyers. This book will greatly assist you in your dealings with the legal profession and with your own attempts to stay current in the areas of law that affect your particular business position. The chapters in this book will, first of all, give you a broad overview of the legal system itself. This will assist you in understanding how laws are created, how they are enforced, and how they are interpreted. At the same time, one needs to bear in mind that even if a given course of action is lawful, it may nonetheless be unethical. To give you some insight with respect to appraising business behavior, we devote a specific chapter to business ethics.

The balance of the text is broken down into chapters that discuss various bodies of law that govern certain types of behavior or transactions. Once you have completed this material, it will be much easier to communicate meaningfully with your attorneys, and to understand articles that appear in such publications as *The Wall Street Journal, Business Week,* or *Money Magazine.* When you take other courses in business school such as marketing or accounting, this material will give you a better understanding of any references to the law.

Civil and Criminal Law

CRIMINAL AS OPPOSED TO CIVIL LITIGATION

The American legal system handles cases in two separate ways—*civil litigation* and *criminal litigation.* The same action may result in both a civil case and a criminal case, but usually a set of facts gives rise to either one or the other.

■ Civil Cases

In a **civil case,** the plaintiff institutes suit against the defendant for some civil wrong allegedly committed by the defendant. Civil suits may be instituted by private citizens, businesses, or the government. The law creates the rights and duties of people. The term *civil law* refers to suits dealing with the rights and duties of people other than those created in the criminal law. The plaintiff often seeks monetary damages in these cases. The goal of the civil system, in general, is to restore the injured party to the position he or she occupied prior to the defendant's wrongful actions. For example, if a person drives a vehicle at an excessive speed and as a result, an accident occurs, that individual probably has committed a civil wrong—a tort. If the injured party broke a leg, the courts would require the defendant to compensate the plaintiff for the damages caused to the plaintiff. By the payment of a certain sum of money, the plaintiff in theory is restored to his or her position before the accident.

■ Criminal Cases

In a **criminal case,** a prosecutor representing either the state or the federal government brings suit against the defendant for an alleged violation of the state or federal criminal laws. The prosecutor, in effect, represents the public at large. The law penalizes a violation of the criminal law with a fine or imprisonment. The victim is not, as a general rule, compensated for the damages done.

The Common Law

A great deal of the law in America today appears in statutes—laws passed by a legislative branch of government such as Congress or a state legislature. Some areas of law, however, are not governed by statute. This law may be found in the decisions of judges in the course of resolving disputes between people—referred to in this text as the common law. When we speak of the common law, we are referring to the entire body of law created by judges when they decide cases. In Chapters 8–10 we discuss two very important areas of common law—contracts and torts.

Some areas, such as the law of contracts, for the most part come entirely from the decisions of judges. Judges also create law, however, by interpreting statutes and other sources of law discussed in this book. For this reason, cases are very important and a considerable portion of this text is devoted to the presentation of decisions of judges.

Analyzing Cases Because cases are a very important source of the law, you should have some systematic method of analyzing them.

It may be useful to you to "brief" the cases in this text. Briefing the cases will assist you in understanding the material dealt with in each case. You should ask yourself the following questions about a case:

1. Who is the party bringing the suit, and who is the party being sued?
2. What are the facts of the case?
3. What issue of law was involved in the case?
4. Which party won the case?
5. Why did the judge rule in the manner he or she did?

Most of the cases in this text include an initial statement concerning the facts of the case. The authors of this text wrote this material. This initial statement generally indicates who brought the suit and which party won the case. The material after the judge's name is the actual language of the judge's report in the real case. This generally deals with the legal issue involved in the case, and it explains the basis of the judge's ruling. You should carefully consider this material in order to develop an understanding of the judge's rationale for his or her decision.

Many cases involve technical issues beyond the scope of this text; therefore, we have edited the cases in this book. We present only the portions of the case that are relevant to the point we are trying to illustrate with the case. The *State Farm Mutual Automobile Insurance Company v. Davis* case is a typical example.

(1) State Farm Mutual Automobile Insurance Company v. Davis

(2) United States Court of Appeals, Ninth Circuit (3) *937 F.2d 1415 (1991)*

(4) Walter Davis, a United States Marine, purchased a 1984 GMC van. State Farm issued Davis (the insured) a policy of automobile insurance covering the vehicle. On November 23, Davis and two other Marines, Brian Painter and David Roberts, were in the GMC van. Painter was driving the van. Davis was riding in the front passenger seat. Roberts occupied the rear seat. While driving on Interstate Highway 5 a Corvette passed them. Davis told Painter to overtake and pass the Corvette. As the van approached the rear of the Corvette, Davis fired his .44 caliber revolver at the Corvette. A bullet struck the driver, Charles Keukelaar, in the back of the head.

In this case, Shellie, a passenger in the Corvette, and Charles Keukelaar sued Davis. Davis's insurer, State Farm, asked the Court for a ruling that it was not obligated to provide coverage for this incident because the shooting did not result from Davis's use of the vehicle. The trial court ruled for State Farm. The Court of Appeals ruled that this shooting did result from the use of the vehicle. It remanded (sent the case back) to the trial court for further consideration of the question of State Farm's obligation to provide insurance coverage to Davis.*

(5) Singleton, Judge

(6)   State Farm argued that it should not have to provide coverage to Davis because the injuries were not caused by an accident resulting from the ownership, maintenance, or use of Davis's car.

The policy which State Farm issued to Davis contains the following relevant language: "We will: 1. pay damages which an insured becomes legally liable to pay because of: bodily injury to others caused by accident *resulting from* the ownership, maintenance, or *use of* your car."

In *State Farm Mutual Automobile Insurance Company v. Partridge,* the Supreme Court of California addressed similar language in an automobile insurance policy. The court found coverage where a gun discharged injuring a passenger while the vehicle was being driven off-road in pursuit of rabbits. The court noted that a "use" of a vehicle need not be the proximate cause of an injury in order to require coverage. It was sufficient if some minimal causal connection existed between the vehicle and an injury.

Davis's shooting of Keukelaar was not merely incidental to his use as a passenger of the GMC van. At the time of the shooting, Keukelaar was proceeding rapidly down the highway in his Corvette. Had Painter not heeded Davis's request to overtake and pass the Corvette, Davis would not have been in a position to shoot at Keukelaar. Further, it is not unreasonable to assume that Davis counted on the speed of the van to escape after the shooting. Under the facts of this case, the van was more than minimally connected with the injuries Keukelaar suffered.

Painter had to chase Keukelaar so that Davis could shoot at him. Davis did not leave the vehicle, but shot Keukelaar while both were traveling down the highway. Finally, Painter had to drive the van into position next to the Corvette, giving Davis the opportunity to fire his gun. The presence of these factors supports our conclusion that the vehicle was more than incidental to this shooting.

In conclusion, we are satisfied that Painter's and Davis's use of the GMC van insured by State Farm had more than a minimal causal connection with the incident leading to Keukelaar's injuries.

(7)   We therefore reverse the decision of the District Court and remand this case in order for that court to consider State Farm's other defenses.

---

*The parties asked the appeals court *not* to consider the question of whether Davis's shooting of Keukelaar was or was not an accident. California law prohibits insurance coverage for losses caused by the willful act of the insured. The question of whether the shooting was or was not intentional had not been resolved at the time of this appeal.

Note the following information about the Davis case.

Section 1 is the name of the case—*State Farm Mutual Automobile Insurance Company v. Davis.* In this particular case State Farm instituted the suit to obtain a determination from the court whether it was obligated to provide insurance coverage in the suit between Keukelaar and Davis. Generally, at the trial court level the plaintiff's name (the party that institutes a suit) is listed first and the defendant's name (the party who is being sued) is listed second. On appeal, the name of the party who filed the appeal is generally listed first. Virtually all of the cases in this text are appellate court decisions.

Section 2 states the name of the court which decided the case. In this case, the United States Court of Appeals for the Ninth Circuit decided the case.

Section 3 contains what attorneys refer to as the case citation. We give a case a citation to enable people to locate the case. The citation system creates an orderly system for categorizing cases. The citation in this case is "937 F.2d 1415 (1991)." The first number refers to the volume of the Federal Reporter in which this case appears. The Davis case may be found in volume 937 of the Federal Reporter. "F.2d" refers to the second set of the Federal Reporter. "1415" refers to the first page on which this case appears in volume 937. "1991" refers to the date this case was decided by the court of appeals.

Section 4 of this case generally includes the names of the parties, the facts of the case, frequently the issue dealt with in the case, and a statement as to who won the case. We see this case involved State Farm, the plaintiff, which filed suit against Walter Davis, the defendant. This case arose out of a shooting incident. Davis shot a bullet into Keukelaar's vehicle. The issue on appeal is whether or not Keukelaar's injuries *resulted from* Davis's use of the car.

Section 5 states the name of the judge who wrote the opinion—in this case, Judge Singleton. Several judges hear each appellate case; the number of judges who participate in any given case varies from court to court. Judge Singleton wrote this particular opinion. Other judges agreed with his reasoning and joined in this opinion; however, we use only the name of the judge who wrote the opinion in this section.

It should be noted that all of the judges on a court may not agree with the thinking of the majority of the judges on the court. In such a case, the judges who disagree with the decision in a case will render a dissenting opinion. In this text, we have included a number of dissenting opinions. Judges also may agree with the decision in the case, but disagree with the reasoning of the majority opinion. Such a judge may write a concurring opinion.

Section 6 states the rationale for the judge's decision. This section, for the most part, is in the judge's own words. This decision represents the thinking of the majority of the judges hearing this case. In this case Judge Singleton states that the accident could not have happened had Davis not been using his vehicle; therefore, the incident arose out of the use of Davis's vehicle.

One may also note that Judge Singleton referred to another, similar case in his opinion—the Partridge case. Judges quite frequently examine other, similar cases in order to determine what should be the proper outcome in a particular case. Judges find it useful to consider the reasoning of other judges. In other cases, judges will look at a variety of other factors in arriving at a decision.

Section 7 indicates that the appeals court overturned the decision of the trial court and sent the case back to the trial court for consideration of other issues that were not considered by the appellate court in this appeal.

An appeals court has a number of options in any case. The appeals court may affirm—that is, uphold—the decision of the trial court. It may instead reverse—that is, overturn—the decision of the trial court. It could also reverse part of the trial court's decision and affirm part of the trial court's decision. Finally, it may do what the appeals court did in this case—reverse and remand. This means that the appeals court is overturning the decision of the trial court and is sending the case back to the trial court for further proceedings not inconsistent with the appeals court's decision.

Case Brief

The clarity of judges' opinions varies. When you begin studying law for the first time, the points judges want to make in their written opinions do not always "jump right out at you." It takes some time to become comfortable reading judicial opinions. For this reason, case briefs may assist you in developing a clearer understanding of the cases.

Briefing a case involves several steps. The first portion of a brief discusses the important facts in the case. Step two requires the student to identify the issue dealt with in the case. The next portion of the brief generally indicates who won the case. Finally, the brief notes the reasons for the judge's decision.

A sample case brief of the Davis case is provided in Figure 1.

State Farm Mutual Automobile Insurance Company v. Davis

United States Court of Appeals, Ninth Circuit *937 F.2d 1415 (1991)*

FACTS: State Farm issued an automobile insurance policy covering Walter Davis's 1984 GMC van. While Brian Painter was driving this van, Davis was riding as a passenger. When a Corvette passed them, Davis told Painter to overtake and pass the Corvette. When Painter reached the Corvette, Davis fired a shot into the Corvette, injuring the driver, Charles Keukelaar. The trial court found that State Farm was not obligated to provide insurance coverage for this incident.

ISSUE: Did Charles Keukelaar's injuries in this case result from Davis's use of Davis's GMC van?

DECISION   Yes.

RATIONALE: The court found that it would not have been possible for Davis to have shot Keukelaar had Davis not been using the van. Therefore, Davis's use of the GMC van had more than minimal causal connection with the incident that led to Keukelaar's injuries. Keukelaar's injuries consequently resulted from Davis's use of Davis's GMC van. As the trial court decided this question incorrectly, the appellate court reversed the decision of the trial court and returned the case to the trial court for further consideration of other issues involved in this case.

■ **FIGURE 1**   Sample Case Brief

Your instructor may require you to brief cases. Even if he or she does not make this a requirement in your class, you will find it useful to brief the cases in this text.

When attorneys prepare a brief for an appellate court, the brief often follows a very similar form—a statement of the facts of the case, a statement of the questions presented by the case, followed by an argument in support of a particular position. Not surprisingly, judges tend to follow a similar approach in writing their opinions in cases.

Where to Find the Law

If you want to locate the original source of some of the material in this text, or to find material in addition to that in this text, consult Appendix A, "Where to Find the Law."

We hope this information will be useful to you in your study of the law.

In this case, some issues still exist that need to be resolved by the trial court before a decision may be made that State Farm must provide Davis coverage under this automobile insurance policy.

1 Part

INTRODUCTION TO THE LEGAL STUDIES OF BUSINESS

1 Introduction to Law and the Legal Studies of Business

Chapter 1

INTRODUCTION TO LAW AND THE LEGAL STUDIES OF BUSINESS

Law and business are inextricably intertwined. Business is the organization of capital and labor to produce a product or service in which each step is regulated by law. Buying and selling, employment practices, and the acquisition of funds are examples of business activities based on law. Every business decision has a legal component and the prudent manager should be aware of it.

However, it is folly to presume that the business manager will be an authority on law, able to evaluate the legal rules, and determine their influence on the problem at hand. Such a task is best left to lawyers. Business managers instead must understand law in the general sense. They must appreciate the nature of the legal environment in which their businesses operate. The law needs to be understood as managers understand other people—what motivates them, angers them, pleases them—without becoming authorities in anthropology, sociology, or psychology.

Characteristics of Law

A law cannot make a person just, sober, or ethical. It cannot make people love their neighbors, nor can it make a business prosper. Many desirable goals cannot be achieved through law. A civilization must have an ethical foundation—something beyond what legal institutions can deliver. Thus, other institutions—the family, church, and community—have major roles to play in the make-up of society. The business manager must understand that the law has limits.

The law provides minimum rules of conduct that society will sanction. In order to be effective, these rules must possess several characteristics such as predictability, flexibility, and reasonable application and coverage. If any of the characteristics is missing, then often the rule will have an inconsequential effect without excessive law-enforcement efforts. In a free society, such an occurrence is intolerable.

PREDICTABILITY

One must be able to predict with some accuracy the legal effect of future conduct. Otherwise no activity would ever be legally safe. In the absence of predictability, a manager would be unable to deal with the following basic questions: Will the contract with ABC, Inc., be enforceable in the courts? Is the seller of the land the owner? If two people want to become partners in a business, how do they do it? An effective law of contracts, property, and business organizations provides answers to these questions. Without such legal predictability, the business manager would be undertaking an enormous risk that adverse legal consequences may arise. Predictability then becomes a prime value for an effective law in this system.

Consider: How much would you recommend that your company pay for a hundred acres of land that the market values at $100,000, if you have no idea whether the seller is the owner of this land? In the alternative, what if the law provides sufficient guidance to assure that the seller is the owner?

Determining how much to offer for the land is a complex business question without tossing in another factor regarding an unpredictable legal environment. Consequently, the more predictable the law is, the more readily one may account for it in making management decisions.

However, predictability does not necessarily mean certainty. Snow falling in Vermont during December and the Chicago Cubs not winning the pennant are predictions of future events that are reasonably assured to occur. However, warm New England Decembers have happened.

Thus, one could imagine that the law may be placed on a *predictability scale*. On one end of the scale are events that have a high degree of legal predictability. An example would be the formation of a corporation. Each state has an incorporation statute outlining the steps that must be followed to form one. Carefully following the requirements assures that the business manager's goal of obtaining a corporate charter will be realized.

On the other end of the scale are events that have no clear legal resolution. The following International Perspective, "German Reunification and Property Ownership," is an example of this problem. It concerns the issue of the ownership of property in East Germany after its unification with West Germany. The legal uncertainty prompted the German government to form a special agency called *Treuhandanstalt* to promptly deal with this question.

Most legal questions have highly predictable answers. In fact, predictability is so important that there is often no *question* in the first place. A driver does not wonder whether or not to stop at a red light. The law's response is quite clear.

What can be bedeviling, however, is whether a high probability prediction based on past practice can be applied to a new circumstance. Or, whether a change in society will also mean that long relied-upon predictions must be reconsidered. For these regularly recurring problems, an effective law must possess an additional attribute—flexibility.

FLEXIBILITY

An effective law must have the capacity to change. This does not mean that it may be amended by a new statute—this can always occur. What flexibility means is that the *same* law can be molded to meet new circumstances. One can envision an effective law, then, as being like a pair of trousers with an elastic waistband. If the wearer's weight changes, the trousers will still fit and the wearer can continue to enjoy the slightly modified version that has always been worn. The wearer does not need to become accustomed to something new but can still use the same, old, comfortable trousers.

Compare these elastic-banded trousers to a pair of jeans. A weight gain means that the jeans are no longer usable and that a new pair must be purchased. The jeans are only good as long as no changes occur in the wearer's shape. Once new jeans are purchased, the wearer never knows about any variables the jeans may have.

An effective law works in the same way as the elasticized trousers. The law's predictability is enhanced because one knows that it has

INTERNATIONAL
PERSPECTIVE

German Reunification and Property Ownership

The fall of the Berlin Wall and the freeing of the East German people from the grip of a totalitarian regime was one of the most breathtaking events of the last part of the twentieth century. The two Germanies, severed at the end of World War II, reunited. No longer were there East or West Germans; all were simply Germans. However, major economic problems loomed, particularly in the east. One of the difficulties was to encourage investment in that area of the country.

However, investors were plagued with uncertainty. Private property had been expropriated in eastern Germany, first by the Nazis and then by the Communist government. After reunification, the original, long-dispossessed owners were laying claims to it. Should they be considered the current owners? How can one be sure about any such claims made after fifty years of use by others? Should the West German government, successor to the Communist regime in the east, instead, be deemed the owner? With the uncertainty over ownership, an investor's risk in buying property was enormous.

Consequently, the German government created an administrative agency, Treuhandanstalt, that was in charge of privatizing properties formerly controlled by the Communist government. Treuhandanstalt's mission was to settle conflicting ownership claims, return the property to its rightful owners, and pay compensation when appropriate. Furthermore, the agency was authorized to exempt buyers from certain environmental clean-up laws. This was a major concern, given the uncertainty of the pollution problems that the former East German government has ignored. During its four years in operation, Treuhandanstalt sold approximately ninety-nine percent of once East German government-owned companies, changing a state-owned Communist economy into a privately held, market-oriented one. Thus, questions of competing claims to the property were settled and investors could rely on the predictability of property ownership.

enough flexibility to cover new events. Further, new and untested laws need not be developed for every change in society that occurs. Old, tried-and-true legal rules can be *adjusted* to provide guidance.

One example of law's flexibility may be drawn from the copyright law. A copyright provides legal protection for original works of authorship or composition. For example, note the copyright statement on the page following the title page of this book. The holder of the copyright owns the work which is considered intellectual property. In order to be copyrightable, the work must show some intellectual creativity and it must not have been plagiarized. Books and musical compositions are common subjects of copyright protection.

Copyright thus provides legal protection to artistic expression. A person who photocopies a best-selling novel and then offers those copies for sale is in violation of the author's copyright unless permission has been granted. Similarly, a musician who records another artist's song on a CD that is later offered for sale will also have copyright problems unless permission is granted. Permissions, of course, are often granted in return for a payment of money so that writers and composers may earn income from their labor.

However, what if a new form of artistic expression is based on prior art? That is, the *new* work quotes from something that is already copyrighted. Shouldn't the original artist have some legal protection? Basing new creations on prior work is of long-standing artistic tradition. Pablo Picasso's early works are clearly based on African art, just as some of Bella Bartok's compositions are based on Hungarian folk melodies.

Consider the Managerial Perspective, "Pretty Woman: Roy or Rap?", concerning a rap version of a classic 1960's rock song. Note how the flexibility inherent in copyright law permitted the Supreme Court to narrow the copyright holder's protection and, thus, not stifle 2 Live Crew's musical expression.

REASONABLE APPLICATION AND COVERAGE

An effective law must be reasonable both in its application and in its subject. In order for the law to have reasonable application, those affected by it must have the opportunity to know its requirements. This concept is contained in the **due process** guarantee in the Constitution of the United States and it is meant to prevent secret laws from being

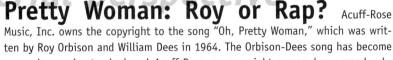

managerial perspective

Pretty Woman: Roy or Rap?
Acuff-Rose Music, Inc. owns the copyright to the song "Oh, Pretty Woman," which was written by Roy Orbison and William Dees in 1964. The Orbison-Dees song has become a popular music standard and Acuff-Rose, as copyright owner, has earned substantial income by licensing it to other musicians who then record the song.

In 1989, Luther Campbell of the rap group 2 Live Crew wrote a rap version of "Oh, Pretty Woman" that he called "Pretty Woman." This version was recorded and released by 2 Live Crew on an album entitled *As Clean As They Want to Be*. Following the release of 2 Live Crew's album, a letter was sent to Acuff-Rose informing it of the rap group's version of "Oh, Pretty Woman." Acuff-Rose refused to grant a license for that use of the song. Nonetheless, *As Clean As They Want to Be* continued to be sold. In 1990 Acuff-Rose sued 2 Live Crew and its recording company for violating its copyright. 2 Live Crew contends that its version of "Oh, Pretty Woman" is a parody, and thus would not violate Acuff-Rose's copyright. Note that under copyright law, parodies may be considered *fair use* to which the copyright owner has no claim. However, a parody must do more than provoke laughter. It must also comment on the original work that is being parodied in order to be protected from copyright infringement. In this way, it is considered fair use, much like criticism or commentary.

In March, 1994, the United States Supreme Court overturned a lower court decision and held that 2 Live Crew's use of "Oh, Pretty Woman" was a parody and thus could be considered fair use under the copyright law. Justice Souter, writing for the Court, found that the rap version ridiculed the original song's naive and sentimentally romantic views by imitating some of its sounds, but changing the lyrics to make a point.

Source: Campbell v. Acuff-Rose Music, Inc., *114 S.Ct. 1164 (1994)*.

applied. However, it does not mean that a person who does not know what the law is need not be concerned with it. As the old maxim states: "Ignorance of the law is no excuse." What the requirement means is that all people must have access to the laws and to legal advisors to assist them in conforming their conduct to existing standards.

An example of law in absence of the reasonable application factor was described in the novel, *The Trial,* by Franz Kafka: "K" was arrested, but he never knew why. He did not know what the accusations were, what the law was that he may have violated, or what he did that prompted his arrest. In addition, there were no known procedures for conducting his trial and, thus, he did not know how to defend himself. Kafka's novel offers a frightening view of law that has no reasonable application. It may also be seen as a prescient view of law in totalitarian regimes.

The subject of an effective law's coverage must also be reasonable. That is, the presumption of what makes a law reasonable in a free society is that the law will reflect social norms. Such laws are readily obeyed because they are consistent with what is deemed to be reasonable. Of course, this concept changes over time and laws that fail to respond will no longer be effective.

Even law that is enacted with the best intentions can be ineffective. A good example is the Volstead Act, in conjunction with the Eighteenth Amendment to the Constitution, which heralded the beginning of Prohibition. Undoubtedly, excessive drinking was, and still is, a national concern and at the time of Prohibition, vast numbers of people supported using the law to combat the problem. (Note the super-majorities under Article V that must approve a Constitutional amendment.)

However, the Prohibition law was ineffective because it was not deemed reasonable. Drinking and alcohol abuse continued as the 1920s became the era of speak-easys, bathtub gin, and the growth of organized crime. By 1933, this legal experiment ended as the Twenty-First Amendment was ratified. Some states, however, carried on with their own Prohibition-style law for decades thereafter, ignoring the corruption, loss of respect for the law, and hypocrisy that it engendered.

Understanding what it takes to make an effective law and having the political will to achieve it are not always synonymous.

HOW LAW AFFECTS BUSINESS

Law can affect business in different ways. Four of these ways are noted. First, the law can create new opportunities, thus, markets can be developed for products or services that could not have existed otherwise. As an example, one can observe the multitude of legal developments overseas caused by the rise of market economies and the deregulation of communications technology. In Europe, for instance, legal changes led to the opening of the television industry beyond the traditional government-owned stations. This created a demand for thousands of hours of new programming. Satellite technology could meet this demand by broadcasting to virtually anywhere in the world—provided the law protects this activity.

The National Basketball Association has embraced these new opportunities. Its broadcast arm, NBA Entertainment, creates basketball shows that are beamed to countries as diverse as Iceland, Japan, and China. This spurred international interest in the NBA and created a new market for sports-related merchandise containing logos of NBA teams. In 1992–93, overseas sales were about $250 million. A change in the law—such as one that would prohibit American events being broadcast to a foreign nation—could radically alter this scenario.

A second effect of law on business is that it may restrict certain business activity. For example, environmental laws limit the amount of pollutants that a factory can emit. Equal employment opportunity statutes affect hiring policies.

In addition, certain laws restrict activity for only selected industries. Note the materials in Chapter 13 on federal securities regulation. It is illegal under federal securities law to buy securities based on important information that is not publicly available. However, the same behavior in the purchase of an antique clock would not be illegal. The scope of permissible conduct in the antiques market is different than that in the securities market. Thus, the law can define the acceptable range of business activities.

A third effect of law on business is that it acts to facilitate the obtaining of certain benefits. For example, assume that a group of investors decides to market snacks in buses and subways. These investors fear that this unique idea may fail and are concerned that creditors may thereafter seek to attach their personal assets. The law contains an organizational form, the corporation, that provides a means by which those investors can limit their losses to the investment in the business. Procedures in their state's incorporation statute will provide a way to form a corporate organization. These legal procedures facilitate the investors, realizing their aim to operate a business in which their personal assets are protected from creditor claims.

Finally, the law acts to formalize and recognize certain private decisions made by business. The primary example of this function is the law of contracts. As will be noted in Chapters 8 and 9, a contract is an agreement that the law recognizes and enforces. Not all agreements meet the standard of a legal contract. But all are the manifestations, at least theoretically, of some bargaining intent of the parties. For example, assume that ABC, Inc. agrees to buy six trucks from XYZ, Inc., with delivery in two weeks. There is no statute or regulation that requires trucks to be delivered within a certain time. However, in the ABC–XYZ example, if the trucks are not delivered as promised, the courts will be available to enforce the bargain, just as if a statute or regulation was in place. Thus, the law acts to provide a formal power to private agreements.

Consider that some laws may have more than one effect at the same time. An environmental regulation, for example, may restrict some firms' activities, while at the same time provide opportunities for those that can design pollution abatement equipment. Thus, it is important to consider not only the various ways that the law affects business but also to assess how changes in the law may also affect economic activity.

Recurring Themes in the Legal Studies of Business

Rules of law, the working of legal institutions, and current issues in the law can all be related to three *themes:* first, historical and social movements influence the development of law; second, the law seeks to control concentrations of power; and third, the law balances conflicting values (see Figure 1.1).

These themes recur continuously throughout the legal environment of business. Consider by analogy, the four-note theme that Beethoven used to open his "Fifth Symphony." These notes served as a pattern on which his masterpiece was woven. Similarly, observing the three legal studies of business themes in this chapter should provide a basis for understanding the chapters that follow.

THEME 1: HISTORICAL AND SOCIAL MOVEMENTS AND THE DEVELOPMENT OF LAW: THE FIRST AMENDMENT AND THE REGULATION OF SPEECH

The First Amendment to the United States Constitution provides that: "Congress shall make no law . . . abridging the freedom of speech,

■ **FIGURE 1.1** Themes in the Legal Studies of Business

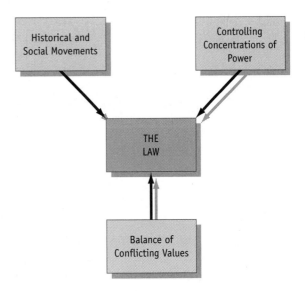

or of the press. . . ." The words of this amendment seem quite clear, but they have never really been taken literally. Since the First Amendment's ratification in 1791, a number of laws have been enacted that affect the freedom of speech. Many of them would be considered unconstitutional today, even though they passed muster for a number of years.

This section will sketch some developments in First Amendment jurisprudence as a way of illustrating that historical and social forces influence the development of law. The historical trends that change society will also influence law. One cannot understand law without appreciating this relationship. Therefore, background discussions of the legal principles are provided throughout this book. The temptation may be to skip them and get to the rule itself. But, understanding the rule and issues that may arise under it requires that one delve into its history. Determining which speech should or should *not* be protected has never been a simple task. A number of cases brought during World War I, under the Espionage Act of 1917, were aimed at anti-war and anti-draft activities that included leafleting, publishing articles in newspapers, and public speaking. The Supreme Court permitted the regulation of the speech if it was found to pose a *clear and present danger*. Similarly, during the 1920's "Red Scare" and the post-World War II anti-communist era, statutes aimed at leftists were enacted that raised free speech questions.

The 1930s was a watershed decade for legal developments during the rest of the century. (Note that some are suggesting current trends in the political arena, and anti-government sentiment may foreshadow another major shift in the law.) The 1930s saw the beginnings of a strong federal government and extensive regulation of business. The Great Depression and the Roosevelt landslide election victory of 1932 contrasted with a more state government-oriented, laissez-faire attitude that had previously prevailed.

Two developments during the 1930s were of particular importance to freedom of speech issues. The first was a shift in the Supreme Court's review of government regulation—regulations that affected personal liberties (including freedom of speech) were to be carefully scrutinized for constitutional infirmities, while economic regulations would be reviewed leniently. The second development was the elevation of free speech to a higher status than any other constitutional provision. Note Supreme Court Justice Cardozo's statement in *Palko v. Connecticut* (1937): "Of that freedom [freedom of thought and speech] one may say that it is the matrix, the indispensable condition, of nearly every other form of freedom."

The 1960s brought major social changes and, in response, a strengthened First Amendment. Its protections were extended to commercial speech (see Chapter 6), symbolic speech (flag burning), and sexually-explicit publications—although what is obscene may still be banned.

The key to determining which speech should be protected is to note the historical context in which First Amendment developments arose: wartime, fear of attacks on the American economic system, and a change in the social climate. Law reacted to those changes, first with statutes that limited speech, and then with court challenges that tested those limits against the First Amendment.

As will be noted in Chapter 10, a trend in the law of torts has been the expansion of business's liability exposure for injuries—although this is changing. Injuries that would have yielded no liability forty years ago, are today the source of damage awards against business. But what if the injury arose from the publication of an advertisement—an activity protected by the First Amendment? Two trends in the law clash in this scenario. Consider the following Thought Problem, "Violence v. Free Speech."

thought problem

Violence v. Free Speech   In January

1985, Michael Savage submitted a personal service advertisement to *Soldier of Fortune* magazine. After several conversations between Savage and *SOF*'s advertising manager, the following advertisement ran in issues from June 1985 through March 1986:

> **GUNS FOR HIRE:**   37 year old professional mercenary desires jobs. Vietnam Veteran. Discrete [sic] and very private. Body guard, courier, and other special skills. All jobs considered.

In late 1984 or early 1985, Bruce Gastwirth began seeking to murder his business partner, Richard Braun. Gastwirth enlisted the aid of another business associate, John Horton Moore. Responding to the *SOF* ad, Gastwirth and Moore contacted Michael Savage in August 1985 to discuss plans to murder Braun.

On August 26, 1985, Savage, Moore, and another individual, Sean Trevor Doutre, went to Braun's suburban Atlanta home. As Braun and his sixteen-year-old son were driving down the driveway, Doutre stepped in front of Braun's car and fired several shots into the car with a MAC 11 automatic pistol. The shots wounded Braun. Braun managed to roll out of the car, but Doutre walked over to him and killed him by firing two more shots into the back of his head as he lay on the ground.

The victim's sons filed a lawsuit against *Soldier of Fortune* magazine seeking damages for the wrongful death of their father. They contended that *SOF* was liable because it had negligently published a personal service advertisement that created an unreasonable risk of the solicitation and commission of violent criminal activity, including murder. *Soldier of Fortune* magazine argued that the First Amendment forbids imposing liability on publishers for publishing an advertisement unless the ad openly solicits criminal activity.

What do you think? Furthermore, do you think that violence in today's society will affect freedom of speech (e.g. content of television programs)?

Source: Braun v. *Soldier of Fortune* Magazine, Inc., *968 F.2d 1110 (11th Cir. 1992).*

THEME 2: THE LAW AND ITS EFFORTS TO CONTROL CONCENTRATIONS OF POWER: DRUG TESTING IN THE WORKPLACE

A second theme in the study of law is how it attempts to limit exploitation by the powerful. Lord Acton, in his letter to Bishop Creighton, aptly characterized this issue: "Power tends to corrupt, and absolute power corrupts absolutely."[1]

Chronicles of this exploitation may be found in innumerable novels. Charles Dickens and Anatole France were writers who illuminated the perils of unregulated power. Philosophers as diverse as John Locke and Karl Marx were concerned about the abuse of power by the king (government) or the capitalist (business). American legal history is replete with examples of laws being enacted to curb activities of the powerful. A prime example is the United States Constitution.

Having freed themselves from the British monarchy that they regarded as tyrannical, the early leaders of the United States established a government with limited powers and divided its functions among three distinct branches. Furthermore, numerous centers of authority were created—the states and the federal government systems—to diffuse government power. Such a division of responsibility may be described as planned organizational inefficiency. The drawback to such a system is that it does not yield prompt action to combat national problems. The advantage is that in times of national hysteria (such as the McCarthy era in the 1950s), a demagogue will be unable to gain control. The Constitution, thus, has fostered individual liberty by creating numerous and competing governmental authorities that inhibit the concentration of power.

However, concentrations of power are not limited to the government. New concentrations of power arose in the late nineteenth century as very large corporations developed. Before the Industrial Revolution, most businesses produced products sold by the maker directly to the purchaser. With the growth of mass production techniques tied to improved delivery systems, the advantages of economies of scale became apparent. Large pools of capital met this need. By the late nineteenth century, the concentration of economic power in such industries as the railroads, oil, steel, and sugar triggered movements in the law to control that power. The platforms of both the Democratic and Republican parties in the 1888 presidential election contained planks that promised solutions to abuses by the moneyed interests.

In 1890, the Sherman Antitrust Act was passed. It was the first nationwide attempt to control economic monopoly. Chapter 18 contains a discussion of the antitrust laws. Additionally, the labor union movement, discussed in Chapter 17, rose out of conflicts between workers and big business. The consumer movement grew from complaints over the relationship between business and the public (see Chapter 15).

Today, drug testing in the workplace is a volatile issue that the law is seeking to control. Drug abuse has become a major concern for both government and private employers. Loss of productivity and increased employee absenteeism have been cited as problems that justify drug-screening programs. One study estimated that this loss may be as high as $60 billion annually. Furthermore, as noted in Chapter 12, expanded employer liability for worker-caused injuries imposes financial risks on corporations that have drug-impaired workers. In 1987, an Amtrak train crashed, killing fifteen people and injuring seventy-five others. The crash was found to have been caused by an engineer who had been smoking marijuana. Lawsuits were filed against Amtrak, which settled for $75 million.

A survey found that, by 1994, eighty-seven percent of American companies were testing for drugs at a cost of about $100 million per year. The survey included both employee and job applicant testing in its figures. A major drug-testing laboratory reported that of the 3.6 million tests conducted that year, more than ninety-two percent did not show drug use.

Compare the current frequency of employment drug testing with a 1987 survey in which only twenty-two percent had drug-testing programs. The reasons for the increase may be attributed to strong government advocacy of drug-testing programs, including federal regulations that affect transportation and defense industry workers. A couple of states offer businesses discounts in their workers' compensation premiums if they institute a drug-testing program. In addition, corporate concern about liability exposure and insurance costs has also been cited in support of drug testing.

Numerous cases have been filed that question the constitutionality of public employee drug-testing programs. Since the employer in these situations is the government, the Fourth Amendment applies to protect employees from unreasonable searches. The United States Supreme Court has upheld some drug-testing programs, although it has not ruled on random testing. During the Reagan Administration, the Customs Service (the agency charged with interdicting the importation of illegal drugs) adopted a policy requiring a drug test of any employee applying for promotion to certain sensitive positions. This urine-testing policy was upheld in *National Treasury Employees v. Von Raab*, as the Supreme Court focused on the compelling government interest in the work of the Customs Service as justification.

But, the effect of the use of this power on innocent individuals should be considered. One customs employee who was compelled to take a drug test stated: "I would say everybody who has taken one either finds it humiliating or asinine. I've been with the Customs Service for eleven years. If they don't know me by now, they're never going to know me. When I arrest somebody I have to respect their rights. I don't see why I should be subject to an indiscriminate test when I haven't done anything."[2] Furthermore, note that the Customs Service had tested 5,300 of its employees as of June 30, 1988. A mere one-tenth of one percent tested positive.

Private employer drug testing also raises concerns. Although constitutional issues generally do not arise, litigation has been filed over the effects of the testing programs. A truck driver, who denied ever using drugs, was fired in 1993 after testing positive for marijuana use. At a hearing for unemployment compensation, the judge found that the laboratory did not establish that the urine it tested was the same sample as that taken from the driver. Thereafter, the truck driver filed a $2 million damage suit against the lab.

In 1988, an oilfield worker was fired after testing positive for drug use. However, the drug test was inaccurate. The worker sued the laboratory that processed the test. He was awarded $4.1 million in damages, most of which was punitive.

Generally, a finding of reasonable private employer conduct (that is, self-restraint in the exercise of power) precludes decisions that favor the employee. *Borse v. Piece Goods Shop, Inc.* is one court's analysis of a drug-screening policy. How might an employer design the policy in order to satisfy the decision?

Borse v. Piece Goods Shop, Inc.

United States Court of Appeals, Third Circuit
963 F.2d 611 (1992)

Sarah Borse was employed as a sales clerk by the Piece Goods Shop for nearly fifteen years. In January 1990, the shop adopted a drug and alcohol policy that required its employees to sign a form giving their consent to urinalysis screening for drug use.

Borse refused to sign the consent form. On more than one occasion, she asserted that the drug and alcohol policy violated her right to privacy. The shop continued to insist that she sign the form and threatened to discharge her unless she did. On February 9, 1990, the shop terminated Borse's employment.

This appeal requires us to decide whether an at-will employee who is discharged for refusing to consent to urinalysis screening for drug use states a claim for wrongful discharge under Pennsylvania law.

Becker, Circuit Judge

Ordinarily, Pennsylvania law does not provide a common-law cause of action for the wrongful discharge of an at-will employee. Rather, an employer may discharge an employee with or without cause, at pleasure, unless restrained by some contract. However, the Pennsylvania Supreme Court recognized the possibility that an action for wrongful discharge might lie when the firing of an at-will employee violates public policy. In order to evaluate Borse's claim, we must attempt to discern whether any public policy is threatened by her discharge.

Our review of Pennsylvania law reveals evidence of a public policy that may, under certain circumstances, give rise to a wrongful discharge action related to urinalysis drug screening. Specifically, we refer to the Pennsylvania common law regarding tortious invasion of privacy. Pennsylvania recognizes a cause of action for tortious intrusion upon seclusion. The Restatement defines the tort as follows: "One who intentionally intrudes, physically or otherwise, upon the solitude or seclusion of another or his private affairs or concerns, is subject to liability to the other for invasion of his privacy, if the intrusion would be highly offensive to a reasonable person."

We can envision at least two ways in which an employer's urinalysis program might intrude upon an employee's seclusion. First, the particular manner in which the program is conducted might constitute an intrusion upon seclusion as defined by Pennsylvania law. The process of collecting the urine sample to be tested clearly implicates expectations of privacy that society has long recognized as reasonable. In addition, many urinalysis programs monitor the collection of the urine specimen to ensure that the employee does not adulterate it or substitute a sample from another person. Monitoring collection of the urine sample appears to fall within the definition of an intrusion upon seclusion because it involves the use of one's senses to oversee the private activities of another.

There are few activities in our society more personal or private than the passing of urine. Most people describe it by euphemisms if they talk about it at all. It is a function traditionally performed without public observation; indeed, its performance in public is generally prohibited by law as well as social custom. If the method used to collect the urine sample fails to give due regard to the employee's privacy, it could constitute a substantial and highly offensive intrusion upon seclusion.

Second, urinalysis can reveal a host of private medical facts about an employee, including whether she is epileptic, pregnant, or diabetic. A reasonable person might well conclude that submitting urine samples to tests designed to ascertain these types of information constitutes a substantial and highly offensive intrusion upon seclusion. Indeed, it may be granted that there are areas of an employee's life in which his employer has no legitimate interest. An intrusion into one of these areas by virtue of the employer's power of discharge might plausibly give rise to a cause of action, particularly where some recognized facet of public policy is threatened.

We hold that dismissing an employee who refused to consent to urinalysis drug testing would violate public policy if the testing tortiously invaded the employee's privacy. The sketchy nature of Borse's complaint makes it difficult to ascertain whether the Shop's drug and alcohol program would constitute a substantial and highly offensive intrusion upon Borse's privacy, however. Although she alleges that the program violates her right of privacy, she fails to allege how it does so. Because we can envision at least two ways in which an employer's drug and alcohol program might violate the public policy protecting individuals from tortious invasions of privacy by private actors, we will vacate the order of the district court dismissing the complaint.

The judiciary is not the only branch of government through which the law acts to control concentrations of power. The legislature is also involved. In the area of corporate drug testing, a number of states have enacted statutes that regulate this practice. Figure 1.2 is an example of how the legislature may restrict the exercise of corporate power. Note the statute's limitations on employer discretion.

THEME 3: THE LAW AS A MEANS OF BALANCING CONFLICTING VALUES

■ Values and Rights

The third theme in the legal studies of business is how the law adjusts competing values. The rules that appear in this book illustrate this. For example Chapter 11 explains that business organizational

■ **FIGURE 1.2** **General Laws of Rhode Island** Chap. 6.5 Urine and blood tests as a condition of employment

> **28-6.5-1. Urine and blood testing generally prohibited.**—No employer or agent of any employer shall, either orally or in writing, request, require or subject any employee to submit a sample of his urine, blood or other bodily fluid or tissue for testing as a condition of continued employment. Nothing herein shall prohibit an employer from requiring a specific employee to submit to such testing if:
>
> (A) the employer has reasonable grounds to believe, based on specific objective facts, that the employee's use of controlled substances is impairing his ability to perform his job; and
>
> (B) the employee provides the test sample in private, outside the presence of any person; and
>
> (C) the testing is conducted in conjunction with a bona fide rehabilitation program; and
>
> (D) positive tests are confirmed by means of gas chromatography/mass spectrometry or technology recognized as being at least as scientifically accurate; and
>
> (E) the employer provides the employee, at the employer's expense, the opportunity to have the sample tested or evaluated by an independent testing facility and so advises the employee; and
>
> (F) the employer provides the employee with a reasonable opportunity to rebut or explain the results.

forms balance the interests of the investors and creditors. The equal employment opportunity laws in Chapter 16 adjust values of a diverse workplace with the autonomy of an employer to choose the most suitable employees.

As certain values become more important, the law will change to reflect them. Note the materials in Chapters 10 and 14. Liability exposure for business has expanded during the twentieth century as the value of compensating victims began to dominate. Thus, the law's adjustment of values is influenced by historical and social forces, the first theme discussed in this chapter.

Rights are values that the law most zealously protects. Freedom of speech, the right to contract, and ownership of property reflect fundamental ideals in the American system. By being considered *rights*, these ideals overrule competing values. One finds rights in the Constitution—in the freedom of assembly clause in the First Amendment, for example. Rights have also been created by statute. An example is the Equal Pay Act which makes it illegal for an employer to pay women and men differently for the same job. The *competing values* were the employer's discretion in setting wage rates and the interests of workers not to have sex discrimination affect that decision.

Courts, too, may be seen as a source of rights. For example, the Supreme Court created the constitutional right of privacy through judicial decision. Furthermore, legal philosophers argue that rights exist independent of any formal government recognition, since all persons have certain natural rights by virtue of being human. The concept of natural rights is very old. It was advanced by Aristotle and by the drafters of the Declaration of Independence. Calls for natural rights or human rights occur when individual freedom is lacking. Totalitarian regimes that jail or kill dissenters, prohibit or discourage religious worship, or arrest people without charge and punish them

The Value of Life: From Whose Perspective?

On July 5, 1884, Thomas Dudley and Edward Stephens, and Brooks, all able-bodied English seamen, and the deceased, an English boy, were cast away in a storm on the high seas sixteen hundred miles from the Cape of Good Hope, and were compelled to put into an open boat. In this boat they had no supply of water and no supply of food, except two one-pound tins of turnips. For three days they had nothing else to subsist upon. On the fourth day they caught a small turtle. On the twelfth day, the remains of the turtle were entirely consumed, and for the next eight days they had nothing to eat. They had no fresh water, except such rain as they from time to time caught in their oil-skin capes. The boat was drifting on the ocean, and was probably more than one thousand miles away from land. On the eighteenth day, when they had been seven days without food and five without water, the prisoners spoke to Brooks as to what should be done if no help came. They suggested that someone should be sacrificed to save the rest. Brooks dissented, and the boy, to whom they were understood to refer, was not consulted.

On July 24, Dudley proposed to Stephens and Brooks that lots should now be cast who should be put to death to save the rest. Brooks refused to consent, and it was not put to the boy, and in point of fact there was no drawing of lots. On that day, the prisoners spoke of their having families, and suggested it would be better to kill the boy that their lives should be saved. Dudley proposed that if there was no vessel in sight by the next morning the boy should be killed.

The next day, no vessel appearing, Dudley told Brooks that he had better get some sleep, and made signs to Stephens and Brooks that the boy had better be killed. The prisoner Stephens agreed to the act, but Brooks dissented from it. The boy was then lying at the bottom of the boat quite helpless, and extremely weakened by famine and by drinking sea water, and unable to make any resistance, nor did he ever assent to his being killed. Dudley offered a prayer asking forgiveness for them and that their souls might be saved. Dudley, with the assent of Stephens, went to the boy, and telling him that his time was come, put a knife into his throat and killed him. The three men fed on the body and blood of the boy for four days. On the fourth day after the act had been committed the boat was picked up by a passing vessel,

—*Continued*

without trial, give rise to the assertion that there are natural or human rights of which no government may deprive its people.

But constitutions, statutes, court decisions, and philosophical ideas are not the sources of our rights. At most, they are their outward manifestations. Constitutions, statutes, and judicial decisions are only words. The concept of natural rights is a philosophical idea. Yet these mere words and ideas represent the real source of our rights—us. Quite simply, we have certain rights in the United States because we, as a nation, want to have them. When we no longer believe in those rights, the law that recognizes them can easily be ignored. Clarence Darrow, the noted trial lawyer, once stated, "It is all right to preserve freedom in constitutions, but when the spirit of freedom has fled from the hearts of people, then its matter is easily sacrificed under law."[3]

■ *Limitations on Rights: Which Value to Choose?*

In a complex and crowded nation, an individual's values may well involve impositions on other people. For instance, if you distribute handbills outlining your disagreement with the current administration, then others are subjected to your standing on the street corner waving the handbills as they pass by. If a newspaper exercises its freedom of the press, then a politician arrested for drunk driving will be embarrassed if named on the front page. Thus, even rights are not without restriction. You may have the right to give a speech for your favorite political candidate. But, you do not have the right to give that speech at 2:00 A.M. outside your professor's bedroom window. Both you and your professor have certain interests: you, to give a political speech; your professor, to be able to sleep undisturbed by loud speeches. If a dispute between you and your professor arises, a court may be called upon to determine the conflict of values.

Rights are not absolute because the values that they represent often clash in a complex society. For example, should a person be able to read any book that is published? Little dispute arises if one is considering the Bible, the works of Shakespeare, or the poetry of Carl Sandburg. However, controversial books such as J. D. Salinger's *Catcher in the Rye* and Mark Twain's *Huckleberry Finn* have been the

—Continued

and the three men were rescued, still alive, but in the lowest state of prostration. If the men had not fed on the body of the boy they would probably not have survived to be picked up and rescued, but would within the four days have died of famine. The boy, being in a much weaker condition, was likely to have died before them.

At the time of the act in question there was no sail in sight, nor any reasonable prospect of relief. Under these circumstances there appeared to the three men that unless they then fed or very soon fed upon the boy or one of themselves they would die of starvation. There was no appreciable chance of saving life except by killing someone for the others to eat. Assuming any necessity to kill anybody, there was no greater necessity for killing the boy than any of the other three men.

Focus on the competing values and then determine whether or not the men should be convicted of murder.

Source: Regina v. Dudley and Stephens, 14 Q.B.D. 273 (England, Queen's Bench Division 1884).

subject of censorship efforts by those who claim the books offend their values. Which values to choose?

The fact that the law makes the choice raises a danger that any limits placed on rights will lead to their loss in practice. This is the central difficulty courts face in deciding disputes that raise such issues as employee privacy, advertising restrictions, and land use regulation.

Totalitarian governments frequently have constitutions that provide many of the same freedoms that exist in the United States. Yet it is clear that their citizens have no such rights in practice. The Constitution of the People's Republic of China, for example, grants its citizens the freedom of assembly and the freedom to demonstrate. The regime, uninfluenced by considerations of law, conveniently ignores these mere words—most notably when its army massacred student demonstrators in Tiananmen Square on June 4, 1989.

The Ethical Perspective, "The Value of Life: From Whose Perspective," illustrates the complexity that sometimes arises when values clash. In addition, the Thought Problem, "What Can Be Done to Safeguard Property?", also shows this situation. The first involves a clash of the most basic values in any civilized society—the value of survival and the duty of a society to prohibit the killing of its members. The second concerns the ownership of property (a right) and whether there are limits in what an owner can do to safeguard it.

For both the Ethical Perspective and the Thought Problem, carefully consider the values that are in dispute. Make sure to note any implications of the decision reached.

thought problem

What Can Be Done to Safeguard Property?
Bertha L. Briney inherited her parents' farmland. Included was an eighty-acre tract where her grandparents and parents had lived. No one occupied the farmhouse. Her husband, Edward, attempted to care for the land. He kept no farm machinery thereon. The outbuildings became dilapidated.

During the next ten years, there was a series of trespassings and housebreakings with loss of some household items and the breaking of windows.

The Brineys, through the years, boarded up the windows and doors in an attempt to stop the intrusions. They posted "no trespass" signs on the land. The nearest one was thirty-five feet from the house. After nothing worked, the Brineys set "a shotgun trap" in the north bedroom. They secured the gun to an iron bed with the barrel pointed at the bedroom door. It was rigged with wire from the doorknob to the gun's trigger so it would fire when the door was opened. The spring gun could not be seen from the outside. No warning of its presence was posted.

Katko lived with his wife and worked regularly as a gasoline station attendant in Eddyville, seven miles from the old house. He had observed it for several years while hunting in the area and considered it abandoned. He knew it had long been uninhabited. The area around the house was covered with high weeds. Katko and his friend, McDonough, had been to the premises and found several old bottles and fruit jars, which they took and added to their collection of antiques. An old organ fascinated Katko. Arriving at the house a second time, they found that the window by which they had entered before was now a solid mass of boards and walked around the house until they found the porch window, which offered less resistance. They crawled through this window. While searching the house, Katko came to the bedroom door and pulled it open, thus triggering the gun, which delivered a charge that struck him in the leg.

Much of his leg, including part of the tibia, was blown away. Only by McDonough's assistance was Katko able to get out of the house. After crawling some distance, he was put in his vehicle and rushed to a doctor and then to a hospital. He remained in the hospital for forty days.

Some weeks after his release from the hospital, Katko returned to work on crutches. He was required to keep the injured leg in a cast for approximately a year and wear a special brace for another year. He continued to suffer pain during this period. There was undenied medical testimony that Katko had a permanent deformity, a loss of tissue, and a shortening of the leg.

Katko knew he had no right to break into the house to steal bottles and fruit jars. He entered a plea of guilty, was fined fifty dollars and costs, and paroled during good behavior from a sixty-day jail sentence. Other than minor traffic charges, this was his first brush with the law.

Focus on the competing values and then determine whether or not Katko should be able to sue the Brineys for his injuries.

Source: Katko v. Briney, 183 N.W.2d 657 (Iowa 1971).

Summary

Law is influenced by culture and history. It is not a thing apart from the values of a society nor does its existence ensure a just world. This chapter outlined the basic attributes that law must possess in a free society. In addition, this chapter noted that law can have multiple effects. There are four ways law can affect business activity: create new opportunities; restrict certain business activity; facilitate in obtaining certain benefits; and act to formalize and recognize certain private business decisions. These factors should be kept in mind as the rest of this text is read. Contract law (Chapters 8 and 9), for example, not only controls certain buying and selling behavior, but it also facilitates market transactions and the efficient allocation of resources.

This chapter also outlined the three themes about which the development of law can be organized: historical influences; control of the powerful; and the balance of values. Consider how these themes work simultaneously to create changes in the law. For example, in Chapter 18 (Antitrust Law) you will read about the Sherman Act which was passed near the end of the nineteenth century. This statute illustrates the combined operation of these three themes. It arose because of the extraordinary changes in the American economy during that century and exemplifies the historical influences theme. Its design was to limit the power of large business combinations and, therefore, illustrates the control of the powerful theme. Finally, the Sherman Act balanced the values of competition and economic efficiency and portrays the balance of values theme.

These themes will surface many times throughout this book. Considering the legal principles from a larger, thematic perspective will help you understand them.

Review Questions

1. Define the following terms:
   a. Predictability in the law
   b. Copyright
   c. Reasonable application of the law
   d. Rights

2. Why does the law act to control or limit the concentration of power and its exercise? Is there a paradox inherent in this control?

3. Why are there no absolute rights?

4. Is there a danger in limitations that the law places on the exercise of rights?

5. Discuss the themes that recur in the law. Give examples other than those mentioned in this chapter.

6. What characteristics must law possess in order for it to be effective in the American system?

7. What are the four effects law may have on business activity? Give an example of each, other than what was noted in this chapter.

8. You are an executive of ABC Corporation, a very large multinational firm. One afternoon you are reviewing the terms of a deal that one of your subordinates has negotiated with XYZ, Inc., a small distribution company. The agreement provides that if XYZ does not sell a certain quota of ABC products, it will pay ABC a penalty of ten times the cost of those products. Without discussing applicable legal rules and based only on the material in this chapter, would you expect a potential problem to arise with such a clause? If so, give reasons.

9. Bill Smith is a highly trained engineer who is in charge of computer design changes at High Tech, Inc. He has been instrumental in developing numerous features of the corporation's line of computers, and he is currently involved in its secret work involving artificial intelligence. AI, Inc., a competitor of High Tech, lures Smith from High Tech in order to organize its newly formed artificial intelligence division. Smith eagerly accepts the new position and High Tech is upset that he is leaving. Without discussing applicable legal rules and based only on the material in this chapter, what are the concerns of Smith and High Tech that could be central to a suit filed by High Tech against Smith?

10. You have been assigned to Hong Kong by your company to head its Far East division. You are in charge of operations in Taiwan, Korea, and Malaysia. Discuss the sources of differences in law between those areas and the United States without focusing on legal rules. How might you begin to understand, or at least appreciate, those differences?

11. Ann Jones is the marketing manager for Sellit, Inc. She supervises fifteen sales representatives. Jones is an avid professional football fan and each year she plans an outing with the representatives as a way to build *team spirit*. Jim Carson, one of the sales representatives, dislikes professional football. He believes it is overcommercialized and panders to primitive violent instincts. One year, he casually mentioned to Jones that he would prefer a different type of group outing, since he has no interest in football. Jones listened but thereafter began to regularly criticize Carson's work. Finally, she fired him. Previously, Carson had been one of the top sales representatives. Without discussing applicable legal rules and based only on the material in this chapter, discuss any legal problems that may arise.

12. Assume you have the opportunity to buy a patent for your company. However, because of a recent change in patent laws, precisely determining who owns the patent is nearly impossible. How will this affect your decision? Why?

13. Assume your company wants to build an office tower in a small city. The tallest building presently located there is four stories high. Thus, no body of law exists in this city that specifically pertains to office towers. However, a number of related laws *do* exist. Does this mean that because of an absence of a specific law that your company should not build the tower? Why or why not?

Notes

[1]John Bartlett, *Familiar Quotations*, 15th ed., E. Black, ed. (Boston: Little, Brown & Co., 1980).

[2]*American Bar Association Journal*, 63 (October 1, 1988).

[3]A. Weinberg, ed., *Attorney for the Damned* (New York: Simon & Schuster, 1977), p. 57.

2

Part

THE AMERICAN LEGAL SYSTEM

Chapter

2

INTRODUCTION TO THE COURTS

In this chapter, the first focus is on the power of the courts to hear a case. Simply because a person files a case in a court does not give the court the power to hear and decide the case—a court must first have jurisdiction over both the subject matter of the case and the people involved in the case.

The second focus of this chapter examines the structure of the American court system. Power in America is shared between the federal government and the fifty state governments. The federal government has a system of courts that is separate from the system of courts operated by the states.

The remainder of this chapter discusses two players in the judicial system—the judge and the lawyer.

The Power to Hear a Case

JURISDICTION

Laura Meyer, who lives in Denver, Colorado, purchased a cellular telephone from Best Cellular Phones in Denver. The telephone did not perform in the manner the salesman promised. Could Laura, if she went on vacation to Florida, file suit against Best Cellular Phones in the county court for Dade County, Florida? No. A person with a legal claim may not simply bring a case to any court in the nation. The court in which the plaintiff files a case must have *jurisdiction*—that is, the power to hear and decide the case.

To begin with, the court must have jurisdiction over the *subject matter* of the case. A court has jurisdiction over a given subject matter if the case is one that the court is authorized to hear. Some state courts are courts of general jurisdiction—they can hear any case arising in the state. For example, a court of general jurisdiction could hear cases involving murders, contract disputes, or traffic offenses.

Other courts are courts of limited jurisdiction—they can hear only certain types of cases. For example, suppose that a judge presides over a probate court in a given state. A *probate* court handles the estates of deceased persons and guardianships. If a person such as Laura Meyer files a breach of contract suit in probate court, the probate judge would be required to dismiss the suit for lack of subject matter jurisdiction. A breach of contract case has nothing to do with the power of the court to hear probate and guardianship matters.

It is not sufficient for a court merely to have jurisdiction over the subject matter of the case. The court must also have power over the person involved in the case. *In personam* jurisdiction over the plaintiff is obtained when the plaintiff files the suit. In personam jurisdiction over the defendant normally is obtained by the service of a summons and complaint on the defendant. A court has jurisdiction over anyone who can be served with a summons and complaint while physically present within the state.

In *Burnham v. Superior Court of California*, the United States Supreme Court reaffirmed the long-standing rule that a court may obtain in personam jurisdiction over a defendant if the plaintiff serves a summons and complaint on the defendant while the defendant is physically present within the state. While the justices of the United States Supreme Court agreed upon this rule, they disagreed on a rationale for the rule. Two of the opinions supporting the decision against Dennis Burnham are explained in *Burnham v. Superior Court of California* to illustrate the different thinking that supports the decision for Francie Burnham.

Burnham v. Superior Court of California

United States Supreme Court
110 S.Ct. 2105 (1990)

Francie Burnham separated from her husband, Dennis, and moved from New Jersey to California with their children. Francie brought a divorce suit in California in June 1988. In late January 1988, Dennis Burnham, who lived in New Jersey, was visiting California on business, after which he went north to San Francisco, where his wife resided, to see the children. Upon returning one of the children to Francie's home on January 24, 1988, he was served with a California court summons and a copy of Francie's divorce petition. He then returned to New Jersey.

Dennis Burnham made a special appearance in California. He alleged that the court lacked personal jurisdiction over him because his only contacts with California were a few short visits to the state for the purposes of conducting business and visiting the children. Dennis argued that the due process clause prohibited California from asserting jurisdiction over him because he lacked "minimum contacts" with the state of California. The California Superior Court held that since he was personally served with the summons and petition in California, there was a valid basis for in personam jurisdiction over him. The United States Supreme Court agreed with the ruling of the Superior Court.

Justice Scalia (announced the judgment of the Court and delivered an opinion)

The proposition that the judgment of a court lacking jurisdiction is void traces back to the English Year Books (1482), and was made settled law by Lord Coke in *Case of the Marshalsea* (1612). Traditionally that proposition was embodied in the phrase *coram non judice*, "before a person not a judge"—meaning, in effect, that the proceeding in question was not a *judicial* proceeding because lawful judicial authority was not present, and could therefore not yield a *judgment*. American courts invalidated, or denied recognition to, judgments that violated the common-law principle long before the Fourteenth Amendment was adopted. In *Pennoyer v. Neff* (1878), we announced that the judgment of a court lacking personal jurisdiction violated the Due Process Clause of the Fourteenth Amendment as well.

Among the most firmly established principles of personal jurisdiction in American tradition is that the courts of a State have jurisdiction over nonresidents who are physically present in the State. The view developed early that each State had the power to hale before its courts any individual who could be found within its borders, and that once having acquired jurisdiction over such a person by properly serving him with process, the State could retain jurisdiction to enter judgment against him, no matter how fleeting his visit. That view had antecedents in English common-law practice, which sometimes allowed transitory actions, arising out of events outside the country, to be maintained against seemingly nonresident defendants who were physically present in England.

Despite this formidable body of precedent, petitioner contends, in reliance on our decisions applying the International Shoe standard, that in the absence of "continuous and systematic" contacts with the forum, a nonresident defendant can be subjected to judgment only as to matters that arise out of or relate to his contacts with the forum. This argument rests on a thorough misunderstanding of our cases.

Nothing in *International Shoe* or the cases that have followed it offers support for the proposition that a defendant's presence in the forum is no longer sufficient to establish jurisdiction. The short of the matter is that jurisdiction based on physical presence alone constitutes due process because it is one of the continuing traditions of our legal system that define the due process standard of "traditional notions of fair play and substantial justice." Where, as in the present case, a jurisdictional principle is both firmly approved by tradition and still favored, it is impossible to imagine what standard we could appeal to for the judgment that it is no longer justified.

Because the Due Process Clause does not prohibit the California courts from exercising jurisdiction over petitioner based on the fact of in-State service of process, the judgment is affirmed.

Justice Brennan (concurring in the judgment)

I agree with Justice Scalia that the Due Process Clause of the Fourteenth Amendment generally permits a State court to exercise jurisdiction over a defendant if he is served with process while voluntarily present in the forum State. Unlike Justice Scalia, I would undertake an independent inquiry into the fairness of the prevailing in-State service rule. I therefore concur only in the judgment.

I believe that the minimum contacts analysis developed in *International Shoe* represents a far more sensible construct for the exercise of State-court jurisdiction than the patchwork of legal and factual fictions that has been generated from the decision in *Pennoyer v. Neff*.

The potential burdens on a transient defendant are slight. Modern transportation and communications have made it much less burdensome for a party sued to defend himself in a State outside his place of residence. Finally, any burdens that do arise can be ameliorated by a variety of procedural devices. For these reasons, as a rule the exercise of personal jurisdiction over a defendant based on his voluntary presence in the forum will satisfy the requirements of due process.

In this case, it is undisputed that petitioner was served with process while voluntarily and knowingly in the State of California. I therefore concur in the judgment.

A difficult problem arises for the plaintiff when the defendant is neither a resident of nor physically present within the state where he or she is to be sued. For many years, the courts adhered to the position that service could be accomplished only by personally serving the nonresident defendant while that person was physically within the borders of the state.

International Shoe Co. v. State of Washington, recognizes the power of the state, in civil suits, to serve a summons and complaint beyond the physical borders of the state. It should be noted that the discussion here applies only to *civil*, as opposed to criminal, suits. This case is of great importance because it permitted the state of Washington to obtain in personam jurisdiction over the International Shoe Company even though the company asserted that it never was physically present in the state. Note that the Supreme Court declares that in personam jurisdiction may, under certain circumstances, be obtained over a person or company not physically present within the borders of the state.

International Shoe Co. v. State of Washington

United States Supreme Court
326 U.S. 310 (1945)

This case deals with a dispute between International Shoe Company and the state of Washington. Though International Shoe's principal place of business was in St. Louis, it conducted business in other states. It was engaged in the manufacture and sale of shoes. International Shoe, the appellant in this case, had no office in Washington, made no contracts there, and maintained no merchandise there. From 1937 to 1940, it employed eleven to thirteen salesmen whose principal activities were confined to the state of Washington. The salesmen exhibited samples and solicited orders in Washington and transmitted the orders to St. Louis for acceptance or rejection.

The state of Washington brought suit against International Shoe for payments it felt International Shoe owed the Washington unemployment compensation fund. In this case, notice of the assessment for the years of 1937 to 1940 was personally served upon a salesman in Washington, and a copy of the notice was mailed by registered mail to International Shoe's home office in St. Louis. International Shoe challenged the power of the courts in Washington to force it to go to Washington to defend this suit. International Shoe claimed that forcing it to defend the suit in Washington would violate the Due Process Clause of the Fourteenth Amendment.

Chief Justice Stone

Appellant insists that its activities within the state were not sufficient to manifest its "presence" there and that in its absence the state courts were without jurisdiction, that consequently it was a denial of due process for the state to subject appellant to suit.

Historically the jurisdiction of courts to render judgment in personam is grounded on their de facto power over the defendant's person. Hence his presence within the territorial jurisdiction of a court was prerequisite to its rendition of a judgment personally binding him. But now due process requires only that in order to subject a defendant to a judgment in personam, if he be not present within the territory of the forum, he have certain minimum contacts with it such that the maintenance of the suit does not offend "traditional notions of fair play and substantial justice."

Since the corporate personality is a fiction it is clear that unlike an individual its "presence" without, as well as within, the state of its origin can be manifested only by activities carried on in its behalf by those who are authorized to act for it.

"Presence" in the state in this sense has never been doubted when the activities of the corporation there have not only been continuous and systematic, but also give rise to the liabilities sued on, even though no consent to be sued or authorization to an agent to accept service of process has been given. Conversely it has been generally recognized that the casual presence of the corporate agent or even his conduct of single or isolated items of activities in a state in the corporation's behalf are not enough to subject it to suit on causes of action unconnected with the activities there. To require the corporation in such circumstances to defend the suit away from its home or other jurisdiction where it carries on more substantial activities has been thought to lay too great and unreasonable a burden on the corporation to comport with due process.

Whether due process is satisfied must depend upon the quality and nature of the activity in relation to the fair and orderly administration of the laws which it was the purpose of the due process clause to ensure. That clause does not contemplate that a state may make binding a judgment in personam against an individual or corporate defendant with which the state has no contacts, ties, or relations.

The activities carried on in behalf of appellant in the State of Washington were neither irregular nor casual. They were systematic and continuous throughout the years in question. They resulted in a large volume of interstate business, in the course of which appellant received the benefits and protection of the laws of the state, including the right to resort to the courts for the enforcement of its rights. The obligation which is here sued upon arose out of those very activities. It is evident that these operations establish sufficient contacts or ties with the state of the forum to make it reasonable and just according to our traditional conception of fair play and substantial justice to permit the state to enforce the obligations which appellant has incurred there. Hence we cannot say that the maintenance of the present suit in the State of Washington involves an unreasonable or undue procedure.

We are likewise unable to conclude that the service of the process within the state upon an agent whose activities establish appellant's "presence" there was not sufficient notice of the suit, or that the suit was so unrelated to those activities as to make the agent an inappropriate vehicle for communicating the notice. It is enough that appellant has established such contacts with the state that the particular form of substituted service adopted there gives reasonable assurance that the notice will be actual. Nor can we say that the mailing of the notice of suit to appellant by registered mail at its home office was not reasonably calculated to apprise appellant of the suit.

Appellant having rendered itself amenable to suit upon obligations arising out of the activities of its salesmen in Washington, the state may maintain the present suit in personam to collect the tax laid upon the exercise of the privilege of employing appellant's salesmen within the state. For Washington has made one of those activities, which taken together establish appellant's "presence" there for purposes of suit, the taxable event by which the state brings appellant within the reach of its taxing power. The state thus has constitutional power to lay the tax and to subject appellant to a suit to recover it. The activities which establish its "presence" subject it alike to taxation by the state and to suit to recover the tax.

As a result of the decision in the *International Shoe Co.* case, states wanted their courts to be able to hear certain types of cases. All states adopted statutes that permit their courts to obtain jurisdiction over nonresident individuals and businesses. These statutes are commonly called *long arm statutes,* and they permit a plaintiff to obtain service of the summons and complaint beyond the physical borders of the state. However, a defendant still may not be required to appear in court in another state if the defendant did not have some minimal contact(s) with the state in question.

Once again, refer to the earlier example involving Laura Meyer and Best Cellular Phones. Best Cellular Phones never had a physical presence within the state of Florida. Did Best Cellular Phones have some minimum contact with the state of Florida so that maintenance of the suit in the state of Florida would not offend traditional notions of fair play and justice? No. Under the facts that were stated, Best Cellular Phones operates only in Denver, Colorado. It had no contacts whatsoever with the state of Florida. Under these circumstances, it would clearly violate the Due Process Clause to force Best Cellular Phones to defend itself in the state court in Florida. If Laura Meyer wants to file suit against Best Cellular Phones, she will probably have to file suit in Denver, Colorado.

When a person wants to file suit against a nonresident who is beyond the physical borders of the state, assuming that the defendant is one over whom the long arm statute would confer jurisdiction, the typical procedure is to file the lawsuit in a state court, sending a copy of the complaint and a summons to the Secretary of State. The Secretary of State then sends this information to the defendant by registered mail. Suppose that Alex, a resident of Montana, collides with Heather in Montana. After the accident, Heather returns to her home in Virginia. If Alex wants to file suit in Montana, he can no longer physically serve the complaint and summons on Heather while she is physically present in Montana. Alex must turn to Montana's long arm statute which will permit him to file suit in Montana and the complaint and summons will be forwarded to Heather in Virginia. The courts will rule that having an automobile accident while in Montana constitutes a minimum contact with the state of Montana so that forcing Heather to return to Montana to defend this suit will not offend traditional notions of fair play and justice.

The International Perspective, "In Which Country Can Suit Be Filed?", discusses how plaintiffs may literally shop around the world for the best forum in which to present their cases.

In Which Country Can Suit Be Filed?

Companies that engage in business throughout the world run the risk that plaintiffs may file suit against them in the country with the law most favorably suited to the plaintiff. In other words, there may be a number of courts throughout the world that have jurisdiction over the same suit—the power to hear and decide a case. For example, the former Prime Minister of Greece, Andreas Papandreou, sued *Time* magazine regarding an article that appeared in *Time's* European edition that tied him to a $200 million bank scandal. Rather than suing in the United States or Greece, Papandreou chose to file in England. English libel law was more favorable to Papandreou than American libel law or Greek law.

Source: "Moving Abroad," *American Bar Association Journal,* September 1989, page 38.

VENUE

Venue deals with the issue concerning which court within a given State is the proper one in which to file the suit. An attorney first needs to make the determination that a suit can be brought in a particular state, then the attorney must examine the state's venue statute to determine where in the state suit may be filed. States generally have courts in each county, except in thinly populated sections of the state. Where this occurs, a state court may be designated for several adjoining counties.

Consider the automobile accident previously mentioned between Alex, the resident of Montana, and Heather, the resident of Virginia. It was concluded that because the accident took place within the borders of Montana, Heather may be compelled to return to Montana to defend a suit brought against her by Alex. Although Alex may file suit against Heather in Montana, he cannot file suit in just any place in the state. For example, Montana might permit suit to be brought: in any county in which the defendant resides; or in any county in which the plaintiff resides if the defendant is served therein; or in the county in which the cause of action arose. Suppose that Alex lives in Great Falls, Montana, and the accident took place in Helena. Suit may therefore be filed by Alex in the county in which Great Falls is located *if* he serves Heather with the summons and complaint while she is in that county—a very unlikely event since she lives in Virginia. Therefore, it is probable that Alex will file suit in the county in which the accident took place—that is, whatever county contains the city of Helena, Montana.

Structure of the Court System

A very general description of the court systems in the United States will provide a foundation for understanding how courts operate. This discussion will describe courts from two different perspectives: first by their jurisdiction (federal or state courts), and second by their function (trial or appellate courts).

THE FEDERAL AND STATE SYSTEMS

Two jurisdictional groups of courts exist in this country: federal courts and state courts. There is one federal court system in the United States, while each state (and the District of Columbia) has its own court system. Discussion of judges, courts, or judicial lawmaking in fact requires generalization about many different and separate court systems.

■ *Federal District Courts*

The federal court system has three major levels of courts (see Figure 2.1). The first level is the federal district courts. Trial courts of the federal system fall in this level. In these courts, juries are impaneled, witnesses are heard, and verdicts are rendered. Federal district courts are generally confined to all or part of one state. For example, two federal districts exist in the state of Indiana: the northern federal district and the southern federal district. Delaware has one federal district while California has four. In addition to the district courts at the trial level of the federal system, some specialized federal courts also exist that are designed to hear cases arising under a certain major area of law. For example, federal bankruptcy courts hear cases arising under bankruptcy law. The federal tax court is empowered to hear cases concerning federal taxation. If a taxpayer disputes the amount of tax the IRS claims is due, the taxpayer may appeal through the IRS and then seek

■ **FIGURE 2.1**   **The Federal Judicial System**

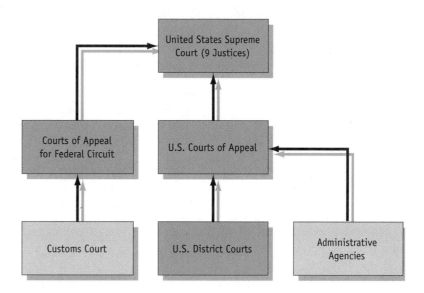

relief in the tax court. Alternatively, the taxpayer may pay the amount in dispute and pursue relief through the federal district court.

Federal courts are limited in the types of disputes they can decide. Article III, Section 2 of the United States Constitution states: "The Judicial Power shall extend to all cases . . . arising under this Constitution, the laws of the United States, and Treaties made . . . under their authority." The Constitution thus gives the federal courts the power to hear cases involving a **federal question**—that is, cases arising at least in part under the United States Constitution, a treaty, or a federal law. If a case deals with a right created by a law adopted by Congress, the federal courts possess the power to hear the dispute. Likewise, a person who alleges that his or her constitutional rights have been violated may ordinarily sue in federal court as well.

In Article III, Section 2, the Constitution also grants the federal courts jurisdiction over what would ordinarily be a State case if there is *diversity of citizenship.* If the plaintiff or defendant are citizens of different states and the amount in controversy being disputed is more than $50,000 then the case may also be heard in federal court. Referring back to the example involving Alex and Heather, note that Heather is a resident of Virginia and Alex is a resident of Montana. If Alex is requesting more than $50,000 he may file suit either in state court in Montana or in federal district court in Montana.

■ *Federal Courts of Appeal*

Within the federal court system, a hierarchy of courts exists—that is, certain courts have control over other courts. The federal district courts are grouped geographically in circuits. For example, the Seventh Circuit contains the federal district courts in Indiana, Illinois, and Wisconsin. The Second Circuit contains the federal district courts in New York, Vermont, and Connecticut. Thirteen federal judicial circuits exist in the United States; eleven contain the district courts from various states. A separate circuit exists for Washington, D.C. A court of appeals exists for the Federal Circuit and each circuit has one court of appeals (see Figure 2.2). The Seventh Circuit Court of Appeals is located in Chicago. The Second Circuit Court of Appeals is located in New York City. A court of appeals is an appellate court, and it does not hear witnesses or preside over trials. Its function is to decide questions that are appealed to it by any party who is dissatisfied with the decision of a district court.

The ruling of a court of appeals is binding **precedent** for all of the federal district courts within that circuit. If another similar case arises in one of the district courts, a prior decision of the court of appeals on the relevant point of law is binding. However, a decision of a court of appeals is not binding outside its circuit.

Suppose that the Ninth Circuit, in considering a labor dispute between a labor union and a company, Magna Corporation, rules that the union may distribute union literature in the Magna Corporation parking lot. The practical effect of a decision suggests that unions in any state in the Ninth Circuit—which includes California, Nevada, Arizona, Alaska, Hawaii, Oregon, Washington, Idaho, or Montana—have the right to distribute union literature in company

■ **FIGURE 2.2 The Thirteen Federal Judicial Circuit Courts**

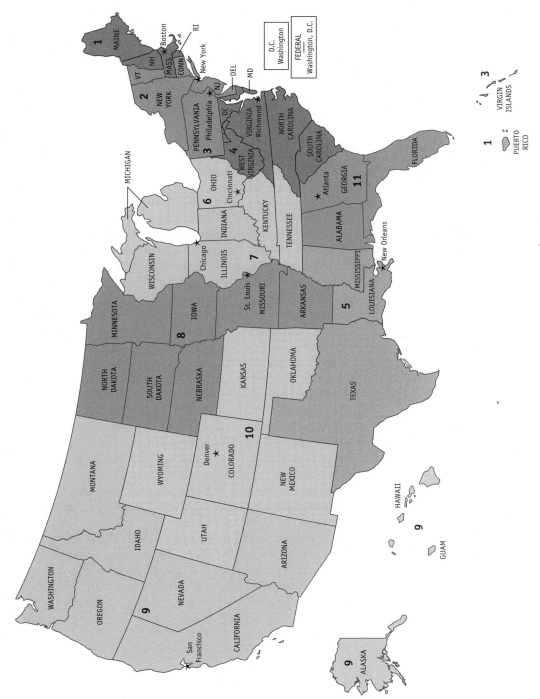

parking lots. However, a decision of a court of appeals is not binding outside the circuit. Suppose that the same issue arises in the Fifth Circuit but this time between another union and the International Corporation. The Fifth Circuit Court of Appeals may place a higher value on the property rights of companies and, therefore, could rule in the opposite manner as the Ninth Circuit. It may hold that the union does not have a right to distribute union literature in company parking lots. In this situation, a different rule exists in the Ninth Circuit and the Fifth Circuit. The Supreme Court often hears cases like this in which the appellate courts disagree on the law. It then resolves the conflict and announces a uniform rule that applies throughout the United States.

■ The Supreme Court

The highest court in the federal court hierarchy is the United States Supreme Court, which is an appellate court. Its work consists of reviewing the work of lower courts to determine if the law is being interpreted and applied correctly. It is the highest court to which an appeal may be taken. The Supreme Court is located in Washington, D.C., and has nine judges—called justices—who, together, decide its cases.

Appeals may be taken to the United States Supreme Court from a number of sources. Typically, a party who lost a case in a federal circuit court of appeals then asks the Supreme Court to review the decision of the court of appeals. It is possible for cases to come to the United States Supreme Court from courts other than the federal circuit court of appeals. For example, some final decisions of state supreme courts may be appealed to the United States Supreme Court. However, the case must involve some federal question. Even though the United States Supreme Court is the highest court in the land, the Constitution restricts the types of cases it is permitted to review. Suppose that a case is tried in a state court in Oregon and is thereafter reviewed by the Oregon Supreme Court. The Oregon Supreme Court then ruled that the manner in which a jury was selected in the case violated the Due Process Clause of the United States Constitution (the Due Process Clause is discussed in Chapter 6). Because the case involves a federal issue—that is, the meaning of the Due Process Clause in the United States Constitution—the United States Supreme Court could review the decision of the Oregon Supreme Court.

At one time the law obligated the United States Supreme Court to hear certain types of cases. Today, all people wishing for the Court to hear their appeals must apply for a *writ of certiorari*—the Court issues this writ if it wishes to hear a case. Whether the Court grants a writ of certiorari is entirely up to the discretion of the nine justices on the Court.

■ State Courts

The federal court system is complemented by the judicial systems of each of the states. These state court systems may differ, making a single, complete description of their structure impractical. Some states do not have an intermediate court of appeals. Those who object to a decision reached at trial appeal directly to the state supreme court.

Some states, especially those with large cities, have different divisions of trial level courts. There may be a criminal division that handles the trial of criminal cases, or a probate division that handles matters dealing with wills and estates, or a family law division that handles divorce and related matters. Furthermore, many states have special courts at a level lower than that of the trial court. These courts are generally limited to very minor disputes, such as minor traffic offenses or disputes involving only a few hundred dollars. Often these courts act more like informal arbitrators, with more relaxed rules of evidence and no jury trials. In fact, in some of these courts the appearance of lawyers for the parties is prohibited. A party who wants to appeal from such a lower level court usually may obtain a *trial de novo* (a total retrial) in the regular trial courts of that state. Figure 2.3 illustrates a typical state court system. Some states have more courts, but this figure is similar to that of most states.

The organization of the courts within a state is very similar to the federal court organization. Trials take place in the trial courts. Decisions of trial courts may be appealed to the state's court of appeals and from there to the highest court in the state—the state's supreme court. Generally, a decision of a state supreme court is final; however, as noted in the prior section on the United States Supreme Court, decisions of state supreme courts may sometimes be reviewed by the United States Supreme Court.

■ **FIGURE 2.3 Typical State Court System**

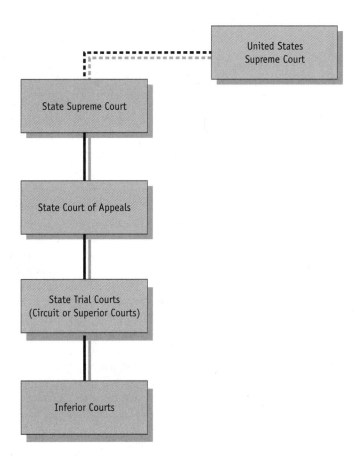

TRIAL AND APPELLATE COURTS

In the previous section, courts were described by their jurisdiction—as state or federal courts. Courts may also be described by function—as trial or appellate courts. Although procedures in one jurisdiction's trial court or appellate court may differ from those in another, the basic function of the courts would be similar.

■ Trial Courts

The *trial court* is the first stage at which the judicial system evaluates a dispute. This court listens to the evidence and renders a verdict or judgment based on that evidence. Trials may be heard by a jury or only by a judge.

The following example illustrates what happens at a typical trial. Mega Builders, a building contractor, agreed to build a five-story office building for the state of South Carolina. Mega Builders hired Acme Electrical Company to do the wiring for this project. After the state workers moved into the building, the building caught fire. The state fire marshall identified the source of the fire as faulty wiring in the building.

The state of South Carolina then filed suit against Mega Builders and Acme Electrical. At trial, the state fire marshall, as well as other experts called by the state, testified under oath as to the source of the fire. Acme Electrical called its own expert, a consultant on electrical wiring, who also testified under oath. Exhibits were shown at the trial. The trial court will determine the facts of the case and will apply the relevant law to these facts, thus resulting in a verdict.

It takes an enormous amount of time, money, and energy to try a case. Most cases that are filed do not even make it to trial. In light of the time, money, and energy considerations, substantial incentives prompt the parties to settle a dispute out of court, rather than going to trial.

■ Appellate Courts

Sometimes a litigant wants to have another judicial review after the trial stage, usually because that party was dissatisfied with the verdict. The party may then file an appeal with the **appellate court** designated to hear such an appeal. An appellate court does not conduct a new trial. It hears no direct evidence in the case. Instead the appellate court reviews the entire record of the case in order to determine whether any errors were made during the trial. The record includes copies of all the pleadings and documents filed in the case, all the exhibits entered as evidence in the case, and a transcript of all the testimony during the trial itself. Both parties in the case also file **briefs.** The briefs are written arguments to the court concerning the points the parties want the court to consider. The party seeking the appellate review (called the **appellant**) will point out the errors in the application of law made by the trial judge and argue that the verdict should be overturned because of these errors. The opposing party (called the **appellee**) will usually argue that no errors were made at trial or that they were minor errors that would have no effect on the outcome of the case. The appellee will argue that the appellate court should simply affirm the decision reached at trial.

In addition to the briefs, sometimes the parties present an oral argument to the court. Appellate oral argument does not involve the questioning of witnesses or the presentation of evidence. Instead, the attorneys are given a certain period of time to argue their position before the court. Frequently, the appellate court justices will interrupt the attorney to ask questions concerning the case, the applicable law, and the attorney's basic argument. Later, the appellate court will render a decision with an opinion discussing the reasons for its decision. These opinions are frequently published and are available in all law libraries. Sometimes a justice may agree with the appellate court's decision but disagree with the reasoning of the court. That justice may then file a separate opinion in the case, called a **concurring opinion.** However, appellate court justices do not always agree concerning the outcome of a particular case. In that event, a separate opinion, called a **dissenting opinion,** may be filed outlining the reasons for the disagreement.

An appellate court's role is considered to be the correction of errors of law made by the trial court judge, not the making of factual determinations. These errors of law may involve, for example, various rulings made by the judge concerning evidence during the course of the case, or they may involve the judge's instructions on the law to the jury.

Personnel in the Judicial System

The judicial system is made up of a variety of different people, each of whom has a role to play in the administration of justice. Two of the most important members of the judicial system—the judge and the lawyer—are the focus of this section.

THE JUDGE

Several different types of judges exist: state court and federal court judges, judges who handle trials, and judges who handle appeals. Some judges hear only one type of legal matter. For example, tax court judges decide only questions dealing with federal taxation, and in some states criminal court judges hear only criminal cases. Although differences exist among the types of work judges do, there are enough similarities to observe some major characteristics of the judiciary.

■ *Function of a Judge in General*

A trial judge must hear evidence as presented by all of the parties in a case. The trial judge determines what evidence is credible and based on what is regarded as credible evidence, the judge then determines the facts of the case (unless a jury is used). The judge also decides the law that applies to a given case.

Consider the Thought Problem, "Judge Criticizes Tobacco Industry," concerning some preliminary matters dealing with a case filed by

Peter Rossi. Rossi filed suit contending that the cigarettes he smoked caused his lung cancer. After filing this suit, Rossi subsequently died. This case had not yet gone to trial.

thought problem

Judge Criticizes Tobacco Industry

Judge H. Lee Sarokin was asked by the lawyers representing Peter Rossi, the plaintiff, to order the defendants to disclose certain documents to the plaintiff. The defendants claimed that the law did not require them to disclose this information. In making a ruling that this information must be disclosed, Judge Sarokin wrote: "Despite some rising pretenders, the tobacco industry may be the king of concealment and disinformation." He also wrote: "All too often in the choice between the physical health of consumers and the financial well-being of business, concealment is chosen over disclosure, sales over safety, and money over morality."

If Judge Sarokin is expected to make a decision concerning what the facts of this case are, why is his statement problematic?

Source: Andrea Sachs, "Judge Forced Off Tobacco Suit," *American Bar Association Journal,* November 1992, page 16.

▪ Judicial Activism

Judicial decision making often involves reviewing the activities of other branches of government. Historically, courts would either find the activity inconsistent with the United States Constitution (unconstitutional) or uphold the action. In effect, the decision would be a yes-or-no type of judgment. The court would use its reviewing power to set limits concerning what other branches of government could do. Today, however, judges frequently find themselves going well beyond merely setting limits on the activities of other units of government. Judges today may require that certain specific action be taken by the government in order to cure a constitutionally defective practice. For example, a lawsuit may be brought by inmates of a prison contending that the conditions of the prison are so poor as to violate their constitutional rights. A court, in finding that the prison indeed violates prisoner rights, may fashion a remedy that involves the court in day-to-day prison decisions.

▪ Judicial Restraint

Judges who believe in judicial restraint think that the primary function of a judge is to interpret the law. They believe that the drafters of the United States Constitution divided power in the United States between the three branches of government in order to give the executive branch of government the power to enforce the law, the legislative branch of government the power to make the law, and the judicial branch of government the power to interpret the law. Such judges believe in adhering to precedent, nor do they believe that it is the role of the judicial branch of government to make social policy and law. Consequently, it is unlikely that a judge who believes in judicial restraint would think that the courts should take over the day-to-day administration of a prison.

In *Kreimer v. Bureau of Police,* the court considers the question of whether or not a library may eject and ban a homeless person from its premises. Is the opinion an example of judicial restraint or judicial activism?

Kreimer v. Bureau of Police

United States District Court for the District of New Jersey
765 F. Supp. 181; 1991 U.S. Dist. LEXIS 7112 (1991)

Richard R. Kreimer is a homeless person. He was ejected from the Joint Free Public Library of Morristown, New Jersey, and subsequently excluded from the library pursuant to a policy adopted by the library that allowed the library staff to ask a person to leave who annoys another person or whose personal hygiene is so offensive to others as to constitute a nuisance. The court examined the policy of the library and enjoined its enforcement because the policy, according to the court, violated the United States Constitution.

H. Lee Sarokin, Judge

Society has survived not banning books which it finds offensive from its libraries; it will survive not banning persons whom it likewise finds offensive from its libraries. The greatness of our country lies in tolerating speech with which we do not agree; that same toleration must extend to people, particularly where the cause of revulsion may be of our own making. If we wish to shield our eyes and noses from the homeless, we should revoke their condition, not their library cards.

The First Amendment to the United States Constitution provides: "Congress shall make no law . . . abridging the freedom of speech, or of the press, or of the right of the people peaceably to assemble, and to petition Government for a redress of grievances." The Amendment applies to the states under the Fourteenth Amendment.

In *Perry Education Assn. v. Perry Local Educators' Association* (1983), the Supreme Court developed a standard by which to examine regulations under the First Amendment. The Court delineated three types of fora: a traditional public forum, a designated or limited public forum, and a nonpublic forum.

Public libraries have traditionally functioned as a public forum for the communication of written ideas. Thus, a public library is not only a designated public forum, but also a "quintessential," "traditional" public forum whose accessibility affects the bedrock of our democratic system. A place where ideas are communicated freely through the written word is as integral to a democracy and to First Amendment rights as an available public space where citizens can communicate their ideas through the spoken word.

Government restrictions on access to a traditional public forum must reasonably serve a significant state interest, the restrictions must be narrowly tailored to serve that interest, and the government must leave open alternative channels of communication. Defendants' argument that the court should afford the policy a presumption of reasonableness and thus defer to the library board is entirely inconsistent with the applicable law.

The library policy in the instant case is not narrowly tailored to serve the stated significant government interest, nor does the policy leave open any alternative means of access to publicly provided reading materials for patrons who may be "denied the privilege of access to the library" under the policy.

Defendants assert that the library policy serves the significant government interest of fostering a quiet and orderly atmosphere in the library conducive to every patron's exercise of their constitutionally protected interest in receiving and reading written communications.

The Supreme Court has consistently recognized the necessity of regulations designed to secure a quiet and peaceful environment.

However, the Court has also consistently held that government must limit time, place, and manner restrictions of a public forum to prohibitions of activity which actually and materially interfere with the peaceful and orderly management of the public space. When subjected to heightened scrutiny, regulations not designed specifically to address disruptive activity are not "reasonable" time, place, and manner restrictions, since they are not responsive to the government's stated purpose of curtailing disruptions, nor are they "narrowly tailored" to serve that purpose.

The library patron policy at issue in this case does not limit itself to prohibitions of actual library disturbance. Under the policy library patrons are excluded from the facility if their behavior "annoys" another person or if their "bodily hygiene is so offensive as to constitute a nuisance to other persons." The policy does not condition exclusion upon an actual or imminent disruption or disturbance as a result of such behavior or hygiene, and hence, the policy does not reasonably effectuate its stated goal of preserving the good order of the library.

According to paragraph 1 of the policy, patrons who sit quietly and peacefully in the library but who are not actively "using library materials shall be asked to leave the building." This restriction has no relation to the library's stated purpose of preserving the peace and quiet of the facility for the benefit of all patrons. Thus, the court concludes the library policy is not a reasonable time, place, or manner restriction which serves the state's significant interest in maintaining the library atmosphere at a level conducive to all patrons' use of the facility.

Expansive judicial decisions—decisions in whose implementation the court has a part—are the source of the current criticism of judges and courts as being too activist. The use of such decisions in constitutional disputes is a major extension of judicial decisions into areas that had usually called for political decisions: decisions based on trade-offs made by the other branches of government. Many people contend that a judge has no expertise in making specific decisions concerning the operation of a prison system or the structure and operation of a school system. Another frequent complaint is that such decisions are most often made by federal court judges who are appointed for life with no direct accountability to the general public who would be affected by their decisions. Traditional court action, such as ordering remedies like specific performance, merely affected parties to the lawsuit. Many of the activist decisions today, however, affect the general public, since tax money often must either be raised or shifted to pay for the court-imposed remedy. Yet the taxpayers have no way to influence that spending decision, since it was mandated by a court in response to a lawsuit.

Other people claim that such judicial activity is necessary in today's complex legal world. Government does many more things for (and to) people today than in the past. Furthermore, today more individual rights are recognized in the law, and people are demanding that those rights be protected. Equal rights under law for people irrespective of race, sex, national origin, or a number of other factors is a very recent development in the law. Segregated public schools were declared unconstitutional barely forty years ago. In addition, certain groups, such as prisoners, welfare recipients, and mental patients, have been found to have basic rights in relation to government activity aimed at them. For a court to say no to government action today may not be enough, especially when the problem is government inaction. When a prison system is so underfunded as to cause unreasonable overcrowding or when school boards do not act to dismantle the vestiges of a once racially segregated school system, a more intrusive remedy may be needed to correct the wrong. Judges may require government to act to fulfill the minimum requirements set out by a statute or by the United States Constitution. Lack of certain government activity may be just as harmful to individual rights as too intrusive of an activity. However, each type of problem may require a different type of judicial solution.

One effect of such judicial activism is, in a sense, to shift some very difficult political decisions from the legislature, where the voters have an influence, to the judiciary (especially the federal courts), where the judges are not accountable to the electorate. For example, politicians may call for harsher penalties and longer jail terms for a wide variety of criminal offenders. However, the same politicians may refrain from making the extremely tough budgetary decision to go along with their anticrime position—namely, funding for more prison facilities to house the additional inmates. This would require either additional taxes or a switch of funds from an already existing program. Neither of these alternatives would be popular. So the politicians may simply enact popular, strict criminal laws that soon begin to increase the prison population. After a time, conditions become so crowded that a lawsuit is brought by a prisoner, and a judge is asked to solve an essentially political question. The only way to solve the problem is to require certain government action, either building additional facilities or releasing prisoners before they have finished serving their time. The judge then catches the political heat. One may not agree with certain activist judicial decisions, but one should realize that such decisions are a product of the increasing role of government in our lives coupled with the greater recognition of individual rights. The legal and political systems have become very complex, often leading to litigation involving not only disputes between parties but also grievances against entire institutions.

As far back as 1968 when Richard Nixon ran for President of the United States and won the race, the promise was made during his election campaign that he would appoint people to the United States Supreme Court who believed in judicial restraint. While most of the justices on the Court in the 1950s and 1960s were activists, President Nixon and his predecessors had a great impact on the overall judicial philosophy of the United States Supreme Court. Figure 2.4 lists the names of the Supreme Court members as of 1997 and roughly where they fit in terms of activist or judicial restraint philosophy.

As Figure 2.4 illustrates, at least four of the current members of the United States Supreme Court can definitely be categorized as falling in the judicial restraint category. As an example of what it means to believe in judicial restraint, consider the words of Justice Sandra Day O'Connor: "I believe in the exercise of judicial restraint. . . . I would not feel free as a judge to . . . expand or restrict a particular statute to reflect my own views of what the goals of sound public policy should

Judicial Restraint	Judicial Activism
Chief Justice William Rehnquist	Justice David Souter
Justice Antonin Scalia	Justice Ruth Bader Ginsburg
Justice Clarence Thomas	Justice John Paul Stevens
Justice Sandra Day O'Connor	Justice Stephen Breyer
Justice Anthony Kennedy	

be . . . I don't believe it is the function of the judiciary to step in and change the law because the times have changed . . . or the social mores have changed."[1]

No one on the Court could really be considered an activist today, but some of the justices could probably be said to have activist leanings at times. The most recent appointees to the Court are Justices Ginsburg and Breyer, both of whom were appointed by President Clinton.

■ *Selection of Judges*

The two general methods of selecting judges are: the election of candidates and the appointment of candidates.

Federal judges are appointed by the President with the advice and consent of the Senate, as provided in the United States Constitution. They serve for life and can be removed from office only by impeachment by the Senate—a power seldom used in the history of this country.

Some states elect their judges in the same manner as any other official. The political parties nominate candidates to fill the judicial positions. The judge is then chosen by the voters in the general election. Some people contend that election of judges is consistent with our form of government in that it ensures that the judicial branch will be held accountable to and be a reflection of the demands of the citizens. Popular control of judges may be seen as highly desirable. Since judges, like all public officials, exercise a great deal of power and control, the people should have a part in selecting the individuals who hold judgeships.

However, others argue that the election of judges risks placing individuals on the bench who are not especially qualified. Candidates for judgeships may be selected in part on the basis of their politics and party loyalty rather than on their judicial qualifications. This political litmus test may be more important than objective criteria in selecting the candidates for the job.

Furthermore, how are voters to determine the most suitable candidates for the judgeships? Much of a judge's work involves only a few members of a community and is not especially newsworthy. Studies have suggested that voters often have little knowledge about candidates for judgeships. If this is so, the argument that the election process makes judges accountable to the public is weakened. Instead, it makes judges accountable to the political party that nominates them. Voters may be expected to show an interest in a judicial election if the candidate for election were involved in a highly controversial matter. The result may be that a judge exercises less independent decision making. The very nature of politics, with campaign contributions, campaign slogans, and advertising, raises problems about the independence of the various judicial candidates.

Yet these elected judges do have a limited term in office and may be removed by the voters. Political parties may use politics as a selection factor, yet the political leaders should be interested in competent candidates, since each candidate reflects and has an effect on the party ticket as a whole. Mistakes made in the election of judges are more easily corrected than mistakes made in the appointment process.

However, the problems inherent in the election of judges, as well as the appearance of political influence on judicial candidates, have led a number of states to move away from the election of judges toward an appointive system, often called the **Missouri plan.** The Missouri plan involves a governor-appointed panel, including a judge, lawyers, and lay members, that recommends suitable candidates for judicial appointment by the governor. Periodically, the appointed judges' names appear on a ballot where voters may vote on whether or not to retain the judges for an additional term. This is not a contest between candidates, but a yes-or-no decision by the voters. The plan removes political parties from the process yet retains periodic voter approval. However, given the general lack of voter knowledge about judges, the removal of poor judges from the bench by this process is unlikely.

Although proponents of this plan contend that it removes the selection of judges from the harmful and partisan effects of the political arena, others argue that it merely changes the type of politics involved. Instead of traditional political party influence, those who seek judgeships are subject to private political infighting between the organized bar and the governor. The governor could be expected to appoint members of the nominating panel and to select judges with compatible political views. Therefore, a judicial candidate may seek political favor from powerful people in the state in order to be nominated by the panel or selected by the governor. It is as if political activity by candidates for a judicial post somehow becomes untainted when it occurs outside of the traditional political system. Another major criticism of the Missouri plan is that the judges who are selected are not necessarily representative of the community at large. Some people contend that the make-up of the selection committees does not reflect the varied interests of the public in general. A political party must develop sensitivity to the community in order to have its members elected to office, but no such pressures exist on the selection committee. The selected judges may be better in terms of objective judicial criteria; however, they may not reflect the make-up of the community.

■ *Accountability of Judges*

The discussion of judges thus far raises two conflicting points—a judge should be independent of influence but at the same time should be somehow accountable to the public; and independence of the judiciary is important in ensuring that judges make decisions based on the law and the facts in dispute.

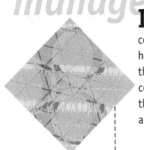

managerial perspective

Improper Remarks by a Judge

In open court during a hearing on a settlement agreement, before trial or any evidentiary hearing, Federal District Court Judge Miles W. Lord made the following remarks to the firm's president, vice president, and general counsel, who were present in court that day. In the agreement, the A. H. Robins Company, the manufacturer of the Dalkon Shield intrauterine contraceptive device, agreed to pay $4.6 million in a products liability suit. Excerpts of his remarks follow:

> Today as you sit here attempting once more to extricate yourselves from the legal consequences of your acts, none of you has faced up to the fact that more than nine thousand women claim they gave up part of their womanhood so that your company might prosper. . . .
>
> If one poor young man were, without authority or consent, to inflict such damage upon one woman, he would be jailed for a good portion of the rest of his life. Yet your company, without warning to women, invaded their bodies by the millions and caused them injuries by the thousands. And when the time came for these women to make their claims against your company, you attacked their characters. You inquired into their sexual practices and into the identity of their sex partners. You ruined families and reputations and careers in order to intimidate those who would raise their voices against you. You introduced issues that had no relationship to the fact that you had planted in the bodies of these women instruments of death, of mutilation, of disease.
>
> Mr. Robins, Mr. Forest, Dr. Lunsford: You have not been rehabilitated. Under your direction, your company has continued to allow women, tens of thousands of them, to wear this device—a deadly depth charge in their wombs, ready to explode at any time. . . . You have taken the bottom line as your guiding beacon and the low road as your route. That is corporate irresponsibility at its meanest. . . .
>
> What corporate officials could learn a lesson from this? The only lesson they might learn is that it pays to delay compensating victims and to intimidate, harass, and shame the injured parties.

The United States Court of Appeals for the Eighth Circuit criticized Judge Lord for his verbal reprimand of the Robins executives. It ruled he had deprived the officials of notice and an opportunity for a hearing.

Judges are not, however, completely independent. One important control on the independence of the judiciary is that of peer and community pressure. Judges want to do a competent job as measured by others. A competent job for a judge is not tied to *who wins* in a given suit. Instead, it is a combination of things that make up the notion of a good judge. Briefly, these things include skill in understanding and applying the law to a given set of facts, fairness and evenhandedness in decision making, and judicial temperament. Judges err, sometimes by making a simple mistake in applying the law. More often, as will be shown in later chapters, the law in question is subject to varied interpretations in a particular case. In these instances, courts of appeal will act to reverse the decision of a judge, showing in their opinion exactly where the judge erred.

In the Managerial Perspective, "Improper Remarks by a Judge," an example is provided showing a case in which the court of appeals felt that Judge Miles W. Lord erred in his handling of a case in front of him.

The power of an appellate court to reverse the decision of a judge because of the appearance of impropriety is illustrated by *Aetna Life Insurance Co. v. Lavoie et al.*

Aetna Life Insurance Co. v. Lavoie et al.

United States Supreme Court
106 S.Ct. 1580 (1986)

Aetna Life Insurance Co. refused to pay the full amount of a hospital bill. The insured brought suit in an Alabama state court for Aetna's alleged bad-faith refusal to pay a valid claim. The jury ruled for the insured. On appeal, the Alabama Supreme Court affirmed the jury verdict in an opinion written by Justice Embry. It was later learned that Justice Embry had two cases pending against insurance companies at the time he wrote the opinion in question, which alleged bad-faith failure to pay claims. Aetna filed a motion challenging Justice Embry's participation in the case. The Alabama Supreme Court denied this motion. Aetna appealed to the United States Supreme Court which ruled that Justice Embry should not have participated in the case.

Chief Justice Burger

It certainly violates the Fourteenth Amendment to subject a person's liberty to the judgment of a court the judge of which has a direct, personal, substantial, pecuniary interest in reaching a conclusion against him in his case.

More than thirty years ago Justice Black, speaking for the Court, reached a similar conclusion and recognized that under the Due Process Clause no judge "can be a judge in his own case or be permitted to try cases where he has an interest in the outcome."

Justice Embry's opinion for the Alabama Supreme Court had the clear and immediate effect of enhancing both the legal status and the settlement value of his own case. When Justice Embry made the judgment, he acted as a judge in his own case. His interest was direct, personal, substantial, and pecuniary.

We conclude that Justice Embry's participation in this case violated Aetna's due process rights. We make clear that we are not required to decide whether in fact Justice Embry was influenced, but only whether sitting on the case then before the Supreme Court of Alabama would offer a possible temptation to the average judge to lead him not to hold the balance nice, clear, and true. The Due Process Clause may sometimes bar trial by judges who have no actual bias and who would do their very best to weigh the scales of justice equally between contending parties. But to perform its high function in the best way, justice must satisfy the appearance of justice.

Because of Justice Embry's leading role in the decision under review, we conclude that the appearance of justice will best be served by vacating the decision and remanding for further proceedings.

LAWYERS

The next section will examine another important actor in the legal system—the attorney. The issue of the growth of the legal profession will first be considered. Secondly, the attorney–client privilege will be discussed. Finally, the question, "How can an attorney represent a guilty person?" will be examined.

■ *Growth of the Legal Profession*

In the 1970s and 1980s, a great number of students suddenly became interested in legal careers. To accommodate the exploding number of applicants to law schools, some universities expanded the size of classes while others created totally new law schools. It seemed like an inexhaustible demand for new law school graduates existed. In the last thirty years, the number of lawyers in the United States exploded.

The enormous bulge created by baby boomers joining the legal profession led to a lot of carping that the United States contains seventy percent of the world's lawyers. In fact, a great number of lawyers exist in the United States. The reality is, however, that many other countries graduate huge numbers of students trained in the law who provide legal advice to businesses and government, although they may not officially be designated as lawyers, as the International Perspective, "Number of Lawyers in Other Countries," illustrates.

Clearly, the United States graduates many attorneys; however, these figures support the argument that an overabundance of lawyers in the United States is not the case when comparing the number of people providing legal services in other countries around the world.

One should recognize that, unlike fifty years ago, the complexity of the law and the frequent changes in the law have created the need for specialized lawyers. While at one time the typical lawyer represented people in all kinds of legal problems, the tendency today is for lawyers to specialize in a field of law. For example, an attorney may engage in just tax law, or labor law, or employment law, and so forth.

INTERNATIONAL
PERSPECTIVE

Number of Lawyers in Other Countries

Japan permits only *bengoshi* to offer commercial legal services. One becomes a bengoshi by attending law school in Japan and then being admitted to the Judicial Research and Training Institute (JRTI). Of the more than thirty-five thousand law school graduates a year in Japan, only roughly 475 pass the JRTI entrance exam. All of those who are admitted to the JRTI graduate. One may naturally wonder: What happens to the other 34,500 law school graduates in Japan? Such people end up providing legal advice in government or in private companies. If one counts all of these *law providers* as lawyers, then Japan has a ratio of 31.71 lawyers per ten thousand people as contrasted with the United States which has roughly 28.45 lawyers per ten thousand people. This suggests that the United States really does not contain many more lawyers than the ratio for Japan shows.

Note the following ratios of law providers in various countries around the world:

Argentina	92.42
France	48.23
The Netherlands	40.99
Mexico	38.06
Switzerland	28.67
United States	*28.45*
Canada	18.43
United Kingdom	16.99
India	10.80
Singapore	6.44
Zimbabwe	2.67

Source: Ray August, "The Mythical Kingdom of Lawyers," *American Bar Association Journal,* September 1992, pages 72–74.

■ *Attorney–Client Privilege*

The attorney–client privilege provides that a client's confidential discussions with an attorney remain confidential. The purpose of the privilege is to encourage client disclosure of all the facts to the lawyer, even those harmful to the client. An attorney cannot adequately represent a client unless all the facts (both favorable and unfavorable) about the matter are known. The information is needed so the attorney may prepare the client's case.

Attorney–client privilege has existed for a long time in the law. Some writers date it to Roman time when advocates were barred from testifying against their clients. Other writers date it to the reign of Elizabeth I of England. At that time, the privilege was based not on the rationale of protection of client's interests but instead on the honor of the lawyer. Trial lawyers were considered gentlemen, and it was a point of honor with gentlemen to keep their confidences. Today, as already shown, the privilege belongs to the client and exists as a matter of law to further the goals of the adversary system rather than for the protection of the attorney's honor.

Of course, at times the existence of the privilege may cause an injustice to occur. A wrongdoer may be set free. A person who breaches a contract may not be held liable. The end result of the privilege is that evidence which may be central to the case may not be used in court if it is privileged information. A case, therefore, may proceed with incomplete information.

Suppose that Brooke Bonner is the President of Super Corporation. Super Corp. sells forty percent of the automobiles sold in the United States. Josef Hamilton is the President of Acme Corporation. Acme sells thirty-five percent of the automobiles sold in the United States. Over lunch one day in Detroit, Brooke and Josef conclude that their companies would make a lot more money if they stopped competing with each other. Their resolution conspired to fix the prices at which they sold their automobiles—a direct violation of antitrust laws.

The government was notified of the conspiracy and brought criminal charges against both Brooke and Josef. Both Brooke and Josef reveal the plot to their respective attorneys, but neither admit anything to the government. At trial, both refuse to testify. They are both acquitted. Because of the attorney–client privilege, their attorneys could not reveal what Brooke and Josef told them. Was justice served in this particular case? The truth was withheld from the court as a result of the attorney–client privilege. The possibility of this result must be balanced against the overall good that may result from the attorney–client privilege.

Clients, even with the existence of the privilege, are reluctant to confide in their attorneys. Often an important task of the attorneys is to gain the trust of the client in order to obtain full information. Few people are eager to confess behavior such as the fact that they conspired with other executives to fix the price of automobiles or that they intentionally discriminated against a prospective employee.

Clients, when discussing very personal and sometimes emotional facts, may try to rationalize their conduct. The privilege is a tool to reassure clients that no court will use their attorneys to bring evidence against them. The privilege, therefore, serves a crucial function in the administration of justice in our legal system. Without it, attorneys would have little hope of gaining the confidence or a truthful statement of the facts from their clients. Consequently, the adversary system would not work properly. The case would be argued and prepared on the basis of false or incomplete facts. (In the law, small factual differences often will cause a change in the way a case is handled by an attorney and perhaps even affect which legal rules are applicable.) The expected result is that clients will most likely not receive a fair trial. Injustice to clients and to the system that relies on the clash in the courtroom in the search for truth would result. The concept of attorney–client privilege is an ideal strongly protected by the courts, since it furthers the search for truth and justice through the operation of our adversary system.

■ *How Can an Attorney Represent a Guilty Person?*

One of the most persistent questions attorneys are asked, and one that troubles many people, is: "How can an attorney represent a guilty person?" A related question is: "How can an attorney, in good conscience, seek to have evidence thrown out of court, resulting in a criminal being set free to prey on other victims?"

This question assumes, of course, that the law itself is just. Would it be morally reprehensible for an attorney in New York in the 1840s to attempt to see that a slave who escaped from an Alabama plantation was not sent back to live the rest of his or her life in slavery? Would it be morally reprehensible for an attorney to represent a woman who illegally attempted to vote prior to the time women were granted suffrage? Consider the Ethical Perspective, "Does the Punishment Fit the Crime?", and ask yourself about the fairness of the punishments administered by the government of Singapore.

The inequity of the law has caused some attorneys throughout history and around the world to attempt to evade the consequences of the law. Even in the United States today, many attorneys regard some American laws as unjust and morally reprehensible. One cannot expect an attorney, representing a person he or she feels is guilty of violating a morally reprehensible law, to feel badly about representing a person guilty of violating such a law.

Attorneys also feel justified in representing a guilty person because their role in the adversary system is to zealously represent clients. The decision-making role rests with the judge or the jury and is not a part of the role given to the attorney in the judicial system.

Furthermore, one could make the argument that a difference exists between *legal* guilt and *moral* guilt. When discussing guilt the average person generally means that the person in question did the act. For example, did the corporation dump toxic waste into the city's water supply? If the corporation, in fact, dumped toxic waste into the city's water supply, the corporation is morally guilty.

However, the legal system's concept of guilt is much broader. In the legal system, guilt means that the government has proved its case against the defendant beyond a reasonable doubt and may punish the wrongdoer. Guilt used in this sense means more than just the simple question of whether or not the defendant did or did not commit the act in question.

ETHICAL
PERSPECTIVE

Does the Punishment Fit the Crime?

Michael Fay, an American teenager living in Singapore along with a group of other teenagers, vandalized fifty cars in Singapore by spray painting the vehicles. For this crime, Michael was sentenced to four months in prison, fined $2,200, and given six lashes with a cane on his buttocks. It should be observed that each stroke of the cane splits the skin and the scars last for a lifetime. Is this a fair penalty for the crime in question?

Nick Leeson was a derivatives trader employed by the 233-year-old British bank, the Barings Bank. While working at a branch office in Singapore, Leeson illegally ran up a loss on derivatives trading totalling more than $800 million. Leeson's derivatives trading losses were so great that the Barings Bank, a venerable British institution, collapsed.

Taking into consideration, firstly, that both of these offenses took place while Fay and Leeson were living in Singapore, and secondly, the sentence handed down to Fay, what would you suggest as the appropriate penalty to be imposed on Nick Leeson?

Nick Leeson was sentenced to six and a half years in prison and no lashes with a cane. Who caused more damage to the economy—Fay or Leeson?

A person, in fact, may have committed the act in question, but the government may not be able to gather enough evidence in order to establish that the accused committed the wrongful act. The burden of proving this fact is on the government. A person is presumed innocent unless the government is able to produce enough evidence to convince a judge or jury, beyond a reasonable doubt, that a crime was committed and the defendant was the person who committed the crime in question. For example, suppose that Mega Corporation, in fact, unlawfully dumped large amounts of mercury into the city's water supply. Mega Corporation is thus *morally* guilty of polluting the city's water supply. If the government brings charges against the corporation, however, the government must establish that an agent acting for Mega Corporation, in fact, dumped the mercury in the water. If no one working for Mega Corporation will make such an admission, and no witnesses exist, Mega Corporation probably will not be convicted. The corporation is legally *not guilty* of the crime of polluting the city's water supply, but at the same time it is morally guilty of that same act.

Summary

Before a court can entertain a suit, the judge needs to determine whether or not he or she has the power to hear the type of dispute involved in the case. This is referred to as a court having jurisdiction over a particular type of dispute (subject matter jurisdiction) or over the parties to the suit (in personam jurisdiction). The United States Supreme Court has ruled that state courts may obtain personal jurisdiction over people who are not physically present within the state. It is also necessary for a suit to be filed in a court in the *correct county*— a matter dealt with in state venue statutes.

In the United States, two court systems exist: a federal court system and a state court system. Trials in the federal system actually take place in federal district courts. In order to file a case in federal court, the case must involve a federal question, or it must involve diversity of citizenship and more than $50,000 must be in controversy. The federal courts of appeals, for the most part, merely review the actions of lower courts and federal administrative agencies. Decisions of a court of appeals are not binding outside of the circuit.

States have courts of limited jurisdiction that can handle only certain types of cases, while courts of general jurisdiction may hear any case that arises in the state. State trial courts, like federal district courts, hear evidence as presented through the testimony of witnesses. State appellate courts, like federal circuit courts of appeals, review the work of lower courts.

The United States Supreme Court reviews the work of appellate courts to determine if federal law was applied correctly to the cases handled in these lower courts. No trials take place in the United States Supreme Court. For the most part, the United States Supreme Court reviews the decisions of federal circuit courts of appeals; however, if a case involves a federal question, the Court may review the decision of a state supreme court.

Understanding the judicial system involves more than gaining an appreciation of its form. It also requires understanding the roles of the major participants in the system—the judge and the attorney. One of the important features of the judicial role is the balance between an independent judiciary and controls on the power that independence brings. Fair decision making is hampered by a judge who is unable to assess a matter free of influence. However, given the powers of a judge, a lack of controls could also cause harm to the administration of justice.

The role of the attorney is another important element of the judicial system. An attorney's task involves zealously guarding a client's interests within the policies and goals of the adversary system. Often, questions concerning the secrecy of client communications with counsel or the representation of a *guilty* client ignore the important functions of the legal system.

Review Questions

1. Define the following terms:
   a. Appellate court
   b. Attorney–client privilege
   c. In personam jurisdiction
   d. Missouri plan
   e. Trial court
   f. Venue

2. What are the major characteristics of the federal judicial system? Can federal courts hear any case that arises? What are the differences and similarities between the federal court system and a state court system?

3. What is the difference between a trial court and an appellate court?

4. Briefly describe the general functions of a judge. What would the effect be on the judicial system if the independence of the judiciary was greatly restricted?

5. In your opinion, what is the best manner for selecting a judge— by election or by appointment? Support your opinion.

6. What is meant by the term *attorney–client privilege?* What is it designed to accomplish?

7. Should an attorney represent a guilty person? What would the effect be on our legal system if attorneys did not represent people who actually committed criminal acts?

8. What is the purpose of the concepts of jurisdiction and venue in the operation of the civil litigation system? Describe problems that may arise if these concepts are removed from the process.

9. While trimming her lawn, Steffey was injured by the electric mower. She purchased it from a retail dealer near her home in Chicago, Illinois. The manufacturer of the mower had its principal place of business in Cincinnati, Ohio. The manufacturer attended trade shows around the country, and it solicited business in all of the states through its advertisements in various trade journals. It sold the

mower that injured Steffey to the dealer in Chicago. Steffey wishes to bring suit against the manufacturer in Illinois. The manufacturer argues that, in light of the fact that it could not be personally served in Illinois, the Illinois courts could not have jurisdiction over it. Who is correct?

10. Shack is a resident of Arizona. Morris is a resident of Oregon. A dispute arose between them, and Morris wants to file suit against Shack. Shack went to Oregon on a vacation. While in Oregon, he was served with a summons and petition. Shack thereafter returned to Arizona. Shack contends that the Oregon courts have no jurisdiction over him because his contacts with the state of Oregon were not continuous and systematic. Is Shack correct?

11. In order to correct the vestiges of unlawful segregation, Judge Clark ordered a number of improvements in the Kansas City Missouri School District. To enable the school district to fund its share of the cost of the desegregation plan, Judge Clark imposed an increase in the property tax levied by the Kansas City Missouri School District. Is this a lawful order? Is Judge Clark acting in accordance with the concept of judicial activism or judicial restraint?

12. The inmates at Cummins Prison Farm and the Tucker Intermediate Reformatory assert that there is a lack of housing, a lack of medical care, infliction of physical and mental brutality, and numerous other abuses of the prisoners. The Eighth Circuit Court of Appeals agreed with the prisoners and took over operation of the prison system. Is the decision in this case an example of activism or judicial restraint?

13. Miller revealed to her attorney, Padgett, in the course of Padgett's representation of her, that she had, in fact, violated antitrust laws. The government now wishes to call Padgett and force her to reveal what Miller told her. Can Padgett be forced to reveal what Miller said?

Note   [1]"When Woman Justice Took Witness Chair," *U.S. News and World Report,* September 21, 1981, page 13.

Chapter 3

CIVIL LITIGATION AND ALTERNATIVE DISPUTE RESOLUTION

A nytime people deal with others, disputes are likely to arise. People tend to handle typical day-to-day disputes themselves, but other, more serious conflicts often require more than just a conversation between two disputants.

The current legal system evolved over hundreds of years. Vestiges of formalities that evolved centuries ago make the legal system far more complex than some of the alternatives to the legal system that are discussed later in the chapter.

The first section of this chapter focuses on the process of *civil litigation*. Civil litigation encompasses all of the trial work in this legal system that does not involve the violation of a *criminal* law. Most areas of the law are affected by the civil litigation process—tort law, contract law, property law, and labor law, for example. The following material examines what happens to the typical business dispute starting with the outset of the conflict through the final resolution of the controversy by the legal system.

In the last decade or so, people in the United States have turned to alternative ways of resolving conflicts other than the process of trying a case in court. Many of these alternative dispute resolution procedures are cheaper, faster, and less formal than the government-operated court system. In the course of your life, you will undoubtedly become involved in a dispute that is resolved through some type of alternative dispute resolution procedure. These procedures are discussed later in this chapter.

Civil Litigation

THE DISPUTE

This part of the text examines the various stages of a typical business dispute as it works its way through the judicial systems operated by the government. Consider this typical business dispute: Suppose that Apex Printing produces commercially printed material for businesses throughout the Midwest. It operates out of a single plant located in Kansas City, Missouri. In the Spring of 1997, a major rainstorm caused the Missouri River to overflow its banks and flooded all of the factories in the West Bottoms—the area of Kansas City where the Apex Printing plant is located. The flood destroyed much of the work in progress, ruined many of the records of the business, and damaged most of its machinery.

When the officers of Apex Printing reviewed their insurance coverage, they discovered that their policy specifically excluded coverage resulting from damage due to floods. The insurance company took this precaution because of the close proximity of the Apex Printing plant to the Missouri River. The loss of the current work in progress damaged Apex's cash flow. It would take months to rebuild. Apex could not afford to rebuild, purchase new machinery, and keep its doors open all at the same time. After just a few months, Apex defaulted on a commercial loan held by the Commercial National Bank. When the bank stopped receiving payments on the loan, it called the officers of Apex into the bank to discuss this loan problem

■ **FIGURE 3.1** Steps in a Typical
Civil Lawsuit

1. Plaintiff serves the defendant with a summons and complaint.
2. Defendant files an answer to plaintiff's complaint.
3. Discovery stage of the lawsuit begins.
4. Jury is selected for trial.
5. Opening statements are made at the trial.
6. Evidence is presented at the trial.
7. Closing arguments are made at the trial.
8. Instructions are given to the jury.
9. Jury deliberates.
10. Jury renders a verdict.
11. Judge enters judgment.
12. Appeal is entered.

and to make a determination about the ability of Apex to resume operations. After a discussion with Apex, the bank officers felt insecure about the capacity of Apex to continue as a viable operation.

The various stages of this conflict will now be considered as it works its way through the judicial system. Note Figure 3.1 that lists the steps in a typical dispute from the filing of the petition to the appeal of the case.

Before discussing the first step—the filing of the complaint—one important consideration should be kept in mind with respect to every conflict—the statute of limitations.

■ *Statute of Limitations*

The law requires that an injured party file suit in a timely manner. Suppose that Blackstone Manufacturing agreed to deliver a hundred thousand bolts to Zenith Automobile Company on or before November 1, 1997. Blackstone failed to deliver the bolts as specified in the contract—which would be a breach of its contractual obligations. May Zenith wait until June 1, 2100, to file a suit against Blackstone? Obviously, waiting more than a century to file suit is unreasonable. If Zenith wishes to file suit, it must do so in a timely manner.

The time period in which suit must be filed is specified in a statute called the *statute of limitations*. The period in which a suit must be filed varies depending on the nature of the suit, the type of document to be filed, and the jurisdiction in which the case is brought. The typical statute of limitations for a contract dispute is five years from the date the cause of action arose. In the dispute between Blackstone Manufacturing and Zenith Automobile Company, therefore, Zenith must file suit against Blackstone within five years of the date in which the contract was breached. If Zenith waits more than five years to file suit, it will be barred from litigating the matter by the statute of limitations. If Zenith files suit, for example, on August 5, 2005, the attorney representing Blackstone would ask the court in which the suit was filed to dismiss the case because Zenith failed to file within the time period specified by the statute of limitations. The court would dismiss the case.

Since the Commercial National Bank intends to file suit only a few months after Apex Printing defaulted on its loan payments, the statute of limitations will not be a factor to its suit.

PLEADINGS

A pleading is a document filed with the court that was written by either the plaintiff or the defendant. The pleadings are also sent to the opposing party. The first pleading to be discussed is the complaint.

■ Complaint

Commercial National Bank wishes to bring suit for breach of the loan agreement. It will refer this matter to the bank's law firm. Undoubtedly, the attorney handling this matter works on cases of this nature on a regular basis. Thus, it will not be necessary for bank employees to spend a great deal of time explaining the situation to the lawyer who handles the case.

To start the suit against Apex Printing, the attorney will draft a *complaint* based on information provided to him by the bank. A complaint is a document, drafted by the plaintiff's attorney, that asks for the plaintiff to be granted some type of relief. Refer to the sample complaint in Figure 3.2. It should be noted that states call this document by other names such as *petition.*

The complaint states, paragraph by paragraph, the nature of the claims the plaintiff has against the defendant and the relief requested of the court. The complaint is filed by the attorney representing Commercial National Bank with the appropriate court. A copy of the complaint is also provided to someone acting on behalf of the defendant, Apex Printing. By reading the complaint, the defendant learns about the nature of the plaintiff's complaint against him or her and what the plaintiff wants the defendant to do or to cease doing. In this case, the bank wants a ruling from the court that Apex Printing has defaulted on its note. The bank will then attempt to collect the note from Apex Printing by doing something such as seizing some of Apex's assets.

■ Summons

In order to institute a suit, the plaintiff requests the court to serve the defendant with a *summons.* A summons is a document issued by the clerk of the court where the complaint is filed. A summons notifies the defendant that suit has been brought against him or her and it specifies the time period in which the defendant must reply to the complaint. The summons and a copy of the complaint filed by the attorney representing Commercial National Bank may be served by the sheriff or other law enforcement personnel on the defendant, Apex Printing. One of the officers of Apex will actually receive the papers on behalf of Apex since the company has no physical existence. In some circumstances, private service may be authorized by a court.

Frequently, the person serving the papers literally hands the summons and a copy of the petition to the defendant. If papers cannot be

■ **FIGURE 3.2** Sample Complaint

IN THE DISTRICT COURT OF DOUGLAS COUNTY, KANSAS

JOHN DOE,   Plaintiff,

v.   Case No. 10011

MARY SMITH,   Defendant.

Proceeding Under K.S.A. Chapter 60

COMPLAINT

COMES NOW the petitioner and states as his cause of action against the defendant.

1. From November 1, 1996, to January 7, 1997, plaintiff occupied, as defendant's tenant, defendant's trailer located at 140 Main, City of Lawrence, State of Kansas.

2. On January 3, 1997, defendant terminated such tenancy by sending a written notice to the plaintiff demanding the trailer be vacated by January 8, 1997.

3. On January 7, 1997, the defendant entered the trailer and took possession of it and all personalty therein.

4. On that date, the following items of personalty in the home were owned solely by plaintiff: a 1996 RCA color television and a Pioneer stereo. The reasonable value of such property on that date was $900.00.

5. At the time defendant took possession of the trailer, she took possession of the plaintiff's property. Plaintiff demanded that the defendant return possession of such personalty to plaintiff, but defendant with willful disregard of plaintiff's legal right to possession of such personalty has refused and failed to surrender possession thereof to plaintiff and still refuses to do so.

6. By reason of defendant's willful conversion of such property with knowledge of plaintiff's legal right to its possession, plaintiff is entitled to compensatory damages in the amount of $900.00.

7. WHEREFORE, plaintiff prays judgment against the defendant for $900.00 compensatory damages for the loss of his personal property, for court costs, and for such other and further relief as to the court may seem just and proper.

DEMAND FOR JURY TRIAL

Plaintiff herein demands trial by jury on all issues of fact contained in plaintiff's petition.

John Matthews
Attorney for plaintiff
100 Tennessee Street
Lawrence, Kansas 66044
1-913-845-0000

delivered to a person, a suit cannot begin. Some people attempt to avoid receiving the summons and petition in order to stall the onset of the suit.

In certain types of cases, it is not necessary to physically serve the papers on the defendant. The law sometimes permits service on the defendant by a simple delivery of the summons and a copy of the complaint to the defendant's home, or by mail, or by publication.

■ *Answer*

After the sheriff serves the summons and a copy of the complaint to an officer of Apex Printing, the officer most likely will sit down and read the documents. The probable next step will be to call the company attorney and inform the attorney of the suit. This enables the lawyer to make a timely response to the complaint as required by the law.

The attorney for Apex Printing will respond to the complaint by filing a document called an *answer* (or reply) with the same court where the complaint was filed. A copy of the answer is also sent to the plaintiff's attorney. A sample answer appears in Figure 3.3.

In an answer, the defendant states his or her response to the plaintiff's allegations. Frequently, the defendant denies all or most of the matters stated in the plaintiff's complaint. Any matter denied must be established by the plaintiff if the case then goes to trial.

Thus far, it has been illustrated that a plaintiff must institute a suit by filing a complaint to which the defendant must respond by filing an answer. Suit must be filed within a certain period of time as specified in the statute of limitations. Once the suit is under way, the discovery phase of the case begins.

DISCOVERY

Discovery, in a civil case, is a process through which opposing counsel may learn, before a trial begins, about information concerning the case. In general, each side must disclose the identity of its witnesses to the other. In addition, opposing sides have the opportunity to

■ **FIGURE 3.3** Sample Answer to a Complaint

IN THE DISTRICT COURT OF DOUGLAS COUNTY, KANSAS

JOHN DOE,   Plaintiff,

v.   Case No. 10011

MARY SMITH,   Defendant.

Proceeding Under K.S.A. Chapter 60

ANSWER

COMES NOW the defendant and for her reply states:

1. That she admits the allegations contained in paragraphs 1–3 of plaintiff's complaint.

2. That she denies each and every other allegation contained in plaintiff's complaint.

John Jones
Attorney for defendant
100 Main Street
Lawrence, Kansas 66044
1-913-100-0000

interrogate those witnesses. Documents relevant to the case are generally disclosed. Briefly, then, the discovery rules permit each side in a civil case to fully learn about the other.

The purpose of discovery is to do away with the element of surprise in a trial and encourage settlement out of court. Once both sides are fully aware of the facts, they can usually reach a negotiated resolution of the dispute.

A number of mechanisms exist for obtaining discovery in civil litigation. Although the discovery rules are designed to operate without court order, the courts do exercise a supervisory role in the process. Courts may limit discovery if they believe it is too burdensome. They may impose sanctions on a party that refuses to permit discovery.

Discovery may be obtained through the interrogation under oath of witnesses and parties to the lawsuit. This discovery technique is called **deposition.** It may be used to preserve the testimony of witnesses who will not be available at trial because of death or illness, or for some other reason. A deposition may also be used to raise questions concerning the truthfulness of a witness at the trial. Consider, for example, that a witness's deposition and trial testimony may conflict. A deposition may also be used as a general tool for having facts revealed about the incident in question and the case of the opposition.

Other discovery tools include the submission of written questions to be answered under oath. The written questions are called **interrogatories.** Documents may also be obtained through the discovery process. Additionally, parties are encouraged to admit to certain portions of the litigation in order to reduce the number of issues to be decided at the trial. This may be accomplished through a request for admissions.

The discovery rules contain a number of techniques that litigants may use to gather facts relevant to the litigation. As a result, such techniques help foster fair, fast, and inexpensive resolution of cases through settlement rather than waiting for a disposition through trial.

The case between Commercial National Bank and Apex Printing involves a relatively simple issue. Apex Printing signed a document (called a note) promising to pay back the money it received from Commercial National Bank. As Apex failed to make payments as specified in the agreement, it probably does not have much of a defense. Even so, the officers of Apex Printing may want to mount some sort of defense in order to stall the bank while they attempt to get their company up and running again. They may, as a defense tactic, encourage their attorneys to engage in the practice discussed in the Ethical Perspective, "The Ethics of Delaying a Case."

ETHICAL
PERSPECTIVE

The Ethics of Delaying a Case

One technique often used by well-financed litigants is the practice of delaying the resolution of the case by prolonging the discovery phase of the case. This is called **dilatory** tactics.

Suppose that Wilson broke her arm in an automobile accident. She filed suit against the driver of the other car, Sullivan. Sullivan's attorney may attempt to drag the case out. Attorneys use such tactics in order to wear the other side down.

As years pass, Wilson may become more amenable to settling the case on Sullivan's terms. The defendant also profits from such a strategy because he earns interest on the money he eventually must pay to the plaintiff up to the moment that Sullivan actually makes a payment to Wilson. If the goal of the justice system is to obtain a speedy and fair resolution to every suit, does it further the interests of justice to engage in such tactics?

MOTION FOR SUMMARY JUDGMENT

After the plaintiff files a complaint, the defendant answers, and the parties have learned something about the facts of the case, one of the parties may believe he or she is entitled to a judgment as a matter of law. Generally, the parties have at least taken the affidavits (sworn statements) of some of the important parties to the case. In some cases, other devices such as depositions may have been obtained.

Essentially, the party making a **motion for summary judgment** is saying that no genuine issue of material fact remains to be decided in the case, and therefore the judge should grant the motion. If any issue of material fact remains, the judge should deny the motion.

Even assuming the judge grants the motion for a summary judgment, he or she still must rule on how the law applies to the facts in question. If the judge thinks the law favors the plaintiff, the judge rules for the plaintiff. If the judge decides that the law requires a verdict on behalf of the defendant, he or she enters a judgment for the defendant. The critical concept here is that no trial is required because all issues of fact have been resolved. This being the case, the judge merely needs to apply the law to the facts.

In the conflict between Commercial National Bank and Apex Printing, Commercial National Bank may make a motion for summary judgment. The bank would present evidence to the judge of the agreement signed by the officers of Apex Printing and evidence establishing that the note was not paid. If Apex does not dispute these facts, the judge may grant the motion for summary judgment. The judge will then, based on the facts, probably rule against Apex unless Apex has a defense or excuse for not making payments as required by the note. Such cases tend to be quite routine.

Trial Procedure

Unlike other places in the world, a sizeable number of cases in the United States are tried in front of a jury. The United States Constitution guarantees people a civil trial in most cases.

The Seventh Amendment to the United States Constitution deals with civil trials. It provides, "In suits at common law, where the value in controversy shall exceed twenty dollars, the right of trial by jury shall be preserved, and no fact tried by a jury, shall be otherwise re-examined in any court of the United States, than according to the rules of the common law."

Take note of the fact that the Seventh Amendment merely *preserves* the right to trial in suits at common law. It does not *create* a right to trial by jury. Without going into detail about common law, suffice it to say that if a matter was regarded as part of the common law at the time of the drafting of the United States Constitution, litigants may request a trial by jury for such issues today. If the case was not a common law matter, no right to a trial by jury exists under the United States Constitution. A right to a jury trial may exist, however, under the applicable *state* constitution.

SELECTION OF A JURY

If the Commercial National Bank/Apex Printing suit goes to trial, one of the parties may think that a jury would serve its interests better than a judge would. Consequently, this party would request a jury. If the parties schedule a trial before a jury, the court will instruct the clerk of the court to call in, on the day set for the trial, a specified number of people—called veniremen—for possible service on a jury in the Commercial National Bank/Apex Printing case. More people than actually needed are called for jury service because some of them, for one reason or another, will be unable to serve on the jury.

■ *Voir Dire*

After dealing with a few preliminary matters, the *voir dire* of the veniremen begins. The purpose of the voir dire is to determine the qualifications of the veniremen to sit as triers of fact in the case and to determine whether they are subject to challenge. During this stage, the judge permits the attorneys to ask the veniremen questions.

Before conducting the voir dire, however, the attorney must do some initial investigation and preparation. The attorney must first learn about the backgrounds of all prospective jurors to determine whether or not he or she wishes to challenge any of them. This will also help to establish the necessary jury rapport. Some of this information may be obtained through various public sources, including the city directory, telephone directory, and other such public listings. Perhaps the best method is simply talking to people who know the juror, such as neighbors and co-workers.

Some states provide information of this type to attorneys prior to trial. In other states, attorneys must search out information about jurors prior to trial or at trial. The juror questionnaire in Figure 3.4 is a typical example of a form prospective jurors may be asked to fill out.

The courts permit two types of challenges to a venireman. The first is a *challenge for cause.* Theoretically, every person called in for possible jury duty could be removed since the courts allow attorneys to bring up an unlimited number of these challenges for cause. If an attorney thinks that a given venireman should be removed from the panel for cause, then the attorney makes this motion to the court. The court then determines whether or not sufficient cause exists to remove that person. The for cause challenge allows an attorney to challenge any venireman on the grounds of bias or prejudice. If the attorney can show that a person is not able to make a fair and impartial decision, the attorney can request the judge to dismiss that person. Likewise, a venireman who is either unwilling or unable to follow instructions or come up with answers to questions can be dismissed for cause.

Attorneys attempt to get people off the jury panel who look as if they may favor the opposing side. While the court may be interested in a fair and impartial jury, the attorneys trying the case attempt to construct jury panels that they hope will be favorably disposed toward their respective clients. Because an attorney gets an unlimited

■ **FIGURE 3.4**   Juror Questionnaire

IN THE SEVENTH JUDICIAL DISTRICT COURT OF THE STATE OF KANSAS
IN AND FOR THE COUNTY OF DOUGLAS

JUROR QUESTIONNAIRE

You have been selected for the privilege to serve as a juror in the District Court of Douglas County. Please carefully read and answer the questions on this form and return it immediately in the enclosed self-addressed, stamped envelope: Questionnaires *must be returned within five days,* whether or not you may expect to be excused from reporting. This questionnaire is for the purpose of determining your qualification for jury duty. Your answers to these questions are for Court use only and will not be made public. Your cooperation and willingness to serve as a juror are appreciated.
PLEASE PRINT OR TYPE YOUR ANSWERS.

1. Name _____ Age _____

2. Residence Address _____ City _____ Zip _____

   Residence Phone Number _____ Work Phone Number _____

3. Years in Residence in Kansas _____ In Douglas County _____

4. Former Residence _____

5. Marital Status _____ Married _____ Separated _____ Widower

   (Please check) _____ Single _____ Divorced _____ Widow

6. Number of Children _____ Ages _____ Can care be provided? _____

7. Have you any ill dependents who require your personal and constant care? __

   If so, give details: _____

8. Occupation _____ Employer _____

   Do you own your business? _____ Number of Employees _____

9. Full Name of Spouse _____ Occupation _____

   Employer _____ Work Address _____ Phone _____

10. If you are not now employed; give your last occupation and employer: _____

    _____

11. Have you ever served as a juror? _____

    Civil Case? _____ When and where? _____

    Criminal Case? _____ When and where? _____

12. Have you or any members of your immediate family been a party to any lawsuit?

    _____

    Criminal? _____ Civil? _____ When and where? _____

    Who in your family was involved? _____

—Continued

number of these for cause objections, the attorney will try, if at all possible, to convince the court to remove all of the veniremen not liked based on some sort of for cause objection. For example, if an attorney could get a venireman to state that he would not rule for the defendant because the defendant is not white, such a person clearly would be excused from jury duty because of for cause purposes.

The Managerial Perspective, "Selecting a Jury," deals with a major antitrust suit brought by MCI against AT&T. It discusses how people, skilled in selecting jurors, can obtain just the type of persons on the jury that the attorney desires.

■ **FIGURE 3.4** Juror
Questionnaire—*Continued*

—Continued

13. Have you ever been convicted of a felony? _____ For what? _____
    Where and when? _____

14. If you believe you have a physical disability which would prevent you from
    serving as a juror, please state what: _____

15. Has any court ever found you to be incompetent or incapacitated? _____
    Where and when? _____ If restored, give date: _____

16. Are you a close friend of, or are you related to any law-enforcement officer?
    If so, please check: ___ Federal ___ State ___ Sheriff's Office ___ City police

17. Do you drive an automobile? _____ Is transportation available? _____
    If you live outside city limits, state mileage one way to city limits: _____

18. Can you read, write, and understand English? _____

19. Please show the extent of your formal education. (Circle highest level completed.)
    Elementary or Secondary School: 1 2 3 4 5 6 7 8 9 10 11 12 College: 1 2 3 4 5 6 7 +

20. Have you had any vocational or professional training? _____
    If so, please state what kind and to what extent: _____
    _____

21. If enrolled in a college or university, please state year and course of study:
    _____

22. If you feel there is any reason you cannot serve as a juror, please state:
    _____
    _____
    _____
    _____
    _____
    _____
    _____
    _____

I affirm that the answers I have given to the above questions are true and correct.

Signed: _____
Dated: _____

At the close of the questioning of the veniremen, a few people always manage to stay on the panel in spite of the best effort of the attorneys to exclude them for cause. At this point, an attorney will avail himself or herself of the *peremptory challenge*—the no cause objection. Peremptory challenge is the second type of challenge to a venireman. Unlike the for cause objection, an attorney is permitted the right to remove only a limited number of veniremen based on the no cause objection.

During the last decade, the United States Supreme Court has applied the Equal Protection Clause of the United States Constitution to the use of peremptory challenges in both civil and criminal cases. The Supreme Court wants to discourage litigants from using group stereotypes in the jury selection process. Litigants may still use peremptory challenges, but they run the risk of violating the Equal Protection Clause if it appears that they based their actions on group stereotypes as was the situation in *J.E.B. v. Alabama ex rel T.B.*

managerial perspective

Selecting a Jury

MCI Communications Corporation brought an antitrust suit against AT&T. At that trial, MCI was awarded $1.8 billion. MCI's attorneys spent a considerable amount of time preparing for every facet of this trial.

One of the factors in which the attorneys were interested was the type of juror who would be of greatest use to MCI. In order to determine this information, attorneys representing MCI hired a public opinion pollster to learn about the attitudes of people in Chicago, the place where the trial was scheduled to take place, toward big business. MCI wanted to determine the type of juror who would keep an open mind about MCI's case.

As a result of the work done by the public opinion pollster, MCI's attorneys developed a profile of the type of person they needed to get on the jury. The poll told them to select self-made people who understood competition, who were first- or second-generation Americans, and who were intelligent enough to understand this rather complex case. Six of the twelve jurors who eventually heard the case had college backgrounds.

Obtaining information of this nature is obviously useful to attorneys in selecting the proper group of people to look for during the voir dire. The size of this verdict suggests that MCI's attorneys selected the jury very astutely.

Source: John A. Jenkins, "Is the Jury Out," *TWA Ambassador*, April 1981, page 64.

J.E.B. v. Alabama ex rel T.B.

United States Supreme Court *114 S.Ct. 1419 (1994)*

T.B., the mother of a minor child, brought a paternity action against J.E.B. in the district court of Jackson County, Alabama. In this case, the court assembled a group of thirty-six potential jurors. When it came time to use the peremptory challenges, the state used nine of its ten peremptory strikes to remove male jurors. This resulted in an all female jury. J.E.B. objected to the state's peremptory challenges because they were exercised against male jurors solely on the basis of gender in violation of the Equal Protection Clause. The trial court rejected J.E.B.'s challenge and empaneled the jury. The jury found J.E.B. to be the father of the child and the court directed him to pay child support. The Alabama Court of Civil Appeals affirmed. The United States Supreme Court reversed the decision of the Alabama Court of Civil Appeals and remanded the case to that court.

Blackmun, Justice

Discrimination on the basis of gender in the exercise of peremptory challenges is a relatively recent phenomenon. Gender-based peremptory strikes were hardly practicable for most of our country's existence, since, until the 19th century, women were completely excluded from jury service. So well-entrenched was this exclusion of women that in 1880 this Court, while finding that the exclusion of African-American men from juries violated the Fourteenth Amendment, expressed no doubt that a State "may confine the selection [of jurors] to males." *Strauder v. West Virginia.*

The prohibition of women on juries was derived from the English common law which, according to Blackstone, rightfully excluded women from juries under "the doctrine of *propter defectum sexus,* literally, the 'defect of sex.'" *United States v.*

De Gross, quoting 2 W. Blackstone, Commentaries. In this country, supporters of the exclusion of women from juries tended to couch their objections in terms of the ostensible need to protect women from the ugliness and depravity of trials. Women were thought to be too fragile and virginal to withstand the polluted courtroom atmosphere.

It is necessary only to acknowledge that our Nation has had a long and unfortunate history of sex discrimination, a history which warrants the heightened scrutiny we afford all gender-based classifications today. Under our equal protection jurisprudence, gender-based classifications require an exceedingly persuasive justification in order to survive constitutional scrutiny.

Far from proffering an exceptionally persuasive justification for its gender-based peremptory challenges, respondent maintains that its decision to strike virtually all the males from the jury in this case may reasonably have been based upon the perception, supported by history, that men otherwise totally qualified to serve upon a jury might be more sympathetic and receptive to the arguments of a man alleged in a paternity action to be the father of an out-of-wedlock child, while women equally qualified to serve upon a jury might be more sympathetic and receptive to the arguments of the complaining witness who bore the child.

We shall not accept as a defense to gender-based peremptory challenges the very stereotype the law condemns.

If conducted properly, *voir dire* can inform litigants about potential jurors, making reliance upon a stereotypical and pejorative notions about a particular gender or race both unnecessary and unwise. Voir dire provides a means of discovering actual or implied bias and a firmer basis upon which the parties may exercise their peremptory challenges intelligently.

A party alleging gender discrimination must make a prima facie showing of intentional discrimination before the party exercising the challenge is required to explain the basis for the strike. When an explanation is required, it need not rise to the level of a "for cause" challenge; rather, it merely must be based on a juror characteristic other than gender, and the proffered explanation may not be pretextual.

OPENING STATEMENT

Once the court has empaneled a group of people who will serve as jurors in the *Commercial National Bank v. Apex Printing* case, the attorneys will present their *opening statements.* In a civil case, the plaintiff's attorney makes his or her opening statement first. In this case, since Commercial National Bank is bringing the action for breach of the loan agreement, its attorney will speak first. Thereafter, the attorney for Apex Printing will give its side of the story.

The purpose of the opening statement is to give the jurors a broad overview of the case. The attorney probably will introduce his or her witnesses, describe their anticipated testimony, stress certain rules of law, tell the jurors what the attorney hopes to prove, and comment on what the other side intends to do. The attorney ought to present plausible reasons why, after hearing the evidence, the jury should find in his or her client's favor. Thus, the opening statement amounts to a broad overview of the trial to come. The jurors are fresh at this point. They listen avidly. Such information may help clarify points in the trial they may misunderstand or fail to hear. The attention span of the jurors surely is best at this point, and for that reason alone the opening statement is of critical importance.

Nothing said during the opening statements is part of the evidence. They are merely statements of what the attorneys expect the proof to be, merely outlines of the case. The decision in a case must be rendered on the basis of the testimony of witnesses who appear at trial. Nonetheless, a good lawyer starts the jury thinking about his or her position in the case during the opening statement and possibly even influences the jurors' thinking at this point.

BURDEN OF PROOF

One matter often discussed in the opening statement is *burden of proof*. The burden of proof is the duty of a party to substantiate an allegation or issue to avoid dismissal of that issue early in the trial or to convince the trier of fact of the truth of the claim and therefore win at trial. In the Commercial National Bank/Apex Printing case, the bank has the initial burden of proof. It must prove, even before Apex is obligated to present any evidence whatsoever, that it had a valid loan agreement with Apex Printing which Apex failed to pay. If the bank fails to establish its burden of proof, the judge will dismiss the case even if Apex Printing, the defendant, never presents any evidence at trial. However, if the bank meets this initial burden of proof, the burden shifts to Apex to challenge the points brought up by the bank. In other words, the defendant automatically loses the case if it fails to meet its burden of proof.

Since this is a civil case, the Commercial National Bank must prove its case by a *preponderance of the evidence*—that is, the evidence presented by the plaintiff must be more convincing than the evidence presented by the defendant in order for the plaintiff to prevail at trial. This does not mean that the trier of fact must be absolutely convinced of the plaintiff's position, but simply that the plaintiff's evidence, on the whole, looks more convincing than the evidence presented by the defendant.

Although criminal law is not discussed in this text, it is important to realize that the burden of proof is different in a criminal case than in a civil case. Unlike a civil case, the government always institutes a criminal case. For the government to win its case, it must convince the jury (or the judge, if a jury is not used) that the defendant is guilty beyond a reasonable doubt—that is, if there is a reasonable doubt in the minds of the jurors about whether or not the defendant committed the crime in question, they should *not* vote to convict the defendant.

RULES OF EVIDENCE

Certain evidence may be admitted at trial while other evidence may not. Certain rules of evidence result in evidence being suppressed (not admitted). A good example is the rule against the admission of hearsay evidence.

Hearsay is evidence that a witness offers not from personal knowledge, but based on a statement made by another person and which is offered to prove the truth of a contested fact. The hearsay rule applies to both oral and written statements. It is subject to a number of exceptions.

Suppose that Jones, an employee of Apex Printing, takes the stand. On the stand Jones testifies that Kyndra Falkner told him that

Ms. Smith, the President of Commercial National Bank, told Kyndra that the signatures on the Commercial National Bank/Apex Printing loan papers are forgeries. Assume that Kyndra is not available to testify at trial, and no one knows where she currently resides. If this statement is offered to prove that the signatures on the note are forgeries, the attorney representing Commercial National Bank may object to this testimony because it is hearsay. Jones is not testifying of his own personal knowledge that the signatures are forgeries but rather based on a statement that he heard from someone else, Kyndra Falkner. The judge, following an objection to the statement, will order the jury to disregard it.

Many other objections exist. Some of them relate to the form of a question—such as the objection that a question is *leading and suggestive*. Suppose an attorney asks a witness, "Were you wearing a beard on June 12, 1997?" Such a question suggests the possible answer an attorney wants the witness to give. A question of this nature should be stated in this manner: "Tell us about your physical condition on June 12, 1997," or some similar wording that does not suggest the desired answer.

CROSS EXAMINATION

If an attorney calls a person to the witness stand and then proceeds to ask that person questions, such questioning is referred to as a *direct examination* of the witness. If the attorney for the opposing side then asks questions of this same witness, such questioning is called a *cross examination* of the witness.

The purpose of cross examining a witness is to permit the opposite party to test what has just been stated by the witness. The attorney tries to demonstrate that the witness's memory is faulty, or that he or she was not in a position to perceive the events in question, or that the witness has not explained the facts clearly.

Referring to the example concerning hearsay, consider the problems posed by allowing Jones to testify that Kyndra Falkner told him that Ms. Smith, the President of Commercial National Bank, told Kyndra that the signatures on the Commercial National Bank/Apex Printing loan papers are forgeries. How can anyone question Kyndra about this statement if she is not present in court at that time? Kyndra may have completely fabricated this story, for example, or may have misunderstood Ms. Smith. There is no way of determining the accuracy of such a statement; therefore, the court probably will exclude the statement as hearsay.

CLOSING ARGUMENTS

Following the close of the defendant's case and after the judge considers any motions made by the parties, each side presents a **closing argument.** In a civil case, the plaintiff has the option of opening. The defendant may then make concluding statements, followed by the plaintiff's response. (Criminal cases operate in the same manner, with the state making the first comments.)

A closing argument really is a review of all the evidence heard during the trial. The attorneys refresh the jurors' memory of important points made during the trial. Generally, some theme exists to the closing remarks that the attorney wishes to convey to the jury. Through this theme he or she tries to analyze and review the testimony. The attorneys also review the instructions of law that the judge will present. They try to explain these instructions so the jurors apply the law correctly. The attorneys must attempt to explain the law because the judge generally just reads the instructions to the jurors.

Quite often, the closing argument is based on pure emotion—in other words, rule for my client because he or she is a very sympathetic person. Such appeals work well in certain tragic or pitiful cases, such as when a child is injured by a truck owned by a large company. The attorney representing the child often tries to convince the jury to rule for the child because the child has been injured—as opposed to deciding the case based on the law and facts presented in court. The following scenario is an excellent example of the use of an appeal to emotion in a closing argument.

The following closing argument was delivered in the case *Burden v. Hornsby* in the Court of Common Pleas at Warrensburg, Missouri, September 23, 1870. The case involved a matter of principle—the death of a man's dog, Old Drum, for which he claimed fifty dollars in damages. The speech was delivered by Senator George Graham Vest. During it, counsel for the defendant sensed the cause was lost. He is rumored to have whispered facetiously to his partner, "We had better get out of the courtroom with our client, else all might be hanged."

Eulogy, to the Dog

Gentlemen of the jury, the best friend a man has in this world may turn against him and become his enemy. His son or daughter that he has reared with loving care may prove ungrateful. Those who are nearest and dearest to us, those whom we trust with our happiness and our good name, may become traitors to their faith. The money that a man has he may lose. It flies away from him perhaps when he needs it most. A man's reputation may be sacrificed in a moment of ill-considered action. The people who are prone to fall on their knees to do us honor when success is with us, may be the first to throw the stones of malice when failure settles its cloud upon our heads. The one absolutely unselfish friend that a man can have in this selfish world, the one that never deserts him, the one that never proves ungrateful or treacherous, is his dog.

Gentlemen of the jury, a man's dog stands by him in prosperity and in poverty, in health and in sickness. He will sleep on the cold ground where the wintry winds blow and the snow drives fierce, if only he may be near his master's side. He will kiss the hand that has no food to offer; he will lick the wounds and sores that come from encounter with the roughness of the world. He guards the sleep of his pauper master as if he were a prince. When all other friends desert, he remains. When riches take wing and reputation falls to pieces, he is as constant in his love as the sun in its journey through the heavens.

If fortune drives the master forth an outcast in the world, friendless and homeless, the faithful dog asks no higher privilege than that of his company to guard against danger, to fight against his enemies. And when the last scene of all comes, and death takes the master in its embrace and his body is laid away in the cold ground, no matter if all other friends pursue their way, there by his graveside will the noble dog be found, his head between his paws, his eyes sad but open in alert watchfulness, faithful and true even in death.

Appeals to emotion can and do work on closing. With the right jury, they may lead jurors to react emotionally as opposed to analyzing the evidence.

INSTRUCTIONS TO THE JURY AND JURY DELIBERATION

Following the closing arguments of the attorneys, the judge in the case will instruct the members of the jury on the law. The attorneys discuss this matter with the judge prior to the time the judge actually reads the instructions to the jury. Generally, when the attorneys make their closing arguments, they will also talk about the instructions so that the jurors understand what law must be applied to the case.

The jury thereafter retires to the jury room at the close of the judge's instructions. The jurors deliberate in secret. They attempt to arrive at a decision. If the jurors fail to arrive at a decision, the judge will declare a *hung jury*—that is, the jurors are said to be deadlocked or unable to reach a decision. The judge will then dismiss the case. Such cases, whether civil or criminal in nature, may be retried.

THE VERDICT

When the jury reaches a decision, the jury foreman fills out the appropriate form provided by the judge. The jurors then return to the courtroom, and the judge or the bailiff announces the jury verdict in open court.

The losing party has an important decision to make following the entry of the judgment. Suppose that Apex Printing loses the case and the court rules in favor of Commercial National Bank. Within a relatively short time frame Apex must make a determination whether to live with the verdict or to appeal.

The Appeal

A decision to appeal generally must be made fairly quickly after the termination of the trial—for example, within thirty days. The costs associated with an appeal often discourage the losing party from appealing the case from the trial court to an appeals court. Unlike the trial court, an appeals court does not actually hear witnesses and admit evidence.

At the appellate level, the appeals court merely examines the record of the trial court to determine if the trial court made any reversible errors. The appeals court often hears oral arguments of the attorneys in the case. It also receives a written discussion of the case—called a brief—from each side, and in certain cases, from other interested parties. The court examines only that part of the transcript provided to it by the parties. It does not review the entire trial transcript. It does not hear witnesses. The appeals court generally considers only issues of law.

If it agrees with the trial court decision, the appeals court affirms the decision. If it finds an error, it may merely reverse the decision, or it may reverse and remand (send the case back to the trial court) for a new trial.

The losing party must evaluate its interests in the case and the expense of the appeal in deciding whether or not to continue with the case. Sometimes a party may think the decision was in error but may lack the money or the interest to pursue the case to a higher court.

SAFE HAVENS

After reading about the complexities associated with a typical trial and appeal, people may wonder: "Is there any place in the nation that I can avoid being sued?" Probably not. However, it is worth noting that people in some regions of the country are far more likely to sue than people in other parts of the nation.

Alternative Dispute Resolution Procedures

Quite often, rather than going through the process discussed earlier in this chapter, the parties resort to some means to bypass or complement the formal legal system. The following material discusses these techniques.

SETTLEMENT

Relatively few legal disputes actually result in a trial; most are settled out of court. There are incentives for litigants to do so. The time and expense of proceeding to trial must be weighed against the advantages of immediate settlement. An injured party may want to collect money damages as soon as possible, thereby hastening an out-of-court settlement. Additionally, settlements may be structured so that payments are made in ways other than in one lump sum—that is, they may be spread over a number of years. This option also makes settlement attractive to the party who must pay damages.

Great delays often occur in getting a case into court, another reason litigants are willing to settle rather than wait for a trial. Then, of course, the risk of loss at trial is always a possibility.

A useful book that a manager may wish to consult regarding negotiation is *Getting to Yes: Negotiating Agreements without Giving In*, by Fisher & Ury (Houghton Mifflin Co., 1992).

The Managerial Perspective, "Compromise or Litigate?", provides one situation to think about concerning the virtues of a good compromise.

ARBITRATION

Arbitration is sometimes used as a substitute for a trial and is quicker and less costly than litigation in a court. The arbitrator—the person who hears and decides the dispute—is selected by the parties. Frequently, the arbitrator is an authority in the area in which the dispute arises. The parties, informally and at convenient times, submit their cases to an arbitrator. The arbitrator, like a judge, weighs the evidence, applies the law, and renders a decision. Arbitration is another practical alternative to the delay and expense associated with the court system. In addition to being quicker and cheaper than trying a case in

managerial perspective

Compromise or Litigate?

During the first half of the twentieth century, Lee de Forest and Edwin Armstrong were engaged in several titanic legal suits regarding who, in fact, discovered certain inventions and thus was entitled to exploit these inventions. Armstrong refused to permit de Forest to use one of his inventions. Armstrong refused to compromise, and de Forest responded by filing suit claiming that he, not Armstrong, was in fact the inventor of the product in question. The case went to the United States Supreme Court in the 1930s and Lee de Forest won. Many scientists at the time argued that Edwin Armstrong should have won the case. One could argue that the moral to this titanic battle is that sometimes it pays to compromise—even when you feel you are in the right. In hindsight, Armstrong probably should have granted de Forest permission to use the product.

court, arbitration has the advantage of being more informal. Furthermore, if the parties desire to keep the matter out of the public eye, arbitration may be used to keep a matter private. This is a major factor in many cases for resorting to arbitration.

Various means may be used to select an arbitrator. Sometimes as many as three arbitrators hear a case. These arbitrators are often provided by an organization such as the American Arbitration Association.

The arbitration is dependent on the parties' agreement to arbitrate rather than litigate the dispute through a court. If they decide to submit the dispute to binding arbitration, a court will refuse to rehear the entire matter. When the parties have signed an agreement that contains a broad arbitration clause, the courts will order the parties to arbitrate any dispute arising under or related to the agreement in the absence of clear evidence the parties did not intend to arbitrate the matter. In general, federal law favors the arbitration of all disputes.

In 1925, Congress adopted the Federal Arbitration Act. It made agreements to arbitrate disputes enforceable. The history of the act indicates a desire by Congress to reject the tendency of courts to refuse to defer cases to nonjudicial personnel. A court must stay its proceedings if the parties agreed in advance to arbitrate disputes and if the matter in question is arbitrable.

In *Shearson/American Express, Inc. v. McMahon*, the United States Supreme Court decided that even statutory claims may be arbitrated. This decision sends an important signal to the courts that the Supreme Court wants to encourage the policy set forth in the Federal Arbitration Act that disputes should be arbitrated, if at all possible.

Shearson/American Express, Inc. v. McMahon

United States Supreme Court
107 S.Ct. 2332 (1987)

Customers of Shearson/American Express filed suit against Shearson and its representative who handled their accounts. They alleged violations of the 1934 Securities and Exchange Act (Exchange Act) and of the Racketeer Influenced and Corrupt

Organizations Act (RICO). Shearson moved to compel arbitration of the claims pursuant to Section 3 of the Federal Arbitration Act. The Court held that both claims were subject to arbitration.

Justice O'Connor

This case presents two questions regarding the enforceability of predispute arbitration agreements between brokerage firms and their customers. The first is whether a claim brought under § 10(b) of the Securities Exchange Act of 1934 (Exchange Act), 48 Stat. 891, 15 U.S.C. § 78j(b), must be sent to arbitration in accordance with the terms of an arbitration agreement. The second is whether a claim brought under the Racketeer Influenced and Corrupt Organizations Act (RICO), 18 U.S.C. § 1961 *et seq.*, must be arbitrated in accordance with the terms of such an agreement.

The Federal Arbitration Act, 9 U.S.C. § 1 *et seq.*, provides the starting point for answering the questions raised in this case. The Act was intended to "revers[e] centuries of judicial hostility to arbitration agreements," *Scherk v. Alberto-Culver Co.,* by "plac[ing] arbitration agreements 'upon the same footing as other contracts.' " The Arbitration Act accomplishes this purpose by providing that arbitration agreements "shall be valid, irrevocable, and enforceable, save upon such grounds as exist at law or in equity for the revocation of any contract." The Act also provides that a court must stay its proceedings if it is satisfied that an issue before it is arbitrable under the agreement, § 3; and it authorizes a federal district court to issue an order compelling arbitration if there has been a "failure, neglect, or refusal" to comply with the arbitration agreement, § 4.

The Arbitration Act thus establishes a "federal policy favoring arbitration." This duty to enforce arbitration agreements is not diminished when a party bound by an agreement raises a claim founded on statutory rights.

Absent a well-founded claim that an arbitration agreement resulted from the sort of fraud or excessive economic power that "would provide grounds 'for the revocation of any contract,' " the Arbitration Act "provides no basis for disfavoring agreements to arbitrate statutory claims by skewing the otherwise hospitable inquiry into arbitrability."

To defeat application of the Arbitration Act in this case, the McMahons must demonstrate that Congress intended to make an exception to the Arbitration Act for claims arising under RICO and the Exchange Act, an intention discernible from the text, history, or purposes of the statute. We examine the McMahon's arguments regarding the Exchange Act and RICO in turn.

The suitability of arbitration as a means of enforcing Exchange Act rights is evident from our decision in *Scherk.* Although the holding in that case was limited to international agreements, the competence of arbitral tribunals to resolve § 10(b) claims is the same in both settings.

We conclude that Congress did not intend for § 29(a) to bar enforcement of all predispute arbitration agreements. In this case, where the SEC has sufficient statutory authority to ensure that arbitration is adequate to vindicate Exchange Act rights, enforcement does not effect a waiver of "compliance with any provision" of the Exchange Act under § 29(a). Accordingly, we hold the McMahon's agreements to arbitrate Exchange Act claims "enforce[able] . . . in accord with the explicit provisions of the Arbitration Act." *Scherk v. Alberto-Culver Co.*

Unlike the Exchange Act, there is nothing in the text of the RICO statute that even arguably evinces congressional intent to exclude civil RICO claims from the dictates of the Arbitration Act. This silence in the text is matched by silence in the statute's legislative history.

Because RICO's text and legislative history fail to reveal any intent to override the provisions of the Arbitration Act, the McMahons must argue that there is an irreconcilable conflict between arbitration and RICO's underlying purposes.

> [W]e find no basis for concluding that Congress intended to prevent enforcement of agreements to arbitrate RICO claims. The McMahons may effectively vindicate their RICO claim in an arbitral forum, and therefore there is no inherent conflict between arbitration and the purposes underlying § 1964(c). Moreover, nothing in RICO's text or legislative history otherwise demonstrates congressional intent to make an exception to the Arbitration Act for RICO claims. Accordingly, the McMahons, "having made the bargain to arbitrate," will be held to their bargain. Their RICO claim is arbitrable under the terms of the Arbitration Act.

Little question exists that an agreement to arbitrate will be enforced in light of the Federal Arbitration Act, the *Shearson/American Express* case, and the state arbitration acts. Courts will compel arbitration if people refuse to arbitrate a matter.

It probably will come as a surprise to many people that an arbitration award generally is final even if the award has an error of law on its face and a substantial injustice results from the arbitrator's decision. In *Moncharsh v. Heily & Blase,* the Supreme Court of California formally adopted this position.

Moncharsh v. Heily & Blase

Supreme Court of California *832 P.2d 899 (1992)*

Philip Moncharsh, an attorney, was hired by a law firm, Heily & Blase. As a condition of employment he signed an agreement that, among other provisions, contained a provision relating to any clients he may take with him in the event he left the firm. The contract provided that Heily & Blase would receive eighty percent of any fee generated from such clients and Moncharsh would receive twenty percent of any fee generated. The contract provided that any dispute arising out of the contract would be subject to final and binding arbitration.

After leaving the firm, Moncharsh continued to represent six clients for whom he had worked while at Heily & Blase. When Blase learned that Moncharsh had obtained fees in these six cases, he demanded eighty percent of the fees generated by Moncharsh. Thereafter, the parties invoked the arbitration clause and submitted the matter to an arbitrator. The arbitrator ruled in Heily & Blase's favor.

Moncharsh petitioned the superior court to vacate and modify the arbitration award. He contended that the arbitrator failed to apply the law correctly. Nonetheless, the Supreme Court of California held that the arbitrator's decision was not subject to review.

Lucas, Judge

We granted review and directed the parties to address the limited issue of whether, and under what conditions, a trial court may review an arbitrator's decision.

The arbitration clause included in the employment agreement in this case specifically states that the arbitrator's decision would be both binding and final. The parties to this action thus clearly intended the arbitrator's decision would be final. Even had there been no such expression of intent, however, it is the general rule that parties to a private arbitration impliedly agree that the arbitrator's decision will be both binding and final. Indeed, the very essence of the term "arbitration" [in this context] connotes a binding award.

It is the general rule that, with narrow exceptions, an arbitrator's decision cannot be reviewed for errors of fact or law. In reaffirming this general rule, we recognize there is a risk that the arbitrator will make a mistake. That risk, however, is acceptable for two reasons. First, by voluntarily submitting to arbitration, the parties have agreed to bear that risk in return for a quick, inexpensive, and conclusive resolution to their dispute.

A second reason why we tolerate the risk of an erroneous decision is because the Legislature has reduced the risk to the parties of such a decision by providing for judicial review in circumstances involving serious problems with the award itself, or with the fairness of the arbitration process. Private arbitration proceedings are governed by title 9 of the Code of Civil Procedure, sections 1280–1294.2. Section 1286.2 sets forth the grounds for vacation of an arbitrator's award. It states in pertinent part: "The court shall vacate the award if the court determines that:

(a) The award was procured by corruption, fraud or other undue means;

(b) There was corruption in any of the arbitrators;

(c) The rights of such party were substantially prejudiced by misconduct of a neutral arbitrator;

(d) The arbitrators exceeded their powers and the award cannot be corrected without affecting the merits of the decision upon the controversy submitted; or

(e) The rights of such party were substantially prejudiced by the refusal of the arbitrators to postpone the hearing upon sufficient cause being shown therefor or by the refusal of the arbitrators to hear evidence material to the controversy or by other conduct of the arbitrators contrary to the provisions of this title."

In addition, Section 1286.6 provides grounds for correction of an arbitration award. That section states in pertinent part: "The court, unless it vacates the award pursuant to Section 1286.2, shall correct the award and confirm it as corrected if the court determines that:

(a) There was an evident miscalculation of figures or an evident mistake in the description of any person, thing or property referred to in the award;

(b) The arbitrators exceeded their powers but the award may be corrected without affecting the merits of the decision upon the controversy submitted; or

(c) The award is imperfect in a matter of form, not affecting the merits of the controversy."

The Legislature has thus substantially reduced the possibility of certain forms of error infecting the arbitration process itself. . . . In light of these statutory provisions, the residual risk to the parties of an arbitrator's erroneous decision represents an acceptable cost—obtaining the expedience and financial savings that the arbitration process provides—as compared to the judicial process.

Although it is thus the general rule that an arbitrator's decision is not ordinarily reviewable for error by either the trial or appellate court, Moncharsh contends that a court may review an arbitrator's decision if an error of law is apparent on the face of the award and that error causes substantial injustice.

We conclude that an award reached by an arbitrator pursuant to a contractual agreement to arbitrate is not subject to judicial review except on the grounds set forth in Sections 1286.2 (to vacate) and 1286.6 (for correction). Further, the existence of an error of law apparent on the face of the award that causes substantial injustice does not provide grounds for judicial review.

We conclude that Moncharsh has demonstrated no reason why the strong presumption in favor of the finality of the arbitral award should not apply here.

The decision in the *Moncharsh v. Heily & Blase* case certainly suggests that a person ought to be exceedingly cautious about signing contracts that require all disputes to be settled by final and binding arbitration. Many courts, like California, take the position that the decision of an arbitrator will not be set aside even if the arbitrator failed to follow the law in arriving at his or her decision.

COURT-ANNEXED ARBITRATION

Unlike a contractual agreement that requires arbitration of disputes, or unlike voluntary agreements to arbitrate after a dispute arises, sometimes courts order a court-annexed arbitration. The courts that utilize this form of alternative dispute resolution compel the parties to certain disputes selected by the courts to engage in nonbinding arbitration of their cases. The judges hope to encourage the parties, after hearing a miniversion of the facts and issues of the case, to resolve the case short of a full-blown jury trial. In this way, the judges attempt to reduce their caseloads by shifting cases to a court-annexed arbitration proceeding. If a party disagrees with the decision of the arbitrator, the case proceeds to a full-blown trial in front of a judge.

Every day it becomes more evident that an increase in arbitration is used to settle conflicts. Arbitration is similar to litigation in the sense that a person possesses the power to make a decision in the case. Other forms of dispute resolution are not perhaps as widely utilized in settling controversies as arbitration. However, they possess certain highly useful attributes not found in arbitration or litigation. These alternative dispute resolution procedures give the parties to a conflict the chance to see and hear, directly from the other side, the shortcomings and strengths of each person's case. The hope is that after hearing this information the parties will *voluntarily* arrive at a mutually satisfactory disposition of their disagreement. However, these forms of alternative dispute resolution procedures do *not* designate anyone as a decision maker who possesses the power to end a dispute, as is the case in arbitration and litigation.

Figure 3.5 graphically depicts the loss of control that all litigation parties experience depending on the type of dispute resolution mechanism utilized to resolve a disagreement. When parties rely on a formal judicial trial, they, in essence, transfer the power to settle their

■ **FIGURE 3.5** Degree of Control That a Party May Exercise over a Dispute

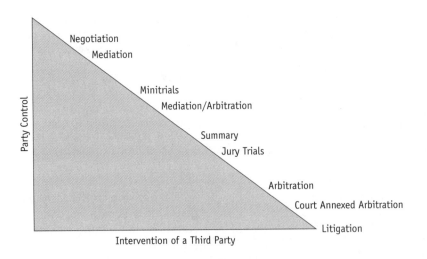

Negotiation

Mediation

Minitrials

Mediation/Arbitration

Summary

Jury Trials

Arbitration

Court Annexed Arbitration

Litigation

Party Control

Intervention of a Third Party

conflict from themselves to someone else. A party involved in a dispute should ask himself or herself: "If I can end this disagreement myself, why should I transfer the power to resolve it to someone else?"

The alternative dispute resolution procedures discussed next may be utilized to assist people involved in a disagreement in the process of resolving the conflict themselves—without the need of resorting to a judge or an arbitrator to do their thinking for them.

MEDIATION

One procedure that is used more and more every day to expedite the resolution of disputes is mediation. Generally, people voluntarily decide on agreeing to mediation. Sometimes, however, a court may forcefully urge the parties to mediate their case, or a court may even force them to resort to mediation. For example, many courts in the United States now require spouses to participate in mandatory mediation before obtaining a divorce.

Mediation, as well as the other alternative dispute resolution procedures, gives a client the chance to hear, from the other side, the shortcomings in his or her position and the strengths of the other side's case.

Unlike an arbitration proceeding in which the arbitrator actually decides the case for the parties, in mediation, the mediator tries to help the parties work out their differences. A mediator searches for ways to satisfy and promote the mutual interests of the parties. Mediation evolved to assist parties who want to maintain a relationship but who are having trouble negotiating. The mediator helps the parties negotiate and at the same time maintain their relationship.

Mediation is thus *consensual.* Mediation is voluntary, as opposed to the coercive, authoritarian approach followed in the judicial system. Mediators have *no power*—other than the mediator's ability to facilitate negotiation. The mediator works with the parties to attempt to facilitate negotiation. The mediator focuses on the parties' *needs*—not on their *rights*. This gets the parties into a problem-solving mode. A judge, on the other hand, must in effect force a decision on the parties based on the parties' rights.

One may argue that mediation is more likely to create and preserve harmonious relationships than the adversary system that evolved in Great Britain. People in many other countries recognize the need for adopting a conflict resolution style that maintains good relations between people. The International Perspective, "Harmonious Relations in India," illustrates this point.

Different mediators employ different styles of mediation. A commonly followed approach is a form of shuttle diplomacy. Following

INTERNATIONAL
PERSPECTIVE

Harmonious Relations in India

Half-way around the globe from the United States, nearly a billion people live in the country of India. Contrary to popular belief in the United States, everyone in India does not speak the same language. A person traveling throughout India would encounter more than twenty-four languages as well as various dialects. Values and religious beliefs vary from region to region. India, rather than being homogeneous, is in fact quite diverse.

In order to deal with this maze of languages, cultural attitudes, customs, and religious beliefs, the people of India developed ways of dealing with this diversity. A business person from the United States may be amazed by the emphasis of the business people of India on creating and 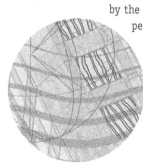 maintaining harmonious relationships. People in a conflict should be encouraged to move in a more harmonious direction by urging them to mediate rather than litigate their disputes.

an opening statement by both sides, the mediator speaks in private with each side and goes back and forth between the parties attempting to arrive at a settlement of the case. In contrast to the deal maker style of mediation, some mediators view themselves merely as orchestrators. Rather than trying to strike a deal, they merely want to facilitate discussion. Orchestrators take a less active role in the process than deal makers.

Not every case is suitable for mediation. Timing is critical. At the outset of discovery, for example, a case may not be ready for mediation. The parties must have a desire to settle the dispute. They must trust each other. If one of the parties wants to create a new precedent in the law, then that party probably will insist on a trial and appeal in order to get a change in the case law.

Unlike in the case of an arbitration proceeding, a decision of a mediator generally may be appealed. If the parties fail to arrive at a settlement of the disagreement, they may proceed on to trial. The parties have much to gain and relatively little to lose by mediating their dispute.

MINITRIAL

Another method of resolving a dispute is the **minitrial.** Corporations sometimes utilize the minitrial to resolve their differences. Each party to a dispute sends a person with decision-making authority to represent it on a panel. These people, along with a neutral third party, serve as a panel whose function is to listen to evidence presented by the parties according to expedited and streamlined procedures. The hope is that after hearing the evidence, the parties will be able to come to some sort of settlement of their dispute. If they do not settle the dispute in this manner, they can always try the case at a later date. Minitrials are currently being extensively used in business litigation.

SUMMARY JURY TRIAL

The **summary jury trial** is the jury equivalent of a minitrial. Many federal judges impanel a regular jury for use in a summary jury trial. The judge may or may not tell the members of the jury that their decision will not be final. In other cases, the parties themselves assemble a group of people to act as jurors. The lawyers representing each side present their cases in a capsulized form. The attorneys then instruct the jury to reach an advisory verdict. The jury members provide the parties with their advisory evaluation of the case. In some jurisdictions, the rules permit the attorneys to question the jurors to explore their reasoning. This helps the parties evaluate the case. To the extent that a summary jury trial simulates the prospective jury trial, the litigants get a pretrial advance view as to the reaction of jurors to the case. One also hears both attorneys expound on the major issues likely to arise at trial. If the summary jury indicates that it views the position of one side as weak, then that party ought to seriously consider compromising its position and settling the case.

SETTLEMENT CONFERENCES

Prior to trial, judges call the parties together for a pretrial conference. This conference, at which the judge is present, may be used to encourage the parties to settle the case. In effect, a judge may act as a mediator at the conference.

EXPERT FACT FINDING

With expert fact finding, the parties employ a neutral third party to make a decision, based either on a limited set of facts or, in some cases, on a set of facts concerning the entire case. Thus, a decision of the expert fact finder may resolve only a few issues rather than the entire case. As the decision of the expert fact finder is similar to an agreement to arbitrate, it probably will be enforced.

PRIVATE JUDGING

More and more parties throughout the country now contract with a referee to hear their dispute. The referee acts just like a judge in a case—and quite often former judges serve as referees. The referee determines the facts of the case and applies the law to these facts in order to arrive at a resolution of the disagreement. These decisions are treated like court decisions and are therefore appealable. A California state statute permits people engaged in civil trials to request that the case be heard by a private referee.

Many people dislike the lottery system by which the government assigns judges to hear a case. With the *Rent a Judge* system, the parties may set their own rules to govern the procedure, meet in any place they desire, and select anyone they want to act as the judge in their case.

Critics argue that the *Rent a Judge* system of resolving disputes encourages the best judges to leave the bench because they earn more money working for private dispute resolution companies. Important cases are handled in secret, and thus the public is kept in the dark about the proceedings. The secrecy of the proceedings troubles many people. Litigants can bypass the long wait for trial in the public court system and receive an immediate airing of their dispute should they so desire it. Furthermore, some states allow the parties to bypass the trial court system entirely and appeal the decision of a private judge to an appellate court. This accelerated access to justice creates a two-tier system of justice in America—one for the affluent and the other for everyone else in the public system.

PRIVATE PANELS

Because certain companies find themselves embroiled in disputes with consumers, it behooves them to set up procedures for handling disagreements. For example, your local Better Business Bureau probably operates a mediation and arbitration procedure in which it attempts to resolve disputes. A consumer with a complaint fills out a complaint form and turns it in to the Better Business Bureau. The

Better Business Bureau then attempts to mediate the dispute. If that fails, the consumer may then resort to arbitration.

MEDIATION/ARBITRATION

This form of dispute resolution combines both mediation and arbitration. The case starts as a conventional mediation proceeding. If the parties are unable to resolve their disagreement through mediation, the case proceeds to *binding* arbitration.

SMALL CLAIMS COURTS

For the average person, the cost of hiring an attorney for representation in a minor matter often exceeds the amount sought. Courts generally refuse to award litigants attorney's fees. This means that if a person sues to recover a small amount, the attorney collects a fee but the client fails to recover anything. The American Bar Association has long recognized the fact that legal services often are out of the reach of the middle class. For this reason, the ABA worked to encourage the states to create small claims courts. Today, all states permit people to file suits in these alternative forums. Most states permit suits for between one thousand and five thousand dollars in their small claims courts.

Suppose that Mary purchases a refrigerator from Acme. A month later, the refrigerator stops working. Acme refuses to repair the machine. Mary cannot afford to pay an attorney fifty to one hundred dollars per hour to litigate this matter. She instead turns to her state's small claims court. Her claim is for five hundred dollars. She fills out a complaint at the court and subpoenas Acme. The firm must then appear or risk a default judgment which means that Mary automatically wins her case if Acme does not appear. The proceedings in small claims court tend to more informal than at a trial. In this case, Mary presents her position, Acme presents its position, and then the judge rules.

ADVANTAGES OF USING ALTERNATIVE DISPUTE RESOLUTION PROCEDURES

As indicated in this chapter, the 1980s were a span of years in which the courts became much more receptive to the use of alternative dispute resolution (ADR) procedures. No doubt the large number of suits flooding some courts contributed to this change in attitude. Courts also have come to realize the substantial advantages associated with settling cases in some manner other than the traditional courtroom battle. These advantages are described next. Figure 3.6 summarizes the advantages and disadvantages of using some form of alternative dispute resolution procedure.

The classic trial takes a great deal of time and money. Delays in cases are legendary. Trials sometimes result in adverse publicity which a firm would like to avoid. Worse yet, many participants in trials often find the entire process to be alienating and frustrating. A judge or jury ends up *imposing* a decision on the parties—a decision that often leaves one side the winner and the other side the loser.

■ **FIGURE 3.6** Pros and Cons
of Using an ADR Procedure

Advantages of Using Alternative Dispute Resolution Procedures

ADR saves time.

ADR saves money.

ADR facilitates a settlement of a dispute.

ADR engages people in the settlement of their own disputes.

ADR proceedings are generally nonbinding.

ADR proceedings are less formal.

ADR proceedings generally permit the parties to select where the dispute is resolved.

Disadvantages of Using Alternative Dispute Resolution Procedures

An ADR proceeding may not work if a party is not willing to keep an open mind.

ADR proceedings are secret.

ADR proceedings prevent a court from creating binding precedents.

ADR proceedings may be creating a two-tier system of justice.

Alternative dispute resolution procedures are designed to try to *facilitate* a settlement, rather than force a decision on people unwilling to come to a voluntary agreement. By involving all of the parties in a dispute, the process facilitates a settlement. The fact that the parties become more involved in the resolution of their dispute, and have a direct role in settling it, encourages them to reach an agreement.

Quite often the participants in an ADR procedure listen to a short presentation of the facts and theories of the case. The parties try to reduce even a major case to just a brief presentation of the crux of the dispute. By getting people to appear at this presentation, even if they are somewhat hostile, the parties hear a succinct version of the case. However, it should be kept in mind that ADR clauses in contracts do not *compel* a party to come to an agreement. The goal of this process is to bring the parties together to try to facilitate a settlement. If a party cannot be persuaded to settle, he or she is always free to insist on a trial. The information presented may persuade the party to settle the matter. In such a case, it may be possible to preserve any business relationship the parties had in the past—as opposed to a trial that ends in a bitter resolution, in which case the parties may even refuse to talk to each other in the future.

Other positive features associated with handling a case in this manner are the fact that such procedures generally are nonbinding and confidential. People have little to lose by listening to this process. If they disagree with the proposed resolution of the dispute, they may generally take the case to trial anyway. Additionally, a settlement at this point prevents most other people from hearing of the dispute. Suppose that the transmission in Acme Automobiles' Victory automobiles tends to fail at twenty thousand miles. If a number of people take their cases to trial, these trials may attract attention in the newspapers and on television. This adverse publicity may encourage other people to file suit. On the other hand, quietly settling these disputes short of trial tends to squelch publicity. This, in turn, may result in very few people learning about experiences of other consumers.

The Pinto automobile serves as an illustration of the dangers of publicity. In the 1970s, some people filed suit over injuries arising from the flange-mounted gasoline tank in the Pinto. Rather than quickly settling the suits, Ford chose to take the cases to trial and then on to the appeals courts. This strategy merely generated more publicity about the defect in the Pinto. In addition to making the corporation look bad, this publicity put ideas in the heads of plaintiffs' lawyers. Numerous suits followed.

United States Federal Rule of Civil Procedure 68 also favors the use of ADR. Rule 68 may be used against a person who refuses to accept a reasonable offer of settlement. This rule permits a judge to assess costs against a person who turned down an offer of settlement and then won less at trial than the amount proposed as a settlement prior to trial.

DISADVANTAGES OF USING ALTERNATIVE DISPUTE RESOLUTION PROCEDURES

Some people feel it is useless to engage in alternatives to a trial in certain instances. For example, if the other side obstinately refuses to cooperate in any fashion, and if he or she agrees to go to an ADR proceeding only as a result of a court order, one may question whether or not such a person would keep an open mind with respect to any proposed settlement that may be suggested. As noted earlier, however, these procedures are designed to *facilitate* settlements. It is possible that even a totally hostile person may profit from participating in such procedures since he or she hears the entire case.

A very serious criticism of such proceedings is they are often conducted in secret. This keeps information about the cases out of the hands of the general public. Furthermore, handling a case in this manner may deprive the courts of an opportunity to handle a matter of great public importance, thus creating a precedent that will govern other similar cases. It could also be argued that the whole process of alternative dispute resolution proceedings is creating a two-tier system of justice—one for the affluent and the other for everyone else in the public system.

ENFORCEMENT

Although a contract may contain a provision for alternative dispute resolution, one of the parties to the agreement may refuse to cooperate in the process. In such a case, the question comes up: "Can a party be *forced* to engage in some form of pretrial alternative dispute resolution procedure?" It seems somewhat questionable at first to force a person to participate in a process that he or she refuses to cooperate in. On the other hand, if a court forces a person to listen to an abbreviated presentation of the facts and issues and to both sides of the case, he or she, no matter how obstinate, may decide on hearing the facts that a trial will be a useless waste of time and money. Furthermore, such a person may see some merit to the other side's position. This may soften his or her resolve. That person may not feel as bad about settling the matter voluntarily as the loser in a trial may feel.

Some question arises about the enforceability of some ADR clauses in contracts because some courts still question the value of forcing a person to participate in a voluntary proceeding. Arbitration clauses, however, are generally enforceable.

The Thought Problem, "Failure to Act in Good Faith," deals with a situation where a party failed to participate in an ADR proceeding in good faith.

thought problem

Failure to Act in Good Faith

Passengers aboard an Eastern Airlines flight to Martinique allege that they were wrongfully ejected from their flight during a stopover in St. Croix. They allege numerous claims against Eastern Airlines, among them breach of contract and negligence. This matter was referred to arbitration. The defendants did not directly appear but rather appeared through their attorneys. The Eastern Airlines attorney presented summaries of Eastern's position and read a few passages from depositions and interrogatories. The arbitrator found that Eastern Airlines did not participate in the arbitration proceeding in a meaningful manner.

What do you think? Should the judge impose any sort of penalty on Eastern Airlines for its failure to participate in good faith? If so, what sort of penalty would you impose?

Source: Gilling v. Eastern Airlines, Inc., United States District Court, District of New Jersey, 680 F. Supp. 169 (1988).

Summary

A suit commences with the filing of a complaint with a court to which the defendant must respond in a timely manner with an answer. Thereafter, the case proceeds to the discovery stage during which the participants learn about each other's case.

If a given case is not settled prior to trial, which is the outcome of some disputes, a party may elect to have a jury trial under certain circumstances. Attorneys to a case are permitted some control over the composition of the jury. They may ask questions of prospective jury members during the voir dire, and depending on the answers received, the attorneys may disqualify certain people from serving on the jury panel. The process of selecting a jury involves a good deal of psychological thinking on the part of attorneys.

A trial gets under way after the opening statements by the attorneys trying the case. The rules of evidence govern which and in what form statements may or may not be admitted. Witnesses may be cross-examined by the opposing side. At the conclusion of the presentation of the evidence, attorneys present their closing arguments, the judge instructs the jury as to the applicable law, and the jury retires to deliberate the case.

After the jury arrives at a verdict, the judge enters the judgment. If a party is disappointed with the decision of the jury, he or she must either live with the decision or file an appeal. The appellate court may then either outrightly reverse the decision of the trial court, affirm the decision, or reverse the decision and remand the case for retrial.

In 1925, Congress passed the Federal Arbitration Act. This act made agreements to arbitrate disputes enforceable. Even so, at one time the courts resisted the attempt by Congress to encourage the arbitration of disputes.

The flood of litigation in recent years has altered the attitude of the courts regarding alternative methods of resolving disputes. Recent United States Supreme Court cases support the enforcement of alternative dispute resolution procedures and, in particular, arbitration agreements. The Court permits compulsory arbitration of even statutory matters, such as those involving the trading of securities.

But contractual agreements today contain many other alternatives to a trial besides arbitration agreements: mediation, court-annexed arbitration, minitrials, summary jury trials, settlement conferences, expert fact finding, private judging, private panels, and small claims courts. Parties use these alternatives to litigation to facilitate a settlement rather than forcing one on a party. These dispute resolution proceedings involve the parties in the resolution of their disagreements. Additionally, these agreements are generally nonbinding and confidential.

The courts today must enforce arbitration agreements, even those dealing with statutory matters. The law is evolving with respect to the enforceability of other types of alternative dispute resolution proceedings; however, many courts will force parties to participate in them. Furthermore, parties often may be penalized if they fail to participate in such proceedings in good faith.

Thus, we clearly are entering a new era in which people will be expected to explore means of resolving their disputes other than the traditional trial in front of a judge or jury.

Review Questions

1. Define the following terms:
   a. Adversary system
   b. Answer
   c. Burden of proof
   d. Complaint
   e. Deposition
   f. Discovery
   g. Expert fact finding
   h. Mediation
   i. Minitrial
   j. Peremptory challenge
   k. Petit jury
   l. Preponderance of the evidence
   m. Private judging
   n. Private panels
   o. Settlement conferences
   p. Small claims court
   q. Statute of limitations

r. Summary jury trial

s. Voir dire

2. Mary was injured in an automobile accident on August 30, 1997. The accident was caused by Tom, who negligently drove his car through a red light and struck the vehicle being driven by Mary. The statute of limitations for filing an automobile negligence lawsuit is two years. When must Mary file her lawsuit? Why does such a rule exist? If Mary files her suit after the date you gave above, are there any additional facts that could be added to this problem that allow Mary to argue that her claim should be allowed to proceed?

3. Laura Stanton, the President of Technet Corporation, thought she had agreed with Jennifer Van, the President of International Corporation, on the merger of the two firms. Laura thinks that Jennifer unlawfully backed out of a valid agreement. How would Laura go about instituting suit against International Corporation? What must International Corporation do in response to any suit brought against it?

4. In the Technet Corporation/International Corporation suit mentioned in question 3, discuss some devices that may be used by Technet Corporation to learn about useful information that International Corporation has in its possession.

5. In the Technet Corporation/International Corporation suit mentioned in question 3, suppose that neither Technet nor International disagree about the facts. If Technet wants an immediate ruling from the judge handling the case, what can Laura suggest that her attorneys do at this point?

6. Suppose that the Technet Corporation/International Corporation dispute mentioned in question 3 goes to trial, and the clerk of the court assembles a group of people to possibly serve as jurors on the case. Laura and her attorneys suspect that a number of these people may favor International Corporation. Is there anything the Technet Corporation attorneys can do to see that these people do not serve as jurors on this case?

7. Do attorneys select people for a jury solely on the basis of whether or not a person appears to be fair and impartial?

8. When it comes time to exercise its peremptory challenges, the International Corporation chooses to strike all of the women from the jury pool. What may the Technet Corporation attorneys want to argue at this point?

9. If the Technet Corporation files suit against International Corporation and is thus the plaintiff in the Technet Corporation/International Corporation suit, who has the initial burden of proof in the case? What does it mean to say that one party has the burden of proof in a case?

10. Is it ever advantageous for the attorney trying a suit to ignore the evidence and simply base his or her closing argument on emotion?

11. International Securities requires that any dispute arising between its customers and its brokers be submitted to arbitration. What is an arbitration proceeding?

12. Rodriguez de Quijas signed a standard customer agreement with Shearson/American Express brokerage house when he set up his stock

account. The contract obligates the parties to settle any controversies through binding arbitration. De Quijas sued Shearson and his broker. He alleged that his money was lost in unauthorized and fraudulent transactions. One of the allegations involved a violation of the 1933 Securities Act. Must de Quijas arbitrate his claim under this act?

13. What are some of the advantages associated with using an alternative dispute resolution proceeding?

14. Are there any disadvantages to employing alternative dispute resolution procedures to resolve a dispute?

15. Acme Brick Corporation enters into a contract with Smith's Pool Company. The contract provides that any dispute between the parties will be submitted to a summary jury. What is a summary jury? Can Smith be forced to participate in this proceeding even if he feels it is a waste of his time?

16. Stevens Construction Company entered into a contract with Acme Electrical Supply. The contract requires the parties to submit any dispute to a private judge. A dispute arises between the parties. Acme appears at the proceeding but presents no evidence. What is a private judge? Can Acme be penalized for its failure to participate?

17. Rockford Corporation entered into a contract with Acme Corporation. The contract provided that any dispute arising out of the contract would be subject to final and binding arbitration. A dispute arose between the parties. Rockford asked for the dispute to be submitted to an arbitrator. After reading the decision of the arbitrator, the president of Acme felt that the arbitrator misunderstood the law. He vowed to take the case to court. Will he be able to get the decision of the arbitrator reversed by a court?

Chapter
4

JUDICIAL REASONING AND
STATUTORY CONSTRUCTION

Astudy of the components of judicial decision making should provide a needed supplement to the legal rules that are presented throughout this text. Determining what the law is in a given situation is far more complex than simply looking up the relevant rules. The people involved in the system also have a major role to play. Understanding how people affect the application of law is a vital component in determining the legal risk of any activity. Consider, then, that the law is comprised of a rule element and a people-who-apply-the-rule element. Judicial decision making provides a clear illustration.

The Judge as a Person: The Personality Factor

A frequently heard saying about our legal system is that it is a system of laws, not of people. As with most folk wisdom—"wind from the west, fish bite the best"—there is an element of truth in it. Our legal system is based on established rules and procedures that apply to all parties equally. For instance, the general rule that contracts for the sale of land must be in writing before they will be enforceable applies to all real estate contracts, whether the parties are rich or poor, black or white, politically powerful or politically weak. In that sense, our system is one of laws. But it is also a system of men and women. Judges are people, not computers or mechanical devices programmed to decide cases on the basis of existing laws or procedures. Judges do not become any less human upon donning their black robes. As a result, the personality of the judge— who the judge is, the background of the judge, the likes and dislikes of the judge—all must be considered in determining how a particular judge will decide a particular case.

When a judge's personality is studied, a major distinction between the law and legal rules becomes apparent. Legal rules, like theorems in geometry, exist in a vacuum—that is, in discussions of their applicability, no mention is made of the effect of a certain person applying them. For example, the rules for applying the tort of negligence are stated as if a *correct* outcome is readily apparent. However, in fact, numerous *correct* outcomes may exist when different people accurately apply those rules.

Throughout this text, cases appear with both a majority opinion (the ruling in the case) and a dissenting opinion. These cases most readily illustrate the application of the personality factor: the same legal rules are being applied. However, the personal characteristics of the judges cause differing opinions. It is this aspect of legal decision making called *the personality factor* that distinguishes the study of legal rules from the study of law.

Without doubt, former President Ronald Reagan appreciated the importance of this factor. In fact, both Reagan and Franklin D. Roosevelt have been accused (or praised, depending on the analyst) of packing the federal judiciary with judges sharing their philosophies. The effect of Reagan's efforts may be seen by the decisions of the United States Supreme Court during the 1988–89 term, which one commentator noted provided the most profound change in legal interpretations in fifty years. A five-justice conservative majority prevailed in decisions ranging from employment discrimination to drug testing in the workplace. Notably, that conservative group determined the Court's holding in more than sixty percent of 5–4 decisions that year.

Former President George Bush continued to appoint conservative judges to the federal courts. By the end of the 1991–92 term, seven of the nine Supreme Court Justices, including Clarence Thomas, could be considered *conservative*. However, during that term, a *swing group* took form with Justice Kennedy often joining moderates Souter and O'Connor. Their votes have kept the Court from overturning certain precedents from the 1960s and 1970s, including the school prayer decision and abortion rights cases. Furthermore, compare President Clinton's appointees, Ruth Bader Ginsberg and Stephen Breyer with the Bush-appointed Clarence Thomas. Their political philosophies are in stark contrast. During the 1994–95 Supreme Court term, the Clinton-appointed justices voted together seventy-nine percent of the time. The Court's most conservative members, Justices Scalia and Thomas, agreed with each other on eighty-three percent of the cases.

However, the personality factor does not suggest that a judge is biased, decides a case before hearing it, or cannot divorce personal feelings from professional efforts. A good judge attempts to keep any personal feelings from affecting the decision in a case. As Samuel Johnson said, "If he [the judge] was such a rogue as to make up his mind upon a case without hearing it, he should not have been such a fool as to tell it."[1] Judges who let bias influence their decisions are beyond the scope of this discussion and are unfit for their jobs.

Judges are not unique in having their individual characteristics affect their decision making. Such characteristics as personal values, social and family background, likes and dislikes, and basic philosophy of life undoubtedly affect a person's decision to, say, become an accountant instead of a teacher. These and other characteristics are involved in legal decision making as well.

A humorous example appeared on a Public Broadcasting System program, imported from England, titled *Rumpole of the Bailey*. Rumpole was a crafty, old barrister (trial lawyer) who had tried many cases in London's courts. Rumpole knew the judges and their personality quirks. In one episode, a young attorney was trying her first case and Rumpole was representing the opposing party. Rumpole, ever the crafty advocate, told the young attorney that the judge was fond of lengthy arguments consisting of citation of legal precedent. In fact, the judge became annoyed if attorneys cited cases as authority in his courtroom. He liked short arguments based on the principle of the case at hand. As expected, the young attorney made a strong, legitimate argument on behalf of her client, citing numerous cases and quoting from the opinions of other judges, while the judge seethed with annoyance. When the young attorney finished, Rumpole made a few comments, and the judge in short order found for Rumpole's client.

The viewer of that television program had no way of knowing whether or not justice was done in that case or whether or not a different argument by the young attorney would actually have changed its outcome. However, it was clear that one style of argument carried very little persuasive weight before that judge.

The Thought Problem, "Pretend You Are the Judge," shows how the personality factor affects decisions made by a judge. Of course, judges realize the effect of personality on their perception of legal issues, legal arguments, and the facts of a case. Therefore, the competent judge will make every attempt to separate personal feelings from a final decision. As just suggested, however, removing personal feelings from the decision-making process does not entirely erase a personality factor, just the most obvious outward manifestations of it.

thought problem

Pretend You Are the Judge

To see how the personality factor works, apply this statute to the facts that follow: "It shall be a criminal offense to willfully damage public property (including trees and vegetation) in public parks." As the judge, you may assess on those who violate this statute any combination of the following penalties:

1. *Jail*—zero to thirty days in the county jail. The judge has the option of deciding which days (for example, weekends only).

2. *Fine*—zero to five hundred dollars.

3. *Probation*—no jail or fine. However, conviction goes on criminal record and defendant must report to a probation officer for six months.

4. *Diversion*—no jail or fine. If the defendant stays out of trouble for one year, then there will be no criminal record.

The following two cases come before you one day while you are performing your duties as a judge. For each case decide: (1) Did the person violate the statute? (2) What penalty should be assessed against the violator?

PROBLEM 1: Mary, who is twenty-one, is a senior in college. Her father and mother are doctors. Mary plans to go to medical school. Her pre-med grades are 3.95/4.00. Mary belongs to the top sorority on campus. She is active in campus events. She is engaged to be married in June.

On the weekend before final exams, Mary's sorority threw its annual Christmas party. This was a traditional event. In the afternoon, the sorority hosted a Christmas party for underprivileged children. Mary was in charge of that event. In the evening, the party would become a celebration of the end of another semester and an outlet before final exam studies began.

When the last child left (about 5:30 P.M.), Mary and her sorority friends began to drink some wine. After the first glass, Mary was a bit giddy and ran from the house laughing and saying, "We need another Christmas tree." She went to a local park and cut down an evergreen. However, a passing police officer stopped her and arrested her. She spent the night in jail.

The next day the local newspapers carried stories concerning Mary's arrest. She was released from jail (pending trial), but was humiliated. She could not face returning to school for finals and took incompletes in all of her classes.

Mary pled guilty to the offense. The tree was worth fifty dollars. She had never even had a parking ticket before.

PROBLEM 2: Leroy, who is twenty-one, dropped out of high school during his junior year. His parents are divorced, and he lives on a farm with his uncle. He is currently unemployed—by choice. Leroy has had a number of jobs: grocery store clerk, farm laborer, gas station attendant. He was fired from each because of his *don't give a damn* attitude. He refuses to help work on his uncle's farm and refuses to look for another job.

Leroy is a 1950s-style hood, although he has never been in trouble with the law. He is clean-shaven and has long hair which he greases back. Leroy dresses in black, keeping his shirt front open. His pleasures consist of driving his souped-up pickup truck around town and playing pool at the local tavern.

Leroy does not attend any church nor does he participate in the community. In short, Leroy does not care about anything.

On the Saturday before Christmas, Leroy was on his way home. He was thrown out of a local tavern for insulting the owner. He was not intoxicated—he had not even finished his first beer. While driving, Leroy decided to stop by a local park. He got out of his pickup truck and chopped down an evergreen—for the heck of it. A passing police officer stopped him and arrested him. He spent the night in jail.

The next day the event was reported in the local newspapers. He was released from jail (pending trial), but did not care. The evergreen was worth fifty dollars.

Make a decision in each case, and compare your decisions and the reasons behind them with those given by your fellow students.

Consequently, an attorney may seek to have a judge removed from hearing a case or may *judge shop*—that is, file the case before a judge whose personality increases the likelihood of success. This does not necessarily mean that attorneys believe that the judge is biased (although this, too, is a reason for an attorney to seek to have a judge removed from a case). It may well mean that the personality of a particular judge may be more (or less) compatible with the client, arguments, or facts to be presented in court.

Sometimes a judge may be concerned that the personality factor may unduly influence the outcome of a pending case. In such a circumstance, the judge may decline to preside. This process is called **recusal.** It usually occurs when the case concerns a factual matter or a party with which the judge is so personally involved as to risk a possible conflict of interest—for example, a case on which the judge has worked on behalf of one of the parties prior to becoming a judge, or a lawsuit against a corporation in which the judge is a shareholder. Recusal reflects two things: first, the judge's realization of the importance of the personality factor and of the possible influence of that factor on the decision; second, where a judge's personal interest may raise questions about the fairness or impartiality of a decision. When a judge's quirks or background unfairly interferes with the professional judgment needed to resolve the dispute, recusal is appropriate.

The International Perspective, "Recusal in a Holocaust Trial," portrays an example of recusal.

Factors in Judicial Decision Making

Decision-making factors are not used by a judge in the same manner that a recipe is used by a chef. A judicial decision does not contain one part history, two parts precedent, and a dash of doing *what is right* (see Figure 4.1). In fact, some judicial decisions may be justified entirely by one factor while others may use two or more. No set rule exists for using or weighing them. The use of factors in justifying a decision is up to the judge.

Recusal in a Holocaust Trial

Adolph Eichmann was in charge of the Nazi extermination of Jews during World War II. He established death camps, such as Auschwitz, as the *final solution* to the Jewish *problem*. After the war, Eichmann escaped from Germany and was given refuge in Argentina. In 1960, Israeli agents captured him and brought him to Israel for trial.

Eichmann's lawyers argued that the three judges who would be hearing the case should recuse themselves. All three judges were Jewish and citizens of Israel, and the attorneys asserted that the horror of the Holocaust would impermissibly prejudice their determination of the validity of the charges against the defendant.

Writing for the court, presiding Judge Laudau rejected that argument: "[W]hen a court of judgment sits to judge, the judge is still a human being, flesh and blood, with feelings and senses, but he is ordered by the law to restrain those feelings and senses, because otherwise there will never be a judge fit to sit in a criminal case where the abhorrence of the judge is aroused, like treason, murder, or any other serious crime. It is true that the memory of the catastrophe and the Holocaust stirs every Jew, but when this case has been brought before us, it is our duty to restrain those feelings when we sit in judgment in this case. And this duty we shall keep."

Source: State of Israel v. Adolph Eichmann, District Court of Jerusalem (April 17, 1961).

HISTORY AND CUSTOM

The law does not exist apart from the world around it. Law evolves as a result of a nation's (or within the United States, even a state's) history. It is based on and derived from the values of the people, and it is a function of all that has affected a nation. Custom is like the historical factor but with a much shorter time span. Frequently, it concerns a type of business practice adopted by a firm or industry that has become standard. Like history, it is a part of law and it can be a major aspect of a judge's decision.

In *Ghen v. Rich* (1881), Provincetown whalers killed a whale and, as generally happens, it floated ashore. Whaling crews used marked lances so their identity could readily be determined when one came across a dead whale. Customarily, the finder of a beached whale would contact the appropriate crew, who would then come to remove the blubber. The finder would receive a small fee. However, the finder in this case sold the whale himself. The court could find no legal rule concerning whale ownership but noted the practice that Provincetown had adopted was widely used in the whaling industry. Thus, based on custom, the court held that the crew who killed the whale was its owner.

BALANCE OF INTERESTS

The statue of justice, a robed, blindfolded woman holding an evenly balanced scale, is a familiar symbol of a court. This statue is a good representation of the next factor to be considered: the balancing of interests. Judicial decisions often affect people other than the parties in the case, or the decision may have major policy implications. Courts are aware of these effects, and so are other interested parties. Often, these other interested parties will file their own written arguments called **amicus curiae briefs**— with the court.

■ **FIGURE 4.1** Components of
Judicial Decisions

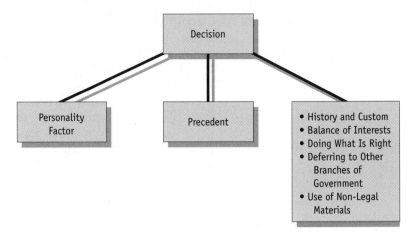

Thus, judges may note the competing interests at stake when deciding a case. Frequently, these balanced interests will be offered as illustrations that the decision is consistent with some applicable legal principle.

Of course, judges may not agree on how to balance the interests. *Moore v. Regents of the University of California,* is an example. It concerns a property ownership question and, like *Ghen v. Rich* previously noted, raised a novel question about ownership. Note the interests (or policies) that concerned the majority and dissenting judges.

Moore v. Regents of the University of California

Supreme Court of California
271 Cal. Rptr. 146 (1990)

John Moore first visited UCLA Medical Center on October 5, 1976, shortly after he learned that he had hairy-cell leukemia. On October 8, 1976, his physician, David Golde, recommended that Moore's spleen be removed. Golde informed Moore that he had reason to fear for Moore's life, and that the proposed operation was necessary to slow down the progress of the disease. On the basis of Golde's representations, Moore signed a written consent form authorizing the splenectomy. Before the operation, Golde and Shirley Quan, a researcher employed by the medical center, made arrangements to study portions of Moore's removed spleen. These research activities were not intended to have any relation to Moore's medical care. However, neither Golde nor Quan informed Moore of the plans to conduct this research or requested his permission.

Moore returned to the UCLA Medical Center several times between November 1976 and September 1983. He did so at Golde's direction and on the advice that such visits were necessary and required for his health and well-being. In fact, defendants were conducting research on Moore's cells and planned to benefit financially and competitively by exploiting the cells and their exclusive access to the cells by virtue of Golde's ongoing physician–patient relationship. Sometime before August 1979, Golde established a cell line from Moore's T-lymphocytes. On January 30, 1981, the regents of the University of California applied for a patent on the cell line, listing Golde and Quan as inventors. By virtue of an established policy, the regents, Golde, and Quan would share in any royalties or profits arising out of the patent.

Moore theorizes that he continued to own his cells following their removal from his body, at least for the purpose of directing their use, and that he never consented to their use in potentially lucrative medical research. Thus, to complete Moore's argument, defendants' unauthorized use of his cells constitutes a **conversion** or wrongful taking of his property. As a result of the alleged conversion, Moore claims a proprietary interest in each of the products that any of the defendants may ever create from his cells or the patented cell line.

Panelli, Justice

To establish a conversion a plaintiff must establish an actual interference with his *ownership* or *right of possession.* Where the plaintiff neither has title to the property alleged to have been converted, nor possession thereof, he cannot maintain an action for conversion. Since Moore clearly did not expect to retain possession of his cells following their removal, to sue for their conversion he must have retained an ownership interest in them.

Moore's novel claim to own the biological materials at issue in this case is problematic, at best. Accordingly, his attempt to apply the theory of conversion within this context must frankly be recognized as a request to extend that theory. While we do not purport to hold that excised cells can never be property for any purpose whatsoever, the novelty of Moore's claim demands express consideration of the policies to be served by extending liability.

Of the relevant policy considerations, two are of overriding importance. The first is protection of a competent patient's right to make autonomous medical decisions. That right is grounded in well-recognized and long-standing principles of fiduciary duty and informed consent. This policy weighs in favor of providing a remedy to patients when physicians act with undisclosed motives that may affect their professional judgment. The second important policy consideration is that we not threaten with disabling civil liability innocent parties who are engaged in socially useful activities, such as researchers who have no reason to believe that their use of a particular cell sample is, or may be, against a donor's wishes.

Research on human cells plays a critical role in medical research. This is so because researchers are increasingly able to isolate naturally occurring, medically useful biological substances and to produce useful quantities of such substances through genetic engineering. These efforts are beginning to bear fruit. The extension of conversion law into this area will hinder research by restricting access to the necessary raw materials. Thousands of human cell lines already exist in tissue repositories. These repositories respond to tens of thousands of requests for samples annually. At present, human cell lines are routinely copied and distributed to other researchers for experimental purposes, usually free of charge. This exchange of scientific materials, which still is relatively free and efficient, will surely be compromised if each cell sample becomes the potential subject matter of a lawsuit.

The theory of liability that Moore urges us to endorse threatens to destroy the economic incentive to conduct important medical research. If the use of cells in research is a conversion, then with every cell sample a researcher purchases a ticket in a litigation lottery. Because liability for conversion is predicated on a continuing ownership interest, companies are unlikely to invest heavily in developing, manufacturing, or marketing a product when uncertainty about clear title exists.

In this case, limiting the expansion of liability under a conversion theory will only make it more difficult for Moore to recover a highly theoretical windfall. Any injury to his right to make an informed decision remains actionable through the fiduciary-duty and informed-consent theories. For these reasons, we hold that the allegations of Moore's complaint state a cause of action for breach of fiduciary duty or lack of informed consent, but not conversion.

Mosk, Justice (dissenting)

The majority claims that a conversion cause of action threatens to "destroy the economic incentive" to conduct the type of research here in issue. In my view whatever merit the majority's single policy consideration may have is outweighed by two contrary considerations. First, our society acknowledges a profound ethical imperative to respect the human body as the physical and temporal expression of the unique human persona. One manifestation of that respect is our prohibition against direct abuse of the body by torture or other forms of cruel or unusual punishment. Another is our prohibition against indirect abuse of the body by its economic exploitation for the sole benefit of another person. Yet the specter of abuse and exploitation haunts the laboratories and boardrooms of today's biotechnological research-industrial complex. It arises wherever scientists or industrialists claim, as defendants claim here, the right to appropriate and exploit a patient's tissue for their sole economic benefit—the right, in other words, to freely mine or harvest valuable physical properties of the patient's body. Such research tends to treat the human body as a commodity—a means to a profitable end. The dignity and sanctity with which we regard the human whole, body as well as mind and soul, are absent when we allow researchers to further their own interests without the patient's participation by using a patient's cells as the basis for a marketable product.

A second policy consideration adds notions of equity to those of ethics. Our society values fundamental fairness in dealings between its members, and condemns the unjust enrichment of any member at the expense of another. This is particularly true when, as here, the parties are not in equal bargaining positions. We are repeatedly told that the commercial products of the biotechnological revolution "hold the promise of tremendous profit." These profits are currently shared exclusively between the biotechnology industry and the universities that support that industry. There is, however, a third party to the biotechnology enterprise—the patient who is the source of the blood or tissue from which all of these profits are derived. While he may be a silent partner, his contribution to the venture is absolutely crucial. But for the cells of Moore's body taken by defendants, there would have been no Mo-cell line at all. Yet defendants deny that Moore is entitled to any share whatever in the proceeds of this cell line. This is both inequitable and immoral.

Biotechnology depends upon the contributions of both patients and researchers. If not for the patient's contribution of cells with unique attributes, the medical value of the bioengineered cells would be negligible. But for the physician's contribution of knowledge and skill in developing the cell product, the commercial value of the patient's cells would also be negligible. Failing to compensate the patient unjustly enriches the researcher because only the researcher's contribution is recognized. In short, if this science has become science for profit, then I fail to see any justification for excluding the patient from participation in those profits.

DOING "WHAT IS RIGHT"

A third decision-making factor is based on ethical considerations. Whether or not a judicial decision is *right* or *just* or *fair* is at the core of its legitimacy. Judges, therefore, use such considerations in formulating their decisions.

Legal philosophers may refer to this factor as **natural law**—that is, an overriding sense of justice or fairness. Natural law is said to arise from God or from the rational sense of the people. It assumes that there is an order in the universe and that the law must reflect it. Its ideals serve to test legal rules against universal principles of justice.

A number of legal doctrines comprise the *doing what is right* factor. The law of equity is based on principles of fairness. The United States Constitution contains the Due Process Clause which has been interpreted to mean fundamental fairness in the American system of justice. The Uniform Commercial Code gives courts the power to modify a contract if it is found to be unconscionable.

Courts have defined **unconscionability** to mean that something is grossly unfair. In addition, consider a contract clause that provides for the removal of the breaching party's little finger. No statute exists that commands a judge to ignore finger-removal clauses. Besides, upholding contract terms is a strong value in the law. Yet, courts will refuse to enforce such a contract because doing so would not be right.

Determining whether or not a legal issue involves this question is not an objective exercise. No list of *what is right* exists, nor is there a foolproof test that will produce the answer. The judge reaches a decision based on experience, social norms, and ethical reasoning.

The Ethical Perspective, "Is a Murderer Entitled to Inheritance?", is meant to place you in the position of a judge. The problem concerns a will—an area of the law where predictability and following the intentions of the deceased are strong values. Should these values be overcome by ethics?

E T H I C A L
P E R S P E C T I V E
Is a Murderer Entitled to Inheritance?

Francis B. Palmer made his last will and testament in which he left small legacies to his two daughters and the remainder of his estate to his grandson, Elmer Palmer. Elmer lived with Francis B. Palmer as a member of his family and at the time of Francis' death, Elmer was sixteen years old. He knew about the terms of the will, but he was concerned that his grandfather may change it, which he had threatened to do on a number of occasions. To prevent this, Elmer Palmer killed his grandfather by poisoning him.

Elmer Palmer intends to claim the property left to him under his grandfather's will. Can he have it?

Source: Riggs v. Palmer, *22 N.E. 188 (New York Court of Appeals 1889).*

DEFERRING TO OTHER BRANCHES OF GOVERNMENT

A court may defer a decision to another branch of government. This factor relates to the structure of American government and the role of each branch (judicial, legislative, executive) as well as that of administrative agencies. Although it may seem that every dispute in American life is ultimately decided in the courts, the judiciary may not be the most effective branch to deal with some of them.

A court has institutional limits. It cannot conduct its own investigation, call witnesses, or hire experts before making a decision. The evidence it considers is what the parties present at trial. The legislature, administrative agencies, or the executive branch of government are better-suited than the judiciary for such tasks. They have staffs to do the work, while a judge, at most, has a law clerk.

Consequently, the limited expertise of the courts may be a primary reason for deferral. For example, one of the most renowned environmental law cases is *TVA v. Hill*, a United States Supreme Court decision from 1978. This was not a case in which the Court created a new doctrine for the protection of the environment, nor did it overturn a major legislative initiative. The Court simply refused to apply *common sense* because it lacked the expertise to have acquired any. It deferred resolution of the problem to the legislature.

In this case, the Tennessee Valley Authority (TVA), a government-owned corporation, had spent more than $100 million of congressionally appropriated money constructing the Tellico Dam. However, before the dam was completed a scientist discovered a new species of fish (a snail darter) whose habitat would be destroyed once the dam began to operate. Four months after this discovery,

Congress passed a statute that required regulations be promulgated to protect any endangered species. Since the snail darter's only known habitat was near the Tellico Dam, regulations were issued that halted its construction.

The Court was asked to apply *common sense* in interpreting the clear statutory language and thereby permit the dam to open. After all, nearly 130-known species of darter existed, ten of which had been discovered in the five years before the case was brought before the Supreme Court.

Chief Justice Burger, writing for the Court, deferred this decision to Congress: "We have no expert knowledge on the subject of endangered species, much less do we have a mandate from the people to strike a balance of equities on the side of the Tellico Dam. . . . Our Constitution vests such responsibilities in the political branches."

CONSIDERATION OF NON-LEGAL MATERIALS

Non-legal materials may play a key role in a judicial decision. For example, economic data may be used to assess the application of a rule of corporate law. Studies in sociology or psychology may influence a decision in a criminal case. In *People v. Collins* (1968), the California Supreme Court overturned a conviction because of flaws in a statistical analysis used by the prosecution. The prosecutor had argued that there was only one chance in twelve million that a couple other than the defendants had the characteristics that were described by witnesses to the crime (black man with a beard, blond woman with a pony tail, seen driving a yellow car). Based on this evidence, the jury convicted the defendants. However, the California Supreme Court overturned it. In an appendix to its opinion, the court, citing statistics books instead of legal sources, corrected the prosecutor's erroneous analysis and showed that, in fact, a probability of more than forty percent supported that another couple with the same profile could have appeared at the time of the crime.

Non-legal materials as a decision-making factor first arose in *Muller v. Oregon* (1908). In an appeal to the United States Supreme Court, Louis D. Brandeis, who was later appointed to that Court, filed a brief that contained extracts from more than ninety social science studies showing that lengthy work days were physically dangerous to women. Brandeis argued that it was, thus, constitutional for a state to make it a crime for employers to require females to work more than ten hours a day. The Supreme Court used these social science studies as the basis for upholding Oregon's statute. This technique for writing briefs is now known as a *Brandeis brief*.

However, the use of non-legal materials by courts, particularly social science studies, has been criticized. The information was not created for use in an adversary system and a concern exists that courts do not use it properly. Furthermore, case holdings are not changed to reflect modifications in social science theory. Those out-dated holdings may still be used as binding precedent in future cases even though their social science underpinnings are no longer valid.

managerial perspective **Football Rules and the Law** A player for the Denver Broncos intercepted a pass intended for Booby Clark of the Cincinnati Bengals. Thereafter, Dale Hackbart of the Broncos attempted to block Booby Clark. After the play was over, Clark hit Hackbart with a forearm to the head causing both players to fall to the ground. This infraction was not seen by the officials, although game film clearly showed what had happened. By the next day, Hackbart was in pain. He sought medical attention, and it was discovered that he had a serious neck fracture.

Hackbart filed a lawsuit against Booby Clark. The issue was whether or not injuries arising from physical contact in a football game were covered by tort law. The court consulted the rules of football in reaching its decision: "The general customs of football do not approve the punching or striking of others. That this is prohibited was supported by the testimony of all of the witnesses. They testified that the intentional striking of a player in the face or from the rear is prohibited by the playing rules as well as the general customs of the game. Punching or hitting with the arms is prohibited. Undoubtedly these restraints are intended to establish reasonable boundaries so that one football player cannot intentionally inflict serious injury on another. Therefore, the notion is not correct that all reason has been abandoned, whereby the only possible remedy for the person who has been the victim of an unlawful blow is retaliation."

Source: Hackbart v. Cincinnati Bengals, Inc. *601 F.2d 516 (Tenth Circuit Court of Appeals 1979).*

The Managerial Perspective, "Football Rules and the Law," is an illustration of a court using non-legal materials. Note how the rules of professional football influenced the application of tort law.

Precedent: The Doctrine of Stare Decisis

The doctrine of stare decisis provides that the principles of law developed in past cases will be used by a court to justify a decision in a current one. These past cases are called *precedents.* When they are rendered by a higher court, they are considered *binding precedents.* For example, assume that the Kansas Supreme Court holds that a person who is barefoot cannot collect damages from injuries caused by walking across broken glass. This decision, by the highest court in the state, would be considered binding precedent in other Kansas courts. Thereafter, the precedent would be applied in Kansas to similar barefoot walker cases. Consequently, the probability of collecting damages from such an injury would be quite low. Predictability in the law would be enhanced.

However, the Kansas precedent would have no binding effect in other states. For example, a Maine court would be free to refer to the Kansas decision, but they would have no obligation to follow its holding. In fact, they could reach the opposite conclusion without even consulting the Kansas case. The doctrine of stare decisis is limited by the geographical boundaries in the judicial system.

PURPOSE, FUNCTION, AND USE OF PRECEDENT

The doctrine of stare decisis provides predictability to our legal system. Of course, in law as in life nothing is ever certain. For example, it is virtually certain that a top-ten basketball team will defeat one with a losing record. It is highly predictable, but upsets do occur.

This situation is similar with the doctrine of stare decisis. Precedent cases are not applied as if they were numbers in a mathematical formula. The other factors in this chapter also influence judicial decision making and thus can affect the predictability of any one body of precedent.

However, predictability is a prime value and judges are, thus, strongly inclined to follow precedent. *Flood v. Kuhn*, illustrates this judicial propensity.

Professional baseball, even twenty-five years ago, was a big business. The issue in *Flood v. Kuhn* was whether or not the antitrust laws should apply to baseball as they do to other professional sports. The United States Supreme Court used precedent, dating from 1922, to reaffirm the judicially created antitrust exemption for baseball. Did another decision-making factor also influence this holding?

Flood v. Kuhn   United States Supreme Court *407 U.S. 258 (1971)*

The petitioner, Curtis Charles Flood, born in 1938, began his major league career in 1956 when he signed a contract with the Cincinnati Reds for a salary of $4,000 for the season. He had no attorney or agent to advise him on that occasion. He was traded to the St. Louis Cardinals before the 1958 season. Flood rose to fame as a centerfielder with the Cardinals during the years from 1958 to 1969. In those twelve seasons, he compiled a batting average of .293. He ranks among the ten major league outfielders possessing the highest lifetime fielding averages. Flood's St. Louis compensation ranged from $13,500 in 1961 to $90,000 in 1969.

At the age of thirty-one, in October 1969, Flood was traded to the Philadelphia Phillies of the National League in a multiplayer transaction. He was not consulted about the trade. He was informed by telephone and received formal notice only after the deal had been consummated. In December, he complained to the commissioner of baseball and asked that he be made a free agent and be placed at liberty to strike his own bargain with any other major league team. His request was denied.

Flood then instituted this antitrust suit in January 1970, in federal court for the Southern District of New York. The defendants (although not all were named in each cause of action) were the commissioner of baseball, the presidents of the two major leagues, and the twenty-four major league clubs. In general, the complaint charged violations of the federal antitrust laws.

Flood declined to play for Philadelphia in 1970 despite a $100,000 salary offer, and he sat out the year. After the season was concluded, Philadelphia sold its rights to Flood to the Washington Senators. Washington and the petitioner were able to come to terms for the 1971 season at a salary of $110,000. Flood started the season but, apparently because he was dissatisfied with his performance, he left the Washington club on April 27, early in the campaign. He has not played baseball since then.

Judge Cooper, in a detailed opinion, held that *Federal Baseball Club v. National League* and *Toolson v. New York Yankees, Inc.* were controlling. On appeal, the Second Circuit felt "compelled to affirm." The United States Supreme Court granted certiorari in order to look once again at this troublesome and unusual situation.

Justice Blackmun

For the third time in 50 years the Court is asked specifically to rule that professional baseball's reserve system is within the reach of the federal antitrust laws.

Federal Baseball Club v. National League (1922) was a suit for treble damages instituted by a member of the Federal League (Baltimore) against the National and American Leagues and others. Mr. Justice Holmes, in speaking succinctly for a unanimous Court, said:

> The business is giving exhibitions of baseball, which are purely state affairs. The restrictions by contract that prevented the plaintiff from getting players to break their bargains and the other conduct charged against the defendants were not an interference with commerce among the States.

Federal Baseball was cited a year later, and without disfavor, in another opinion by Mr. Justice Holmes for a unanimous Court. In the years that followed, baseball continued to be subject to intermittent antitrust attack. The courts, however, rejected these challenges on the authority of *Federal Baseball*.

In *Toolson v. New York Yankees, Inc.* (1953), *Federal Baseball* was cited as holding "that the business of providing public baseball games for profit between clubs of professional baseball players was not within the scope of the federal antitrust laws." . . . The emphasis in *Toolson* was on the determination, attributed even to *Federal Baseball,* that Congress had no intention to include baseball within the reach of the federal antitrust laws.

In view of all this, it seems appropriate now to say that with its reserve system enjoying exemption from the federal antitrust laws, baseball is, in a very distinct sense, an exception and an anomaly. *Federal Baseball* and *Toolson* have become an aberration confined to baseball. It is an aberration that has been with us now for half a century, one heretofore deemed fully entitled to the benefit of stare decisis, and one that has survived the Court's expanding concept of interstate commerce. It rests on a recognition and an acceptance of baseball's unique characteristics and needs.

Accordingly, we adhere once again to *Federal Baseball* and *Toolson* and to their application to professional baseball. If there is any inconsistency or illogic in all this, it is an inconsistency and illogic of long standing that is to be remedied by the Congress and not by this Court. Under these circumstances, there is merit in consistency even though some might claim that beneath that consistency is a layer of inconsistency.

And what the Court said in *Federal Baseball* in 1922 and what it said in *Toolson* in 1953, we say again here in 1972: the remedy, if any is indicated, is for congressional, and not judicial, action.

WHEN PRECEDENT IS NOT FOLLOWED

The decision in *Flood v. Kuhn* was not a foregone conclusion because the doctrine of stare decisis is not rigid. It provides that precedent may be ignored if a current case is distinguishable or if conditions have changed since the precedent decision was rendered. Stare decisis is not a straight jacket. It allows change in the law. Thus, attributes of predictability *and* flexibility are contained in the doctrine.

As an illustration, consider *Flagiello v. Pennsylvania Hospital* (1965). A patient broke her ankle because of negligence by two hospital employees. The hospital, citing precedent, argued that as a charitable institution, it was immune from liability. This was an accurate statement of the law existing at that time known as the *charitable immunity doctrine.* The court found that the precedent was outdated and held that the charitable immunity doctrine was no longer legally justified. Note how the court used a metaphor to explain its decision: "Stare decisis channels the law. It erects lighthouses and flies the signals of safety. The ships of jurisprudence must follow that well-defined channel which, over the years, has been proven to be secure and trustworthy. But it would not comport with wisdom to insist that, should shoals rise in a heretofore safe course and rocks emerge to encumber the passage, the ship should nonetheless pursue the original course, merely because it presented no hazard in the past. The principle of stare decisis does not demand that we follow precedents which shipwreck justice."

Of course, most decisions usually do not present such either/or propositions—that is, either follow past cases (as in *Flood v. Kuhn*) or reject them outright (as in *Flagiello v. Pennsylvania Hospital*). Often the court is given a choice as to which precedent to apply. Both parties cite cases that support a finding in their favor. Consequently, two questions arise:

1. Which case will have precedential effect?

2. What is the legal principle of the precedent case?

Attorneys are adept at citing cases that support a line of reasoning. This does not involve trickery or misrepresentation to the court. Enough factual differences usually exist between precedent cases and the current dispute making it possible to distinguish precedents that are unfavorable and place emphasis on others. In *Flood v. Kuhn*, for example, it was likely that Curt Flood's attorneys sought to distinguish the current business environment of baseball from what existed when the precedent cases were decided. Instead, they would cite cases from other professional sports that supported their position. The issue for the court was, which cases would be considered precedent? Would they be the old cases that concerned baseball? Or, would they be the ones that focused on other professional sports in the modern business world?

In addition to this issue, one must determine what principle the precedent case represents. In some judicial opinions, the court makes remarks about the law that are not precisely at issue. In *Parker v. Foote*, a leading easements case from the early nineteenth century, adjoining landowners were in dispute over a building addition one of them had constructed. This addition blocked the light and air that had been flowing without obstruction into the other's home. This party contended that he had a right to the continued and uninterrupted flow of light and air. The issue in the case was whether or not the jury or the judge should decide the dispute. The court, in addition to resolving this issue, went on to discuss whether or not American law would permit a landowner to acquire the right to light and air merely because of its long-term enjoyment. It was this *extra* judicial discussion that today is considered the precedential effect of that case.

A discussion of this kind is called **dicta**. Dicta are not considered to have precedential effect. However, it is not always easy to predict what a court will consider dicta from a past opinion or what legal ruling will deserve precedential value. Sometimes, as with *Parker v. Foote,* a case is read in such a way as to give precedential effect to what are usually considered dicta.

Furthermore, a court may also comment on an issue beyond what is necessary for its decision. This may be the judge's opinion of the ramifications of the ruling on a closely related issue. It too is considered dicta and is not the rule of the case that has precedential value. However, a court may use it as precedent supporting a decision in a future case. One of the best-known instances of such dicta was Justice Stone's footnote number 4 in *United States v. Carolene Products Co.* (1938). The United States Supreme Court at that time was, after enormous pressure, beginning to uphold various controls of economic activity enacted by Congress as part of Roosevelt's New Deal. The footnote in *Carolene Products* suggested that the Court may continue very strict constitutional review of legislative attempts to regulate liberty rights even though it was loosening its review standard for legislation that regulated property rights. The footnote, which was merely an opinion about the Court's standard of constitutional review for certain legislative restrictions, was the starting point for the development today of the distinction between property rights and liberty rights treatment by the courts.

Statutory Construction

Judges interpret statutes. Once a statute is enacted, the legislature does not provide updates or a running commentary. Nor does a legislature clarify the language that it used. These tasks fall to the courts. Thus, understanding statutes not only involves reading them, but also involves consulting judicial opinions in which they are applied. Together the statute's words and its judicial construction form a legal rule.

Not all statutes, of course, become subject to judicial scrutiny. For instance, a statute that prohibits driving on an expressway faster than sixty-five miles per hour is clear: no difficulty arises in interpreting the amount of speed that will create a violation. A person arrested for driving seventy miles per hour cannot argue that the statute should be construed to allow seventy miles per hour within its terms. Judges, in interpreting statutes, simply do not have the right to do whatever they like. Even if the judge believes that a sixty-five-miles-per-hour limitation is foolish or unwise, the judge may not simply ignore the statutory command. In fact, this principle is so accepted that no one will argue that the court should substitute its own miles-per-hour standard for that imposed by the legislature.

Not all statutes are as straightforward as the speed limit example. Sometimes the terms of a statute seem ambiguous or outdated. Perhaps applying the statute creates a great injustice or defeats its purpose. Technology may have changed so that the wrong the statute sought to correct is being done in a way not contemplated by its exact words. If so, then a court will be called on to interpret those words. The Thought Problem, "Applying a Statute," is an example of how statutes sometimes need to be treated on a case-by-case basis.

thought problem

Applying a Statute
Assume that a statute enacted in 1876 states, "It is unlawful to walk across or drive a vehicle across a public flower garden." Apply this statute to the following facts. Does the conduct violate the statute?

1. A person runs across a public flower garden.

2. In 1881, a person drives a horse and buggy across a public flower garden.

3. A doctor, while strolling in the park, sees a child fall from a tree and becomes seriously injured in the middle of a public flower garden. The doctor walks across the garden to administer aid to the child.

4. In 1997, a person drives a car across a public flower garden.

Literary studies often involve interpreting poems or novels. The investigation into the *true* meaning of those works is similar to what a court does when construing a statute. The writer and legislator put their ideas into words. The English professor and the judge analyze those words. Observe the dictionary definitions of *front, fence,* and *frog.* Sometimes the same word has multiple meanings or may mean different things depending on the context in which it is used. Furthermore, a single literary work may have a number of meanings depending on the interpretation technique that is applied.

Consider Herman Melville's novel, *Moby Dick.* If only the words of the book are examined, one may read it as an adventure story about whaling. If Melville's life and times are added to the analysis, a different interpretation may arise. If one looks for symbolism or some underlying theory behind the work, additional meanings will be forthcoming. Thus, the same book may have multiple interpretations depending on how one approaches it.

With all of this disagreement, how can one decide on what *Moby Dick* means? Would it not be best to simply ask what the author intended when he wrote it? Unfortunately, Herman Melville is not available to either tell us or respond to any of the various interpretations that have arisen. Furthermore, even if he could, one wonders if it would be all that enlightening. Perhaps, he wrote the book only to make money. Maybe he intended for the book to be ambiguous. Besides, what he would tell us would have to be in words, too, and how should *those* be interpreted? All that we have is the book, *Moby Dick.* So, we ask instead, "What does that book *mean?*"

This is the same question used in statutory interpretation. Judges are unable to divine legislative intent, other than to look at the final product—the statute. What would such an *intent* be, anyway? A crucial legislator's votes may have been swapped for support on an unrelated bill, or votes may have been cast because of political pressure. In neither instance was a particular intent expressed about the statute.

In addition, the topic covered by the statute may be so technical that innumerable questions are raised about how a statute regulates it. Tax laws are an example, as well as federal securities laws. Stocks, bonds, and debentures are common types of securities, but what about orange groves and beauty products? Neither orange groves nor beauty products, at first glance, are the type of debt or equity interests one commonly associates with securities. However, cases have found them to be securities under peculiar circumstances. Nonetheless, it is doubtful that Congress considered them when selecting the words it used in the 1934 Securities and Exchange Act.

In addition, word definitions may change after the statute was enacted. Note the 1876 (hypothetical) garden protection statute in the previous Thought Problem. The term, *vehicle*, changed meanings between 1876—when there were no cars—and 1997 when an automobile drove across the garden. The *intent* of the legislature could, thus, not have included a vehicle that did not exist. However, the mischief that the legislature sought to control would be ostensibly caused by errant motorists as well as horse and buggy drivers.

Finally, some statutes contain intentionally vague or ambiguous provisions. Sometimes this was required in order to garner enough votes to pass the bill. Or, several key legislators may need, for political reasons, to interpret a provision differently. Vague language is a legislative decision to let the courts work out the details.

Furthermore, ambiguous statutes discourage loophole finding—staying within the terms of the statute but violating its spirit. The Uniform Commercial Code contains numerous examples. Many of its provisions require commercially reasonable conduct. Nowhere does the statute precisely outline the type of conduct that will meet the reasonableness test. Undoubtedly, if a series of clear guidelines were presented, someone could conform to those guidelines but, under the particular facts of a case, exercise unreasonable conduct. Courts are given the leeway to interpret *reasonableness* in the statute, and people are notified to exercise caution, at least in sharp business practices.

A final reason for deliberate ambiguity is the circumstances that the statute is created to regulate are so varied that more particularized language may be impossible to insert. For example, Section 2-205 of the Uniform Commercial Code provides that a "firm offer," unless otherwise stated, will remain open for acceptance for a commercially reasonable time not to exceed three months. A "firm offer" to sell a crate of just-picked strawberries and a "firm offer" to sell a crate of books may be the same thing legally, but the facts of each situation make the length of time such an offer could remain open very different. That is, since strawberries will rot, a commercially reasonable time will be much shorter for them than for a crate of books.

Courts use a number of techniques to determine what the words of a statute mean. The next section outlines three of these techniques: legislative history; construing the meaning of the words of the statute; and inquiry into the spirit or purpose of the statute (see Figure 4.2).

LEGISLATIVE HISTORY

The English language is not so precise an instrument as to always convey ideas clearly. Sometimes in order to understand a statement, a reader must consult additional source material. The judge, in consulting legislative history, acts in much the same way. By doing research into the deliberations of the legislature, the judge may be able to better understand the statute. **Legislative history** consists of

■ **FIGURE 4.2** Statutory
Interpretation Techniques

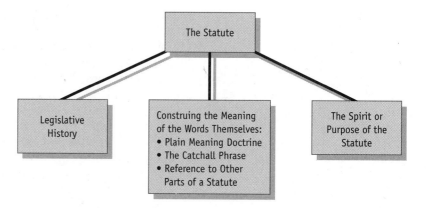

reports, studies, speeches, statements, committee findings, and similar materials that were created at the time the statute was drafted.

Use of legislative history, although a solid research technique, has been criticized. It assumes that only one meaning for the statute exists and that if the judge searches hard enough in the background documents, that one meaning will appear. Statutory construction involves judicial interpretation, and a statute, like a piece of literature, may be interpreted in different ways by different readers.

More practically, actually finding the legislative purpose through a review of the statutory history may be very difficult. How can the study of the statements of a few legislators and the reports of a committee or two enable a judge to determine that the legislature as a whole passed the statute with a certain purpose in mind? Maybe the deciding vote was cast because of political pressure or as part of an agreement that delivered legislative support on a wholly different issue. Some writers argue that use of legislative history by a court may encourage a legislator to create a historical record of a particular interpretation of an act, which in fact is not the one most fellow legislators would have agreed on.

Use of legislative history involves judgment, as does use of historical materials by a scholar writing about, say, the presidency of Thomas Jefferson. Which *historical* material should be considered reliable and which unreliable? If the documents clash, how are the inconsistencies to be resolved? How much documentation is enough to allow one to safely make a conclusion concerning the historical background? Use of legislative history may not produce a clear answer.

CONSTRUING THE MEANING OF THE WORDS THEMSELVES

The **plain meaning doctrine** is the most straightforward of statutory interpretation techniques. The court will look solely to the ordinary and usual meaning of the words in order to determine what the statute says. In a sense, this technique is akin to reading *Moby Dick* as a whale-hunting adventure story. Frequently, judicial opinions that use this technique refer to normally accepted usage or simply cite a dictionary definition of the terms.

Sometimes a *catchall phrase* has been inserted after a series of specific terms in a statute. Courts interpret the catchall phrase to include the same kind of items that had been specifically listed before it. For example, assume that last year the legislature amended the previously discussed 1876 garden protection statute to prohibit crossing public flower gardens by "car, bicycle, motorcycle, van, truck, bus, or other vehicle." If someone drives a moped across a flower garden, the court would need to determine whether or not the statute applies. The catchall phrase, *other vehicle*, would likely be construed to include *moped* because it is similar to the types of vehicles that the statute specifically lists.

A court may also *refer to other parts of a statute* when seeking the meaning of a particular term. Readers do this all the time. For example, if a person does not know the definition of a word in a novel, its meaning may sometimes be gleaned from the accompanying subject matter. Sometimes, the same word will have different meanings depending on the context in which it is used. The term, *hard rock*, will be understood differently if one is reading about popular music instead of gemstones. Similarly, a court may look at the whole statute to gain understanding about what certain words mean in the specific provision being reviewed. In that way, the provision is construed consistently with the entire enactment.

THE SPIRIT OR PURPOSE OF THE STATUTE

Statutes are passed for a reason. Thus, they are more than just a mere collection of words. All have a purpose, whether it is protection of the environment, disclosure of information to investors, or prohibiting discrimination in employment. Sometimes, the statutory language does not further that purpose. Its application may have results that the legislature neither contemplated nor would likely endorse. Sometimes, application of the statutory language would yield an illogical result or one that has little connection to the reason the statute was passed. In such circumstances, a court may ignore the language and render a decision based on the purpose of the statute.

Consider the International Perspective, "Immigration Law: Purpose or Language?" Hiring a minister from overseas was clearly illegal under the terms of the immigration act. But this was not the problem Congress had been aiming to regulate. Applying the statute (as written) to the case would have been inconsistent with its purpose.

Immigration Law: Purpose or Language?

The Church of the Holy Trinity hired a minister from England to lead its congregation. The church was located in New York, and the new minister would be required to live there. A federal immigration statute made it illegal for anyone to assist an alien in migrating to the United States when, upon arrival, the alien would be contractually bound to perform some service. The statute exempted certain types of jobs, including actors, singers, and domestic servants. However, no exemption for ministers existed.

Under the language of the statute, the church's contract was illegal. Its minister was English and was hired to move to the United States and lead a congregation. However, this was not the type of problem the immigration act was enacted to remedy. No indication that Congress had ever considered the hiring of foreign ministers existed when the statute was being debated. The legislature had been concerned about large American businesses hiring huge numbers of foreign laborers under contracts in which the employer would pay passage to the United States and the workers would accept low wages for a set time. The effect was to drive wages down thereby harming all laborers. The practice had become so widespread and the worry about income contraction so great that Congress prohibited it.

In light of this purpose, the United States Supreme Court held that the church's contract was not covered by the immigration statute. "[W]e cannot think Congress intended to denounce with penalties a transaction like that in the present case. It is a familiar rule, that a thing may be within the letter of the statute and yet not within the statute, because it is not within its spirit, not within the intention of its makers."

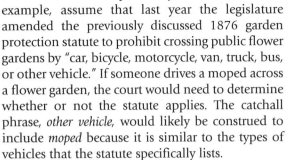

Source: Church of the Holy Trinity v. United States, *143 U.S. 457 (United States Supreme Court 1892).*

Refer to the garden protection statute discussed earlier in this chapter, for another example. Recall that the language of the statute prohibited *walking* across public gardens. What if someone ran instead? The purpose of the statute was to prevent gardens from being trampled. Yet, the plain meaning of the word *walk* does not include the act of running. Under this analysis, one may consider that running is within the letter of the law, but violates its spirit. Consequently, it is highly predictable that a court would construe the statute consistent with its purpose and find the runner in violation.

Statutes, through such interpretation, remain vital in an ever-changing world. Legislators could not hope to cover with precision, all of the behavior they intend to regulate and exempt that which they do not. Courts perform a *flexibility* function through their construction of statutes.

Consider *Lennon v. Immigration and Naturalization Service*. Note how both the majority and dissenting opinions used different statutory construction techniques. Can you identify which ones?

Lennon v. Immigration and Naturalization Service

United States Court of Appeals, Second Circuit *527 F.2d 187 (1975)*

On October 18, 1968, detectives from the Scotland Yard drug squad conducted a warrantless search of John Lennon's apartment at 34 Montague Square, London. There, the officers found a half an ounce of hashish inside a binocular case and thereupon placed Lennon under arrest. Lennon pleaded guilty to possession of cannabis resin in Marylebone Magistrate's Court on November 28, 1968; he was fined £150.

On August 13, 1971, Lennon and his wife, Yoko Ono, arrived in New York. They had come to this country to seek custody of Mrs. Lennon's daughter by a former marriage to an American citizen.

The immigration and Nationality Act § 212(a) lists thirty-one classes of "excludable aliens" who are ineligible for permanent residence. Among those excludable is "any alien who has been convicted of a violation of any law or regulation relating to the illicit possession of marihuana." Since John Lennon's conviction appeared to render him excludable, the Immigration and Naturalization Service (INS) specifically waived excludability. The Lennons were then given temporary visas valid until September 24, 1971; the INS later extended the expiration date to February 29, 1972.

The day after Lennon's visa expired, March 1, Sol Marks, the New York District Director of the INS, notified the Lennons by letter that, if they did not leave the country by March 15, deportation proceedings would be instituted. On March 3, Lennon and his wife filed third preference petitions. In response to these applications, the INS instituted deportation proceedings three days later.

In March, April, and May 1972, deportation hearings were held before Immigration Judge Fieldsteel. The Immigration judge filed his decision on March 23, 1973. Since Yoko Ono had obtained permanent resident status in 1964, he granted her application. But, because he believed that John Lennon was an excludable alien, the immigration judge denied his application and ordered him deported.

Kaufman, Chief Judge

We have come a long way from the days when fear and prejudice toward alien races were the guiding forces behind our immigration laws. The Chinese exclusion acts of the 1880s and the "barred zone" created by the 1917 Immigration Act have,

thankfully, been removed from the statute books and relegated to the historical treatises. Nevertheless, the power of Congress to exclude or deport natives of other
countries remains virtually unfettered. In the vast majority of deportation cases, the
fate of the client must therefore hinge upon narrow issues of statutory construction.
To this rule, the appeal of John Lennon, an internationally known "rock" musician,
presents no exception. We are, in this case, called upon to decide whether Lennon's
1968 British conviction for possession of cannabis resin renders him, as the Board of
Immigration Appeals believed, an excludable alien under § 212(a)(23) of the Immigration and Nationality Act (INA), which applies to those convicted of illicit possession of marihuana. We hold that Lennon's conviction does not fall within the ambit
of this section.

We base this result upon our conclusion that Lennon was convicted under a law
which in effect makes guilty knowledge irrelevant and such a law does not render
the convicted alien excludable.

The language of the British statute under which Lennon was convicted is decep-
tively simple: "A person shall not be in possession of a drug unless . . .
authorized. . . ." But around this concise provision, judicial interpretation has created a scholastic maze as complex and baffling as the Labyrinth at Knossos in
ancient Crete. However, we conclude, from analyzing British law as it existed in
1968, that Lennon was convicted under a statute which made guilty knowledge irrelevant. Under British law a person found with tablets which he reasonably believed
were aspirin would be convicted if the tablets proved to contain heroin. And a man
given a sealed package filled with heroin would, if he had had any opportunity to
open the parcel, suffer the same fate—even if he firmly believed the package contained perfume.

The general purpose of § 212(a)(23) is, of course, to bar undesirable aliens from
our shores. There is also, we note, some indication that Congress, in enacting
§ 212(a)(23), was far more concerned with the trafficker of drugs than with the
possessor. We do not believe that our holding will subvert these Congressional ends.
Virtually every undesirable alien covered by the drug conviction provision would also
be barred by other sections of the statute. Moreover, addicts are barred. Finally, our
holding will not, of course, give any comfort to those convicted in the United States
of drug violations.

Given, in sum, the minimal gain in effective enforcement, we cannot imagine that
Congress would impose the harsh consequences of an excludable alien classification
upon a person convicted under a foreign law that made guilty knowledge irrelevant.

Before closing with the traditional words of disposition, we feel it appropriate to
express our faith that the result we have reached in this case not only is consistent
with the language and purpose of the narrow statutory provision we construe, but
also furthers the intent of the immigration laws in a far broader sense. The excludable aliens statute is but an exception, albeit necessary, to the traditional tolerance
of a nation founded and built by immigrants. If, in our two hundred years of independence, we have in some measure realized our ideals, it is in large part because
we have always found a place for those committed to the spirit of liberty and willing
to help implement it. Lennon's four-year battle to remain in our country is testimony
to his faith in this American dream.

Accordingly, the denial of Lennon's application for adjustment of status and the
order of deportation are vacated and the case remanded for reconsideration in
accordance with the views expressed in this opinion.

Mulligan, Circuit Judge (dissenting)

That statute would exclude any alien who has been convicted of a violation of any
law or regulation relating to the illicit possession of narcotic drugs or marihuana.
Since the statute applies to any alien it makes no difference whether he be John
Lennon, John Doe or Johann Sebastian Bach.

The undisputed fact however is that Lennon did plead guilty to the possession of cannabis resin, and while this may have been convenient or expedient because of his wife's pregnancy and his disinclination to have her testify in court, it is elementary that we cannot go behind the plea.

The majority here concludes that the Congress was more concerned with trafficking in drugs than in possession and their opinion does not cover the trafficker who obviously is fully aware of the nature of the business he is pursuing. The statute however bars the possessor as well as the trafficker. If there were no users there would be no trafficking. It must also be emphasized that the vast majority of those who are arrested with illicit drugs in their homes or on their persons are users who are fully aware of their presence and their properties. It is the unusual case where contraband such as this is surreptitiously planted in one's reticule of blue jeans pocket. Yet by disregarding convictions under the British statute or any other foreign counterpart, the majority would admit to the United States those who knowingly possessed any illicit drugs. This holding seems to me to conflict with INS § 212(a)(23), which plainly bars those who have been convicted of a violation. Lennon's guilty plea here puts him within the statute.

Summary

Judicial decision making is made up of seven factors. One of these, the personality factor, is unacknowledged, but is vital for understanding the others. The other six factors reflect important policies in the law: history and custom; balancing of interests; doing what is right; deferring to other branches of government; consideration of non-legal materials; and the doctrine of stare decisis.

Note the breadth of the factors. Courts are influenced by such divergent forces as ethics, community standards, and the structure of the legal system. Together, they embody vital attributes of law, such as predictability and flexibility.

However, judicial decisions do not merely concern the common law. Often they require interpretation of a statute. Such a task delves into the meaning of the statute's language, and courts use a number of techniques to do so. Three of them were outlined in this chapter: the use of legislative history; a focus on the meaning of the words themselves; and a concern for the spirit or purpose for which the statute was enacted.

Review Questions

1. Define the following terms:
   a. Brandeis brief
   b. Recusal
   c. Stare decisis
   d. Plain-meaning doctrine

2. Justices of the United States Supreme Court place their assets in a **blind trust**. A blind trust is a legal device by which a person is appointed to invest the property of the justice. However, the nature of those investments is kept secret. Why is this done? Assuming that no dishonest justices exist, why is this necessary?

3. Brewing, Inc., is a beer manufacturing corporation. It agreed to supply the Dew Drop Inn with five barrels of beer per month. A barrel is defined by statute as containing thirty-one gallons. After a few

months, managers of the inn noticed that they seemed to be receiving barrels containing fewer than thirty-one gallons. Upon checking, they learned that the barrels ranged from thirty-one gallons to 29.7 gallons. In the beer industry, as a barrel ages, it holds less and less liquid because the hoops that hold the barrel together must be driven closer to the center in order to keep them tight. Over time, this reduces the size of the barrel. The Dew Drop Inn sues Brewing. What might the corporation argue in defense?

4. You are an executive with the XYZ Corporation. The corporation has been sued by a disgruntled supplier. Counsel has informed you that five cases that discuss the issue in the lawsuit have been found in your jurisdiction. All five cases support the position of the supplier. How might you expect the issue to be resolved?

5. Given the facts in question 4, under what circumstances would you expect the opposite outcome?

6. Grace and Sam Stamos are an elderly couple who recently moved to the United States from Greece. They understand only a little English. Richards visited them at home in order to sell them a freezer. At first, they were not interested, since they did not have a great deal of money. However, Richards discussed the matter with them for ten hours that day. Finally they agreed to purchase a freezer and signed a fifteen-page contract. The contract was written in English, with complex legal terminology, and was in very small print. No one explained the terms of the contract to the Stamoses. One provision provided that if they were late making a payment on the freezer, all of their other property could be taken by the seller and sold to pay their debt. The freezer was worth three hundred dollars. The contract required a thirty-dollars-per-month payment for five years.

Without discussing applicable legal rules, if the seller attempts to enforce the contract against the Stamoses and a court rules in their favor, how might the court justify its decision?

7. Grades seem to be an almost indispensable part of college life. However, at Veritas College, a proposal has been made to abolish the school's grading system. Based on some or all of the factors raised in this chapter, what justifications could be made by a decision maker either for refusing to abolish the grading system or for retaining it?

8. Late one winter afternoon two people, Jack and Sally, slip on some unshoveled snow in a retail store's parking lot. Jack is a transient, unemployed by choice. He makes ends meet by occasional thefts. He had planned to go into the retail store to warm himself. Sally is a CPA who was hurrying into the store to make a major purchase. She has been a valued customer there for a number of years. Sally is married with three children, and is active in charitable organizations. Both Jack and Sally have the same type of injury. For each choose among the following (or a combination):

   a. The store is not liable to pay damages for their injuries.

   b. Each injured party will receive the same amount in damages for his or her injuries.

   c. There is no requirement that Jack and Sally be treated alike in whether the store is liable for the amount of damages.

Justify your decision and base your reasons on the materials in this chapter.

9. Use statutory interpretation techniques to discuss how the statute involved in the following problem should be interpreted. Make sure you can identify the technique urged on the court by each party in the dispute.

Glen filed a lawsuit against the United States government. He represents a class of plaintiffs who are terminally ill with cancer and would like to use the drug Laetrile as part of their treatment. The United States government would not permit the interstate shipment and sale of Laetrile since it was not approved by the secretary of the Department of Health, Education, and Welfare pursuant to the Food, Drug, and Cosmetic Act. The act will not permit the distribution of any new drug without such approval. The act defines a *new drug* as "any drug not generally recognized, among experts qualified by scientific training and experience to evaluate the safety and effectiveness of drugs, as safe and effective for use under the conditions prescribed, recommended, or suggested in the labeling."

Scientific experts have determined that Laetrile is not generally recognized as safe and effective as a treatment for cancer since no adequate studies exist that demonstrate the drug's safety or effectiveness. Remarks made in Congress at the time of the act's passage show that lawmakers were concerned about drugs being place on the market before adequate testing was done, the danger being the harm that their use could cause to people. Furthermore, Congress was concerned about fraudulent cures being offered as drugs to people who were ill. However, terminally ill patients may be distinguished from the general population because there is no cure leading to recovery from their disease.

10. Use statutory interpretation techniques to discuss how the statute involved in the following problem should be interpreted. Make sure you can identify the technique urged on the court by each party in the dispute.

A jury returned a verdict for Baker against Jacobs. Immediately thereafter, Baker treated the jury to cigars at a local hotel as a gesture of appreciation. Upon learning of this, Jacobs sought to have a court set aside the verdict rendered by the jury. He relied on the following statute: "If a party obtaining a verdict in his favor shall, during the term of the court in which such a verdict is obtained, give to any of the jurors in the case, knowing him to be such, any victuals or drink, or procure the same to be done, by way of treat, either before or after such verdict, on proof thereof being made the verdict shall be set aside and a new trial granted."

11. You are an executive with the XYZ Corporation. The corporation is involved in the landscaping business. A major part of its business is supplying plants and seeds. A statute reads as follows: "No flower, vegetable, bush, or other plant may be imported into the United States without approval from the USDA." You learn that a unique variety of tree, found only in Japan, is available for your corporation to import into the United States. However, the delay and cost in obtaining approval for importing the special trees would make them

too expensive to import. Must the corporation obtain approval before importing the trees? Give reasons.

12. A statute reads as follows: "No business may keep a large, vicious dog on its premises." The statute was enacted after several children were attacked by guard dogs that broke loose from the businesses they were protecting. During consideration of the bill, several representatives filed reports showing similar incidents throughout the country. Many argued that innocent citizens, especially children, should not have to fear attack from beasts. A few noted that alarm systems, if properly installed, would adequately protect any business.

You own a small business that has been robbed several times. After reading the statute just referred to, you buy a mountain lion to keep at your business to deter burglars. Are you in violation of the statute? Give reasons.

Note   [1]James Boswell, *The Life of Samuel Johnson* (1791), p. 958.

Chapter

5

THE LEGISLATURE,
EXECUTIVE BRANCH, AND
ADMINISTRATIVE AGENCIES

The Legislature

CONTEXT IN WHICH THE LAWMAKING OCCURS

Recall that courts make laws on a case-by-case basis. However, a judge is not a roving *do-gooder* sitting on the bench and solving all of society's problems. For example, if no cases arise involving tort law, then there can be no judge-made tort law. Even if a particular judge is convinced that a doctrine should be modified, that judge may not simply change it. The legal rule can only be changed within the context of a dispute brought before the court. Furthermore, as noted in Chapter 4, courts have no power to investigate independently the facts and gather information that may be helpful in rendering a decision. Courts generally are limited to the facts presented to them by the parties at trial.

Compare the work of the courts with that of the legislature. First of all, statutes are not enacted to settle private disputes. The legislature is not the appropriate body to consider them. Nonetheless, individual concerns may result in legislative action. For example, assume that a constituent is worried that a new recording technology will permit users to record copyrighted material without paying the owner for the privilege. No *dispute* exists here that can be heard by a court. Yet a clash of interests occurs between copyright owners and users that needs some legal review. This review could entail a revision of the copyright statute, or perhaps it may best be handled either through a recorder license requirement or by one of the scores of other proposals. The courts are not freewheeling enough to consider them. Only the legislature if capable of this type of lawmaking.

The legislature has mechanisms: committees, subcommittees, and investigative panels that study the effect of the new recording technology on copyright protection. Institutionally, the legislature may seek out expert opinions on the matter. Witnesses may be required to appear and answer questions. Staff may accumulate data and prepare reports. In short, the legislature may gather information to determine how best to deal with the issue. Because of the need to acquire such information, the legislative branch has broad investigative powers.

Some congressional investigations have been highly publicized. In the early 1950s, Senator Joseph McCarthy claimed to have uncovered communist infiltration into American life. His bombasting and witch-hunt tactics gave us the term *McCarthyism* which is applied when character-destroying, unsupported allegations are leveled against someone.

In the 1970s, Senator Sam Ervin's Watergate investigation uncovered corruption in the Nixon White House that led to the only resignation of a U.S. President in American history. During the mid-1980s, the Iran-Contra Committee catapulted a witness, Oliver North, into the national spotlight. A decade later the Whitewater investigation explored President Clinton's ties to a failed Arkansas savings and loan.

These examples of legislative investigations are well-known. Of course, most investigations are not so noteworthy. Their goal is merely information gathering in order to alert and put the legislative process into action.

Thus, the context of lawmaking is vastly different between courts and the legislature. While the courts are limited to information the litigants provide, legislators have no similar boundaries. This reflects the broader, more general scope of statutory lawmaking as compared to the narrower context of judicial decision making.

■ Relationship to the Past of Any Newly-Made Law

Review the doctrine of stare decisis as discussed in Chapter 4. Courts work within that doctrine when applying past decisions to current disputes. Thus, predictability and flexibility in the law are furthered.

No similar constraint is placed on the legislative branch. Statutes may be written without regard to past law. However, the value of predictability is such that a connection is often made anyway. For example, the New Mexico legislature's Solar Rights Act protected access to sunlight needed for operating a solar energy collector. Before the statute was enacted, New Mexico only protected such access if the sunlight user purchased an easement. An easement is a right to use another person's land. Here, it would be the right to prohibit others from occupying a defined swath of airspace.

The New Mexico legislature chose a bold and radical departure from this past law. Its statute granted rights to continued, unobstructed sunlight to whomever first used a solar collector. No requirement that one acquire an easement existed as under prior law.

Although this seemed innovative, the new statute connected to past law as a means of ensuring continuity and predictability. The New Mexico Solar Rights Act was built on rules of civil procedure that provided the mechanism to enforce the new solar right—rules governing the transfer of property rights, and principles of eminent domain (the power of government to take private property for public use).

Additionally, the Act was patterned after New Mexico's water law which existed for years and had innumerable cases arise under it. Thus, acquiring a solar right was designed to be similar to the way one acquired a water right. Furthermore, the legislature used terms in the Solar-Rights Act that had accepted meanings in water law—*prior appropriation* and *beneficial use.* These precedents enhanced the predictability of the new statute.

Legislation may also connect to the past by being patterned after another state's statute. That way, the experiences of that state and its judicial opinions may provide guidance about the meaning of the new statute. For example, if the Kansas legislature planned to change its corporation law, it could pattern the new statute after one already existing in Missouri. Or, the Kansas legislature may use that act as a model and refine the language to remove problems that Missouri courts have had to confront. Although no formal stare decisis principle governs legislation, the doctrine's policies do influence how statutes are drafted. Being able to use a past statute as a guide to understanding a new one promotes predictability.

Before the end of the nineteenth century, most American law (e.g., torts, commercial contract, and property) was common law—a body of cases from which legal principles may be derived. Throughout that century, precedents included both American and British decisions. Statutes merely filled the gaps or overturned some undesirable cases.

Near the end of the nineteenth century, a codification movement arose that proposed drafting one statute for each area of law (e.g., sales of goods or partnerships). This statute would clear up confusion that existed because of conflicting precedent cases. Thus, predictability and clarity would be enhanced. The first legal area to undergo codification was civil procedure—the mechanical rules of bringing a case to court.

Committees drafted uniform laws that were based on the common law. For example, the Uniform Sales Act, enacted in most states, codified certain common law contract principles. In the 1950s, the Uniform Sales Act was replaced by the Uniform Commercial Code, a more comprehensive statute governing commercial transactions.

Today, much of the common law has been codified.

THE LEGISLATIVE PROCESS

Most business law is based on statutes, from organizing a firm, to borrowing money, to hiring employees, to selling a product. Chapter 4 discussed judicial interpretation of statutes. The next section will outline the way statutes are created. See the Ethical Perspective, "Big Labor, Big Business, and Influencing Legislation."

The legislative process converts political policies into law, thus, materially affecting business activity. For example, in 1964, Congress enacted the Civil Rights Act which prohibited racial or sexual discrimination in employment. It also created the Equal Employment Opportunity Commission (EEOC), an agency to oversee the statute's operations. Thereafter, business personnel practices changed since job applicants could no longer be treated differently based on race or sex.

But the reach of the statute extended far beyond this initial activity. Courts interpreted the Act. The EEOC drafted administrative regulations and brought cases to enforce them. Affirmative action and sexual harassment charges arose and became issues that businesses needed to confront or risk liability under the Civil Rights Act, even though neither was specifically provided for in the statute.

Thus, the way statutes are created and evolve is of great interest to business. An obscure clause in a tax bill may save a firm millions of dollars. A technology-forcing provision in environmental legislation may require that a company spend money to clean the air rather than, say, build a factory.

Figure 5.1 shows the path of a bill from the drafting stage to actually becoming law. Note the many steps the bill must take before it is enacted.

ETHICAL
PERSPECTIVE
Big Labor, Big Business, and Influencing Legislation

During 1995, Big Business PACs made $50 million in political contributions while Big Labor PACs gave over $11.2 million. The following pie charts show how the money was divided between the Democratic and Republican parties.

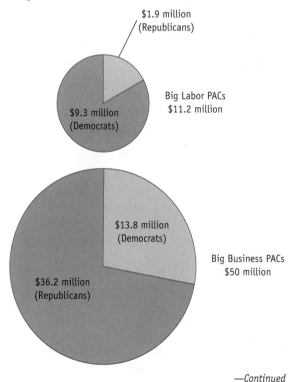

$1.9 million (Republicans)

Big Labor PACs $11.2 million

$9.3 million (Democrats)

$13.8 million (Democrats)

Big Business PACs $50 million

$36.2 million (Republicans)

—Continued

—*Continued*

Far more money will likely be spent in the 1996 elections. In the spring of 1996, the AFL-CIO decided to spend $35 million. Initial expenditures created advertisements that took aim at freshman Republicans on minimum wage and Medicare issues. In response, the U.S. Chamber of Commerce began to coordinate efforts to keep Congress in pro-business hands, seeking $20 million to target a number of Congressional districts. Further efforts were also planned. In addition, the Business Industry Political Action Committee was drafting a manual to show groups how to legally influence elections.

Source: Phil Kuntz and Glenn Burkins, "Business Groups, Worried by AFL-CIO's Plan for Election Spending, Ready Own War Chest," *Wall Street Journal,* May 10, 1996, Section A, page 12.

Note, too, the diversions. It is unlikely that the statute will bear much resemblance to its initial draft. It is often reworked to reflect the compromises and political bargains that are needed to garner enough votes to pass it. Redrafts, modifications, and tying the bill to related issues are common. As Figure 5.1 illustrates, the process is not very tidy. Looking at the chart brings to mind a quotation that is often attributed to Otto von Bismarck, the great German Chancellor of the late nineteenth century: "People who love sausage and respect the law should never watch either one being made."

Business plays an important role during the legislative process. From providing financial support to candidates, to lobbying for particular bills, to supplying information to legislators, businesses act aggressively to protect their interests. And, why not?

Statutes are inherently political documents that translate policy ideas into law. For example, the Republican Party's "Contract with America," introduced prior to the 1994 Congressional election, was seen as *just politics.* Its themes were traditional ones for that party—lower taxes and less government regulation of business. Of course, the contract would have remained a mere political statement except that the Republican party won control of both houses of Congress that year. Representative Newt Gingrich who devised the contract became Speaker of the House of Representatives. Thereafter, this *political statement* became the blueprint for Republican-sponsored legislation. Lobbyists were very active in drafting some of these bills, and corporate money flowed into Republican party coffers. Business interests supporting these policies saw their ideas championed.

Note how politics were translated into law making. The key is to appreciate the connection between policy formation, lobbying, political activity, and legislation. Those who wait on the sidelines and assume that *good* (i.e., their interests) will prevail in the legislature are often disappointed.

Of course, to note the connection between politics and legislation belabors the obvious. However, statutes are often considered as if they were handed down by some higher authority instead of being the creations of politicians. Frequently, the legislator never reads the bill before voting, although the committee report may be consulted. That legislator's vote may be based on directions from party leadership, public opinion, the advice of an aide who has studied the bill, or the arguments made by a lobbyist. In fact, the bill itself is most often drafted by aides or lobbyists and not by any individual legislator.

The most effective efforts to influence legislation occur during the political stages of the legislative process. One of the most common means is through campaign contributions. These contributions are designed to influence the legislator or to reinforce a legislator's voting

FIGURE 5.1 Course of a Bill through the Kansas Legislature. A bill may originate in either the House of Representatives or the Senate. The chart shows the course of a bill introduced into the house. The procedure for a bill introduced into the Senate would be the same by changing *House* to *Senate,* and other words appropriately.

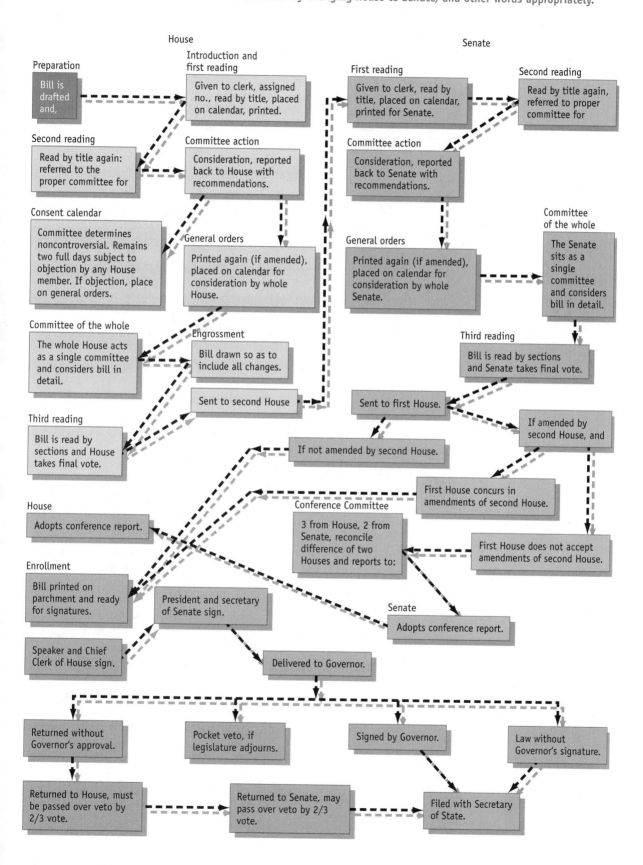

managerial perspective
Money and the Legislative Process

Corporate political contributions follow the election returns. The party in power is in a position to further the legislative goals of the contributors. As the balance of power shifts, so does the funding.

The 1994 Congressional elections marked a major shift in power between the Democrats, who had long controlled Congress, and the Republicans, who gained control of both the House and Senate. Corporate campaign contributions made a similar shift. The following corporate PAC contributions illustrate this shift:

■ AT&T: In 1993–94, nearly $1.3 million was contributed to House and Senate candidates with about 41 percent going to Republicans. Of the more than $380,000 contributed in the first eleven months of 1995, more than 59 percent went to Republicans.

■ Phillip Morris: In 1993–94, more than $650,000 was contributed to House and Senate candidates with about 38 percent going to Republicans. Of the nearly $200,000 contributed in the first eleven months of 1995, nearly 78 percent went to Republicans.

■ Federal Express: In 1993–94, more than $810,000 was contributed to House and Senate candidates with about 31 percent going to Republicans. Of the more than $180,000 contributed in the first eleven months of 1995, nearly 70 percent went to Republicans.

Source: New York Times Sunday Magazine, January 7, 1996, page 12.

record that has been beneficial to the donor. Common types of contributions are those made to members of a key committee that oversees bills directly affecting the business of the donor. These donations are made usually without regard to the political leanings of the legislator or whether or not the legislator needs the funds to wage an electoral campaign against a tough opponent. Frequently, newly elected legislators will receive contributions from donors who did not support them during the election. These funds are not necessarily from businesses and individuals in the legislator's district. Instead, they are from those who are interested in the outcome of certain policy debates. See the Managerial Perspective, "Money and the Legislative Process."

Donors hope that the contributions will at least provide access to the legislator. Given the legislator's limited time, access permits the donor to make arguments and provide information that may be persuasive.

The political arena is a vital component of the legal environment of business. Once a statute is enacted, the role of the legislature ceases (except to possibly modify the statute at some point in the future). The courts are then charged with interpreting the statutory language.

The Executive Branch

Under classic separation of powers theory, the legislature makes the law, the courts interpret it, and the executive branch enforces it. Implementing court orders and carrying out statutory mandates are examples of this executive branch role. However, precise delineation of their separateness is not an accurate description. The process of lawmaking, for example, entails overlapping between the three branches.

Although throughout this section, the executive branch of government will be referred to as the presidency; this branch includes many officials besides the president (see Figure 5.2). The executive branch also contains a number of agencies called executive agencies. Examples include the Department of Agriculture, the Department of Commerce, the State Department on the federal level, the office of the prosecutor, and the police department on the state or local level. Note the discussions later in this chapter concerning administrative agencies that are applicable to executive agencies as well.

RELATIONSHIP OF THE EXECUTIVE WITH OTHER BRANCHES OF GOVERNMENT

The three branches of government act to check and balance one another, so that no one branch or individual acquires too much power. Both the Congress and the courts act as checks on the president and are at the same time dependent on the president. Congress relies on the executive branch for the implementation of the laws it enacts. A president who supports certain legislation will most likely vigorously enforce it. However, a president who does not agree with a statute may frustrate its purposes by having a weak enforcement program. An example from the 1980s was the Reagan Administration's enforcement policies in a number of regulatory areas—for example, antitrust and environmental protection. By not enforcing the legislation as did prior administrations, the Reagan Administration in fact was changing the *law*, even though no formal legislative or regulatory modifications occurred. Thus, the antitrust law factor was less significant in corporate merger decisions under Reagan than under Carter, Ford, or Nixon. The risk of government interference in such activities, being less, lowered the *cost* of executives' acquisition decisions. Note that the Bush and Clinton Administrations increased the enforcement effort in both antitrust and environmental protection. Thus, the legal environment changed again.

Congress, however, does have leverage over the executive branch and can certainly frustrate the plans and policies of a president. Its ultimate control is the power to impeach and remove the president from office. However, other congressional powers act more regularly as checks on the executive branch. Congress has control over the appropriation of federal funds and may either underfund or refuse to fund an executive's key programs. Congress also has the power to refuse to consent to certain presidential appointments. The Senate's rejection of Robert Bork, one of President Reagan's nominees to the Supreme Court, was an example. Bork, unquestionably, had superb credentials; however, his positions on key issues that could come before the Court led to the Senate refusing to consent to the appointment. Lastly, Congress has the ability to shape legislative programs.

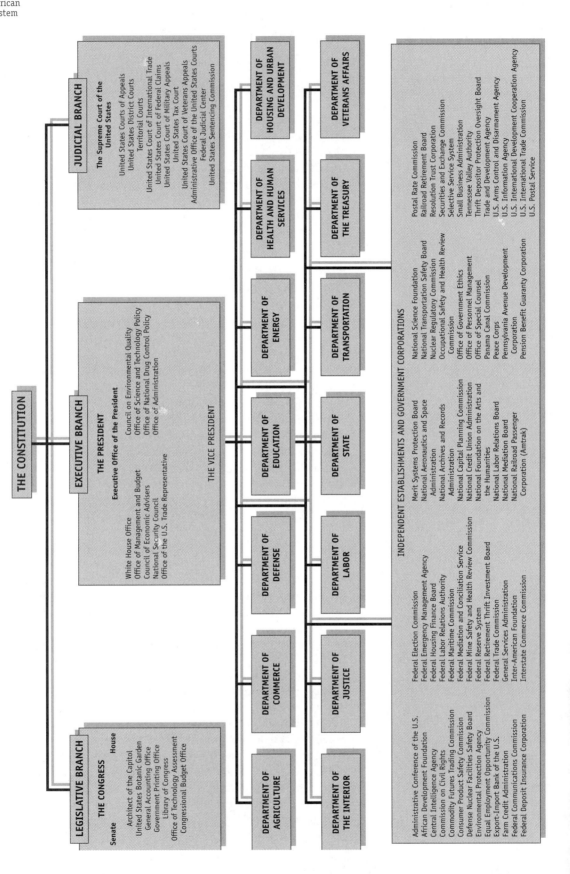

■ **FIGURE 5.2   The Government of the United States**   Source: *The United States Government Manual 1994–95.* Office of the Federal Register/National Archives and Records Administration. Revised July 1, 1994. Washington, DC: U.S. Government Printing Office.

THE CONSTITUTION

LEGISLATIVE BRANCH

THE CONGRESS

Senate   House

Architect of the Capitol
United States Botanic Garden
General Accounting Office
Government Printing Office
Library of Congress
Office of Technology Assessment
Congressional Budget Office

EXECUTIVE BRANCH

THE PRESIDENT

Executive Office of the President

White House Office
Office of Management and Budget
Council of Economic Advisers
National Security Council
Office of the U.S. Trade Representative

Council on Environmental Quality
Office of Science and Technology Policy
Office of National Drug Control Policy
Office of Administration

THE VICE PRESIDENT

JUDICIAL BRANCH

The Supreme Court of the United States

United States Courts of Appeals
United States District Courts
Territorial Courts
United States Court of International Trade
United States Court of Federal Claims
United States Court of Military Appeals
United States Tax Court
United States Court of Veterans Appeals
Administrative Office of the United States Courts
Federal Judicial Center
United States Sentencing Commission

DEPARTMENT OF AGRICULTURE

DEPARTMENT OF COMMERCE

DEPARTMENT OF DEFENSE

DEPARTMENT OF EDUCATION

DEPARTMENT OF ENERGY

DEPARTMENT OF HEALTH AND HUMAN SERVICES

DEPARTMENT OF HOUSING AND URBAN DEVELOPMENT

DEPARTMENT OF THE INTERIOR

DEPARTMENT OF JUSTICE

DEPARTMENT OF LABOR

DEPARTMENT OF STATE

DEPARTMENT OF TRANSPORTATION

DEPARTMENT OF THE TREASURY

DEPARTMENT OF VETERANS AFFAIRS

INDEPENDENT ESTABLISHMENTS AND GOVERNMENT CORPORATIONS

Administrative Conference of the U.S.
African Development Foundation
Central Intelligence Agency
Commission on Civil Rights
Commodity Futures Trading Commission
Consumer Product Safety Commission
Defense Nuclear Facilities Safety Board
Environmental Protection Agency
Equal Employment Opportunity Commission
Export-Import Bank of the U.S.
Farm Credit Administration
Federal Communications Commission
Federal Deposit Insurance Corporation

Federal Election Commission
Federal Emergency Management Agency
Federal Housing Finance Board
Federal Labor Relations Authority
Federal Maritime Commission
Federal Mediation and Conciliation Service
Federal Mine Safety and Health Review Commission
Federal Reserve System
Federal Retirement Thrift Investment Board
Federal Trade Commission
General Services Administration
Inter-American Foundation
Interstate Commerce Commission

Merit Systems Protection Board
National Aeronautics and Space Administration
National Archives and Records Administration
National Capital Planning Commission
National Credit Union Administration
National Foundation on the Arts and the Humanities
National Labor Relations Board
National Mediation Board
National Railroad Passenger Corporation (Amtrak)

National Science Foundation
National Transportation Safety Board
Nuclear Regulatory Commission
Occupational Safety and Health Review Commission
Office of Government Ethics
Office of Personnel Management
Office of Special Counsel
Panama Canal Commission
Peace Corps
Pennsylvania Avenue Development Corporation
Pension Benefit Guaranty Corporation

Postal Rate Commission
Railroad Retirement Board
Resolution Trust Corporation
Securities and Exchange Commission
Selective Service System
Small Business Administration
Tennessee Valley Authority
Thrift Depositor Protection Oversight Board
Trade and Development Agency
U.S. Arms Control and Disarmament Agency
U.S. Information Agency
U.S. International Development Cooperation Agency
U.S. International Trade Commission
U.S. Postal Service

The judicial branch also interacts with the executive. Judges do not seize property, keep people in jail, or make sure a school is integrated on a day-to-day basis. A judge may order that any of these things occur, but the judge does not execute the orders. Their implementation is left to the executive branch. However, at the same time that the court relies on the executive, the court also has the power to set the limits of the executive's power, as illustrated under the discussion of executive orders.

LAWMAKING POWERS OF THE EXECUTIVE BRANCH

Traditional executive branch lawmaking involves setting the policy agenda for the legislature and sending it bills to consider. Giving initial shape to the debate, establishing legislative priorities, and lobbying to get measures passed gives the president a strong voice in lawmaking.

However, this is not a constitutional mandate. During the nineteenth and early twentieth centuries, the legislature set its own agenda and crafted new bills, too. These were times of powerful congressional leaders, and the president's role, at least when it came to lawmaking, was more of an administrator than an initiator. However, the rise of the *strong executive branch* helped to create the modern tradition. This may be observed in the federal government from FDR's first term in the early 1930s and the storied one hundred days, in which he sent a flurry of bills to the heavily Democratic Congress, until the mid-term election of 1994 when the Republican party gained control of both Houses of Congress and set the agenda thereafter. Whether the president will regain the policy initiative is, today, an open question.

However, there are more direct ways that the executive branch makes law. One way is through executive orders. Another way is by how it enforces the law.

■ *Executive Orders*

The president has the power to issue **executive orders,** which may have the same force and effect as statutes enacted by the Congress or regulations promulgated by an administrative agency. Often these orders are merely housekeeping rules—setting government job categories at certain salary levels, authorizing the creation of boards or committees to coordinate compliance with a statute. However, executive orders may have a much greater effect. Executive orders have controlled wages and prices, set curfews, and made energy policy.

One of the most noteworthy executive orders was former President Lyndon Johnson's 1965 executive order requiring affirmative action in hiring by contractors who did business with the federal government. This was an important and far-reaching rule in that it, in effect, regulated business practices of a large number of firms throughout the United States. Johnson's executive order went far beyond any existing policy to remedy racial discrimination. This executive order was the source of an employment discrimination claim brought by women and minority group members against Harris Trust & Savings Bank. The bank was considered a federal contractor because it held federally-insured deposits; thus, its activities were governed by the executive order. Harris Bank settled the claim for $14 million. It also agreed to modify its hiring policies as well as enhance its training programs to provide advancement opportunities for women and minority group employees.

The president, however, does not have unrestrained power to create law through executive order. That power is limited by the Constitution and by legislation. For example, the president would not have the authority to make an executive order prohibiting federal courts from applying the antitrust laws. Although a president may support such a limitation, the Constitution confers that power solely on Congress. Additionally, executive orders must be drafted within the confines of the express or implied powers set by Congress. A president does not have the ability to draft executive orders to fit any situation that may come to mind.

Thus, lawmaking by the executive branch is more limited than that of the legislature or even the judiciary. Executive orders may only be issued under authority granted by the Constitution or the legislature. Only certain topics may be affected by executive order. When a dispute arises, the courts determine whether or not the order is effective.

To illustrate, former President Harry Truman ordered the steel mills seized during the Korean War because of a labor dispute. Truman argued that he had this power both under constitutional authority and as implied by a number of war-related statutes. Article 2, Section 3 of the United States Constitution requires that the president "take care that the laws be faithfully executed." Truman contended that his executive order was necessary to carry our wartime legislation concerning material procurement and wage and price stability. The United States Supreme Court found neither congressional nor constitutional support for Truman's action. Justice Black, writing for the Court, noted: "The President's order does not direct that a congressional policy be executed in a manner prescribed by Congress—it directs that a presidential policy be executed in a manner prescribed by the President. . . . The Constitution does not subject this lawmaking power of Congress to presidential or military supervision or control."

Figure 5.3 displays an executive order concerning the North American Free Trade Agreement (NAFTA), the free trade agreement between the United States, Canada, and Mexico.

■ Lawmaking through Enforcement

How the executive branch decides to implement a statute or carry out a judicial order makes *law*. Of course, this does not mean that the executive branch may amend statutes or revise court orders at will. The executive branch has no such powers. However, the effect may be similar in practice, although formally, the law remains the same.

Consider this example. Assume that a stretch of highway is posted at fifty-five miles per hour. On either side of it, the speed limit is sixty-five miles per hour. The statutory mandate is clear. However, the speed one travels on that highway will more likely be influenced by how the executive branch allocates its enforcement resources. If it

■ **FIGURE 5.3** Executive Order 12915 of May 13, 1994

Federal Implementation of the North American Agreement on Environmental Cooperation

By the authority vested in me as President of the Constitution and the laws of the United States is hereby ordered as follows:

Section 1. Policy

The North American Agreement on Environmental Cooperation shall be implemented consistent with United States policy for the protection of human, animal or plant life or health, and the environment. The Environmental Cooperation Agreement shall also be implemented to advance sustainable development, pollution prevention, environmental justice, ecosystem protection and biodiversity preservation in accordance with the North American Free Trade Agreement (NAFTA).

Section 2. Implementation of the Environmental Cooperation Agreement

(a) *Policy Priorities.* In accordance with the Environmental Cooperation Agreement, it is the policy of the United States to promote consideration of the following priorities:

(1) the environmental impact of goods throughout their life cycles, including the environmental effects of processes and production methods and the internalization of environmental costs associated with products from raw material to disposal;

(2) pollution prevention techniques and strategies, transboundary and border environmental issues, the conservation and protection of wild flora and fauna (including endangered species), their habitats and specially protected natural areas, and environmental emergency preparedness and response activities;

(3) implementation of Environmental Cooperation Agreement provisions and the exchange of information among the United States, Canada, and Mexico concerning the development, continuing improvement, and effective enforcement of and compliance with, environmental laws, policies, incentives, regulations, and other applicable standards.

(b) *Environmental Effects of the NAFTA.* Pursuant to the Environmental Cooperation Agreement, the Administrator of the EAP shall work actively within the Council to consider on an ongoing basis the environmental effects of the NAFTA and review progress toward the objectives of the Environmental Cooperation agreement.

The White House   *William J. Clinton*
May 13, 1994

regularly patrols the fifty-five mile per hour stretch, one can expect adherence to the limit. If it does not, drivers will most likely ignore it. This does not mean that the speed limit has been raised. One could still be ticketed for driving at fifty-eight miles per hour. However, *in practice,* a change has occurred because of executive branch enforcement decisions.

Appreciating the interplay between rules and how they are enforced, provides an understanding of legal risk. The legal environment for business is more than a series of rules that provide an academic perspective. It also involves the legal system in which the executive's enforcement policies play a large role. If the justice department—an executive branch agency—de-emphasizes prosecution of, say, gambling crimes, then, in practice, the legal environment of gambling has changed. No gambling law has to be modified nor any judicial decision rendered. It is the enforcement decision of the executive branch that *made law*. The discussion of the Reagan Administration's antitrust law policy in the previous section is also germane here.

The Constitution provides powers to the president that may also be categorized as lawmaking ones. The president has the right to veto any bill passed by Congress. The possibility of a veto will often move Congress to draft legislation compatible with the president's goals. In addition, the president has the power to appoint federal judges (with the advice and consent of the Senate). The overwhelming majority of the appointments are confirmed. Thus, by selecting judges with similar political philosophies, a president may influence the law for years after leaving office. Furthermore, the president may bypass the judiciary by pardoning a person from criminal acts or change a judicial decision by commuting a sentence imposed by a court.

However, the legal system consists of more than the traditional judicial, legislative, and executive branches. Administrative agencies play a major role, too.

Administrative Agencies

An administrative agency is a governmental body other than a court or a legislature. Agencies exist at all levels of government and affect businesses through rule making, adjudicating disputes, and enforcing laws that have been delegated to them. In the past thirty-five years, administrative agencies have become increasingly involved in various aspects of American life. They have affected the ways in which the largest corporations conduct day-to-day business. Their ability to dispense government funds has affected even the poorest individuals' lives.

Administrative agencies control broad areas of the law. Such diverse legal topics as air and water pollution, safety in the workplace, product safety, and equal employment opportunities are covered by different administrative agencies. Volumes may be written on the workings of just one agency. Therefore, rather than review new legal rules that happened to be produced by the administrative law system, this section will focus on several general issues concerning the administrative agency in the American legal system.

IMPORTANCE OF AGENCIES

Administrative agencies are not new to our form of government. The first agencies were established by Congress in 1789. They were created to affix duties on foreign imports (the forerunner of today's customs office) and to provide pensions for the soldiers who were disabled in the Revolutionary War (the forerunner of today's Veterans' Administration).

The First Congress created those agencies for practical reasons. Processing applications for disability benefits and administering duties on imported products would take an enormous amount of time. The decision-making bodies established by the Constitution were not appropriate for handling such matters, and specialized bodies were necessary to carry out the policy. The practical rationale that led the First Congress to establish those agencies is still the driving force behind new ones being created today.

Administrative agencies exist at all levels of government. Federal agencies regulate such areas as the environment, workplace safety, and civil rights, as well as distribute social security payments. State government is also filled with administrative agencies. Such state offices as the division of motor vehicles, workers' compensation department, and the fish and game control board are examples. Local government also contains a number of administrative agencies—police and fire departments, zoning commissions, and park boards.

Virtually no business decision may be made without complying with an agency regulation. For example, personnel questions in business often involve regulations of the Equal Employment Opportunities Commission (EEOC). Business decisions about finance or capital accumulation may involve regulations of the Securities and Exchange Commission (SEC). The workplace and its design often involve the Environmental Protection Agency (EPA) or the Occupational Safety and Health Administration (OSHA). Marketing products may be regulated by the Federal Trade Commission (FTC) or the Federal Reserve Board (Fed). State or local regulation may also affect these business decisions. Administrative regulation of business is a pervasive force in the legal system and in the business world. Some writers call agencies the fourth branch of government even though they are not mentioned in the Constitution.

The International Perspective, "Japanese Ministries and a Call for Reform," is an example of the important role of administrative agencies in Japan.

Administrative agencies are creations of the legislature. Their lives are begun through the enactment of a statute, called an **enabling act,** which outlines the desired policy goals. Often, however, the specific implementation provisions for these goals are not included in the statute. Instead, the agency is charged with the responsibility of carrying out the intention of the legislature. Note that the legislature need not create a new agency to administer the areas it chooses to regulate. Frequently, an existing agency is given the authority.

Two of the most important features of an administrative agency are its expertise and its ability to monitor regulatory programs. Agencies are staffed with experts in the area over which the agency has jurisdiction. They can provide the technical skills needed to carry out the policies that led to the agency's creation.

INTERNATIONAL
PERSPECTIVE

Japanese Ministries and a Call for Reform

Ministries wield substantial power in Japan. The best students, who must pass a difficult exam, vie for places in the bureaucracy. Although these positions do not pay well, they provide the power to make laws and set policy virtually unencumbered by the political process. The Japanese bureaucrat is not accountable to the prime minister, the cabinet, or the party leaders. As a result, the ministries have been criticized as being in their own world, oblivious to the needs of the Japanese people.

Recently major scandals have shaken these ministries and moves have been made to shift their power into the hands of politicians and voters. For example, Health Ministry bureaucrats long ignored warnings about the potential of an AIDS-contaminated blood supply. In addition, these bureaucrats resisted importing sterilized blood. The result was death from AIDS for about four hundred Japanese people who were given tainted blood. Thousands more may be infected with the virus. The Ministry had hidden documents showing that they knew of the risks of AIDS-contaminated blood, but nonetheless banned imports. A panel recently gave the public access to other documents.

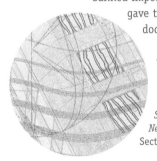

With public support waning for the ministries, changes may be in the works.,

Source: Sherly WuDunn, *The New York Times,* May 5, 1996, Section A, page 6.

FUNCTIONS OF AN AGENCY

The doctrine of separation of powers places the legislative, the judicial, and the executive powers in separate branches. This doctrine was an important element in the Constitution's plan to minimize the risk of too much power being concentrated in one governmental body. However, administrative agencies have all of these functions.

The agency is able to legislate—that is, to draft rules that serve as guidelines for following the regulatory scheme. Agencies may also exert the power of the executive. An agency may investigate whether or not the rules it enacted have been followed. Some agencies are empowered to assess fines against those who violate their rules as well as file complaints in court against them. Finally, an administrative agency is able to perform the same tasks as the judiciary by deciding cases in the area of its expertise.

The National Labor Relations Board (NLRB), for example, is a very active adjudicator. Its decisions are published in bound volumes, much the same as court decisions, and the NLRB uses its past decisions as precedent in current cases. Most interestingly, the NLRB rarely drafts regulations. Instead, it relies on its case decisions to create rules of conduct under the National Labor Relations Act (NLRA), the statute governing labor-management relations in the private sector.

The law controls the activities of administrative agencies. Courts exercise review. The legislature also has tools available to check the agency. Since the legislature created the agency, the legislature can abolish or change the agency in virtually any way it sees fit. Furthermore, since the legislature controls funding, subtle pressures may be exerted during the time that funding decisions are being made for the next fiscal year.

Congress has enacted general statutes that affect the activities of administrative agencies. The Administrative Procedure Act sets forth procedures that an agency must follow in its rule-making and adjudication functions. These standards are due process protections. Hearing procedures must contain the general processes similarly available to parties in a judicial hearing. Rule making requires public notice and the opportunity for interested or affected parties to comment. Sunset legislation abolishes an agency after a set period of years, unless the legislature re-creates it.

However, legislative oversight of agency activities primarily occurs indirectly. Use of the budgetary process to forbid the expenditure of funds for certain programs or to designate that funds be used in a certain way may channel agency activity. Furthermore, agency commissioners generally owe their appointments (and reappointments) to Congress. Unless the president makes those decisions a major part of his policies, that leverage remains with Congress. Finally, hearings and investigations of agency activities are used by legislators to influence those activities and to thwart unwanted policy initiatives. Thus, agencies generally consult Congress informally before undertaking policy initiatives.

■ *Executive Function of Administrative Agencies*

INSPECTION AND DATA GATHERING   An administrative agency could not function without the ability to gather and analyze information. Information is vital to the agency in its tasks of rule making and adjudication. One of the reasons that agencies are created is to have experts available to study and respond to a problem that the legislature seeks to regulate.

Most of the information received by agencies is voluntarily transmitted to them. Private parties respond to requests by the agency to produce documents and other data. Some agencies also inspect public records. However, agencies are not dependent upon cooperation. In fact, the first administrative agencies created by Congress in 1789 had the power to order that records be kept. Administrative agencies may also subpoena witnesses and documents. This power is important as a means of gathering information for a hearing or as a part of the rule-making process. Business managers often complain about this function of administrative regulation. Record keeping and reporting are both costly and time consuming, especially when a business is required to do so by several agencies. Some critics question whether or not the need for this information outweighs the burden placed on businesses.

An agency may also inspect a business's books and records or visit the premises. For example, local health and safety regulation for housing would be difficult to enforce without the agency's having the ability to inspect premises covered by the regulation. Spot inspections by OSHA investigators determine if workplace safety rules have been violated. Although inspections are an important form of law enforcement, they need to be balanced against the general rights provided in the Constitution.

The United States Supreme Court, in *Marshall v. Barlow's, Inc.* (1978), upheld a challenge to a warrantless administrative search. A corporation, Barlow's, Inc., sought to injoin OSHA from conducting warrantless searches for safety hazards and other violations of the Occupational Safety and Health Act. Justice White, writing for the majority, stated: "The businessman, like the occupant of a residence, has a constitutional right to go about his business free from unreasonable official entries upon his private commercial property. The businessman, too, has that right placed in jeopardy if the decision to enter and inspect for violation of regulatory laws can be made and enforced by the inspector in the field without official authority evidenced by a warrant."

GIVING ADVICE   One of the most common activities of an administrative agency is giving advice. Inquirers are often seeking information concerning how to comply with the agency's regulations. In most cases, the information received from the agency is reliable and can be followed.

However, the agency is not bound by the advice given by one of its employees. Of course, when that happens the result may be devastating.

Yet, if such advice could bind the agency, there would be a danger that the agency could begin to assume powers that the legislature did not wish it to have solely because of its inability to disavow acts by its employees. In a sense, this doctrine, although sometimes unfair, controls agency powers. *Federal Crop Insurance Corp. v. Merrill,* is an example.

Federal Crop Insurance Corp. v. Merrill

United States Supreme Court
332 U.S. 380 (1947)

The Federal Crop Insurance Corporation is a government-owned corporation created for the purpose of insuring wheat producers against crop losses due to unavoidable causes, including drought. The corporation promulgated and published in the *Federal Register* regulations specifying the conditions on which it would insure wheat crops, including a provision making "spring wheat which has been reseeded on winter wheat acreage" ineligible for insurance. The corporation accepted an application for insurance from a wheat grower, who, without knowledge of the provision, informed the local Federal Crop Insurance Corporation agent that most of the wheat to be insured was being reseeded on winter wheat acreage. Later, most of the wheat on the reseeded acreage was destroyed by drought. The corporation, after discovering that the destroyed acreage had been reseeded, refused to pay the loss, and this litigation was begun in one of the lower courts of Idaho. The Supreme Court of Idaho affirmed the judgment of the lower court, in effect adopting the theory of the trial judge: since the knowledge of the agent of a private insurance company, under the circumstances of this case, would be attributed to, and thereby bind, a private insurance company, the government-owned corporation is equally bound. The United States Supreme Court reversed.

Justice Frankfurter

We assume that recovery could be had against a private insurance company. But the Corporation is not a private insurance company. It is too late in the day to urge that the Government is just another private litigant, for purposes of charging it with liability, whenever it takes over a business theretofore conducted by private enterprise or engages in competition with private ventures. Government is not partly public or partly private, depending upon the governmental pedigree of the type of a particular activity or the manner in which the Government conducts it. The Government may carry on its operations through conventional executive agencies or through corporate forms especially created for defined ends. Whatever the form in which the Government functions, anyone entering into an arrangement with the government takes the risk of having accurately ascertained that he who purports to act for the Government stays within the bounds of his authority. The scope of this authority may be explicitly defined by Congress or be limited by delegated legislation, properly exercised through the rule-making power. And this is so even though, as here, the agent himself may have been unaware of the limitations upon his authority.

Congress has legislated in this instance, as in modern regulatory enactments it so often does, by conferring the rule-making power upon the agency created for carrying out its policy. Just as everyone is charged with knowledge of the United States Statutes at Large, Congress has provided that the appearance of rules and regulations in the Federal Register gives legal notice of their contents.

Accordingly, the Wheat Crop Insurance Regulations were binding on all who sought to come within the Federal Crop Insurance Act, regardless of actual knowledge of what is in the Regulations or of the hardship resulting from innocent ignorance. The oft-quoted observation in that "Men must turn square corners when they deal with the Government," does not reflect a callous outlook. It merely expresses the duty to all courts to observe the conditions defined by Congress for charging the public treasury. The "terms and conditions" defined by the Corporation, under authority of Congress, for creating liability on the part of the Government preclude recovery for the loss of the reseeded wheat no matter with what good reason the respondents thought they had obtained insurance from the Government. Indeed, not only do the Wheat Regulations limit the liability of the Government as if they had been enacted by Congress directly, but they were in fact incorporated by reference in the application as specifically required by the Regulations.

■ *Judicial Function of Administrative Agencies*

An administrative agency not only investigates rule violations, but it also hears complaints brought before it. **Agency adjudication** of a dispute is very similar to that of a court. Witnesses are heard, evidence is submitted, the law and policy are applied, and a decision is reached. The Administrative Procedure Act codifies traditional court practices to provide fair procedures in administrative hearings. For example, the act requires that notice of an agency complaint be provided to the affected party, who is then given the opportunity to respond and to have counsel. The conduct of a hearing is similar to a court proceeding. Witnesses are called and examined. The opposing party may cross examine them. In addition, certain agencies have adopted their own hearing rules, which are published in the *Federal Register,* the official public notice organ of federal administrative agencies.

An agency hearing is presided over by a hearing examiner who performs functions similar to those of a judge. The hearing examiner conducts the hearing and rules on motions raised by the parties. The examiner also renders a decision based on the evidence presented. Usually this decision is written and accompanied by findings of fact.

However, some major differences exist between court and agency hearings. Agency hearings never use a jury. The decisions are made solely by a hearings examiner. As a result, the evidentiary rules designed to insulate juries from unreliable evidence are not applied as strictly in an administrative hearing. Furthermore, since some agencies use the adjudicative process more as a rule-making than a dispute-settling mechanism, they are more willing than courts to accept general evidence about the issues. The National Labor Relations Board (NLRB) is an example of such an agency.

DOCTRINES OF JUDICIAL REVIEW OF AGENCY ADJUDICATIONS Courts review agency decisions on the following four levels, focusing on questions of law and constitutional procedure:

1. Whether the agency exceeded the authority that was granted to it by the enabling act;

2. Whether the agency's interpretation of the law was correct and whether it applied the law accurately;

3. Whether the hearing was fair and, thus, in keeping with constitutional due process requirements; and

4. Whether the agency acted reasonably and not arbitrarily during the hearing and decision making.

The judicial review is not a trial de novo, which would entail a court rehearing all of the evidence as if for the first time. It is like an appellate review in that the hearing record will be examined to determine whether or not it comports with the four levels of review, as previously listed. Courts usually will not substitute their views of the facts for those of the agency.

The Thought Problem, "Reviewing a Finding of Deceptive Advertising," is an example of a court's review of Federal Trade Commission (FTC) hearing. Note how the deceptive advertising law is a function of legislation, judicial decision making, and administrative agency enforcement.

thought problem

Reviewing a Finding of Deceptive Advertising

Colgate-Palmolive Company sold a shaving cream called "Rapid Shave." Television commercials purported to give visual proof that the shaving cream could soften sandpaper so that it could be shaved. Unknown to the viewer, the apparent sandpaper was plexiglass to which sand had been applied. This prop was shaved immediately after being doused with shaving cream. Actual sandpaper would require an eighty minute soaking before it would be softened enough to shave. Was this deceptive under federal statute?

In 1914, Congress created the Federal Trade Commission (FTC). This agency was charged with regulating "unfair or deceptive acts or practices in commerce." Because of the broad scope of the terms, the FTC was given latitude in applying them to the cases that came before it. Courts afforded great weight to the commission's findings in this area.

The FTC, after a hearing, decided that the Rapid Shave advertisement was a deceptive practice that violated the law because the use of plexiglass in the simulation was not disclosed. Colgate-Palmolive argued that it would be impractical to explain to television viewers that they were not being shown an actual demonstration.

If Colgate-Palmolive sought judicial review of the FTC decision, what do you think a court may do?

Furthermore, review the advertisement itself. Is it fair not to inform viewers about such simulations? Or, should we expect a certain level of skepticism or sophistication from the television viewing public that would make such a disclosure unnecessary?

Source: Federal Trade Commission v. Colgate-Palmolive Co., *380 U.S. 374 (United States Supreme Court 1965).*

■ *Legislative Function of Administrative Agencies*

Administrative agencies make rules that are called *regulations.* These regulations may be compared to statutes. They set forth general guidelines that parties must follow. Often, the enabling act that created the agency is vague, and more specific guidance is required. Regulations are promulgated to fill in those gaps. Agency regulations, then, may have more practical influence on conduct than on the language of the statute. Some commercial law areas that require disclosure of information—for example, agency-drafted business forms—will assure compliance with regulatory requirements.

The Administrative Procedure Act outlines the rule-making procedures that federal agencies must follow. The goal is fairness, and the following three steps are required:

1. The agency must give notice of its rule making in the *Federal Register;*

2. Interested parties must be provided an opportunity to participate. The agency may limit input to written comments, although it is free to schedule oral testimony, too. However, the agency is not constrained by this information source. Like a legislature, it can acquire information on its own. The purpose of the participation requirement is to give the public a voice in the process; and

3. The final rule must be published in the *Federal Register* at least thirty days before it is to become effective.

JUDICIAL REVIEW OF AGENCY REGULATIONS A regulation need not be approved by other government agencies before it is effective. Agencies are relatively independent in this regard. For example, the Securities and Exchange Commission need not submit its proposed regulations to Congress or the White House for pre-publication approval. However, this does not mean that regulations are not subject to review. They may come under the scrutiny of the judicial branch.

Courts use similar techniques to review regulations that they do for agency hearings. Their focus is on whether or not the agency has followed the law and the Constitution. The following three techniques may be noted:

1. **The regulation must be consistent with the statutory authority granted to the agency.**

Agencies are creatures of their enabling acts, limited in scope and power by their terms. Courts will overturn regulations that are outside of this scope. For example, the Environmental Protection Agency (EPA) was created to control pollution problems. It has no authority to regulate discrimination in employment even though that is an important issue, too. If the EPA promulgated such a regulation, the courts would find it to be inconsistent with the agency's statutory authority.

A decision by the Fourth Circuit Court of Appeals, *Forging Industry Association v. Secretary of Labor* (1984), illustrates this concept. OSHA adopted an interim regulation that sought to reduce the exposure of employees to high levels of noise. The amount was to be calculated over time, which included both workplace and non-workplace hours. The court vacated this regulation as being outside the scope of OSHA's power. "[T]he hearing conservation amendment clearly imposes responsibilities on employers based on non-work-related hazards. Under the amendment, an employer whose workers are unaffected by workplace noise may be subject to numerous requirements simply because its workers choose to hunt, listen to loud music, or ride motorcycles during their non-working hours. Hearing loss caused by such activities is regrettable, but it is not a problem that Congress delegated to OSHA to remedy."

managerial perspective

Challenging Pay Cable Television Regulations

The Federal Trade Commission (FTC) created a number of regulations concerning pay-per-program or pay-per-channel cable television. The regulations dealt with programming and included an advertising ban. The FTC's purpose was to prevent the pay channels from taking away popular programming that had been on over-the-air (free) television. The regulations were challenged and were found to be arbitrary and capricious.

The court found that the FTC failed to justify why it considered cable television to be merely a supplement to broadcast television instead of its equal. Without this justification, its artificially narrow focus for cable television was arbitrary. In addition, no factual information before the commission showed that cable's siphoning of programming from broadcast television would be harmful to the public interest. All that existed was information showing that championship boxing matches were shown only on closed-circuit television and that Evil Knievel decided to show his Snake River jump in the same manner.

Furthermore, the FTC's reliance on protecting the poor from programming loss was also without support. No documentation was provided to illustrate this and, given the FTC's ban on advertising, cable firms would have no ability to creatively link user fees and advertising to make such programming available. The court stated: "We are thus left with the conclusion that, if the Commission is serious about helping the poor, its regulations are arbitrary; but if it is serious about its rules, it cannot really be relying on harm to the poor."

Source: Home Box Office, Inc. v. Federal Communications Commission, *567 F.2d 9 (United States Court of Appeals, District of Columbia Circuit 1977).*

2. The agency's rule-making procedures must be fair.

A court will overturn a regulation if it finds that the agency did not comply with the Administrative Procedure Act or the Constitution's due process requirement in issuing the regulation. Sometimes, procedures will also be outlined in an agency's enabling act and these, too, must be followed. Under this technique, the court does not examine the rule itself but rather how the agency created it.

For example, assume that the Equal Employment Opportunity Commission (EEOC) promulgated a new regulation dealing with sexual harassment in the workplace. However, the public was given no opportunity to comment during its rule-making process. A court would overturn this regulation because the agency did not comply with the Administrative Procedure Act.

3. The regulation must be reasonable and not have been arbitrarily made.

A court will overturn a regulation if the facts that the agency considered do not support it. Such regulations will be found to have been made arbitrarily rather than reasonably. For example, assume that the Federal Trade Commission (FTC) issued a regulation that bans certain sales tactics as deceptive. However, the FTC had no factual basis for the regulation. Instead, the concept arose during an idle lunch time chat by the commissioners. This regulation was made arbitrarily. The FTC had no informational background from which the regulation was derived, and it based the regulation solely on the commissioners' personal opinions.

In addition, the agency rule-making record will be reviewed to determine whether or not a rational relationship exists between the regulation and the agency's enabling act. Similarly, a rational relationship must exist between the regulation and the information before the agency. An agency cannot selectively consider some facts and ignore others. Its record must be a complete one. In a sense, the court *tests* the agency to make certain that it had sufficient background to come up with its regulation.

The Managerial Perspective, "Challenging Pay Cable Television Regulations," illustrates this standard of review. Note how the Court of Appeals examined the agency's facts and found that they did not support its regulatory conclusions.

Summary

This chapter examined the legislature, executive branch, and administrative agencies. Although a legal studies course usually focuses on the judicial branch, the other branches of government also have a major effect on business. Most law today has been codified (the legislature) and current calls for its reform resound in the political arena. If legislators respond as they did to the tort reform movement (see Chapter 10), new statutes will certainly be enacted.

Observe current debates in your state legislature, and consider how proposed statutes relate to the law as it already exists. A close relationship between a law and its current applications will provide more predictable results and make the new statute easier to comply with. Furthermore, note the lobbying—which interest groups are making the arguments, and how much are they spending in doing so? Lobbying is inextricably tied to the legislative process.

The executive branch, often referred to as the *presidency* in this chapter, has a broader lawmaking role than the classic separation of powers theory provides. Its lawmaking power comes through executive orders and through decisions about how to enforce the law. Compare the power of law enforcement with the personality factor of a judge, as discussed in Chapter 4. The *personality factor* of the executive branch has a similar effect on the law.

Problems needing expertise and efficiency that fall outside the institutional limits of other branches of government led to the creation of administrative agencies. Within the limits specified by their enabling acts, they were deliberately granted all the powers that the Constitution had carefully divided among the three branches of government. The agency may make rules and regulations—that is, act like a legislature. The agency may also hold hearings to determine whether or not its rules have been violated or to resolve disputes concerning them. This function is like that generally associated with the judiciary. Finally, the agency is empowered to enforce the rules and laws in the area of its jurisdiction—in effect, to act like the executive branch of government.

However, administrative agency activities are not without limitation or review. The legislature, which created the agency, has powerful tools available to control agency activity. Courts also play a major role in reviewing the work of administrative agencies. Agency-hearing decisions and regulations must comply with the relevant enabling act, statutes concerning administrative procedures, and fundamental notions of due process. Although administrative agencies are powerful government bodies, their activities may be restrained by other branches of government.

Review Questions

1. Define the following terms:
   a. Codification
   b. Lobbying
   c. Executive order
   d. Enabling act

2. Compare lawmaking by the legislature with lawmaking by judicial decision.

3. Does business have more influence in lawmaking by the legislature or in lawmaking by the courts? Explain.

4. Discuss the lawmaking powers existing in the executive branch of government.

5. Congress enacted general statutes concerning the importance of wage and price stability in this country. They specifically prohibited the president from ordering wage and price controls. However, the president has the power to enter into contracts on behalf of the government to carry out the appropriation-of-funds decisions made by Congress. Assume that the president drafts an executive order requiring all companies that do business with the government to freeze their prices and wages on pain of losing future government contracts if they do not comply. Is that executive order within the power of the president to make?

6. What are the three main functions of an administrative agency? Discuss each function.

7. Compare and contrast hearings before an agency with hearings before a court.

8. An administrative agency properly promulgated the following regulation: "All applications for variances and exceptions to the rules of this agency must be filed by March 15 of the year for which such variance or exception is sought." On March 10, Mary Smith called the local office of the agency and asked an employee when an application for a variance must be filed. Smith was told that all applications must be on file no later than April 4 to qualify for a variance that year. If Mary Smith files her variance on April 3, will she be able to rely on the information given to her by the agency employee if the agency cites the regulation as grounds for denying her variance application?

9. Bill Jones owns a small manufacturing business. The by-product of the manufacturing process includes some toxic chemicals. The Environmental Protection Agency (EPA) regulates the disposal of

those chemicals. One afternoon an investigator from the EPA appears at the factory to inspect its chemical disposal process. No one from the EPA had received a court warrant to search the business. Must Jones permit the investigator to inspect the factory? Give reasons.

10. The Securities and Exchange Commission (SEC) is a federal administrative agency created and authorized by Congress to regulate securities (e.g., stocks, bonds) and securities markets. In July, the SEC filed suit claiming that XYZ, Inc., had discriminated against its female employees by not paying them at the same rate as male employees holding comparable jobs. The SEC based its suit on a regulation it recently made forbidding discrimination in employment. What argument may be raised by XYZ, Inc., in response to that suit?

11. Assume the SEC rule in question 10 was drafted without any public opportunity for comment and was promulgated without providing any notice. Furthermore, the rule was never published before it was applied to the XYZ matter. What additional arguments may XYZ, Inc., make based on these facts?

12. The Federal Trade Commission (FTC) promulgated a regulation that prohibited the use of sugar in breakfast cereals. The stated purpose for the regulation was to protect children from health problems that may be caused by too much sugar consumption. However, studies presented to the agency showed that presweetened cereals were eaten primarily by adults. Children usually added their own sugar to unsweetened breakfast products. Furthermore, the FTC had no information that sugar consumption was harmful (except statements by commission members complaining about tooth decay that their children experienced). Discuss how a court may review this regulation.

Chapter

6

CONSTITUTIONAL LAW
AND BUSINESS

All laws in the United States must conform to the provisions of the United States Constitution. For example, if a law passed by a state legislature conflicts with a provision in the United States Constitution, the state law is invalid. The Constitution, consequently, is a very important document in the United States.

At the beginning of this chapter, a serious problem is discussed, and how the drafters of the Constitution solved the problem is explained: the concentration of too much power in the hands of too few people. Thereafter, this chapter examines how much power the government has to regulate business. The first question addressed is—to what extent may the federal government regulate business? The next issue considers the related topic of the power of state governments to regulate business and some of the limitations on the power of states to pass laws regulating business.

Finally, this chapter concludes by briefly examining one of the most important amendments to the United States Constitution—the First Amendment. Among other things, the First Amendment guarantees individuals and businesses the right of free speech—the focus of the discussion on the First Amendment.

The United States Constitution

The United States celebrated the bicentennial of the Constitution of the United States not so very long ago. When the colonists originally separated from the United Kingdom, they initially adopted a document called the Articles of Confederation which Americans followed for a few years. It quickly became apparent, however, that the Articles of Confederation created a federal government that was too weak. In 1791, the current Constitution took the place of the Articles of Confederation. This extraordinarily well thought out document has served this country admirably for more than two hundred years and has been the model for other constitutions throughout the world.

In the Appendix at the end of this textbook, a complete version of the United States Constitution is located. Note its two major functions. First, the articles of the Constitution set forth the basic structure of the government. Many of the amendments pertain to government organization (for example, the Twenty-Second Amendment places limits on the number of terms a president may serve). The next section of this text examines the structure of the government.

The second major function of the Constitution is to provide for individual rights. Most often, the provisions of the Bill of Rights—the first ten amendments of the Constitution—are cited as performing this function. However, individual freedoms, such as the right to a trial in a criminal case (Article III, Section 2), are also provided in the articles of the Constitution and in other amendments. For example, the Civil War Amendments—the Thirteenth, Fourteenth, and Fifteenth Amendments—were the constitutional basis for the legal battle for civil rights.

Structure and Organization of the United States Government

Prior to the American Revolution in 1776, the United Kingdom governed the American colonies. The colonists engaged in an armed insurrection against British rule. The colonists differed with the British over how the colonies should be governed, and they risked their lives and the lives of their families and friends in a successful attempt to throw off one form of government in favor of a radically different way of governing.

In the late eighteenth century, Britain still placed a great deal of power in the hands of the monarchy. The monarch at that time was King George III. King George III ruled an empire that spanned the entire globe. He managed to keep a firm grip over the British empire even without access to computers, e-mail, fax machines, cellular telephones, beepers, telegraph wires, and transportation methods, such as jet airplanes, railroads, or automobiles. With such momentous difficulties in communicating with the governed, it is not surprising that the King chose to rule through the exercise of autocratic power—rules that were developed in England and transmitted to underlings in far away places such as the American colonies.

As with all autocratic systems, power in the colonies was exercised in a manner with which the governed did not always agree. For a more contemporary example of the excesses of the exercise of totalitarian power, think about the ethical considerations posed by the actions of the Chinese government in the International Perspective, "Abuse of Governmental Power."

The people who wrote the United States Constitution benefitted from studying thoughts of the great thinkers of their time. Or, as Sir Isaac Newton once observed: "I accomplished so much because I stood on the shoulders of giants." These thinkers recognized the great dangers posed to everyone by the excessive concentration of power in the hands of just a few people. Reconsider the earlier discussion in Chapter 1 concerning the issue of concentrations of power.

INTERNATIONAL PERSPECTIVE

Abuse of Governmental Power

In an attempt to come to grips with its burgeoning population, the Chinese government adopted a one-child-per-family policy. It mandates forced abortions in order to achieve this policy goal.

Some children, nonetheless, make it to orphanages. Dr. Zhang Shuyun, a former doctor at the Shanghai Children's Welfare Institute, revealed that a program of state-sponsored extermination—called *summary resolution*—operates in the orphanages. Pursuant to this policy, children are regularly selected for death, particularly those with special problems, in summary resolution meetings. These children are then denied food and care until they die.

The Wall Street Journal observed, in an editorial on this issue: "For a government that mandates forced abortion, it isn't such a huge step to kill the recently born. Especially when the government is a totalitarian one. . . . [T]he cruelest acts of our age have been committed by governments with unlimited power driven by monstrous arrogance."

What do you think? Can the actions of the Chinese government be justified through adoption of a cost/benefit analysis—or by arguing that more people will benefit through the deaths of these children than will be harmed by their deaths?

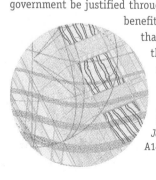

Source: "China's Deadly Orphanages," *The Wall Street Journal*, January 11, 1996, page A14.

SEPARATION OF POWERS

The colonists who wrote the United States Constitution devised a solution to the problem created by totalitarian regimes. In the Constitution, they created three separate branches of the federal government to carry out its basic functions: Article I created the legislative branch; Article II created the executive branch; and Article III created the judicial branch. Each branch of government has been provided certain powers, that, when combined, empower the government. The legislative branch was given the power to make laws and to control the funds of the government; the executive branch was granted general administrative power to carry out the laws passed by Congress; and the judicial branch was created to decide controversies arising under the laws of the United States. The branches of government seem to have very separate and distinct functions. However, the work of the branches overlaps.

The principle of separation of powers was crafted into the Constitution to ensure that the main functions of government—adjudicating, legislating, and executing laws—did not combine. Such a combination of powers, it was feared, would give rise to a tyrannical form of government. However, the three branches were not set apart as autonomous units. Instead, a system of checks and balances was created to minimize the risk of the accumulation of power in a single branch.

Federal Power to Regulate Business

The **commerce clause** is of great significance with respect to the power of the federal government to regulate business. This clause appears in the United States Constitution in Article I, Section 8, Subsection 3. It reads as follows: Congress shall have the power "To regulate Commerce with foreign Nations, and among the several States, and with the Indian Tribes." The commerce clause serves not only as a source of congressional power to regulate commerce, but also as a limitation on the power of the states to enact legislation that regulates commerce.

This clause gives Congress three areas over which it can regulate commerce—that involving the Indian tribes, commerce with foreign nations, and commerce among the states. We will leave the matter of trade with the Indian tribes to another course. The latter two areas are very important to business.

FOREIGN COMMERCE

Throughout the history of the United States, there has never been any question that the federal government has the exclusive right to regulate foreign commerce and that this power extends to all aspects of foreign trade. Chief Justice Marshall in 1824 so held in *Gibbons v. Ogden*. The states and local governments therefore may not interfere in any way with foreign trade. Suppose that a city wished to bar the importation of goods from Russia. If it passed an ordinance to this effect, such an ordinance would be struck down in a court as beyond the power of the city. The commerce clause reserves the power to pass such legislation exclusively to the federal government.

COMMERCE AMONG THE STATES

Most legislation passed by Congress related to business must be within Congress's power under the commerce clause in order for a court to uphold the legislation. This clause is a major source of congressional power, although by no means the only source of power. For example, some legislation has been held to be within the power of Congress to pass because of its taxing power. The commerce clause, however, is the most significant source of congressional power. As interpreted today, this clause grants enormous power to the federal government.

The United States Supreme Court, in examining this grant of power to Congress, initially adhered to one interpretation of the clause. In the classic case *Gibbons v. Ogden* (1824), the Court took a very broad view of the meaning of this phrase. The Court regarded *commerce* as activity that concerns or affects more than one state. This was the *commerce* that constitutionally could be regulated by Congress.

A New York statute gave Ogden a monopoly to run a steamboat on a New York river. The federal government enacted a statute awarding Gibbons the right to operate a steamboat on the same waterway. Ogden initially obtained an injunction prohibiting Gibbons from operating his steamboat on the waterway. The Supreme Court decided, in light of the federal statute, that the grant given to Ogden by New York must fall. The commerce clause gave Congress the power to regulate this activity. Article VI of the Constitution (the supremacy clause) provides that the Constitution, laws, and treaties of the United States "shall be the supreme law of the land." As the New York statute conflicted with a statute lawfully enacted by Congress pursuant to the commerce clause, the United States law prevailed because of the supremacy clause.

As time passed, the Court moved away from the interpretation expressed in *Gibbons v. Ogden*. The Court chose to interpret the clause more restrictively, essentially saying that the commerce clause dealt with physical, interstate movement. This made it more difficult for Congress to lawfully pass regulations involving purely local acts.

In the 1930s, the United States found itself in the midst of the Great Depression. Franklin D. Roosevelt assumed the office of the presidency in 1933. He immediately proposed statutes, which were enacted by Congress as part of the New Deal, that were aimed at pulling the United States out of the Depression. The Supreme Court held that much of the New Deal legislation was outside Congress's commercial clause power. For example, in *Schechter Poultry* (1935), the Court ruled that Congress lacked the power to regulate the chicken-processing industry under the commerce clause. The Court also refused to uphold federal legislation dealing with prices, working hours, and wages.

These cases caused a major confrontation between President Roosevelt and the Court. In the wake of the controversy over Roosevelt's proposal to change the composition of the United States Supreme Court by increasing its membership, the Supreme Court reversed its long-held interpretation of the commerce clause. In *N.L.R.B. v. Jones & Laughlin Steel Corp.* (1937), it laid to rest the idea that Congress cannot reach intrastate activities:

> Although activities may be intrastate in character when considered separately, if they have such a close and substantial relation to interstate commerce that their control is essential or appropriate to protect that commerce from burdens and obstructions, Congress cannot be denied the power to exercise that control.

Since the decision in 1937 by the Supreme Court in *N.L.R.B. v. Jones & Laughlin Steel Corp.*, the United States Supreme Court consistently has ruled against every challenge to the exercise of congressional power under the commerce clause—that is, until *United States v. Lopez*, was decided. This case suggests that at least some limits on the exercise of power of Congress exist under the commerce clause.

United States v. Lopez

United States Supreme Court *115 S.Ct. 1624 (1995)*

Alfonso Lopez, Jr., a high school student, carried a .38 caliber handgun onto the school grounds of Edison High School in San Antonio, Texas. Lopez was arrested for violating a federal statute—the Gun-Free School Zones Act of 1990. The trial court convicted him of violating this act, and he challenged his conviction based on the theory that Congress exceeded its power to legislate under the Commerce Clause by enacting this statute. The Court of Appeals for the Fifth Circuit agreed with his argument, and it reversed his conviction. The United States Supreme Court affirmed.

Rehnquist, Chief Justice

In the Gun-Free School Zones Act of 1990, Congress made it a federal offense "for any individual knowingly to possess a firearm at a place that the individual knows, or has reasonable cause to believe, is a school zone." 18 U.S.C. § 922(q)(1)(A) (1988 ed., Supp. V). The Act neither regulates a commercial activity nor contains a requirement that the possession be connected in any way to interstate commerce. We hold that the Act exceeds the authority of Congress "[t]o regulate Commerce . . . among the several States. . . ." U.S. Const., Art. I, § 8, cl. 3.

Jones & Laughlin Steel, Darby, and *Wickard* ushered in an era of Commerce Clause jurisprudence that greatly expanded the previously defined authority of Congress under that Clause. In part, this was a recognition of the great changes that had occurred in the way business was carried on in this country. Enterprises that had once been local or at most regional in nature had become national in scope. But the doctrinal change also reflected a view that earlier Commerce Clause cases artificially had constrained the authority of Congress to regulate interstate commerce.

But even these modern-era precedents which have expanded congressional power under the Commerce Clause confirm that this power is subject to outer limits.

We have identified three broad categories of activity that Congress may regulate under its commerce power. First, Congress may regulate the use of the channels of interstate commerce. Second, Congress is empowered to regulate and protect the instrumentalities of interstate commerce, or persons or things in interstate commerce, even though the threat may come only from intrastate activities. Finally, Congress' commerce authority includes the power to regulate those activities having a substantial relation to interstate commerce, *i.e.,* those activities that substantially affect interstate commerce.

Within this final category, admittedly, our case law has not been clear whether an activity must "affect" or "substantially affect" interstate commerce in order to be within Congress' power to regulate it under the Commerce Clause.

We conclude, consistent with the great weight of our case law, that the proper test requires an analysis of whether the regulated activity "substantially affects" interstate commerce.

If § 922(q) is to be sustained, it must be under the third category as a regulation of an activity that substantially affects interstate commerce.

We have upheld a wide variety of congressional Acts regulating intrastate economic activity where we have concluded that the activity substantially affected interstate commerce. Examples include the regulation of intrastate coal mining; intrastate extortionate credit transactions; restaurants utilizing substantial interstate supplies; inns and hotels catering to interstate guests; and production and consumption of home-grown wheat.

These examples are by no means exhaustive, but the pattern is clear. Where economic activity substantially affects interstate commerce, legislation regulating that activity will be sustained.

Even *Wickard,* which is perhaps the most far-reaching example of Commerce Clause authority over intrastate activity, involved economic activity in a way that the possession of a gun in a school zone does not.

Section 922(q) is a criminal statute that by its terms has nothing to do with "commerce" or any sort of economic enterprise, however broadly one might define those terms. Section 922(q) is not an essential part of a larger regulation of economic activity, in which the regulatory scheme could be undercut unless the intrastate activity were regulated. It cannot, therefore, be sustained under our cases upholding regulations of activities that arise out of or are connected with a commercial transaction, which viewed in the aggregate, substantially affects interstate commerce.

Congress may regulate even an activity that is purely intrastate in character when the activity, combined with like conduct by others similarly situated, affects commerce among the states or with foreign nations. For example, even if a particular restaurant engaged in purely intrastate sales, Congress still may regulate its activities if, when combined with conduct by other restaurants, such activity affects commerce among the states or with foreign nations.

It is not only the federal government that may regulate business; state governments may do so also. In the next section this power of state governments is addressed.

State Power to Regulate Business

The power of the states to regulate is referred to as the police power of the states. The states reserved this power when they banded together to form the United States. The states, in turn, have delegated some of their power to regulate to local governments.

The power of the states to regulate is not without limitation. As noted earlier, the commerce clause is not only a source of congressional power to regulate commerce, it also is a limitation on the power of the states to enact legislation that regulates commerce.

NATIONAL UNIFORMITY

If a state passes legislation that is local in character, that legislation may still be held to be unconstitutional under certain circumstances. Some areas of regulation are deemed to be areas in which only the federal government can regulate. These are areas where uniformity on a nationwide basis is essential. A famous example of this involved an attempt by the state of Arizona to limit the length of passenger trains to fourteen cars and the length of freight trains to seventy cars. The United States Supreme Court in *Southern Pacific R.R. v. Arizona* ruled

Cigarette Smoking

Rose Cipollone began smoking in 1942. She died of lung cancer in 1984. In a suit she filed prior to her death and carried on by Rose's son following her death, she claimed that the cigarette manufacturers were liable for her illness and subsequent death. Rose based her suit on the argument that the cigarette manufacturers should be liable for their failure to warn her of the dangers posed by smoking cigarettes.

In 1965, Congress adopted a statute that, in Section 4, made it unlawful to sell or distribute a cigarette package unless it bore the following label: "CAUTION: CIGARETTE SMOKING MAY BE HAZARDOUS TO YOUR HEALTH." The statute in Section 5, captioned "Preemption," provided that no other statement shall be required on any cigarette package and that no statement shall be required in any advertising of any cigarettes. In 1969, Congress strengthened this warning.

The United States Supreme Court considered the question of whether or not the 1965 law preempted Rose Cipollone's claims against the cigarette manufacturers. The Court ruled that Congress included a provision in the act that explicitly deals with the issue of preemption. This provision prohibited state and federal rule-making bodies from requiring any cautionary statements on cigarette labels or in cigarette advertising other than the warning specified in the federal statute.

Source: Cipollone v. Liggett Group, Inc., *112 S.Ct. 2608 (United States Supreme Court 1992).*

that even though Congress had not passed any legislation pertaining to the length of trains, Arizona could not limit the length of trains passing through the state of Arizona. The Court reasoned that if train length were to be regulated at all, then national uniformity would be necessary and could be prescribed only by Congress.

STATUTORY PREEMPTION

A second area in which states may not regulate commerce is those situations where Congress has preempted an area. By **preemption,** the courts mean that Congress has completely occupied a field. Sometimes Congress will expressly state in an act that it intends to preempt the field. Consider the Managerial Perspective, "Cigarette Smoking," which deals with the power of Congress to preempt an area of law.

PREEMPTION BY IMPLICATION

If congressional legislation is extensive in a particular area, the courts may find that Congress has preempted the area by implication. A good example of this may be found in *City of Burbank v. Lockheed Air Terminal, Inc.* This case dealt with an ordinance passed by the city of Burbank, California, that attempted to prohibit aircraft from taking off between the hours of 11:00 P.M. and 7:00 A.M. After examining the extensive federal regulation of aircraft takeoffs, the Court concluded that even though Congress never expressly preempted this area, it had preempted the area by implication. Such a decision makes sense in light of the chaos that would be created if every town could create its own rules relating to aircraft takeoffs and landings.

managerial perspective

Preemption

Karen Silkwood was a laboratory analyst for Kerr-McGee at a plant engaged in fabricating plutonium fuel pins for use as reactor fuel in nuclear power plants. Karen was contaminated by plutonium from the Kerr-McGee plant. Thereafter, she was killed in an unrelated automobile accident.

In this case, the United States Supreme Court considered the question of whether or not a state punitive damages award of $10 million against Kerr-McGee was preempted by the various federal acts regulating nuclear energy. The Court was not persuaded by the fact that the federal government had extensively regulated the field of nuclear energy. It held that there must be some evidence of an irreconcilable conflict between federal and state law, or evidence that imposition of the state law would frustrate the objectives of the federal law in order to justify setting aside the punitive damages award. The Court found no such conflict or frustration in the circumstances of this case; therefore, it upheld the $10 million punitive damages award against Kerr-McGee.

Source: Silkwood v. Kerr-McGee Corporation, *104 S.Ct. 615
(United States Supreme Court 1984).*

The Managerial Perspective, "Preemption," deals with the issue of whether or not the federal government's extensive regulation of the field of nuclear energy precludes a state court from rendering a punitive damage award.

OTHER LIMITATIONS

Assuming Congress has not preempted a field, and it is not one deemed to be an area in which only Congress may pass regulations, then a state, pursuant to its police power, may pass legislation that regulates business. However, some limitations on state power still exist.

For example, a state law may not be in irreconcilable conflict with a federal law. In the event of such an irreconcilable conflict, the Supremacy Clause of the United States Constitution requires that the state law be struck down. For example, suppose a federal law requires that turkeys be labeled to show the net weight of the stuffed bird. If a state adopts a law that says the net weight of the stuffed bird could not appear on the label, the federal law and the state law would be in direct conflict. Because federal laws are the supreme law of the land, when a conflict of this nature exists, the state law will be invalidated.

The Constitution also prohibits state laws that discriminate in favor of intrastate commerce. States cannot pass legislation that favors local businesspeople at the expense of out-of-state businesses. The *Dean Milk* case is a classic illustration of such a law. In this case, the city of Madison, Wisconsin, passed a law that made it unlawful to sell any milk as pasteurized unless it had been processed and bottled at a plant within a radius of five miles from the central square of Madison. Obviously, the city has an interest in the health of its citizens and, thus, some justification for such an ordinance exists. What this law does, however, is it erects an economic barrier that protects a local industry from competition located outside of the city. The Supreme

Court struck this law because, in light of the fact that other alternatives were available that the city could have used to make certain that milk sold in Madison was safe for consumption, this law discriminates against interstate commerce. *Dean Milk Co. v. City of Madison, Wisconsin*, 340 U.S. 349 (1951).

Consider the Thought Problem, "Importation of Fish," that deals with the issue of discrimination against interstate commerce by a state government.

thought problem

Importation of Fish

The state of Maine, by statute, prohibited the importation of live baitfish into Maine. The golden shiner, a species of minnow, is commonly used as live bait in sport fishing. Robert Taylor, who operated a bait business in Maine, arranged to have 158,000 live golden shiners delivered to him outside the state. He was arrested for violating the Lacey Act, which makes it a federal crime to import fish in violation of any state law. Taylor argued that the indictment should be dismissed because Maine's import ban unconstitutionally burdens interstate commerce, and therefore could not form the basis for a federal prosecution under the Lacey Act. In order to justify its law, Maine must establish that its statute serves a legitimate local purpose and that this purpose could not be served as well as available nondiscriminatory means.

What do you think? Suggest reasons that may be put forth by the state of Maine that indicate a legitimate local purpose in keeping live baitfish out of Maine.

Source: Maine v. Taylor, *106 S.Ct. 2440 (United States Supreme Court 1986).*

Figure 6.1 summarizes the limitations on the state power to regulate.

Limitations on Governmental Power

The drafters of the United States Constitution realized that government power could be abused. Consequently, they placed some limits on the exercise of government power in the Constitution. In particular, they were concerned about the intrusion of the government on the rights supposedly retained by the people at the time the United States government was formed.

■ **FIGURE 6.1** Limitations on the State Power to Regulate

National Uniformity	If uniformity of laws on a nationwide basis is necessary, states may not regulate business.
Express or Implied Preemption	If the federal government has completely occupied a field, states may not pass laws in this area.
Irreconcilable Conflict	If a state law directly conflicts with a federal law, the state law is invalid.
Discrimination against Interstate Commerce	If a state law favors businesses located within the state, this law is invalid.

STATE ACTION REQUIREMENT

The Constitution of the United States provides protection for individual rights. As originally drafted, the Constitution did not contain many protections of individual freedoms. Some of our most cherished rights were added by amendments (for example, freedom of speech, freedom from unreasonable search). The articles in the original document did contain a few basic provisions protecting individual rights, but during the ratification process many of the states were concerned that protections of additional rights were not explicitly contained in the document.

The concern for individual rights was genuine and arose from recent experiences. When the country was under British rule, troops were placed in homes without permission and searches were made without warrants. However, the British government was not the only source of rights violations. Some of the states under the Articles of Confederation also abused individual rights. Certain state legislatures passed bills of attainder, sentencing certain individuals to death without the benefit of a jury trial. At least one state levied a tax that was so burdensome to newspapers as to severely limit freedom of the press.

The drafters of the constitutional rights guarantees were concerned with abuse by government, not abuse by various individuals. The actions of the British colonial government and the governments of the states under the Articles of Confederation gave rise to practical concern by many leaders in the late eighteenth century that individual rights had to be expressly protected from abuse by the government. This is the foundation of an important idea behind the protection of constitutional rights—the concept of *state action*. Purely private and individual activity is not covered by the Bill of Rights. It is against the government and the power of the government, with its attendant danger to the freedom of all, that the individual is protected by the Bill of Rights. For example, it is not constitutionally prohibited for an individual to refuse to invite a classmate to a party solely because that person wrote poetry. It may not be a decision one would approve, but it does not violate the Constitution. However, the government may not pass a statute prohibiting poets from attending parties. The statute would be stricken as having a *chilling effect* on First Amendment freedoms.

There are constitutional protections for individual rights other than those contained in the first ten amendments. These protections may be found, for the most part, in the Civil War Amendments (the Thirteenth, Fourteenth, and Fifteenth Amendments), which were enacted between 1865 and 1870. These amendments provided the constitutional foundations for the revolution in civil rights law and criminal procedure that has occurred in this country in the last forty-five years. Of those amendments, the most influential is the Fourteenth Amendment, with its Due Process and Equal Protection clauses.

DUE PROCESS CLAUSE

Section 1 of the Fourteenth Amendment provides that no state shall "deprive any person of life, liberty, or property, without due process of law." A similar provision applicable to the federal government is contained in the Fifth Amendment. Although this phrase has a nice ring to it, what does it mean? What is the liberty and property of an individual that the state may not take away without due process? Furthermore, what exactly is *due process*—that is, what procedures must a state provide before it can deprive a person of life, liberty, or property? These questions have been raised and litigated in countless cases. Quite frankly, there is no clear answer.

Today, due process analysis is, for the most part, a guarantee of procedural protection against unfair or intrusive government behavior. It does not refer to what the government may *do* to people; it concerns itself with *how* the government may do it. Due process is a general term stipulating that government owes duties of fairness in its treatment of individuals.

A few general principles of due process must be observed before people are deprived of life, liberty, or property. One principle is that the affected individuals must have notice of the government activity being taken against them. Notice allows the individuals to prepare a defense or challenge to the government's activity. It eliminates the horror of being subjected to government processes without knowing the basis for the action.

A second principle involves various components of a fair hearing. Merely knowing the basis of the government's action would be valueless if the individual could not effectively challenge that action. A fair hearing involves a neutral, unbiased decision maker who renders a judgment on the evidence presented at the hearing. This is an important factor in that it requires the government to justify its activities to the decision maker. It also provides a forum in which the individual may raise a defense. Additional factors include the rights to present evidence and to test the evidence of the government at the hearing.

In *Connecticut v. Doehr*, the state of Connecticut failed to provide for either notice of a pending government activity concerning the defendant or a hearing. This case deals with a matter previously considered by the United States Supreme Court in a number of other cases—the circumstances under which a plaintiff may seize the assets of a defendant prior to a decision of the trial court in favor of the plaintiff.

Connecticut v. Doehr

United States Supreme Court *111 S.Ct. 2105 (1991)*

John DiGiovanni submitted an application for an attachment in the amount of $75,000 on Brian Doehr's home in Connecticut. DiGiovanni sought the prejudgment attachment of Doehr's home in conjunction with a civil action he had filed against Doehr for assault and battery. Connecticut law allowed prejudgment attachment of real estate without first giving the person whose property is subject to attachment notice or the opportunity for a prior hearing (referred to as **ex parte** attachment). The statute did not require DiGiovanni to post a bond. A judge could order the attachment after making a finding, based on the plaintiff's oath, that there was probable cause to sustain the validity of the plaintiff's claims. After the sheriff attached Doehr's home, Doehr received notice of the attachment. At this point, the statute gave Doehr a right to a hearing.

Doehr challenged the constitutionality of this statue under the Due Process Clause of the Fourteenth Amendment. The United States Supreme Court ruled that the Connecticut statute violated the Due Process Clause.

Justice White

With this case we return to the question of what process must be afforded by a state statute enabling an individual to enlist the aid of the State to deprive another of his or her property by means of the prejudgment attachment or similar procedure. Our cases reflect the numerous variations this type of remedy can entail.

These cases underscore the truism that due process, unlike some legal rules, is not a technical conception with a fixed content unrelated to time, place and circumstances.

Prejudgment remedy statutes ordinarily apply to disputes between private parties rather than between an individual and the government. Such enactments are designed to enable one of the parties to make use of state procedures with the overt, significant assistance of state officials, and they undoubtedly involve state action substantial enough to implicate the Due Process Clause. Nonetheless, any burden that increasing procedural safeguards entails primarily affects not the government, but the party seeking control of the other's property. For this type of case, therefore, the relevant inquiry requires, first, consideration of the private interest that will be affected by the prejudgment measure; second, an examination of the risk of erroneous deprivation through the procedures under attack and the probable value of additional or alternative safeguards; and third, principal attention to the interest of the party seeking the prejudgment remedy, with, nonetheless, due regard for any ancillary interest the government may have in providing the procedure or forgoing the added burden of providing greater protections.

We agree with the Court of Appeals that the property interests that attachment affects are significant. For a property owner like Doehr, attachment ordinarily clouds title; impairs the ability to sell or otherwise alienate the property; taints any credit rating; reduces the chance of obtaining a home equity loan or additional mortgage; and can even place an existing mortgage in technical default where there is an insecurity clause. Nor does Connecticut deny that any of these consequences occurs.

Our cases show that even the temporary or partial impairments to property rights that attachments, liens, and similar encumbrances entail are sufficient to merit due process protection.

We also agree with the Court of Appeals that the risk of erroneous deprivation that the State permits here is substantial.

Permitting a court to authorize attachment merely because the plaintiff believes the defendant is liable, or because the plaintiff can make out a facially valid complaint, would permit the deprivation of the defendant's property when the claim would fail to convince a jury. . . . The potential for unwarranted attachment is self-evident and too great to satisfy the requirements of due process absent any countervailing consideration.

Finally, we conclude that the interests in favor of an *ex parte* attachment, particularly the interests of the plaintiff, are too minimal to supply such a consideration here. Plaintiff had no existing interest in Doehr's real estate when he sought the attachment. His only interest in attaching the property was to ensure the availability of assets to satisfy his judgment if he prevailed on the merits of his action. Yet there was no allegation that Doehr was about to transfer or encumber his real estate or take any other action during the pendency of the action that would render his real estate unavailable to satisfy a judgment. Our cases have recognized such a properly supported claim would be an exigent circumstance permitting postponing any notice or hearing until after the attachment is effected. Absent such allegations, however, the plaintiff's interest in attaching the property does not justify the burdening of Doehr's ownership rights without a hearing to determine the likelihood of recovery.

We believe that the procedures of almost all the States confirm our view that the Connecticut provision before us, by failing to provide a preattachment hearing without at least requiring a showing of some exigent circumstances, clearly falls short of the demands of due process.

EQUAL PROTECTION CLAUSE

Section 1 of the Fourteenth Amendment also provides that no state shall "deny to any person within its jurisdiction the equal protection of the laws." As with due process, it is not quite clear what this section of the amendment means. Its meaning has changed during the one-hundred-plus years since its adoption. As noted in Chapter 1, the language did not always prohibit legislated segregation of the races. Such an interpretation is a recent phenomenon. In fact, the use of the Equal Protection Clause to attack government-imposed discrimination based on a host of individual characteristics (such as race, sex, wealth, alienage) is also a rather recent development.

The **Equal Protection Clause** does not prohibit the law from treating different groups of people differently. What it does is to require that the state show that such differential treatment serves an interest of the state. The Supreme Court, in interpreting the clause, employs a sliding scale of interests that the government must demonstrate are furthered by the classification. Certain government classifications are examined by the Court under a *strict scrutiny test*. This test requires government classifications to be closely related to the furtherance of a government purpose and that no less discriminatory alternative means of achieving the government's aims be available. For example, racial classifications are considered by the Court to be *suspect*, and to require the strictest standard of judicial review. Any legislation that treats people differently on the basis of race does not meet the equal protection standard, unless the government can show that it had a compelling interest in making that classification, which could not be served in any other way. This is a very difficult standard to meet.

The minimum review standard, generally applicable to regulation of business, is whether or not the legislature had some reasonable basis for the classification. This is referred to as the *rational basis test*. Government classifications must have a rational relationship to the achievement of a valid government objective. In general, the courts tend to defer to the legislature's judgment, as is illustrated in *State by Humphrey v. Ri-Mel, Inc.*

State by Humphrey v. Ri-Mel, Inc.

Court of Appeals of Minnesota
417 N.W.2d 102 (1987)

Minnesota required that for-profit health clubs post a bond. The bond was required to protect members from losses arising if the club were to go out of business. Such a bond was *not* required for nonprofit health clubs. Ri-Mel argued that the bond requirement violated the Equal Protection Clause. The court of appeals found that the bonding requirement was rationally related to a legitimate state goal of reducing losses experienced by people who belonged to for-profit clubs.

Forsberg, Judge

Appellants claim the standard of review to be applied in analyzing the constitutionality of the Act is the strict scrutiny standard or an intermediate standard because the Act limits the fundamental right to enter into contracts, and impermissibly restricts the contractual relationship between health clubs and its members. However, in *Essling v. Markman* the Supreme Court explained that freedom of contract has not been recognized as a fundamental right sufficient to invoke strict judicial scrutiny, and thus minimum judicial scrutiny is appropriate. Under the "rational basis" test an Act should be upheld as constitutional if the record shows the Act is rationally related to achievement of a legitimate government purpose. There is a presumption in favor of the constitutionality of legislation and a party challenging constitutionality has the burden of demonstrating beyond a reasonable doubt a statute violates a provision of the constitution.

Appellants assert the legislative distinction between for-profit and nonprofit health clubs is not rationally related to the purpose of the Act and bears no relation to the question whether prepayments by club members require the security of a bond.

The purpose of the Club Contracts Act is to protect consumers by preventing the collection by corporations of large "prepayments" to capitalize the venture and then closing their business without providing services or making refunds. The Act achieves this purpose by requiring for-profit clubs to post surety bonds to protect members from loss of money if the club should cease doing business unexpectedly without adequate funds to make refunds to consumers.

The Minnesota Attorney General's Office argues it is unaware of any nonprofit health club in Minnesota ever going out of business after taking consumer prepayments. There has been no showing that the harms sought to be protected against by the Act have occurred in nonprofit organizations or clubs offering health or fitness facilities. Nonprofit health clubs do not have the same incentive to use high pressure sales tactics or to take large prepayments to maximize profits.

The Club Contracts Act distinction between profit and nonprofit organizations is a permissible one, rationally related to the legitimate purpose of minimizing potential harms which have occurred in for-profit clubs. Therefore, the Act is not unconstitutional on its face as a violation of equal protection guarantees.

In between the strict scrutiny test (as it is applied to race) and the rational basis test (as it is applied to business), a number of different standards of review exist, depending on the type of classification. For example, discrimination based on sex, the right to travel, and the right of access to justice have different standards of equal protection review. Classifications based on gender, for example, must serve important governmental objectives and must be substantially related to achievement of those objectives.

Figure 6.2 summarizes the standards that are applied in equal protection cases. The government is also limited in its power to restrict the freedom of speech by people, as is discussed in the next section.

■ **FIGURE 6.2** **Equal Protection Standards**

Strict Scrutiny Test	The government classifications must be closely related to the furtherance of a government purpose, and no less discriminatory alternative means of achieving the government's aims are available.
Gender Test	Classifications based on gender must serve important governmental objectives and must be substantially related to achievement of those objectives.
Rational Basis Test	A government classification must have a rational relationship to the achievement of a valid government objective.

The First Amendment and Business

The First Amendment to the United States Constitution reads as follows: "Congress shall make no law respecting an establishment of religion, or prohibiting the free exercise thereof; or abridging the freedom of speech, or of the press, or the right of the people peaceably to assemble, and to petition the government for a redress of grievances."

This section of the chapter concerns that portion of the First Amendment that governs freedom of speech, with an emphasis on business. Freedom of speech is one of the most important guarantees in the United States Constitution. The free exchange of information helps ensure the preservation of democracy. The drafters of the Constitution believed that through the free and open exchange of ideas the truth, sooner or later, would be exposed. Once the citizens know the truth, they are able to make more intelligent decisions.

The core of the First Amendment clearly deals with the protection of political expression. The people who wrote the Constitution were deeply upset by the numerous historical instances in which people around the world have been prevented from criticizing their governments—even when such criticisms were completely legitimate. They wanted to make certain that people in the United States felt safe in objecting to the activities of those in control of the government. On the other hand, it is debated to this day just how literally to take the words *no law* in the First Amendment.

Consider the Ethical Perspective, "Free Speech of Publishers," concerning the free speech rights of publishers.

ETHICAL PERSPECTIVE

Free Speech of Publishers

Paladin Press has published some of the following books: *Kill Without Joy, Improvised Explosives, 21 Techniques of Silent Killing, Hit Man: A Technical Manual for Independent Contractors, Homemade C-4,* and *Anarchist's Cookbook.* People dealing with bombing suspects indicate that they routinely find Paladin books in the possession of suspects.

The owner of Paladin Press, Peder Lund, made the following statement: "As a human, I feel sorry for anyone who's put through physical suffering. As a publisher and a pragmatist, I feel *absolutely* no responsibility for the misuse of information."

What do you think? Should publishers such as Paladin Press have a right to produce books that may fall into the hands of people such as the person who bombed the federal office building in Oklahoma in 1995, killing more than a hundred people? Is Mr. Lund correct when he states that he has no responsibility for the misuse of such information? Should such publishers even have a right of free speech?

Source: Erik Larson, "Libraries of Killers Often Include a Book or Two from Paladin," *The Wall Street Journal,* January 6, 1993, page 1.

WHAT IS "FREEDOM OF SPEECH"?

Many rules have been found in the First Amendment that a person could not find by looking at the literal language of the amendment. What is speech? Is slander speech? Is threatening another person speech? Are pornographic statements speech? Are agreements to fix prices speech? If so, how can Congress regulate or prohibit such speech? The Constitution, after all, says Congress may pass *no* law. It does not say Congress may restrict pornography, or threats to other people, or slander.

To obtain a *workable* reading of the First Amendment, the justices read certain things into the language of the Constitution that a literal reading would not permit. This is true not only of the First Amendment but of the rest of the Constitution, treaties, statutes, contracts, and so on. The ability to *interpret* the law gives judges considerable discretion to determine what the law is. By the same token, the more imprecise and vague that language used in a document is, the more open to varying interpretations it is.

Instead of using extremely precise terms, the drafters of the United States Constitution elected in many places to use phrases that left the courts considerable discretion in interpreting the Constitution. The drafters hoped to create a document that would last this country for many generations. By drafting the Constitution in imprecise terms in certain places, they created a flexible Constitution that could be reinterpreted according to the needs of the times.

Nowhere is this flexible approach more obvious than in the area of freedom of speech. One could interpret this language, by reading it literally, as prohibiting any form of restriction on pure speech whatsoever. Former Supreme Court Justices Black and Douglas probably came closest to adopting such an interpretation. Other justices sitting on the United States Supreme Court have been more inclined to permit restrictions on speech. For example, Justice Holmes once wrote that a person does not have the right to yell "fire" in a crowded theatre.

Justice Holmes' position seems rational. Very few people support the idea that speakers should be able to exercise their right of free speech in such a manner as to endanger the lives of other people. Most justices over the years have supported some restrictions of one nature or another on speech. In general, the Court permits the government to place reasonable time, place, and manner restrictions on the exercise of free speech.

Suppose that Jennifer attended a state university and took business law in room 405 of Anderson Hall from 10:00–11:20 A.M. on Tuesdays and Thursdays. While her instructor, Debra Hamilton, was speaking, Jason Hamilton rushed in the room, pushed Debra away from the podium, and began to lecture the students on the virtues of communism. A speech dealing with communism is clearly a political speech and as noted earlier, political speech is at the very heart of the First Amendment. On the other hand, is this the best time and place for the exercise of Jason's right of free speech? In light of the fact that the classroom has already been designated for business law at that time, and the fact that Jason could make the same speech in other places on campus such as on the sidewalks or in a park without interfering with the rights of other people, the courts would rule that while Jason may be able to give a speech on communism on campus, giving it during the business law class would not be the right time or place for Jason to exercise his right of free speech.

People have suggested over the years that restrictions should be set on the free speech of businesses. Do corporations have the same First Amendment rights as human beings?

BUSINESS AND FREE SPEECH

The United States Supreme Court, as explained in *First National Bank of Boston v. Bellotti* (1978), clarified the issue of whether or not a corporation, as well as a private citizen, may exercise the right of free speech.

First National Bank of Boston v. Bellotti

United States Supreme Court
435 U.S. 765 (1978)

A Massachusetts statute prohibited corporations from making contributions or expenditures "for the purpose of . . . influencing or affecting the vote on any question submitted to the voters, other than one materially affecting any of the property, business, or assets of the corporation." It specifically prohibited such contributions or expenditures on votes relating to taxation. The statute provided for penalties of fines and imprisonment. Appellants, the bank, wanted to spend money to publicize their views on a proposed constitutional amendment relating to a graduated income tax. They sought to have the law declared unconstitutional. The Supreme Court of Massachusetts upheld this act. The United States Supreme Court ruled that the statute violated the United States Constitution.

Justice Powell

The referendum issue that appellants wish to address falls squarely within the First Amendment. In appellants' view, the enactment of a graduated personal income tax, as proposed to be authorized by constitutional amendment, would have a seriously adverse effect on the economy of the State. The importance of the referendum issue to the people and government of Massachusetts is not disputed. Its merits, however, are the subject of sharp disagreement.

The question in this case, simply put, is whether the corporate identity of the speaker deprives this proposed speech of what otherwise would be its clear entitlement to protection. We turn now to that question.

We find no support in the First or Fourteenth Amendment, or in the decisions of this Court, for the proposition that speech that otherwise would be within the protection of the First Amendment loses that protection simply because its source is a corporation that cannot prove, to the satisfaction of a court, a material effect on its business or property. The "materially affecting" requirement is not an identification of the boundaries of corporate speech etched by the Constitution itself. Rather, it amounts to an impermissible legislative prohibition of speech based on the identity of the interests that spokesmen may represent in public debate over controversial issues and a requirement that the speaker have a sufficiently great interest in the subject to justify communication.

The Act permits a corporation to communicate to the public its views on certain referendum subjects—those materially affecting its business—but not others. It also singles out one kind of ballot question—individual taxation—as a subject about which corporations may never make their ideas public. The legislature has drawn the line between permissible and impermissible speech according to whether there is a sufficient nexus, as defined by the legislature, between the issue presented to the voters and the business interests of the speaker.

In the realm of protected speech, the legislature is constitutionally disqualified from dictating the subjects about which persons may speak and the speakers who may address a public issue. Especially where, as here, the legislature's suppression of speech suggests an attempt to give one side of a debatable public question an advantage in expressing its views to the people, the First Amendment is plainly offended.

COMMERCIAL SPEECH AND THE RIGHT TO RECEIVE INFORMATION

Listeners often benefit from hearing all sides of a story. The more information presented to the public, the more likely members of the public are to make intelligent decisions. This clearly is the case for political speech. Does the public also benefit from hearing commercial speech as well?

For a long period in American history, the Supreme Court did *not* recognize a right to engage in commercial speech. In fact, the court explicitly ruled that businesses do not have a constitutionally protected right of free speech. In 1976, the Supreme Court finally reversed itself and decided that, in fact, speech which does no more than propose a commercial transaction is protected by the First Amendment as well as political speech. The Court based its decision on the need of the public to hear commercial information.

COMMERCIAL SPEECH BY PROFESSIONALS

Just as businesses had no right to engage in purely commercial speech, professionals, such as physicians, accountants, engineers, and attorneys also had no constitutionally recognized right to engage in commercial speech. Just as the Court changed its mind with respect to commercial speech by businesses, it reversed itself with respect to commercial speech by professionals.

The Court in 1977 considered the questions of advertising by two attorneys for the purpose of increasing their business—clearly commercially motivated speech. In *Bates v. State Bar of Arizona,* two Arizona attorneys, John Bates and Van O'Steen, had decided to advertise in order to attract the volume of business necessary to sustain their legal clinic. They reasoned that it would be necessary to advertise to attract a large number of clients.

The clinic performed only routine services, such as uncontested bankruptcies, uncontested divorces, uncontested adoptions, and changes of names. To attract more business, the clinic placed an advertisement in the *Arizona Republic,* a daily newspaper of general circulation in the Phoenix metropolitan area (see Figure 6.3). The advertisement stated that the clinic offered "legal services at very reasonable fees," and the fees for certain services were listed. This advertisement violated the Arizona rules governing the practice of law under which attorneys were forbidden to advertise.

The Court decided that the First Amendment of the United States Constitution invalidated the prohibition on advertising by attorneys. A majority of the members of the Court concluded that a state may

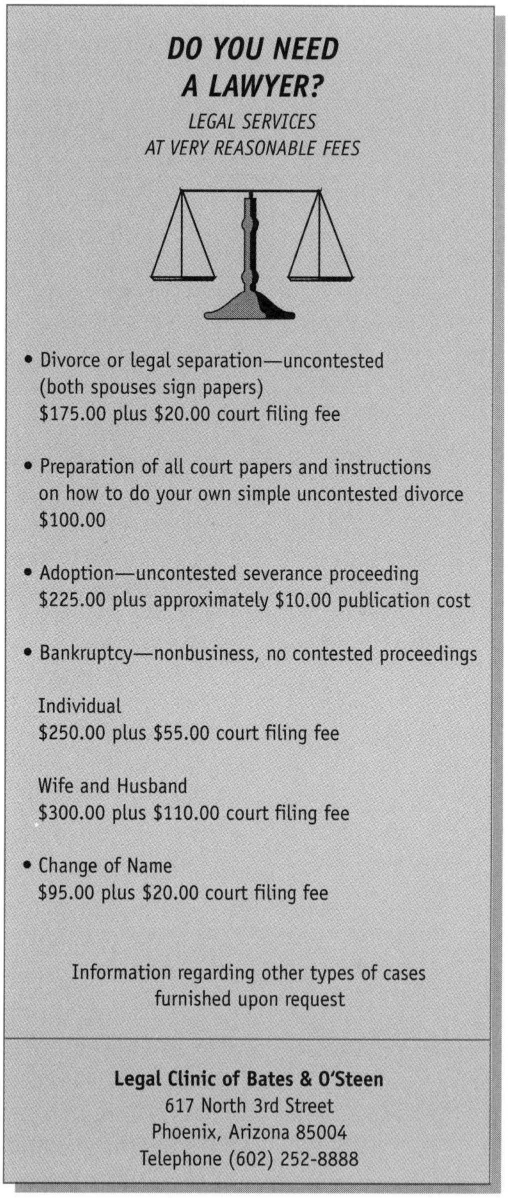

■ **FIGURE 6.3** Legal
Advertisement from *Bates v. State
Bar of Arizona*

**DO YOU NEED
A LAWYER?**
*LEGAL SERVICES
AT VERY REASONABLE FEES*

• Divorce or legal separation—uncontested
(both spouses sign papers)
$175.00 plus $20.00 court filing fee

• Preparation of all court papers and instructions
on how to do your own simple uncontested divorce
$100.00

• Adoption—uncontested severance proceeding
$225.00 plus approximately $10.00 publication cost

• Bankruptcy—nonbusiness, no contested proceedings

Individual
$250.00 plus $55.00 court filing fee

Wife and Husband
$300.00 plus $110.00 court filing fee

• Change of Name
$95.00 plus $20.00 court filing fee

Information regarding other types of cases
furnished upon request

Legal Clinic of Bates & O'Steen
617 North 3rd Street
Phoenix, Arizona 85004
Telephone (602) 252-8888

not prevent the publication in a newspaper of a truthful advertisement concerning the terms and availability of routine legal services. The state may regulate advertising by attorneys, but it may not prohibit advertising outright. The Court listed some permissible limitations: false, deceptive, or misleading advertising may be restrained, and reasonable restrictions on the time, place, and manner of advertising may be required.

Summary

In addition to providing individuals with basic rights, the Constitution of the United States created the general structure of American government. The government structure is one of relationships between sources of power. The Constitution provided that the legislative, executive, and judicial powers be confined to separate units of the federal government.

The Constitution grants extensive power in the commerce clause to the federal government. This power has been used to pass innumerable rules that control the conduct of business in America. The states get their power from the police power. They also extensively regulate the activities of businesspeople. Both the power of the states and the power of the federal government are limited by various provisions in the United States Constitution.

Provisions for protecting individual rights from government infringement may be found in a number of places in the Constitution. The Bill of Rights and the Civil Rights Amendments are prime sources of those protected individual freedoms.

One of the most important areas of constitutional protection for business is the First Amendment's freedom of speech guarantee. Corporations are protected by this provision, and recently the concept of speech has been interpreted by the Supreme Court to include business advertising or commercial speech.

Review Questions

1. Define the following terms:
   a. Commerce clause
   b. Commercial speech doctrine
   c. Due Process Clause
   d. Equal Protection Clause
   e. Separation of powers

2. Explain the concept of *state action* in constitutional law.

3. Should business speech be protected by the First Amendment?

4. The city of Columbus, Ohio, wishes to require that any product from a communist country be labeled with the country of origin. Is it within the power of the city to pass such a regulation?

5. Dirks wishes to plant one hundred acres of corn. The federal government orders him to plant only twenty acres of corn. Dirks argues that because he intends to use the corn only to feed the cattle on his farm, his activities are purely intrastate and thus cannot be regulated by Congress. Is he correct?

6. The state of Oklahoma wants to pass a law that requires local utility companies to use oil produced in the state of Oklahoma. The state wants to pass this statute to help support local oil producers. Would such a statute be within the state's power under the United States Constitution?

7. Warren, a man, wishes to join a local garden club that restricts its membership to women. The club refuses to take him as a member. Warren asserts that the club's action violates the Equal Protection Clause of the Constitution. What could the club argue in its defense?

8. Wisconsin passed a statute that permitted creditors to seize debtors' wages without first giving the debtors a hearing. If the debtors wish to challenge this statute, what could they argue?

9. A state legislature wishes to pass a statute that treats one race of people differently from another race. Is such a statute ever lawful under the Equal Protection Clause?

10. An association of coal producers challenged the constitutionality of the Surface Mining Control and Reclamation Act of 1977. The act was passed by Congress to protect the environment from the adverse effects of surface coal mining operations. Congress held extended hearings in both houses concerning the effects of surface mining on the environment. The House committee documented the adverse effects of surface coal mining on interstate commerce as the source of damage to 11,000 miles of streams, the loss of forests, the destruction of wildlife habitat, and the sedimentation of river systems. Is the application of this act to the coal companies a lawful exercise of congressional power under the commerce clause? Would it be useful for the coal producers to argue that they were engaged in local activities only?

11. Minnesota banned the retail sale of milk in plastic, nonreturnable, nonrefillable containers. Minnesota permitted the sale of milk in other nonreturnable, nonrefillable containers, such as paperboard. The state was concerned about solid waste management problems posed by plastic containers. Clover Leaf Creamery alleged that the act violated the Equal Protection Clause of the Constitution. Is Clover Leaf correct?

12. Oklahoma passed a statute prohibiting the sale of 3.2 percent alcohol beer to males under the age of twenty-one and to females under the age of eighteen. In determining whether or not such a statute violates the Equal Protection Clause, would the Court apply the reasonable basis test?

13. Ollie's Barbecue was located in Birmingham, Alabama. Ollie refused to serve African-Americans in direct violation of the 1964 Civil Rights Act that prohibits racial discrimination by a restaurant. In light of the fact that this restaurant has a largely local clientele, can the restaurant be forced to comply with this law?

3
Part

ETHICS AND THE LEGAL ENVIRONMENT OF BUSINESS

7 Ethics: Its Relationship with Legal Studies
and Business Decision Making

Chapter 7

ETHICS: ITS RELATIONSHIP WITH LEGAL STUDIES AND BUSINESS DECISION MAKING

thics is the study of what is right or good. Traditionally, it was the province of philosophers. Today, it plays a major role in evaluating business conduct. But, ethics is more than a dispassionate scholarly inquiry. It is at the heart of many business decisions, and managers who ignore ethics risk creating serious problems for their firms. One of these risks has to do with the legal environment.

The law often acts to capture unethical conduct. It does so in three ways: first, legal rules often have an ethical component; second, application of a rule is influenced by the ethics of the parties in the dispute; and third, damage awards may be a response to unethical conduct (see Figure 7.1).

Read the following two examples and compare how unethical conduct may trigger special provisions in the law:

1. Jack installed a fence around his back yard that is ten feet high because he likes the look of an enclosed space. As a result, much of his neighbor's yard is shaded during the afternoon, and the garden she cherishes is ruined.

2. Bill installed a fence around his back yard that is ten feet high because he dislikes his neighbor and knows the fence will annoy her greatly. After the fence is installed, much of his neighbor's yard is shaded, and the garden she cherishes is ruined.

Who should prevail when incompatible uses are advanced by adjoining landowners? If the gardener prevails, then the fence must be torn down. But, if the fence owner wins, destruction of the neighbor's garden will not be compensated.

The law provides that no one has a right to an uninterrupted flow of sunlight even if it has been enjoyed for a long time; otherwise, productive uses of neighboring land would be stymied by claims of *wrongful shading*. A well-known case provides an example which involved adjoining beachfront hotels—businesses that rely on sun-filled premises to attract customers.

In *Fontainebleau Hotel Corp. v. Forty-Five Twenty-Five, Inc.* (1959), the Fontainebleau's newly constructed high-rise addition blocked the sun to the Eden Roc's pool and sunbathing area. The Eden Roc sued to have the obstruction removed. The court, applying the law noted previously, held that the Eden Roc had no right to unobstructed sunlight. Thus, the high-rise addition to the neighboring hotel remained.

Reread the fence construction illustrations presented earlier in this chapter and apply the legal rule. Do you see a difference between

■ **FIGURE 7.1** Ethical Influences on Law

them? Is either of them distinguishable from the situation in the Fontainebleau case?

Bill's fence should stand out as being different. His fence was not constructed for a legitimate reason such as needed privacy, aesthetic taste, or even personal whimsy. This fence was built to annoy his neighbor, which was a base and nasty purpose.

Under the general rule, the gardener must suffer the consequences; but because Bill acted with ethically suspect motives, a corollary legal rule applies—one dealing with *spite fences.* Under the *spite fence rule,* the motives of the fence builder are examined. If the motives are like Bill's, then the neighbor (the gardener in this example) has the right to have the sunlight obstruction removed. Thus, the *spite fence rule* may be described as an ethics-based corollary to the general rule of rights to sunlight.

Recall the material on judicial reasoning and decision making in Chapter 4, particularly the *personality* and *doing "what is right"* factors. It was noted how numerous factors comprise the decisions. Given the flexibility that such decision making affords, ethically repugnant conduct may influence the application of the law. Thus, the same legal rule may provide a different outcome when ethical concerns about a party's behavior exist. The hypothetical example in Chapter 4 regarding Mary and Leroy illustrates this point.

When punitive damages are awarded to the plaintiff in civil cases, they are meant to punish a defendant. In contrast, other civil damage measures (e.g., lost wages, pain and suffering, medical expenses) are designed to compensate the victim. Punitive damages arise only when the defendant's conduct has been found to be reprehensible— that is, conduct so unethical that financial retribution should be exacted. The following examples illustrate this point:

> 1. Jane scraped the side of a car as she tried to park in a space at a shopping mall. She thought she had enough room to maneuver but misjudged the distance. She caused $1,000 in damage.

> 2. Mary noticed a bumper sticker that offended her on a parked car. She pulled her car next to it and maneuvered so that her bumper scraped the side of the parked car. "That will show the scum!" she exclaimed. The damage to the car was $1,000.

In both illustrations, the damage to the car was the same. But, consider the circumstances in each case as to why the damage occurred. It is due to these circumstances that punitive damages may arise. Jane mistakenly scraped the car. Although the law makes her responsible for the consequences, her motives were not ignoble. Contrast Jane's motives with Mary's intentions. Mary purposefully damaged a car because she did not like the bumper sticker. Ethics condemns conduct whose aim is to cause injury. The law also enforces punishment in situations like this, and Mary could be assessed punitive damages. Note, then, how her unethical conduct may enhance the award that a court enters against her.

In short, the law is filled with trapdoors and tripwires that may ensnare people whose conduct is ethically suspect. Business managers, therefore, not only must appreciate the legal environment in which their companies operate, but they must also look to ethical norms for guidance. The purpose of this chapter is to develop the connection between these two concepts.

What Is Business Ethics?

COMMON MISUSES OF THE TERM

The term *business ethics* is often misused. Consider one common definition—a business acts ethically when it earns profits while inflicting the last possible harm on society. This is not a definition of ethics. It is merely a different way of tallying costs and benefits, and an inordinately complex one at that.

For example, do social injuries occur to employees who are furloughed in recessionary times? Or would social injuries occur to shareholders if the firm refused to reduce its workforce in a recession, thereby jeopardizing its financial position? Should noncorporate members of the community who are affected by corporate decisions be included in its sphere of responsibility? (For example, worker layoffs may hurt the business of a local movie theater.) Should there be an ordering of the groups that may be injured by a corporate decision? Even though such social injuries may occur, apparently a value must be attached to them to balance against corporate dollars otherwise lost. This seems simple, but how are social injuries to be so weighted? Placing a numerical value on the social injury to an unemployed worker is a vague approximation at best. As H. L. Mencken wrote: "Explanations exist; they have existed for all time. There is always a well-known solution to every human problem—neat, plausible, and wrong."[1]

A second misuse of the term *business ethics* is that an ethical business undertakes voluntary, socially beneficial activities for nonbusiness reasons. The marginal return for these expenditures would be less than an alternative business-related expenditure of the same funds. This is not a definition of business ethics, either. No definition of business ethics exists that requires firms to lose money.

Suppose that ABC, Inc., gave $1,000 to the community ballet company. If the contribution garners a great deal of *free* publicity for the corporation and contributes to the quality of life in the community, thereby making it more attractive to employees, the return from that contribution may be much greater than any alternative business use of the funds (such as purchasing advertising or offering bonuses to key employees). Whether or not this is an ethical decision is independent of how the ballet company's contribution affected the business. Labeling a decision as *ethical*, based on such cost-benefit evaluations, confuses different ways of evaluating problems.

A third misuse of the term *business ethics* divides firms into ethical or unethical categories. If ABC, Inc., manufactures parts for nuclear weapons, then the firm may be condemned as *unethical*. On the other hand, if XYZ, Inc., does not test its consumer products on animals, then this firm is praised as being ethical. However, this is not business ethics. This confuses a decision-making process with certain answers or tests, and it is often used to advance some political agenda. The only value of this characterization is that it clarifies the speaker's position on certain social issues. It provides no definition of the term *business ethics*.

A PROPOSED DEFINITION OF BUSINESS ETHICS

Ethical business decision making is a search for the good. It is a process of reasoning, a way to evaluate problems. It is not a certain result. Good-faith, ethical decision making may yield different conclusions.

The key to this definition of business ethics is the word *search*. Using the model that is proposed later in this chapter (as Figure 7.2) will constitute this search. Decisions arising from it will be as close to *good* as one could expect. *Good* is an ethereal concept that is undefinable and perhaps even unattainable. This is why the focus must be on the search. To focus on good as an end in itself is to forget that ethics is a means to make decisions. Ethics is the intellectual journey—not the destination.

CONSIDERING COMMON MISCONCEPTIONS ABOUT ETHICS

Believing that ethics provides *answers* is a source of common misconceptions about its study. In fact, by focusing on *the good*, from the earlier definition, one may easily become so bogged in the depths of its meaning as to throw up one's hands in surrender. This surrender is often preceded by the adherence to confused ideas about ethical decision making. This section will consider some of them.

The first misconception to be discussed is that ethics is merely a question of personal values—that is, what is right or wrong in any business situation depends on who is asked for an opinion. Of course, since everyone has an opinion, in the final analysis, it all boils down to my opinion versus your opinion. In a business setting (the cynic argues), the opinion that will prevail is the one held by the person of highest rank.

The mix-up here is based on two distinct ideas: preference and process. Indeed, everyone has an opinion (preference). Thus, one

■ FIGURE 7.2 Ethical Decision Making

Universal Principle: All human beings have intrinsic worth, and they are, thus, not to be considered as a mere means to an end.

Application:
Reflection
  1. Possible decision alternatives considering the areas of responsibility
  2. Selection of an alternative based on overall benefit provided

Identifying Areas of Responsibility
  1. The business itself
  2. Members of the business organization (e.g., employees, investors)
  3. Customers of the business
  4. The community

person may prefer Mozart while another likes Garth Brooks. This is fine, and in fact, on the level of preference, there is no way to choose between them. The concept reflects purely subjective taste. Ethics, however, is something different. It is the process of reaching a decision. Much like musicologists can evaluate composition techniques to rank quality of compositions (Mozart will win without question), the ethicist uses a model to reach a decision. The incidental fact that some prefer Garth Brooks or would prefer a different outcome to a business problem has no bearing on the issue at all.

A related misconception about ethics is that given disagreements of opinion, there is no way to choose which is best. Consider the following example. Assume that XYZ, Inc., has devised the perfect crime—one that can never be detected or proved so that no legal liability will arise. XYZ has decided to have the sales forces of all its competitors murdered. In this way, XYZ will quickly become the dominant firm in its market. Now, also assume that two people's opinions differ—one argues that XYZ's plan is unethical, while the other states that it is ethical. Under this misconception, there would be no way to choose, ethically, between the opinions. Thus, murdering competitors would be the ethical equivalent to not murdering them.

Absurd, isn't it? But this misconception does have some power. Not all problems that arise provide such a clear-cut scenario as the XYZ plan. What if, instead, XYZ's decision involved the production of inexpensive handguns or popular music with violent lyrics? Or, consider the problem facing Johnson & Johnson executives as noted in the Managerial Perspective, "Tylenol Poisonings and Ethical Business Decision Making." Evaluate the solutions offered by the Food and Drug Administration and the FBI. These, too, could be justified ethically. Finding the easy *right* answer suddenly becomes elusive.

However, such problems do not mean that ethics is unworkable. Instead, these kinds of problems illustrate that ethical analysis may produce alternative solutions—none of which are intrinsically better than another. What makes one solution preferable to another is the perspective of the evaluator. In any event, the solution that is chosen will have survived an ethical evaluation which makes it superior to one that did not.

Note that outcomes with multiple *right* answers exist in other fields, too. Law is an example; yet, the law is workable. Executives frequently make business decisions where the application of a legal rule is uncertain or where sound, legal analysis yields multiple solutions. A number of these situations are discussed in future chapters.

Refer to the *Moore v. Regents of the University of California* case in Chapter 4. Both the majority and dissenting opinions accurately applied the law, but different conclusions were reached. Clearly, this does not mean that no law exists or that disagreements in law are irreconcilable. It simply means that the legal problem was a difficult one to solve. The same situation relates to ethics.

A final misconception is that ethics is irrelevant to practical business concerns, such as profitability, cost efficiency, producing a quality product, and survival in the marketplace. Such a misconception

managerial perspective

Tylenol Poisonings and Ethical Business Decision Making

In 1982, seven people in the Chicago area died after taking cyanide-laced Tylenol capsules. Investigators found that someone unknown (and never found) had tampered with the capsules. Tylenol is made by Johnson & Johnson, and this specific product accounted for approximately fifteen percent of the corporation's $468 million in net earnings the previous year. It held an approximately thirty-five percent share of the $1.2 billion painkiller market.

Immediately, consumers throughout the country stopped using Tylenol in both capsule and tablet form. The price of Johnson & Johnson stock dropped eighteen percent in one week. Tylenol users stated that they would never again use the product. Should the product continue to be sold?

A variety of responses to this crisis was considered. Food and Drug Administration officials urged that no mass recall be undertaken, fearing that such an action would increase the national panic over the Chicago deaths. The FBI argued that a recall, which would be very expensive, would encourage terrorist groups to use similar tactics as a means to attack major corporations.

Nonetheless, corporate officials decided to recall the thirty-one million boxes of Tylenol capsules in stores throughout the country at a cost of $50 million. The corporation fully cooperated with the investigation, and its CEO appeared on television programs to discuss the incident. Within ten weeks, the product was again on the market, this time in triple-seal tamper-resistant packaging. Eighty million Tylenol coupons, each worth $2.50, were provided to consumers. Within a year, Tylenol had regained most of its lost market share and customer confidence.

relegates ethical analyses to textbooks and the classroom. Perhaps, an argument could be stated that ethics is appropriate for clergy or professors, but in the real world it is fruitless because the race is won by the strong, the swift, and the cunning. In other words, nice guys finish last.

The next section will help in correcting this misconception.

Why Should a Business Act Ethically?

ETHICAL EXPECTATIONS OF TODAY'S BUSINESSES

Expectations about businesses' ethical duties have changed throughout American history. In the early nineteenth century, for example, corporations were created to have both an economic and a public interest purpose. These firms were akin to utilities in that they operated turnpikes or canals that were vital community services. During this era, ethical duties owed to the general public mixed naturally with profit-making concerns.

As the industrial revolution progressed, expectations about business ethics were reevaluated to meet economic development demands. For example, a business was deemed to owe only those duties mandated by law. Profitmaking for the shareholders overrode concerns for the public. It was believed that public benefits would naturally accrue through the operation of the marketplace.

The following quotation is illustrative of that era. During the mid-1930s, Du Pont Corporation tried to convince General Motors to use its newly developed safety glass in General Motors cars. Alfred P. Sloan, President of General Motors, responded: "It is not my responsibility to sell safety glass. . . . You can say, perhaps, that I am selfish. We are not a charitable institution—we are trying to make a profit for our shareholders.[2]

Today, the demarcation between profitmaking and charitable purpose is not so apparent. Ethical expectations of business have expanded to include community interests, as well as those of the shareholders. The Managerial Perspective, "Ethical Expectations and Donations to a University," illustrates how the law has expanded to encompass this expectation.

Corporate law requires that boards of directors make decisions that are in the best interest of the shareholders. After all, the board is working with the shareholders' investments (see the discussion of fiduciaries' duties in Chapter 12). For example, if the board of directors buys lottery tickets with corporate money, then the shareholders will have a legal claim against them. Shareholder's interest is not furthered by squandering corporate funds. But, what about giving company money to a university? Where is the profitability in this action?

Ethical expectations for business may be justified in two ways. First, ethical duties that apply to individuals do not disappear when they form a business organization. Thus, arguing that ethics and business do not mix is like asserting that group actions are immune from ethical expectations. If so, then one cannot expect groups to abide by ethical norms that govern individuals. Consider the implications. If Jack Jones is acting alone, it is expected that he has ethical duties. But, if Jack Jones joins a street gang, then he does not have ethical duties. This is absurd.

Consequently, organizations are held to ethical norms just as the individuals who comprise them. Of course, this does not mean that businesses will automatically act ethically. It does not mean that individuals will act ethically, either. But, consequences for failing to fulfill ethical expectations do exist.

How would you evaluate the following two hypothetical examples? Give practical advice. Keeping promises is an ethical expectation; however, note in both examples that the *law* does not require that the promise be kept.

1. Bill invites Mary to go to a movie with him on Saturday at 8 P.M. She accepts. At the appointed time, Mary has something better to do, and she is not home when Bill arrives. Undaunted, Bill later makes a date for the next weekend. Mary stands him up again. Still determined, Bill tries again, but Mary stands him up a third time. If Bill asks you whether or not he should ask Mary for a date on the coming weekend, what would you recommend?

managerial perspective

Ethical Expectations and Donations to a University

A. P. Smith Manufacturing Company made a donation to Princeton University. Shareholders filed a lawsuit claiming that this donation was a misuse of business funds. The court found that the donation was consistent with a business purpose. In upholding the corporate gift to Princeton, Judge Stein removed a legal impediment that otherwise would have prevented an expansion of the ethical expectations of business. Quoting from the decision:

> I cannot conceive of any greater benefit to corporations in this country than to build, and continue to build, respect for and adherence to a system of free enterprise and democratic government, the serious impairment of either of which may well spell the destruction of all corporate enterprise. It is no answer to say that a company is not so benefited unless such need is immediate. A long-range view must be taken of the matter. A small company today might be under no imperative requirement to engage the services of a research chemist or other scientist, but its growth in a few years may be such that it must have available an ample pool from which it may obtain the needed service.
>
> It must also be remembered that industry cannot function efficiently or enjoy development and expansion unless it has at all times the advantage of enlightened leadership and direction. The value of that kind of service depends in great measure upon the training, ideologies and character of the personnel available. All of these considerations must lead the reflecting mind to the conclusion that nothing conducive to public welfare, other than perhaps public safety, is more important than the preservation of the privately supported institutions of learning which embrace in their enrollment about half the college-attending youth of the country.
>
> What promotes the general good inescapably advances the corporate weal. I hold that corporate contributions to Princeton and institutions rendering the like public service are, if held within reasonable limitations, a matter of direct benefit to the giving corporations, and this without regard to the extent or sweep of the donors' business.

Source: A. P. Smith Manufacturing Company v. Barlow, *97 A.2d 186 (Superior Court of New Jersey 1953).*

2. Jane needs to have the plumbing fixed in her house. She contacts ABC Plumbing, Inc., to get an estimate. Jane works from 8 A.M. until 5 P.M., so she asks the company to stop by her house at 7:30 A.M. on Monday morning. The company agrees, but on Monday morning no one comes and Jane has to hurry to get to work on time. She calls ABC Plumbing again, and the company agrees to come by her house Wednesday at 7:30 A.M. But, on Wednesday no one shows up. Jane tries for Friday, but still no one comes. If Jane asks you whether or not she should contact ABC Plumbing another time, what would you recommend?

Compare your recommendations and the reasons behind them with those of your classmates. Are there consequences for failing to keep promises?

A second justification for the ethical expectations of business is that a market economy requires an ethical underpinning. A fundamental precept of a market is that individuals may make contracts that further their interests (see Chapters 8 and 9 for discussions on contract law).

A contract is a type of promise that the legal system will enforce. Note the connection between the ethical (keeping promises) and the legal (contract law). Imagine what would happen if no ethical expectation existed for individuals who make promises but do not keep them. In such a world, contracts would be breached if the expected benefits from doing so would outweigh the risk that the law would impose damages. What may happen to a market economy? Refer to the Thought Problem, "Applying Ethical Expectations," as an example of expectations involving ethical considerations.

thought problem

Applying Ethical Expectations

Jack ordered a new sweatshirt from the university bookstore on Monday. He paid $20 for it and expects the bookstore to send it to him by Friday.

■ Under a market economy that includes ethical expectations, describe the steps that Jack and the bookstore will take in making this transaction. Thereafter, what would you expect to happen if the sweatshirt is delivered and Jack discovers an unrepairable rip on an inside seam?

■ Now, consider a market *without* ethics, and determine whether or not you would change your responses given above.

■ Finally, in a market without ethics, what would the effect be of a sweatshirt seller who kept promises and who could be relied upon to act ethically?

First of all, contracts would become more elaborate documents since promises would be kept only if convenient. Only the law (and the detailed language of the contract) would discourage breaches. Resources that a company could use for productive purposes instead would be spent on self-protective contract clauses or strategic devices for getting around them. Consequently, the transaction costs of contracts would increase—the more complex the document, the higher the cost of formalizing the bargain.

In addition, parties would turn to the courts more frequently for enforcing promises rather than for relying on the ethical behavior of others. Since litigation is expensive and produces neither goods nor services, one would see another unproductive use of resources.

Today's ethical expectations mean that businesses risk negative consequences when they do not meet these expectations. But, practical business reasons for a firm to act ethically do not constitute the entire picture. A close connection between ethics and legal liability risk also exists.

THE ROLE OF ETHICS IN THE LEGAL ENVIRONMENT

A reason must exist for a business manager to consider ethics as an important aspect of each decision that is made. The law provides it. After all, civilization will not crumble if a manager concludes that a short-term capture of market share is an acceptable rationale for a business decision, even though doing so means using unethical tactics. Furthermore, the market system will survive that executive's rejection of ethical values. In fact, in the short term, the manager's firm may prosper. Thus, one needs more than a *good business rationale* to justify ethical decision making.

One law-related justification for ethical business decision making is provided by government regulation. Look at the table of contents in this book for these general categories: Securities Regulation (Chapter 13); Consumer Law and Environmental Law (Chapter 15); Employment Discrimination Law (Chapter 16); Labor Law (Chapter 17); and Antitrust Law (Chapter 18). Certain features are common to each of these categories. All were created by statute, and all of them have administrative agencies to carry out their goals. Increased costs are imposed on business to comply with their mandates, and they add liability risks beyond what previously existed. Finally, each imposes requirements to contract law that diminishes parties' ability to construct bargains freely. The reason is that ethical expectations for market behavior were not met, and the political environment responded with regulation. Irrespective of one's views about the wisdom or workability of government regulations, ethically suspect behavior created political impetus for a solution.

Consider the Truth in Lending Act discussed in Chapter 15. It requires that certain disclosures be formally made to individuals who are seeking credit. Prior to this act, it was not unusual for creditors to fail to divulge the annual interest rate or the total amount of interest to be paid on a loan. What was *sold* to the debtor was simply the *affordable* monthly payment. Since the legitimate interests of debtors were ignored by this practice, the political climate acted and consumer credit is now regulated. Note how this increased the transaction cost of consumer loan contracts. Truth in Lending added requirements that must be met for a contract to be valid. Penalties are imposed if those requirements are not followed.

Another example is the *Boomer v. Atlantic Cement Company* case in Chapter 15. In this case, the court refused to prohibit a factory's pollution on the basis of the common law doctrines of nuisance and trespass. One may suggest that the factory ignored the legitimate interests of adjoining landowners to use their property unhindered by someone else's waste. What followed a few years after this case were the environmental laws that changed how all such factories did business.

Of course, making ethically based decisions may also be costly. Forty years ago an executive who concluded that polluting a river with factory waste was unethical would have had a very difficult time convincing the board of directors to spend millions of dollars on an alternative waste disposal system. No immediate incentive would have been thought to exist for the firm to act responsibly (in absence of regulatory mandate) if none of its competitors were. This is a common argument about why environmental regulation is necessary. However, consider that decision making in business should not lead to either/or propositions, such as pollute the river or spend millions not to pollute the river.

Ethical decision making may generate alternatives. Since the decision either to continue polluting the river or to prompt the inefficient spending of money ignores legitimate interests of both the community or the shareholders, creativity is needed to accommodate both sides of the issue. For example, what if the company decided to develop less-polluting technology? Any discoveries would serve to enhance its competitive position. Since environmental regulation did, in fact, occur, compliance would have been easier. Perhaps a new business that supplies low-pollution technology could have resulted. Also, if there had been no environmental laws, the company would have benefitted by generating less waste and thus, become a more cost-efficient producer.

The law also provides *short-term* links to ethical decision making—that is, actions that are ethically suspect are more readily covered by the law. Legal rules often have an ethics component. As an example, consider the promissory estoppel material in Chapter 8. Pay particular note to the Managerial Perspective involving the Hoffmans and Red Owl Stores. Promissory estoppel is an ethics rule of contract law. In this Managerial Perspective the formal elements of a legal contract (e.g., offer, acceptance, consideration) did not exist. Formalistically, there should not be any contractual liability. However, for ethical reasons, the contract doctrine of promissory estoppel treats the parties as if they had a contract. Thus, executives who consider law to be formalistic may easily be confused by its ethical components. Those who do understand may limit future legal liability risk.

Truth, a fundamental ethical value, is also factored into the law. Spreading false information about a competitor may cause legal problems. For example, in the 1980s, Corona Extra Beer, which is imported from Mexico, had sudden and enormous success at cracking the American market. For some time, it was considered a *yuppie* beer since upscale young people made a point of ordering it (with a customary wedge of lime). In 1987, Corona Extra faced declining sales following a rumor that the beer was contaminated with human urine. Barton Beers, Inc., Corona's importer, filed suit against a beer wholesaler whom it contended had defamed Corona Extra. The wholesaler sold only Heineken Beer, Corona's main competitor in the imported beer market. The suit was settled a month and a half later after the wholesaler agreed to state publicly that Corona Extra was not contaminated.

Not only do legal rules contain an ethical component, but their application is also influenced by such considerations. Recall from Chapters 1 and 4 that flexibility and judicial personality are important for assessing the legal risk of any business decision. One attribute of those factors is ethics.

In the cases *Tennant Company v. Advance Machine Company* and *Millison v. E. I. du Pont de Nemours & Company*, ethically suspect decision making encouraged the courts to expand the law to fit the situations. In *Tennant Company v. Advance Machine Company*, the common law of ratification was an issue. Ratification occurs when a company approves or accepts the benefits of an employee's act that it had not authorized. Thereafter, the company becomes legally responsible. In spite of no direct evidence of corporate approval, the court in *Tennant Company v. Advance Machine Company* found that the corporation had ratified the illegal act.

The *Millison v. E. I. du Pont de Nemours & Company* case involved interpreting a statute. Workers' compensation acts were designed to compensate employees for job-related injuries through administrative procedures. Employers are immune from lawsuits. However, the court for *Millison v. E. I. du Pont de Nemours & Company* created an exception to this employer immunity when unethical conduct led to an employee's injury. The case was tried and a jury awarded six of the workers $1.4 million.

Tennant Company v. Advance Machine Company

Minnesota Court of Appeals
355 N.W.2d 720 (1984)

Tennant and Advance are competitors in manufacturing and marketing floor-cleaning equipment. From Fall 1978 through Spring 1979, certain Advance employees rummaged through the trash in a dumpster behind Tennant's Western regional sales offices in California. The raids uncovered some confidential sales information that George McIntosh, an Advance employee, forwarded to other Advance sales representatives and to company officers. McIntosh, who reported directly to Jerry Rau, Advance's Vice-President for Industrial Sales, sent Rau memos summarizing information stolen from the Tennant documents.

Rau testified that when he learned of the clandestine activity, he handled it very lightly because he did not consider it a terrible thing. He considered it a joke. Jerry Pond, President of Advance, learned about this activity from Rau early in 1979. Pond also handled it in a very light manner until this lawsuit was commenced in early 1980. Then, he discharged McIntosh. When asked whether he thought raiding the dumpster and rifling through a competitor's trash was unethical, Pond equivocated by saying that he did not have enough information to make a judgment on those practices.

The jury determined that Advance engaged in unlawful business practices, and that Tennant was entitled to $100,000 in compensatory damages and $400,000 in punitive damages.

Parker, Judge

California law imposes punitive damages to deter employment of unfit persons for important positions. It reflects certain policy judgments about corporations, primarily that top management sets the company's ethical tone. Accountability of the principal is necessary to enforce corporate responsibility: If we allow the master to be careless of his servants' torts we lose hold upon the most valuable check in the conduct of social life. In this case the president of Advance, who personally hired the individuals responsible for illegal activity, was indifferent to the ethics of their behavior.

Anything which convincingly shows the intention of the principal to adopt or approve the act in question is sufficient to establish ratification and therefore liability. It may also be shown by implication. Where an agent is authorized to do an act, and he transcends his authority, it is the duty of the principal to repudiate the act as soon as he is fully informed of what has been thus done in his name, else he will be bound by the act as having ratified it by implication. Both the president and vice president of Advance, Pond and Rau, were aware of McIntosh's activities early in 1979. Rau had discussed the matter directly with McIntosh. He also received memos containing the illegal information. The obviously sensitive nature of the material would have caused suspicions about their source. Pond had been informed by Rau and received the same memos when Rau was recovering from his heart attack.

Advance officers took no action against McIntosh until nearly one year after the fact. The failure to discharge or even reprimand an agent for illegal activity is evidence of the principal's approval. Pond never repudiated the act by informing Tennant of its occurrence. In fact, he was equivocal about the ethics of the activity.

While there was no direct evidence of ratification, the jury nonetheless had ample circumstantial evidence to sift through.

Millison v. E. I. du Pont de Nemours & Company

Supreme Court of New Jersey
501 A.2d 505 (1985)

Plaintiffs-employees are all past or present workers at defendant du Pont's Chamber Works or Repauno plants. Both plants are involved in the manufacture of chemicals; each contains an extensive amount of piping through its facilities. As asbestos was often used for insulation purposes, the pipes in these plants were, at one time, surrounded by asbestos. It is therefore reasonably inferable that certain employees at the Chamber Works and Repauno plants were exposed to the asbestos insulation and inhaled asbestos fibers.

Plaintiffs allege that du Pont and the company physicians fraudulently concealed from plaintiffs the fact that company medical examinations had revealed that certain plaintiffs-employees had contracted asbestos-related diseases. They assert that each year the du Pont doctors would give employees complete physical examinations, including chest X rays, pulmonary function tests, electrocardiograms, urine analyses, and blood tests. Plaintiffs contend that the results of these physical exams indicated that plaintiffs-employees had contracted serious pulmonary and respiratory abnormalities associated with exposure to asbestos. They further maintain that, rather than provide medical treatment for these ailing employees, defendants fraudulently concealed plaintiffs' asbestos-related diseases and sent them back into the workplace, where their initial infirmities were aggravated by additional exposure to asbestos. Plaintiffs claim that the time from defendants' first knowledge of an employee's condition to the time when the employee was told of the danger was as long as eight years.

It is undisputed that plaintiffs' injuries, if proven, are compensable under the Workers' Compensation Act. The controversy presented, however, calls for a determination of whether or not the legislature intended that the Compensation Act should serve as a worker's sole and exclusive remedy under circumstances such as those alleged.

Clifford, Justice

We acknowledge a certain anomaly in the notion that employees who are severely ill as a result of their exposure to asbestos in their place of employment are forced to accept the limited benefits available to them through the Workers' Compensation Act. Despite the fact that the current system sometimes provides what seems to be, and at times doubtless is, a less-than-adequate remedy to those who have been disabled on the job, all policy arguments regarding any ineffectiveness in the current compensation system as a way to address the problems of industrial diseases and accidents are within the exclusive province of the legislature.

Plaintiffs have, however, pleaded a valid cause of action for aggravation of their initial occupational diseases under the second count of their complaints. Count two alleges that in order to prevent employees from leaving the workforce, defendants fraudulently concealed from plaintiffs the fact that they were suffering from asbestos-related diseases, thereby delaying their treatment and aggravating their existing illnesses. Du Pont's medical staff provides company employees with physical examinations as part of its package of medical services. Plaintiffs contend that although plaintiff's physical examinations revealed changes in chest X rays indicating asbestos-related injuries, du Pont's doctors did not inform plaintiffs of their sicknesses, but instead told them that their health was fine and sent them back to work under the same hazardous conditions that had caused the initial injuries.

These allegations go well beyond failing to warn of potentially dangerous conditions or intentionally exposing workers to the risks of disease. There is a difference between, on the one hand, tolerating in the workplace conditions that will result in a certain number of injuries or illnesses, and, on the other, actively misleading the employees who have already fallen victim to those risks of the workplace. An employer's fraudulent concealment of diseases already developed is not one of the risks an employee should have to assume. Such intentionally deceitful action goes beyond the bargain struck by the Compensation Act. But for defendants' corporate strategy of concealing diseases discovered in company physical examinations, plaintiffs would have minimized the dangers to their health. Instead, plaintiffs were deceived—or so they charge—by corporate doctors who held themselves out as acting in plaintiffs' best interests. The legislature, in passing the Compensation Act, could not have intended to insulate such conduct from tort liability. We therefore conclude that plaintiffs' allegations that defendants fraudulently concealed knowledge of already contracted diseases are sufficient to state a cause of action for aggravation of plaintiffs' illnesses, as distinct from any claim for the existence of the initial disease, which is cognizable only under the Compensation Act.

Under our holding, all degrees of negligence continue to be subject to the "exclusive remedy" bar of compensation. Thus, these plaintiffs now face the unenviable burden of proving a deliberate corporate strategy to conceal plaintiffs' asbestos-related diseases that were discovered by defendants-doctors in corporate physical examinations. Proof that the doctors negligently misdiagnosed plaintiffs' X rays or estimated poorly concerning the seriousness of plaintiffs' maladies will be insufficient to establish a cause of action outside the Compensation Act. If, however, plaintiffs can in fact prove their allegations of fraudulent concealment of known diseases by defendants-doctors, we think it wholly proper that defendants be held to answer for their misconduct. Those corporations that would use their medical departments as a tool to prevent employees from learning of known injuries that are substantially certain to be aggravated by lack of disclosure must be deterred from embarking on such a course of conduct.

Note the large damage awards in the *Tennant Company v. Advance Machine Company* and *Milliston v. E. I. du Pont de Nemours Company* cases. The *Tennant Company* jury awarded punitive damages that were four times greater than the sum they awarded as compensation. Ethics played a role and thus, acting without regard to ethical principles risks greater penalties being assessed. In addition, consider the Federal Sentencing Guidelines which provide a formula for assessing criminal penalties for business crimes. One aspect states that a company that has a strong, well-managed ethics program will receive more lenient treatment than if such a program did not exist. For example, a $1 million fine could be reduced by more than ninety percent for a company that cooperates with the prosecutor and has an in-house ethics program.

How to Make Ethical Business Decisions: An Analytical Model

The model that is offered for making ethical business decisions should be considered in the context of this textbook. First of all, it is not the only model that can be used to make ethical decisions. Numerous philosophers have suggested systems through which one may make ethical choices. Of course, other philosophers have pointed out the flaws, drawbacks, and ways each of the systems may be manipulated. So be it. This is not a philosophy text. The purpose of this model is to illustrate the value of ethical decision making and to provide a means by which a manager may accomplish it. If you have taken an ethics course (if not, you are urged to do so) and prefer another model, we have no qualms in encouraging you to use it in your professional career. We would also make the same arguments, as previously stated, about its value as a means to limit legal risk.

In addition, we do not intend to survey the great ethical thinkers or summarize their ideas. This is a legal studies textbook and the purpose is to illustrate the connection between law and ethics. What this model will do is provide a means to evaluate business problems by emphasizing this connection.

Of course, there are ways other than ethics to analyze problems. You have probably encountered them in other courses. It is important that you distinguish these models from ethical reasoning.

"SELF-INTEREST" IS NOT ETHICS

Under a self-interest model, individuals act rationally to maximize their own interests. The assumption is that efficient allocation of resources will occur if these individuals are free to pursue their own ends with minimal restraint. This is a basic, albeit abbreviated, tenant of economics. It does not seek to provide an ethical perspective.

Thus, it is important not to confuse the two. Analyses based on a self-interest model are not the same ones that would arise using an ethical analysis, nor will the conclusions necessarily be the same. In his book, *Economic Analysis of Law 2d*, Richard Posner, using the self-interest model, argued that the sale of babies should be legalized. The reason for this, he noted, is because an imbalance exists in the supply and demand for babies due to the wide availability of contraception and cumbersome adoption policies. He asserted that this baby shortage was caused by government regulation, and he suggested a free-market solution—the legalization of private baby sales. By legalizing baby sales, the baby shortage could be solved in the same way as a shortage of toasters. High prices would encourage self-interested producers to enter the marketplace until equilibrium is reached.

Posner's proposal is not an ethical analysis. It is one that uses a self-interest model.

LEGAL REASONING IS NOT ETHICS

Something that is legal is not necessarily ethical. Nor will a legal analysis always yield the same conclusion as an ethical analysis would yield. Law reflects the values of a society. If these values are sound, then the law will be just, and abiding by the law will often be a shorthand for acting ethically.

Compare a self-interest analysis with a legal one by reconsidering the baby-selling example previously mentioned. Assume that the law prohibits selling babies. A legal analysis of the issue would conclude that a mother and father should not sell their children because it violates the law. Self-interest in, say, making a profit has no bearing on evaluating a problem based on law. However, if baby sellers were frequently caught and the penalty was great, both the self-interest and the legal analysis would yield the same conclusions, but for different reasons. Irrespective of the conclusion, the problem would be evaluated differently. The legal analysis perspective would be questioned as: what are society's rules?

Consider, however, a society that enacts unjust laws or one in which unethical conduct is not prohibited by law. Abiding by the law will not yield ethical conduct. Just the opposite may occur. Review the International Perspective, "Recusal in a Holocaust Trial," in Chapter 4. Had Adolph Eichmann and others *disobeyed* the rules, they would have been acting ethically. As another illustration, keeping promises *is* an ethical value. But, the law of real estate contracts requires that promises to buy land be made in writing. Thus, reneging on an oral promise to buy land does not constitute a legal issue even though it raises an ethical issue. Although legal analysis is important (especially in this textbook), it is not ethics.

WHAT IS ETHICAL DECISION MAKING?

Ethical decision making seeks to apply a universal principle unencumbered by self-interest or legal considerations. Figure 7.2 provides the model that will be used as our universal principle. Thus, one does not inquire about how certain outcomes will affect personal interests nor does it question if outcomes are permitted by law. The universal principle is meant to distinguish what is right from what is wrong regardless of other factors. If they happen to coincide, then this is convenient. But, there is no requirement or expectation that they coincide.

Consider, then, our universal principle—all human beings have intrinsic worth, and they are, thus, not to be considered as a mere means to an end.

What does this mean, and how can it be applied? First, note how using this principle poses a different perspective on the baby-selling example. Babies are valuable in and of themselves. Therefore, ignoring their interests to further a goal of self interest (e.g., profitmaking or efficient allocation of resources) violates this principle. In addition, inquiring about the legality of baby selling does the same thing. Babies have intrinsic value, whatever the law says. Of course, this distinction does not offer a solution to the problem, but it does separate ethical reasoning from other types.

Try to apply the ethical principle to the baby-selling issue. Assume, in addition, that some children are ignored and mistreated by their parents and that other families want to adopt children, but none are available. Can you suggest alternatives to the supply and demand problem for babies based on ethical reasoning?

To make our universal principle more readily applicable to business (and usable in your legal studies course), a few guidelines will be proposed.

■ *Ethics as a Thinking Process: Reflection*

Applying our ethics principle requires the reflection on how a decision may affect those to whom a company owes a duty. To do so, one must ignore self-interest conclusions and what the law dictates. Of course, in the final analysis these are connected. Consider that it is in a company's self interest to use ethical reasoning because the decisions will have a lower risk of legal liability than other means of decision making. This argument was discussed earlier in this chapter. It directly ties ethics to legal studies.

Reflection takes place in two steps. First, the executive should devise alternatives, taking into account how each will affect the company's areas of responsibility. This is an inherently creative process. No multiple-choice list exists from which to choose. The key is that in seeking solutions this way, no one to whom ethical duties are owed will be left out nor will their legitimate interests be ignored. Thereafter, one may select the alternative based on the overall benefit it provides. Several very good alternatives may exist. Irrespective which one is chosen, the business manager can feel confident that it has been developed based on ethical reasoning.

Consider this a brainstorming exercise, but with a focus on areas of responsibility. In the Thought Problem, "Ethics and Christmas Displays," determine who was affected by the Christmas holiday decorator's decision and whether or not their interests were considered.

thought problem

Ethics and Christmas Displays

Alvin Copeland always decorated his home for the Christmas holiday. Over the years, the display grew to include extravagant light designs—some that were shaped into reindeer, a star, snowmen, angels, and Santa Claus. Huge tapestries and figurines were erected on his property, and music was piped outdoors to accompany the display. Copeland operated his Christmas extravaganza from early December until after the first of the year. The display began at dusk and ended at 11 P.M. on weekdays and at midnight on weekends.

Copeland's home was located in a limited-access residential neighborhood. Even so, gigantic crowds came to see his Christmas display. The traffic congestion diminished Copeland's neighbors' access to their own homes. The crowds brought noise and public urination and property damage began to occur.

What do you think? Apply our ethical principle to this scenario, and suggest alternatives that Copeland may consider.

Source: Rodrigue v. Copeland, 475 So.2d 1071 (Louisiana Supreme Court 1985).

■ *Duties Owed to Whom: Identifying Areas of Responsibility*

Areas of responsibility are not endless. Ethical decisions could never be made if a manager owed duties to everyone, no matter how remote they were from the business. As an illustration, consider the effect of dropping a pebble into a pond. Small circles appear and grow larger, then they get fainter as they spread beyond the place where the pebble hit the water. Effects of the dropped pebble could be measured well beyond where the last ring appeared on the pond's surface. However, some of them would be so small that they would require enormous effort to detect.

Similarly, with areas of ethical responsibility, a business only owes duties to those within its spheres of control. Its decisions have a direct effect on them and thus, their interests must be taken into account under our ethical principle. These spheres of control are the company's areas of responsibility. They are the business itself, the members of the business organization, customers of the business, and the community where the business operates or has influence.

Note how closely the first three areas of responsibility relate to traditional business school studies: profitability, employee relations, and total quality management. These concerns are not foreign to ethical decision making. Consider an executive who makes a decision only to increase his salary. This is clearly a self-interest decision. Since the executive chose to ignore the interests of others (e.g., the company, its employees, and so on), the decision does not satisfy our ethics principle. Undoubtedly, such a decision would not satisfy sound management principles, either.

FOCUS: ON THE BUSINESS ITSELF   The primary area of responsibility pertains to the business itself. Making a decision that ignores profitability, market share, and cost structure (as examples) will be ethically suspect. So would one that fails to consider the long-term health of the enterprise. This does not mean that rate of return is an ethical yardstick. Instead, ethics requires that such concerns should not be ignored. Business firms, after all, are comprised of people. Their economic well-being is tied to the success of the firm.

Consider the following example which describes the fate of the Johns-Manville Corporation. Decisions were made that ignored the long-term effects on the enterprise. The consequences were devastating.

The Johns-Manville Corporation sold asbestos, a fiber that is used for insulation. Since the 1930s, management knew the health hazards of this product. Asbestos caused lung cancer in those who inhaled it. Nonetheless, management continued to sell and promote the product with neither warnings nor an effort to protect those who may inadvertently be exposed to it.

As expected, product liability suits were filed. Since the disease took years to develop, it wasn't until the 1980s that the litigation became overwhelming. More than four hundred new lawsuits were filed each month. Enormous damages were sought. In 1982, because of mounting legal liabilities, the Johns-Manville Corporation filed for reorganization under Chapter 11 of the Bankruptcy Act. Until then, management continued to promote asbestos as a product. In fact, in 1981, the company earned more than $38 million in total sales of $138 million. Under the bankruptcy procedures, a settlement was reached with current and future asbestos-injured litigants.

However, the company that emerged from the bankruptcy proceeding was a far different entity from the pre-products liability

Johns-Manville. In 1977, its stock sold for $300 per share. In June 1989, the stock could be purchased for $8. Most of the stock (eighty percent) was transferred to a special trust created to compensate injured parties. The original shareholders hold only about two and a half percent of the shares. Further, Johns-Manville was ordered to pay $75 million annually to the trust, with an additional twenty percent of its profits going to the trust beginning in 1992.

Taking into account the interests of the business itself is an important area of responsibility. The next two sections continue this traditional business-oriented focus.

FOCUS: ON MEMBERS OF THE BUSINESS ORGANIZATION A second area of responsibility pertains to the members of the organization—primarily employees and investors. Consider the investor in a corporation, for example. Money is provided for the business by the investor to use, and a return is expected. However, the investor/shareholder relinquishes control over this money and has no input into how it is being spent. Such decisions are made by management. The investors expect that their interests will not be ignored, and not as a means of furthering some personal interest of the CEO. Ethics supports this expectation just as the law does (see Chapter 12 for a discussion of fiduciary duties).

Employees' interests also need to be considered when making ethical decisions. Business problems related to working conditions, hiring and promotion practices, and downsizing, for example, raise ethical issues. Considering such questions in merely cost-benefit terms (a self-interest, decision-making model) equates human beings with dollars. It ignores the fact that individuals have intrinsic worth and that they are not to be used as a means to an end (e.g., cost-cutting practices).

Of course, this does not mean that downsizing efforts are not ethical. This conclusion is not based on the decision, but rather on how one has reached it. As an illustration, consider what happened when James F. Mullin retired from Pfizer, a drug-manufacturing company.[3]

Mullin had worked at Pfizer for thirty-four years. A few months before he decided to retire, he asked company officials if any plans for offering a bonus program to entice employees to voluntarily leave the firm existed. Such plans, called the *golden handshake,* are designed to soften a company's decision to downsize. Mullin was told that Pfizer had no such plan under consideration. He retired as planned.

Six weeks later, Pfizer announced a *golden handshake* plan that had been under serious consideration when Mullin inquired about it. Should company officials have told him?

Under a self-interest model, the company should not because, while the plan was being considered, employees who would have ordinarily left probably would not do so. The result would be a higher cost for the *golden handshake.* In addition, the law was unsettled concerning a company's duty to disclose such plans before they become effective. But, what about the ethical considerations in this situation? Analyze the situation and list your reasons.

Mullin, feeling betrayed by the breach of trust, sued Pfizer—a highly profitable company. In September 1995, a jury entered a verdict in Mullin's favor, finding that Pfizer made misrepresentations to Mullin.

FOCUS: ON CUSTOMERS OF THE BUSINESS   A third area of ethical responsibility pertains to the customers of a business. An elementary business-school maxim is that financial problems await firms that ignore their customers. As the following example illustrates, the customers' interests include the credibility of management.

In the mid-1970s, three major corporations were competing in the baby food market: Gerber Products, Beech-Nut Nutrition, and H. J. Heinz. To gain an edge, in 1977, Beech-Nut began to market a product it labeled as apple juice that contained no apple juice. During the next five years it sold $60 million worth of its falsely labeled juice. Beech-Nut also saved substantial money because the raw materials for its mixture were cheaper to purchase than apple juice. As investigators began to uncover this fraud, Beech-Nut refused to cooperate and shipped its phony apple juice inventory to a location where the investigators had no jurisdiction. Finally, the corporation was charged with violating the Food, Drug, and Cosmetics Act. It pled guilty and was fined $2 million. Its president and vice-president of operations were convicted of similar charges. Beech Nut's market share fell from 19.7 percent in 1987, when the case ended, to the current 15 percent.

Concern for customers also means providing a quality product or service. (Note how a customer focus is at the heart of total quality management theories in business schools.) Consider the International Perspective, "Selling Products Overseas."

The Managerial Perspective, "Hot Coffee and a Concern for the Customer," is another example of a customer focus. The *hot coffee case* against McDonald's is often used as an illustration of a legal system run amok. But, consider McDonald's act from a customer-focus perspective. A jury awarded $2.8 million to a customer who had been burned by spilled coffee. A judge reduced the amount to $480,000 and McDonald's thereafter settled for an undisclosed sum.

FOCUS: ON THE COMMUNITY   The final area of ethical responsibility pertains to the community. This section focuses on the interests of those who are not a part of businesses' traditional constituency. There are two components: first, the regions where the company does business, has operations, or wields influence. As an example, consider the Managerial Perspective "Should the Ballpark Have Lights?" in Chapter 12. This Managerial Perspective is based on a case regarding a Chicago

INTERNATIONAL PERSPECTIVE

Selling Products Overseas

ABC, Inc., is a major American pharmaceutical company. Its products are sold world-wide through wholly owned subsidiaries. Three years ago, ABC, Inc., received government approval to begin selling XY-123, a heart disease drug, in the United States. Although ABC, Inc.'s pre-sale product testing indicated that the product was safe, a number of patients who took the drug had life-threatening reactions.

A number of lawsuits were filed, and large product liability judgments were rendered based on American law. Note that the product liability law in the United States is substantially more consumer-oriented than in other countries. Thus, product-caused injuries leading to company liability in the United States would not necessarily do so overseas.

Because of what seems to be high product liability exposure in the United States, ABC, Inc., withdraws XY-123 from the market. However, the substantial investment in XY-123 has not been recovered.

What do you think? Should ABC, Inc., begin selling XY-123 in overseas countries that have less strict product liability laws than in the United States? Would it matter if the country was a wealthy industrialized nation or a poor third-world country? What do you think were the emphasized areas of responsibility, and which areas were ignored by ABC, Inc.?

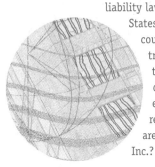

managerial perspective

Hot Coffee and a Concern for the

Customer
Stella Liebeck received third-degree burns after spilling a cup of coffee she had purchased from McDonald's. McDonald's coffee, by company policy, was served at 180 degrees—twenty degrees hotter than their competitors. Coffee, at such a temperature, could cause serious burns in a few seconds.

In the past decade, nearly seven hundred other coffee burns had been reported to McDonald's. Some of them were serious, and the company had paid more than $500,000 in settlements. An executive testified that although McDonald's knew that its coffee had caused serious burns, it never consulted a burn expert. McDonald's also decided against warning customers even though few would think such an injury could be possible. In addition, the executive testified that the company did not intend to change the temperature of the coffee. Finally, a company-hired statistician called the coffee injuries *insignificant* when compared to the number of cups McDonald's sold each year.

After the trial, one of the jurors said: "The facts were so overwhelmingly against the company. They were not taking care of their customers." Another juror stated that the issue was about McDonald's "callous disregard for the safety of the people."

Source: A. Gerlin, "A Matter of Degree," *The Wall Street Journal,* Section A, page 5 (September 1, 1994). (The quotations were taken from this article.)

Cubs' management decision not to install lights in Wrigley Field. A community factor—the effect of lights on the neighborhood—played an important part in the decision. Note that the court rejected a shareholder challenge to the *no lights* policy. Can you identify other areas of ethical responsibility that were considered by the Chicago Cubs' management?

Although lights have now been erected at Wrigley Field, compromise with the neighborhood was essential to bringing night baseball to Chicago Cubs' fans. The team promised to limit the number of night games it plays and to start the games at an earlier time than what is typical for the rest of the major league.

The second component involving the community pertains to the individuals who may be affected directly by the decision. The practice of hiring *sound alikes* to make commercials has long been common in advertising. The copyright law, which protects property interests in musical compositions, generally prohibits the use of any song without its owner's permission. A particular musician's interpretation of the song, however, was considered to fall outside the copyright law's protection. As a result, advertisers would acquire rights to a song and then seek an unknown performer to mimic the style of a famous rendition.

In 1970, a court rejected a claim by Nancy Sinatra against the use of a sound-alike version of "These Boots Are Made for Walking" in a tire commercial. Sinatra's recording of that song had been very popular. Thus, the self-interest and legal analysis models of decision making provide an obvious answer to whether or not a company should

ETHICAL
PERSPECTIVE

Do You Want to Dance, Ethically?

Ford Motor Company and its advertising agency, Young & Rubicam, Inc., promoted Lincoln Mercury automobiles with a campaign aimed at the *yuppie* market. The goal was to create an emotional connection with the cars by invoking memories from when the target buyers were in college. Songs from the 1970s were used to do so.

One of these songs was "Do You Want to Dance?", a popular song taken from Bette Midler's 1973 album, *The Divine Miss M*. Midler refused to perform the song for the commercial. Thereafter, Young & Rubicam, Inc., hired a former Midler backup singer to cut a *sound-alike* version. The result was so impressive that Midler's friends thought she was singing in the commercial.

Midler did not write "Do You Want to Dance?", and Young & Rubicam, Inc., had acquired a license to use it from the composer. The commercial did not make any reference to Bette Midler or to her 1973 recording.

Midler filed suit and was awarded $400,000 in damages. In the process, a new type of property was recognized—the right to a particular singing style.

What do you think? How might an ethically-based decision by the advertisers have changed the outcome? Be creative in your suggestions.

Source: Midler v. Ford Motor Company, *849 F.2d 460 (Ninth Circuit Court of Appeals 1988).*

use *sound alikes.* See the Ethical Perspective, "Do You Want to Dance, Ethically?", and apply the ethics model to determine if there is another perspective.

Summary

Ethics is a major component of the law. After all, law is designed to provide justice, and *justice* is an ethical concept. Consequently, ethically suspect business decisions are bound to raise legal questions. In fact, greater legal risk arises when questionable decisions are made.

This chapter noted three ways in which ethics affects legal risk: first, legal rules are frequently written with an ethical factor included. The doctrine of *promissory estoppel*, discussed in the contracts chapters that follow, is an example. Second, application of law is influenced by the ethics of the parties in the dispute. Materials in Chapter 4 on *judicial reasoning* introduced this concept. Third, the damages awarded may be influenced by the ethics of the parties involved in litigation. Note how often punitive damages were awarded in the examples provided in this chapter where ethical decision making was lacking.

Ethics is a decision-making process, not a particular outcome. Ethics may be distinguished, as it was in this chapter, from a self-interest model and from legal analysis. The key is to apply a universal principle that is unaffected by personal considerations or legal rules. This chapter outlined a universal principle that requires the consideration of the effects of a decision on certain areas of ethical responsibility.

Review Questions

1. Analyze the following case using the suggested ethical decision-making model discussed in this chapter. XYZ, Inc., operates a hospital. The hospital is a profit-making business. The relevant legal rule, in this case, concerns the duty to rescue. Under the common law, which is applicable here, a person has no obligation to rescue another person in distress. For example, if A notices that B is drowning, A has no legal duty to rescue B even if what would be required of A (tossing B a life preserver) would not endanger or inconvenience A. Additionally, assume that for-profit hospitals have no legal duty to treat anyone who seeks assistance.

Margaret O'Neill awoke at 5:00 A.M. and saw her husband standing at the window, rubbing his arms and chest. His mouth was open, and he was trying to get as much air as he possibly could. He was perspiring, and his face was white as contrasted with his normally ruddy complexion, and he complained of severe pains in his chest and arms. With Mrs. O'Neill's assistance, John O'Neill dressed and walked to XYZ's hospital which was three blocks away. The O'Neills did not own an automobile, and no taxis were available at that time.

The hospital maintained an emergency room. When the O'Neills arrived, they were directed to the nurse in charge. Mrs. O'Neill told the nurse that her husband was very ill. She explained the symptoms she observed and stated that she thought he was having a heart attack. She requested the services of a doctor. At that point, John O'Neill mentioned that they were members of the Health Insurance Plan (HIP). Thereupon, the nurse, following corporate policy, stated that the XYZ hospital had no connection with that insurance plan and did not, therefore, care for HIP patients. She did allow Mr. O'Neill to telephone an HIP doctor, who informed Mr. O'Neill that HIP services would be available at 8:00 A.M.

Mrs. O'Neill asked the nurse to have a doctor examine her husband anyway, since it was an emergency. The nurse refused. Thereafter, the O'Neills left the hospital and returned home. They walked, pausing occasionally to permit John O'Neill to catch his breath. After they arrived at their apartment, and as Mrs. O'Neill was helping her husband undress, he fell to the floor and died before any medical attention could be obtained.

2. General Motors Corporation (GM) has its headquarters in Detroit, Michigan. GM, like other major American automobile concerns, has a number of factories in the Detroit area that produce a large number of cars. In the spring of 1980, General Motors notified the city of Detroit that it would close one of its major Detroit plants within three years. Detroit, like many other old northern industrial communities, had for some time experienced deteriorating economic conditions.

General Motors' decision to close the plant would inevitably worsen the economic problems—more than six thousand jobs would be lost directly, as well as millions of dollars in tax revenue, and the effect on other businesses would make the loss even more costly to the city. GM, therefore, offered to build the replacement facility in Detroit if a suitable site could be found. Otherwise, the plant would be built in another part of the country.

A number of sites were considered by the city, but none were suitable, except a 465-acre tract that included an area known as Poletown. Poletown was an ethnic neighborhood consisting primarily of Polish-American families. The city of Detroit condemned the 465-acre tract, including the Poletown area, so that it could be cleared, converted into an industrial park, and then conveyed to General Motors. The condemnation action affected approximately three thousand people, sixteen churches, and one hundred businesses. The area was not a slum.

Was General Motors' decision to build in the Detroit area on the Poletown site an ethical one, given the loss of Poletown? Use the decision-making process discussed in this chapter to support your answer.

3. Dunes Park is an ecologically sensitive area. It consists of fifty acres of lakefront property. The land is sandy, and large hills dot the area. Few shrubs and trees grow in the sandy soil, providing a unique landscape. It is a very popular area. Dunes Park is not protected under federal environmental legislation. However, it is a state park, having been dedicated in 1920. During the past ten years, various environmental groups have attempted to have the federal government take over the park and bring it under its control. However, there is no interest on behalf of the federal government to do so. The standard response given to the groups was that "there are a number of other dune areas under federal environmental protection and there is no reason to add another."

Last year the state's budgetary problems became virtually insurmountable. While searching for new sources of revenue, the state received a report from a university geologist that predicted that Dunes Park contained large quantities of natural gas. However, the report also noted that current natural gas-drilling technology, if used, would severely strain the environmental capacity of the park. In fact, there was a great danger that the ecological make-up of the park would be destroyed. Nonetheless, the state decided to offer natural gas-drilling permits to various corporations with the expectation that a discovery would lead to improved financial conditions for the state.

You are an executive with XYZ, Inc., an energy development firm. You are contacted by the state concerning a possible bid for drilling rights in Dunes Park. You are aware of the university geologist's report that confirms a number of internal exploration reports. In fact, internal reports project that huge reserves of natural gas may be found beneath the park. During the past five years, the natural gas reserves of XYZ have been greatly depleted. New discoveries have not kept pace with the removal of gas from existing fields. As a result, the stock price of XYZ has been decreasing. Industry analysis paints a grim picture for energy firms that fail to replace the resources they use. One of the firms so pictured is XYZ. Environmental groups are expected to vigorously protest any move to explore for gas in Dunes Park. This may well result in unfavorable publicity for the firm that does the exploring.

On the basis of the ethical decision-making model discussed in this chapter, should XYZ seek to drill for natural gas in the park? Justify your decision.

4. XYZ, Inc. manufactures automobiles. The industry is very competitive, and the corporation has lost twenty percent of its market share over the last ten years. Furthermore, its current share is being threatened by lower-priced cars being produced overseas and imported to the American market. Therefore, XYZ has become very cost conscious. Labor, materials, and design features for the cars must be cost effective.

You are the senior project manager for the production of the new low-priced car being produced by XYZ. Sales of the car are scheduled to begin in approximately eighteen months. Currently, the goal is to be able to produce a high-quality small car to effectively compete with the imports. Already the corporation is advertising its determination to "drive the imports from the highways." Your responsibility is to make absolutely certain that the car will be profitable when sold in the intended $9,000 range. Additionally, the car must be a high-quality product.

Company engineers recommend that the gasoline tank system be redesigned for the car. The current design made the tank somewhat vulnerable to puncture (and explosion) during rear-end collision tests that were conducted. In order to meet their suggested specifications, an additional $20 million would need to be invested in the car. Doing so would make the $9,000 price impossible to meet. Furthermore, company actuaries estimate that the current design would produce $10 million in damage awards that the corporation would have to apy as a result of exploding gasoline tanks. This figure is already factored into overall costs that go toward computing the $9,000 sales price.

What decision should you make? Justify your decision. Would your decision be different if the design change would not affect the $9,000 price? Would your decision be different if you and members of your family would be driving the car?

5. You are the vice-president of marketing for a major corporation. Every regional sales manager reports directly to you. One of your jobs is to determine which, if any, of the sales representatives should be promoted to regional manager. These positions open only occasionally, and selecting a top person for that job is of vital concern to the company. The industry is very competitive, and the regional manager is key in keeping current customers satisfied and in working with the representative in garnering new customers.

Last week one of the regional managers retired, and you have been studying the pool of sales representatives, seeking a replacement. The most qualified person, by far, is Mary Smith. In fact, her performance to date has been among the strongest ever recorded for the corporation. However, you know that three of your major customers in that region have serious misgivings about dealing with women in business settings. You heard one customer mention that women are unsuited for responsible sales management positions.

Should you promote Mary Smith? Base your evaluation only on the materials provided in this chapter.

6. You are an executive with ABC, Inc. The corporation manufactures a very popular jet ski. Although the market for this recreational product is quite competitive, your firm's design has proved to be the winner. This morning, ABC's engineers deliver a report to you that states that certain uses of the jet ski, given its design, may be very dangerous. These uses are not atypical for jet skiers. You also have a report that states that recreational products users are quite concerned about safety and will quickly turn on a once-popular product that they discover risks injuries.

What, if anything, should you do? Base your evaluation on the materials provided in this chapter.

7. You are an executive with a very large company. Six years ago you began to deal with a small supplier of rubber fittings that are used

in the production of your firm's products. Your firm has become virtually the sole customer of this supplier. Because of your demands for quickly delivered inventory, the small supplier has borrowed heavily to redesign its operations. In fact, one may consider the survival of the supplier to be tied to its contract with your firm.

Last year your firm signed a ten-year contract with the supplier. The price per unit was designated. However, the economic climate has become uncertain. You would like to cut costs here and there. One of your assistants suggests that you simply withhold payment from the small supplier. When the supplier is sufficiently squeezed financially, the assistant assures you, it will readily accept a renegotiation of the contract.

What do you think? Should you use this strategy? Base your evaluation on the materials provided in this chapter.

Notes

[1] H. L. Mencken, *Selected Prejudices* (New York: Octagon, 1926), p. 67.
[2] Dan Cordtz, "Detroit's Catch-22," *Financial World* 36, June 27, 1989.
[3] From J. Rabinovitz, "Companies Find That Keeping 'Golden Handshakes' Secret Has Its Price," *The New York Times* October 22, 1995, section 1, page 16.

4

Part

THE COMMON LAW

Chapter

8

INTRODUCTION TO CONTRACTS—THE ESSENTIAL ELEMENTS

People in business enter into contracts on a regular basis. A businessperson needs to recognize when his or her actions may lead to the creation of a binding agreement—otherwise, a person may inadvertently create a contract. In this chapter, a discussion on what the law means by the term *contract* is provided. Then, we look at the sources and history of contract law.

Every businessperson needs to recognize that knowing something about how to negotiate increases the likelihood of getting the best possible deal. Everyone in the business world negotiates on a regular basis. In both this chapter and Chapter 9, a few negotiation principles are mentioned that a person ought to keep in mind while creating and performing a contract.

The heart of this chapter concerns the essential elements necessary to create a valid contract—offer, acceptance, consideration, capacity, and legality.

Meaning of the Word *Contract*

Each day people throughout the United States enter into contracts. Quite often, the people involved fail to recognize that a contract ever came into existence. The average person probably enters into hundreds of contracts a year without realizing it. Buying clothing, purchasing groceries, and subscribing to a magazine are just a few examples of the many contracts people enter into every year.

A person not trained in the law often assumes that a contract must be drawn up in a formal written document drafted by an attorney. In fact, contracts may result, without either party signing a formal written agreement, from the exchange of letters between people, from conversations, or even from the actions of people who have neither written nor said anything.

Suppose that today you decide to purchase a candy bar. You go to a vending machine, deposit some change, and out comes your selection. Even though you never signed anything or spoke to anyone, your actions created a contract between the seller and yourself. If the machine fails to give you a candy bar after you deposited your money, the contract created by the deposit of money has been breached.

To understand how these actions created a contract, it is first necessary to know what a contract is.

WHAT IS A CONTRACT?

In the law, **contract** refers to a transaction in which two or more people have entered into an agreement that is legally enforceable. Quite often, the parties first engaged in some discussion of their differences before arriving at an agreement.

In arriving at a technical definition of the term *contract*, the courts sometimes rely on the **Restatement of Contracts.** The *Restatement of Contracts* is *not* the law in any state. It is an effort of legal scholars, sponsored by the American Law Institute, to analyze existing judicial decisions and to distill from them some sound principles of contract law. The *Restatement* has often been relied on by the courts as a guide in resolving cases involving contracts.

The drafters of the *Restatement of Contracts* suggest the following definition of a contract: "A contract is a promise or set of promises for breach of which the law gives a remedy, or the performance of which the law in some way recognizes as a duty." The next question, then, is: What is a promise? A **promise** is a voluntary commitment by one person to another person to perform in some manner or refrain from some action in the future.

Often it is helpful to approach contract law by focusing on the promises of the parties. Consider the following example. Acme Drugstore enters into an employment contract with Janice Hartman. Hartman agrees (or promises) to work for Acme and Acme agrees (or promises) to pay Hartman. According to this agreement, Hartman is obligated to work for Acme and has the right to receive payment for her work. Acme has the right to receive Hartman's services and is obligated to pay her for these services. Thus, a contract may be thought of as an agreement that consists of a promise or set of promises that creates legal rights and obligations.

Sources of the Rules of Contracts

THE COMMON LAW

In order to locate the rules of contract law, attorneys must turn, for the most part, to cases (see Figure 8.1). Case law consists of the rules of law announced in court decisions. Each decision in a case dealing with contracts becomes part of the law in this area, and the ruling serves as a precedent that binds courts in the future. The common law controls such matters as service contracts, employment contracts, and real estate contracts. For example, suppose that Arthur sold his gasoline station to Wilbur and thereafter refused to comply with his obligations under the contract. An attorney researching the law concerning breach of contracts must examine judicial opinions to find an answer to any questions that arise.

Not all of the law of contracts may be found in judicial decisions. The provisions of the Uniform Commercial Code govern certain types of contracts.

THE UNIFORM COMMERCIAL CODE

■ The Uniform Commercial Code in General

The **Uniform Commercial Code** (UCC) covers many areas of commercial law. Before the twentieth century, the law came primarily

■ **FIGURE 8.1** Sources of the Rules of Contracts

The Common Law—the law found in cases

Article 2 of the Uniform Commercial Code—a statute dealing with the sale of tangible, movable goods

Other Sources of Contract Law—state and federal governments have passed special statutes dealing with certain types of contracts from cases, and the laws dealing with commercial transactions varied greatly from state to state. In order to simplify the law, model statutes (codes) were drafted covering several areas of commercial law. These codes were enacted by the legislatures in a number of states. Based on the experience gained in these early attempts at simplifying the law, the National Conference of Commissioners on Uniform State Laws and the American Law Institute set about drafting new codes that would eliminate some of the problems associated with the earlier codes.

This effort culminated in what is now called the Uniform Commercial Code. This model code, consisting of ten articles, deals with the sale of goods, commercial paper, secured transactions, and other commercial activities.

Though the UCC is merely a model code, all of the states have enacted it (except Louisiana, which adopted parts of it, but not Article Two, dealing with the sale of goods). States have generally followed the language that appears in the model version. Some states have altered the language of the model code in certain places. The following discussion of the UCC will be confined to that part of it dealing with the sale of goods.

■ *Article Two of the UCC*

Unlike the law of contracts covering items other than the sale of goods, in which the primary source of law is cases, the law dealing with the sale of goods is embodied in Article Two of the UCC. It is still necessary, of course, for the courts to decide cases to elaborate the meaning of the UCC, but the code itself is the primary source of law. Judges and attorneys turn first to the UCC to resolve legal disputes dealing with contracts for the sale of goods.

Section 2-105(1) of the UCC defines goods as all things that are movable at the time of identification to the contract for sale.

For example, Patrick O'Connor goes to Salina Marine and purchases an eighteen-foot bass boat. The boat is tangible and movable. The provisions of Article Two of the UCC govern its sale. Suppose that Patrick purchases a home located in a subdivision later in the day. A contract for the sale of a house is *not* a contract for the sale of goods because the house is permanently attached to the ground—it is *not* movable. That evening, Patrick hires a painter to paint his new home. The common law of contracts governs this agreement as well, because the employment contract does not deal primarily with the sale of goods but rather is a sale of services.

OTHER SOURCES OF CONTRACT LAW

While most of the law of contracts comes either from the common law or from Article Two of the UCC, state and federal statutes add additional rules to those found in these two sources. For example, special statutes apply to transactions involving consumers. In Chapter 15, Consumer and Environmental Law, some of these rules are addressed.

The principles of the law of contracts as we know them today developed to a great extent in the nineteenth century, and the rules are a product of the economic, social, and political thought of that era. In examining the basic requirements of a contract, bear in mind the forces that produced these rules. The law of contracts is still evolving. The next section describes the forces at work in society today that are contributing to a change in the attitude of the courts and legislatures as to the nature and enforceability of contracts.

Historical Look at Contract Law Development

ENFORCEMENT OF PROMISES

If the courts failed to enforce contractual promises, the system of business would collapse. Buyers and sellers count on the delivery of goods and services from the other parties to a contract. Because the courts enforce contractual promises, businesses are assured of the delivery of goods and services.

Yet this was not always the case in contract law. In the early development of the law of contracts in England, the courts recognized liability only for a faulty performance of a promise and declined to penalize a failure or refusal to perform a promise. By the sixteenth century, the courts had begun to enforce promises made by parties to a contract.

Later, such British writers as Adam Smith (1723–1790) and John Stuart Mill (1806–1873) pleaded for the courts to enforce contractual promises. They believed that once a buyer and seller signed a contract, each person needed to be able to count on the other person's promise to deliver or accept these goods and services in the future.

John Stuart Mill, a major writer of the nineteenth century, advocated the freedom of the individual to guide his own destiny unimpeded by government. Only through individual freedom, he believed, could the greatest human development occur. Mill believed in the school of *laissez-faire* economics. To Mill and his followers, laissez-faire economics permitted the full development of the individual and permitted production and trade to follow their natural courses unimpeded by government. Followers of this theory believed that the government should interfere with free trade only to the minimum extent necessary to preserve order.

Advocates of laissez-faire economic theory, who believed that a contract represented the free choice of individuals, influenced the nature of contract law. This stress on individualism and free choice was manifested in the widespread belief that freedom to contract was essential to the development of the economic system. They encouraged government, by and large, to let the economy operate free of government intrusion.

FREEDOM OF CONTRACT

■ Complete Freedom?

The courts never have recognized *complete* freedom of contract. For example, no court has ever been willing to enforce a contract that contemplates the commission of a crime. Today, such contracts are called *illegal agreements.*

Suppose that Sludge, Inc., entered into a contract with Acme Transportation Company. The contract required Acme to accept delivery of certain radioactive materials and to dump them in the river from which the city draws its water supply. If Acme changed its mind after signing the contract, could Sludge get a court order requiring Acme to live up to the promises it made? No. If a court were to enforce such a contract, it would encourage other people or companies to violate the law.

■ *Contract Law in the United States*

Laissez-faire economic thinking, with its great emphasis on the freedom of individuals to contract, greatly influenced the development of the law in the United States during the nineteenth century.

For example, American courts generally followed the doctrine of **caveat emptor**—let the buyer beware—at that time. The courts expected buyers to look out for themselves. They assumed people would exercise a high degree of caution before entering into any transaction. If a person entered into a contract and then became unhappy with the bargain, the courts rarely permitted the party to escape from the contract. Even today, courts rarely permit a person to escape from a contract. In 1972, in the *Flood v. Kuhn* case discussed in Chapter 4, the United States Supreme Court refused to uphold a challenge to the contract signed by Curtis Flood, a baseball player. Flood signed the contract at age eighteen without the assistance of an attorney. The contract, in effect, bound him to its terms for his life as a baseball player.

Although courts rarely permit a person to escape from a contract today, the law changed significantly as the nineteenth century unfolded. American society changed radically after the Civil War, and many large industrial enterprises flourished. Some of the industrialists became enormously wealthy. Protest movements took root in response to this concentration of economic power. Doubt began to arise among people in the United States about the wisdom of freedom of contract.

Legislators pushed through legislation dealing with needed reforms in the workplace, but judges were reluctant to change with the times. In the late nineteenth century, Congress and the state legislatures tried to adopt restrictions on the concept of freedom of contract, but the courts routinely struck down such statutes on a variety of grounds—one of which being the right to freely contract. The following example illustrates this view.

Lochner, a bakery owner, was convicted of violating a New York state statute that prohibited making employees work more than sixty hours in a week or more than ten hours per day. The bakery owner challenged the right of the state of New York to prevent him from asking his employees to work more hours than the statute permitted.

The United States Supreme Court looked at the Fourteenth Amendment to the United States Constitution. This amendment prohibits the government from depriving anyone of life, liberty, or property without due process of law. The Court recognized the right to sell labor as a protected liberty. It ruled that no reasonable ground existed for interfering with the liberty of a person or with the right of free contract. Therefore, it struck down the New York statute because it deprived the employees and Lochner of their right to freely contract.[1]

THE TWENTIETH CENTURY

■ Inequality of Bargaining Power

What the courts were overlooking was the *inequality of bargaining power* between the parties. They wrote about freedom of contract between two knowledgeable, intelligent, and equally positioned people. But large companies, perhaps the only employment in town, frequently drafted one-sided contracts that required people to work long hours in unsafe working conditions for unreasonably low wages. Workers accepted the terms offered by the industrialists, but the resulting contracts were hardly freely and voluntarily negotiated agreements.

The courts gradually began to recognize the gross inequality of bargaining power that is present in many bargaining situations, particularly in contracts between consumers and businesses. The more powerful party, often the seller, presents the other party with a choice: Either sign the printed contract presented or go elsewhere. The agent of the seller negotiating the deal often lacks the power to alter the terms of the printed form. The seller deprives the buyer of the opportunity to read the contract. In some cases, the buyer needs additional background to understand the terms of the contract. Even if he or she does have the time and understanding, the buyer lacks the bargaining power to force the other party to alter the terms of a written contract. As a practical matter, the buyer cannot go elsewhere because other businesses use the same terms. Gradually, as the belief in unrestrained individualism and liberty declined, the legislatures, Congress, and the courts began to erode the doctrine of freedom of contract.

By the beginning of the twentieth century, the courts had become more receptive to social legislation. The courts started to sustain social legislation that restricted the number of hours women and children could work. They upheld minimum wage laws and many other restrictions on the ability of an employer to dictate the terms of employment.

With the election of Franklin D. Roosevelt as president and his implementation of the New Deal, Congress made further inroads on the right to freely contract. Congress passed legislation regulating many facets of the economy. Eventually the United States Supreme Court upheld most of this legislation.

Non-Legal Considerations

Before we launch into a technical discussion of the law of contracts, let us look at one non-legal consideration that influences the parties' behavior during the bargaining process. This non-legal consideration often shapes the relationship between the parties far more than simple legal rules.

NEGOTIATION

In order to get a good deal and not get taken, think about the entire process of bargaining.

■ One-Time Transactions as Opposed to Continuing Relationships

It makes a difference how a person approaches a bargaining session and whether or not he or she contemplates further dealings with the other party to the contract. Suppose that Christina, an executive at the Acme Corporation, wants to dispose of some of Acme's older personal computers. She advertises them for sale. Shawn, a person Christina does not know, contacts her to obtain more information about the computers. If she never intends to deal with Shawn in the future, then Christina may decide to take a more competitive approach to the negotiations.

On the other hand, suppose that Christina intends to hire Shawn's company to handle the payroll for the Acme Corporation. In this situation, Christina contemplates a continuing business relationship with Shawn. Creating a cooperative bargaining atmosphere may be in her best interest as she must deal with Shawn in the future. If Shawn thinks Christina took advantage of him in negotiating the contract or cheated him, he may try to *even the score* in some manner when he performs his obligations under the contract. For example, Shawn may choose to be less helpful than he otherwise would have been when Christina calls to obtain information.

The International Perspective, "Japanese Negotiations," discusses the issue of the importance of a relationship in contracting.

People in business spend a large amount of time negotiating deals. As the examination of contract law is discussed, we will return from time to time to the issue of how best to negotiate a contract. The rules that must be observed in order to create a valid contract is the topic of the next discussion.

Contract Requirements—The Essential Elements

IN GENERAL

In considering the following material, bear in mind that the law of contracts varies from state to state to some degree, particularly in the area of consumer contracts. The following remarks are generalizations about the state of the law across the United States.

1. Offer—a manifestation by the person making the statement of a desire to enter into a contract

2. Acceptance—a manifestation of assent to the terms of an offer in the manner required or authorized by the offer

3. Consideration—something of value given in exchange for something received from the other party

4. Capacity—the ability to enter into a legally binding agreement

5. Legality—the contract must have a lawful purpose or object to be valid

As suggested at the beginning of this chapter, a contract essentially is an agreement the court will recognize and enforce. Figure 8.2 outlines the elements necessary to fulfill the legal requirements for a *valid* contract.

Each of these requirements is discussed later in this chapter. In addition, the parties must have truly assented to the agreement. Finally, certain types of contracts must be in writing to be enforceable. The last two topics are covered in Chapter 9.

The following material is a very general, simplified discussion of the basic provisions necessary to create a contract. The law of contracts is complex, but this material is presented to give you a broad overview.

PRELIMINARY NEGOTIATIONS

Prior to actually getting to the point when a negotiator makes an offer, a considerable amount of information generally must be exchanged between the parties. After all, a person needs to know exactly what the seller is offering before he or she develops an opinion about whether or not to enter into an agreement and on what terms. People in business spend a lot of time in this stage of the bargaining process—discussing exactly what a person is offering and on what terms. The more complex the transaction, the more time must be invested learning about the proposed deal.

Suppose a major corporation wishes to dispose of some, but not all, of its properties located in Los Angeles. An officer of the corporation then decides to write a letter to other corporations that the president thinks may be interested in the properties. The president's letter merely states: "We are considering selling some of our commercial properties located in Los Angeles. Please write us if you are interested in acquiring property in the Los Angeles market." A recipient of this letter could not write back and state: "I accept your offer." The recipient cannot accept because no offer has yet been made. The parties are in the preliminary negotiations stage. The negotiations between the parties may give rise to a specific offer at a later date.

No offer exists in this example because the letter was too indefinite. The recipient of the letter would not know which properties were being offered, or the terms of the offer, or the price. Until these and perhaps some other matters are specified by the seller, no offer to sell has been made. The seller in this instance has merely invited other businesses to indicate their interest in acquiring these properties.

Negotiation Note: **Ask about a Person's Needs**

When a party engages in the preliminary negotiations phase of bargaining, he or she finds out information little by little regarding both the proposed transaction and the counterpart in the deal. One useful piece of information to gain from the process is what the other party needs. This is not always obviously apparent and people, for a variety of reasons, may be reluctant to state their true desires.

For example, suppose William Bagley, a hard-driving high school dropout, built up a huge chain of pizza restaurants. Giant Corporation wants to buy out Bagley's company. While Bagley, of course, wants a *fair* price for his company, he may also want something else—such as a seat on the board of directors of Giant Corporation. Bagley may directly make this a condition of the sale. On the other hand, for reasons of personal pride, he may not want to directly bring up the seat on the board because he does not want to be embarrassed if the Giant Corporation rejects his proposal. The Giant Corporation may, for example, reject his request because of his lack of education. However, knowing Bagley's need to sit on the board of directors at Giant Corporation may be a very useful bit of information.

Negotiators try to learn about all of the aspirations of the other party through such techniques as skillful questioning. Once a negotiator knows what the other party wants, it becomes easier to construct an offer that appeals to that person. In the Giant Corporation situation, Giant Corporation may include the offer of a seat on the Giant Corporation board along with a dollar figure for Bagley's company. Since Bagley wants this position, the offer possibly will look much more attractive to him than one for more money but without a seat on the board.

The Managerial Perspective, "Negotiation Note: Ask about a Person's Needs," involves an important negotiating consideration—the *needs* of the parties.

OFFER

An **offer** is a manifestation by the person making the offer of a desire to enter into a contract. The person making the offer is called the **offeror,** and the person to whom the offer is made is referred to as the **offeree.**

Figure 8.3 summarizes the three requirements that must be met in order for a statement to constitute a valid offer. Each of the three elements of a valid offer will be discussed next.

■ *Intention to Contract*

Consider the earlier example dealing with the sale of real estate by a corporation located in Los Angeles. In that example, no intention to contract could be implied. The corporation merely wanted to learn of the interest of other parties in purchasing Los Angeles property. In order to determine if a statement or writing indicates an intent to

■ **FIGURE 8.3** Elements of a Valid
Offer

1. The statement must indicate an intention to enter into a contract.
2. The statement must be certain and definite.
3. The statement must be communicated to the person to whom the offer is made—the offeree.

contract, the conduct or words used by the offeror must suggest to the offeree that the offeror genuinely desires to enter into a contract.

A court bases its decision as to whether or not the words in question manifest an intent to contract by employing an objective test: Would a hypothetical reasonable person have thought that the offeror intended to make an offer? Courts consider such factors as the language of the statement or writing, the surrounding circumstances, and the relationship of the parties in applying this test. Offers made in anger, jest, or undue excitement may or may not constitute a serious offer on the part of the offeror. Courts try to determine the response such words would evoke in a reasonable person hearing these words under the given circumstances.

Suppose that the queen of the United Kingdom said to a British subject, "I will trade my throne for a new car." Would a reasonable person think the queen of England actually intended to trade her title for an automobile? On the other hand, consider Richard III's famous plea: "A horse! A horse! My kingdom for a horse!" With an army closing in on the king, and the prospect of imminent death growing quite near, the exchange of even an old nag for the British crown probably seemed to King Richard, under those circumstances, a fair trade.

The Thought Problem, "Was It an Offer?", deals with the question of the seller's intent to contract.

thought problem

Was It an Offer?   On December 20, 1952, Lucy went with an employee to Zehmer's restaurant in McKenney. Lucy had known Zehmer for more than fifteen years and was familiar with the Ferguson farm. Lucy asked Zehmer if he had sold the Ferguson farm. Zehmer said no, and then Lucy replied: "I bet you wouldn't take $50,000 for that place." Zehmer replied: "Yes, I would too. You wouldn't give fifty." Lucy said he would and he asked Zehmer to write up an agreement. Zehmer wrote on the back of a restaurant check: "We hereby agree to sell to W. O. Lucy the Ferguson farm complete for $50,000.00, title satisfactory to buyer." Both Mr. and Mrs. Zehmer signed their names to the check. Zehmer later claimed that the writing was a bluff or a dare to force Lucy to admit that he did not have $50,000 in cash. Zehmer claimed that the whole matter was a joke.

What do you think? Did the Zehmers' actions manifest an intent to contract such that Lucy could create a binding contract by accepting the offer? Would the following additional facts change your mind? When Zehmer arrived at the restaurant at 8:30 P.M. Lucy was fairly high. The parties then had another drink. Thereafter, the discussion in question took place.

Source: Lucy v. Zehmer, Supreme Court of Appeals of Virginia, 84 S.E.2d 516 (1954).

▨ *Certain and Definite*

To constitute an offer, the statement or writing must cover enough terms so that a contract could be enforced. At the minimum, the following terms must be included in the offer for a common law contract to be certain and definite: who the offeree is; the subject matter of the contract; the price; and the terms of payment, delivery, or performance.

Offers involving the sale of goods, which are covered under Article Two of the Uniform Commercial Code, do not need to be as precise as those governed by the common law rules. If a contract fails to mention such terms as the price of goods, the time for performance of the agreement, or the time the seller must deliver the goods, then specific provisions that the scholars included in the UCC will be used. These provisions instruct a judge about how to fill in such missing terms. These provisions enable a court to fill in missing terms for virtually any agreement for the sale of goods in order to create a contract. The Code only requires that a person offering goods for sale manifest an intent to contract to the offeree and that a certain quantity of goods is being offered for sale. Suppose that International Rakes sends the following letter to Hardware Corporation. "Dear Sirs: We will sell your company one thousand units of the International model number 105 rake for a price of $7 per rake." This is a valid offer although it says nothing about such matters as credit terms, the time for payment or delivery, and so forth. Very few offers dealing with the sale of goods fail on account of indefiniteness.

Most advertisements are not certain and definite with respect to the terms on which an item is being offered for sale. Courts generally treat the typical advertisement not as an offer but as an invitation to negotiate and make an offer.

In *Chang v. First Colonial Savings Bank*, the Changs argued that the advertisement placed by First Colonial Savings Bank created an offer when the bank placed the advertisement in the newspaper.

Chang v. First Colonial Savings Bank

Supreme Court of Virginia
410 S.E.2d 928 (1991)

First Colonial Savings Bank placed the following advertisement in a Richmond, Virginia newspaper. It stated in part:

You Win 2 Ways with First Colonial's Savings Certificates.

1. Great Gifts

2. High Interest

Saving at First Colonial is a very rewarding experience. In appreciation for your business we have Great Gifts for you to enjoy NOW—and when your investment matures you get your entire principal back PLUS GREAT INTEREST. . . . Plan B: 3½ Year Investment. Deposit $14,000 and receive two gifts—a Remington Shotgun and a GE CB Radio OR an RCA 20" Color-Trac TV—and $20,136.12 upon maturity in 3½ years. Substantial penalty for early withdrawal. Allow 4–6 weeks for delivery. Wholesale cost of gifts must be reported on IRS Form 1099. Rates shown are 8¾% for Plan B. All gifts are fully warranted by manufacturer.

DEPOSITS INSURED TO $100,000 BY FSLIC. Interest can be received by monthly check.

The Changs saw this advertisement. Relying on the advertisement, they deposited $14,000 at Colonial. They received the gifts. When they returned three and a half years later to cash in the CD, Colonial informed them of an error in the advertisement. They should have deposited $15,000 to receive $20,136.12. They were never informed of the error in the advertisement until this time. First Colonial did display in its lobby pamphlets that contained the correct figures when the Changs made their deposit. The Changs argued that under these circumstances the advertisement constituted an offer which when accepted was binding. The trial court rules for Colonial. The Supreme Court of Virginia reversed and ruled for the Changs.

Hassell, Justice

The general rule followed in most states, and which we adopt, is that newspaper advertisements are not offers, but merely invitations to bargain. However, there is a very narrow and limited exception to this rule. "Where the offer is clear, definite, and explicit, and leaves nothing open for negotiation, it constitutes an offer, acceptance of which will complete the contract."

In any event, there can be no doubt that a positive offer may be made even by an advertisement or general notice. . . . The only general test which can be submitted as a guide is an inquiry whether the facts show that some performance was promised in positive terms in return for something requested.

Applying these principles to the facts before us, we hold that the advertisement constituted an offer which was accepted when the Changs deposited their $14,000 with the Bank for a period of three and one-half years. A plain reading of the advertisement demonstrates that First Colonial's offer of the television and $20,136.12 upon maturity in three and one-half years was clear, definite, and explicit and left nothing open for negotiation.

Even though the Bank's advertisement upon which the Changs relied may have contained a mistake caused by a typographical error, under the unique facts and circumstances of this case, the error does not invalidate the offer. First Colonial did not inform the Changs of this typographical error until after it had the use of the Changs' $14,000 for three and one-half years. Additionally, applying the general rule to which there are certain exceptions not applicable here, a unilateral mistake does not void an otherwise legally binding contract.

Accordingly, we will reverse the judgment here in favor of the Changs.

Reversed and final judgment.

■ *Communicated to the Offeree*

An offer must also be communicated to the offeree. A person cannot accept an offer about which he or she has no knowledge. For example, suppose that terrorists drive Mr. Rich's limousine off the road and seize him. Mr. Rich's company, Moneybags, Inc., offers a reward of $1 million for his return—alive. Kay Marks never heard about the reward. As she was jogging down the street, she heard someone yell from a nearby house. Kay rushed over to the house, broke the door down by striking it with her foot, and subdued the terrorists. Kay's actions are not an acceptance of the Moneybags' offer because the offer was not communicated to her. Had Kay known of the offer, her actions would have created an acceptance of the offer and created a contract.

■ **FIGURE 8.4** Ways an Offer May
Be Terminated

1. By the Offeror	By revocation of the offer
2. By the Offeree	By rejecting the offer, or by making a counter-offer
3. By Operation of the Law	Offer terminates automatically after a reasonable period of time passes

■ *Termination of the Offer*

Figure 8.4 lists some of the various ways discussed in this textbook that an offer may be terminated.

■ *Termination by Offeror*

The person who makes an offer, the offeror, may terminate the offer by communicating to the offeree the withdrawal of the offer. In general, an offer may be terminated *(revoked)* at any time before the offer has been accepted. A revocation is not effective until it has been received by the offeree. Suppose that on January 1, Acme Automobiles agreed to purchase 10,000 automobile batteries from Safe Start, Inc. Acme mailed this offer to Safe Start, Inc., on January 1. On January 2, an executive at Acme faxed a revocation of the offer to Safe Start, and the fax was received by Safe Start that day. On January 3, Safe Start received the original purchase order. It is not possible for Safe Start to create a contract by accepting the original offer at this point because Acme effectively revoked its offer on January 2.

Several exceptions exist to the rule that an offer may be withdrawn any time until it has been accepted. One exception is when the parties have signed an *option contract*. If the offeree gives something of value to the offeror in order to keep the offer open for a certain period of time, then the offer may not be revoked during the time period agreed upon by the parties. Suppose that on January 1, Robert Vess, a real estate developer, gave a property owner $50,000 for an option on the property. The property owner promised to give Vess six months in which to accept her offer to sell the property, and she agreed not to sell the property to anyone else during this six-month period. In this situation, the parties entered into an option contract. The property owner may not sell the land in question to anyone other than Vess for six months.

Consider the Ethical Perspective, "Employer Offers Job," that deals with several offers of employment.

ETHICAL
PERSPECTIVE

Employer Offers Job

Hiliary Claxton received an offer of employment on November 1 from the Acme Corporation to work as an accountant for $30,000 per year. The offer stated that it must be accepted in writing by Hiliary by November 15, or Acme Corporation would revoke its offer at that time and would offer the position to another student. The job market was tight, and Hiliary hated to pass on a definite offer. However, she hated the people she met during the job interview at the Acme Corporation.

Hiliary had already gone to a second office visit with Vista Corporation—a company with wonderful, pleasant, happy workers. Vista also paid $35,000 per year for the same job. Vista Corporation is located in Hiliary's hometown, a place she really wants to return to since her fiancé currently works there. The Acme job is located a thousand miles away from her hometown. Unfortunately, Vista indicated that if it made Hiliary an offer at all, the offer would not be made until the company finished interviewing in mid-January.

What do you think? Would it be wrong for Hiliary to accept the Acme offer now, but then accept Vista's offer if it came at a later date? (Hiliary would notify Acme that she would not be working for them if she accepted the Vista offer.)

■ *Termination by Offeree*

An offer may be terminated by an express rejection by the offeree. Suppose that Sharon offers a job to Marc. Marc replies, "No thanks."

This constitutes an express rejection by the offeree. Marc's actions terminate the offer. Unless Sharon renews the offer to Marc, Marc no longer possesses the power to accept. Therefore, the next day when Marc says to Sharon, "I will take the job you offered me yesterday," no contract is created because Marc no longer has the power to accept the offer.

Suppose, instead of expressly rejecting the job, Marc stated: "I will take the job if you agree to pay me $10 per day more than you offered." Such a statement is a **counter-offer.** A counter-offer is an attempted acceptance that varies the terms of the original offer. It operates in effect as a rejection of the original offer. The person making the counter-offer is treated as having made a new offer. An acceptance generally must be in exactly the same language as the offer. The courts refer to this as a **mirror-image rule.** A counter-offer terminates the power of acceptance by the offeree. After making such a statement, Marc may no longer accept the original offer unless Sharon renews it.

The UCC, which controls contracts for the sale of goods, permits an acceptance that varies the terms of the offer under certain circumstances. This is covered in Section 2-207 of the UCC. Because it is a rather complex provision, we will not discuss it; merely note that the UCC permits acceptances that alter the terms of an offer under certain specified conditions.

In several situations, an offer terminates automatically, although the parties fail to take any action. One such situation is when the offer states it will terminate at a particular time. An offer that states that it must be accepted on January 1, automatically terminates at that time. Suppose that Skates Belting offers to sell river-dredge belting at a bargain price. The Skates Belting offer states that the offer will terminate on July 1. River, Inc., could not accept the offer on August 1 because the offer would have automatically terminated on July 1.

■ *Termination by Operation of the Law*

Offers do not always state a definite time in which they will terminate. In this case, an offer will terminate after a reasonable period of time. What constitutes a reasonable period of time depends on the circumstances. Suppose that on January 15, 1997, the Area Map Company offers to create a map for the Public Works Department for the city of Los Angeles for a cost of $30,000. The Public Works Department could not call the Area Map Company on September 1, 2005, and accept the offer to create the map. A court would rule that Area's offer terminated automatically due to the passage of time.

■ *Making the Offer*

It was previously noted that a thoughtful negotiator ought to consider the relationship between the parties and the needs of the other party in constructing his or her offer. In the Managerial Perspective, "Negotiation Note: Who Should Make the Offer?", another important negotiating concern is addressed.

managerial perspective

Negotiation Note: Who Should Make the Offer?

The prudent negotiator always tries to get his or her counterpart to make the initial offer. As a general proposition, the person who makes the initial offer occupies the weaker bargaining position. Suppose that Limited Partners, a real estate group, wants to purchase a shopping center owned by Hy Income. Hy Income will try to get Limited Partners to make the initial offer. Hy Income may say something like, "How much do you want to pay?" Hy Income hopes that Limited Partners will respond with a very large figure—a figure much higher than what Hy Income is willing to sell. For example, Hy Income may be willing to sell the shopping center for $15 million but Limited Partners may offer $18 million. If Limited Partners offers a figure that is too low, Hy Income will simply reject their offer.

Consider another situation. Suppose that Limited Partners purchases the shopping center and takes out fire insurance on it with Fire Insurance, Inc. A year later, a major fire breaks out at the shopping center causing extensive smoke, water, and fire damage. The insurance company will ask Limited Partners to file an estimate of its losses. In effect, the insurance company is asking Limited Partners to make an offer of settlement. If it looks cheap, Fire Insurance, Inc., probably will pay the claim. If the claim appears to be too high, Fire Insurance, Inc., will insist that the parties negotiate over the actual settlement figure. It works to the advantage of Fire Insurance, Inc., to make Limited Partners—the insured—file a claim, as opposed to Fire Insurance, Inc., initially proposing a settlement figure to Limited Partners.

A job interview poses a similar situation. Employers want to get employees at the lowest possible salary. An interviewer often says to the prospective employee: "How much are you currently making?" This gives the interviewer some idea of how much the job applicant wants. A person looking for work should avoid divulging such information. Instead, let the employer make the initial offer.

ACCEPTANCE

An acceptance is a manifestation of assent to the terms of an offer in the manner required or authorized by the offer. Only the offeree, the person to whom the offer has been made, has the power of acceptance.

The person making an offer may specify the manner of acceptance. He or she may indicate a desire for acceptance in a particular manner (by mail, for example), within a specified time period (by June 1, for example), and at a particular place (perhaps at his or her place of business).

Suppose that on March 30 Zenith Envelopes sends an offer to sell its number 14 envelope for a given price. The offer states that only acceptances received by Zenith Envelopes at its home office in San Francisco by May 1 will be honored. In this situation, if Acme Office Supply places an order on April 29, but Zenith receives it on May 2, no contract comes into existence as a result of the exchange of these letters.

If the offer does not place any restrictions on the acceptance, then any kind of acceptance that takes place within a reasonable period of time will create a contract. However, in any nongoods transaction, acceptances must not change the terms of the offer. If they do, the acceptance is treated as a counter-offer and will automatically terminate the offer.

Suppose that Acme Builders offers to rent ten thousand square feet in the Hillcrest Shopping Center at $15 per square foot to the Corner Pharmacy. Corner Pharmacy responds by accepting the offer to rent ten thousand square feet of space at a rate of $12 per square foot. Corner Pharmacy's acceptance will be treated as a counter-offer.

If the offer does not state that the acceptance will not be effective until it is received, the moment an acceptance is sent by an authorized means a contract is effective. Courts call this the **implied agency rule** (or the mailbox rule). In general, the same means or a faster means of communication than that by which the offer was made will be authorized. For example, if the offer was made by mail, an acceptance by mail is effective when the letter of acceptance is deposited in the mailbox—assuming the letter is properly addressed and stamped.

Consider the following situation. Morris offers by mail to sell his home to Anne. The offer is clear and definite in every respect. On June 1, Anne deposits a properly stamped and addressed letter of acceptance in the mailbox. Louise, on June 1, after Anne mails her letter of acceptance, meets with Morris personally. She offers to purchase the home, and Morris accepts because he does not know of Anne's acceptance of his offer. On June 2, Morris receives Anne's letter. In this situation, a contract between Morris and Anne came into existence on June 1—the date the letter of acceptance was deposited in the mail. Unfortunately for Morris, he also created a contract on June 1 with Louise. Thus, he has sold his home twice! Clearly, Morris cannot deliver the home to both women. Therefore, the person to whom he fails to deliver the home may sue him for breach of contract.

This example illustrates the pitfalls associated with the mailbox rule. Morris could have protected himself in this example by stating in the original offer to Anne that the acceptance would not be effective until it was received. In that scenario, when he sold the home to Louise, he could have called Anne on June 1 and withdrawn the offer—even after she had deposited her acceptance in the mailbox on June 1. This is true because, under these circumstances, her acceptance would not be effective until it was received.

If the offeree accepts by an unauthorized means, the acceptance is not effective until received. Suppose that on June 1 Acme Paints sends a telegram to a chemist in which it offers to employ the chemist. On June 3, the chemist sends Acme Paints a letter of acceptance through the mail. Acme receives the letter on June 6. Since the chemist used a slower means of communication than a telegram, his choice of communication was unauthorized. No contract would come into existence until the date in which Acme Paints received the acceptance, June 6. In this situation, Acme Paints could have revoked its offer any time prior to receiving the chemist's letter on June 6.

CONSIDERATION

■ *Bargain and Exchange*

The parties to a contract must have bargained with each other and exchanged something for something else. The courts will not enforce a mere gift promise. Suppose that an executive at Apex Drug Company learns of the charitable works with AIDS patients performed by the City Hospital. The executive, wanting to help the hospital, offers to give a hundred thousand syringes to City Hospital. Since the City Hospital has not promised to give Apex Drug Company anything in return for the hundred thousand syringes, no consideration exists to support this agreement.

In addition to a bargain and an exchange, the agreement must impose a **legal detriment** on the **promisee** (the person to whom a promise is made) or the **promisor** (the person making the promise) must receive a **legal benefit.**

A promisee may incur a legal detriment by doing something that he or she was under no prior obligation to do. For example, suppose that Paul, a free-lance journalist, agreed to write an article for a magazine. As Paul was not previously obligated to write an article for anyone, he agreed to do something that he had no prior obligation to do. Alternatively, a promisee may incur a legal detriment by refraining from doing something the person was not previously obligated to refrain from doing. Suppose that Paul agreed not to submit his article in handwritten form as opposed to typewritten. In this case, Paul has agreed to refrain from doing something that he was not previously obligated to refrain from doing.

A promisor may obtain a legal benefit by obtaining something that he or she had no prior legal right to obtain. Suppose that the magazine in the prior example agreed to pay Paul $400 for his article. The magazine, the promisor, thus will receive something that it was not otherwise entitled to receive—Paul's article. A promisor may also benefit when the promisee refrains from doing something that he or she otherwise had a legal right to do. The magazine, the promisor, by promising to pay Paul for the article only if he agreed not to submit it in handwriting, obtained a benefit because Paul must refrain from doing something he had a legal right to do—submit the article in his own handwriting.

A promisee who merely agrees to perform a preexisting duty is not doing anything that he or she was not previously obligated to do anyway. Thus, the promisee has not incurred a legal detriment. Suppose that Bill and Frances Fuller enter into a contract with a home builder. The builder agrees to build them a home according to specifications drawn up by their architect in return for $300,000. During the construction of the home, the builder threatens to stop work on the project unless the Fullers agree to pay an additional $35,000. The Fullers agree to pay $35,000 more, and the builder completes the home. If the Fullers refused to pay any more than $300,000 the builder will be unable to collect the additional $35,000. There was no legal benefit to the Fullers because they got only what they were contractually entitled to receive. Likewise, there was no legal detriment to the builder because the builder did not do anything that he was not already contractually obligated to perform. The builder should have agreed to do something other than what he was obligated to do under the contract with the Fullers in return for the extra $35,000.

In *Jennings v. Radio Station KSCS*, the court found both a legal detriment to the promisee and a legal benefit to the promisor.

Jennings v. Radio Station KSCS

Court of Appeals of Texas, Forth Worth *708 S.W.2d 60 (1986)*

Steve Jennings, a prisoner in Texas, filed suit against Radio Station KSCS. He alleged that his only contact with the outside world was through the radio. Jennings claimed that the radio station had a policy to play "at least three in a row, or we pay you $25,000. No bull, more music on KSCS." He contacted the station on several occasions after the station failed to play at least three consecutive songs, but the station refused to pay him $25,000. The station moved for a summary judgment. It argued that there can be no enforceable contract because there was no consideration flowing to the station as offeror. The trial court granted the station's motion for summary judgment denying Jennings' right of recovery. The court of appeals reversed.

Ashworth, Justice (retired, sitting by assignment)

It is elementary contract law that a valuable and sufficient consideration for a contract may consist of either a benefit to the promisor or a loss or detriment to the promisee. Thus when a promisee acts to his detriment in reliance upon a promise, there is sufficient consideration to bind the promisor to his promise. In the instant case, appellant's petition alleged that he stopped listening to KSCS when appellee refused to pay him $25,000.00. Implicit in this statement is an allegation by appellant that he listened to KSCS *because* appellee promised to pay him $25,000.00 if he could catch the radio station playing fewer than three songs in a row. Appellant thus relied to his detriment. He could have listened to *any* station, but he listened to KSCS because of the promise. Appellee also benefitted by the promise. KCSC gained new listeners, like appellant, who listened in the hope of winning $25,000.00. We hold that appellant's petition sufficiently alleges a cause of action sounding in breach of contract to necessitate a trial on the merits.

We reverse the summary judgment and remand the cause to the trial court.

■ *Adequacy of Consideration*

The items in a bargained for exchange do not need to be of equal value. Courts refer to this as the adequacy of consideration exchanged between the parties. Suppose that Hard Brick, Inc., agrees to sell twenty-five thousand bricks to a building contractor for five cents per brick—forty five cents less than its standard selling price. Hard Brick, Inc., cannot ask a court at a later date to *set aside* the contract because the consideration exchanged was not adequate. In general, the courts will not examine the adequacy of consideration exchanged.

■ *Promissory Estoppel*

Sometimes a party may enforce an agreement even when no consideration to support a contract exists. A promise is binding on a party if, at the time of making the promise:

1. he or she should have expected that the promise would induce some sort of action on the part of the person to whom the promise is made, and

2. the person to whom the promise is made does, in fact, take some sort of action in reliance on the promise, and

3. injustice may be avoided only by enforcement of the promise.

Suppose that Stacy, a wealthy graduate of the University of Kansas, promises to donate $10 million to the University of Kansas in order to build a new science building. Looking at this example from Stacy's position, she did not receive anything in exchange for her promise to donate $10 million to the University of Kansas. Since the parties did not bargain and exchange anything, no consideration to support a contract exists. On the other hand, when Stacy entered into such an agreement, she should have expected that her promise would induce the University of Kansas to take some sort of action—for example, the University enters into a contract with a builder to construct the science building. If the University, in fact, enters into such a contract with a builder, a court most likely would take the position that injustice can be avoided only by enforcement of Stacy's promise. This means that even though no valid contract exists, a court would force Stacy to keep her promise to the University.

In the Managerial Perspective, "Buyers Attempt to Purchase Store," the court recognized a contract binding on Red Owl Stores. It is a well-known illustration of the rule of promissory estoppel.

CAPACITY

The parties to a contract must have the capacity to contract. Some people are legally regarded as lacking the capacity to contract. One such group of people are the mentally incompetent. A second important group is minors. The term *minor* is defined by state law. Virtually all states consider a person a minor until he or she reaches the age of eighteen, although a few states require the person to reach twenty-one years of age before he or she has the capacity to contract.

■ *Mental Incompetency*

If a court finds a person unable to care for himself or herself, the court may declare that person to be mentally incompetent. The court then appoints someone to take care of that person's contractual affairs. Such a person lacks the capacity to contract. If a person who has been declared legally incompetent should enter into a contract, the contract would be treated as *void*—that is, the agreement would be treated as never having had any legal effect from the outset because one of the requirements of a valid contract (capacity) is missing.

Suppose that Charlie successfully operated a publishing house for years. At the age of eighty, his children finally concluded that his

Buyers Attempt to Purchase Store

Lukovitz, acting on behalf of Red Owl Stores, promised the Hoffmans that, for the sum of $18,000, they could acquire a Red Owl store. In June, Lukovitz encouraged the Hoffmans to sell their grocery store fixtures and inventory because they would be in their new store by the fall. Red Owl Stores thereafter increased the amount the Hoffmans had to pay to $24,000. In November, the Hoffmans sold their bakery building and purchased a lot in another town based on Red Owl's assurance that this was the last necessary step before the deal was finalized. Red Owl Stores then increased the amount the Hoffmans had to pay to $26,000. Thus, a number of promises were made by Lukovitz on behalf of Red Owl on which the Hoffmans relied and acted upon to their detriment.

The court looked at the facts and concluded that an injustice would result in this case if it did not recognize that a contract existed between Red Owl Stores and the Hoffmans. It ruled that Red Owl Stores must pay damages to the Hoffmans since it breached the contract that existed between the parties.

Source: Hoffman v. Red Owl Stores, *133 N.W.2d 267 (Supreme Court of Wisconsin 1965).*

advanced state of senility required them to ask a court for an order declaring him to be incompetent. His daughter was named guardian over Charlie and moved him to a nursing home a block away from his company. A week later, Charlie simply walked off the premises of the nursing home and returned to his office. No one saw him enter his old office. At that moment, a salesman from the Popular Paper Company dropped by to show Charlie a new line of paper. The salesman knew nothing about Charlie's mental state, and Charlie seemed stable at the time. He agreed to purchase $100,000 worth of paper from the salesman. This contract is void from the outset because Charlie had been found in a court of law to be mentally incompetent.

Contracts involving people who are mentally incompetent, but who have not yet been legally declared so, are treated slightly different. Such contracts are said to be *voidable*—that is, the agreement is said to be binding against the competent party but may be voided by someone representing the incompetent party. Suppose in the prior example that Charlie's children have not yet received a court order declaring Charlie to be incompetent, but he nonetheless is in the advanced state of senility. After purchasing the paper from the salesman, Charlie's daughter could get a court order voiding the sale on the grounds that Charlie was incompetent at the time of signing the contract.

■ *Minors*

Contracts entered into by minors also are treated as voidable. A minor may disaffirm (avoid) his or her contract any time up to the time that he or she reaches the age of *majority* (the age specified by the state when a person has the capacity to contract), or a reasonable time thereafter. The law protects minors and the incompetent because they clearly could be exploited by unethical people.

■ *Necessaries*

It should be noted that contracts by minors for necessaries are generally enforceable. Necessaries are things such as food, clothing, and medical services, if they are not already being provided for the minor. For example, suppose that Jack, who is fourteen years old, runs away from home because his parents *bug him*. He moves to Los Angeles and starts living on the streets. Jack purchases a $75 leather jacket on credit because he thinks it makes him look *cool*. In light of the fact that no one is providing clothing for Jack, the contract is an enforceable agreement. His minority status will not be a defense.

One method of protecting a person dealing with a minor is for that person to require a financially responsible adult, as well as the minor, to sign the contract. In the event that the minor disaffirms, the adult would be bound by the provisions of the contract. Suppose Jack decides that he needs a $12,000 motorcycle to use around Los Angeles. The motorcycle dealer asks both Jack and his friend, Pete, who is twenty-one years old, to sign the purchase agreement. While Jack may be able to disaffirm the purchase contract until he reaches the age of majority or a reasonable time thereafter, Pete cannot disaffirm the agreement. If Jack disaffirms the agreement, the motorcycle dealer may collect the contract price from Pete.

LEGALITY

A contract must have a lawful purpose or object to be valid. The general rule is that if the parties enter into an illegal bargain, the courts "leave the parties where it finds them." This means the courts will do nothing to assist either party to an illegal agreement. Some exceptions to this rule exist, but in most cases, a party that enters into an illegal bargain may not petition a court for relief.

For example, people who sell real estate must receive a license from the state to engage in this profession. If a real estate agent sells real estate in a state in which he or she is not licensed, the agent cannot collect a commission on the sale. A good illustration of this may be found in *Massie v. Dudley*, 3 S.E.2d 176 (1939). Massie, who had been a licensed real estate agent, let his license lapse. Massie arranged the sale of a farm. State law required people to have a license in order to sell real estate. Massie found a buyer for the farmer's land, but the farmer refused to pay Massie for his work. The court ruled that Massie was not entitled to compensation for his services.

Gambling contracts are a classic example of illegal contracts. Until recently, virtually every state outlawed *all* forms of gambling. For centuries, courts have refused to enforce such bargains. In 1710, Queen Anne of England signed the Statute of Anne. Parliament passed this statute, designed to invalidate notes given in payment of gambling debts, in order to protect the landed gentry in England. It made all gambling debts unenforceable. The puritanical settlers in the United States passed similar antigambling statutes which made gambling debts uncollectible. In most cases, because such contracts are illegal, the courts "leave the parties where it finds them." Interestingly, although gambling has been legal for years in Nevada, until 1983 gambling debts were not enforceable by the courts in Nevada. In 1983, the Nevada legislature finally permitted the enforcement of gambling debts.

Suppose that Tony went to the Ridge Country Club men's lounge. While there, he became involved in a high stakes poker game. Tony lost $25,000 at the club that night. Since he did not have $25,000 with him at the time, Tony told the winner, Frank, that he would pay Frank the next week. Could Frank file suit in court demanding that Tony pay him the $25,000? No. Courts "leave the parties where it finds them." Suppose Tony *had* paid the $25,000 that night to Frank. Could Tony file suit in court demanding a return of the money? No— for the same reason.

▤ *Contract of Adhesion*

Just as courts generally refuse to enforce gambling debts on the grounds of illegality, they also will refuse to enforce a contract of adhesion. A contract of adhesion is an extremely one-sided contract with provisions that favor only the drafter, which is presented on a take-it-or-leave-it basis to a party in a very weak bargaining position. The courts refuse to enforce such agreements on the basis of illegality.

Two other theories on which courts refuse to enforce contracts will now be considered: public policy and unconscionability.

▤ *Public Policy*

A court may refuse to enforce a contract that has been found to be contrary to public policy. Alternatively, a clause within a contract may be ruled contrary to public policy, and the court may elect to enforce all of the contract except the offensive clause.

WHAT COURTS MEAN BY PUBLIC POLICY   In general, conduct that conflicts with generally accepted standards of conduct in the community violates public policy. By examining the applicable statutes and judicial precedents, a judge determines what these community standards are. There is no precise rule or formula for a judge to determine what is and what is not contrary to public policy. As social, economic, moral, and ethical values change, the concept of public policy also changes.

Public policy has recently evolved into another concept. Today, the courts will refuse to enforce contracts not only if they are illegal or contrary to public policy, but also if they are unconscionable. The concept of unconscionability is an evolution of judicial thinking, building on the ideas of illegality, contracts of adhesion, and contracts that are contrary to public policy.

▤ *Unconscionability*

The doctrine of unconscionability is just as unclear as the concept of public policy. The courts recognize unconscionability as a ground for invalidating contracts under both the common law and the Uniform Commercial Code.

What courts typically mean by an unconscionable contract is a grossly unfair agreement entered into by a person with minimal bargaining power. The contract must have been unconscionable at the time it was entered into by the parties, as opposed to a contract that, at a later date, becomes unfair because of some event the parties had not anticipated.

The failure to adequately define the term *unconscionable,* or to at least set up more precise standards to guide the courts, has given judges broad authority to remake contracts. This provision conveys to judges a vast power and discretion to tamper with the provisions of a contract negotiated between private parties.

TYPICAL CASE   Generally, it would seem that the party in the best position to assert the doctrine of unconscionability as a defense is a person who was not engaged in business (for example, a consumer), who did not regularly enter into contracts, and who had a limited education, especially in business affairs. This party probably dealt with a businessperson who presented a form contract drafted by an attorney in such a manner that it unfairly favored the businessperson over the consumer. The contract probably was presented on a take-it-or-leave-it basis, and the consumer had few other places to go to obtain the goods or services. Generally, the purchaser had little time to examine the terms of the contracts. Very possibly he or she had been pressured into signing *at once* without being given the opportunity to reflect on the terms.

Consider the Thought Problem, "Valid Contract or Unconscionable Agreement?", and decide whether or not a judge ought to find it to be unconscionable.

thought problem

Valid Contract or Unconscionable Agreement?

The Reynosos and a Spanish-speaking salesman representing Frostifresh Corporation entered into a contract for the sale of a refrigerator freezer. During their conversation, Mr. Reynoso told the salesman that he had only one week left on his job, and he could not afford to purchase the appliance. The salesman distracted and deluded the Reynosos by advising them that the appliance would cost them nothing because they would be paid bonuses or commissions of $25 each on the numerous sales that would be made to their neighbors and friends. Thereafter, the Reynosos signed a contract written entirely in English. The contract was neither translated for them nor explained to them. In the contract, a cash sales price was stated and set forth as $900. To this price, a credit charge of $245.88 was added, totalling $1,145.88 to be paid for the appliance. The cost to Frostifresh for the freezer was $348.00.

What do you think? Is this an unconscionable agreement? How much of a markup do appliance dealers normally get on the appliances they sell? Would it make any difference if the contract had been written in Spanish? How much of a bonus do you think the Reynosos received?

Source: Frostifresh Corporation v. Reynoso, *274 N.Y.S.2d 757 (District Court of Nassau County, New York, Second District 1966).*

UNCONSCIONABILITY—BUSINESSPEOPLE While unconscionability enables consumers on occasion to avoid their contractual obligations, businesspeople fare poorly under this doctrine. By and large, the courts tend to reject unconscionability as a ground for escaping contracts when people in business assert it.

The reasons for declining to apply this doctrine to business contracts essentially are: (1) the parties generally are knowledgeable, sophisticated corporations; (2) the negotiations leading up to the consummation of the contract are deliberate and detailed; (3) the contracts are not presented on a take-it-or-leave-it basis but are generally negotiated transactions; and (4) usually the parties have the assistance of legal counsel or are aware they could use legal counsel. Such contracts rarely involve a person who is unaware of his or her legal rights and has very little bargaining power. The parties rarely have been oppressed or surprised by the terms.

Typically, the businessperson asserting unconscionability as a defense simply made a bad deal and is looking to the courts for relief from the consequences of his or her bad judgment. The courts, in light of the unusual negotiations and awareness of the terms of the contract, are quite unlikely to be receptive to the argument of unconscionability in the business context. The case, *Potomac Electric Power Co. v. Westinghouse Electric Corp.*, is typical of the treatment of businesspeople who assert unconscionability as grounds for not enforcing the contract.

Potomac Electric Power Co. v. Westinghouse Electric Corp.

United States District Court, District of Columbia *385 F. Supp. 572 (1974)*

After several years of contract negotiations, in the summer of 1970, a turbine-generator was placed in commercial operation in Maryland. A few months later, a malfunction developed, causing substantial damage to the turbine. As a consequence, the unit was out of service for six months.

Potomac Electric Power Co. (PEPCO) seeks compensatory and punitive damages from Westinghouse Electric Corp. arising from an alleged contract breach for the manufacture and sale of the steam turbine-generator. The complaint alleges negligence, gross negligence, misrepresentation, breach of contract to repair or replace, breach of warranties, breach of express guarantees, and unconscionability. In response to the complaint, Westinghouse relies on various defenses and contends that PEPCO is estopped from asserting any claim and has waived any right to consequential damages by virtue of the express provisions of the contract.

Parker, Judge

The rights and obligations of the parties are contained in a fully detailed and integrated written contract. Under the first subsection the defendants expressly warranted that the equipment would be of the kind and quality described in the contract and would be free of defects in workmanship or material for one year. In the event of a breach of this warranty, upon notification of the defect and substantiation of proper maintenance and operation, the defendant was only required to repair or replace the nonconforming part at its expense. The parties further agreed that there were no other warranties, express or implied, or merchantability, fitness for purpose, or other warranties. This last provision of the warranty was conspicuously underlined. The liability limitation subsection of the contract also specifically provided that the defendant would in no event be liable ". . . for special, or consequential damages, such as, but not limited to, damage or loss of other property or equipment, loss of profits or revenue, loss of use of power system, cost of capital, cost of purchased or replacement power, or claims of customers of Purchaser for service interruption. . . ."

Within the framework of this commercial transaction the Court perceives no valid legal reason why PEPCO should not be held to the clear and express provisions of the written agreement between the parties. Warranty and limitation of liability clauses such as found in the present contract, which restrict PEPCO's remedies to the repair and replacement of nonconforming parts and limit Westinghouse's liability, regardless of its negligence in causing such nonconformities, are valid and enforceable and have been consistently upheld by the courts. They are also consistent with Sections 2-316(4) and 2-719(1)(a) and (3), Uniform Commercial Code. Provisions such as those precluding PEPCO from recovering consequential damages have likewise been upheld as valid and enforceable.

Finally, plaintiff raises the issue of the unconscionability of the exculpatory clauses. The negotiated agreement between these parties was not a contract between two small unknowledgeable shop keepers but between two sophisticated corporations each with comparable bargaining power and fully aware of what they were doing. The negotiations leading to the consummation of the contract were deliberate, detailed and consumed more than two years. PEPCO's representatives were experienced and the final agreement was reviewed by their corporate legal staff. While the evidence shows that other than Westinghouse, there was only one other domestic manufacturer with the capability of marketing the turbine-generator, there is nothing to indicate that PEPCO was precluded from contracting with that manufacturer or even foreign manufacturers. Nor is there any evidence in the record showing that PEPCO was a reluctant and unwilling purchaser, overreached and forced to yield to onerous terms imposed by Westinghouse.

In short, the facts have been sufficiently developed and the Court finds that there is no genuine issue as to any material fact and concludes that the law clearly supports the defendant.

■ Covenants Not to Compete

One type of anticompetitive restraint that is sometimes justified as a *reasonable* restraint of trade is the covenant not to compete. This is an agreement restricting the right of a person to practice a trade or profession or to operate a particular kind of business, but this agreement or promise not to compete is just one part of a larger, lawful agreement. Courts often enforce these ancillary agreements even though they do restrain trade.

Enforceable covenants not to compete are common in employment contracts and contracts involving the sale and purchase of a business. In these and similar contexts the covenant not to compete may serve a very useful function.

In order for a covenant not to compete to be enforceable, the restriction must be necessary to protect the legitimate interests of one of the parties to the contract and the restriction must not be excessive given this legitimate need. Courts often focus on whether or not the agreement is reasonable in scope. Specifically, they focus on the dimensions of the restriction in terms of time and territory.

There are many cases holding that restrictions for a year or two are reasonable. In some employment cases, however, courts have refused to enforce restrictions for shorter durations, expressing concern for

managerial perspective

Covenant Not to Compete

H & R Block, Inc., is a corporation that franchises individuals and other concerns to operate a business solely for the preparation of income tax returns under the name of H & R Block.

Earl Lovelace, of Yates Center, Kansas, entered into such a franchise agreement with H & R Block. As part of that agreement, he agreed to not enter into competition with H & R Block for five years should he cease operating an H & R Block franchise. Several years after entering into the agreement, Lovelace terminated the agreement and opened a tax preparation business under his own name at the same location in Yates Center where he had operated under the H & R Block name.

H & R Block felt that it should be entitled to prevent Lovelace from engaging in the tax preparation business for five years. While restrictive covenants of this nature are frequently enforceable, they must be reasonable in the area and the time restrained. The court ruled that an agreement preventing a person from competing with H & R Block anywhere for a five-year period was an unreasonable restraint on competition and was not enforceable.

Had H & R Block limited the restrictive covenant to cover only Yates Center for a period such as two years, the agreement would probably have been enforceable. However, a restrictive covenant that prevents a person from engaging in a business for an unreasonable period of time or in an unreasonable area will not be enforceable.

the employee's inability to earn a livelihood and the imbalance between the restrictive burden on the employee and the employer's need for protection. Some restrictions for periods considerably longer than two years have been upheld, especially in connection with the sale of a business.

In the Managerial Perspective, "Covenant Not to Compete," the court grapples with the question of whether or not the restrictive covenant used by H & R Block, Inc., was enforceable.

When combined with reasonable time periods, territorial restrictions that cover small areas, such as "within a one-mile radius" or "within the city of Beverly Hills, California," have nearly always been upheld; though some exceptional cases to the contrary exist. Under appropriate circumstances restrictions involving considerable territories may be enforced.

No hard-and-fast rules exist regarding what is reasonable. Reasonableness depends on the totality of circumstances in a given situation.

■ Exculpatory Clauses

An exculpatory clause is a provision in a contract that attempts to relieve a party of liability for negligence. For example, a stable may ask the owner of a horse to agree by contract not to hold the stable owner liable for any injury to the horse that arises from a natural disaster such as a fire.

The courts tend to view a contractual provision in a negative light if the provision relieves a party of liability for its negligence. For example, suppose the International Amusement Park asks visitors to its park to sign the following agreement: "It is agreed that neither International Amusement Park nor any of its employees will be liable for harm caused to park visitors due to the negligence of International Amusement Park or its employees." If someone challenges such a contractual provision, he or she probably will argue that enforcement of such a provision is contrary to public policy because such an exculpatory clause may have the effect of causing park employees to act less cautiously in their dealings with people coming into the park. Courts tend to focus on the facts of the case when determining whether or not to give effect to such a provision.

The *Huber v. Hovey* case deals with the question of whether or not a person who signed a document releasing a racetrack of liability may recover damages from the racetrack for his injuries. The trial court in this case ruled on behalf of the defendants. The Supreme Court of Iowa affirmed.

Huber v. Hovey   Supreme Court of Iowa *501 N.W.2d 53 (1993)*

Dale Huber entered the pit area at the Winneshiek County Fairground racetrack. While standing in the pit, a race car's wheel struck and injured him. Both the trial court and the Supreme Court of Iowa ruled for the defendants.

Neuman, J.

On September 2, 1989, Dale went to the racetrack to watch a friend race. He had been to races before, though not at this track. Dale saw that spectators were going to the grandstand, instead of the pit area, but he followed his friend to the pit area anyway. He paid the $10 admission fee and was told to add his signature to a printed form. The form, captioned "Release and Waiver of Liability and Indemnity Agreement," provided:

> IN CONSIDERATION of being permitted to enter for any purpose any RESTRICTED AREA . . . including . . . pit areas . . . EACH OF THE UNDERSIGNED . . . 1. HEREBY RELEASES, WAIVES, DISCHARGES AND COVENANTS NOT TO SUE the promoter, participants . . . track operator, track owner, officials, car owners, drivers, pit crews, any persons in any restricted area . . . owners and lessees of premises used to conduct the event . . . for the purposes herein referred to as "releasees", from all liability to the undersigned, his personal representatives, assigns, heirs, and next of kin for any and all loss or damage, and any claim or demands therefor on account of injury . . . whether caused by the negligence of the releasees or otherwise while the undersigned is in or upon the restricted area. . . .
>
> EACH OF THE UNDERSIGNED expressly acknowledges and agrees that the activities of the event are very dangerous and involve the risk of serious injury. . . .
>
> THE UNDERSIGNED HAS READ AND VOLUNTARILY SIGNS THE RELEASE AND WAIVER OF LIABILITY. . . .

The words "I have read this release" were printed in red above each signature line.

Feeling pressured to keep the line behind him moving, Dale signed the form without reading it and entered the pit area. He was standing about ten feet behind a protective "wheel fence," watching the race, when one of the cars lost a wheel and axle. The wheel tore through the fence, striking and injuring him. Dale sued for damages.

Huber claimed several parties were negligent: Dennis Hovey, the car's driver; Nordic Speedway, Inc. (Nordic), the lessee of the track; and the Winneshiek County Fairground Board and the Winneshiek County Agricultural Association, owner and operator of the racetrack property. The defendants jointly moved for summary judgment based on Dale's release.

Dale asserts that racetracks have a nondelegable duty to ensure their patrons' safety, and that any attempt to insulate themselves from liability violates public policy. We find no merit in this argument. Although track owners and operators have a duty to provide safe premises we have repeatedly held that contracts exempting a party from its own negligence are enforceable, and are not contrary to public policy.

Dale also seeks to avoid the effect of the release on the ground he did not read it. It is well settled that failure to read a contract before signing it will not invalidate the contract. Absent fraud or mistake, ignorance of a written contract's contents will not negate its effect.

Dale next asserts the release is unenforceable against spectators as a matter of law. He argues releases are only valid when signed by a party knowledgeable and informed about the risks. While conceding that participants are presumed knowledgeable, and do not have a reasonable expectation of safety, he argues that spectators are unaware of the risks of pit areas, and cannot sign away their reasonable expectations without being informed of such risks.

We disagree. We believe there is no valid legal distinction between a release signed by a spectator permitted entry into a restricted area, and a release signed by a participant. Courts throughout the country have upheld such releases.

We therefore hold the district court was correct in refusing to recognize a distinction between spectator releases and participant releases, and in granting summary judgment to Hovey, Nordic, and the fairground board and agricultural association on Dale's claims.

Summary

The law of contracts has evolved over hundreds of years into the court-enforced laws of today. Over a period of centuries, the courts gradually accepted the notion that they should enforce a contract freely entered into by the parties. Nineteenth-century philosophers, many of whom espoused the doctrine of freedom of contract, argued that the free enterprise system depended on the willingness of the courts to enforce every contract. The courts, persuaded by this thinking, developed the doctrine of caveat emptor—let the buyer beware. For many years few people succeeded in escaping their contractual obligations.

More recently, the courts have moved away from this doctrine because of the harsh consequences associated with enforcing certain contracts. The courts have come to recognize that many contracts are not the product of the free will of individuals, as John Stuart Mill believed, but rather are the product of an inequality of bargaining power between the parties. This inequality of bargaining power often gives the stronger party the opportunity to insert unfair clauses into a contract. Today, the courts are inclined to set aside unfair contracts.

Before any contract comes into existence, certain requirements must have been fulfilled. The person seeking the transaction must manifest a desire to enter into a contract, referred to as an offer. The person to whom this offer is made must manifest an assent to the terms of the offer in a manner required or authorized by the offer, referred to as an acceptance. The entire transaction must be supported by consideration—that is, the contract must have been the product of a bargain and exchange between the parties to the contract. Finally, no contract will be enforced if the parties to the contract lack the capacity to contract or if the bargain in question is illegal.

Businesspeople spend a lot of time negotiating contracts. They need to recognize certain facts about the negotiation process. A person who wants to maintain a good relationship with his or her counterpart needs to think about the consequences of his or her negotiating techniques on the long-term relationship between the parties. In negotiating a contract, a person should bear in mind the needs of the other party, as well as his or her own desires. Finally, it frequently is in a person's best interest to let his or her counterpart make the opening (initial) offer.

Review Questions

1. Define the following terms:
   a. Caveat emptor
   b. Contract
   c. Contract of adhesion
   d. Promise
   e. Promissory estoppel
   f. Public policy
   g. Unconscionability
   h. Uniform Commercial Code

2. Why did the concept of freedom of contract develop as part of contract law?

3. Why did John Stuart Mill think it was important for the courts to enforce a contractual promise?

4. Can Sheila enforce a contract if she accepts an offer that was not made to her?

5. Is the meaning of the term *unconscionability* understood by everyone?

6. Under what circumstances will a court enforce a contract even when it is *not* supported by consideration?

7. Acme Corporation decides to divest itself of one of its subsidiary corporations, a soft drink bottling company. While at the country club, the president of Acme mentions to another member, Peter West, that Acme intends to sell its bottling plant. On hearing this information, West responds "sold." Does this statement create a contract between Acme and West?

8. K-Mart places an advertisement in the *Chicago Tribune* showing an RCA color television and a price of $700. Janice Bradwell appears at the K-Mart store the next day. Can she create a contract merely by saying, "I accept your offer to sell the RCA color television for $700"?

9. On June 1, Franklin offered to sell an office building to Miller. Miller wanted more time to make up her mind. She paid $1,000 to Franklin for an option contract that expired August 1. On July 1, another buyer agreed to buy the building. Can Franklin sell the building to the new buyer?

10. Rawls offers to sell her house to Jackson for $150,000. Jackson responds, "I will take your house for $150,000 if you agree to first repaint all of the walls inside the house." Does Jackson's statement create a contract? Suppose that Rawls refuses to repaint the walls in his house, and Jackson thereafter says: "I will take your house for $150,000." Does his second statement create a contract?

11. On March 1, 1974, Padgett offers to sell her home to Blackburn. The offer does not state a definite time in which it will terminate. On March 1, 1994, Blackburn accepts the offer. Does this create a contract?

12. Wong offers to sell his hundred-acre farm to Walters. Wong sends an offer by telegram to Walters on September 1. Walters receives the telegram on September 1. On September 2, he mails Wong a letter of acceptance. Wong receives Walter's letter of acceptance on September 5. On what date is a contract formed? Would it make a difference if Walters telegraphed back an acceptance on September 2?

Suppose, instead, that on September 2, Walters mails a letter of acceptance. On September 3, Wong telegraphs a revocation to Walters, which Walters receives that day. Wong thereafter receives Walter's letter of acceptance on September 5. What would be the outcome in this situation?

13. Pareja thinks very highly of her neighbor Cohen. One day Pareja offers to give Cohen her brand new refrigerator for free. Cohen says, "Thank you. I accept." When Cohen comes to pick up the refrigerator, Pareja informs her that she no longer wants to give the refrigerator to Cohen. Is there an enforceable bargain between Pareja and Cohen?

14. Acme Corporation entered into a contract with Giant Construction. Giant Construction contractually agreed to erect a new plant for Acme Corporation at a cost of $8 million. Midway into the project, the builder threatened to stop work on the plant unless Acme agreed to pay an additional $300,000. Acme agreed to pay the extra money. Is there any consideration to support Acme's promise to pay the extra money?

15. Tina goes into the Alaskan Fur store. She selects a $25,000 mink coat. Tina signs an agreement to pay $25,000 for the coat. Tina is seventeen years old. Is this contract enforceable? Is it ethical to purchase a mink coat?

16. Quick Lubrication Corporation sells a store to Bill Drews. The store is located in Los Angeles, California. The agreement between Quick Lubrication Corporation and Drews forbids Drews, should he ever terminate his relationship with Quick Lubrication Corporation, from ever opening a competing lubrication shop anywhere in the world for the rest of his life. What is such an agreement called? Is it enforceable?

17. In 1898, Congress passed a law prohibiting employers from requiring employees, as a condition of employment, to agree not to join labor unions. Adair required his employee, Coppage, to sign such an agreement and fired him when he joined a union. In the absence of a valid contract between the parties, may Congress make it a crime for Adair to fire Coppage without just cause?

18. McConnell entered into a contract with Commonwealth Pictures. The contract obligated Commonwealth Pictures to pay McConnell for obtaining the distribution rights for certain pictures. McConnell negotiated these rights, but Commonwealth Pictures refused to pay for his services because McConnell procured the rights by bribing a representative of the company. Is this contract legal and thus enforceable?

19. Capitol sued Mary for the $406 balance due under a contract for household goods. The merchandise was valued at $595 plus $18 sales tax. The credit charge for purchase over a two-year period equaled $219. The cost of the goods to Capitol was $234. Mary claimed that the goods were grossly overpriced, that she had already paid their fair market value, and that the contract terms were unconscionable. Are the contract terms unconscionable?

20. Janell McNearney's college contacted her about making a donation to the school. Janell offered to give the school $100,000. Relying on her statement, the school entered into a contract to build a $4 million building. Janell now refused to give the school the $100,000. She contends it was a mere gift promise, unsupported by consideration. Is there any way the school can compel her to pay the $100,000?

21. Marie Bredemann worked for the Vaughan Manufacturing Company for a number of years. The president of Vaughan Manufacturing Company orally promised to pay her $375 per month for life when she retired. In reliance on his statement, she retired. Several years later, the company, which had been paying her $375 per month, stopped making payments. It argued that no consideration to support the alleged contract between Vaughan and Bredemann exists. What could Bredemann argue?

22. Hunter rented a trailer and hitch from American Rentals. While driving his car, the hitch broke, causing Hunter's car to overturn. At the time of renting the hitch and trailer, Hunter had signed a contract that absolved American Rentals from any responsibility for this type of injury. What is such a clause in a contract called? Should it be enforceable or not?

Note   [1]*Lochner v. New York*, United States Supreme Court, 198 U.S. 45 (1905).

Chapter

9

CONTRACTS—OTHER IMPORTANT CONSIDERATIONS

n Chapter 8, the origin and sources of contract law were examined. During the Industrial Revolution, the courts gave a great deal of weight to the idea of freedom of contract, but as the twentieth century progressed, the courts began to accept the idea of more and more governmental intervention in the contracting process. Chapter 8 discussed the elements that must be present in order to have a valid contract—offer, acceptance, consideration, capacity, and legality.

In this chapter, the idea of genuine assent is examined. If the parties to a contract did not freely and voluntarily assent to its terms, a court will not enforce the contract. Courts also refuse to enforce certain types of contracts if the parties failed to reduce their oral agreement to a writing. The various types of contracts that must be in writing to be enforceable will be discussed.

Although offers and acceptances must be certain and definite, ambiguous terms sometimes slip into an agreement. When this occurs, someone must interpret the *true* meaning of the contract. A judge often performs this role.

Parties perform their obligations pursuant to a contract most of the time. If one of the parties fails to abide by his or her contractual duties, a termination of the contract may result. The breaching party may be responsible to the aggrieved party for damages. In other situations, the aggrieved person may ask the court to compel the performance of the contract. Note that courts sometimes impose contractual liabilities on people who have not intentionally made a contract.

In conclusion, this chapter examines one interesting negotiating strategy—the win-win approach to negotiating a contract.

Genuine Assent

Sometimes people will agree to a contract, but the agreement will not have been freely and voluntarily arrived at by one of the parties. Figure 9.1 summarizes the situations in which a person failed to enter into an agreement out of his or her own free will. When one of these situations is present, the courts may refuse to enforce an agreement.

MISTAKE

Sometimes a person enters into a contract because of a mistake. If the mistake was material—that is, if it involved a fact that induced the party trying to avoid the contract to enter into the bargain—it may be possible to set aside the contract.

■ **FIGURE 9.1** Situations in Which Assent Has Not Been Freely and Voluntarily Given

Mistake—one or both of the parties enter into an agreement because of some mistake pertaining to a material fact

Fraud—the false representation of a material fact made willfully to deceive or recklessly that was justifiably relied upon by the injured party and which caused damage to that person

Misrepresentation—the false representation of a material fact that was justifiably relied upon by the injured party and which caused damage to that person

Undue Influence—one party's stronger will overwhelms the willpower of another party causing that party to enter into an agreement

Duress—a person, through a wrongful act or wrongful threat, coerces another party to enter into a contract

The courts examine whether only one person to the contract was in error, or whether all parties to the contract were operating under a mistaken belief. A mistake is *unilateral* if only one party held a mistaken belief; it is *bilateral* if both parties were mistaken.

If the mistake is a unilateral mistake of fact, the courts generally will enforce the contract. On the other hand, if one party knew or should have known of the unilateral mistake by the other, that party will not be able to take advantage of the mistake by enforcing the contract. For example, suppose that Acme Construction solicited bids from several companies. One bid that Acme Construction received was much lower than all of the other bids for no apparent reason. In such a case, a court would not permit Acme Construction to take advantage of the obvious mistake.

If both parties make a material mistake, the contract is voidable. Suppose that Wilson and Petry enter into a contract for the sale of a rare book. At the time they enter into the contract, neither Wilson nor Petry is aware that the book has been destroyed in a fire. Such a contract will not be enforced by a court, on the grounds of mutual mistake.

The Ethical Perspective, "A $1,188 Mistake," shows a situation where the seller of a baseball card made an eleven hundred dollar mistake.

FRAUD

If a party makes a false representation of a material fact—either intentionally or recklessly—and the other party justifiably relies on this representation, thus resulting in damage to him or her, such a representation will be regarded as fraudulent. A fact is material if the person trying to avoid the contract would not have entered into the contract had he or she known of the misrepresentation. If the other party does, in fact, rely on such a statement, and if this causes an injury, the person may bring an action to rescind (set aside) the contract. The misrepresentation must be of a present or past fact. False statements as to events in the future are not actionable.

Statements of opinion usually may not be used as the basis of a fraud or misrepresentation case. Suppose that a sales representative for Lighting Fixtures, Inc., said to a retail store owner: "Our lamps are the most attractive lamps on the market today." Based on this statement, the retailer purchased some lighting fixtures. If the store's customers found the lamps unattractive, could this statement be the basis for a fraud suit? No. The law treats the salesman's remark as a mere statement of opinion.

Contrast this situation with the following scenario. The owner of the Jewelry Shop intentionally misrepresented to her customer, Kathy

ETHICAL PERSPECTIVE

A $1,188 Mistake

Twelve-year-old Bryan Wrzesinski purchased a 1968 Nolan Ryan rookie card at Joe Irmen's Ball-Mart store in Chicago, Illinois for $12. Bryan did not know the true value of the card—more than $1,100—but he realized he was getting a good deal. Bryan owned more than fifty thousand baseball cards. When Joe Irmen asked him to return the card because his clerk misread the "1200" price tag as $12.00 in selling the card to Bryan, Bryan refused. Joe then sued Bryan in small claims court. Does the mistake by Joe's clerk entitle him to rescind the contract of sale? Before the judge ruled in the case, the parties settled the dispute. In this case, Bryan could have argued that the store made a unilateral mistake, and therefore he was not obligated to return the card. On the other hand, the store could have argued that Bryan knew of the store's mistake; thus, the contract was voidable. The law aside, one may ask whether or not it is *ethical* to snap up the baseball card knowing the store had made a pricing mistake.

Meyers, that the diamonds in a bracelet were v.v.s. grade. If Kathy bought the bracelet and the diamonds turned out to be less than v.v.s. grade, Kathy Meyers could sue the jeweler based on fraud. Why? If the person making the misrepresentation has superior knowledge, such as the statement of an expert, the person to whom it is made may rely on this statement of opinion. The court addresses this point in the *Vokes v. Arthur Murray, Inc.* case that appears later in this chapter.

In general, silence is not fraudulent, although in some instances the law does impose a duty to speak. If a person chooses to speak, he or she must tell the whole truth. Deceptive partial disclosures probably will be treated as fraudulent. For example, suppose that Phyllis Grant offers her warehouse for sale. The buyer, noting the close proximity of the warehouse to the river, asks her: "Has the warehouse ever flooded?" Phyllis replies: "Yes, last year." In fact, the warehouse flooded every year for the last ten years. Phyllis' failure to reveal the whole truth is fraudulent.

The Thought Problem, "Typing Skills No Ticket to a Job," deals with a dissatisfied student.

thought problem

Typing Skills No Ticket to a Job

In 1988, Blane was a thirty-four-year-old housewife and a part-time cook with a ninth-grade education. While watching television, she heard about Riley Business College. Blane spoke with a representative, Linda Brown, and expressed concern about her inability to type. Brown assured Blane of her ability to learn, explaining that the course was twenty-six weeks long and that thirteen weeks were devoted solely to typing instruction. Brown told Blane that the policy of Riley Business College was to require each student to pass a typing proficiency test at thirty-five words per minute before the student could receive a diploma. According to Brown, the test was designed to qualify students to compete in the job market. Blane passed the final proficiency examination with a score of forty-six words per minute and nine errors. Blane graduated from the course in May 1989. Blane applied for approximately fifteen clerical positions to no avail. She then sued Riley Business College for breach of contract, fraud, and educational malpractice.

What do you think? Blane thought she had been defrauded. Did Riley Business College explicitly misrepresent anything?

Source: Blane v. Alabama Commercial College, Inc., *585 So.2d 866 (Supreme Court of Alabama 1991).*

Fraud sometimes occurs in the sale of real estate. For example, the seller may fail to disclose information that he or she should reveal. Suppose that Ryan Barton owns a small office building with a leaky roof. He shows the building to Diane Anderson on a clear day and fails to disclose the condition of the roof to Diane prior to the sale. This type of unethical behavior naturally leaves the defrauded person feeling *taken*. In measuring the legitimacy of such conduct, Barton (the seller) may ask himself: If I were in the position of the buyer, would I want the seller to disclose this information to me? If so, how can I ethically neglect to reveal the condition of the roof to my buyer?

Regrettably, some people feel little compunction about engaging in cheating their associates. Today, disgruntled buyers frequently turn to a court when they think the seller failed to make material disclosures about the property being sold. Many real estate agents, as well as state statutes in certain states, now require sellers to disclose all known defects in the property in question. Different types of questions may appear on a seller's disclosure statement. These forms vary widely around the country. In places like California, the form may include questions about mud slides and earthquakes, whereas a form for Florida may ask about information concerning termites. When sellers make such disclosures, a much lower likelihood of a subsequent suit by a buyer exists because the buyer knows in advance about all of the defects in the property.

Strawn v. Canuso deals with the question of whether or not a developer or the developer's real estate broker had a duty to disclose the existence of a nearby closed landfill. The court of appeals found that such a duty of disclosure exists, and the Supreme Court of New Jersey affirmed the decision of the appeals court. The failure of these parties to reveal the presence of this landfill to prospective purchasers was fraudulent.

Strawn v. Canuso

Supreme Court of New Jersey *140 N.J. 43; 657 A.2d 420; 1995 N.J. LEXIS 54 (1995)*

The Canuso Management Corporation built homes in Voorhees Township, New Jersey. The Canuso company built these homes near a hazardous-waste dump site, known as the Buzby Landfill. Fox & Lazo, Inc. was the selling agent for the development. The plaintiffs, representing more than a hundred-fifty homeowners, brought suit against Canuso and Fox & Lazo, Inc., based on fraud, negligent misrepresentation, and the New Jersey Consumer Fraud Act. In this case, the court ruled that the builder-developer and the real estate broker had a duty to disclose to prospective buyers the presence of the hazardous-waste dump site.

Justice O'Hern

The Buzby Landfill consists of two tracts of property, a nineteen-acre portion owned by RCA and a contiguous thirty-seven-acre parcel now owned by Vorhees Township. Those two tracts were the site of a landfill from 1966 to 1978. Although the Buzby Landfill was not licensed to receive liquid-industrial or chemical wastes, large amounts of hazardous materials and chemicals were dumped there. The landfill was also plagued by fires.

Plaintiffs allege that the developers [and real estate brokers] knew of the Buzby Landfill before they considered the site for residential development. Plaintiffs contend that although defendants were specifically aware of the existence and hazards of the landfill, they did not disclose those facts to plaintiffs when they bought their homes. A 1980 EPA report warned: "The proposed housing development on land adjacent to the site has all the potential of developing into a future Love Canal if construction is permitted." A copy of the EPA report was in the defendants' files.

The doctrine of caveat emptor survived into the first half of the twentieth century. Generally speaking, the principle of caveat emptor dictates that in the absence of an express agreement, a seller is not liable to the buyer or others for the condition of the land existing at the time of transfer.

Whatever its origins or purposes, the rule of caveat emptor has not retained its original vitality. With time, and in differing contexts, we have on many occasions questioned the justification for the rule.

The question is whether our common-law precedent would require disclosure of off-site conditions that materially affect the value of property. By its favorable citation of California precedent, the court establishes that a seller of real estate or a broker representing the seller would be liable for nondisclosure of on-site defective conditions if those conditions were known to them and unknown and not readily observable by the buyer. Such conditions, for example, would include radon contamination and a polluted water supply.

The silence of the Fox & Lazo representatives and the Canuso Management Corporation's principals and employees created a mistaken impression on the part of the purchaser. Defendants used sales-promotion brochures, newspaper advertisements, and a fact sheet to sell the homes in the development. That material portrayed the development as located in a peaceful, bucolic setting with an abundance of fresh air and clean lake waters. Although the literature mentioned how far the property was from malls, country clubs, and train stations, neither the brochures, the newspaper advertisements, nor any sales personnel mentioned that a landfill was located within half a mile of some of the homes.

The fact that no affirmative misrepresentation of a material fact has been made does not bar relief. The suppression of truth, the withholding of the truth when it should be disclosed, is equivalent to the expression of falsehood. The question under those circumstances is whether the failure to volunteer disclosure of certain facts amounts to fraudulent concealment, or, more specifically, whether the defendant is bound in conscience and duty to recognize that the facts so concealed are significant and material and are facts in respect to which he or she cannot innocently be silent. Where the circumstances warrant the conclusion that the seller is so bound and has such a duty, equity will provide relief.

Is the nearby presence of a toxic-waste dump a condition that materially affects the value of property? Surely, Lois Gibbs would have wanted to know that the home she was buying in Niagara Falls, New York, was within one-quarter mile of the abandoned Love Canal site. See Lois M. Gibbs, Love Canal: My Story (1982) (recounting residents' political struggle concerning leaking toxic-chemical dump near their homes). In the case of on-site conditions, courts have imposed affirmative obligations on sellers to disclose information materially affecting the value of property. There is no logical reason why a certain class of sellers and brokers should not disclose off-site matters that materially affect the value of property.

The duty that we recognize is not unlimited. We do not hold that sellers and brokers have a duty to investigate or disclose transient social conditions in the community that arguably affect the value of property. In the absence of a purchaser communicating specific needs, builders and brokers should not be held to decide whether the changing nature of a neighborhood, the presence of a group home, or the existence of a school in decline are facts material to the transaction. Rather, we root in the land the duty to disclose off-site conditions that are material to the transaction. That duty is consistent with the development of our law and supported by statutory policy.

We hold that a builder-developer of residential real estate or a broker representing it is not only liable to a purchaser for affirmative and intentional misrepresentation, but is also liable for nondisclosure of off-site physical conditions known to it and unknown and not readily observable by the buyer if the existence of those conditions is of sufficient materiality to affect the habitability, use, or enjoyment of the property and, therefore, render the property substantially less desirable or valuable to the objectively reasonable buyer. Whether a matter not disclosed by such a builder or broker is of such materiality, and unknown and unobservable by the buyer, will depend on the facts of each case.

Ultimately, a jury will decide whether the presence of a landfill is a factor that materially affects the value of property; whether the presence of a landfill was known by defendants and not known or readily observable by plaintiffs; and whether the presence of a landfill has indeed affected the value of plaintiffs' property. Location is the universal benchmark of the value and desirability of property. Over time the market value of the property will reflect the presence of the landfill. Professional builders and their brokers have a level of sophistication that most home buyers lack. That sophistication enables them better to assess the marketability of properties near conditions such as a landfill, a planned superhighway, or an office complex approved for construction. With that superior knowledge, such sellers have a duty to disclose to home buyers the location of off-site physical conditions that an objectively reasonable and informed buyer would deem material to the transaction, in the sense that the conditions substantially affect the value or desirability of the property.

The judgment of the Appellate Division is affirmed.

■ *Lying*

Whenever a person enters into a contract, he or she should be alert to the fact that some people may actually plan, from the outset of their negotiations, to defraud the people with whom they are dealing. One technique of defrauding people is to lie to them.

Consider the Ethical Perspective, "Sandman Electrocutes Racehorse," that deals with insurance fraud.

MISREPRESENTATION

A misrepresentation occurs when a person, by words or acts, creates in the mind of another person an impression that is not in accordance with the true facts. Can you tell when another person is not representing things truthfully? Consider the Managerial Perspective, "Negotiation Note: Body Language," as an example.

Unlike fraud, in a case that is based on misrepresentation as a theory of recovery, it is not necessary to establish that the person making the misrepresentation did so intentionally. A person who unintentionally makes a false statement may be sued based on misrepresentation. For example, suppose that Dawn Hall states during her sales pitch to Laurie Rawlings, the owner of a mail order company, that the International envelope stuffing machine can insert 2,000 letters into envelopes every minute. Hall and International believe this statement to be true. The machine actually delivered to Rawlings is capable of stuffing only 1,500 letters into envelopes each minute. Rawlings could have the contract for the purchase of the machine set aside based on misrepresentation even though Hall believed the

Sandman Electrocutes Racehorse

Kelli Adams, a millionaire rancher, owned a stable of valuable racehorses. She kept one horse, Streetwise, insured for $1 million. Adams faced serious cash flow problems so she hired Tommy Burns, the "Sandman," to electrocute the horse. Electrocution mimics death from colic. Streetwise, an otherwise perfectly healthy horse, was insured for death by colic. Adams plans to tell the insurance company that Streetwise died from colic and thus collect the $1 million.

It is a regrettable fact, but everyone in business needs to recognize that some people lie. In fact, lying is not uncommon in business. In this respect, consider the following comment from the *Harvard Business Review*:

> Most executives from time to time are almost compelled, in the interests of their companies or themselves, to practice some form of deception when negotiating with customers, dealers, labor unions, governments, or even other departments in their companies. By conscious misstatements, concealment of pertinent facts or exaggerations—in short, by bluffing—they seek to persuade others to agree with them. I think it is fair to say that if the individual executive refuses to bluff from time to time, if he feels obligated to tell the truth—he is ignoring opportunities permitted under the rules and is at a heavy disadvantage in his business dealings.*

—Continued

managerial perspective

Negotiation Note: **Body Language**

In negotiating a deal, a person needs to pay careful attention to what one's counterpart says or fails to say. In the negotiating process, by asking pointed questions, making statements, listening to the other's responses, and watching for physical reactions, a person may acquire information about the other person's desires. Body language reveals a lot as well. Do not just look at a person's face—it is, in fact, the most controlled portion of the body. Instead, watch a person's arms, legs, and feet. All provide clues about a person's psychological state.

Consider the previous example dealing with the electrocution of Streetwise. Suppose that when the insurance investigator comes to question Kelli Adams about the sudden death of her horse from colic, Adams starts to cough, clear her throat, shift her position in the chair, and cover her mouth when she speaks. All of these actions could be signs that she is lying when she tells the investigator that the horse died of colic.

---

statement regarding the machine's capacity to be true at the time she made it to Rawlings.

Vokes v. Arthur Murray, Inc., deals with a misrepresentation by dance instructors at Arthur Murray's School of Dancing.

UNDUE INFLUENCE

Undue influence is present if a person agrees to a contract because of the stronger personality or will of the other party. Undue influence differs from duress from the standpoint that, in the case of duress, a person yields his or her assent because of fear, whereas in the case of undue influence, the person assents to the contract because he or she is unable to hold out against the dominating personality of the other party. Suppose that John lived on his parents' farm in Iowa all of his life. When his parents turned eighty, John told them that he intended to move off the farm and go work for John Deere unless his parents sold the farm to him for $50,000—far less than the true value of the farm. His parents consented to the sale, not out of their own free will, but because they feared what would happen to them without John there to run the farm. Such a contract could be set aside based on undue influence.

When a person finds himself or herself in a vulnerable position, it may be a good idea to get someone else involved to do the negotiating—a point discussed in the Managerial Perspective, "Negotiation Note: Employing a Third Party."

—Continued

While the author of the *Harvard Business Review* article is not suggesting that people commit insurance fraud, as in the example with Kelli Adams, he does suggest that something considerably less than complete candor may be expected in the business world. From there, it is a small step over the line to outright fraud as in the electrocution of Streetwise.

A person contemplating such behavior ought to ask himself or herself: "Would I lie to myself? If not, how can it be ethical to treat other people (or businesses) in a way that I would not treat myself?" The German philosopher Immanual Kant (1724–1804) held that there was an absolute moral law that could never be compromised by expediency. His *categorical imperative,* in contrast to the above quotation, maintains that it is unethical to lie.

Needless to say, Kant would undoubtedly find the practice of faking the death of a racehorse in order to collect insurance benefits, and then lying about it, highly unethical.

---

*Albert Carr, "Is Business Bluffing Ethical?" in *Harvard Business Review* (January–February 1968), page 144.

Source: Marcia Chamers, "Sua Sponte," *The National Law Journal,* December 14, 1992, page 15.

Vokes v. Arthur Murray, Inc.

District Court of Appeal of Florida
212 So.2d 906 (1968)

Audrey E. Vokes filed an action to rescind (set aside) her contracts entered into with Arthur Murray, Inc., alleging fraud and undue influence on the part of agents of this business. Vokes entered into more than $31,000 in contracts with the defendant. The trial court dismissed her complaint for failure to state a cause of action. The court of appeals disagreed, stating that Vokes had stated enough facts to merit a trial, and reversed the trial court's finding.

Pierce, Judge

Defendant Arthur Murray, Inc., a corporation, authorizes the operation throughout the nation of dancing schools under the name of "Arthur Murray School of Dancing" through local franchised operators, one of whom was defendant J. P. Davenport, whose dancing establishment was in Clearwater.

Plaintiff Mrs. Audrey E. Vokes, a widow of 51 years and without family, had a yen to be "an accomplished dancer" with the hopes of finding "new interest in life." So, on February 10, 1961, she attended a "dance party" at Davenport's "School of Dancing," where she whiled away the pleasant hours, sometimes in a private room during which her grace and poise were elaborated upon and her rosy future as "an excellent dancer" was painted for her in vivid and glowing colors. She was sold eight one-half-hour dance lessons to be utilized within one calendar month therefrom, for the sum of $14.50 cash in hand paid, obviously a baited "come-on."

Thus, she embarked upon an almost endless pursuit of the terpsichorean art during which, over a period of less than sixteen months, she was sold fourteen "dance courses" totalling in the aggregate 2,302 hours of dancing lessons for a total cash outlay of $31,090.45, all at Davenport's dance emporium. All of these fourteen courses were evidenced by execution of a written "Enrollment Agreement—Arthur Murray's School of Dancing" with the addendum in heavy black print. "No one will be informed that you are taking dancing lessons. Your relations with us are held in strict confidence," setting forth the number of "dancing lessons" and the "lessons in rhythm sessions" currently sold to her from time to time, and always of course accompanied by payment of cash of the realm.

At one point she was sold 545 additional hours of dancing to be entitled to award of the "Bronze Medal" signifying that she had reached "the Bronze Standard," a supposedly designation of dance achievement by students of Arthur Murray, Inc.

Later she was sold an additional 926 hours in order to gain the "Silver Medal," indicating she had reached "the Silver Standard," at a cost of $12,501.35.

At one point, while she still had to her credit about 900 unused hours of instructions, she was induced to purchase an additional 24 hours of lessons to participate in a trip to Miami at her own expense, where she would be "given the opportunity to dance with members of the Miami Studio."

She was induced at another point to purchase an additional 126 hours of lessons in order to be not only eligible for the Miami trip but also to become "a life member of the Arthur Murray Studio," carrying with it certain dubious emoluments, at a further cost of $1,752.30.

At another point, while she still had over 1,000 unused hours of instruction she was induced to buy 151 additional hours at a cost of $2,049.00 to be eligible for a "Student Trip to Trinidad," at her own expense as she later learned.

Also, when she still had 1,100 unused hours to her credit she was prevailed upon to purchase an additional 347 hours at a cost of $4,235.74, to qualify her to receive a "Gold Medal" for achievement, indicating she had advanced to "the Gold Standard."

On another occasion, while she still had over 1,200 unused hours, she was induced to buy an additional 175 hours of instruction at a cost of $2,472.75 to be eligible "to take a trip to Mexico."

Finally, sandwiched in between other lesser sales promotions, she was influenced to buy an additional 481 hours of instruction at a cost of $6,523.81 in order to "be classified as a Gold Bar Member, the ultimate achievement of the dancing studio."

All the foregoing sales promotions, illustrative of the entire fourteen separate contracts, were procured by defendant Davenport and Arthur Murray, Inc., by false representations to her that she was improving in her dancing ability, that she had excellent potential, that she was responding to instructions in dancing grace, and that they were developing her into a beautiful dancer, whereas in truth and in fact she did not develop in her dancing ability, she had no "dance aptitude," and in fact had difficulty in "hearing the musical beat." The complaint alleged that such representations to her "were in fact false and known by the defendant to be false and contrary to the plaintiff's true ability, the truth of plaintiff's ability being fully known to the defendants, but withheld from the plaintiff for the sole and specific intent to deceive and defraud the plaintiff and to induce her in the purchasing of additional hours of dance lessons." It was averred that the lessons were sold to her "in total disregard to the true physical, rhythm, and mental ability of the plaintiff." In other words, while she first exulted that she was entering the "spring of her life," she finally was awakened to the fact there was "spring" neither in her life nor in her feet.

The complaint prayed that the Court decree the dance contracts to be null and void and to be canceled, that an accounting be had, and judgment entered against the defendants "for that portion of the $31,090.45 not charged against specific hours of instruction given to the plaintiff." The Court held the complaint not to state a cause of action and dismissed it with prejudice. We disagree and reverse.

Defendants contend that contracts can only be rescinded for fraud or misrepresentation when the alleged misrepresentation is as to a material fact, rather than an opinion, prediction or expectation, and that the statements and representations set forth at length in the complaint were in the category of "trade puffing," within its legal orbit.

It is true that "generally a misrepresentation, to be actionable, must be one of fact rather than opinion." But this rule has significant qualifications, applicable here. It does not apply where there is a fiduciary relationship between the parties, or where there has been some artifice or trick employed by the representor, or where the parties do not in general deal at "arm's length" as we understand the phrase, or where the representee does not have equal opportunity to become apprised of the truth or falsity of the fact represented. As stated by Judge Allen of this Court: ". . . A statement of a party having . . . superior knowledge may be regarded as a statement of fact although it would be considered as opinion if the parties were dealing on equal terms."

It would be reasonably supposed here that defendants had "superior knowledge" as to whether plaintiff had "dance potential" and as to whether she was noticeably improving in the art of terpsichore. And it would be a reasonable inference from the undenied averments of the complaint that the flowery eulogiums heaped upon her by defendants as a prelude to her contracting for 1,944 additional hours of instruction in order to attain the rank of the Bronze Standard, thence to the bracket of the Silver Standard, thence to the class of the Gold Bar Standard, and finally to the crowning plateau of a Life Member of the Studio, proceeded as much or more from the urge to "ring the cash register" as from any honest or realistic appraisal of her dancing prowess or a factual representation of her progress.

Even in contractual situations where a party to a transaction owes no duty to disclose facts within his knowledge or to answer inquiries respecting such facts, the law is if he undertakes to do so he must disclose the whole truth. From the face of the complaint, it should have been reasonably apparent to defendants that her vast outlay of cash for the many hundreds of additional hours of instruction was not justified by her slow and awkward progress, which she would have been made well aware of if they had spoken the "whole truth."

In *Hirschman v. Hodges* it was said that ". . . what is plainly injurious to good faith ought to be considered as a fraud sufficient to impeach a contract," and that an agreement may be avoided ". . . because of surprise, or mistake, *want of freedom, undue influence, the suggestion of falsehood, or the suppression of truth.*" (Emphasis supplied.)

We repeat that where parties are dealing on a contractual basis at arm's length with no inequities or inherently unfair practices employed, the Courts will in general "leave the parties where they find themselves." But in the case sub judice, from the allegations of the unanswered complaint, we cannot say that enough of the accompanying ingredients as mentioned in the foregoing authorities, were not present which otherwise would have barred the equitable arm of the Court to her. In our view, from the showing made in her complaint, plaintiff is entitled to her day in Court.

DURESS

If a person by a wrongful act or threat, coerces someone else to agree to the provisions of a contract, the person is entitled to use the defense of duress. He or she assented to the contract because of an extreme fear that precludes the exercise of free will and judgment.

A classic example of duress is depicted in the movie *The Godfather*. In this movie, Don Corleone, the Godfather, is alleged to have held a gun to a bandleader's head and said to him: "Either your brains or your signature will be on this paper." Needless to say, the bandleader signed the agreement. Under such circumstances, the bandleader would not be able to exercise his free will and judgment. He would be overcome with fear of the consequences associated with *not* entering into the contract. The law would refuse to recognize the contract should the bandleader wish to contest it at a later date.

The Statute of Frauds

It is not generally necessary for a contract to be in writing to be valid. Many oral contracts are perfectly enforceable. When a person purchases candy, the purchase constitutes a sale of goods which the law treats as a contract. A contract for the sale of goods need not be evidenced by a writing if the price of the goods is less than $500.

Certain types of contracts, however, must be evidenced by a writing to be enforceable. The requirement of a writing has its origins in the British statute of frauds enacted by Parliament in 1677. The British statute was designed to prevent perjury—false testimony under oath. The British thought that certain types of contracts were likely to give rise to perjured testimony in the absence of a writing. To remedy this problem, the British Parliament required proof of certain types of contracts in writing. If the person claiming a contract could not produce a writing reflecting the agreement between the parties, the agreement would not be enforced.

Every state has passed a statute of frauds, and the terms of these statutes vary from state to state. Most of these statutes prevent the types of contracts listed in Figure 9.2 from being enforced in the absence of a written document.

For example, if Peters says to Swanson, "I will pay Harvey's debt if Harvey fails to pay you," such a statement must be evidenced by a writing to be enforceable. If Peters agrees to purchase a home from

Negotiation Note: Employing a Third Party

Sometimes it helps to employ a third party to bargain for you. If nothing else, he or she may remain emotionally detached from the situation, even a situation that is highly stressful. Attorneys spend a lot of time representing clients for just this reason.

In baseball, for example, few (if any) players negotiate their own deals because they recognize the value associated with employing a detached, knowledgeable third party to act on their behalf. The negotiator may drive a hard bargain—and may even engage in insults and name calling if the bargaining process falls to that level. The player could not do the same without jeopardizing his relationship with the team.

■ **FIGURE 9.2** Types of Contracts Which Must Be in Writing to Be Enforceable

> **Common Law Contracts**
> 1. Contracts to be liable for another person's debts
> 2. Contracts involving a sale of land or an interest in land
> 3. Contracts that cannot, by their terms, be performed within one year from the date the contract was entered into by the parties
>
> **Contracts Governed by the Uniform Commercial Code**
> All contracts for a sale of goods for a price of $500 or more must be evidenced by some writing sufficient to indicate that a contract of sale has been made

Anderson, because such a contract involves a sale of real estate, it must be in writing to be enforceable. If Peters asks his bank to extend the time during which he can pay his note to the bank by two years, a contract to extend the note for two years cannot be performed within one year therefore it must be evidenced by a writing to be enforceable.

A contract that has been fully performed by both parties to the contract is not subject to the statute of frauds. For example, suppose that John Bersford Tipton, a multimillionaire, orally agrees to sell his office building in downtown New York City to Donald Trump for $75 million. Trump pays the money and takes title and possession of the building. Neither Trump nor Tipton may get out of this contract on the basis of the statute of frauds because both parties have fully performed.

Contracts involving the sale of goods are subject to a separate statute of frauds found in Article Two of the Uniform Commercial Code. The UCC states that contracts for the sale of goods for a price of $500 or more are not enforceable unless they are evidenced by some writing sufficient to indicate a contract of sale has been made.

Suppose that Jones, a farmer, calls Decatur Elevator on the telephone to inquire about the price of wheat that day. The elevator employee indicates that they are paying $3.50 per bushel of wheat. Jones then states that he will sell his entire crop of wheat—a thousand bushels—to Decatur Elevator for that price. The employee accepts his offer. Such an agreement, because it concerns the sale of goods for a price of more than $500, must be in writing to be enforceable.

As with the common law statute of frauds, the Uniform Commercial Code statute of frauds is subject to exceptions.

TYPE OF WRITING REQUIRED

A formal writing drafted by an attorney is not required for a contract to be enforceable. Generally all that is required is a written document that covers the basic terms of the agreement and that is signed by the party against whom enforcement is sought.

THE PAROL EVIDENCE RULE

The parol evidence rule prohibits the use of any oral agreement or written statement entered into prior to or at the time the written contract was signed if the written contract was unambiguous. Such evidence will not be used as evidence at trial if it adds to, alters, or varies the terms of the written contract. This rule establishes that where parties reduce their agreement to a detailed, complete written contract, only the written contract should serve as evidence of their agreement.

The following example shows how the parol evidence rule operates in practice. Four students rent an apartment for $400 per month. One of the students moves out, and the remaining three students locate another person, Chuck, who agrees to move into the apartment. He visits with the manager of the apartment complex. Chuck asks the manager if he will be responsible for only one-fourth of the rent, or $100. The manager confirms this. No one else hears the conversation, and Chuck signs a contract that includes a clause he does not understand: "In the event the premises are rented to one or more individuals, each of the individuals shall be jointly and severally liable for the rental due under this agreement and the performance of the terms and conditions of this agreement." Soon thereafter, the other three students decide they dislike Chuck, and they vacate the apartment. The manager then informs Chuck that he must pay the entire rent of $400. The parol evidence rule creates a serious problem for Chuck. The clause in question makes him individually responsible for the entire rent of $400. The parol evidence rule prohibits the introduction at trial of what the manager told him.

The parol evidence rule focuses on promises that were made prior to the signing of the written contract or at the same time as the signing of the written contract. The parol evidence rules does not affect an agreement entered into subsequent to the signing of the written contract. Such a modification of an existing agreement, of course, may in its own right require a writing under the provisions of the statute of frauds, and may also require its own separate consideration.

■ Rationale for Rule

The underlying rationale is that if a written contract is produced to establish or memorialize an agreement, the written contract should be considered to be an embodiment of all the terms that were agreed on at the time. The practical significance of this rule is clear—if you have a written contract, make sure it includes all of the important terms.

EXPLICITLY COVERING ALL ASPECTS OF THE AGREEMENT IN WRITING

After negotiations are completed and a bargain has been struck, the time comes to present the agreement to an attorney for the formal drafting of a contract. A client typically has a general idea for an agreement—one that the client wants written out into a formal contract. At this point, the client's attorney will have various provisions to suggest that the client has not considered. More often than not, the final document drafted by the attorney will strike the client as a needlessly complex and detailed agreement filled with arcane language. Why do lawyers draft such complex documents?

One reason is that attorneys prefer to use terms in their agreements that have been judicially interpreted. The use of such terms or phrases adds certainty to the agreement. Many of these phrases are clear to attorneys but not necessarily to the general public.

U.S. lawyers also know from experience that problems arise in business transactions. They tend to believe that the best way to address this fact is to draft a document that, at the outset, spells out the relationship between the parties so they know exactly what the deal is between them. Spelling out the agreement in crystal-clear language will reduce the possibility of misunderstandings in the future. It also tends to make the agreement more complex.

The International Perspective, "Contracting in Japan," contrasts the U.S. approach to that followed in Japan.

Asians prefer flexible agreements that enable them to work out differences without damaging the relationship between the parties. However, another good reason exists for opting in favor of a somewhat vague agreement. In the course of drafting a very explicit agreement, an attorney may raise issues that the parties to the contract never thought of—issues that, in fact, may never come up during the life of the agreement. Then the question arises: Should a contract include provisions that may be totally academic?

The negotiations must then be reopened and may become bogged down in haggling over seemingly insignificant or irrelevant terms. Of course, attorneys want to reduce risk. Complex terms may seldom make a difference, but if things go wrong, these provisions may be critical. The real question in a business transaction is: How much risk are you willing to undertake? A businessperson may view the whole transaction on a *risk continuum*. If a person insists on a document that reduces his or her legal risk to zero, the other side may refuse to sign.

DUTY TO READ

In complex deals, it may take months or even years to arrive at an agreement. At this stage, the parties probably feel pretty tired and

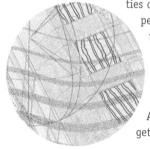

INTERNATIONAL
PERSPECTIVE

Contracting in Japan

As previously noted, U.S. attorneys like to pin every point down in an agreement. Japanese people, and other Asians, take a radically different approach towards contracting. They prefer to build a relationship with a person before entering into an agreement with him or her. Because Japanese people plan on a long-term relationship that benefits all of the parties, the precise dimensions of the agreement are less important to them than the quality of the relationship.

If problems arise in the course of performing an agreement, Americans tend to look to their contract to determine the *rights* and responsibilities of the parties. Japanese people, on the other hand, take the position that things may be worked out at the time problems arise. They do not favor the very explicit agreements that American attorneys try to get their clients to sign.

worn down. They may be tempted to skip actually reading the agreement. It is an error to sign a contract without first reading it. Why? If a person signs an agreement without first reading it, he or she runs the risk of being bound by its terms even though the signer was ignorant of the terms of the writing or of its proper interpretation.

A person contemplating signing a contract should always assume that he or she will be bound by whatever is in the writing. One should always read a contract before signing it. If anything about the agreement is unclear, give serious consideration to the idea of having an attorney review the transaction before signing the agreement.

■ *Rationale for Rule*

By enforcing a contract against someone who failed to read a document or failed to comprehend it, the courts lend certainty to the law of contracts. No one could rely on a signed document if the other party could avoid the transaction by saying he or she had not read or did not understand the writing. If the courts let a person out of a contract under these circumstances, all predictability and certainty of business contractual relationships would be destroyed. Parties to a contract would never be certain whether the contract would be enforced or not. The way to avoid the harsh results that may flow from the doctrine of the duty to read is to read contracts before signing them.

Interpretation of Contractual Provisions

Once the parties have entered into a valid contract, problems may still arise over the meaning of the contract language itself. The English language, even when the words are carefully chosen by competent attorneys representing all of the parties, is subject to varying interpretations.

WHO INTERPRETS THE WORDS IN A CONTRACT?

A contract is a privately negotiated agreement. Attorneys or judges are called upon to *interpret* a contract only when the parties choose to avail themselves of these sources of interpretation.

In most situations, the parties never utilize the services of a lawyer or a judge to interpret a contract. Even when a law firm or in-house legal staff drafts an agreement, in the final analysis the parties to the contract end up interpreting the agreement. Quite often, for various reasons, they bypass the legal staff and simply give their own interpretation to a document—perhaps a meaning the attorneys who drafted it never intended. The parties may actually guess what they think the document means, especially if they find themselves pressed for time and the words or phrases in question deal with a relatively trivial matter.

If a dispute arises over the correct interpretation of the language in a contract, whose interpretation is likely to prevail—that of the person in the more powerful bargaining position or that of the weaker party? The Managerial Perspective, "Negotiation Note: Bargaining Power," addresses this question.

Negotiation Note: Bargaining Power

Scott and Allison Schmidt lived in Fort Lee, New Jersey. When Allison's company transferred her to Denver, the Schmidts made arrangements to purchase a home in Denver and to sell their home in Fort Lee. They hired a mortgage broker in Denver to locate a lender to finance their new home. Just as the workers finished packing the moving van for the shipment of the furniture to the Schmidts' new home in Denver, the mortgage broker called the Schmidts to tell them their loan had fallen through. The Schmidts thought they had complied in every respect with the requirements of the lender and ought to be given the loan. In such a situation, are the Schmidts in a strong position to attempt forcing the lender to give them the money? Probably not. Most likely, the Schmidts will agree to any substitute loan the mortgage broker can arrange for them on such short notice—at a higher interest rate of course.*

Bargaining power, of course, also makes a difference in the actual negotiation of the original terms of the contract. A party that lacks bargaining power has to settle for whatever the other side offers.

Suppose that Mogul Records asked a band, the Blues, to sign a record contract. The Blues consulted with an attorney, who suggested various changes in the contract. Will Mogul Records modify this contract for an unknown group like the Blues? Suppose, instead, that at the height of their fame, the Beatles had asked for a similar change in their contract. Would they have gotten it?

Hollywood contracts tend to be very one-sided agreements. Consider the following passage from the book *Indecent Exposure*:

> In analyzing Hollywood's abuses, the truly sophisticated experts tend to focus not so much on the occasional instances of flagrant illegality as on the more prosaic standard terms and conditions of the average Hollywood contract—perfectly legal terms and conditions—that give the studio or the network enormous advantages over the actor, director, writer, or small production company. The powerful and arrogant few tend to take full advantage of every situation, and the lure of working in the industry is so strong that the fearful mass of prospective employees will sign just about anything to do so—often to their later regret. Hollywood is full of people who argue, *after* a film or TV series becomes a hit, that they deserve more money and are being cheated, when in fact they signed a legal contract—onerous perhaps, but legal nonetheless—that entitles them to no more than they are getting.**

A good example of this scenario pertains to the author of the book that served as the basis for the tremendously successful movie, *Forest Gump*. *Forest Gump* grossed more than $657 million world-wide. Winston Groom, who wrote the book, entered into a contract with Paramount Pictures to receive a flat fee plus an additional fee based on the *net profits* of the film. As of the end of 1994, six months after the film's release, Paramount reported *Forest Gump* had lost $62 million. Obviously, Winston Groom would not get anything more in this situation. On the other hand, the star of the film, Tom Hanks, received between $30–$40 million because he received a percentage of Paramount's *gross receipts*. Why did Tom Hanks get a percentage of the gross profits, while Winston Groom received a percentage of the net profits? Presumably, Tom Hanks had more bargaining power.***

*Earl Gottschalk, Jr., "Picking the Wrong Mortgage Broker Can Become a Homeowner's Nightmare," *The Wall Street Journal,* March 26, 1992, page C1.

**David McClintock, *Indecent Exposure* (New York: William Morrow & Co., 1982), p. 514.

***John Lippman, "Author of 'Gump', Paramount in Talks Over 'Net Profit'," *The Wall Street Journal,* May 26, 1995, page C12.

Powerful people often get what they want. A party may protect himself or herself from unfair behavior by one's counterpart during the course of performance of an agreement by insisting that a contract use precise language. The greater the need for interpretation, the more discretion an attorney places in the hands of the interpreter. Suppose that an employer promised his employee a *fair share* of the profits. Such a clause simply gives too much discretion to the employer. The more explicit the agreement, the less room that exists for an incorrect or unfair reading of the document—assuming the parties, in fact, read the contract and know its contents. Suppose instead that the employer agreed to pay his employees "five percent of the gross profits of the business" such a provision would have left little room for the employer to attempt to shortchange his employee.

When parties disagree about the meaning of contract language, they may be forced to turn to a court for interpretation of the agreement, as is illustrated by *Burroughs v. Metro-Goldwyn-Mayer, Inc.*

Burroughs v. Metro-Goldwyn-Mayer, Inc.

United States District Court, Southern District New York
519 F.Supp. 388 (1981)

Edgar Rice Burroughs wrote the book *Tarzan of the Apes* in 1912. He later transferred his interest in this book to Edgar Rice Burroughs, Inc. In 1931, MGM acquired the right to use the Tarzan character and other characters appearing in Burroughs's works in an original story to be created by MGM as a screenplay for a motion picture. MGM also acquired the right to produce remakes of the first film. Any remake had to be based substantially on the first MGM film, without material changes or material departures from the original MGM story line. MGM released the first film in 1932. It issued a remake of the film in 1959. By 1980, MGM had begun work on yet another Tarzan film. The heirs of Burroughs brought suit to enjoin release of the new MGM film. They contended this new film, starring Bo Derek, was a material departure from the original film. After viewing all three films in question, the court concluded that MGM had not breached the contract.

Werker, District Judge

The 1931 agreement provides as follows:

> . . . Metro agrees . . . that all "remakes" of the first photoplay produced by it hereunder, as well as all other photoplays produced by it hereunder subsequent to the making of said first photoplay, shall be based substantially upon the same story as that used by Metro in connection with said first photoplay and that in such subsequent remakes and/or additional photoplays there will be no material changes or material departures from the story used in connection with said first photoplay . . .

After viewing the films in question, I must conclude for the reasons that follow that MGM's 1981 remake of the film "Tarzan, The Ape Man" is based substantially on the 1931 photoplay and that there are no material changes or material departures from the story used in that photoplay. My analysis will focus on the storyline as well as the portrayal of the characters and their relationships.

The 1931 photoplay is based on the story of an explorer James Parker, whose daughter Jane joins him in Africa. The movie opens with Jane's arrival and her father's decision shortly thereafter to set off on a safari in search of the fabled "elephants' graveyard" for ivory. In this film, Parker is portrayed as a strong man and Jane as his admiring daughter. There is a suggestion of sexuality in their relationship. The expedition consists of Parker, Jane, Parker's partner Harry Holt, and several natives. On the journey, the party is faced with nearly insurmountable struggles with nature. For example, Jane almost falls off a cliff in the scene of the party crossing the escarpment and Holt is nearly devoured by crocodiles as the party crosses a river on rafts. It is the scene where the party crosses the escarpment that Tarzan's cry is heard for the first time.

After the party crosses the river, Jane is terrorized by an attacking animal and Tarzan appears from the jungle to rescue her. He carries her off and at this point, Jane discovers that Tarzan is human. She gradually begins to trust him and they appear to fall in love. After a brief stay with Tarzan in which Jane seems quite content, she is found by her father and Holt. They are exceedingly distrustful of the ape-man. She rejoins the safari and the group sets out again for the elephants' graveyard. While enroute, the party falls prey to a tribe of pygmies and they are threatened with death when they are thrown into a pit with a huge gorilla. Tarzan, of course, comes to their rescue. Holt, Parker, Jane and Tarzan then follow a wounded elephant to the elephant's graveyard, where Parker dies. Jane decides to stay with Tarzan and Holt returns to civilization.

In the 1981 film, the story similarly opens with Jane's arrival at her father's camp in Africa. This time, however, Parker is a professional adventurer rather than an explorer. He is a strong man and a bit more eccentric than in the first film. Jane, though admiring, is more hostile toward her father. There again is an element of sexuality in their relationship. As in the 1931 photoplay, shortly after Jane's arrival, Parker, Holt, Jane and some natives set out on an expedition to find the elephants' graveyard. While on the journey, the group hears Tarzan's cry and in contrast to the 1931 film, this time Parker speculates that his is the famed 100 foot ape-man. Jane again is imperilled by wild animals enroute and rescued by Tarzan. Holt and Parker are highly distrustful of Tarzan as they were in the original film, but Jane again perceives that he is human. Although his initial encounter with Jane is brief, Tarzan clearly is fascinated by her. He later captures her while she is swimming in a river. She gets away from him, but is then attacked by a snake. As in the original photoplay, Tarzan comes to her rescue. It is at this point that Jane becomes enamored of Tarzan. After what seems to be a couple of days, Parker finally finds his daughter and she rejoins the safari. The group is soon attacked by an African tribe, however, and Tarzan comes to their rescue. Parker nevertheless dies at the hands of the ivory king and Jane and Tarzan leave Holt to live together in the wild.

While there are some differences between the films in the jeopardies and dramatic sequences employed, as well as in the emphasis accorded different elements of the story, they are insufficient to warrant the conclusion that this Tarzan movie is not based substantially upon the 1931 story. The use of the phrase "based substantially" contemplates some deviation from the original story. In addition, the fact that the contract prohibits only material departures and material changes demonstrates that changes and departures were in fact contemplated by the parties.

Plaintiffs argue that the changes and departures in the 1981 photoplay are material. Their principal contention is that the film is no longer suitable for young children. Considering the shift in social mores over the half century from 1931 to 1981, I simply cannot agree that a change of the nature complained of constitutes a material change from the 1931 photoplay. Indeed, the 1931 film itself contained scenes which for its time were rather suggestive.

Since the overall theme of the 1981 film, development of the plot, order of sequence and locus of the 1981 photoplay as edited conform to the 1931 photoplay, I can only conclude that the storyline in the 1981 film is based substantially on the 1931 film and does not contain material departures or changes from that photoplay.

Since I have concluded that the 1981 film as edited is based substantially on the 1931 film and does not contain material changes or material departures from the 1931 film, an injunction permanently restraining release and distribution of the film will not be issued.

Burroughs v. Metro-Goldwyn-Mayer, Inc. demonstrates the fact that two people, looking at the *same* language within a contract, may arrive at differing interpretations of the meaning of the contract. Even words carefully selected by a skilled attorney may lead to differences of opinion.

The heirs of Burroughs regarded the book *Tarzan of the Apes* and the original photoplay based on that book as wholesome, family entertainment. When they saw the 1980 film starring Bo Derek, the heirs thought that the new film lacked the wholesome quality of the original photoplay. In the absence of this attribute, they alleged that MGM had breached its obligation to base the new film "substantially on the same story" as the 1932 film. MGM took the position that the contract permitted it to deviate, in minor respects, from the original story.

The inability of the parties to come to an agreement on the meaning of the terminology "based substantially on the same story" forced the parties to resort to a court for a definitive interpretation of the agreement. In interpreting the meaning of a contractual phrase, a court may attempt to inquire what the parties to the contract intended to accomplish through the use of the particular language that appears in the contract. In this case, the death of Edgar Rice Burroughs made it impossible to ask for his opinion of the contract. Quite likely, the other parties involved in the drafting of the agreement either had also died or had forgotten what they intended to accomplish.

Refer back to Chapter 4, "Judicial Reasoning and Statutory Construction." In that chapter, a number of factors that judges acknowledge in making decisions were discussed. One of those factors was "doing what is right." The judge in this case probably in effect was attempting to "do what is right." In this task, the judge needed to rely on his subjective judgment of the proper resolution of this dispute since there was little else to guide him in resolving this case. A more explicit contract may have not only assisted the judge in his role as interpreter of this contract, it may have eliminated the need to go to court in the first place as the contract may have been clear on its face as to what type of remake was permitted.

Rights of Third Parties

In most situations, only the parties to a contract have any rights in the contract. However, two situations exist in which someone who was not a party to a contract may have an interest in a contract: (1) by assignment, or (2) as a third-party beneficiary.

ASSIGNMENTS

An **assignment** is a transfer by one party to a contract of his or her rights under the contract to someone who was not a party to the original contract. The party who transfers the rights is called the **assignor**. The party to whom rights are transferred is called the **assignee**. As a general rule, a party may assign all of his or her rights under a contract.

Suppose that Lawrence Heating and Cooling sells an air-conditioning unit to Janice Brooks for $1,700. Lawrence needs money immediately in order to keep its business running, so it assigns its right to payment from Brooks to the First National Bank. First National Bank pays Lawrence $1,500 for the contract. Lawrence is the assignor of the right to receive money from Brooks. First National Bank is the assignee. The bank now has a right to receive $1,700 from Brooks.

When an assignment is made, the assignee takes whatever rights the assignor possessed. The assignee also takes the contract subject to any defenses that exist against the assignor. The assignee in effect "steps into the shoes of the assignor." In the prior example, suppose that Lawrence defrauded Brooks. When First National Bank attempts to collect from Brooks, Brooks could assert the defense of fraud against First National Bank.

While it is generally true that an assignor may assign all of his or her rights under a contract, exceptions do exist. Sometimes it is not possible to assign rights under a contract without the consent of the other party to the contract to such an assignment. For example, if a contract is highly personal in nature—one that involves a relationship of special confidence or trust—the contract cannot be assigned. Suppose that Mildred Smith hires Jack Lansky to paint her portrait. Smith may not assign her rights under this personal service contract to Hoffman.

Further, a contractual right cannot be assigned when the assignment would place an additional burden or risk on the original party obligated to perform under the contract. Suppose that a corporation in St. Louis agrees to deliver goods to a buyer in Chicago. The buyer in Chicago could not assign its rights to another business in Honolulu and expect that St. Louis seller to deliver the goods to Honolulu instead.

DELEGATION OF DUTIES

In general, if a person's duties under a contract do not involve personal skill or a relationship of trust and confidence, and the contract does not expressly prohibit the delegation of duties, a person may delegate his or her duties under a contract. Delegation of a contractual duty does not relieve the original party of responsibility for the competent performance of that duty. Suppose that Smith agrees to paint Jones's home. Smith delegates his duty under this contract to Akins. Akins does a very poor job of painting Jones's house. In this situation, Jones could recover damages from Smith.

THIRD-PARTY BENEFICIARIES

A contract may confer benefits on a person who was not a party to the original contract. The person who receives such benefits is called a **third-party beneficiary.** There are two broad categories: intended beneficiaries and incidental beneficiaries.

■ *Intentional Benefit*

A third party who benefits from a contract is an **intended beneficiary** if a major purpose of one of the contracting parties was to benefit the third party. For example, suppose that John Johnson purchases a life insurance policy from Acme Insurance. Johnson names his daughter, Christina, as the beneficiary of the life insurance policy. Even though Christina was not a party to the contract between Acme Insurance and her father, she can require the company to pay her the benefits due under the policy in the event that her father dies.

■ Incidental Benefit

Sometimes parties enter into a contract which, if the contract is performed, will also benefit a person who is not a party to the contract. The parties did not intend to discharge a debt owed to this third party, nor did they intend to confer a gift on this person. The parties did not intend to benefit this person at all. Such a person, called an *incidental beneficiary*, does not have any rights under the contract and is not permitted to sue for the nonperformance of the contract. Suppose that Acme Construction contracts to build a thousand-unit apartment complex in which it agrees to install Whirlpool appliances. Acme instead installs General Electric appliances. Although this contract would have benefitted Whirlpool, Whirlpool has no right to sue the builder for not using its products in the apartment complex.

Termination of a Contract

METHODS OF DISCHARGE

Figure 9.3 lists the various manners in which contractual obligations may be discharged.

■ Performance

The vast bulk of contracts are terminated by the parties to the contract performing their obligations under the contract. When the law requires no further performance from the parties, their obligations are said to be discharged.

■ Agreement

Sometimes a contract is discharged through an agreement of the parties to terminate the original contract. The agreement to terminate a contract by mutual consent must be supported by consideration. Suppose that Jackson Transportation entered into a contract to employ Mike Walters as a manager. Walters thereafter learns of a better employment opportunity, and Jackson locates a person who appears better qualified than Walters. In such a situation, the parties may mutually agree to terminate the original employment contract.

■ **FIGURE 9.3** Ways to Discharge Contractual Obligations

> Performance—the parties to the contract do everything that is required of them under the agreement
>
> Agreement—the parties assent to terminating the original contract
>
> Operation of Law—under certain circumstances, a rule of law may result in the discharge of parties from a contract

■ *Operation of Law*

A contract may be discharged by operation of law. Various legal rules exist that will cause contractual obligations to be discharged under certain circumstances. For example, courts will discharge the parties from a contract if a change in the law makes performance of the contract illegal. Suppose that a person enters into a contract to sell alcohol and then the state legislature outlaws such sales. The courts will discharge the parties from their contractual obligations.

CONDITIONS OF PERFORMANCE

As previously noted, at some point in time the parties to a contract no longer have any obligations under the contract. In most cases, the parties are discharged when they perform the acts specified in the contract. For example, Acme Construction agrees to dig a trench for Southwestern Bell for $25,000. The contract will be discharged after Acme Construction digs the trench and Southwestern Bell pays Acme $25,000.

The performance obligation may also be discharged by the occurrence or failure of a *condition* on which the contract is based. A condition is an expressly stated or implied event on which the performance of a contract is dependent. If the condition is not satisfied, the parties are excused from fulfilling what would otherwise have been their obligations. Thus, the parties may *condition* their performance on the occurrence or nonoccurrence of some facts or events.

For example, suppose that Richard Brownley obtained fire insurance for his office building from Fire Insurance, Inc. Two years later, a fire breaks out on the second floor causing extensive damage to the entire building. Most fire policies require the insured—in this case, Richard Brownley—to notify the insurance company within ten days that a fire has occurred. This means that if Brownley should fail to provide the requisite notice to Fire Insurance, Inc., within ten days of the fire, the insurance company does not need to pay him for his loss.

Sparacino v. Pawtucket Mut. Ins. Co. deals with a condition in an insurance policy. In this case, the court considered the question of whether or not Pawtucket Mutual Insurance Company had a duty to defend the Newspaper and Mail Deliverers' Union of New York and Vicinity in a case arising from the action of one of the union members. The district court ruled that the insurance company had no such duty.

Sparacino v. Pawtucket Mutual Insurance Company

United States Court of Appeals for the Second Circuit *50 F.3d 141; 1995 U.S. App. LEXIS 5988; (1995)*

Frank Sparacino, President of the Newspaper and Mail Deliverers' Union of New York and Vicinity, asked for a declaration that Pawtucket Mutual Insurance Company had a duty to defend and indemnify the union in a case brought against the union. The union had failed to notify Pawtucket Mutual Insurance Company in a timely fashion of a possible claim against the union as is required by the union's insurance policy with Pawtucket Mutual Insurance Company. The United States Court of Appeals for the Second Circuit ruled that the union was excused under the circumstances of this case from reporting its loss in a timely fashion to the insurance company.

Heaney, Senior Circuit Judge

The underlying personal injury action arose when union member Robert J. Boyle, who was picketing at a job site, hurled a rock through a bus window. The rock struck Gary Lee Mauney in the skull and severely injured him. Boyle later pleaded guilty to second degree assault and possession of a deadly weapon. Approximately one year after the incident, Mauney brought an action against the Union alleging negligent supervision of the picketers and ratification of Boyle's assault upon Mauney.

To obtain coverage under its insurance policy, the Union must establish that it complied with Section IV.2 of the policy. Under this section the Union has a duty to notify the insurer "as soon as practicable of an 'occurrence' or an offense which may result in a claim."

Under New York law, compliance with a notice-of-occurrence provision in an insurance policy is a condition precedent to an insurer's liability under the policy. An insured's failure to give timely notice to its insurer may be excused by proof that the insured had a reasonable belief of nonliability. The test for determining whether the notice provision has been triggered is whether the circumstances known to the insured at that time would have suggested to a reasonable person the possibility of a claim.

Did the Union have a good faith, reasonable belief that it was not covered?

The Union reported the rock-throwing incident to its insurance broker, Richard Dovner, shortly after it occurred. A couple of days later Dovner informed the Union in writing that the policy did not cover any injuries in connection with this incident.

As the court recognized in *Universal Underwriters Ins. Co. v. Patriot Ambulette, Inc.,* it is reasonable for an insured to rely on the statements of an insurance broker. The Union here relied on its broker's broad and unequivocal statement that "the general liability policy with Pawtucket Mutual only covers the Labor Union Office for bodily injury and/or property damage" and "will not pick up any coverage for the rock-throwing incident." Although the broker was apparently mistaken in his interpretation of the scope of the insurance contract, it was reasonable for the Union to rely on the statement and to believe that the policy did not cover any aspect of the rock-throwing incident. We conclude that the Union's belief in noncoverage was reasonable under the circumstances presented here.

In light of all the circumstances, we find that the Union's delay in providing notice to Pawtucket of the rock-throwing incident is excused by the Union's reasonable belief in noncoverage under the policy. Accordingly, we reverse the summary judgment in favor of Pawtucket and remand for further proceedings on the merits.

DEGREES OF PERFORMANCE

As noted earlier, most contracts are terminated by the parties to a contract performing their obligations under the contract. Sometimes, however, a party fails to live up to its contractual obligations—that is, the party breaches the contract. Courts recognize three degrees of contract performance as noted in Figure 9.4.

■ *Complete Performance*

A complete performance occurs when parties have fully and perfectly performed their contract duties. Obviously, if this occurs, the performing parties' obligations are discharged, and they are entitled to enforce their rights under the contract.

■ **FIGURE 9.4**   Degrees of Contract Performance

> Complete Performance—the parties have fully performed their contractual obligations
> Substantial Performance—the parties have fully performed their contractual obligations with minor deviations
> Material Breach—one of the parties to a contract has substantially failed to perform his or her contractual duties

■ *Substantial Performance*

Substantial performance occurs when parties essentially perform their contractual obligations, but with minor deviations. Because there are minor deviations, a breach of contract exists.

Some contract obligations are of such a nature that it is not unusual for actual performance to fall short of complete performance. Often this is the case with construction contracts that involve performance according to a detailed set of plans and specifications. No matter how conscientious the builder may be, it is understandable that the finished work may deviate from the plans and specifications in minor respects. In a contract of this kind, when a party renders substantial performance (i.e., involving a relatively minor breach), the other party's obligation ordinarily will not be discharged as a result of the breach.

Consider the following example. Rush Builders entered into a contract with Amy and Frank Jam for the construction of a $300,000 home. The contract specified that the builder would use a particular grade of Du Pont Stainmaster carpet. Because of circumstances beyond the builder's control, he was unable to purchase this brand of carpet, so he substituted a carpet of similar price and quality. Since the builder's failure to comply with the contract was minor and done in good faith, Rush Builders will be held to have substantially complied with its obligations under the contract. The buyers are not permitted to refuse to take the home because Rush breached the contract. Rush is entitled to the contract price of $300,000 minus any damages that the buyers are able to establish were caused by the breach of contract.

■ *Material Breach*

A material breach occurs when a party fails to substantially perform contract duties. When a material breach occurs, the nonbreaching party is discharged, is excused from further performance, and has a right to damages caused by the breach. Suppose in the prior example that Rush Builders promised to include a kitchen in the home. Owing to an oversight, it failed to build the kitchen. In such a case, Rush Builders could not force the Jams to accept the home. Furthermore, the Jams would be entitled to damages because Rush did not deliver the home it contractually promised to them.

The next example deals with a controversial topic—should a party ever intentionally breach a contract? When a party begins to question a deal, he or she may ask: "Should I *intentionally* breach the contract even though I freely and voluntarily entered into it in the first place?" Instances may arise in which the law imposes small penalties for breaching a contract, but great benefits may be realized by breaching it. In such a case, society in general may obtain more economic benefit if the party breached the agreement than if he or she complied with the provisions of the agreement.

It could be argued that the law ought to be structured in such a way that encourages businesses to engage in *value-maximizing behavior*—even if that includes occasionally breaching a contract. For example, suppose that Acme Steel agrees to sell a thousand tons of steel to Superior Motors. In the meantime, Zenith Motors, which needs steel desperately because of a great surge in demand for its cars, offers to pay more for this same thousand tons of steel. In such a case, if Zenith Motors offers enough for the steel, it may actually pay Acme Steel to breach the agreement with Superior Motors. The damages a court forces Acme Steel to pay for breaching the agreement with Superior Motors may be smaller than the increased income it derives from the sale to Zenith Motors. Of course, in practice, Acme Steel must take into consideration the effect of the breach on its business relationship with Superior Motors and other matters.

Looking at the typical contract from a practical standpoint, one should ask: Even if one of the parties to the contract willfully breaches the contract, will the other party file suit? If the parties contemplate a continuing contractual relationship, the aggrieved party probably will not file suit. If they do not contemplate a continuing contractual relationship and one of the parties inflicts a serious injury on the other, the aggrieved party quite likely will file suit.

Suppose that Acme Mowers supplies mowers to a major retailer. This contract represents a major portion of Acme's business. The retailer has flagrantly violated the contract in the past, and now and then it refuses, without excuse, to take mowers that Acme Mowers delivers. In light of the uncertainty caused by this arrangement, Acme Mowers may attempt to charge more for its products if it is able to do so. However, because Acme Mowers wants the business of the retailer very much, it probably will overlook even flagrant violations of the contract—assuming of course that the cost/benefit analysis works out.*

Not everyone takes contractual obligations as lightly as the cost/benefit analysis seems to suggest. The divorce settlement entered into between Robert E. Lucas, Jr., and Rita C. Lucas provides an excellent example of a person who believes a deal is a deal. Paragraph 6 of the Lucas' property settlement agreement dated January 23, 1989, stated: "Wife shall receive 50 percent of any Nobel Prize." This agreement was due to expire on October 31, 1995. In mid-October of 1995, Lucas won the Nobel Prize in economics for his theory of "rational expectations." When asked about the agreement, Lucas replied: "A deal is a deal. It was her idea. Maybe if I'd known I'd win, I would have resisted the clause."[1]

---

*For a more thorough discussion of this line of thinking, see Richard Posner, *Economic Analysis of Law*, 2nd ed. (Boston: Little Brown & Co. 1977), and other law and economics books and articles.

INTERNATIONAL
PERSPECTIVE
McDonald's Leases Building in Beijing

McDonald's built a restaurant in the Wangfujing area of Beijing in mainland China. In 1994, the government of China ordered McDonald's to vacate the site in order to make room for a new development by Hong Kong investor, Li Ka-shing. Apparently, McDonald's misunderstood what rights accompany a twenty-year lease in China. Business consultants report that the fallout from the McDonald's case is that foreign investors are asking a lot more questions about their land rights. To some foreign investors, it sounds a lot like the Chinese disregarded a binding contract and thus, they must proceed more cautiously in dealing with the Chinese government in the future.

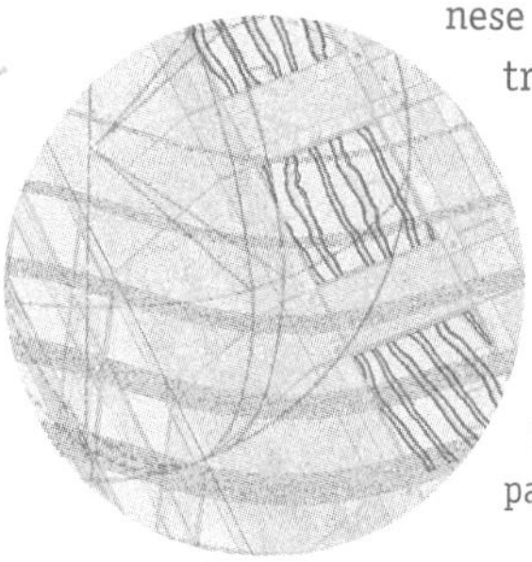

South China Morning Post, "Investors Wary over Land Rights," October 12, 1995, page 3.

Adopting a "deal is a deal" philosophy also helps bolster one's reputation. Not many businesses desire to cultivate a reputation for reneging on their contractual obligations because this simply makes people more cautious in dealing with such a business in the future. It just makes doing business all the more difficult. The International Perspective, "McDonald's Leases Building in Beijing," is an example of a binding contract not taken seriously.

IMPOSSIBILITY

Another way a contract may be terminated is if one of the parties is unable to perform the contract prior to the date set for performance. If an unforeseeable event occurs that makes it impossible for one of the parties to perform, the parties will be released from their obligations under the contract. Generally, what is required is that the promisor cannot legally or physically perform the contract, such as when one of the parties becomes seriously ill and his or her personal performance is required. For example, if Dr. Kelly is scheduled to perform an operation and has a heart attack, she would be excused from her obligation to operate.

Remedies

DAMAGES

When one of the parties to a contract fails to perform properly under the contract, this is a breach of the agreement. In such a situation, the injured party may sue for any damages he or she sustained as a result of the breach of contract.

TYPES OF DAMAGES

Figure 9.5 lists the four types of damages that a plaintiff may obtain in a breach of contract suit.

■ **FIGURE 9.5** Damages Available in Breach of Contract Suits

> Compensatory Damages—those damages that will pay for the injury directly resulting from the breach of contract
> Consequential Damages—damages that flow indirectly from the breach of contract
> Nominal Damages—a token sum awarded to the winning party
> Punitive Damages—damages awarded to punish the breaching party; these are not generally available in a breach of contract suit

■ Compensatory Damages

Certain damages compensate the injured party only for the injury suffered and caused by the breach of contract. For example, Kroeger hires Shin to work for the month of June. Shin is to perform certain services in return for the sum of $1,000. Kroeger wrongfully cancels the contract. Shin is unable to find work during June. Shin may sue Kroeger for breach of contract and collect $1,000 as compensatory damages.

■ Consequential Damages

Damages that do not flow directly from the acts of a party but arise only indirectly are said to be consequential damages. They are caused by special circumstances beyond the contract itself. The nonbreaching party may not recover for such damages unless a reasonable person could have foreseen those damages at the time of contracting.

A famous illustration of this rule is found in *Hadley v. Baxendale*, a case arising in England in 1854. The crankshaft in the Hadleys' flour mill in Gloucester broke, causing the mill to close. The Hadleys delivered the crankshaft to Baxendale, who operated a transportation company. Baxendale promised to take the crankshaft to the foundry on the following day. The delivery of the crankshaft was delayed by some neglect. The Hadleys did not receive the new shaft until several days after they could have reasonably expected to receive it. The Hadleys sued Baxendale for the profits lost during the additional days the flour mill was closed. The court refused to permit the Hadleys to recover for their lost profits because it was not reasonable to anticipate that a broken shaft would cause the mill to close. Most mills at that time kept more than one crankshaft on hand to deal with such as emergency. Thus, a loss would not have occurred under ordinary circumstances. The special circumstances—the fact that the Hadleys had only one crankshaft—were never communicated to Baxendale; therefore, the loss of profits as a consequence of a breach of contract could not have been reasonably contemplated by the parties when they entered into the contract.

■ Nominal Damages

A very small sum of money may be awarded if a plaintiff is unable to prove substantial loss. For example, a court may rule that the defendant technically violated the contract, but in light of the plaintiff's inability to establish a loss, the court awards the plaintiff $1. **Nominal damages** are a classic example of a Pyrrhic victory.

■ Punitive Damages

Sometimes damages are awarded to the plaintiff in order to punish the defendant so as to deter conduct of this nature in the future. It is extremely rare for a party to collect **punitive damages** in a breach of contract case unless fraud or some other kind of willful or tortious conduct exists.

DUTY TO MITIGATE DAMAGES

While it is true that a party that is injured by a breach of contract has a right to collect damages, the injured party has a duty to limit the losses that result from the breach. The obligation to limit the losses as much as possible is known as **mitigation of damages.** Suppose that a person rents an apartment for one year. After living in the apartment only a month, the tenant moves out. While it is true that the landlord is entitled to damages resulting from the wrongful breach of the contract by the tenant, the landlord nonetheless must try to rent the apartment. If the landlord succeeds in finding another tenant, the damages owed by the first tenant are reduced by whatever rent the landlord receives from the substitute tenant.

This does not mean that the landlord must rent to anyone who comes along simply to reduce the first tenant's losses. The landlord certainly could refuse to rent to someone with a poor credit history, for example, even if this person was willing to take over the apartment in question. Similar problems arise in the employment context. If an employee who is working under a contract is wrongfully fired, he or she has an obligation to find employment elsewhere. This does not mean, however, that the worker must take just any job. Courts generally require the employee only to take comparable work.

Equitable Remedies

The general goal of the courts when handling a breach of contract is not to punish the wrongdoing party but rather to attempt to restore the injured party to the same position that he or she would have occupied had the contract not been breached in the first place. This is generally accomplished by awarding the aggrieved party a certain sum of money.

In addition, *equitable remedies* are available when the remedy at law—that is, monetary damages—is not adequate to fully compensate the aggrieved party. Two frequently used equitable remedies are the decree of specific performance and the injunction.

Figure 9.6 lists two equitable remedies that are available in a breach of contract suit.

SPECIFIC PERFORMANCE

Sometimes the plaintiff wants the defendant to perform the acts called for in the contract, but the defendant refuses to perform its obligations under the contract. In such a case, the aggrieved party may ask a court for a decree of **specific performance.** A decree of specific performance is a court order requiring a party who is guilty of a breach of contract to perform its obligations under the contract. A person who fails to obey such a court order may be imprisoned for contempt of court.

As a general rule, the courts will not require the defendant to perform the acts specified in the contract if the payment of damages

■ **FIGURE 9.6** Equitable Remedies

> Specific Performance—a court order requiring a party to do something specified by the court
>
> Injunction—a court order requiring a party to refrain from engaging in a particular activity

would adequately compensate the injured party. Courts generally permit a party to request specific performance of a contract if the subject matter of the contract is unique or if the contract involves the sale of real estate. For example, suppose that an art collector purchases a famous painting by Renoir. The seller thereafter refuses to deliver the picture to the collector. In such a case, as the Renoir painting is unique, a court will order the seller to deliver the painting to the buyer.

INJUNCTION

A court issues an **injunction** for the purpose of requiring a party to refrain from engaging in a particular act or activity. Suppose that Mike Waters signs a three-year contract to play baseball for the Kansas City Royals at $2 million per year. In the contract he agrees that if he does not play baseball for the Royals, he will not play for any other baseball team during the contract period. Soon after signing the contract, he realizes that the Chicago Cubs are willing to pay him $3 million per year. If Waters even attempted to start playing for the Cubs, the Royals could go to court and obtain an injunction ordering Waters to stop playing for the Cubs or any other ball team.

Win-Win Negotiating Strategy

The win-win negotiating strategy is a particularly useful style of negotiating contracts, as shown in the Managerial Perspective, "Negotiation Note: The Win-Win Negotiating Style."

Summary

Even if all of the requirements for a valid contract have been met—offer, acceptance, consideration, capacity, and legality—the contract will still not be enforceable if the parties did not freely and voluntarily enter into the agreement. Furthermore, the courts will not enforce certain contracts if they are not evidenced by a writing. Before signing a contract, a person should take care to make certain that the written contract actually reflects the oral agreement entered into between the parties. The parol evidence rule may create serious problems for a party if the final written contract does not reflect the oral agreement between the parties.

Even a contract that seems clear at the outset must be interpreted. First the parties to the contract give their own interpretation to the contract terms. If they cannot come to an agreement as to what these terms mean, they may be forced to go to court to get an official interpretation of the language used in the contract.

A contract may be terminated in a variety of ways, but most commonly it is terminated by the parties to the contract performing their contractual obligations. If one of the parties to the contract does not comply with his or her obligations, the law provides various remedies to the nonbreaching party.

Whenever negotiating with another party, give some consideration to the win-win strategy of negotiation. It is possible that you will come up with an agreement that satisfies the needs of both parties

managerial perspective

Negotiation Note: The Win-Win Negotiating Style

People employ a host of negotiating styles and techniques. When you bargain with other people, keep in mind the *win-win style* of negotiating. A person employing this strategy hopes to conclude the deal with all parties feeling pleased with the outcome of the negotiating process. Each side must come out of the deal with a sense of gaining something valuable.

For example, suppose that a professor's tenants broke a house lease in September, just three months after signing for a year's rental. The tenants found the home of their dreams, bought it, and moved out. In an academic town, most people secure their rentals by August for the coming school year, so the professor was afraid he would be unable to locate suitable new tenants. In such a situation, anger could easily dominate the professor's reactions. But a "take no hostages" posture of winning at all costs is emotionally wearing and often self-defeating. Moreover, it overlooks the tenants' perspective. Is it unreasonable that the tenants want to move into a home of their own?

A better strategy would be for the professor to resist the temptation to release his anger on the tenants. Instead, he should use the win-win approach. The professor occupies a powerful negotiating position—after all, the tenants agreed to pay rent until the following August. He should call the tenants and firmly, but politely, point out to them that he intends to hold them to their contract. However, at the same time, he should suggest that if they locate someone else to take over their lease, he will release them from their obligations. This gives the tenants some incentive to find a substitute party. Through pointing out to the tenants not the landlord's needs, but rather the tenants' own need to resolve the matter to avoid a suit, and by adopting a flexible attitude, the professor ensures that both parties are likely to come out of the transaction as winners.

and at the same time helps maintain a good working relationship between them.

Review Questions

1. Define the following terms:
   a. Assignee
   b. Assignor
   c. Incidental beneficiary
   d. Intended beneficiary
   e. Material breach
   f. Mitigation of damages
   g. Parol evidence rule
   h. Statute of frauds
   i. Substantial performance

2. Does a person have a duty to read a contract before signing it? Is that person bound by the contract if she or he fails to read it before signing?

3. Darla Paxton operates an antiques store. She hires Neil Clark to fill in for her at times. Daphne Martin, a collector with more than two hundred rare dolls, asks the price of a particular doll. Neil misreads the price tag and informs her it costs $15 rather than $1500 that Darla marked on the tag. Daphne purchases the doll. Thereafter Darla asks for it back because of Neil's mistake. Must Daphne return the doll? If she knew of the mistake, is it ethical to take advantage of Neil's error?

4. Verlyn Fuller spoke with a representative of the Acme Trucking School. The representative told him that he would learn to drive a truck and the training he would receive was designed to qualify a student to compete in the job market. After Verlyn graduated from the school, he was unable to locate a job. Is Acme Trucking School guilty of fraud?

5. On June 1, Donna Mello spoke with Phyllis Miles. Donna orally agreed to sell her home to Phyllis. They agreed on all of the terms necessary to create a binding contract. The next day, Neil Delacruz offered Donna $5,000 more for her home. Can Donna sell her home to Neil? Why or why not?

6. Parker, a thirty-seven-year-old bachelor, entered into a series of contracts with Arthur Murray for dancing lessons. During the lessons, he was told he had "exceptional potential to be a fine and accomplished dancer." The contracts he signed stated in bold type at the bottom. "Noncancellable Contract," and also stated, "I understand that no refunds will be made under the terms of this contract." He was thereafter severely injured in an automobile accident and was incapable of continuing his dancing lessons. At that time, he had contracted for a total 2,734 hours of lessons. He contends that he should be released from these contracts on the basis of impossibility. Should he win?

7. Christopher Kitsos claimed that he was offered an oral contract for lifetime employment by the Mobile Gas Service Corporation. The company fired him. When sued by Kitsos, the company argued that this contract had to be in writing in order to be enforceable. Is the company correct?

8. Chen Wang recently moved to the United States. Wang spoke with an agent for a shopping center about leasing a restaurant in the center. The restaurant occupied two buildings in the center. Wang inquired whether or not he could cancel the lease on one of the buildings if business in the restaurant turned out to be poor. The agent said yes. The contract Wang signed was for ten years for both buildings. It said nothing about a right to cancel the lease. Business turned out to be very poor. Can Wang cancel the contract?

9. Vargas is an artist, and a native of Peru. He has lived in the United States for more than thirty years. He entered an employment contract with the publishers of *Esquire* magazine, after having looked at and signed it. The contract was written in plain English. Vargas now wishes to cancel the contract on the ground that he failed to read and understand its contents when it was signed. Is this a good defense to a breach of contract claim?

10. Smith signed a contract with Standard Oil to sell a piece of property. In a suit to enforce the contract against Smith, Smith argued that she was unable to read the contract when it was presented for signature because of her faulty eyesight. She did not have eyeglasses with her, so she signed the contract only on the assurances given to her by Standard Oil. As soon as she arrived home, she put on her glasses and discovered that the contract did not contain a provision that she was led to believe was in it. Can she have the contract set aside?

11. Kilroy owes Acme Corporation $5,000. Acme needs money to continue operating so it assigns its right to the $5,000 to First National Bank. It later develops that Kilroy has a claim of breach of warranty against Acme. In this example, which party is the assignor and which is the assignee? Is it possible to assign such an obligation? May Kilroy assert his defense against First National Bank?

12. On June 1, Richard's home caught fire, causing substantial damage. The insurance contract required him to notify the company of a loss within ten days. Richard did not call the company for three months. What is the clause in the contract called? Does it make any difference that Richard waited three months to call the company?

13. Carolyn Kenyon hired a contractor to build a home for her at a cost of $425,000. The contract required the builder to use Kohler plumbing fixtures. Because of a strike, the builder was unable to purchase Kohler fixtures. The builder substituted plumbing fixtures of equal quality and value. When Carolyn saw the completed house, she refused to pay the builder because he failed to comply with the contract. She viewed his actions as a material breach of contract, thus discharging her from any obligations under the contract. Is she correct?

14. Book Company's printing press stopped working because of a defective part. The company contacted the manufacturer of the press, which agreed to repair the part in two days. The manufacturer assumed that Book Company had a spare part it could use in the meantime. The actual repair took three weeks. Book Company wants to recover from the manufacturer the lost profits it would have made during this time period. What types of damages are these? Can Book Company recover these damages?

15. Marc Stanfield was the president of a medium-size computer company working under a three-year contract. The company wrongfully fired him after two years. As a condition of collecting the last year of salary under his contract, does he have an obligation to look for work elsewhere? If he learns of a job as a cashier at the local McDonald's, must he take this job?

Note

[1]"Great Divide: Split the $1 Million," *The Kansas City Star,* October 21, 1995, pages A1 and A19.

Chapter
10

ASSESSING EXTERNAL
COSTS OF DOING BUSINESS:
TORT LIABILITY

Business activity may cause harm—outperforming a competitor to such an extent that their business closes is one example; laying off employees is another example. Sometimes a person is injured or property is damaged because of business activity. However, a business is not legally liable for every harm. Whether or not it will be held responsible is the subject of tort law.

What Is Tort Liability?

DISTINCTION BETWEEN TORT AND OTHER FORMS OF LIABILITY

Torts are legally compensable wrongs other than breaches of contract. They are administered by the civil justice system even though some of the behavior may also be considered criminal. Recall the discussion of contract law in Chapters 8 and 9, and note the following distinctions between a contract breach and a tort.

First, the scope of the *wrongs* is different. A contract breach involves one person not keeping a promise made to another person. Thus, failure to perform the contract as agreed on only commits a wrong against the other party. As an illustration, assume that Bill agreed to pay Tom $1,000 for painting his house. After Tom finished the work, Bill refused to pay him. The *wrong* is Bill's failure to keep his promise to Tom, and only Tom would have the right to enforce their contract. No one else was harmed by Bill's action.

Torts arise from human foibles. Thus, failure to live up to one's duties risks liability to whomever has been injured. No relationship between the wrongdoer and the injured person is required. Assume that Mary's errant driving caused an accident. Her *wrong* was that she did not drive the car consistent with the standards society has set. Therefore, damages that she caused—even to a stranger—would be assessed against her under tort law.

A second difference between tort and contract liability is reflected by the remedies they provide. In contract law, the damages must be tied to the agreement. If ABC, Inc., failed to deliver frames as promised to Mary's Hobby Shop, ABC, Inc., will be assessed the difference between what it had agreed to sell the frames for—$5,000— and the price Mary had to pay when she bought substitutes—$6,000. Total damages would be $1,000. However, what if Mary, who is quite high-strung, also loses three nights of sleep and she has an upset stomach for a week? Even though she was *injured* in this way by ABC, Inc.'s breach, contract law does not provide a remedy.

Contrast this situation with tort law. Tort remedies are determined by the injury that has occurred. This is the case even if the injury was unexpected, or like Mary's situation, based on an unforeseen condition. As an example, assume that Joe gently tossed his book across a crowded classroom. What are the damages you may expect? Perhaps someone's nose would be bloodied or a pair of glasses knocked to the floor. But, what if the book hit a student with an atypically sensitive skull who must be rushed to the hospital as a result? Even though

managerial perspective

Yellow Pages Advertisements: Contracts or Torts?

Eugene DeLanney owned a real estate business and contracted with Southwestern Bell to place an advertisement in their Yellow Pages. Prior to the directory's publication, DeLanney's wife asked Southwestern Bell to make changes in the listing. Bell agreed. However, when doing so, the DeLanney real estate advertisement was deleted by mistake.

A tort claim was filed against Southwestern Bell claiming that they failed to exercise reasonable care by omitting DeLanney's advertisement from the directory. The court held that the *wrong* committed was not a tort, but rather a breach of contract. It asserted that Southwestern Bell only had a duty to publish the advertisement because of the contract with DeLanney. In addition, the only damages arose from Southwestern Bell's failure to perform the contract and what DeLanney sought to recover was the benefit of his bargain with Southwestern Bell.

Source: Southwestern Bell v. DeLanney, *809 S.W.2d 493 (Supreme Court of Texas 1991).*

such an injury may be rare, tort law would make Joe financially responsible.

Tort law covers a far broader (and less definitive) array of conduct than does contract law. Nonetheless, as the distinctions previously stated note, a breach of contract is not a tort. Consider the Managerial Perspective, "Yellow Pages Advertisements: Contracts or Torts?" The customer was injured by the telephone company, but the wrong was a broken promise (contract breach) rather than a lapse of a general standard of care.

Tort liability is also different from criminal liability even though the same conduct (for example, punching someone in the nose) may give rise to both. A tort is a wrong against an individual, and that person has the right to seek compensation. Claims must be pursued through the civil justice system. Thus, if Mary had punched Tom, he could file a tort claim against her seeking damages for his injured nose. Punishing Mary is not the aim of this proceeding.

Concurrently, the state could file a criminal complaint against Mary. Unlike a tort, this is not an action taken by the victim, but rather by the state. Community conduct standards formalized in the criminal code were breached, and the law will punish Mary for her transgression. A criminal proceeding will not compensate Tom.

PURPOSES OF TORT LAW

Tort law has three purposes (see Figure 10.1): first, to provide compensation for those injured by the actions of another; second, to allocate risk of loss between those who are injured and those who cause harm; and third, to provide incentives for changing behavior.

The compensation purpose of tort law is to provide a monetary award reflecting the damage that has been inflicted. The person who caused the injury is responsible for paying the award. The law takes

■ **FIGURE 10.1** Purposes of Tort Law

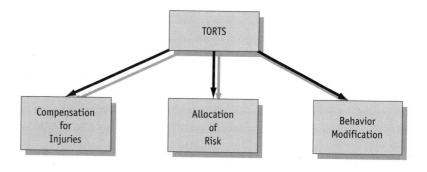

into account a number of factors in determining this compensation. Both current damages and future losses are considered. Commonly used factors include:

■ *Economic damages:* Lost wages and diminished capacity to earn future income are typical measures. For a business, lost profits would provide a similar figure. These damages may be computed.

■ *Expenses:* Specific costs incurred because of the tort are also common measures of compensation. Medical bills are an example.

■ *Intangible damages:* Injuries that are impossible to accurately assess, nonetheless, they are compensable under tort law. Pain and suffering for a physical injury, and harm to a businesses' reputation are both examples.

As an illustration, Jack was injured by a tort committed by ABC, Inc. As a result, he was away from work for a month and lost $4,000 wages. In addition, he will only be able to work part-time for the next three years and will lose $35,000 in future income. Jack's hospital and doctor bills totalled $15,000. So far, Jack has incurred $54,000 in damages. However, his injury also caused substantial pain and great inconvenience. Although these are highly subjective factors, they were caused by ABC, Inc.'s tort, and the law makes the company responsible. Thus, a jury could award Jack an additional $126,000 for these losses. In this case, his total compensation would amount to $180,000.

However, Jack will not receive that sum because he has legal fees to pay. In tort cases, the plaintiff's attorneys work on a contingency fee basis—they receive a percentage (usually one-third) of any award. If no award is granted, the attorneys get no fee. In addition, the plaintiff's lawyer frequently advances expenses needed to prepare the case. Typical expenses are expert witness fees and investigation costs. Assume that in Jack's case, the expenses totalled $10,000. This sum will be subtracted from the award and if there is no award, usually the law firm absorbs the loss.

Jack's $180,000 award could be reduced by $60,000 due to his attorney's fee, and an additional $10,000 is needed to reimburse his lawyer for advancing expense money. Consequently, Jack would receive $110,000.

The second purpose of tort law is to allocate risk. The question is, who should bear the loss—the person who is injured or the one who caused the injury? In the previous example, the risk belonged to ABC, Inc., who caused Jack's injury. The $180,000 award to Jack reflected this liability. However, if a revised tort law assigned the risk to Jack, he would receive no compensation for his injuries. He alone would absorb the loss.

Tort law's answer to this allocation of risk question has not always been the same. The allocation is influenced by social and economic forces. In the early nineteenth century, the United States had primarily an agrarian economy. Tort law focused on intentional harms usually arising out of physical violence. But, as the machine age began, and especially as railroads spread throughout the country, a large number of machine-related injuries began to occur. These were serious injuries that no one meant to have happen.

The doctrine of negligence, which was not well developed until that time, became a major force in tort law. In fact, the first major book on the subject was not published until 1850. The Industrial Revolution not only changed the way people lived and how they worked, it also influenced the development of tort law. As the legal historian, Lawrence Friedman, wrote: "The modern law of torts must be laid at the door of the Industrial Revolution, whose machines had a marvelous capacity for smashing the human body."[1]

However, the same machines that smashed bodies also created wealth, provided jobs, and became the key to economic growth. Railroads opened the West by linking wilderness and farm areas to cities and markets. Tort liability risk did not stand in the way. Nineteenth-century courts were sympathetic to the interests of industry and created a number of doctrines that made it difficult for the injured to collect damages. These rules were applied by the judge and, thus, kept tort liability decisions away from the jury. Juries were assumed to be more sympathetic to the injured party than to a wealthy corporate defendant.

Consider the Thought Problem, "Limiting Tort Law Risk," and the effect of the court's decision on the railroad industry in the nineteenth century. The case affected the railroad's costs in two ways: first, the railroad company was not assessed damages for the injuries its train caused Haring; and second, there was no incentive to make safer crossings. Company funds could be spent on other projects.

thought problem

Limiting Tort Law Risk
Haring was riding in a fast-moving sleigh that was hit by a train. High embankments near the crossing where the road and tracks intersected made it impossible to see an approaching train from the road. The railroad had not created clear sight-lines when it laid the tracks. Haring's widow sued. The court held that Haring, a passenger in the rapidly moving sleigh, did not use reasonable care. Nothing was done to determine whether or not a train was coming and the sleigh had rushed, heedlessly, onto the tracks. Therefore, any railroad negligence was canceled out, and Haring absorbed the loss. This decision was made by the court, not by the jury.

As Justice Barculo explained:

It is contended by the counsel for the plaintiff, that the question of negligence should have been submitted to the jury. But when, upon the plaintiff's own showing, he has defeated his claim by his own misconduct, there can be no propriety in requiring the jury to pass upon the evidence. We cannot shut our eyes to the fact that in certain controversies between the weak and the strong and between a humble individual and a gigantic corporation, that the sympathies of the human mind naturally, honestly, and generously, run to the assistance and support of the feeble, and apparently oppressed; and that compassion will sometimes exercise over the deliberations of a jury, an influence which, however honorable to them as philanthropists, is wholly inconsistent with the principles of law and the ends of justice. There is, therefore, a manifest propriety in withdrawing from the consideration of the jury, those cases in which the plaintiff fails to show a right of recovery.

Change the facts to increase the sleigh-rider's probability of winning this case.

Source: Haring v. New York and Erie Railroad, *13 Barb. 9 (Supreme Court of New York 1852).*

Of course, the damage caused by the sleigh and train accident did not vanish. Tort law merely assigned the risk between Haring and the railroad, both of whom were at fault. Even at the time, cases like this one were not met with universal approval.

As the nineteenth century ended and the success of the Industrial Revolution was made manifest, pressures arose for reform. For example, legislation was enacted that removed workplace injuries from the tort law system (see Chapter 17 and the discussion of Workers' Compensation Acts). Courts also created exceptions to the rules that kept injured people like Haring from being awarded compensation. The risks of tort liability began to shift by the turn of the century.

By the 1970s, the burden was clearly on business. Injuries that would have been uncompensated a hundred years before were now yielding jury awards. The Thought Problem, "Injury on the Ski Slopes," illustrates an example. Compare how this decision affected costs to the ski industry with how the Haring case affected the railroads.

thought problem

Injury on the Ski Slopes James Sunday,

who was twenty-one years old, was a novice skier. He was seriously injured while using the beginner's trail at Stratton's Ski Resort. This ski area was carefully maintained and designed to accommodate the low skills of its users. Sophisticated equipment was used for this purpose. In addition, obstructions were removed from the beginner's trail, and grass was planted to provide a smoother surface. Furthermore, the snow base on the beginner's trail was the best-maintained area at the resort. The resort advertised a world-wide reputation for trail maintenance, grooming, and snow cover.

At the time of Sunday's accident, the resort had a fifty-two-person patrol force at work and a crew that regularly checked the trails for hazards. Nonetheless, while skiing along the beginner's trail at the pace of a fast walk, Mr. Sunday's skis became entangled in a small bush that was concealed by loose snow. The bush was within the limits of the trail, and neither he nor his companion saw it before the accident.

The injury left James Sunday a quadriplegic. He endured eight operations. He was in a coma, and he had a severe drug reaction during his treatment. He requires special equipment to live. His care, by others, takes three and a half hours each morning. It is expected that Sunday will require about two months of hospitalization each year for the rest of his life (which is projected to be another fifty years). He can neither work nor father children.

A jury awarded Sunday $1.5 million in his suit against the ski resort. This verdict was upheld on appeal. The court stated: "It is clear from the evidence that the passage of time has greatly changed the nature of the ski industry. . . . [T]he timorous no longer need stay at home. There is a concerted effort to attract their patronage and to provide novice trails suitable for their use. This is the state of the evidence in this case; none of it was calculated to show the bush to be a danger inherent in the use of a novice slope as laid out and maintained by the defendant. Like many other fields, the 'art' has changed vastly."

Change the facts to increase the ski resort's probability of winning this case.

Source: Sunday v. Stratton Corporation, *390 A.2d 398 (Vermont Supreme Court 1978).*

The questions accompanying the previous two Thought Problems illustrate the third purpose of tort law—to modify behavior. By making certain conduct more risky, one may expect more care being taken by those engaged in it. The Haring decision and the Stratton Ski Resort's liability would influence the behavior of other sleigh drivers or operators of novice ski trails.

As another example, note that corporations have been found liable for torts committed by employees who had become intoxicated at company picnics. The effect of these awards has been to increase the risk of serving alcohol at these functions. Consequently, companies have an incentive to review liability-prone picnic policies. Possible solutions include that liquor may be banned or more closely monitored. The goal is to reduce the liability risk.

But, what if tort law risk causes a company to reconsider more efficient manufacturing processes? Maybe the company would be reluctant to develop new tools. In addition, a large damage award could harm a firm that has been providing a needed service, not to mention jobs. How should the risk be balanced then? A broad liability scope could financially cripple companies and damage the national economy. On the other hand, a narrow scope could result in the inevitable misfortunes of a complex and highly industrialized society borne by an unlucky few who are injured.

TORT LAW: INSURANCE AND REFORM

The stark choice between a destitute, injured person denied tort law recovery or a company ravaged by a damage claim needs to be viewed in light of insurance. An injured person may have health or income disability insurance that cushions the loss, although fewer people are covered each year. However, this compensation does not off-set a tort damage award. Thus, if Jack (who was entitled to a sizable tort damage award from ABC, Inc., in the earlier example) had insurance coverage, the jury would not have been told, and his $180,000 award would not be affected. Furthermore, the sum would not be reduced by the payments he received from his insurance company.

There are two reasons for this. First, people or companies like ABC, Inc., who commit torts should not benefit from the good fortune of having the injured person be someone like Jack, who was well insured. Second, those with insurance should not be penalized for their foresight. However, is it fair for Jack to collect twice? Tort reform legislation has changed the outcome in a few states.

In addition, most companies purchase insurance to guard against the risk of tort suits. Thus, a firm may manage its potential tort claims without putting its assets at risk. The insurance premium is a predictable cost of doing business. Furthermore, the insurance company may require changes in business procedures as a condition of coverage, or it may charge a lower premium if those changes are made. Consequently, both the allocation of risk and behavior modification factors are affected by insurance.

Insurance also provides a ready source of compensation from which damage judgments may be satisfied. A tort award is not bankable—it must be collected. Defendants with neither assets nor insurance coverage are considered *judgment proof.* They are not able to pay the award, and the injured party will receive no money. Insurance thereby furthers the compensation purpose of tort law.

Nonetheless, placing greater liability on business meant that larger tort-related costs were demanded either through insurance premiums or through the risks that tort liability posed directly. This problem led to a reform movement, and state legislatures responded and continued to consider changes. Statutes were enacted that limited damage awards or modified tort law doctrine. In addition, tighter regulation of insurance companies also occurred.

Since 1986, nearly every state has enacted such legislation. Most states changed the Joint and Several Liability Rule. Under the old rule, a damage award could be collected from any defendant found liable, irrespective of the amount of fault. For example, assume that three companies were found to have caused injury to Jane Doe: LMN, Inc., had been seventy-five percent at fault; XYZ, Inc., had been fifteen percent at fault; and Acme, Inc., had been ten percent at fault. Jane's damage award against the three companies totalled $100,000. Under the Joint and Several Liability Rule, she could collect the money from any one of the companies. Thus, if LMN, Inc., and XYZ, Inc., were bankrupt, then Acme, Inc., would absorb the entire loss even though it was only ten percent liable. Reform tied financial loss to a defendant's degree of fault. Thus, Acme, Inc., would now be assessed only $10,000, the portion of Jane's damages that it caused.

In addition, ceilings on punitive and non-economic awards (e.g., pain and suffering) were also widely enacted. Illinois, for example, capped non-economic damages at $500,000. Furthermore, a few states required that tort damages be reduced by other compensation that an injured person received. Note how this reduction may change the amount that Jack receives in the hypothetical example discussed earlier.

Although none of the changes affected the basic principles of tort law (to be discussed in the next section), they did remove some of the liability risk businesses faced. Tort case filings decreased six percent from 1991 through 1993. Furthermore, jurors have been siding with defendants more often lately. For example, in 1989, plaintiffs won at trial sixty-three percent of the time. By 1992, this figure had dropped to fifty-two percent. In addition, the amount of the awards has been decreasing. Only thirty percent of the awards were above $200,000 in 1992—two percent less than in the previous year.

Nonetheless, two questions remain:

1. How does (or should) society compensate those who have been injured?

2. How can business best guard against tort liability risk?

These are issues still seeking resolution. See the International Perspective, "Tort Risk: An International Comparison," for a different example of tort risk.

Regulating Purposeful Conduct: Intentional Torts

An intentional tort arises when the purpose of an act is to cause an injury. Such acts have serious ethical implications and, thus, may lead to an award of punitive damages in addition to those damage awards intended to compensate the victim. An intentional tort may also lead to criminal charges being filed against the wrongdoer.

For example, assume that Mary was fired from her job with an investment firm. For revenge, she told others in the firm that her supervisor embezzled money from the company. This was false, but it harmed her supervisor anyway. A promotion was postponed as a result. Note the connection between Mary's actions and the expected outcome—she lied about her supervisor in order to inflict injury. Mary committed an intentional tort.

The close connection between the act and its expected consequences is a key characteristic of an intentional tort. However, such torts are not limited to those like Mary's situation, whose act had a malicious factor. The legal standard is broader:

> Would a reasonable person in the position of one who committed the act believe that the injury that occurred was certain to follow?

Clearly, this standard applies to Mary. A reasonable person would believe that her supervisor would be harmed as a result of her lies.

But, the standard would also apply to actions undertaken without a malevolent motive. For example, assume that a practical joker pulled a chair out from underneath a person who was about to sit down. As a result, the victim fell to the floor and was injured. It was unlikely that the practical joker wanted to cause harm. Most likely, getting a few laughs as a result of the stunt was the joker's aim. However, the intentional tort standard does not focus on a practical joker's motives, but rather on a reasonable person's belief about the connection between the act

INTERNATIONAL
PERSPECTIVE

Tort Risk: An International Comparison

The American tort system has been accused of imposing a $300 billion *tax* on American business through damage awards, attorney's costs, and the efforts undertaken by business solely to avoid tort liability. Furthermore, because of liability concerns, American business was said to be reluctant to innovate. The conclusion was that the tort law system hampered the ability of American companies to compete internationally, because foreign firms did not face similar liability risks at home. These arguments were used to justify calls for narrowing the scope of tort doctrines, capping damage awards, or making it more difficult for injured parties to sue.

A number of studies, however, raised questions about these criticisms and suggested that the *remedies* urged by the critics were misguided. One of the studies compared the American liability system with those of six Western European nations. As expected, the damage awards in Europe were smaller and more predictable than in the United States. Further, litigation was found to be more expensive in the United States primarily because of the amount spent on attorney's fees. However, the study

—Continued

and the injury arising from it. Causing someone to fall inevitably led to an injury.

The standard similarly applies to a business's intentional tort. Review the *Millison v. E. I. du Pont de Nemours & Company* case in Chapter 7. Undoubtedly, corporate management did not conceal the asbestos problems in order to cause disease, but a reasonable person would have expected such a result.

The following sections will review some common intentional torts. Note how the examples discussed meet the standard.

BATTERY

Battery is a purposeful touching of a person without consent. Although batteries are commonly thought of as violent assaults—knifings, punchings, kickings, and so on—the tort of battery is not so limited. *Any* unpermitted contact with another person may suffice, even if no physical injury arises. Thus, spitting in someone's face may be considered battery. Cases raising battery issues have also been filed against smokers. In one case, a radio talk-show host blew cigar smoke in the face of an anti-smoking advocate who was appearing as a guest on another program at the station. The court held that the conduct was a battery if it could be proven that the smoke was intentionally aimed at the plaintiff (*Leichtman v. WLW Jacor Communications, Inc.* [1994]).

—Continued

also noted major legal and social differences between the United States and Western Europe. European nations have a vast network of government entitlements (e.g., national health care, and income security programs) that do not have counterparts in the United States. Consequently, injured Europeans do not need to resort to tort law litigation for monetary relief. Note, however, that the study found that European accident victims, like their American counterparts, expected compensation for their injuries. The difference was the source: Americans seek a party to *blame* via tort litigation; Europeans have a social program safety net. Thus, the study concluded that no tort law *crisis* has arisen in Europe because the countries, using tax revenues, provide benefits that injured Americans must seek through the tort law system.

The broad scope of this tort may be traced to its common law origins. Battery was considered a means to keep the peace. It was a substitute, provided by the legal system, for retribution. Thus, a nineteenth-century gentleman who was slapped with a glove would have a legal claim of battery against the wrongdoer, as opposed to resorting to the traditional private remedy—a duel at dawn. Consequently, when damages are assessed today for a battery claim, the element of indignity is given great weight. One does not need to have sustained physical injuries in order to be compensated.

Battery has three elements: first, the defendant's act must be voluntary; second, the defendant must have intended either to harm the plaintiff or to otherwise impart an offensive touch; and third, the touching must have produced a physical injury or an offense to a reasonable person's sense of dignity.

Assume that George was trying to walk across a crowded room. He tapped Sam lightly on the shoulder so he could get by. Would this be considered battery? Although George did voluntarily touch Sam without permission, no intentional tort would arise. There was no intent to injure or offend Sam. Social convention permits such touching as a means to request that someone move aside. Furthermore, even if Sam was greatly offended by the touch, a reasonable person—given social convention—would not be offended. Consequently, neither the second nor third element of a battery could be established.

However, if George had tackled Sam in order to clear a path through the crowded room, a battery would have occurred. Tackling is not an acceptable way of moving through crowds, and a reasonable person would be offended by it. Then again, if George and Sam were playing football, and Sam was racing for the goal line, George's tackle would not be tortious.

Thus, one needs to consider battery—and the concept of lack of consent to being touched—to be affected by circumstances, time, and place. See the *Manning v. Grimsley* case as an example. Do you think a battery would arise if, instead, Grimsley had thrown a *wild pitch* that went into the stands?

Manning v. Grimsley Court of Appeals, First Circuit *643 F.2d 20 (1981)*

On September 16, 1975, a professional baseball game was being played at Fenway Park between the Baltimore Orioles and the Boston Red Sox. Ross Grimsley was a pitcher for the Orioles. Some spectators, including Manning, were seated behind a wire-mesh fence in bleachers located in right field. Grimsley, during the first three innings, had been warming up in the bullpen located near the right field bleachers. The spectators in the bleachers continuously heckled him. On several occasions, Grimsley looked directly at the hecklers, and not just into the stands. At the end of the third inning, Grimsley faced the bleachers and wound up as though he was going to pitch in the direction of the plate toward which he had been throwing. But the ball travelled from Grimsley's hand at more than eighty miles an hour, at an angle of 90 degrees, from the path of the pitcher's mound to the plate and directly toward the hecklers in the bleachers. The ball passed through the wire-mesh fence and hit the plaintiff.

Wyzanski, Senior District Judge

We, unlike the district judge, are of the view that from the evidence Grimsley was an expert pitcher, and on several occasions, immediately following heckling, he looked directly at the hecklers, not just into the stands. The ball he threw travelled at a right angle to the direction in which he had been pitching and directly at the hecklers. Thus, the jury could reasonably infer that Grimsley intended (1) to throw the ball in the direction of the hecklers, (2) to cause them imminent apprehension of being hit, and (3) to respond to conduct presently affecting his ability to warm up and, if the opportunity came, to play in the game itself.

The foregoing evidence and inferences would have permitted a jury to conclude that the defendant Grimsley committed a battery against the plaintiff. An actor is subject to liability to another for battery if intending to cause a third person to have an imminent apprehension of a harmful bodily contact, the actor causes the other to suffer a harmful contact. The whole rule and especially that aspect of the rule which permits recovery by a person who was not the target of the defendant embody a strong social policy including obedience to the criminal law by imposing an absolute civil liability to anyone who is physically injured as a result of an intentional harmful contact or a threat thereof directed either at him or a third person. It, therefore, was error for the district court to have directed a verdict for defendant Grimsley on the battery count.

DEFAMATION

Defamation is a communication that causes unwarranted harm to another's reputation. No physical injury occurs—the damage is done with *words*. For example, assume that Bill is a stockbroker. Jan started a rumor by telling some of his clients that Bill brags about the money that he has swindled. These rumors were false, but they destroyed Bill's business. His worried clients changed brokers. Injury resulted even though no physical harm occurred.

When a company is defamed, honesty, creditworthiness, or the quality of its product(s) is often targeted. Recall the Corona Extra Beer example in Chapter 7. False rumors were spread about the beer being contaminated with human urine, and a defamation suit followed.

Prior to the eighteenth century in England, defamation cases were heard in ecclesiastical courts because such conduct was considered to be a sin. The church was the forum for such a claim, and it was remedied by penance. Even when the common law courts began to hear defamation cases, those that did not cause a specific injury were returned to the church for remedy.

A tort of defamation has three elements:

1. The defamatory statement(s) must have been communicated to a third party orally, in writing, or through the media.

2. The fact that such communication occurred must have been intended by the defendant. Thus, if a third party eavesdropped or accidentally picked up a phone conversation between the plaintiff and defendant, the intent-to-communicate criterion would not have been met.

3. The third party must have understood that the statements were derogatory.

In a defamation action, the plaintiff does not need to show that the statements were false. The burden is on the defendant to prove that the statements were true. If so, no defamation occurred.

On November 17, 1992, during its *Dateline* program, NBC reported on the dangers of General Motors (GM) pickup trucks that had been built between 1973 and 1987. More than three hundred people had been killed in crashes in which the truck's gasoline tank had caught fire. A staged crash of a GM pickup truck was shown on the program. Its gasoline tank caught fire.

General Motors denied that its pickup trucks were unsafe. It received a tip that NBC's crash simulation had been rigged to ensure that a fire occurred. GM investigated and learned that NBC had attached incendiary devices to the fuel tank of the pickup truck used in its simulation. This was not revealed to the *Dateline* audience. General Motors sued NBC for defamation. The case was soon settled. NBC admitted that its staged crash was misleading and they apologized. It also agreed to pay General Motors for any investigation expenses that were incurred.

The International Perspective, "Defamation in Cyberspace," is an example of defamation in an international law context.

FALSE IMPRISONMENT

False imprisonment is the wrongful restraint of a person's mobility. Locking someone in a closet would be an example of false imprisonment. However, if a second door existed by which an easy exit could be made, no false imprisonment would arise because the ability to move about freely was not impaired.

However, false imprisonment is not limited to incarcerations. The word *imprisonment* in the tort's name is misleading—that is, preventing another's freedom of movement by imposing physical barriers that do so are not required. Thus, a threat of violence that causes someone to stay put against his will would constitute false imprisonment. Furthermore, no length of time is required for the tort to occur. A brief period of time would be sufficient. Consider the following hypothetical situation.

Tom was walking along the street. Jim and Mary stopped him. They informed Tom that if he moved from that spot within the next ten seconds, they would beat him up. Tom was afraid of the consequences and so he did as they ordered. This would be one example of false imprisonment. Tom's freedom to move about at will was impeded by Jim and Mary's credible threats. Even though he was not physically injured, and ten seconds is a very short time, Tom would still be able to collect damages if he sued. The compensable harm was Tom's lost freedom of movement.

Furthermore, the person who claims a false imprisonment must have been restrained unwillingly. For example, if Andy agreed to be locked in a closet in order to show off his escape-artist skills, there would be no false imprisonment. Even though Andy was prevented from moving about, he willingly consented to it. Consider the case of *Hardy v. LaBelle's Distributing Co.* (1983). Debra Hardy, an employee of LaBelle's Distributing Co., was accused of stealing a watch. She was taken into an office filled with police officers and management personnel. The door was closed behind her, and when she was confronted with the allegation, she denied it and offered to take a lie detector test. She was not ordered to stay in the room. Later, she testified that she had wanted to remain there and clarify the matter. The court rejected her false imprisonment claim, finding that she was not detained against her will.

The *Great Atlantic & Pacific Tea Co. v. Paul* case also raised a false imprisonment issue. How does it differ from the Hardy case?

Defamation in Cyberspace

David Rindos was an anthropology professor at the University of Western Australia. In 1993, he underwent a tenure review, and the committee recommended that tenure not be granted to him. In June of that year, he was dismissed from the university. Later that month, a message criticizing the university for this decision appeared on a worldwide computer network bulletin board. The message was placed by Hugh Jarvis, an American anthropologist.

Gilbert Hardwick, a colleague of Rindos, responded on the network. In his message, Hardwick stated that Rindos' professional reputation was not based on legitimate academic research but on an ability to berate others about his own theories. In addition, Hardwick alleged that Rindos had engaged in sexual misconduct.

Rindos filed a lawsuit that Hardwick failed to defend. The court found that the statements were seriously defamatory in that they denigrated Rindos' academic competence and implied that his denial of tenure and dismissal were tied to academic and sexual misconduct. In addition, the court found that the statements had been published throughout the world on the network.

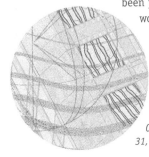

The court awarded Rindos $40,000 in damages.

Source: Rindos v. Hardwick, No. 1994 of 1993, unreported judgment 940164 (Supreme Court of Western Australia, March 31, 1994).

Great Atlantic & Pacific Tea Co. v. Paul

Court of Appeals of Maryland
261 A.2d 731 (1970)

John Joseph Paul, a retired police officer suffering from a recent heart condition, went shopping at his local A & P store. His heart attack was so recent that this was one of the first times he had ventured outside. Due to heavy crowds in the store, Mr. Paul left his cart at the end of one aisle and slowly proceeded to examine carefully the labels of various articles of food to make certain they complied with his strict post-cardiac diet. Having examined and selected a particular item, he would then return to his cart, deposit the goods, and go in search of other merchandise.

John Parker, the second assistant manager, considered this method of shopping somewhat unusual. His attention having been attracted, Parker observed Mr. Paul's shopping techniques for approximately twenty minutes. On completion of his observation, Parker came to the conclusion that Mr. Paul had taken a can of flea and tick spray and placed it in his coat pocket with the apparent intention of shoplifting.

Mr. Paul testified that Parker accosted him in the middle of an aisle and demanded in a loud voice to know what he had done with the spray. When Mr. Paul said he did not have such an item, Parker replied, "Don't tell me, you goddamn thief. You got it in your coat." Mr. Paul further testified that when this encounter occurred, approximately twenty-five to thirty customers in the immediate vicinity of the aisle turned and stared, and continued to watch as Parker roughly frisked him, knocking over a display of cans, and loudly repeating his accusation of thievery. Parker then grabbed Mr. Paul by the arm and forced him to march to the manager's office at the front of the store, therefore, attracting the attention of shoppers waiting at the check-out counters. No flea spray or any other item belonging to A & P was found on Mr. Paul's person.

Mr. Paul testified that the incident aggravated his heart condition—causing him physical pain and suffering—as well as creating personal humiliation.

The jury returned a verdict for Mr. Paul.

Diggs, Judge

Great Atlantic & Pacific Tea Co. claims error was committed in the false imprisonment phase of the case. The necessary elements of a case for false imprisonment are a deprivation of the liberty of another without his consent and without legal justification.

Any property owner, including a storekeeper, has a common law privilege to detain against his will any person he believes has tortiously taken his property. This privilege can be exercised only to prevent theft or to recapture property, and does not extend to detention for the purpose of punishment. This common law right is exercised at the shopkeeper's peril, however, and if the person detained does not unlawfully have any of the arrester's property in his possession, the arrester is liable for false imprisonment.

Parker testified he did not see Paul place any merchandise in his coat and did not check the shelf to see if the "missing" item had been returned, although if he had, these activities would not have necessarily constituted probable cause. He further testified he stopped Paul in an aisle before Paul had given any indication of leaving the store, even though customers could not pay for any item until they reached the check-out counters at the front of the store. In a self-service store we think no probable cause for detention exists until the suspected person actually attempts to leave without paying unless he manifests control over the property in such a way that his intention to steal is unequivocal. Construing all the evidence in a light most favorable to the defendant, there is no showing of probable cause here.

We will affirm the judgment entered for Paul.

Regulating Careless Conduct: The Tort of Negligence

Torts of negligence arise from careless or heedless actions. The focus is on the *conduct* and not on the reasons behind it. Thus, torts of negligence are distinguishable from intentional torts.

To illustrate, assume that Jerry had been watering his front lawn. When he was finished, he forgot to move the hose which stretched across the sidewalk. If a passerby tripped over the hose, fell, and was injured, Jerry would be liable because of his negligence. It did not matter *why* Jerry had left the hose on the sidewalk. The inquiry would be whether doing so was reasonable.

There are four elements in a tort of negligence:

1. *Duty.* Everyone has a duty to act as a reasonable person. For example, assume that ABC, Inc., manufactures children's toys. In all aspects of its operations, ABC, Inc., will be judged by the reasonable person standard.

2. *Breach of duty.* Behavior that fails to meet the reasonable person standard is said to breach the duty. If ABC, Inc., fails to test a toy for possible design defects, it will have breached its duty because a reasonable person would have done so.

3. *Causation.* The breach of duty must cause an injury. Even though ABC, Inc., breached its duty above, it would not face tort liability if one of its customers fell out of a tree. The negligent toy testing did not cause the fall. If instead, the customer was injured because of the faulty design of the toy, then the causation element would have been met.

4. *Injury.* Some person or property must be damaged. If ABC, Inc.'s, toy had not sold, or if it did sell but was placed in the bottom of a toy box and never played with, it could cause no injury. Thus, even though ABC, Inc.'s, behavior did not comply with its legal duty, it would have no liability. In sports lingo this would be called "no harm, no foul."

Consider the Ethical Perspective, "Torts and Sleep." See if you can identify the elements of tort. Do any elements exist that are particularly difficult to apply? Thereafter, evaluate it based on the ethics materials provided in Chapter 7.

STANDARD OF CARE

Negligence arises when one's actions fall below what are considered as community expectations. An old English case provides a good definition: "Negligence is the omission to do something which a reasonable man, guided upon those considerations which ordinarily regulate the conduct of human affairs, would do, or doing something which a prudent and reasonable man would not do."[2]

Compare this standard with the definition of ethics that was provided in Chapter 7. Ethics refers to what a person *ought* to do. The

---

ETHICAL
PERSPECTIVE

Torts and Sleep

Tony LeMaster worked for Norfolk & Western Railway Company. On October 11, he reported for work at 7:00 A.M. At midday, LeMaster (and other employees) were taken to a derailment site to clean and repair the area. This was an emergency and required strenuous manual labor. After working continuously until 10:00 P.M., LeMaster told his foreman that he was tired and wanted to go home. The foreman told him that he could not leave. At 1:00 A.M., LeMaster was given a lunch break—the first time he had eaten since noon the day before. Thereafter, he returned to work until 9:00 A.M., when he informed his foreman that he could no longer work.

LeMaster was told that he could go home, and he got a ride back to his car which was parked at the Railway Company Office, located about fifty miles from where he lived. While driving home, LeMaster fell asleep and caused an accident. A lawsuit was filed against the railroad company by the injured person.

After evaluating the problem using both tort and ethical principles, can you make any suggestions to Norfolk & Western Railway Company?

Source: Robertson v. LeMaster, 301 S.E.2d 563 (Supreme Court of West Virginia 1983).

reasonable person test focuses on what a person is *required* to do. Of course, determining such a standard is an imprecise formulation influenced by social and moral considerations. The conduct required to satisfy a standard of reasonable care may change over time. Furthermore, it may impose different behavior standards depending on the relationships between the parties involved.

Carefully review *Weirum v. RKO General, Inc.* and *Bearman v. University of Notre Dame*—two cases that focus on the legal duty the defendant owed to the injured person. Note how the courts took the reasonable person standard and tied its expectations to the facts of the cases.

Weirum v. RKO General, Inc.

Supreme Court of California
539 P.2d 36 (1975)

Radio station KHJ is a successful Los Angeles broadcaster with a large teenage following. In order to attract an even larger portion of the available audience and thus increase advertising revenue, KHJ inaugurated in July of 1970 a promotion entitled "The Super Summer Spectacular." Among the programs included in the "spectacular" was a contest broadcast on July 16, 1970, the date of the accident explained below.

On that day, "The Real Don Steele," a KHJ disc jockey, traveled in a conspicuous red automobile to a number of locations in the Los Angeles metropolitan area. Periodically, he apprised KHJ of his whereabouts and his intended destination, and the station broadcast the information to its listeners. The first person to physically locate Steele and fulfill a specified condition would receive a cash prize.

In Van Nuys, seventeen-year-old Robert Sentner was listening to KHJ in his car while searching for The Real Don Steele. On hearing that The Real Don Steele was proceeding to Canoga Park, he immediately drove to that vicinity. Meanwhile, in Northridge, nineteen-year-old Marsha Baime heard and responded to the same information. Both of them arrived at the Holiday Theater in Canoga Park to find that someone had already claimed the prize. Without knowledge of the other, each decided to follow the Steele vehicle to its next stop and thus be the first to arrive when the next contest question or condition was announced.

For the next few miles the Sentner and Baime cars jockeyed for the position closest to the Steele vehicle, reaching speeds of up to eighty miles an hour. About a mile and a half from the Westlake offramp, the two teenagers heard the following broadcast: "11:13—The Real Don Steele with bread is heading for Thousand Oaks to give it away." The Steele vehicle left the freeway at the Westlake offramp. Either Baime or Sentner, in attempting to follow, forced Ronald Weirum's car onto the center divider, where it overturned, killing Weirum. Baime stopped to report the accident. Sentner, after pausing momentarily to relate the tragedy to a passing peace officer, continued to pursue Steele, successfully located him, and collected a cash prize.

Weirum's wife and children brought an action for wrongful death against Sentner, Baime, and RKO General, Inc., as owner of KHJ. Sentner settled prior to trial. The jury returned a verdict against Baime and KHJ in the amount of $300,000. Baime did not appeal.

Mosk, Justice

The primary question for our determination is whether defendant owed a duty to Ronald Weirum, the decedent, arising out of its broadcast of the giveaway contest. Any number of considerations may justify the imposition of duty in particular circumstances, including the guidance of history, our continually refined concepts of morals and justice, the convenience of the rule, and social judgment as to where the loss should fall. While the question whether one owes a duty to another must be decided on a case-by-case basis, every case is governed by the rule of general application that all persons are required to use ordinary care to prevent others from being injured as the result of their conduct. However, foreseeability of risk is a primary consideration in establishing the element of duty.

We conclude that the record amply supports the finding of foreseeability. These tragic events unfolded in the middle of a Los Angeles summer, a time when young people were free from the constraints of school and responsive to relief from vacation tedium. Seeking to attract new listeners, KHJ devised an "exciting" promotion. Money and a small measure of momentary notoriety awaited the swiftest response. It was foreseeable that defendant's youthful listeners, finding the prize had eluded them at one location, would race to arrive first at the next site and in their haste would disregard the demands of highway safety. It is of no consequence that the harm to decedent was inflicted by third parties acting negligently. Here reckless conduct by youthful contestants, stimulated by defendant's broadcast, constituted the hazard to which decedent was exposed.

It is true, of course, that virtually every act involves some conceivable danger. Liability is imposed only if the risk of harm resulting from the act is deemed unreasonable. We need not belabor the grave danger inherent in the contest broadcast by defendant. The risk of a high-speed automobile chase is the risk of death or serious injury. Obviously, neither the entertainment afforded by the contest nor its commercial rewards can justify the creation of such a grave risk. Defendant could have accomplished its objectives of entertaining its listeners and increasing advertising revenues by adopting a contest format which would have avoided danger to the motoring public.

The judgment and the orders appealed from are affirmed.

Bearman v. University of Notre Dame

Court of Appeals of Indiana
453 N.E.2d 1196 (1983)

On October 27, 1979, Mr. and Mrs. Bearman attended a football game at the University of Notre Dame. The Bearmans left the game shortly before it ended. As they were walking through a parking lot toward their car, they observed two men who appeared to be drunk. The men were fighting, one of them fell down, and then they walked away from each other. One of the men walked past the Bearmans. A few moments later, the man fell into Mrs. Bearman from behind, knocking her to the ground. Mrs. Bearman suffered a broken leg from the fall. There were no ushers or security people in the area when the incident occurred.

Staton, Judge

Generally, the operator of a place of public entertainment owes a duty to keep the premises safe for its invitees. This duty includes a duty to provide a safe and suitable means of ingress and egress, and a duty to exercise ordinary and reasonable care to protect a patron from injury caused by third persons. However, the invitor is not the insuror of the invitee's safety. Before liability may be imposed on the invitor, it must have actual or constructive knowledge of the danger.

The University is aware that alcoholic beverages are consumed on the premises before and during football games. The University is also aware that "tailgate" parties are held in the parking areas around the stadium. Thus, even though there was no showing that the University had reason to know of the particular danger posed by the drunk who injured Mrs. Bearman, it had reason to know that some people will become intoxicated and pose a general threat to the safety of other patrons. Therefore, Notre Dame is under a duty to take reasonable precautions to protect those who attend its football games from injury caused by the acts of third persons.

WHAT CAUSED THE INJURY?

■ *The Defendant's Negligence*

The causation element requires that a link be established between the defendant's negligence and the plaintiff's injury. Assume that Tom, while driving negligently, sideswiped Susan's car. The connection between the car damage and Tom's negligent driving is direct. Thus, the causation element would be satisfied.

However, the more tenuous this link, the less likely that causation may be established. Assume that a twenty-year-old university student on a biology class field trip drank heavily during dinner, became disoriented, and wandered away from the campsite. She was injured when she fell over a cliff. The professor supervising the trip had never given the student the instructions about camping skills that were required by university rules for field trips. Even so, it would be hard to see how this omission could have contributed to her accident. Without a connection between the professor's failure to instruct and the student's injury, there would be no tort liability. *Beach v. University of Utah* (1986).

A "but for" test is often used to evaluate the causation link—that is, "but for" the defendant's negligence, the plaintiff would not have been injured. Consider the damage to Susan's car in the previous example. "But for" Tom's negligent driving, Susan's car would not have been damaged. In this situation, Tom caused the injury.

Apply the "but for" causation test to the Thought Problem, " 'But for' the Poor Equipment, Could He Have Been Saved?"

thought problem

"But for" the Poor Equipment, Could He Have Been Saved?

Jerome Ford worked on a fishing boat that had left Boston Harbor. This night, as he was ascending a short flight of stairs on deck, the boat rolled, he was thrown overboard, and he immediately disappeared into the water. No cry was heard, and no clothing was seen on the water's surface. Ford was not seen again.

When he was noticed missing, a rescue boat was lowered into the water. However, the rescue boat had been tied to the deck rather than suspended above it at the ready, and ropes had to be cut before it could be launched. Furthermore, only one oar was on board, so maneuvering the boat was quite difficult.

Assess the Ford family's claim for negligence based on the duty to keep rescue equipment accessible.

Source: Ford v. Trident Fisheries Co., *122 N.E. 389 (Massachusetts Supreme Court 1919).*

A defendant is not liable for every injury that may be tied to a negligent act. Consider the Great Chicago Fire as an example. Mrs. O'Leary negligently left a lantern where her cow could kick it over. The cow did so and her barn caught on fire. Soon, adjoining buildings were burning and before the fire was extinguished, the City of Chicago was in ruins. Apply the "but for" test. "But for" Mrs. O'Leary's negligence, a building ten blocks away would not have been destroyed. Should she be liable for that damage?

Although Mrs. O'Leary's carelessness *caused* the loss, she would not be held legally responsible for it. The law limits her responsibility to injuries that were reasonably foreseeable. Stated another way, the damage must be a "natural and probable" consequence of her negligent conduct. The law calls this causal limitation doctrine *proximate cause.* Thus, Mrs. O'Leary would not be liable for the far-away damaged buildings because the loss was not "proximately caused" by her negligence.

Who, then, could successfully bring a claim against Mrs. O'Leary—perhaps a neighbor or two, but at some point *proximate cause* will draw an arbitrary line, and her liability would end. Thus, consider causation to have two elements: the first element, illustrated by the "but for" test, requires that the negligence be tied to the injury; and the second element, *proximate cause,* is a practical limitation on the scope of liability.

Consider *Palsgraf v. Long Island R. Co.* as an example. It is a classic illustration of proximate cause. Note how difficult it is to apply the doctrine, as shown by the majority and dissenting opinions.

Palsgraf v. Long Island R. Co.

Court of Appeals of New York
162 N.E.99 (1928)

Palsgraf was standing on a platform of defendant's railroad after buying a ticket to go to Rockaway Beach. A train stopped at the station, but was bound for another place. Two men ran forward to catch it. One of the men reached the platform of the car without mishap, though the train was already moving. The other man, carrying a package, jumped aboard the car but seemed unsteady, as if about to fall. A guard on the car, who had held the door open, reached forward to help him in, and another guard on the platform pushed him from behind. In this act, the package was dislodged and fell upon the rails. It was a small package, about fifteen inches long, and was covered with newspaper. In fact it contained fireworks, but there was nothing in its appearance to give notice of its contents. The fireworks exploded when they fell. The shock of the explosion threw down some scales used for weighing at the other end of the platform many feet away. The scales struck the plaintiff, Palsgraf, causing injuries for which she sued.

Cardozo, Chief Justice

The conduct of the defendant's guard, if a wrong in its relation to the holder of the package, was not a wrong in its relation to the plaintiff, standing far away. Nothing in the situation gave notice that the falling package had in it the potency of peril to persons thus removed. Negligence is not actionable unless it involves the invasion of a legally protected interest, the violation of a right. "Proof of negligence in the air, so to speak, will not do." If no hazard was apparent to the eye of ordinary vigilance, an act innocent and harmless, at least to outward seeming, with reference to her, did not take to itself the quality of a tort because it happened to be a wrong, though apparently not one involving the risk of bodily insecurity, with reference to some one else. "In every instance, before negligence can be predicated of a given act, back of the act must be sought and found a duty to the individual complaining, the observance of which would have averted or avoided the injury." "The ideas of negligence and duty are strictly correlative."

One who jostles one's neighbor in a crowd does not invade the rights of others standing at the outer fringe when the unintended contact casts a bomb upon the ground. The wrongdoer as to them is the man who carries the bomb, not the one who explodes it without suspicion of the danger. Life will have to be made over, and human nature transformed, before prevision so extravagant can be accepted as the norm of conduct, the customary standard to which behavior must conform.

The risk reasonably to be perceived defines the duty to be obeyed, and risk imports relation; it is risk to another or to others within the range of apprehension. Here, by concession, there was nothing in the situation to suggest to the most cautious mind that the parcel wrapped in newspaper would spread wreckage through the station. If the guard had thrown it down knowingly and willfully, he would not have threatened the plaintiff's safety, so far as appearances could warn him. His conduct would not have involved, even then, an unreasonable probability of invasion of her bodily security. Liability can be no greater where the act is inadvertent.

Negligence is not a tort unless it results in the commission of a wrong, and the commission of a wrong imports the violation of a right.

Andrews, Justice (dissenting)

Negligence may be defined roughly as an act or omission which unreasonably does or may affect the rights of others, or which unreasonably fails to protect one's self from the dangers resulting from such acts.

There must be both the act or the omission, and the right. It is the act itself, not the intent of the actor, that is important.

Where there is the unreasonable act, and some right that may be affected there is negligence whether damage does or does not result. That is immaterial. Should we drive down Broadway at a reckless speed, we are negligent whether we strike an approaching car or miss it by an inch. The act itself is wrongful. It is a wrong not only to those who happen to be within the radius of danger, but to all who might have been there—a wrong to the public at large.

Due care is a duty imposed on each one of us to protect society from unnecessary danger, not to protect A, B, or C alone.

Negligence does involve a relationship between man and his fellows, but not merely a relationship between man and those whom he might reasonably expect his act would injure; rather, a relationship between him and those whom he does in fact injure. If his act has a tendency to harm some one, it harms him a mile away as surely as it does those on the scene.

The proposition is this: Everyone owes to the world at large the duty of refraining from those acts that may unreasonably threaten the safety of others. Such an act occurs. Not only is he wronged to whom harm might reasonably be expected to result, but he also who is in fact injured, even if he be outside what would generally be thought the danger zone.

As we have said, we cannot trace the effect of an act to the end, if end there is. Again, however, we may trace it part of the way. An overturned lantern may burn all Chicago. We may follow the fire from the shed to the last building. We rightly say the fire started by the lantern caused its destruction.

A cause, but not the proximate cause. What we do mean by the word "proximate" is that, because of convenience, of public policy, of a rough sense of justice, the law arbitrarily declines to trace a series of events beyond a certain point. This is not logic. It is practical politics.

We look back to the catastrophe, the fire kindled by the spark, or the explosion. We trace the consequences, not indefinitely, but to a certain point. And to aid us in fixing that point we ask what might ordinarily be expected to follow the fire or the explosion.

This last suggestion is the factor which must determine the case before us. The act upon which defendant's liability rests is knocking an apparently harmless package onto the platform. The act was negligent. For its proximate consequences the defendant is liable. If its contents were broken, to the owner; if it fell upon and crushed a passenger's foot, then to him; if it exploded and injured one in the immediate vicinity, to him also as to A in the illustration. Mrs. Palsgraf was standing some distance away. How far cannot be told from the record—apparently 25 to 30 feet, perhaps less. Except for the explosion, she would not have been injured. We are told by the appellant in his brief, "It cannot be denied that the explosion was the direct cause of the plaintiff's injuries." So it was a substantial factor in producing the result—there was here a natural and continuous sequence—direct connection. The only intervening cause was that, instead of blowing her to the ground, the concussion smashed the weighing machine which in turn fell upon her. There was no remoteness in time, little in space. And surely, given such an explosion as here, it needed no great foresight to predict that the natural result would be to injure one on the platform at no greater distance from its scene than was the plaintiff. Just how no one might be able to predict. Whether by flying fragments, by broken glass, by wreckage of machines or structures no one could say. But injury in some form was most probable.

Under these circumstances I cannot say as a matter of law that the plaintiff's injuries were not the proximate result of the negligence.

■ *What If the Injured Person Was Negligent, Too?*

As noted in the Thought Problem, "Limiting Tort Law Risk," presented earlier in this chapter, Haring's negligence canceled the liability of the railroad even though it, too, was negligent. This rule is called the doctrine of contributory negligence. It is an *all-or-nothing* proposition—that is, if the plaintiff (Haring) was even slightly negligent, thereby contributing to his own injury, then no recovery is permitted.

Contributory negligence first appeared in an early nineteenth-century English case, *Butterfield v. Forrester* (1809). In this case, a pole had been negligently left in a roadway. A swiftly moving horseback rider struck the pole and was injured. However, the pole was visible from a hundred yards away and it could have been avoided. In denying recovery to the rider, the court noted that plaintiffs, too, must act reasonably and exercise care to protect themselves. Failure to do so precludes holding someone else liable for their injuries.

Contributory negligence was widely cited in the United States in the nineteenth and most of the twentieth centuries. It protected industry from damage awards arising from their negligent activity, and thus fit well with legal trends in the nineteenth century. But even so, courts were concerned about the harshness of denying any recovery to even slightly negligent plaintiffs. In the late nineteenth century, a few states (e.g., Illinois and Kansas) rejected the doctrine but then re-embraced it a few years later. Thereafter, exceptions were created that mitigated the effect of the doctrine.

By the early 1970s, the legal climate had changed. As noted earlier, the tort law risk was heightened for defendants (primarily businesses) and lowered for injured parties. The doctrine of contributory negligence changed to fit this trend, too. Rather than *all-or-nothing* approach, the law provided that negligent plaintiffs should have their damage awards reduced. This new rule is known as comparative negligence, and it has replaced contributory negligence in virtually every state.

Comparative negligence grants a proportional recovery to the injured party based on a comparison of the plaintiff's negligence with that of the defendant. Thus, if Haring had been forty percent negligent because of failure to take precautions at a train crossing, and the railroad had been sixty percent negligent for failing to remove sight obstructions, damages of $100,000 would be reduced by forty percent. The railroad would be responsible only for the amount that its negligence caused Haring's injury, or $60,000.

No-Fault Liability: Strict Liability in Tort

Not all tort liability risk arises from fault. An employer may be liable for the torts of its employees even though the employer acted neither negligently nor with malicious motives. This is the doctrine of vicarious liability, and it will be discussed in Chapter 12. In addition, a manufacturer of a defective product may be held liable even though nothing the manufacturer did may be faulted. Product liability will be discussed in Chapter 14. Furthermore, there are statutory schemes that impose liability for workplace injuries without a finding of fault. These statutes are called Workers' Compensation Acts, and they will be discussed in Chapter 17.

In common law, a similar rule is known as strict liability. Under this principle, tort liability will be found even though the defendant may have been morally blameless and acted as a reasonable person. Strict liability surfaces when activities may be classified as either inappropriate for the location or abnormally dangerous.

Strict liability was first applied in the English case *Rylands v. Fletcher* (1866). In this case, a coal mine flooded when an adjoining landowner's water reservoir, which was inappropriate for the location, on adjoining land burst. No negligence was established, but liability was found because of the abnormality of creating a reservoir on that land. By choosing to use his property in that unusual way, the landowner assumed the risk that damage may occur to a neighbor.

The Rylands approach was not accepted in the United States during the nineteenth century. Imposing such a burden on high-risk, hazardous enterprises was thought to impede industrial growth that was vital to the country. Instead, the risk of loss was placed on those individuals in the vicinity of that activity, unless, of course, they could establish that their loss was caused by a business's negligence.

Today, by way of contrast, strict liability is widely applicable. It makes an injured party's claim for compensation easier to establish.

Neither negligence nor a wrongful intent need to be found. The focus is on the defendant's conduct and whether it is *out of place* or abnormally dangerous. If so, the defendant is liable. A couple examples of strict liability follow:

1. *Out-of-place activities.* A person who does something that is unsuited for the location in which it is done is strictly liable for injuries that arise from it. Compare the following:

- ABC, Inc., was excavating a lot in a city's business district. It used a small amount of explosives to do so. Even though ABC, Inc., took every possible precaution, flying debris damaged an adjacent building.

- XYZ, Inc., used a small amount of explosives while building a road in a remote, isolated area. Even though XYZ, Inc., was careful, flying debris destroyed the tent of a nearby camper.

ABC, Inc., would be strictly liable for the damaged building, while the camper would need to show that XYZ, Inc., had been negligent. The legal reasoning focuses on the different locations where the blasting occurred. The question is whether it is *out-of-place* for a small amount of dynamite to be used in a crowded city or in a secluded area. Strict liability does not prohibit ABC, Inc., from using explosives in the city—it simply imposes higher risk on the company for doing so.

Another example of strict liability follows:

2. *Abnormally dangerous activities.* Strict liability may also apply to activities that are ultra-hazardous. In the example above, assume that XYZ, Inc., used a huge amount of explosives to clear land for a roadbed. This would be such a dangerous scenario, that even though it will occur in an isolated area, XYZ, Inc., would face strict liability. The Managerial Perspective, "Explosion in Alaska," further illustrates this point. In addition, compare the following:

- Mary owned a large, vicious, and ill-tempered dog. The beast escaped from her yard and bit a neighbor.

- Jane owned a friendly little puppy that slipped from its collar and, inexplicably, bit a neighbor.

Mary would face strict liability for her neighbor's injury while Jane would not. Keeping a vicious dog puts neighbors in peril and creates a high degree of risk that someone will be attacked. Although Mary was not forbidden to own such a beast, she would be strictly liable for damages that occur as a result.

As a third example of strict liability, consider *T&E Industries v. Safety Light Corporation* (1991). In 1974, T&E Industries purchased land that it thereafter learned was contaminated with radioactive waste that had been dumped on the premises by a previous owner. The court upheld T&E Industries' claim against the former owners based on strict liability. Dumping radioactive waste was an abnormally dangerous activity.

"Explosion in Alaska" emphasizes that not only is the storage of a large amount of explosives ultra-hazardous, but its location, given the amount of explosives, would be *out-of-place.*

managerial perspective

Explosion in Alaska

Yukon Equipment, Inc., kept 80,000 pounds of explosives in a storage magazine on a 1,870-acre tract of land in the suburbs north of Anchorage, Alaska. The nearest building was 3,820 feet away. In the past, the magazine had been broken into, and explosives had been taken. In the early morning hours of December 7, 1973, thieves again broke in, but this time they set a charge to conceal their crime. The magazine exploded with such force that buildings were damaged within a two-mile radius, and the ground concussion from thirty miles away measured 1.8 on the Richter Scale.

Strict liability was held to apply. The amount of explosives was found to have created a great risk of major harm that even reasonable care could not eliminate it. Furthermore, storage of high explosives in such quantity is not commonly done. Finally, the location was not appropriate given both the large quantity of explosives and the damage that occurred at such a great distance. These factors showed that Yukon Equipment, Inc., was engaged in ultra-hazardous activity, and thus they should be strictly liable. Furthermore, even though the explosion was set by thieves, Yukon Equipment, Inc., would still be liable. Setting charges to hide wrongdoing is not extraordinary criminal behavior. The risk-shifting policy of strict liability was too strong to be overcome by criminal intervention.

Justice Matthews wrote: "As between those who have created the risk for the benefit of their own enterprise and those whose only connection with the enterprise is to have suffered damage because of it, the law places the risk of loss on the former. When the risk created causes damage in fact, insistence that the precise details of the intervening cause be foreseeable would subvert the purpose of that rule of law."

Source: Yukon Equipment, Inc. v. Fireman's Fund Insurance Co., *585 P.2d 1206 (Alaska Supreme Court 1978).*

Summary

Tort law allocates risk between those who cause harm and those who are injured. This allocation is influenced by a number of policies: compensation of victims; the desire to influence behavior; and concerns about how any liability affects economic development. Over the years, the risk has shifted between businesses and individuals. This chapter compared the late nineteenth and twentieth centuries to illustrate this shift.

To account for the effects of liability risks, recall one of the themes discussed in Chapter 1: the law is affected by historical and social forces. These forces were the source of the change in tort law between the centuries. Consider, too, what is happening today with the increase in international trade and the competitive pressures entailed. Tort law is undergoing yet another shift that current issues are influencing.

Most tort law doctrines deal with fault. In fact, a person who commits a tort is often called a *wrongdoer*. Both intentional torts and torts of negligence reflect this interpretation. In an intentional tort, the key is with the motives behind the action. Negligence requires that a duty of reasonable care be breached. Intentional torts and torts of negligence focus on a defendant's unacceptable conduct. However, tort law creates liability risk without a question of fault. Strict liability shifts liability risk for abnormally dangerous activities. The risks for undertaking such activities include liability for injuries even if all conceivable precautions may have been taken to prevent them.

1. Define the following terms:
   a. Comparative negligence
   b. Intentional tort
   c. Negligence
   d. Strict liability

2. ABC, Inc., agreed to sell 10,000 custom-made transistors to XYZ, Inc. These transistors are key components in XYZ, Inc.'s high-tech products. ABC, Inc., knew this, but it failed to deliver what it had promised. As a result, XYZ, Inc., went bankrupt. Does XYZ, Inc., have a tort claim against ABC, Inc.?

3. What are the purposes of tort law?

4. Mary Jenkins was seriously injured by ABC, Inc.'s tort. She incurred medical bills of $30,000 and lost six months from work. Her annual salary is $40,000. Furthermore, she has difficulty doing everyday tasks or even sleeping some nights because of the discomfort. Which, if any, of these factors would influence her award of damages?

5. Discuss the relationship between tort law and insurance.

6. If the *Mary Jenkins v. ABC, Inc.,* case had been brought in a state such as Illinois that has instituted *tort reform* measures, how may an award of damages be changed?

7. Sandra brought suit against a grocery store, alleging that the manager of the store included a dead rat as a practical joke with the groceries that were delivered to her home. When the groceries arrived, the delivery person stated, "The store manager said you had better open the package while I am here." When Sandra opened the package, she saw the dead rat, whereupon she fainted, fell to the floor, and was injured.

What type of tort should Sandra allege took place? Would your answer change if a rat from a grocery store's storage area had simply crawled into the package without the knowledge of anyone in the store? Could it be said that a tort still exists?

8. A concert by a popular group has just been announced. Their concerts always sell out so a long line formed at the ticket window on the first day that tickets were sold. Bill decided to cut in line near the front. When he did so, he was pushed around by others in the line and beaten. May Bill pursue a tort claim against the attackers for his injuries?

9. Jack was enraged when the expensive compact disc player he purchased did not reproduce the music at the high-quality level, as advertised. He picketed the manufacturer's offices that were located on a busy street. Leaflets that he handed out stated: "XYZ, Inc., makes inferior compact disc players, and they lie about it! They are unethical in their relationships with their customers to the point of being criminal!" Does Jack face a tort liability risk?

10. Mary is convinced that her neighbor, Tom, has been sneaking into her yard and stealing her prize tomatoes from the vines. She then invites Tom into her garage on the pretext of showing him a new lawn mower. When Tom arrives, she shut all the doors and locked them so he could not leave. Then, she said: "You're not leaving here until you confess, you thief!" Does Mary risk tort liability?

11. What are the major differences between a tort of negligence and an intentional tort? Give an example of each.

12. Tom owned a fast-food restaurant business. The restaurant sold sandwiches. It stocked a table with ketchup, mustard, and relish for customers to use. One afternoon while filling the mustard container, Tom accidentally spilled mustard on the floor. Before he had a chance to clean it up, a customer entered the restaurant. Tom promptly waited on the customer but forgot about the mustard on the floor. A few hours later, another customer entered the restaurant, slipped on the mustard, fell, and broke a leg. Does the injured customer have a tort claim against Tom? Explain.

13. The ABC Corporation owned a delivery business. One of its trucks was parked negligently on a steep incline in neutral gear with the parking brake only partly engaged. That evening, the truck rolled downhill and struck a car causing the car to hit a telephone pole. The pole fell to the ground and demolished a fire hydrant. Water began to spray. Before the hydrant could be turned off, Smith's basement was flooded. Does Smith have a tort claim against the ABC Corporation?

14. Mary Jones was jogging. She was wearing headphones with the volume nearly on maximum and was concentrating more on the music than on where she was running. As a result, she entered a busy intersection against the light and a clearly noted "Do Not Walk" sign. She was struck by a speeding car that was travelling nearly fifteen miles per hour over the speed limit. If Mary brings a tort action against the driver of the car, what defense could be used? First, assume the case arose in a state that retained its nineteenth-century tort law doctrines, and note the arguments. Thereafter, assume the state has adopted doctrines in line with a majority of other states today, and note the arguments anew.

15. Susan often grills out during the summer, and she spends considerable money on charcoal lighter fluid. This year, she decided to buy a 200-gallon drum of the fluid. It would save her money, and she may keep it in her backyard. Mary lives in a wooded, suburban neighborhood. Does Mary have a tort liability risk even though she takes numerous precautions with the lighter fluid?

16. Assess current developments in the American economy. Assume that they presage long-term changes. Then, review some of the tort law doctrines in this chapter, and suggest possible modifications that may arise. Note the materials in Chapter 1. One theme in the legal environment is that it reflects social and historical movements.

Notes

[1]Lawrence Friedman, *A History of American Law* (New York: Simon & Schuster, 1974), p. 409.

[2]*Blyth v. Birmingham Waterworks Co.*, 156 Eng. Rep. 1047 (1856).

5

Part

THE LEGAL ENVIRONMENT OF BUSINESS ORGANIZATIONS AND THEIR OPERATION

Chapter

11

LEGAL ASPECTS OF BUSINESS ORGANIZATIONAL FORMS

In this chapter, the legal structures of business organizations will be examined. These forms are the sole proprietorship, the partnership, the limited partnership, the corporation, and the limited liability company. Each structural form facilitates certain combinations of labor, capital, and management. Together they provide the legal framework in which a business operates.

More than 15 million sole proprietorships, over 3.8 million corporations, and more than 1.5 million partnerships exist in the United States today with far fewer limited partnerships (about 270,000) and limited liability companies (approximately 50,000). However, the number of limited liability companies is likely to increase in the near future.

Legal organizational forms fit all types of businesses from small one-person operations to multinational behemoths. They are suitable for manufacturers, service providers, or any combination of the two. In addition, the same business may be operated as a corporation by one group of investors, while another group may have selected the partnership form as a mode of operation. The law does not dictate that a certain type of business must use one particular form.

What the law does is provide an array of *benefits* associated with each form. Which form is best depends on how one compares or views those benefits. Comparison is subjective, however, based on the collective values of those making the choice. Thus, one group of executives may find a partnership to be the best structure for their consulting firm because a right to share profits is very important to them. Another group of executives may have different goals in mind—such as limited liability—that make the corporate form their preference for such a business. Neither group would be *wrong*, even though they may find the other group's choice of organizational form questionable.

As an example, consider the following:

1. Mozart and Salieri intend to pool their resources to begin a computer software company. Each wants to have the legal right to share in the profits and to exercise direct management and control of the software company's operations.

2. Hemingway and Fitzgerald intend to invest in a cattle ranch. Neither knows anything about ranching, but they believe, in the long run, that the venture will provide a healthy return on their money. Thus, they plan to hire an expert to manage the ranch. Furthermore, since ranching is a rather volatile business, neither Hemingway nor Fitzgerald wants to risk more than the initial investment.

Note the differences between the goals of the two groups. The investors in the first scenario want to manage their investment with a legal right to share in profits. The second pair of investors seek protection of their assets beyond what was invested and intend to disassociate themselves from day-to-day concerns. The law of business organizational forms helps each pair meet their goals by providing a number of choices regarding how to structure their businesses. This chapter outlines the basic features of each choice. When you have finished reading this chapter, choose the form that best serves the needs of the investor groups.

Evaluating Organizational Forms on the Basis of Business Interests

All businesses have common features—they need capital, they have assets and liabilities, and they try to satisfy their customers. Someone must be in charge of day-to-day activities; there is an owner with the power to take charge in making final decisions for a business.

These general features exist irrespective of the structure of the business. However, they may have different legal implications depending on the form under which the business operates. For example, although having investors is a common feature, their legal status differs in a partnership (investor as partner), a corporation (investor as shareholder), or a limited partnership (investor as limited partner). One difference is that investing as a partner creates a greater risk of personal liability for business debts than investing as a corporate shareholder or limited partner. Consequently, Firm A operating as a partnership may have more difficulty convincing Jane Jenkins to invest than would Firm B (a corporation), if Jenkins is adverse to taking such a risk.

The focus on legal forms of business organizations provided in this textbook is on the comparative benefits the forms provide. For example, Jane Jenkins would only be interested in the partnership or corporate forms to the extent that they would affect her aversion to personal liability. These benefits will be organized under four principles—limited liability, profit share, management rights, and control. Table 11.1 outlines how the principles of business interest compare among legal organizational forms.

LIMITED LIABILITY PRINCIPLE

Limited liability means that investors are not financially responsible for their businesses' debts. In other words, their "liability is limited" to the amount they have invested. This principle provides that business creditors may only attach a company's assets and recover under its insurance policy. Once these assets are depleted, no further sources may be used to satisfy an unpaid balance. In absence of a limited liability protection, these creditors would have been able to seek additional money from the personal assets of the company's investors.

For example, assume that Jack Barnes invested $10,000 in a company whose structure provided him with limited liability. A

■ **TABLE 11.1** Organizational
Forms and Business Interests

	BUSINESS INTEREST			
Business Form	**Limited Liability**	**Profit Share**	**Management Rights**	**Control**
Sole proprietorship	No	Yes	Yes	Yes
Partnership	No	Yes	Yes	Yes
Limited partnership	Only for limited partners	Yes	Only for general partners	Only for general partners
Corporation	Yes	No	No	No
Limited liability company	Yes	Yes	Yes	Yes

combination of falling sales and tort suit judgments depleted the company's reserves and far-outstripped its insurance coverage. Even after the company was liquidated, the creditors were still not fully paid. However, since investors such as Jack Barnes have limited liability, they are immune to those creditors' claims. All Barnes lost was his investment of $10,000—that was his *limited liability*.

Consider that the limited liability principle lessens an investor's risk. Jack Barnes knew that the most he could lose was $10,000. Thus, he would more likely be willing to invest in a risky enterprise because he knew at the outset that the worst-case financial scenario may be the loss of his $10,000.

As noted in Table 11.1, however, not all organizational forms provide their investors with limited liability. The International Perspective, "Limited Liability Overseas," provides a list of countries and the legal organizations that provide limited liability for investors.

INTERNATIONAL PERSPECTIVE
Limited Liability Overseas

A number of overseas countries have legal organizational structures that also provide limited liability for investors. The following list is a sample:

Denmark: the Aktieselskaber (ApS)

France: the Société Anonyme (SA)

Germany: the Aktiengesellschaft (AG)

Greece: the Anonymos Eteria (AE)

Italy: the Società per Azioni (SpA)

Spain: the Sociedad Anonima (SA)

PROFIT SHARE PRINCIPLE

The profit share principle concerns an investor's right to a share of the firm's profits. Merely knowing that the XYZ Company had an excellent year and that after all expenses a significant surplus remains, tells nothing about how much—if anything—the investor will receive. It is possible that the investor will receive nothing; and to make matters worse, the market value of the investment may be less than it was the year before.

An organizational structure that does not provide a profit share right separates profitability from the return on an investment—which was the case with XYZ Company. Usually, a highly profitable XYZ Company will mean that its investors will do well, too, but no legal right guarantees it. The guarantee is only effective if XYZ Company has a legal structure that provides a profit share right to its investors (see Table 11.1).

MANAGEMENT RIGHTS PRINCIPLE

Some investors demand *hands on* decision making in their firms. By doing this, their skills may be used to help make the firm a success and, of course, to increase the value of their investments simultaneously. For these investors, a right to participate in management is important. This is the *management rights principle*.

Note the Mozart and Salieri example at the beginning of this chapter. Management rights will be an important factor in their selection of an organizational form. Business structures that do not provide investors with management rights separate the capital providers from the firm's operation. These investors are passive, relying on someone else to make decisions. Hemingway and Fitzgerald, also portrayed at the onset of this chapter, fit this model. Neither has any expertise in managing a cattle ranching operation. They merely want their investment money to work for them.

CONTROL PRINCIPLE

The control principle reflects whether or not an investor has input in the strategic decisions of a company. Unlike the management rights principle, the control principle does not envision the investor as a hands on, day-to-day player. Instead, the situation is more like *investor as boss*.

Consider this distinction even further by using ABC Company as an example. Investor Jane Jenkins exercises her management rights by hiring employees, selecting advertising outlets, and pricing the products that ABC Company sells. In all of these tasks, Jenkins is carrying out ABC Company's policies. This exemplifies the management rights principle. By way of contrast, consider that ABC Company's policies are set by those in control. If the investors in the company also have a control right, Jane Jenkins—along with other investors—will set company policy. This is the *control principle*.

Note the Thought Problem, "Choosing an Organizational Form," while studying Table 11.1. Business organizational forms are tools that may be used to further the goals of limited liability, profit share, management rights, and control. They are best considered in relation to one another.

thought problem

Choosing an Organizational Form

Bill Jones, Mary Thomas, and Charles Smith are considering organizational forms for their software and network development company. Jones is wealthy and intends to invest a substantial sum in the business. Although he wants a say in the direction that the firm takes, he has no time for day-to-day management details. Thomas plans to invest her retirement savings in the business. She believes that huge profits may be made. As a result, Thomas hopes to be able to retire early and live comfortably, thereafter. Smith, by contrast, has very little money to invest. However, the product ideas belong to him. Without his involvement, it is unlikely that the business could survive.

Which of the organizational forms meet the needs of Jones, Thomas, and Smith? Furthermore, once you have finished this chapter, review this Thought Problem and refine your answer.

The Sole Proprietorship

The *sole proprietorship*, the least complex form of business organization, consists of one owner—the proprietor. No legal formalities precede its creation. A sole proprietorship may be any size, although most are small businesses. In fact, the sole proprietorship does not need to have employees. Consequently, the owner could be the only one involved in the business. Of course, most sole proprietors take on employees, and once this occurs, the principles discussed in Chapter 12 regulate the sole proprietor–employee relationship.

As an example, assume that Mary Johnson's environmental protection company was a sole proprietorship. As owner, Mary will have control of the business and will make all of the management decisions. In order to start the company, she secured a loan from a local bank using her home as collateral. She selected the firm's equipment and worked at its offices throughout the day. Although her conduct is regulated by certain bodies of law (e.g., contract law in her dealings with clients, licensing requirements of the state and local governments, and so on), she was not required to follow any legal procedure for becoming a sole proprietor. If the environmental protection company is successful, Mary Johnson will reap the benefits. If it fails, then she will be responsible for its losses. There is no legal distinction between Johnson and her business.

As a result, no separate body of *sole proprietorship law* exists. Since there is only one owner, no special legal rules are needed to regulate co-owner relations. Furthermore, since the sole proprietor (without employees) is also the manager of the business, no legal rules are necessary to govern the separation between the control and management functions of the business. The sole proprietor and the business have a single identity. Therefore, the *law of sole proprietorship* encompasses the laws of contracts, torts, and agency, as well as government regulations applicable to any business.

But, what if more than one person owns the same business? Refer, again, to the intentions of Mozart and Salieri or Hemingway and Fitzgerald. A number of questions arise with them that were of no concern to Mary Johnson. For example:

- Which of the co-owners will make management decisions?
- Who will exercise control?
- How will profit sharing be determined (if profit sharing exists at all)?
- Will either person be liable for unpaid claims against the business?

The forms of business organization—partnership, limited partnership, corporation, and limited liability company provide a framework by which such questions may be answered.

The Partnership

Consider two sole proprietors who decide informally to merge their businesses. Each would retain three attributes of a sole proprietor—management rights, profit share, and personal liability for business losses. But, problems suddenly appear. No longer would either sole proprietor have unfettered control of the business. Furthermore, the management rights, profits, and liability risks will need to be shared. The legal aspects of this sharing may be called the *law of partnership*. It is a business organizational form with its own body of law.

The use of a partnership organization for a profit-seeking business may be traced to arrangements among ancient Babylonian sharecroppers. The arrangement also was used in ancient Greece and Rome, where it was called a *societas*. A more direct ancestor of current American partnership law is the Law Merchant, a body of informal rules that derived from business practices during the Middle Ages. The Law Merchant was international in scope and was initially developed apart from the formal legal rules created by any country's government. In the sixteenth and seventeenth centuries, England merged the Law Merchant into its common law. Thereafter, it (and the law of partnership) grew with the common law.

In both England and the United States, the nineteenth century was a time of significant use of the partnership form. This reflected heightened business activity in both countries as well as the difficulty in securing corporate charters. By the end of that century, confusion among common law principles (judicial opinions would disagree) led to a movement to codify the law of partnership. The English Parliament enacted the Partnership Act of 1890. In the United States, statutes were passed by individual states following a model called the Uniform Partnership Act which was drafted in 1914. This act and its successor, the Revised Uniform Partnership Act, are the current sources of American partnership law.

CREATION OF A PARTNERSHIP

A partnership is defined as an association of two or more persons as co-owners, a business for profit. If a business organization fits within this definition, it will be considered a partnership. No formal action is needed to create the form. Consider Mary Johnson and her environmental protection business from the perspective of this definition.

First, according to the definition, another person will need to be involved in the business. That person, Ted Short, is a product designer and, thus, Johnson and Short will combine their talents in environmental protection and product design. Of course, this arrangement alone will not make them partners. A number of other legal arrangements (employer–employee, for example) could yield the same result. Consequently, something more will be needed for a partnership to develop between Johnson and Short.

A second part of the definition requires that Johnson and Short be co-owners of the business. Attributes of co-ownership may be gleaned from the operation of the firm which include investment of capital, sharing of management, sharing of profits, and responsibility for any business losses. If Johnson and Short's business exhibits these attributes, each will be considered co-owners and, thus, partners in the eyes of the law.

This is all Johnson and Short will need to do. No formal legal procedures are required to form a partnership. Nothing needs to be filed with a state office. No documents or contracts need to be signed by the partners. Having one's business fit within the definition is sufficient. In fact, the law of partnership acts as a stopgap when people operate a business as co-owners without having considered the law of organizational forms. The *Zajac v. Harris* case illustrates such a situation.

Partnership contracts that regulate certain aspects of partner relations are not prohibited. In fact, the astute partner may seek to customize the partnership arrangement. As noted in Chapters 8 and 9, contracts are a means by which parties may legally enforce their expectations. Although people think of contracts as a necessity when buying or selling things, they are also an important component of business organization. For example, Mary Johnson may want a larger share of the profits than Ted Short may want. Or perhaps, Short would like to have a greater say in the firm's management. In absence of a partnership agreement, partnership law provides that each will have equal legal rights to profits, management, and control. Consequently, Johnson and Short may want to draft a partnership agreement that specifies their particular needs at the time they begin doing business together.

The *Zajac v. Harris* case illustrates a number of the points previously mentioned. First, this case is an example of how courts determine whether or not a certain business arrangement is a partnership. Note the confusing facts of this case. Real-life business arrangements do not always follow textbook-perfect models. Second, reflect on the importance of an agreement being negotiated at the outset of a business relationship. If Zajac and Harris intended to be partners, a written partnership agreement could have clarified their relationship. Similarly, an employer–employee relationship could also have been formalized. In its absence, their dispute led to litigation.

Zajac v. Harris   Supreme Court of Arkansas *410 S.W.2d 593 (1967)*

George Harris brought this suit to compel Carl A. Zajac to account for the profits and assets of a partnership that he asserted existed between the parties for two years. Zajac denied that a partnership existed, insisting that Harris was merely an employee in a business owned by Zajac.

Smith, Justice

At first blush the testimony appears to be in such hopeless conflict that the controlling issue at the trial must have been one of credibility. Upon reflection, however, we arrive at a somewhat different view of the case. The business association that is known in the law as a partnership is not one that can be defined with precision. To the contrary, a partnership is a contractual relationship that may vary, in form and substance, in an almost infinite variety of ways.

These two laymen went into business together without consulting a lawyer or attempting to put their agreement into writing. It is apparent from the testimony that neither man had any conscious or deliberate intention of entering into a particular legal relationship. When the testimony is viewed in this light the conflicts are not so sharp as they might otherwise appear to be. Our problem is that of determining from the record as a whole whether the association they agreed upon was a partnership or an employer–employee relationship.

Before the two men became business associates Zajac had conducted a combination garage-and-salvage company, filling station, and grocery store. In the salvage operation now in controversy the parties bought wrecked automobiles from insurance companies and either rebuilt them for resale or cannibalized them by reusing or reselling the parts. Harris testified that he and Zajac agreed to go into business together, splitting the profits equally—except that Harris was to receive one fourth of the proceeds from any parts sold by him. Harris borrowed $9,000 from a bank, upon the security of property that he owned, and placed the money in a bank account that he used in buying cars for the firm. The profits were divided from time to time as the cars were resold, so that Harris's capital was used and reused. He identified checks totaling more than $73,000 that he signed in making purchases for the business.

Zajac, by contrast, took the position that Harris was merely an employee working for a commission of one half the profits realized from cars that Harris himself had bought. Zajac denied that he had ever agreed that Harris would spend his own money in buying cars. "I told him, when you go out there, when you bid on a car, make a note that I will pay for it." We have no doubt, however, that Harris did use his own money in the venture and Zajac knew that such expenditures were being made.

Zajac and his wife and their accountant had charge of the books and records. No partnership income tax return was ever filed. Harris was ostensibly treated as an employee, in that federal withholding and Social Security taxes were paid upon his share of the profits. The firm also carried workmen's compensation insurance for Harris's protection. In our opinion, however, any inference that might ordinarily be drawn from these bookkeeping entries are effectively rebutted by the undisputed fact that Harris, apart from being able to sign his name, was unable to read or write. There is no reason to believe that he appreciated the significance of the accounting practices now relied upon by Zajac. They were unilateral.

Zajac paid Harris one half of the profits derived from cars that Zajac bought with his own money and sold by his efforts. Zajac has insisted from the outset that Harris was working upon a commission basis, but that view cannot be reconciled with Harris's admitted right to receive his share of the profits derived from business conducted by Zajac alone.

Harris invested, as we have seen, substantial sums of his own money in the acquisition of cars for the firm. Zajac concedes that Harris was entitled to a share of the profits from transactions that Harris certainly did not handle on a commission basis. When the testimony is reconciled, as we have attempted to do, it does not appear that the judge in the court below was wrong in deciding that a partnership existed.

LIMITED LIABILITY PRINCIPLE

Partners do not have limited liability. Thus, if unpaid claims remain after all business assets have been spent and the firm's insurance coverage has been exhausted, the partners will be required to use their own property to satisfy the claims. Personal liability has recently become a substantial problem for large accounting partnerships.

More than four thousand lawsuits are filed each year against accounting firms. This is more than twice the number of lawsuits filed just ten years ago. Furthermore, the amount of damages has been increasing, too. In 1992, an Arizona jury awarded a claimant $338 million against Price Waterhouse. Insurance covered only about one third of that amount. Although the verdict was reversed, its magnitude risked driving the firm—and its partners—into bankruptcy. Consequently, the Big Six accounting firms spend approximately nineteen percent of their audit and accounting revenues protecting their practices.

Because of large damage awards and increased risks to personal assets, large professional partnerships have lobbied state legislatures for changes in the law so that a partner's personal assets will be protected. An impetus for this activity was the demise of a former Big Eight accounting firm, Laventhol & Horwath. Some former partners in the bankrupt accounting partnership were assessed $400,000 each to pay the firm's creditors. Approximately a dozen former partners filed bankruptcy hoping to shelter some of their personal assets from creditor claims. The Managerial Perspective, "A New Twist to Partnership Liability," illustrates this change in the law.

managerial perspective

A New Twist to Partnership Liability

The jury award of $338 million against Price Waterhouse illustrated a dangerous pitfall for large partnerships. Price Waterhouse has approximately one thousand partners located in offices throughout the world. A claim arising from the activities of a few accountants in one office could make all partners in the firm personally liable. In the Price Waterhouse example, an audit conducted by its Arizona office led to the lawsuit.

Twenty states (including New York) have enacted legislation to limit partners' liability exposure for malpractice claims committed by other partners in the firm. Only the partners involved in the wrongdoing would be personally liable. However, the partners' personal liability arising from other claims (e.g., breach of contract) were not affected by this legislation.

Firms that choose to operate with this malpractice liability protection are called *limited liability partnerships*. All of the Big Six accounting firms have done so.

Business executives must consider the liability disadvantage when evaluating the partnership organizational form. Although insurance and company assets may act as buffers, the ultimate sources for unpaid claims are the partners. However, compensating advantages exist that make the partnership an attractive organizational form for some executives.

PROFIT SHARE PRINCIPLE

Partners have a legal right to a share of business profits. Assume, at the end of the year, that the Jones, Thomas, and Smith partnership earned $150,000 in profits. (Refer to the Thought Problem, "Choosing an Organizational Form," earlier in this chapter.) Each partner would receive an equal share in the amount of $50,000. However, is this fair? Charles Smith would question this. His ideas and talents led to the profits. Perhaps, he should receive a greater share. If the others agreed, a contract could be drafted to reflect that amount. Smith would prefer two-thirds ($100,000) for himself and one-sixth ($25,000) each for Jones and Thomas. Of course, Jones and Thomas may have different opinions. Nonetheless, private agreement allows partners to customize their profit share.

Becoming a partner in a large professional partnership has been synonymous with earning a large income. It is not uncommon for such partners to earn annual salaries with a six figure income. Although personal liability is a risk with this form of business, a successful arrangement may produce huge gains for a partner. Note in *Zajac v. Harris* that George Harris sought to have the business declared a partnership. Most likely, the profitability of the business showed that his partnership share would far exceed what he was paid in *wages*.

MANAGEMENT RIGHTS PRINCIPLE

Partners have a legal right to manage their business. Consequently, another advantage of this business organizational form is that the partners have input in the operation of the business. In theory, then, one may assume that by careful management, partners may limit the risk of personal liability that is a part of the organizational form. Today's litigation climate, however, somewhat belies that theory (see the discussion of the changes and trends in the scope of tort liability in Chapter 10).

However, not all partners want to have an active role in the operation of the business. Some may have special areas of expertise. Once again, note the Thought Problem that appears earlier in the chapter. If Jones, Thomas, and Smith become partners, they will have equal rights to manage. However, Jones has no interest in management, and Smith is the key to the firm's success. Consequently, an agreement may be drafted that reflects this option.

CONTROL PRINCIPLE

Partners are co-owners of the business. As such, their work for the partnership is not compensated by wages or a salary. Instead, they work for a share in the profits. Furthermore, as co-owners, each partner has the same right to vote on issues affecting the firm. Unless specified otherwise in the partnership agreement, this equal right to control is unaffected by the amount a partner has invested in the business or the skills and experience a partner may possess. Control is a fundamental attribute of the partnership form.

Thus, if Jones, Thomas, and Smith operate their business as a partnership, each will be considered one-third owner. This will be true even if Jones invested more money than the combined amount of Thomas and Smith. An agreement may change this equal control, perhaps to reflect Jones' greater investment or to recognize the importance of Smith's software development skills.

Although a partner's right to control, manage, and share profits in the business make the partnership an attractive form, the risk of personal liability always must be considered. Of course, a firm with ample assets and impressive insurance coverage will insulate a partner from that risk. But, as previously noted, the risk may never fully be alleviated. Thus, a need exists for an organization in which a person may invest money, share in the profits, but have no risk of personal liability. This form is called the *limited partnership*.

The Limited Partnership

The **limited partnership** may be traced to the *commenda* in the Middle Ages. In principle, the commenda was much like today's limited partnership, in which the investor (the commendator) provided funds for a business that was managed by another person (the commendatarius). Most of the profits would go to the commendator, but no liability for losses would attach.

Limited partnership law in the United States arose in the early nineteenth century as a response to concerns about partners' personal liability risk, as well as to the difficulty of obtaining a corporate charter. In 1822, New York became the first state to enact a limited partnership statute. It was based on the French Commercial Code of 1807. Chancellor Kent, in *Commentaries on American Law*, described it as the first instance in which non-British law was adopted in the United States. Today, limited partnership law in the U.S. is based primarily on one of two model statutes—the Uniform Limited Partnership Act or the Revised Uniform Limited Partnership Act.

Unlike a partnership, a limited partnership is not formed by operating a business in a certain way. Some formal steps required by statute must be taken, including filing a document with the state. As the next section on *business interests* notes, more rigidity occurs with this type of organization than with a partnership. Investors are categorized as limited or general partners, and their roles in the firm are thereafter circumscribed.

Consequently, a typical business (e.g., a manufacturing company or a consulting group) usually will not operate using the limited partnership form. Only when investors fit the roles of general or limited partners will that form be suitable. This often occurs when the type of business is quite risky, and only a few of the investors have an interest in managing it.

Broadway shows, professional sports franchises, and oil explorations are examples of the types of businesses that frequently involve limited partnerships. The risk of loss is high, but the possibility of enormous profit exists also. In addition, investors in a speculative real estate development, for example, may take advantage of gains, yet still be protected by limited liability. The Managerial Perspective, "Professional Baseball and Limited Partnerships," illustrates the type of business that uses the limited partnership form.

BUSINESS INTERESTS AND THE LIMITED PARTNERSHIP

The key characteristic of a limited partnership is in the designation of investors—some investors are limited partners, while others are general partners. Consult Figure 11.1 as you review the limited liability, profit share, management rights, and control principles discussed next.

■ Limited Liability, Management Rights, and Control Principles

The limited liability, management rights, and control principles are tied together in limited partnerships. As noted in Figure 11.1, general partners have the same status as partners in a partnership. The general partner's assets may be seized to satisfy unpaid claims against the business. Furthermore, the general partner has the right to manage the business, and he has control over it.

Limited partners, by way of contrast, have limited liability as long as they refrain from participating in the management and control of the business. Their role is like a passive investor. The reward for passivity is a share in the profits and limited liability. However, the limited partners do not need to be inert. The approval process involving

managerial perspective

Professional Baseball and Limited Partnership

The New York Yankees baseball team is a limited partnership with eighteen limited partners. George Steinbrenner owns fifty-five percent of the team, and he is the managing general partner. The partners' arrangement provides that Steinbrenner may veto the sale of even the smallest share of the team held by the others. The Steinbrenner-led investors purchased the Yankees in 1973 from CBS for $10 million. In 1993, they were offered $500 million for the team.

In the spring of 1995, one of the limited partners, Harvey L. Leighton, placed an advertisement in *The Wall Street Journal* offering one percent of the team for sale. His asking price was $2.95 million, which was discounted from what the share would have fetched if the team had been sold in 1993.

However, even if Leighton found a buyer, he could not sell his share without Steinbrenner's approval. As one former limited partner said: "There's nothing more limited than a limited partner in the Yankees." Nonetheless, Leighton praised Steinbrenner as a "great guy," who is tough, but with whom an investor could make a lot of money. "When I die," Leighton said. "I'd like to come back as George Steinbrenner."

Source: Kirk Johnson, "For Sale: A Piece of the Yankees," *The New York Times,* March 8, 1995, page B1.

■ **FIGURE 11.1** Limited Partnership

	General Partners	**Limited Partners**
Limited Liability	No	Yes, unless a limited partner participates in management or control
Profit Share	Yes	Yes
Management Rights	Yes	No, but a limited partner risks losing limited liability if he or she participates in management
Control	Yes	No, but a limited partner risks losing limited liability if he or she exercises control

new general partners and limited partners joining the firm and occasional consulting with the general partner are examples of activities that will not threaten their limited liability.

■ *Profit Share Principle*

Both the general and limited partners have a right to share in the profits from the business. Thus, one may see how this form is attractive for risky businesses. On one hand, investors (as limited partners) know that they will lose no more than their initial investment. On the other hand, if the venture is successful (e.g., a discovery of a huge oil field), then the profits pass to the investors.

Refer to the Thought Problem, "Choosing an Organization Form," involving Jones, Thomas, and Smith from earlier in this chapter. A limited partnership may hold some attractions for each person. Jones has a high personal net worth, so he would want limited liability protection. He also has no management interests. Thus, his needs fit the limited partner profile quite well.

In addition, neither Thomas nor Smith has wealth, so even if they were subject to personal liability, it is unlikely that a claimant would bother to pursue them. After all, since they have few assets, any judgment would be uncollectible. Furthermore, Smith has the key skills that are needed to operate the business. Therefore, Thomas would best fit the company as a general or limited partner, while Smith would be a general partner.

Of course, if their business is successful, both Thomas and Smith may opt for limited liability protection. If this is the situation, perhaps a corporation should be considered.

The Corporation

A **corporation** is a legal entity. The law considers it to be a person, having its own rights, duties, and responsibilities. The concept of an organization of individuals having a single personality has deep historical roots. Some writers date this idea to primitive societies; others contend that the seeds of the modern business corporation may be found in ancient Greece. Still others submit that it was first developed in Rome. Under Roman law, a corporation was empowered to do many things that an actual person could do—hold and convey property, inherit land and goods, and acquire assets or incur liabilities. Early Christian societies continued to use a corporate concept of organization. These forms of incorporation greatly influenced the development of English law, which became the basis for American corporate law.

The direct antecedents of American corporations, however, were the joint stock companies that were begun in sixteenth-century England. At first, these were temporary arrangements, organized for single overseas trading expeditions. Later, a more permanent structure was developed. One of the most well-known was the Governor and Companies of Merchants Trading in the East Indies (the British East India Company). Organized by charter granted by Elizabeth I in 1600, the British East India Company thrived for more than two hundred years.

Many other joint stock companies were chartered in England; some of them played an important role in colonizing North America. In 1607, for example, the Virginia Company of London settled Jamestown, Virginia. The Massachusetts Bay Company, chartered in 1629, settled New England. This joint stock company was unique in that the colonists were its controlling members instead of merely its employees. Note that these companies were more than simple commercial enterprises. They also governed the settlements that they established.

The first corporation in the American colonies was chartered in 1768, in what would become the state of Pennsylvania. The company was called the Philadelphia Contributionship for Insuring Houses from Loss by Fire. As the name implies, it was an insurance company and was the only corporation organized in this country before the

Revolution. Thereafter, a number of American businesses received corporate charters. Most of these companies were involved in banking or insurance or in establishing the country's system of overland turnpikes, toll bridges, and canals.

Early American corporations were granted their charters by state legislatures, a time-consuming and expensive process. Of course, before the Industrial Revolution, the United States had primarily an agrarian economy. Thus, little need or demand arose for a simplified incorporation process. New York, in 1811, was the first state to enact an enabling act for manufacturing companies. An enabling act provides an administrative procedure that relieves the legislature of the task of acting on each corporate charter application. However, the New York statute was quite restrictive. Not until New Jersey's General Corporation Act of 1875 did enabling acts reject strict state control over corporate formation and activities. The New Jersey act may be seen as the prototype of today's corporate organization statutes.

These statutes outline a procedure that must be followed in order for a corporation to come into existence. Generally, this includes filing articles of incorporation with the secretary of state. If the filed documents meet the requirements of the enabling statute, the secretary will issue a certificate of incorporation signifying the formal beginning of a corporation's legal existence. Thereafter, bylaws must be adopted, directors and officers elected, and shares of stock issued. Additionally, regular meetings of directors and shareholders must occur. Compare these formalities with the simple and uncomplicated way that a partnership organization may be created.

CHARACTERISTICS OF THE CORPORATE FORM

The corporation is a unique form of business organization. Legally, it is a separate entity—a person in the eyes of the law, distinguishable and apart from any of its members. The separate entity concept of the corporation was described by Chief Justice John Marshall of the United States Supreme Court in the famous case of *Dartmouth College v. Woodward* in 1819:

> A corporation is an artificial being, invisible, intangible, and existing only in contemplation of law. Being the mere creature of law, it possesses only those properties which the charter of its creation confers upon it, either expressly or as incidental to its very existence. These are such as are supposed best calculated to effect the object for which it was created. Among the most important are immortality, and if the expression may be allowed, individuality.

■ *Individuality*

A corporate individual cannot be seen or touched. It is an intangible organizational idea that is given life, personality, and an existence by the law. It is solely a creature of the law, being formed pursuant to statute. Corporations have many of the legal characteristics of any natural person. For example, the corporation may sue and be sued. It may own property and invest it. A corporation may make money, lose money, and go bankrupt. Corporations may enter into contracts.

Since a corporation has no physical form, its individuality is obviously limited. A corporation may act only through agents (see Chapter 12). Agents are people (workers, managers, vice-presidents, and so on) who are empowered to do certain tasks on behalf of the corporation. For example, when General Motors first produced the Corvette, the corporation legally used its capital and resources to design the new sports car. However, people acting on behalf of General Motors (its agents) actually produced the car. Corporate agents made decisions concerning all aspects of design and production. Other agents built the car, tested it, and developed its unique features. Nonetheless, the corporation is bound by the contracts those agents created on its behalf and may be liable for torts committed by them. Thus, a contract negotiated by a General Motors executive to buy steel from Inland Steel Corporation for use in constructing the sports car will bind General Motors. In addition, if the braking system was negligently developed by people in the company's design department, the corporation—General Motors—may be liable for injuries caused by the defect.

■ *Compartmentalization of Business Roles*

The key feature of a corporation is that it compartmentalizes business roles that in other organizational forms (the partnership) are performed by one person (see Figure 11.2). Investors in an incorporated business are the shareholders. The people who perform management functions are the officers and executives. Control of the corporation rests with the board of directors.

Although the corporate roles are separated, the same person may occupy more than one role. Refer, again, to the Thought Problem earlier in this chapter involving Jones, Thomas, and Smith. If they decide to incorporate their business, Charles Smith (as an investor) would be a shareholder. He could also be elected to the board of directors and could hold an executive position as well.

SHAREHOLDERS (INVESTOR ROLE)   The shareholders in a corporation are considered to be its owners. They invest money in the enterprise through the purchase of stock. However, shareholders do not participate in the management or operation of the corporation unless they occupy some position other than shareholder—for example, shareholder–director or shareholder–division manager. The only control that shareholders exercise is through the election of the

■ **FIGURE 11.2** Business Roles within the Corporation

control that shareholders exercise is through the election of the board of directors.

Generally, each share of common stock is entitled to one vote. Thus, the shareholders who control sufficient shares may indirectly control the corporation through the election of a board of directors who will carry out those shareholders' aims. The other shareholders, although able to vote, will have no effective voice in corporate affairs. In large, publicly held corporations, shareholders who are dissatisfied with management may simply sell their shares on the market. But in small, privately held corporations in which no market for the shares exists, this is not an alternative.

BOARD OF DIRECTORS (CONTROL ROLE)   The board of directors, which is elected by the shareholders, controls the corporation. However, to do so, the directors must act as one. Individual board members have no power to make independent decisions on behalf of the corporation.

Assume in the aforementioned Thought Problem, that all three investors—Jones, Thomas, and Smith—were elected to the board of directors. To be effective, decisions concerning the corporation need to come from the three of them as a board. If Thomas decided that it would be best for the corporation to enter an alliance with another computer software maker, she would have no power to act on the corporation's behalf. The authority of any board member is limited to the activities of the group.

Furthermore, membership on the board does not mean that the person has management rights. For example, Thomas would have no power to negotiate contracts, hire employees, or do anything else associated with the day-to-day activities of the business. She would need to have a management position, in addition to her directorship, to do so.

BUSINESS INTERESTS AND THE CORPORATE FORM

■ Limited Liability Principle

Corporate shareholders have limited liability. Thus, they are not liable for unpaid claims of the business. Consequently, if Jones, Thomas, and Smith form a corporation, their investment as shareholders will be the most money they could lose even if the firm became insolvent.

Although the limited liability principle today is synonymous with the corporate form, this has not always been the case. Corporate charters in the early nineteenth century rarely provided for limited liability. In this situation, corporate investors were treated in the same manner as if they were operating the business as a partnership.

In 1816, New Hampshire began granting limited liability to corporate shareholders. However, this practice was not adopted in all of the other states in the Union. For example, before 1830, Massachusetts and Rhode Island did not provide limited liability to shareholders. On the other hand, two nearby states—Maine and New Hampshire—did grant limited liability to shareholders. Nonetheless, as Philip I. Blumberg noted in this four-volume treatise, *Corporate*

Groups and Enterprise Liability, little evidence of differing economic activity existed among the four states.

In 1847, Rhode Island was the last state to adopt limited liability; but uniformity among the states still did not exist. Until 1931, California provided that shareholders were liable, pro rata, for debt incurred by the corporation. Today, both New York and Wisconsin refuse to extend shareholder limited liability to wage claims by corporate employees. Thus, the limited liability is not a natural consequence of corporate individuality. It was a political response to investor interests.

Corporations in the early nineteenth century rarely had the power to own shares in other corporations. Thus, a business's organizational structure was reasonably simple—individual shareholders owned the corporation, which, in turn, owned the business. Beginning with New Jersey in 1888, corporations were permitted to own shares in other corporations. Therefore, the business enterprise itself could be divided into a group of corporations with interlocking interests and ownership, but with central control.

The railroad corporations were the first to use this *enterprise organization*. A single railroad company would be transformed into an amalgam of parent and subsidiary corporations. Today, enterprise organization is a common form by which large *corporations* do business. Mobil, for example, operates its business through more than five hundred corporate subsidiaries. British Petroleum Corporation operates through more than one thousand corporate subsidiaries.

The law, however, did not create new doctrines for these multicorporate business organizations. It simply extended the limited liability concept to them, even though they are quite different from the simple corporate organization model from which limited liability arose.

Consequently, investors were granted limited liability whether they were acting as individuals or other corporations. As noted in Figure 11.3, this meant firms could create *fire walls* between various

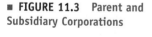
FIGURE 11.3 Parent and Subsidiary Corporations

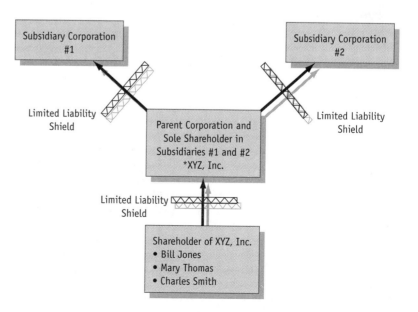

aspects of their business, so that a financial disaster in one area would not harm the entire enterprise.

However, courts have begun to treat individual corporate shareholder cases different from those involving parent–subsidiary relationships. They are more willing to ignore the limited liability of parent corporations for incidents that, theoretically, should only involve a subsidiary. For example, using Figure 11.3, assume that claims against Subsidiary Corporation #1 far-outstripped its assets and insurance coverage. Under the limited liability principle, the shareholder—XYZ, Inc.—would not be responsible for these losses. However, courts recognizing the unity factor of a *business enterprise* often hold XYZ, Inc. liable, too.

■ *Profit Share, Management Rights, and Control Principles*

In a corporate organization, management rights and profit share concepts are inextricably intertwined. Both are driven by the issue of control or, more directly, by the actions of the person who has the legal power to make decisions for the corporation.

The concept of a profit share is different in a corporation than it is in the other organizational forms reviewed thus far. No member of a corporate organization has a right to its profits. How those profits are used is a decision that is vested in the board of directors. Consequently, a highly profitable corporation may choose to invest all of its profits in new factories or equipment. Conversely, it may distribute the money to the shareholders in the form of dividends. Of course, comparable decisions may also be made in partnership and limited partnership organizations. The distinguishing feature, however, is that unlike the partners in a partnership or the general and limited partners in a limited partnership, corporate shareholders have no legal right to any of the profit. In those other organizations, the profit right would need to be relinquished. This is not the case with the corporation. Thus, the key *profit share* decisions in a corporate form involves control of the board of directors.

A similar relationship exists for the management rights principle. The board of directors elects corporate officers who then hire executives and staff. The key is to focus on the selection of the corporate board.

The board of directors is elected by a majority vote of the shareholders. Thus, the investor who owns fifty percent plus one of the shares *controls* the corporation. In large corporations where ownership is diffused and not all shareholders vote, this control may be obtained by a much smaller percentage. Compare this with the partnership form. In the partnership form, each investor, irrespective of the amount contributed, retains a right to share in the profits as well as the management rights.

A concern, therefore, becomes apparent for the minority shareholders—their investment in the organization may leave them disenfranchised. But, how this affects a particular investor will depend on whether the corporation is a close corporate or a publicly traded one. The next discussion will sketch out this distinction.

A **close corporation** has few shareholders, and its shares of stock are not traded on any organized market. Often a close corporation is a small, family-owned business. The local bakery, dry-cleaner, and auto shop are examples. But *smallness* is not a requirement. Hallmark, a greeting card company based in Kansas City, is a close corporation that has worldwide operations.

However, examine a more typical close corporation. Assume that Mozart and Salieri, in the example that opened this chapter, formed a corporation that issued one hundred shares, none of which are traded on a public market. Mozart invested $51,000, thereby receiving fifty-one of the company's issued shares. Salieri invested $49,000, thereby receiving forty-nine shares of stock. Mozart and Salieri are also members of the board of directors, by unanimous vote of the shareholders. Each also holds an officer position, by unanimous vote of the board. Additionally, both work every day in the business. Since Mozart and Salieri are friends, they jointly decide all issues involving the business.

Note the similarities between this typical close corporation, as an operating business and a partnership. In both, the investors manage the company as a partner or by serving on the board. Their friendship fosters joint control which would include a determination about the distribution of company earnings. In practice, then, the operation of Mozart and Salieri's business would differ little, whether it is a partnership or a corporation.

Now, consider the Ethical Perspective, "The Squeeze Out."

The issue of control has a particular meaning for the close corporation. However, in a large, publicly traded corporation, additional factors to be considered in a discussion of control also exist.

A *publicly traded corporation* is one whose shares are bought and sold in an organized marketplace, such as the New York Stock Exchange. Publicly traded corporations often have thousands of employees, scattered operations, and shareholders that change almost by the minute. Frequently, such corporations are international in scope. Although the basic principles of corporate law apply—shareholders elect the directors who elect the officers, some practical differences do exist.

First, a relatively small percentage of the shares will control the corporation, since few shareholders actually vote in director elections. Second, management generally will be in control of those shares' votes—either through ownership or through an alliance with the owners. Third, the directors will be selected by management and will

ETHICAL PERSPECTIVE

The Squeeze Out

Mozart and Salieri begin to feud. The disagreement escalates. At the next shareholders' meeting Mozart refuses to vote to renew Salieri's membership on the board of directors. Instead, he uses his majority of fifty-one votes to elect Cosima to the board. The new board consists of Mozart and Cosima. Their first duty is to cut corporate costs. As a result, Salieri also loses his job with the company. Mozart and Cosima share his tasks and also substantially raise their salaries. Further, they refuse to pay any more dividends. Salieri's investment has been rendered worthless to him.

However, one may ask: Why can't Salieri simply sell his stock to someone else, since shares of stock are freely transferable property? Two reasons come to mind. First, no organized market exists for close corporate shares. Salieri would need to find a buyer for his particular investment. Second, it is unlikely that anyone would buy his minority shareholder interests, which provide neither income nor the likelihood of market appreciation (since there is no market).

What happened to Salieri is called a *corporate squeeze out*. It is a source of bitter litigation in close corporations. However, courts review close corporation squeeze-outs on the basis of certain *duties* that the majority shareholders would owe the minority shareholders. These duties arise from a concern for the majority's position of control and its potential for abuse.

Recall the materials on ethics in Chapter 7. Apply the ethical principle to Mozart's squeeze out of Salieri. Furthermore, Chapter 12 discusses a legal rule (the fiduciary duty) which is directly applicable.

then be offered to the shareholders to approve, disapprove, or abstain. Invariably these director candidates will prevail. Only in the rare event of a contest for control will shareholders have a choice in the slate of directors.

The realities of the publicly traded corporation raise complex issues. Corporate legal theory suggests that management is selected by the board which is chosen by the shareholders. Yet, for the most part, in publicly traded corporations, management is the key and the directors are beholden to management for their positions. Although directors owe fiduciary duties to the shareholders (see Chapter 12 for a discussion of these duties), corporate critics frequently point to the lack of shareholder democracy as a source of corporate ills. One well-known criticism is leveled at the enormous income levels of top management at publicly traded American corporations—levels far exceeding what is earned by their Japanese and European counterparts. The board of directors, of course, sets the top executive salary level.

What is a noncontrolling shareholder in such a corporation to do? The typical response is to sell the shares. Since an organized public market exists, this dissatisfied investor is not stuck to the company, as was Salieri in the earlier example. Another response is to pressure management. Of course, this will not work for the owner of only one hundred shares. But a trend in share ownership suggests that pressure may become a powerful device. Many individuals who invest in public companies do so through institutions such as mutual funds and pension plans. These large institutions are beginning to use their clout to pressure certain corporate managements to be more responsive to shareholder interests. The question of stratospheric executive salaries is one of those interests. The implicit threat, of course, is that the mutual fund or pension plan will sell its shares or support an insurgent who seeks to oust current management.

In any event, the concept of corporate control for the business executive is tied more to the nature of the corporation than to legal theory. The complex issues go far beyond the brief survey in this chapter and merit an additional course of their own.

The Limited Liability Company: An Emerging Organizational Form

Each of the traditional legal business organizational forms (partnership, limited partnership, and corporation) has unattractive features. A partnership imposes a risk of personal liability on its partners. In a limited partnership, limited partners cannot manage the firm. In a corporation, management and profit share are tied to control.

Recently, a new organizational form—the limited liability company—has been made available for investors. The first state to enact a limited liability company statute was Wyoming in 1977, reportedly at the behest of an oil company. By the summer of 1995, forty-eight states (and Washington, D.C.) had followed suit. A similar business organizational form exists in some overseas countries including Brazil, Germany, Portugal, and Saudi Arabia.

As noted in the next section, the limited liability company combines the best features of the other business organizational forms. As an added attraction, in 1988, the Internal Revenue Service issued a revenue ruling that indicated it would treat limited liability companies as partnerships for income tax purposes—that is, the business organization itself would not be a taxable entity. Consequently, the limited liability company organizational form has generated substantial interest.

As recent as 1993, only eighteen states had enacted limited liability company statutes. Today, only two have not done so, and each has the matter under study. Furthermore, the number of businesses that have organized as limited liability companies exceeded the predictions of even the most enthusiastic supporters. By the summer of 1995, fifty thousand limited liability companies had been formed.

Just as with the corporation and limited partnership, investors who intend to use the limited liability company form must comply with some statutory formalities. This includes filing a document with the state.

BUSINESS INTERESTS AND THE LIMITED LIABILITY COMPANY

■ Limited Liability Principle

Investors (known as *members*) in a limited liability company have limited liability. Like shareholders in a corporation and limited partners in a limited partnership, the most money they may lose is what they have invested in the business. However, members have an advantage over corporate shareholders under the profit share principle.

■ Profit Share Principle

Limited liability company investors (*members*) have a right to share in the profits. Thus (as shown in Figure 11.1), they are like limited partners in a limited partnership. However, note the difference under the next principles.

■ Management Rights and Control Principles

Investors (*members*) in a limited liability company have a right to both manage and exercise control in the business without affecting their profit share or limited liability. However, the members are not required to be active in the business. They may select an outsider as a manager or permit some members to opt out of such responsibilities.

Contrast this aspect with the limited partner in a limited partnership. A limited partner who manages the business will risk losing the limited liability benefit. But, this is not true for members of limited liability companies.

Refer to the Thought Problem at the beginning of this chapter involving Jones, Thomas, and Smith. Note how the limited liability company would meet their needs:

■ Jones would have limited liability to protect his personal fortune, and he would have the right to control the business. However, he could opt out of day-to-day management responsibilities.

■ Thomas, on the other hand, is most interested in sharing the profits to which she has a right as a member of a limited liability company.

■ Smith, the investor whose ideas form the basis of the company, would be able to act as manager without jeopardizing his limited liability protection.

Thus, in this situation, the limited liability company seems to offer the most advantages. Although few legal developments exist regarding this organizational form, with widening availability, a trend may occur where limited liability companies replace the partnership form and, in some instances, become preferable to the corporation.

Limited liability companies may be particularly attractive for start-up, risky, entrepreneurial ventures. Investors may provide funding, lend their expertise in management, and share in the wealth that is generated without exposing noninvested assets to loss. The limited liability company clearly illustrates how the law may be used to facilitate business conduct.

Summary

Five legal forms under which a business may be operated were discussed in this chapter—the sole proprietorship; the partnership; the limited partnership; the corporation; and an emerging form, the limited liability company. For the business executive, these are more than mere legal technicalities. Each could have profound implications for any business that chooses to operate under one of the forms. In fact, failing to choose could lead to one being presumed by the law— partnership. Consequently, it is important that the executive select the form that best meets certain business interests.

Legal organizational forms may be distinguished in many ways. This chapter focused on four of the most basic—the limited liability principle, the profit share principle, the management right principle, and the control principle. The business executive should evaluate the relative importance of these interests before deciding which organizational form to use. Each legal form tends to favor certain interests over the others.

All business organizational forms are governed by state law. Thus, one may expect some differences between them. Nonetheless, since the partnership, limited partnership, and corporation have had a long history of use, their contours should be relatively easy to predict. This is not the case with the limited liability company, a new and untested organizational form. Its widespread availability as a legal form of business is a recent phenomenon. Nonetheless, the limited liability company offers an interesting alternative that must be considered by executives seeking an organizational form.

Review Questions

1. Define the following terms:
   a. Limited liability
   b. Partnership
   c. Limited partnership
   d. Close corporation
   e. Parent–subsidiary corporation

2. Mary and Sam would like to become co-owners of a bike shop. Discuss whether or not they may do so under the sole proprietorship form of doing business.

3. Tom and Bill are involved in a bakery business. Bill invested all of the money. They share gross income, by agreement: twenty percent to Tom and the balance to Bill, who pays all the expenses of the business from his share. Since Tom is a master baker, he makes all decisions concerning breads, cookies, and cakes. Do Tom and Bill have a partnership?

4. Under what circumstances would you suggest that a partnership form would be least attractive to a business executive?

5. George and Susan own an oil well under the limited partnership form of business organization. George is the limited partner, and Susan is the general partner. If the business cannot pay $1 million in creditor claims, how much may the creditors seek from George? How much could they seek from Susan?

6. Would your answer to question #5 change if George were closely involved in making management decisions for the oil well business?

7. Jack and Molly decide to operate their restaurant as a corporation. They begin to call each other "shareholder" and put a sign out in front that says "Eats, Inc." However, they do not file any documents with the state. Have they created a corporate organizational form?

8. For a birthday gift, Jim's uncle gives him two shares of stock in XYZ, Inc., a publicly traded corporation that does business throughout the world. In yesterday's newspaper, Jim reads that XYZ, Inc., is insolvent and has millions of dollars of unpaid bills. Should Jim be concerned that the creditors will seek contribution from him?

9. Betty is an investor in small risky businesses. She has been very successful because many of these businesses have become quite profitable. The state in which she does business does not currently recognize the limited liability company form. If a proposed statute is being considered by the legislature, should she lobby in favor or against it?

10. Bill and Jane would like to jointly own a bookstore. Neither has any interest in managing the business, but each would like to have a share in the profits. Which of the business organizational forms fit their needs?

11. June and Sam intend to begin a deep-sea diving and salvage company. Since both are expert divers, they intend to be active in the business and jointly make all management decisions. However, neither wants to risk any of their personal assets, beyond what they invest in the business. Which of the business organizational forms fit their needs?

12. Tom and Mary would like to open a custom-made automobile shop. Since both are experts in auto design and construction, they intend to have a personal involvement in all aspects of production and jointly make all management decisions for the business. Further, they believe that this business may produce huge profits, and each would like the legal right to a share. Which of the business organizational forms fit their needs?

13. May and June each have net worth in the hundreds of millions of dollars. Their friend George, though penniless, is a computer design genius. He has shown them his new ideas, which are revolutionary. May and June would like to invest in George's new design ventures. However, they know nothing about computers and are too busy to bother with managing the business. They want to share in its profits, but are emphatic that their personal fortunes should not be placed at risk. Which of the business organizational forms fit their needs?

14. Compare the concept of control in a partnership with control in a corporation.

15. Tom and Jane operate a business together. Jane invested $10,000 in the business; Tom invested $8,000. What added risk would Tom have if the business was a corporation instead of a partnership?

16. Bill decided to invest $10,000 in a Broadway show. The show was being operated as a limited partnership. The investors were the limited partners, and the producers of the show were general partners. Unfortunately, the show was a flop, and after all the assets were liquidated, $200,000 was still owed to various creditors. Is Bill liable for all or any portion of that debt? Note that there are twenty limited partners in this organization.

17. Maude invested $5,000 in a limited partnership. There were three other limited partners and one general partner. The limited partnership was engaged in growing and marketing avocados. After two years, with no return on her investment, Maude became rather concerned. She visited Jack, the general partner, and demanded his resignation. Instead, he agreed, at her urging, to allow her to co-sign all checks the firm issued. Thereafter, she had input into all expenditures of the limited partnership. Within six months the firm was bankrupt, and $40,000 remained in unpaid debts. Do the creditors have claims against the limited partners?

18. How would you evaluate Bill's Broadway show business (in question 16), and Maude's avocado business (in question 17), if they had been organized as partnerships, corporations, or limited liability companies?

19. What are the roles of a shareholder and a director in a corporation?

Chapter

12

*MEMBERS OF BUSINESS
ORGANIZATIONS:
REGULATION OF THEIR
ACTIVITIES THROUGH
AGENCY AND FIDUCIARY
DUTY PRINCIPLES*

he laws of agency and fiduciary duty regulate relationships among members of business organizations (e.g., employees, managers, investors) and also between those members and *outsiders*. These laws facilitate the creation of contracts, give legal meaning to organization members' powers, and impose duties beyond what is ordinarily required.

Furthermore, business management theories are built on the framework that agency and fiduciary duty law provides. For example, how is it that organizational charts work to divide tasks? What gives a manager control over subordinates? Agency and fiduciary duty law are at the core of theories that attempt to explain such questions.

In addition, agency and fiduciary duty laws expand some of the basic ideas that were discussed in the contracts chapters (Chapters 8 and 9) and the torts chapter (Chapter 10). Review these chapters and then consider the following:

■ Why do sales representatives' contracts bind their employers? After all, the business organizations are not directly involved. No investors or managers took part in the negotiation. Only the employee–sales representatives were in contact with the third parties.

■ How can a corporation be liable for a tort? The organizational form requires that individuals act on the corporation's behalf and, thus, those individuals are the ones who may commit torts. Yet, the law imposes liability on the corporation. Why?

■ If employees mismanage a firm, does an investor have legal recourse against them? Recall from Chapter 11 that some investors take no part in operating their business. Thus, trust in those who do run the business is essential. Are there any consequences if that trust is violated?

These questions are answered by agency and fiduciary duty laws. An understanding about how these laws act as the *connectors* between contract and tort principles and the practical nature of business organizations is essential.

The Agent–Principal Relationship

AGENCY RELATIONSHIPS THAT ARE CREATED THROUGH CONTRACT

The law of agency may be traced to ancient Rome where *agents* were actually slaves who had no legal status under Roman law. Their legal identities were absorbed into the Roman families they served. Since the master—the male head of the household—represented the family in the eyes of the law, he also became liable for the actions of his slaves. Today, the law of agency carries forward the legal consequences of the Roman relationship, even though the relationship no longer exists in its original form.

An agency relationship is created by the consent of two people—*agent* and *principal*. The most common agent–principal relationship is between employee and employer. Thus, when Mary Smith hires Jack Jones to manage her firm's sales operations, an agency relationship is created. Smith is the principal and Jones is the agent. Their relationship is based on their contract.

However, not every consensual contractual relationship between two people creates an agency relationship. For example, buyer and seller relations are contractual, but the parties are not each other's agent and principal. All that is consented to is the transfer of property rights for a price. A debtor–creditor relationship is also based on a contract, but the only *consent* between them is tied to their loan. They, too, are not agent–principal.

An agency relationship needs to be distinguished from those that are merely contractual. The following two factors are distinguishing:

1. *Power:* The agent must have been granted the power to act on behalf of the principal. Consider the Smith–Jones agency relationship just mentioned. When Mary Smith hired Jack Jones, she empowered him to act in her place as sales operations manager. Smith granted this right to Jones under their contract.

However, not all such contracts create an agency relationship. For example, assume that ABC, Inc., hired The Accounting Firm to audit its warehouse operations. Even though The Accounting Firm is acting on behalf of ABC, Inc., they are not agent and principal. All that occurred is that ABC, Inc., purchased a result—the audit—and The Accounting Firm promised to provide it. Thus, agency requires something more than merely agreeing to perform a task on behalf of another.

2. *Control:* In an agency relationship, the principal has the right to control the work activities of the agent. Therefore, under an agency contract, the principal buys more than simply a result. The principal also buys the right to tell the agent how to get it. Referring to the ABC, Inc., example, the only requirement imposed on The Accounting Firm is for them to deliver its audit report to ABC, Inc. The auditors are not required to be on the job at certain times, report to ABC, Inc., on its progress, or submit to ABC, Inc.'s supervision. Furthermore, The Accounting Firm most likely has numerous other audit projects in the works. In addition, if ABC, Inc., decided to have its marketing department also audited, another bargain needs to be struck with The Accounting Firm. ABC, Inc., will not be able to simply reassign the auditors.

The relationship is similar to a buyer–seller relationship—ABC, Inc., is buying a service while The Accounting Firm is providing it. Although ABC, Inc., has empowered the accountants to do the audit on its behalf, it exercises no control over The Accounting Firm's work. The Accounting Firm is an *independent contractor.*

Now, consider the Mary Smith–Jack Jones agency relationship again. Jones is Smith's employee. His time on the job is set by Smith, and she supervises him. She may change his duties. Thus, the Smith–Jones contract grants Mary Smith the right to control how Jack Jones carries out the tasks she has empowered him to assume. They are principal and agent.

Whether a worker is classified as an agent or an independent contractor may have important consequences for a business. Note the Thought Problem, "The Status of Newspaper Carriers," that raises this issue. If the carrier is an agent, then the newspaper will be liable for the injuries he caused. This concept, called *vicarious liability,* is discussed later in this chapter.

thought problem

The Status of Newspaper Carriers

John Lane was a newspaper carrier. He solicited and collected subscriptions for the Sunday *Topeka Daily Capital* in Delia, Kansas. He made the deliveries using his own car. When he sold a subscription, he handed the new customer a card containing the name of the newspaper and his name, "Carrier, J.A. Lane." He was never under the direct supervision of the *Topeka Daily Capital* during any of his work. The newspaper sent Lane the number of Sunday papers he requested, and then he made the deliveries to the customers he had solicited.

One Sunday, while delivering the *Topeka Daily Capital,* Lane's car collided with an automobile containing Michael Hurla who was severely injured.

What do you think? Was Lane an agent of the *Topeka Daily Capital?* If not, change the facts of this situation to make him one.

Source: Hurla v. Capper Publications, Inc., *87 P.2d 552 (Kansas Supreme Court 1939).*

AGENCY RELATIONSHIPS WITHIN BUSINESS ORGANIZATIONAL FORMS

A second source for agency relationships is the organizational form a business takes. As previously noted, all employees are agents. However, other members of the organization are considered its agents, too. This relationship arises from the organizational structure. No separate contract is required to create it.

Table 12.1 identifies organizational agents and principals. In addition, this table provides a way of distinguishing organizational forms other than those discussed in Chapter 11.

In a partnership, the partners are considered agents and principals of each other. Thus, if Bill Jones, Mary Thomas, and Charles Smith (the three investors discussed in the previous chapter) form a partnership, they will automatically become agents and principals of each other. Each will have the power to act on behalf of the others (as their agents), and each will retain control (as principals). Recall from Chapter 11 that partners have the right to control and manage their businesses.

■ **TABLE 12.1** The Agency Relationship and Business Organizational Forms

	AGENCY RELATIONSHIP	
Business Form	**Who Are Agents?**	**Who Is the Principal?**
Sole proprietorship	Employees*	Sole proprietor
Partnership	Partners	Partners
Corporation	Corporate officers†	Corporate entity
Limited partnership	General partner	Other general partners and the limited partners
Limited liability company	Members	Company

*Employees of any organizational form are considered agents.
†Only officers elected by directors, as required by enabling acts, since they are distinct from being mere corporate employees.

In a limited partnership, only the general partner has agency powers. (Note that limited partners are not agents, and their role in the organization does not include a management and control right.) The principal here is the *limited partners* (and any other general partners). Since a limited partnership, like the partnership, is not a legal entity, unsatisfied claims arising because of agent (or general partner) actions may be collected from the general partner.

Assume that Jones, Thomas, and Smith created a limited partnership, with Charles Smith as the general partner. Bill Jones and Mary Thomas would be the limited partners. Smith would be an agent, and Jones and Thomas would be the principals. However, their *control* would be limited to selection of the general partner. If Jones and Thomas exercise control over the business, they would lose their limited liability status.

A corporation provides a contrast. Its agents are the officers (president, vice-president, secretary) elected by the board, with powers as described in the corporate bylaws. The principal is the corporation. Since the corporation is a legal entity, it is the party for whom the agents work. Members of the board of directors are not agents—unless they serve the corporation in some other capacity. Board members have no power to act individually. Their power exists solely from their decisions as a collective group.

If investors Jones, Thomas, and Smith form a corporation, none of them would be either agent or principal unless they undertake a role, other than as shareholders, in the firm. If Mary Thomas was hired as production manager, she would be an agent because she is an employee. The corporation would be the principal. Alternatively, if the board of directors elected Thomas as corporate president, she would also become an agent because of the structural requirements (officer elections) of the corporate form. Her principal would be the corporation.

In a limited liability company, the members who manage the firm are agents. The company is the principal. Not all members need to have a management role, and only those that do are called agents. If Jones, Thomas, and Smith form a limited liability company, they will only be its agents if they undertake management roles. As members, they have the right to manage. Therefore, all of them could be agents.

Business Consequences of the Agency Relationship

An agency relationship has two consequences that do not exist if an independent contractual relationship is created instead.

First, the principal is liable for its agent's torts that are committed within the course and scope of the business. This is called the *doctrine of respondeat superior,* or *vicarious liability.* It expands a business's (principal's) tort risk. Thus, an injured party would have a claim against the principal even if the principal was blameless.

Second, an agent's contracts bind the principal. This body of law focuses on the agent's authority and facilitates day-to-day operations of business organizations.

TORTS AND VICARIOUS LIABILITY

A business's tort liability risk arises from two sources:

- the torts that the business has committed (Review the materials in Chapter 10 to recall this risk.)

- the torts committed by employees under the doctrine of vicarious liability

Consider the Thought Problem, "Business Liability Risk." Note that the painter–employee's tort was so far removed from the nature of his job that the doctrine of vicarious liability was not even raised. However, the employer was still liable based on its own negligence.

thought problem

Business Liability Risk
Gore Properties, Inc., owned the Ritz Apartments. The Ritz's manager hired Harry Porter to paint Codie Whitman's apartment. Codie Whitman was a single woman who lived alone and kept two locks on her door for security.

The apartment manager did not know Harry Porter nor did he obtain any references before hiring him. In fact, the manager made no investigation of Porter at all. Nonetheless, the manager let Porter into Whitman's apartment when she was not at home and left him there unsupervised. Furthermore, the manager provided Porter with a key to Whitman's apartment.

The day after Porter began to paint Whitman's apartment, he strangled her to death with a painter's towel. The court held that with these facts, the plaintiff created a prima facie case of negligence against Gore Properties, Inc.

Reviewing the materials in Chapter 10, would you come to the same conclusion? Furthermore, note that the apartment manager was an agent of Gore Properties, Inc. After reading the material that follows, consider whether or not the manager's negligence was within the course and scope of Gore Properties, Inc.'s business.

Source: Kendall v. Gore Properties, Inc., *236 F2d. 673 (United States Court of Appeals, District of Columbia 1956).*

At first, the doctrine of vicarious liability may seem at odds with the notions of fairness and justice. After all, this doctrine imposes liability on someone who is blameless. However, the doctrine may be justified in the following two ways:

- *The Downside of Agency Law:* Agency law creates the framework under which principals may have others act on their behalf. The law considers an agent a *substitute* for the principal. Principals would be liable if they commit torts while acting on their own behalf. They should similarly be liable for their *substitute's* torts.

- *Loss Spreading:* An injured party will be more likely to receive compensation from the principal—a business with assets or insurance—than from the agent who committed the tort. Imposing a liability risk on businesses in this way will make them use greater care in supervising their agents. Furthermore, businesses may spread the risk by factoring the risk of agent tort liability into their pricing policies. Thus, the *cost* is distributed among all customers, rather than being imposed solely on the unlucky person injured by an agent's tort.

The doctrine of vicarious liability has been a part of the common law for nearly three hundred years. It was first created by Justice Holt, in England, in the case of *Jones v. Hart* in 1698. However, vicarious liability is not unique to American and English common law. Legal systems influenced by the French Napoleonic Code also use the principle. In fact, the French legal writer Domat was urging such a rule for France at about the same time Justice Holt decided *Jones v. Hart*. The Code Napoléon of 1804, with some modifications, adopted Domat's ideas. As an aside, in the 1804 Code Napoléon, teachers were held to be vicariously liable for damages caused by their students during the time they were under the teachers' supervision. Fortunately for today's professors, this was never a principle of the common law. It has also been changed in France, by amendment to the code in 1937.

A principal is liable for an agent's tort only if it was committed within the course and scope of the business. Thus, if the tort was not connected to the agent's job, then no vicarious liability exists. As an example, assume that Tom Jenkins worked as a delivery driver for Acme, Inc. If Jenkins negligently causes an accident while taking a shipment of computer chips to a customer's factory, Acme, Inc., would be vicariously liable. Jenkins's tort is closely tied to his job as a delivery driver; therefore, it would be within the course and scope of Acme, Inc.'s business.

However, if Jenkins decided to go to a baseball game on his day off, and negligently caused an accident on the way, Acme, Inc., would not be vicariously liable. There is no connection between this tort and Jenkins's job. Thus, the tort would not be within the course and scope of Acme, Inc.'s business.

More complex scenarios often arise. For example, what if Jenkins negligently caused an accident after departing from a direct delivery route so that he could stop at home and feed his cat? In this scenario, elements that are both job-related and personal are mingled. A clear-cut determination of whether or not a tort is within the course and scope of Acme, Inc.'s business would not be easy to make.

Nonetheless, factors may be identified that aid in determining whether or not a tort is within the course and scope of the business. The following factors are pertinent in this determination:

1. Were the agent's action common among other employees? For example, if Acme, Inc.'s delivery drivers often ran personal errands while on company business, the *scope* of their jobs may be expanded to include them. This would especially be so if the employer permitted it.

2. When and how did the tort occur? If it happened during normal business hours, at the place of business, or if it was committed using property owned by the business, a number of job-related ties may be established. For Jenkins, the accident occurred during business hours and while he was using the business's truck.

These factors are cited in what are known as *frolic* cases (such as the Jenkins cat-feeding illustration). The issue is whether or not the employee's *frolic* is significant enough to overcome job-related aspects surrounding the tort. The Managerial Perspective, "Vicarious Liability and Frolics," further illustrates this topic.

managerial perspective

Vicarious Liability and Frolics

Amos Carter owned a business in New York City. He sent an employee with a truck-load of merchandise from Manhattan to Staten Island. The employee was directed to return to the company garage on the West Side after making the delivery.

Instead, after leaving Staten Island, the employee drove to the East Side to visit his mother. A carnival was in progress in the neighborhood, and the driver joined in the fun. He permitted boys to climb all over the truck and gave them a tour of the neighborhood.

Later, the driver stopped in front of a pool hall to visit a friend. As he was about to drive back to his employer's garage, one of the boys climbed back onto the truck and was injured as it drove away. The court held that the driver was not within the course and scope of his employer's business when the accident occurred.

What do you think? Since the business was not found to be vicariously liable, what legal alternatives remained for the boy?

Source: Fiocco v. Carver, *137 N.E. 309 (New York Court of Appeals 1922).*

Another complex vicarious liability scenario arises when someone is injured by an employee's intentional tort. Another evaluation factor often comes into play—was the employee's act unexpected by the employer? Expectation is tied to the nature of the job. For example, a person would be more likely to expect a physical assault on a customer coming from a nightclub bouncer than from a clothing store sales clerk.

Consider the *Williams v. Community Drive-In Theater, Inc.* case in which a drive-in theater patron was shot by an employee. Note how the court used the expectation factor in determining whether or not the incident was within the course and scope of the employer's business.

Williams v. Community Drive-In Theater, Inc.

Kansas Supreme Court
520 P.2d 1296 (1974)

Jerry Williams was a patron at the theater operated by defendant—Community Drive-In Theater, Inc. Donna McKenna, a theater employee, testified that at the time of the incident she was sixteen years of age and had been working at the Community Drive-In Theater for about three weeks. She worked at the concession stand; she sometimes helped close the theater. On April 7, 1970, at about 10:30 P.M., while she was still working at the cash register, the assistant manager, Mr. Robertson, asked her if she would help him close the theater. She agreed. Robertson parked his car close to the entrance so he could view the movie and also see if anyone tried to get in without paying. While sitting there, Donna McKenna saw the plaintiff's car come into the drive-in and go to the concession stand. Robertson drove his car to the concession stand and spoke with one of the three men who was in the plaintiff's car. Donna McKenna accompanied Robertson and then went to her car to get her husband's .410-gauge shotgun. Since there were three men against Robertson, she thought the shotgun would give him a little more authority. After retrieving the gun, she walked behind the plaintiff as they moved toward the manager's office. The men stopped. She then put the gun against the plaintiff's shoulder and told him, "Let's go to the other side of the building." The plaintiff turned as if to walk in front of her. The shotgun slipped so she grasped it tighter, which probably released the trigger. The plaintiff was shot.

The manager, Mr. Barnhardt, testified as to the duties of various drive-in employees. The assistant manager, Robertson, was in charge that night after Barnhardt had left. Robertson was expected to investigate any disturbance, maintain discipline among patrons, watch and protect property, and take appropriate action. Robertson had obtained a deputy sheriff's commission and a deputy sheriff's shirt to use on occasions when deemed necessary. Robertson also obtained a permit to carry a gun and carried one at times while on duty. Security was needed on weekends and when the drive-in had large crowds. Fights occurred and people threw beer cans. It was a pretty rough place and, on those occasions, the manager would try to break up disturbances with the use of force. On several occasions the police were called. Leon Barker, a doorman, carried a gun and once "put a gun to a guy's head for throwing gravel." The incidents mentioned occurred prior to the night in question. The manager was certain that Robertson knew Donna McKenna had the shotgun in her car because everyone knew that her husband owned a shotgun. The manager had never told Donna McKenna to leave the gun at home.

Harmon, Commissioner

If an assault by an employee is motivated entirely by personal reasons such as malice or spite or by a desire to accomplish some unlawful purpose and does not have for its purpose the furtherance of the employer's business, it will be considered personal to the employee and not such as will make the employer answerable. If the assault is committed by the employee while furthering the employer's interest in some way, the employer is liable. Thus, we see the relation of the act to the employer's business becomes an important criterion in determining the employer's liability.

In the case at bar the trial court in reaching its decision apparently regarded the employee in question as merely a concession stand employee. We think the record indicates she was more than that. She was specifically requested to remain after the concession stand closed and assist in closing the theater. Part of those duties consisted of preventing unauthorized entry after the ticket office had closed. Despite the fact she may not later have been paid by her employer for her services that night, she was the drive-in's employee at the crucial time. Although she may have used poor judgment in her actions, her own testimony indicates she was motivated by a desire to further theater interests rather than personal reasons such as malice or spite. She was shepherding two apparent intruders to the assistant manager for investigation when the shotgun discharged. There was evidence that the fact she had the gun on the premises was known to that individual, who himself carried a gun. The facts presented indicate certain employment at the drive-in was of a nature where the display and use of guns was contemplated in the furtherance of the employer's business in preserving order. We think the facts bearing upon whether she acted within the scope of her employment were such as to raise an issue requiring jury determination. Accordingly it must be held the trial court erred in granting summary judgment for the theater. The judgment is reversed and the cause remanded with directions to proceed with trial of the action.

The risk of tort liability may affect management decision making. Careful selection, supervision, and training of employees, for example, may lessen this risk in three ways:

1. It may limit the occurrence of torts in the first place. Consider the *Williams v. Community Drive-In Theater, Inc.,* case. The patron was injured because the gun accidentally discharged. Training employees about security techniques would limit such incidents. Fewer torts would mean less liability.

2. It may lessen the risk that the employer will be found negligent. Note the Thought Problem, "Business Liability Risk," from earlier in this chapter. The employer failed to use reasonable care in the selection and supervision of the painter. Thus, the employer's own tort would create a liability risk.

3. It may help define "the course and scope of the business" under vicarious liability. Consider the Managerial Perspective, "Vicarious Liability and Frolics," from earlier in this chapter. Management defined the driver's task as making a delivery on Staten Island and then returning to the company garage. The driver's deviation from the schedule created the scenario for the *frolic*. Thus, the employer was not found to be vicariously liable.

Of course, management of liability risk is not without expense. Employee-training programs and careful hiring procedures may add substantial costs to a business's operations. Purchasing insurance even costs money. No set formula exists for balancing the risk of liability with management costs. After all, a company may be lucky and rarely or never have torts arise. Nonetheless, since people cannot always count on luck, practical decisions must be made. See the Thought Problem, "Company Picnic Policies," as an example of a company's liability risk being put to test.

thought problem

Company Picnic Policies Anthony Bara-

jas was employed by the Trojan Fireworks Company. On December 21, the company held a Christmas party at its plant from noon until 4:00 P.M. All employees were required to attend. Alcoholic beverages were served, and a number of employees drank heavily, including Barajas. He became intoxicated. Nonetheless, after the party, he attempted to drive home. He caused an accident in which one person was killed and two others were injured.

Assess Trojan Fireworks Company's liability risk. If you were an executive for Trojan Fireworks Company, how would you manage future company parties?

Source: Harris v. Trojan Fireworks Company, 174 Cal. Rprt. 452 (California Court of Appeals 1981).

CONTRACTS AND AGENT AUTHORITY

An agent may make contracts that bind only the principal. Assume that Mary Smith, an employee of XYZ, Inc., purchased computer screens on behalf of her employer from ABC Suppliers. As an agent, Smith is empowered to act in XYZ, Inc.'s stead. Thus, the parties to the computer screen contract would be her employer, XYZ, Inc., and ABC Suppliers. Mary Smith is not a party to that contract. She is like a copper wire that the contract flows along between her employer and the computer seller.

Agency contract rules facilitate the operation of a business. Imagine an organization where the principal was required to sign every

■ **FIGURE 12.1** Contracts by Agents

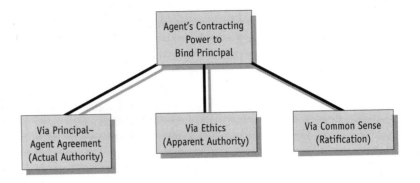

contract on behalf of the firm. This may be feasible for a small company, but the trouble of doing so would soon become overwhelming. In addition, this would be impossible if the firm was a corporation. A corporation is merely a legal idea, and no person is in charge of occupying the role as *principal*.

Three doctrines regulate an agent's power to bind a principal to a contract—actual authority, apparent authority, and ratification (see Figure 12.1).

The doctrine of *actual authority* requires that the principal has given expressly or by implication some specific contracting powers to the agent. Determining whether or not an agent has actual authority requires a review of the directions given by the principal to that agent. If the agent's power is definite and precise, the agent is considered to have express authority. For example, if the principal directs the agent to purchase a certain brand of computer software for the business, the agent—when purchasing the software—is using the express authority given by the principal.

However, not all instructions given to the agent will be so unequivocal. Sometimes the agent will be assigned a job with a general description—computer supplies manager—or the agent will be given somewhat vague directions—"Buy some computer software for the business." Although the principal has empowered the agent to perform a function, its exact contours have not been stated. Nonetheless, the agent still has actual authority. However, to determine the scope of that authority will require that assumptions be made about the nature of the business and the intent of the principal. In short, the inquiry is to determine what may be inferred from the general grant of authority. This doctrine is called *implied authority*.

Implied authority is practical. No principal could be expected to precisely convey every action for the agent to take. Furthermore, some contracting activities may require choices to be made that may readily be delegated to the agent. Thus, the doctrine of implied authority works together with express authority to describe the contracting rights given by the principal to the agent.

Consider the following example. Warren was recently hired by ABC, Inc., as a warehouse manager and is therefore its agent. His job description grants him the power to "hire employees and generally manage the warehouse." If Warren hires a forklift operator, he will be acting with express authority. That is, Warren has expressly been given the right to hire warehouse workers on behalf of ABC, Inc. Therefore, his principal—the corporation—is bound by the employment contract. Now, assume Warren hired a local pest control firm to rid the warehouse of vermin. Nothing in his job description expressly states that he is empowered to hire pest control firms. However, his position as warehouse manager and the general language of his grant of authority, to "generally manage the warehouse," clearly implies that authority was granted to him by ABC, Inc.

A second doctrine concerning agents and contracts with third parties is known as *apparent authority*. Apparent authority arises in the absence of actual authority. It is based on an ethical evaluation of the principal. The principal should have alerted the party with whom the agent dealt about the agent's lack of authority, but it did not do so. Recall the materials in Chapter 7 and note the ethics standard—all human beings have intrinsic worth and they are, thus, not considered a means to an end. Principals who ignore the interests of those with whom their agents deal risk being bound to contracts under apparent authority.

Apparent authority has two elements. First, the principal must have created the impression that the agent had the authority to enter into the contract. Second, the third party must have reasonably relied on an agent's having the authority. For example, assume that Jill has the actual authority to negotiate spare automobile parts contracts worth no more than $10,000; that is, she has been given an express limit on her actual authority. Jill, however, enters into a contract on behalf of her principal to purchase $11,000 in spare automobile parts. Under the doctrine of apparent authority, she would have the power to bind her principal to that contract.

By granting Jill the actual authority to enter into automobile parts contracts, her employer created the impression that she was empowered to enter into the contract at issue. The employer would have had to give notice of Jill's authority limitation for the contract to be voidable. Failing to do so established the appearance that Jill's actual authority did not have an express dollar ceiling. Furthermore, the party with whom Jill contracted had no way of knowing about the $10,000 limitation. The additional $1,000 in parts would hardly seem unusual or out of line.

Apparent authority may thus be seen as a fairness device designed to protect the interests of third parties contracting with agents. Principals cannot escape liability for the misimpressions of agent authority they allow to reasonably exist.

A final doctrine concerning agents and contracts is **ratification.** Ratification binds the principal to an agent's contract in the absence of either actual or apparent authority. If the principal accepts the benefits of an unauthorized contract, or in some other way affirms that contract, then the principal is bound. For example, assume in the previous example that Jill signed a promissory note borrowing $5,000 from a bank. She had no actual authority since she was limited to purchasing spare automobile parts. Furthermore, she had no apparent authority because the principal created no impression that she was empowered to borrow money for the firm. However, if the principal were to take the $5,000 and use it for business, then the contract would be ratified and the principal would be bound by it. The doctrine of ratification is based on common sense. If the principal accepts the benefits of the contract, then the obligations of that contract should also apply.

The *Lind v. Schenley Industries, Inc.,* case shows the operation of the authority doctrines. Note that multiple doctrines of authority may often be raised simultaneously. On any one of them being established, the principal will be bound to the terms of the contract.

Lind v. Schenley Industries, Inc.

United States Court of Appeals, Third Circuit
278 F.2d 79 (1960)

Lind had been employed for some years by Park & Tilford. In July 1950, Lind was informed by Herrfeldt, then Park & Tilford's vice-president and general sales manager, that he would be appointed assistant to Kaufman, Park & Tilford's sales manager for metropolitan New York. Subsequently, Lind received a communication, dated April 19, 1951, signed by Kaufman, informing Lind that he would assume the title of "district manager." The letter went on to state: "I wish to inform you of the fact that you have as much responsibility as a State Manager and that you should consider yourself to be of the same status." The letter concluded with the statement: "An incentive plan is being worked out so that you will not only be responsible for increased sales in your district, but will also benefit substantially in a monetary way."

Lind assumed his duties as district manager for metropolitan New York. During the weeks following Lind's new appointment, Lind frequently inquired of Kaufman regarding what his remuneration would be under the incentive plan. Lind was informed that details were being worked out. In July 1951, Kaufman informed Lind that he was to receive one percent commission on the gross sales of the men under him. This was an oral communication and was completely corroborated by Kaufman's former secretary. On subsequent occasions, Lind was assured by Kaufman that he would get his money. Lind was also informed by Herrfeldt, in the autumn of 1952, that he would get a one percent commission on the sales of the men under him. Early in 1955, Lind negotiated with Brown, then president of Park & Tilford, for the sale of Park & Tilford's New Jersey Wholesale House, and Brown agreed to apply the money owed to Lind by reason of the one percent commission against the value of the goodwill of the Wholesale House.

Was Park & Tilford bound by its employees' representations to Lind?

Biggs, Chief Judge

The problems of "authority" are probably the most difficult in that segment of law loosely termed "Agency."

From the evidence it is clear that Park & Tilford can be held accountable for Kaufman's actions on the principle of "implied authority." Kaufman was Lind's direct superior, and was the man to transfer communications from the upper executives to the lower. Moreover, there was testimony tending to prove that Herrfeldt, the vice-president in charge of sales, had told Lind to see Kaufman for information about his salary and that Herrfeldt himself had confirmed the 1 percent commission arrangement. Thus Kaufman, so far as Lind was concerned, was the spokesman for the company.

Testimony was adduced by Schenley tending to prove that Kaufman had no authority to set salaries, that power being exercisable solely by the president of the corporation, and that the president had not authorized Kaufman to offer Lind a commission of the kind under consideration here. However, this testimony, even if fully accepted, would only prove lack of actual or implied authority in Kaufman but is irrelevant to the issue of apparent authority.

However, the court, below, concluded as a matter of law, that Lind could not reasonably have believed that Kaufman was authorized to offer him a commission that would, in the trial judge's words "have almost quadrupled Lind's then salary." But Lind testified that before he had become Kaufman's assistant in September 1950, he had earned $9,000 for the period from January 1, 1950 to August 31, 1950, that figure allegedly representing half of his expected earnings for the year. Lind testified that a liquor salesman can expect to make 50 percent of his salary in the last four months of the year owing to holiday sales. Thus Lind's salary two years before his appointment as district manager could have been estimated by the jury at $18,000 per year, and his alleged earnings, as district manager, a position of greater responsibility, do not appear disproportionate. On the basis of the foregoing it appears that there was sufficient evidence to authorize a jury finding that Park & Tilford had given Kaufman apparent authority to offer Lind 1 percent commission of gross sales of the salesmen under him and that Lind reasonably had relied upon Kaufman's offer.

It must be remembered that when dealing with internal corporate management matters an employee must be able to rely on the word of his superiors, or their apparent spokesmen, lest operation of such organizations becomes impossible. A salesman cannot check every promise made to him by a superior with the president and the board of directors of the corporation.

Although agency contract doctrines are beneficial to business, pitfalls may also arise, as previously noted. The scope of the authority granted to an agent may have flexible boundaries. Furthermore, agents may ignore their authority; yet, the principal may still be bound to the contract under apparent authority. Consequently, business managers need to be aware of and deal with those risks. Two ways of assessing risks may be suggested. Of course, they have costs that must be considered:

- *Use of Contract:* Careful delineation of the power granted to an agent may limit the exposure to unwanted contracts. For example, actual authority may be limited by a monetary ceiling on contracts or on what may be purchased. Compare the actual authority of an employee hired by an automobile manufacturer as a *"buyer of inventory"* with an employee whose role is limited to "purchasing inventory costing less than $15,000 for compact cars."

- *Agent Relations:* Careful selection, supervision, and training of agents may limit circumstances where agents will exceed their actual authority limits, yet, create binding contracts under apparent authority. For example, it is unlikely that Jill (in the earlier text example) would have purchased $11,000 in spare parts if she had been trained and supervised about the limits of her power. In addition, the hiring process could have been used to screen employees, like Jill, who are more likely to ignore management directives.

Reconsider the *Lind v. Schenley Industries, Inc.* case. What could Park & Tilford have done to limit the risk that their employees' representations to Lind would be binding? Would it have benefited Park & Tilford to do so?

The Law of Fiduciary Duty

A fiduciary is vested with power and authority over another person's property and is charged with managing that property for the other person's benefit. This other person, therefore, places trust and confidence in the work of the fiduciary, hoping to benefit from that work. A fiduciary relationship, then, is one of power and dependence. Thus, agents owe fiduciary duties to their principals.

■ *Agent Power:* The principal empowers an agent to act on his or her behalf. As previously noted, this includes the power to create contracts and to face the risk of liability arising from an agent's torts. Therefore, an agent's activities may have a substantial effect on the principal's property.

■ *Principal Dependence:* The principal must rely on the person selected as agent to take care of creating contracts and performing other business functions. Misplaced reliance may lead to unwanted contracts and unexpected tort liability. Furthermore, the principal must trust his agent. The principal realizes that by having power the agent may be tempted to use it for his own benefit rather than for the principal's benefit.

An agent's fiduciary duty has two components that are tied to the power-dependence relationship noted earlier. The first component is the fiduciary duty of care that imposes a burden of diligence, attention, and informed decision making. For example, an employee negotiating a contract must do so with skill, while keeping the best interests of the employer in mind. This duty balances against the employer's risk that the employee may, through careless action, bind the employer to an unwanted or unfavorable contract.

The second component is the fiduciary duty of loyalty. Once the principal–agent relationship has been created, the agent must make the interests of the principal paramount. Given the power that is vested in the agent, the temptation may arise to use it for personal benefit rather than on the principal's behalf.

Consider the Ethical Perspective, "Duties at the Races." Note that people who owe fiduciary duties are held to a higher, more ethical standard than that which is usually expected in the law.

ETHICAL PERSPECTIVE

Duties at the Races

A racehorse named Grace was entered by its owner, Shaw, in the Kentucky Futurity, a prestigious trotting race. Not only was the purse substantial, but the winning horse would also increase in value as would its sire, mare, and siblings. Mike McDevitt, a jockey, was hired by Shaw to ride Grace.

W.E.D. Stokes owned a stock farm where he bred and raised horses. Grace's sire and a couple of siblings were owned by Stokes. Thus, if Grace won the Kentucky Futurity, then Stokes would see the value of these horses increase.

Even though McDevitt (the jockey) was already employed by Shaw, W.E.D. Stokes offered him an additional $1,000 if he won the Kentucky Futurity while riding Grace. Because of McDevitt's skill, Grace won.

What do you think? What is McDevitt's fiduciary duty? May he collect the $1,000 from Stokes? Evaluate this problem based on the ethics materials in Chapter 7. How does your answer compare with a fiduciary duty analysis?

Source: McDevitt v. Stokes, 192 S.W. 681 (Kentucky Court of Appeals 1917).

FIDUCIARY RELATIONSHIPS WITHIN BUSINESS ORGANIZATIONS

Fiduciary duties also arise within business organizational forms. As previously noted, employees owe fiduciary duties. However, other members of the organization also owe these duties. They arise from the organizational structure and no employer–employee relationship is required. Table 12.2 identifies these intra-organizational fiduciary relationships.

■ **TABLE 12.2** The Fiduciary Relationship and Business Organizational Forms

Business Form	FIDUCIARY RELATIONSHIP	
	Who Owes a Fiduciary Duty?	To Whom Is the Fiduciary Duty Owed?
Sole proprietorship	Employees*	Sole proprietor
Partnership	Partners	Partners
Corporation	Directors and officers	Shareholders
Limited partnership	General partner	Other general partners and the limited partners
Limited liability company	Members who manage	Members

*Employees of any organizational form owe fiduciary duties.

INTERNATIONAL PERSPECTIVE

British Directors and Singapore Courts

The Barings family started a bank in England in 1762. It survived revolution and world war and, by the late twentieth century, had become one of the leading financial institutions in the world. But in 1995, because of wildly speculative trading by one of Barings Bank's Singapore employees, Nick Leeson, the venerable establishment crashed. The remnants were purchased by ING, a Netherlands institution.

Nick Leeson was charged with violating Singapore law and pled guilty in early December 1995. He was sentenced to six and a half years in prison. The sentencing judge commented that the activities of Barings Bank put the integrity of the Singapore financial market at risk. Richard Wu, the finance minister, suggested that increased regulation may be considered.

The Singapore government had commissioned a report on the fall of Barings Bank. When it was issued, the report raised questions about whether or not the London directors of the bank, who claimed they were ignorant of Leeson's activities, had exercised sufficient care in overseeing them. The report concluded that the directors—if they indeed did not know—were either grossly negligent or voluntarily chose not to know. Therefore, a major lawsuit is a possibility.

The legal fallout over Barings Bank, perhaps including questions about its directors' duties, may not be finished.

Source: Jean-Claude Pomonti and Marc Roche, "L'affaire Barings pourrait rebondir et impliquer d'anciens dirigeants de la banque," *Le Monde,* December 5, 1995, page 17.

Partners owe fiduciary duties to each other. Note how the power-dependency concepts arise in a partnership. Each partner, as an agent, may enter into contracts on behalf of the firm; torts committed by the partner may be binding on the firm. Further, note that the partners have a risk of personal liability for unpaid claims against their business. Consequently, each partner has a great deal of power in relation to the property of the others. As a result, the partners are dependent and, by necessity, have placed trust in each other when they entered into the relationship.

Similarly, in a limited partnership and limited liability company, those who manage the firm owe fiduciary duties. In a limited partnership, the general partner owes the duties to the limited partners. Since the limited partners are precluded from management and control of the firm, they must rely on the skills of the general partner for the operation of the business. Thus, the legal restrictions on the limited partner create the need for such a duty to arise.

In a limited liability company, those members who manage the firm owe fiduciary duties to the other members since, as managers, they are empowered to make business decisions that affect the others' investments.

Within a corporation, the board of directors and officers owe a fiduciary duty to the shareholders. The International Perspective, "British Directors and Singapore Courts," is an example of this situation. Note that under corporate law the shareholders do not have a role in managing the firm. Their influence is *indirect*—they elect the board of directors, which in turn elects officers. Therefore, the shareholders rely on others to manage the firm. Under corporate law, the board of directors is vested with this power.

managerial perspective

Should the Ballpark Have Lights?

A shareholder filed suit against the board of directors of the Chicago Cubs National League Ball Club, Inc. During the years of 1961–1965, the Cubs lost money from their baseball operations. The shareholder attributed those losses to inadequate attendance at their home park, Wrigley Field. The Cubs were the only major league team without ballpark lights. Thus, no home games were played at night.

The shareholder contended that because the directors refused to install lights in order to be able to schedule night games, the Cubs would continue to lose money. The shareholder questioned the board's rationale for this decision—night games would have a deteriorating effect on the neighborhood around Wrigley Field. Whether or not the team would benefit financially was not paramount. The shareholder considered this to be an improper motive under the directors' fiduciary duty of care.

The court disagreed. Neighborhood quality, it held, could affect fans' interest in attending a game and, in the long run, could decrease the value of Wrigley Field. Furthermore, the court noted that the Cubs' financial losses could be tied to reasons other than their no-lights policy. Therefore, the court was unwilling to insist that the board forego its judgment simply because all of the other teams had decided to install lights. No fiduciary duty breach occurred.

Source: Shlensky v. Wrigley, *237 N.E.2d 776 (Illinois Court of Appeals 1968).*

THE FIDUCIARY DUTY AND DIRECTOR–SHAREHOLDER RELATIONSHIPS

The fiduciary duty that corporate boards of directors owe to the shareholders has been the subject of much litigation and development in the law. Consequently, it provides a good source of information about the fiduciary duty. However, the precise contours of any fiduciary's obligations are driven by the specific nature of the relationship.

■ Fiduciary Duty of Care

A board of directors' duty of care focuses on its decision-making and oversight functions. The law requires directors to use the amount of care that an ordinarily prudent person in a like position would use given similar circumstances. This is neither an easy nor a precise standard to apply.

Nonetheless, it is clear that a board of directors' duty of care requires that they use prudent procedures when making decisions on behalf of the corporation. The duty does not guarantee that the decision be correct, but merely that it was carefully considered. In addition, the directors must be vigilant in their oversight of corporate operations. They must stay abreast of business developments and cannot ignore unfavorable information.

The Managerial Perspective, "Should the Ballpark Have Lights?", concerns the decision-making function of the board of directors. A board's fiduciary duty is not related to the wisdom of its decision. After all, a court is not necessarily wiser about business matters than a group of executives. The fiduciary duty focuses on the process by which that decision was made. If it was a sound and thoughtful process, then the directors have fulfilled their obligation to the shareholders.

As previously noted, a board of directors' oversight function is also subject to fiduciary duty review. The *Bates v. Dresser* case illustrates this point. This case involves a bank fraud and claims that the fiduciaries violated their duty of care by not detecting the fraud before it became a disaster. The duty of care was applied differently to the board of directors than it was to the president—who also owed a fiduciary duty. Although each owed the shareholders a fiduciary duty of care, their positions in the day-to-day operation of the bank were different. Thus, the diligence each board member needed to exercise on behalf of the corporation was found to be factually different.

Bates v. Dresser   United States Supreme Court *251 U.S. 524 (1920)*

The bank was a small establishment in Cambridge, Massachusetts, with a capital of $100,000 and average deposits of about $300,000. Coleman, who made the trouble, entered the service of the bank as messenger in September 1903. In January 1904, he was promoted to bookkeeper.

In November 1906, he began the thefts that come into question here. Having a small account at the bank, he would draw checks for the amount he wanted, exchange checks with a Boston broker, get cash for the broker's check, and, when the checks came to the bank through the clearinghouse, abstract his own from the envelope, enter the others on his book, and conceal the difference by a charge to some other account or a false addition in the column of drafts or deposits in the depositors' ledger. He handed the cashier only the slip from the clearinghouse that showed the totals. The cashier paid whatever appeared to be due, and thus Coleman's checks were honored. So far as Coleman thought it necessary, in view of the absolute trust in him on the part of all concerned, he took care that his balances should agree with those in the cashier's book.

By May 2, 1907, Coleman had abstracted $17,000, concealing the fact by false addition in the column of total checks and false balances in the deposit ledger. Then, for the moment, a safer concealment was effected by charging the whole to the inactive account of Dresser, then the bank's president. Coleman adopted this method when a bank examiner was expected. Of course, when the fraud was disguised by overcharging a depositor, it could not be discovered except by calling in the passbooks, or taking all of the deposit slips and comparing them with the depositor's ledger in detail. By February 21, 1910, when the bank closed, the amount taken by Coleman was $310,143.02.

The directors considered the matter in September 1909, but concluded that the falling off in deposits was due in part to the springing up of rivals whose deposits were increasing, but was parallel to a similar decrease in New York. An examination by a bank examiner in December 1909 disclosed that nothing was wrong.

In this connection, it should be mentioned that in the previous semi-annual examinations by national bank examiners, nothing was discovered pointing to malfeasance. The cashier was honest, and everybody believed that they could rely on him, although in fact he relied too much on Coleman, who also was unsuspected by all. If the cashier had opened the envelopes from the clearinghouse and had seen the checks, or had examined the deposit ledger with any care, he would have found out what was going on. The scrutiny of anyone accustomed to such details would have discovered the false addition and other indicia of fraud that were on the face of the book. But it may be doubted whether or not anything less than a continuous pursuit of the figures through pages would have done so except by a lucky chance.

Justice Holmes

The question of the liability of the directors in this case is the question whether they neglected their duty by accepting the cashier's statement of liabilities and failing to inspect the depositors' ledger. The statements of assets always were correct. Of course liabilities as well as assets must be known to know the condition and, as this case shows, speculations may be concealed as well by a false understatement of liabilities, as by a false show of assets. But the former is not the direction in which fraud would have been looked for, especially on the part of one who at the time of his principal abstractions was not in contact with the funds. A debtor hardly expects to have his liability understated. Some animals must have given at least one exhibition of dangerous propensities before the owner can be held. This fraud was a novelty in the way of swindling a bank so far as the knowledge of any experience had reached Cambridge before 1910.

We are not prepared to reverse the finding of the master and the Circuit Court of Appeals that the directors should not be held answerable for taking the cashier's statement of liabilities to be as correct as the statement of assets always was. Their confidence seemed warranted by the semi-annual examinations by the government examiner and they were encouraged in their belief that all was well by the president, whose responsibility, as executive officer; and, knowledge from long daily presence in the bank, were greater than theirs. They were not bound by virtue of the office gratuitously assumed by them to call in the pass-books and compare them with the ledger, and until the event showed the possibility they hardly could have seen that their failure to look at the ledger opened a way to fraud. We are not laying down general principles, however, but confine our decision to the circumstances of the particular case.

The position of Dresser, the president, is different. Practically he was the master of the situation. He was daily at the bank for hours, he had the deposit ledger in his hands at times and might have had it at any time. He had had hints and warnings in addition to those that we have mentioned, warnings that should not be magnified unduly, but still would have induced scrutiny but for an invincible repose upon the status quo. In 1908 one Fillmore learned that a package containing $150 left with the bank for safe keeping was not to be found, told Dresser of the loss, wrote to him that he could but conclude that the package had been destroyed or removed by someone connected with the bank, and in later conversation said that it was evident that there was a thief in the bank. He added that he would advise the president to look after Coleman, that he believed he was living at a pretty fast pace, and that he had pretty good authority for thinking that he was supporting a woman. In the same year or the year before, Coleman, whose pay was never more than twelve dollars a week, set up an automobile, as was known to Dresser and commented on unfavorably, to him. There was also some evidence of notice to Dresser that Coleman was dealing in copper stocks. In 1909 came the great and inadequately explained seeming shrinkage in deposits. No doubt plausible explanations of his conduct came from Coleman and the notice as to speculations may have been slight, but taking the whole story of the relations of the parties, we are not ready to say that the two courts below erred in finding that Dresser had been put upon his guard.

In accepting the presidency Dresser must be taken to have contemplated responsibility for losses to the bank, whatever they were, if chargeable to his fault. Those that happened were chargeable to his fault, after he had warnings that should have led to steps that would have made fraud impossible, even though the precise form that the fraud would take hardly could have been foreseen.

■ *Fiduciary Duty of Loyalty*

The fiduciary duty of loyalty regulates the relationship between an individual board member and the corporation. Although the duty is

■ **FIGURE 12.2**   Fiduciary Duty of Loyalty Differs from Acceptable Market Conduct

> A corporate board member (fiduciary) may not use certain information or property to gain personal market advantage.
>
> A corporate board member's contracts with the firm are carefully scrutinized for fairness.
>
> Business opportunities that may interest the board member belong to the corporation if it, too, has an interest.

owed to the shareholders, the focus is on potential conflicts of interest between what is best for the business and what is best for the individual director. Directors are required to promote the interests of the corporation without regard to their personal interests.

Consider the power that corporate directors have. Board members are privy to confidential business plans. Individually, they may influence management policy. The concern is that they may abuse their position of trust by taking advantage of it for personal gain. The fiduciary duty of loyalty requires conduct that is different from what is acceptable (and perhaps laudable) for a participant in a market economy. Figure 12.2 highlights these differences.

USE OF INFORMATION OR PROPERTY   Using corporate information or property for personal benefit without regard to the effect on the company would be a breach of a board member's duty of loyalty. Assume that Jack Smith is on the board of directors of XYZ, Inc. At a meeting, he learns about XYZ, Inc.'s new marketing strategy. A booklet outlining the plan was distributed to the board members. Smith's fiduciary duty of loyalty would prohibit him from giving that booklet to the marketing director of his own company, Smith Enterprises, even if his firm would benefit greatly from it. The marketing strategy belonged to XYZ, Inc. Smith learned about it in his role as director. Thus, he is bound to use that information only to benefit XYZ, Inc.

Recall the *Bates v. Dresser* case from earlier in this chapter. Although Coleman—the employee charged with the theft—was merely an employee, he, too, owed a fiduciary duty. Did he breach it?

MAKING CONTRACTS   Corporate board members are not prohibited from making contracts with their own company. Thus, Jack Smith's company, Smith Enterprises, may sell component parts to XYZ, Inc., where Smith is on the board of directors. However, a breach of loyalty may occur since Smith would have information that his company could use to get an *insider's advantage*. Furthermore, he may be able to influence XYZ, Inc., to accept his company's terms.

Consequently, such contracts are reviewed for fairness. For example, if the component supplies were ordered from a catalog that Smith Enterprises sent to prospective buyers nationwide, there would be no advantage that Smith's board position would have. The contract would be *fair*. Alternatively, Jack Smith could make a full disclosure to the full board of XYZ, Inc., of all aspects of the deal, including the value of the property or services involved, the amount of profit to be made, and any add-ons. Unlike a typical contract offer and acceptance, Smith's burden as a member of the board of directors would be to ensure that XYZ, Inc., knew about the defects in his company's component supplies proposal.

BUSINESS OPPORTUNITIES   A director's right to pursue profit-making business opportunities is limited by the fiduciary duty of loyalty. Thus, a director may not compete. Referring, again, to the Jack Smith and XYZ, Inc., example just mentioned, assume that XYZ, Inc., owned a chain of fast-food restaurants. Smith's duty of loyalty prohibits him from operating a drive-through hamburger franchise that is owned by ABC, Inc., a competitor.

In addition, a director cannot invest in new business opportunities that his corporation may be considering. Assume that XYZ, Inc., has decided to acquire land to expand its operations. If Jack Smith is offered the opportunity to acquire a site that seems to fit XYZ, Inc.'s needs, he may not acquire it unless XYZ, Inc., rejects the opportunity to buy it.

Apply these duty of loyalty principles to the Ethical Perspective, "A Chance to Acquire Pepsi: For the Investors or for Oneself?"

ETHICAL
PERSPECTIVE

A Chance to Acquire Pepsi: For the Investors or for Oneself?

Guth was the chief executive officer of Loft, Inc., a firm that operated soft-drink and candy outlets. The firm had been dissatisfied with what it had to pay Coca-Cola Company for the syrups it used to make soft drinks for its stores. Guth learned that the secret formula of another syrup manufacturer, Pepsi, was available, so he bought the formula for himself, using Loft, Inc., funds to finance part of the purchase. Guth then formed a new business, called it the Pepsi-Cola Company, and made liberal use of Loft, Inc.'s employees and capital to develop it. Loft, Inc., knew nothing of his activities. Guth's new company then sold the syrup to Loft, Inc., for use in its stores.

Guth's Pepsi-Cola Company became a success and when his actions became known, he denied that Loft, Inc., had any stake in it. In a lawsuit brought by Loft, Inc., the court disagreed and ordered him to transfer all of his shares of stock in Pepsi—worth millions of dollars—to it.

Why did the court do this? What suggestions would you have proposed to Guth when he first discovered that Pepsi was for sale? Use an ethical decision-making process.

Source: Guth v. Loft, 5 A.2d 503 (Delaware Chancery Court 1939).

Summary

Business organizations are operated by individuals. In Chapter 11, the forms of those organizations were explored. Here, the powers and duties that the law provides to people within the organizations were discussed. Note how basic legal environment concepts, as discussed in Chapter 1, are illustrated by these materials: first, the legal environment facilitates the operation of the business organizations (the law of agency); second, the legal environment controls the power that it grants to agents (the law of fiduciary relationships).

An agent–principal relationship is not limited to that of an employee and employer. Although that is its most common identity, it also has other identities within each of the organizational forms. For example, partners are agents and principals of each other. Corporate officers are agents; the corporate entity is the principal. In any event, agents are empowered to act on behalf of the principal. Two major aspects of this power were explored—the ability of agents to create contracts on behalf of the principal, and the liability risk to the principal arising from torts committed by the agent.

In addition, while granting agents these powers, the law also imposes a fiduciary duty on them. Fiduciaries owe their beneficiaries duties of care and loyalty that exceed standards normally imposed by the legal environment. The fiduciary duty extends not only to agents and their principals, but to other organizational relationships as well—corporate director-shareholder is an example. In fact, any relationship with an imbalance of power and dependence is a candidate for fiduciary duty regulation.

Review Questions

1. Define the following terms:
   a. Agent
   b. Principal
   c. Apparent authority
   d. Vicarious liability
   e. Fiduciary duty

2. Under what circumstances could a person who owns shares in ABC, Inc., be considered an agent of ABC, Inc.?

3. While on vacation, Jack is approached by an artist who has a booth where he sketches portraits. Jack agrees to have a drawing made but insists that it be of his left side and that only a blue pencil be used. Do Jack and the artist have a principal and agent relationship?

4. Mary and Jane are partners in a bookstore. Bill is an employee whose job role is limited to buying used books from wholesalers. One afternoon, Bill purchases a big-screen television set, charging it to the bookstore. When the set is delivered, the partners install it against a wall and show advertising videos to their customers. Would the partnership be bound to Bill's contract? If so, why? If the bookstore did not use the television set, would the partnership still be bound to Bill's contract?

5. Jack is a shareholder in ABC, Inc., a publicly traded company that manufactures mobile homes. It is his only role in the firm. One day, while visiting a furniture store, Jack orders custom-made items to be used in ABC-manufactured mobile homes. He negotiated an excellent price. However, ABC, Inc., does not want that furniture. Is ABC, Inc., bound to the contract?

6. Bill works for a sole proprietor. He has a written job description that lists "to purchase computers as needed by the business" as one of his responsibilities. Would Bill have the authority to purchase a printer—assuming the business needed one?

7. Mary is an auditor with the Smith & Jones partnership. She was assigned to audit the books of a major client but thought a few days on the beach would be more exciting. So instead of following office audit procedures, she fabricated the numbers. If the client suffers a financial loss because of this audit, does the Smith & Jones partnership face any risk of liability?

8. Jim is a member of the XYZ, Inc., board of directors. The firm intends to expand its office space but has been unable to secure the needed land. If the opportunity is presented to Jim to purchase a site that would be perfect for XYZ, Inc.'s needs, must he offer it first to the corporation?

9. Do partners owe the same duties toward each other that limited partners owe to general partners?

10. George is on the board of directors of ABC, Inc. He attends meetings only occasionally. When he does, he often dozes through most of them. He also does not bother to read reports prepared for the directors, instead relying on management to keep him informed. In fact, he supports anything that management proposes. Does this behavior increase George's risk of legal liability?

11. Smith, Inc., received an offer to purchase its assets in September for $500 million. The offer was made after months of negotiations and evaluation of the assets of the corporation. However, the deal was never consummated. On December 18, another offer of $500 million was received. The offer must be accepted or rejected by December 21. A special meeting of the board of directors was called to consider the offer. The directors met for one hour and heard a report roughly outlining the offer. They neither asked questions nor requested that corporate experts be called to advise them concerning its soundness. Furthermore, general inflation had increased by ten percent in the last quarter of the year. The directors accepted the offer. Have the directors fulfilled their duty to the shareholders?

12. Mary is a member of the board of directors of XYZ, Inc., which operates a popular restaurant in the city. In February, the directors met to discuss the possibility of expanding the restaurant onto the vacant lot next to it. However, because interest rates were high, the board deferred action on the proposal. In April, Mary was approached by the owner of the lot who offered Mary an excellent deal, including low-interest financing, to purchase the lot. Mary immediately agreed. Discuss this problem with relation to Mary's duty to the shareholders of XYZ, Inc.

13. Tom was the sole proprietor of a grocery store. He hired Jane to stock the shelves in his store. One afternoon, Jane was putting bars of soap in a large basket located in an aisle of the store. She was bored with the task so to make it more enjoyable, she invented a game in which, for each bar of soap placed in the basket, the next one would have to be tossed in from one step farther away. A bar of soap missed the basket and skidded down the aisle. A customer stepped on the soap, fell, and was injured. Would Tom be liable for that tort?

14. Jim began working at Harry's Book Shop. His job was to sell books to customers. One Thursday afternoon, a bedraggled old professor was browsing through the shelves and noticed an early edition of Walt Whitman's poetry. The price marked on the book was $150. Jim approached the professor, and they began to speak and haggle about the price. They agreed, finally, that the professor could purchase the book for $128. When the professor attempted to pay for the book, Harry refused to accept the agreed-upon $128 and insisted on the full $150. Must Harry sell the book for the price negotiated by Jim? (Assume that negotiating over the price of books is standard practice in many used-book stores.)

15. Jane Jones is the sole owner of a small business that manufactures pencils. She is also a member of the board of directors of XYZ Corporation. May Jones legally enter into a contract to sell pencils manufactured by her business to XYZ Corporation? If so, may she negotiate with XYZ Corporation to the same extent she is able to do so with all other pencil buyers?

Chapter
13

LEGAL ASPECTS OF CAPITAL ACQUISITION: CONTRACT, PROPERTY, AND SECURITIES REGULATION

Capital acquisition is facilitated by law. Some managers may seek capital through loans (contract and property law). Others may decide to sell parts of their companies instead (securities regulation). A number of business factors influence this decision—interest rates, lender concerns, and public demand for new shares of stock (see Figure 13.1).

However, one of the most important factors is the law. The law not only facilitates the transactions, but it imposes costs and liability risks that arise depending on which capital acquisition method is used. Some laws, for example, impose new regulatory burdens on the firm. Others inhibit certain uses of business property. Undoubtedly, the *legal factor* is a vital element in capital acquisition decisions.

Recall the Thought Problem, "Choosing an Organizational Form," in Chapter 11 involving Bill Jones, Mary Thomas, and Charles Smith. Assume that they decided to organize their business as a corporation. After a few years of operation, JTS, Inc., needed capital for expansion. According to Figure 13.1, the law provides a number of ways capital may be acquired:

■ JTS, Inc., could borrow what it needs from a bank, promising to repay the money with interest by January 1, 2005. This would raise contract law principles (as discussed in Chapters 8 and 9).

■ Before the bank would agree to make the loan, it may require assurances beyond JTS, Inc's promise to repay. Consequently, JTS, Inc., could offer the bank a lien on some of its property. The loan would now entail principles of both contract and property law—topics that will be discussed later in this chapter.

■ JTS, Inc., could bypass the bank and seek numerous *creditors* for the loan it seeks—that is, JTS, Inc., could sell bonds. Assume the corporation needs $10 million for its expansion plans. It could break up that large indebtedness into small chunks of $1,000 each and sell them to the general public. Thereafter, JTS, Inc., would be obligated to repay the loan (plus interest) to the ten thousand *creditors* who bought a part of its indebtedness. This plan raises a new legal issue—securities regulation.

■ As an alternative to borrowing money, JTS, Inc., could seek new investors. Since JTS, Inc., is a corporation, it could offer new shares of stock. This plan also raises securities regulation issues.

■ **FIGURE 13.1**　Seeking Capital

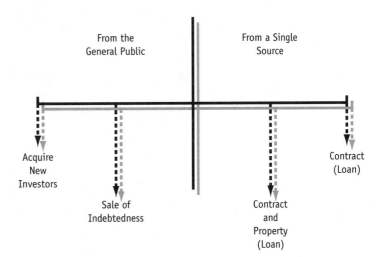

managerial perspective

Raising Capital to Fund Lawsuits

Companies like WBX Partners invest in intellectual property lawsuits. These suits arise when an inventor claims that his patent has been infringed. An inventor who satisfies the *originality* tests of the United States Patent Office is granted a patent. A patent is a formally recognized property right, and it grants sole ownership of an invention to the patent holder. No one may use the invention without the permission of the patent holder. Using another person's invention without permission risks an infringement lawsuit.

Unlike the pursuit of personal injury claims, attorneys are reluctant to undertake patent infringement suits on a contingency fee basis. They consider patent cases to be too time consuming and costly. Consequently, an aggrieved inventor would need to have substantial assets to afford such a claim.

WBX Partners had an idea. It created a limited partnership to fund claims that a waterbed patent had been infringed. Investors—as limited partners—provided the capital to pay the legal expenses of enforcing the patent rights. More than $1 million was raised in this way. To date, more than $9 million has been recovered from infringers. Thirty additional cases have been filed. Without this source of capital, the waterbed's patent holder—who became a limited partner—would have been unable to afford the litigation costs, and the infringers would have escaped scot-free.

Review the materials in Chapter 11 and then determine what attributes of a limited partnership made it an attractive form for WBX Partners to use?

Source: L. Himmelstein, "Investors Wanted—For Lawsuits," *Business Week*, November 15, 1993, page 78.

Which of these capital acquisition methods should JTS, Inc., choose? The answer depends on market conditions, the size of JTS, Inc., and whether or not more debt (or additional shareholders) fits the needs of the business. Such issues are the focus of finance courses, and their consideration will be left for that venue. What the law does is facilitate the choice that JTS, Inc.'s management makes. In doing so, however, the law also imposes duties and burdens that may affect JTS, Inc.'s choice in the first place. The Managerial Perspective, "Raising Capital to Fund Lawsuits," illustrates a creative way in which the law facilitated capital acquisition.

Securing Capital from a Single Source

THE UNSECURED LOAN AND PRINCIPLES OF CONTRACT LAW

An unsecured loan is a contract between a debtor and a creditor in which the creditor lends money to the debtor, and the debtor promises to repay it. The law of contracts provides the framework in which the debtor and the creditor may structure their agreement. Refer to the example in this chapter involving JTS, Inc. The first option was for the corporation to acquire capital through an unsecured loan. The bank would lend JTS, Inc., the capital it needed. JTS, Inc., would promise to pay it back.

Review the contract law materials in Chapters 8 and 9. Then, consider the following discussion.

Offer and Acceptance

A valid contract, including an unsecured loan, must satisfy the offer and acceptance requirements imposed by contract law. Imagine the negotiations that took place between JTS, Inc., and the bank. Offers were made; counter-offers were proposed in response. At some point, JTS, Inc., offered to pay 12.75 percent interest on a three-year, $500,000 loan with payments to be made monthly. The bank accepted this proposal. Thus, contract law's offer and acceptance requirements were met.

Note, however, that the terms of an unsecured loan may be far more elaborate than what JTS, Inc., and the bank negotiated. Executives for each party may use the document to manage risks that may arise during the term of the loan. Some of their concerns could include:

- *Changing Market Conditions:* Both the bank and JTS, Inc., may be worried about interest rates. In a year or two, the market may change, and interest rates may be 8 percent (or 15 percent) on a comparable loan. If neither party is confident that the 12.75 percent rate will hold, they may insert a clause in their contract that provides for a *floating* rate based on a market index they choose.

- *Hedging the Risk of Loss:* The bank may want to hedge its risk of losing money in the event JTS, Inc., fails to pay as agreed (defaults on the loan). A contract clause may require JTS, Inc., to keep $50,000 in an account at the bank. This sum would be readily accessible by the bank in the event that JTS, Inc., defaults.

Creating an unsecured loan may be a creative process that makes ample use of the flexibility of contract law. But, doing so costs money. The more negotiation and customized contract provisions that exist means the more the loan transaction will cost. Consequently, pre-printed forms are often used as a cost-cutting method. These forms contain clauses that will usually benefit the party supplying the form. Provisions that meet JTS, Inc.'s concerns will not appear if the bank's pre-printed forms are used. A trade-off exists—costs of customization versus pre-printed forms that may not protect a company's interests. How to balance the trade-off is a business decision, not a legal decision.

Consideration

The law requires that contracts, including unsecured loans, be made for consideration. In the JTS, Inc., loan example, the bank committed itself to provide $500,000 to JTS, Inc., and the corporation promised to repay that sum plus 12.75 percent interest. Therefore, this element of contract law is also satisfied.

Breach

The party who breaches a contract is liable to the other party for damages. The most likely scenario of a breach of contract would be for

JTS, Inc., to default. The bank's remedy would be to file a lawsuit against JTS, Inc., that would lead to a damage award if the lawsuit is successful. Under contract law theory, the bank's interests have been protected. However, can you think of any practical problems with this remedy?

- *Time and Cost:* Lawsuits are slow and expensive. Review the material in Chapters 2–4. From the bank's perspective, the delay and the legal fees required to pursue contract remedies may make such a course unattractive. For example, it may take a year for the bank to receive a judgment; during that time, it cannot expect payments on the $500,000 it lent to JTS, Inc. In the meantime, the bank's attorneys will still need to be paid.

- *Collectibility of Judgment:* JTS, Inc., may have neither the funds nor the property to satisfy the bank's judgment. Merely because a court awards damages does not mean that the bank will receive any money. The judgment must be collected from JTS, Inc. If JTS, Inc., could not afford its loan payment, then it is unlikely that it can pay whatever the court may order. Furthermore, by the time the bank's lawsuit is filed, JTS, Inc.'s assets may have been sold, or other creditors may have been able to get to these assets first.

Consequently, from the bank's perspective, contract law has limitations. If the bank could describe something better, it may say that it would prefer reimbursement without having to resort to litigation, and it would like a reserved source of property to acquire if JTS, Inc., defaults. What the bank should then consider is a *secured* loan.

THE SECURED LOAN: PRINCIPLES OF CONTRACT AND PROPERTY LAW

A secured loan provides the creditor with a hedge against the risk of debtor default. Of course, sound business practices aim for the same thing. Pre-loan screening techniques may be used to separate likely defaulters from those with good payback histories. However, a secured loan provides even additional assurances. It makes a debtor's continued ownership of specific property subject to full repayment of the loan.

Two areas of law converge when a secured loan is created—contracts and property. In addition to promising the repayment of the loan, the debtor transfers an interest in some of its property as *security* for that promise. If the debtor defaults, the creditor may repossess the property. However, before secured loans are explored further, an understanding of the fundamentals of property law is necessary.

■ Fundamentals of Property Law

Property law is a system that allocates scarce resources. In a market economy, those resources are said to be comprised of *rights*. The person with all of the rights is the owner. But, more than one person may hold rights to the same property. This is what occurs in a secured loan—the owner (debtor) and creditor both have rights in the property.

The Ethical Perspective, "A World without Property," illustrates the need for a resource allocation system, which the law of property provides.

PROPERTY RIGHTS HAVE TWO ELEMENTS   Property rights define a relationship between people that is recognized and enforced by the government. Thus, the owner of an acre of land or a machine has certain powers pertaining to those items that other people do not possess. These *powers* provide the owner with choices that may be made freely and that all others are obliged by law to honor. The power to sell the land or the machine, to lease them to a neighbor, or to use them as collateral for a loan are examples. These powers are called *property rights*.

Consider this example. In Daniel Defoe's novel, *Robinson Crusoe*, the setting shows Crusoe shipwrecked alone on a deserted island. During that time, he captured and raised a herd of goats. Because no one else lived on the island, Crusoe could neither sell the goats to others nor use them as collateral for a loan. Furthermore, no disputes could arise regarding who could use the goats, since Crusoe was alone. There was no need to allocate the animals and, therefore, it cannot be said that Crusoe had property rights to them. In this circumstance, no need existed for defining how the goats could be allocated.

Later in the novel, another person named Friday appeared on the island. With Friday's appearance, a need to allocate the goats surfaces. The problem is how would this be done? What if Crusoe decided either to sell a goat to Friday or to loan him a few for beginning his own herd? There is nothing *automatic* about Friday accepting a subordinate position regarding those animals. Perhaps, Friday may consider that all of the goats belonged to him and that Crusoe should pay him *rent* for using them. Who is correct, and how would you decide?

- Should property rights be based on the fact that Crusoe was the one who initially captured the goats?
- What if Friday is the better herdsman?
- Maybe the stronger of the two people should own the goats.

The latter would certainly settle the matter and, thereafter, their relationship concerning the goats would be set. However, to settle the matter in this way would not be a property rights issue. It would merely be a personal matter between Crusoe and Friday.

What is missing from this scenario is a system of allocation on the island—that is, for property to exist, a government (or the law) must rule on any claims that Crusoe and Friday may have concerning the goats. Therefore, if Crusoe's *deserted* island was located just a few miles from the California coast and is actually a part of that state, then California's property law would apply. The question exists of whether or not either person had rights in the matter of owning the goats. If so, defining those rights would be a matter of the law.

ETHICAL
PERSPECTIVE

A World without Property

Twelve families live in a village. Each family is rather poor and has only one cow. Located on the edge of the village is a five-acre meadow—no one owns it nor does anyone take care of it. The meadow seems to take care of itself. All families in the village graze their cows in the meadow without harming it at all. They have been doing this for years.

Recently, a thirteenth family moved to the village. They are from the city and are prosperous. When they learn about the nearby grazing meadow, they invest all of their money in a herd of cattle (because the market for beef is very strong) and drive the cows to the meadow each day.

Because of the large number of animals, the meadow is soon stripped bare of grass. Why? Which of the families, if any, will reseed the meadow? Do you have any suggestions for the villagers? Would your response change if all people acted ethically?

Williams v. Weisser illustrates the two elements of property—a relationship among people that is recognized and subsequently enforced by law. This case involved a college professor and his claim of ownership to his lectures.

After reading this case, determine what you would recommend to the note-taking company for lessening the risk of a professor making a property rights claim to his lectures.

Williams v. Weisser   California Court of Appeals *78 Cal. Rptr. 542 (1962)*

Plaintiff is an assistant professor in the Anthropology Department at UCLA. Defendant's business, Class Notes, in Westwood, California, sold outlines for various courses given at UCLA. The defendant paid Karen Allen, a UCLA student, to attend plaintiff's class in Anthropology 1, to take notes from the lectures, and to type up the notes. Allen delivered the typed notes to defendant, and defendant placed a copyright notice thereon in defendant's name, reproduced the typed notes, and offered them for sale. Plaintiff objected. Defendant did not cease these activities until served with summons, complaint, and temporary restraining order. Plaintiff seeks a permanent injunction, general damages, and punitive damages.

One of the grounds on which the judgment was based was that the defendant infringed on the plaintiff's common law copyright (property right) to his lectures.

Kaus, Presiding Judge

The oral delivery of the lectures did not divest plaintiff of his common law copyright to his lectures. Nothing tangible was delivered to the students. The principle which pervades the whole of that reasoning is, that where the persons present at a lecture are not the general public, but a limited class of the public, selected and admitted for the sole and special purpose of receiving individual instruction, they may make any use they can of the lecture, to the extent of taking it down in shorthand, for their own information and improvement, but cannot publish it. It is defendant's position that, copyright aside, he was privileged to publish the notes and to use plaintiff's name in connection with such publication because "[p]laintiff intentionally placed himself in the public eye when he undertook his employment as an instructor."

An author who owns the common law copyright to his work can determine whether he wants to publish it and, if so, under what circumstances. Plaintiff had prepared his notes for a specific purpose—as an outline to lectures to be delivered to a class of students. Though he apparently considered them adequate for that purpose, he did not desire a commercial distribution with which his name was associated. Right or wrong, he felt that his professional standing could be jeopardized. There is evidence that other teachers at UCLA did not object to representatives of Class Notes being in the classroom; indeed some cooperated with defendants in revising the product of the note takers. Plaintiff considered the Anthropology 1 notes sold by defendant as defective in several respects, chiefly because of certain omissions. Any person aware of the cooperation given by other faculty members could reasonably believe that plaintiff had assisted in the final product. We think that these considerations easily bring the case within the ambit of *Fairfield v. American Photocopy*. There the defendant used the plaintiff's name in advertising a certain product. He was said to be one of the many satisfied users of the product. He had been a user, but had returned the product to the defendant. The court held that defendant's conduct was "an unauthorized and unwarranted appropriation of plaintiff's personality as a lawyer for pecuniary gain and profit." We think that the *Fairfield* case is indistinguishable from the one at bar.

HOW THE LAW CLASSIFIES TYPES OF PROPERTY   The law classifies types of property, or places them in *boxes*, to use a metaphor. Three *boxes* should be considered—real property (land), tangible personal property (moveable items), and intangible personal property (ideas). Once a classification is made, certain laws become applicable. The laws that apply depend on the *box* in which the property has been classified.

For example, the legal rules associated with the transfer of land require more formalities than those concerning the transfer of a compact disc player. Procedures for establishing ownership in a song or an invention are more heavily regulated than those for establishing ownership in a jacket. But, the same thing is happening in each example. In the first example, property rights are being transferred. In the second scenario, an owner's claim is being recognized. The law effectuates these general concepts based on the practical nature of the property. The classifications take a practical view of property.

Is It Real or Personal Property? Something may be classified as either real property (land and anything firmly attached to it) or personal property (everything else). Personal property may be either tangible (it may be seen, felt, or touched—it has a physical existence) or intangible (ideas, accounts receivable, or other items with economic value but without a physical existence). When a person buys a new home, that purchase is considered real property. The land and the house (which is firmly attached to the land) are transferred to the buyer. This textbook, shoes, the songs heard on the radio, and a new short story are all examples of personal property. Such types of personal property may be tangible (the textbook or the shoes) or intangible (the song or the short story). If someone steals a textbook, the owner has a claim against the thief. Similarly, if another band records a songwriter's work without permission, or a company publishes a story without the author's consent, the songwriter or author would have claims for property rights infringement even though the song and the short story by themselves do not have a physical existence. The have a physical existence only when placed on a CD or printed on paper.

Note the definitions of real and personal property in the preceding paragraph. Which of the following things may always be placed in one category or the other?

1. A house

2. A painting

3. Fertile topsoil

4. A rug

The answer is none of them. Normally, of course, the items may be readily classified, but the law of property, at times, requires a more focused review of the definitions. The legal environment makes each item of property subject to factual evaluation, rather than relying on general notions of what is normal. Thus, consider the painting from the list. Typically, it would be a framed canvas and would be personal property. But *typically* does not include the mural painted on the side of a three-story building. A painting of this nature is an indivisible part of the building and thus would be considered a part of the real property.

The classification of atypical types of property has its own set of guidelines and is known as the *law of fixtures.* Note the practical nature of these guidelines, as they seek to assist in the classification. They illustrate the flexible nature of the definitions of real and personal property.

A **fixture** may be defined as personal property that is so attached to or used with real property that it is considered to be part of that real property (see Figure 13.2). For example, a doorknob at the hardware store is personal property. It is stacked on a shelf and is in no way connected with the land or the building. But as soon as a home owner purchases the doorknob and affixes it to the front door, that item of personal property has been transformed into a part of the house as part of the real property.

The *reasonable person* legal standard applies to fixtures questions— that is, would a reasonable person familiar with the community and with the facts and circumstances of the case be justified in assuming that the person attaching or using the personal property with the real property intended the item of personal property to become a fixture and therefore part of the real property? Courts have developed four guidelines to determine what this mythical reasonable person would do. One is whether or not there is a written agreement labeling an item as a fixture. The written agreement shows intent and is a strong but not conclusive factor in determining whether or not something is a fixture.

Courts will also analyze the facts concerning the relationship of the item of personal property to the real property. These facts revolve around three general concepts. The first is the degree of attachment or annexation of the item of personal property to the real property. The greater the attachment means the more a part of the real property the item appears to be. Certainly a brick that becomes part of the wall of a building is more solidly affixed to the real property than a throw rug lying on one of the room's floors. Second, courts analyze the ease or difficulty of removing the item of personal property, and whether or

■ **FIGURE 13.2** Fixtures

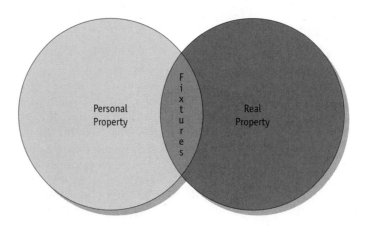

Personal Property

Fixtures

Real Property

not such removal would damage the real property or the item of personal property. Ease of removal suggests that the item is not a part of the real property. Removing the brick from a wall in the building would result in damage to the wall and probably also result in damage to the brick. Since the throw rug could easily be rolled up and carried out of the room there would be no damage occasioned by its removal. The third fact that courts analyze is the appropriateness of the use of the personal property item with the real property—that is, by its use alone, should the item of personal property be considered part of the real property? For example, the throw rug may fit into this category if it was custom designed to fit wall to wall in an unusually shaped room—perhaps a room shaped as a star—as well as being a necessary part of the particular decor of that room. In such a case, the easy-to-remove, unaffixed throw rug begins to appear to have been intended to be a part of the real property.

The Thought Problem, "A House as Personal Property," provides an example of an unusual application of the fixture rules. Is a house considered to be real property? Ordinarily, one could safely answer *yes*. But the special (and practical) nature of that house may change the response.

thought problem

A House as Personal Property

For nearly seventy years, the Wilmore family owned a large tract of waterfront land known as Robinson's Beach. The Wilmores leased portions of this land to tenants who constructed bungalows on it. These beachhouses were only used during the summer. The tenants paid for their use of the land, and they were responsible for maintaining it and carrying insurance on the bungalows they had constructed. The tenants made repairs and remodeled as necessary. Occasionally, a tenant would sell a bungalow, and the Wilmores did not interfere with the sale or the new tenant.

The beachhouses were simple structures. They had no basements, and their foundations consisted of cinderblocks that had been set firmly on the ground. In fact, if the water and electrical connections were removed, these houses could easily be moved without damaging them or the land.

One spring, the Wilmores agreed to sell their land. The contract provided that they would transfer Robinson's Beach to the buyer. After that summer, the tenants attempted to move their beachhouses. However, the company that purchased the land from the Wilmores contended that they owned the buildings, too. After all, they had purchased the Wilmore's real property.

The court held that the tenants owned the beachhouses. The houses were not part of the Wilmore's land and, thus, they would be considered personal property. The bungalows had been erected as temporary structures with no intention of making them part of the land—they could readily be moved, and the tenants were responsible for the upkeep. Therefore, the beachhouses were not included in the land sales contract between the Wilmores and the buyer.

What should the buyer company have done during negotiations with the Wilmores to better protect its interests? Review Chapters 8 and 9 for clues.

Source: Sigrol Realty v. Valcich, 212 N.Y.S.2d 224 (New York Supreme Court, Appellate Division 1961).

Intellectual Property and Its Growing Importance for Business. Personal property, as previously noted, may be classified as either tangible or intangible. Basic industries that produce goods—steel, automobiles, and textiles, for example—create wealth through the production of tangible personal property. These industries were the heart of the American economy from the late nineteenth century and throughout most of the twentieth century. Not only were their products protected by laws of property, but as foreign competition increased, various protectionist devices were instituted to salvage their market share. Although this development is beyond the scope of this text, it illustrates the importance of tangible personal property to the economy.

Of perhaps even greater importance in today's post-industrial economy is intangible personal property. It has no physical existence, but that does not mean that it is not real or that it cannot have extraordinary value. As was noted in *The Ramayana:* "There are three things which are real: God, human folly, and laughter. Since the first two pass our comprehension, we must do what we can with the third."[1] Perhaps then, one may consider intangible personal property as having a heightened or more sophisticated reality than tangible personal property.

Accounts receivable and business goodwill are common forms of intangible personal property that have long been important to business. But, also growing in importance to the economy is a type of intangible personal property called *intellectual property.* Intellectual property includes patents, trademarks, copyrights, and trade secrets. Each are areas of law designed to protect original ideas ranging from computer programs, to production processes, to corporate logos, to the persona of a celebrity. Microsoft and Netscape are examples of companies whose stock-in-trade is intellectual property.

However, in absence of property rights status, original ideas would be available for any company to use. Furthermore, originating firms would have little incentive to develop new ideas, since the products they produced could easily be pirated by competitors. Thus, in the last fifteen years, the legal environment protecting intellectual property has been strengthened.

Computer software is subject to patent protection. In 1982, Congress created a new federal circuit court of appeals designed to hear intellectual property disputes. This new court has upheld eighty percent of the asserted patents, while only thirty percent were previously upheld when challenged by competitors. Royalty payments from intellectual property have grown as a source of corporate revenue. For example, licenses granted by patent holders—so others could use their ideas—routinely provided a one percent royalty on sales. In 1987, Texas Instruments raised its charge to five percent, and its licensing revenues increased by $281 million over the next two years. Lawsuits over intellectual property have also proliferated.

The *Midway Mfg. Co. v. Artic International, Inc.,* case involved intellectual property. The court was asked to define the relationship between Midway Manufacturing Company and Artic International, Inc., as it related to Midway's copyright—that is, does Midway's intellectual property preclude Artic's modified use of it?

After reviewing the case, consider what Artic International, Inc., may have done to lessen the risk that Midway Manufacturing Company would raise copyright infringement questions.

Midway Mfg. Co. v. Artic International, Inc.

United States Court of Appeals, Seventh Circuit *704 F.2d 1009 (1983)*

Midway Manufacturing Co., the plaintiff, makes video game machines. Inside these machines are printed circuit boards capable of causing images to appear on a television picture screen and sounds to emanate from a speaker when an electric current is passed through them. Each machine may produce a large number of related images and sounds. These sounds and images are stored on the machine's circuit boards. How the circuits are arranged and connected determines the set of sounds and images the machine is capable of making. Playing a video game involves manipulating the controls on the machine so that some of the images stored in the machine's circuitry appear on its picture screen and some of its sounds emanate from its speaker.

Artic International, Inc., the defendant, sells printed circuit boards for use inside video game machines. One of the circuit boards the defendant sells speeds up the rate of play—how fast the sounds and images change—of "Galaxian," one of the plaintiff's video games, when inserted in place of one of the "Galaxian" machine's circuit boards. Another one of the defendant's circuit boards stores a set of images and sounds almost identical to that stored in the circuit boards of the plaintiff's "Pac-Man" video game machine; thus, the video game that people play on machines containing the defendant's circuit board looks and sounds virtually the same as the plaintiff's "Pac-Man" game.

Midway Manufacturing Co. sued Artic International, Inc., alleging that Artic's sale of these two circuit boards infringes its copyrights in its "Galaxian" and "Pac-Man" video games.

Cummings, Chief Judge

Midway Manufacturing claims that its "Pac-Man" and "Galaxian" video games are "audiovisual works" protected under the 1976 Copyright Act. However, there is a difficulty that must be overcome if video games are to be classified as audiovisual works. Strictly speaking, the particular sequence of images that appears on the screen of a video game machine when the game is played is not the same work as the set of images stored in the machine's circuit boards. The person playing the game can vary the order in which the stored images appear on the screen by moving the machine's control lever. That makes playing a video game a little like arranging words in a dictionary into sentences or paints on a palette into a painting. The question is whether the creative effort in playing a video game is enough like writing or painting to make each performance of a video game the work of the player and not the game's inventor. If so, then the games are not "audiovisual works" as protected by the Act.

We think it is not. Television viewers may vary the order of images transmitted on the same signal but broadcast on different channels by pressing a button that changes the channel on their television. The creative effort required to do that did not make the sequence of images appearing on a viewer's television screen the work of the viewer and not of the television station that transmitted the images. Playing a video game is more like changing channels on a television than it is like writing a novel or painting a picture. The player of a video game does not have control over the sequence of images that appears on the video game screen. He cannot create any sequence he wants out of the images stored on the game's circuit boards. The

> most he can do is choose one of the limited number of sequences the game allows him to choose. He is unlike a writer or a painter because the video game in effect writes the sentences and paints the painting for him; he merely chooses one of the sentences stored in its memory, one of the paintings stored in its collection.
>
> Thus we affirm the district court's order that enjoins the defendant from manufacturing or distributing circuit boards that can be used to play video games substantially similar to those protected by the plaintiff's copyrights.

Today, the legal environment is working to define intellectual property rights that are vital to high-tech industries. Patent protection has been made available for genetically engineered life forms. The earliest example of this was a patent granted for a form of bacteria. A mouse that was engineered to have a defective immunity system similar to that which is caused by the AIDS virus has also received patent protection. The holders of these patents have property rights in their discoveries.

Computer technology raises additional issues. As information is transferred digitally, perfect copies may be made. This creates challenges to the property law system. At one time, intellectual property, such as books, music, or films, could only be accessed in tangible form (e.g., purchasing a book or compact disc, or renting a film). Distribution was easily controlled by the owner. But, once music is digitalized, it may be put on-line and easily accessed by a computer. Although this technology creates interesting programming, mini *publishing houses* may begin making perfect, yet unauthorized copies. Recall the example of the villagers and the grazing meadow at the beginning of this chapter. What risk(s) may occur?

This issue is not an idle fear for owners of intellectual property. It has already happened. When a telecommunications company made high-speed digital telephone lines available to business customers, one of the first uses was to make perfect copies of musical compact discs onto digital audio tape. Note that the problem is not limited to the United States and its legal system. International concerns also exist. Movies, computer programs, and musical recordings are often copied and sold in countries that have inadequate protections for intellectual property (or who fail to enforce the laws that they have). The International Perspective, "The Beatles for Free?", illustrates this situation.

The Beatles for Free?

Japanese law protects the copyright (ownership) of music for fifty years. However, copyrights for recordings made prior to 1971 are not recognized in Japan. Thus, recordings by popular musicians, such as the Beatles and Elvis Presley, have been copied and sold in Japan with neither permissions nor royalty payments being made to their owners. It is estimated that the recording industry in the United States loses approximately $500 million per year in this way.

In February 1996, both the United States and the European Union filed complaints against Japan with the World Trade Organization, claiming that an international treaty governing intellectual property rights was being violated. This treaty became effective on January 1, 1996. Although various treaties for the past one hundred years have protected intellectual property, this treaty was the first one in which a dispute-settling mechanism was included. This treaty also covers computer software, books, and trademarks.

If a settlement between the United States, Europe, and Japan cannot be reached, a World Trade Organization panel may be formed to decide the matter. Under the treaty, the panel has the power to impose trade penalties if its decision is not complied with.

Source: B. Bahree, "U.S., European Union Turns to WTO," *The Wall Street Journal,* February 12, 1996, page A10.

■ Using Property Rights as Collateral for a Loan

Refer, again, to the JTS, Inc., loan example from earlier in this chapter. Recall that the bank is seeking *security* before it agrees to lend

$500,000 to JTS, Inc. Property rights may provide it. Since property is legally a *bundle* of rights, JTS, Inc., may transfer one of these rights to the bank. All other rights will remain with JTS, Inc.

The bank's *security* right provides it with the option to acquire all of the rights to the item of property if JTS, Inc., defaults. For example, if the corporation used a machine as collateral for its loan, the bank may become owner of the machine if JTS, Inc., does not repay its debt.

By taking collateral, the bank hedges its possible default loss in two ways:

1. The bank is able to salvage something from JTS, Inc.'s bad debt. The property taken as a *security* right is the source of that guarantee.

2. The threat of repossession may spur JTS Inc., to find money to repay the loan. After all, without the machine, JTS, Inc.'s entire production line may shut down.

However, the use of secured loans is not limited to creditor interests. Debtors may offer *security* as a means of enticing a creditor to make a loan (or to provide more favorable terms). Thus, JTS, Inc., may provide property rights to its building and machines as a part of its offer–counter-offer strategy when negotiating with the bank.

Finally, if JTS, Inc., does repay the loan, then the bank relinquishes its property right. Figure 13.3 illustrates how this transaction works.

The legal steps that JTS, Inc., and the bank must take in creating a secured loan are determined by the type of property being used. Note the classification of property materials previously discussed.

- *Real Property:* If the collateral is land, then the real property mortgage principles must be followed. Thus, if JTS, Inc., used its factory as collateral, the bank will have a formally recorded *right* in that factory to secure its loan. If JTS, Inc., defaults, the bank may repossess the factory, thus, becoming its owner.

- *Personal Property:* Both tangible and intangible personal property may be used as collateral for a loan. However, different legal rules (e.g., the Uniform Commercial Code) than those imposed for land must be used in order to transfer personal property rights to the bank. Therefore, JTS, Inc., may use its computers (tangible personal property) and its accounts receivable (intangible personal property) as collateral for the loan.

Even though the practical effect is the same for personal property as for real property—the bank hedges its risk by acquiring a property

■ **FIGURE 13.3** Using Property as Collateral

Step One
JTS, Inc., owns an item of property. (Bundle of Rights: JTS, Inc.=5; the bank=0)

Step Two
JTS, Inc., transfers a "security interest" right to the bank, retaining the others. (Bundle of Rights: JTS, Inc.=4; the bank=1)

Step Three
Possibility #1: JTS, Inc., repays the loan. The bank's right will return to JTS, Inc. (Bundle of Rights: JTS, Inc.=5; the bank=0)
Possibility #2: JTS, Inc., defaults. The bank acquires all of the rights. (Bundle of Rights: JTS, Inc.=0; the bank=5)

right—the legal means of doing this are different. Following the wrong procedure will result in no legal right being transferred to the bank. This is an example of the complexity and formality of the law. It emphasizes why business managers need to rely on competent legal counsel for reaching their goals.

See the Thought Problem, "Seeking Capital," which is an exercise in creatively negotiating a loan in order to raise capital.

thought problem

Seeking Capital

ABC, Inc., intends to acquire $200,000 in capital. It is negotiating a loan with a lender. The lender has evaluated ABC, Inc., and concluded that the corporation has a good credit record. ABC, Inc., also has enough expected income to repay the loan.

ABC, Inc., owns the following property:

■ an undeveloped piece of land on the outskirts of town, worth $20,000

■ a building on Main Street (where ABC, Inc., has its business), worth $100,000

■ the contents of the building (e.g., machinery, office furniture, computers), worth $30,000

■ a patent on its unique manufacturing process, worth $10,000

In addition, note the loan market conditions. Interest rates for a $200,000 loan range between 7.25 percent and 8.43 percent. Furthermore, such loans may vary in length from one to four years.

You and a classmate should assume the roles of executives with ABC, Inc., and the lender. Structure acceptable transactions that may provide ABC, Inc., with the capital it seeks, as well as satisfy the lender.

Acquiring Capital from the General Public: The Securities Markets

A second major source for capital acquisition is the general public. A company may offer the public the chance to buy its debt or a piece of the business itself. These offerings are called *securities* and are specially regulated by both state and federal law. Additionally, with important securities markets overseas (e.g., London, Tokyo), international regulations are also pertinent. The *general public* is not limited to Americans—anyone in the world may be involved.

JTS, Inc., is still seeking to acquire capital. The following additional choices may be considered by the corporation:

■ *Debt Securities:* JTS, Inc., may offer bonds for sale. A bond is a piece of JTS, Inc.'s indebtedness, in which the bondholder is a *creditor* of JTS, Inc. The bond may be secured with property, or it can merely be a promise by the corporation to repay the money. Rather than having one creditor handle a $500,000 loan, JTS, Inc., could carve that sum into $1,000 pieces and have five hundred bondholders.

■ *Equity Securities:* JTS, Inc., may sell shares of its stock. Unlike debt, the buyers—who would be the investors—have no claim to be repaid. Their relationship with JTS, Inc., is as its shareholders. Consult the material in Chapter 11 regarding the attributes of corporate shareholding.

In either scenario, a contract is made between JTS, Inc., and the buyer of either its bonds or shares of stock. However, this contract is not the same as the simple common law contract that was discussed in Chapters 8 and 9. JTS, Inc.'s contract to sell securities must also comply with complex federal regulations. Failure to do so risks legal liability.

Federal securities regulation began during the Great Depression with the enactment of two congressional statutes—the Securities Act of 1933 (1933 Act) and the Securities and Exchange Act of 1934 (1934 Act). These statutes remain at the heart of securities regulation in the United States.

However, the regulation of securities long preceded this development. In Great Britain, for example, securities regulation surfaced as early as 1285 when Edward I authorized the Court of Aldermen to license London brokers as a means of controlling the developing capital markets. The early part of the eighteenth century represented vast speculative investments fueled by the success of a few British trading companies in the New World. Many of the investments were dubious schemes. One morning, a thousand investors paid two guineas, each as a first installment, for the purchase of a share in a company whose business was considered to be of major importance, but no one knew what this business entailed. Available speculative investments, at one point, exceeded the value of all of the land in Britain. As a result, in 1720, Parliament passed the *Bubble Act* which was designed to eliminate abuses. Thereafter, many of the schemes collapsed, causing major investors losses. During the nineteenth century, various securities regulation statutes were enacted in Britain, reflecting its maturing industrial economy.

Interest in securities regulation arose later in the United States. In 1903, roughly one-third of the transactions on the New York Stock Exchange were estimated to be a result of attempted manipulation of the market. Federal legislation was proposed in the late nineteenth century, but the first regulations began to appear in the states. In 1911, Kansas enacted the first major securities regulation statute which reflected the strong Populist current of the times; the moneyed Eastern interests were exploiting the honest tillers of the soil. By 1913, twenty-two states had followed suit.   .

However, these state **blue sky laws** were not particularly effective. The laws were limited to the states of their enactment, while the scope of the capital markets was national in character. Furthermore, not all states had such laws, and often no proper enforcement mechanism was available where regulations existed. Nonetheless, at the time, federal intervention was not considered a proper course.

Political philosophies changed by the early 1930s. The Great Depression had begun, heralded by the stock market crash in 1929. In the autumn of that year, the value of the securities traded on the New York Stock Exchange was $89 billion. By 1932, the value had fallen to $15 billion. The Roosevelt administration had taken office, and federal intervention into economic activity was the byword. Furthermore, revelations about market abuses during the 1920s combined with the other factors to create the political climate for the enactment of federal securities laws. For example, a report of the House of Representatives noted that approximately one-half of the securities issued during the 1920s were worthless.

The Securities Act of 1933 and the Securities Exchange Act of 1934 were enacted to regulate the securities markets (see Figure 13.4). However, Congress did not intend to create a system of insurance to protect bad investments or to cushion the shock of market fluctuations. Instead, the acts were designed to limit market abuses. The acts protected investors from potentially unfair and manipulative practices in the securities markets. They also provided that investors not have less information than corporate insiders when analyzing potential securities transactions.

■ **FIGURE 13.4** **Goals of Securities Regulation**

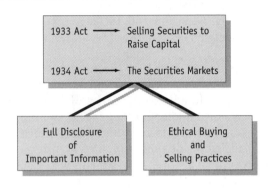

INITIAL ISSUANCE OF SECURITIES

If JTS, Inc., decided to sell bonds or shares of stock, then it would need to comply with the 1933 Act— sometimes called the *truth-in-securities act*. This act's name reflects its purpose, which is to ensure full disclosure of all material information about the new security to the investing public. The information is contained in filings that must be made by the issuer of the securities to the *Securities and Exchange Commission (SEC)*, the administrative agency created to implement and monitor the federal securities laws. These filings are called a *registration statement*. A summary of its contents is called a *prospectus* and must be provided to the investors. The SEC reviews the filed registration statement for full disclosure purposes. It does not judge the wisdom or the soundness of the investment being proposed. Rather, the 1933 Act imposes that responsibility on the individual investor. Securities markets operate more efficiently, and investors are able to make rational investment decisions if they have the necessary information.

Failure to make this disclosure is considered a fraud. However, *fraud*, under the 1933 Act, does not require an intent to conceal the truth. Instead, it arises when the registration statement contains a misstatement or omission of a material fact.

Material facts are those pertinent things that would be of interest to the ordinary, prudent investor. For example, assume that JTS, Inc., filed a registration statement regarding its newly issued stock. The financial information in the registration statement failed to indicate that JTS, Inc., was on the verge of insolvency. Instead, the data merely indicated that its fortunes had waned. Furthermore, in the registration statement's listing of the board of directors, Mary R. Thomas was erroneously listed as Mary Q. Thomas.

Note that two misstatements of fact occurred in JTS, Inc.'s registration statement—first, the financial picture that was presented; and second, the error in Thomas's name. However, the 1933 Act and its full disclosure policy are not concerned with information that would not be of interest to investors. Thus, the only registration statement fraud would be JTS, Inc.'s failure to disclose its precarious financial position. No investor would be influenced by the misspelling of Thomas's name.

Liability for fraud in the registration statement may be imposed on a number of parties involved in its preparation. These parties include:

- *The Issuer:* The corporation that offered the securities. JTS, Inc., would face liability if its registration statement failed to make full disclosure.

- *Corporate Directors:* Since Bill Jones, Mary Thomas, and Charles Smith were the directors of JTS, Inc., they, too, would face 1933 Act liability.

- *Outside Experts:* Accounting firms prepare certified financial statements for the registration statement. Material errors in or omissions from those documents could lead to 1933 Act liability. However, an accounting firm would not be liable for mistakes in portions of the registration statement that others had prepared.

A claim of fraud in the registration statement may be overcome by the due diligence defense. However, this defense is not available to the issuer, nor could JTS, Inc., raise this issue. The other parties (corporate directors and outside experts) would prevail if they could show that they had reasonable grounds to believe that the disclosed information was accurate and that nothing important was omitted. The due diligence defense, in short, provides that taking care in the providing of full disclosure is all that is expected. Merely because inaccurate information appeared in the registration statement is not enough to impose liability.

The *Escott v. BarChris Construction Corp.* case is the leading judicial opinion of the 1933 Act. It is also the most lengthy (and probably the most complex) case in this book. Nonetheless, this case provides an excellent primer on the 1933 Act. While reading it, find the answers to the following questions:

- What were the false statement(s) and errors that appeared in BarChris Construction Corporation's registration statement?

- Why did District Judge McLean find that not all of these statements were material?

- Do you think the judge's decision would have been different if BarChris Construction Corporation's securities had been a highly rated, conservative investment instead of a speculative, growth-oriented one?

- Why was BarChris Construction Corporation found liable? Could it assert the due diligence defense?

- Why would Escott have bothered to file claims against the directors and the accounting firm when he could get a judgment against BarChris Construction Corporation?

- Why did Auslander face 1933 Act liability? Did he meet his due diligence defense?

- Why was Peat, Marwick a party to this lawsuit when the mistakes were made by one of its employees? (Consult the material in Chapter 12 for clues.)

- Do you think Peat, Marwick would have met its due diligence defense if its employee had followed generally accepted auditing procedures?

Escott v. BarChris Construction Corp.

United States District Court, Southern District of New York
283 F. Supp. 643 (1968)

BarChris Construction Corp. was engaged primarily in the construction of bowling alleys, referred to here as *bowling centers.* These were rather elaborate affairs. They contained not only a number of alleys or *lanes,* but also, in most cases, bar and restaurant facilities. The introduction of automatic pin-setting machines in 1952 gave a marked stimulus to bowling. It rapidly became a popular sport, with the result that bowling centers began to appear throughout the country in rapidly increasing numbers. BarChris benefited from this increased interest in bowling. Its construction operations expanded rapidly. It is estimated that in 1960 BarChris installed approximately three percent of all lanes built in the United States.

In general, BarChris's method of operation was to enter into a contract with a customer, receive at that time a comparatively small down payment on the purchase price, and proceed to construct and equip the bowling alley. When the work was finished and the building delivered, the customer paid the balance of the contract price in notes, payable in installments over a period of years. BarChris discounted these notes with a factor and received part of their face amount in cash. The factor held back part as a reserve.

In 1960, BarChris began a practice that is referred to throughout this case as the *alternative method of financing.* In substance, this was a sale and leaseback arrangement. It involved a distinction between the *interior* of a building and the building itself—that is, the outer shell. In instances where this method applied, BarChris would build and install what it referred to as the *interior package.* Actually, this amounted to constructing and installing the equipment in a building. When it was completed, BarChris would sell the interior to a factor, James Talcott Inc. (Talcott), who would pay BarChris the full contract price therefor. The factor then proceeded to lease the interior either directly to BarChris's customer or back to the subsidiary of BarChris. In the latter case, the subsidiary in turn would lease it to the customer.

Under either financing method, BarChris was compelled to expend considerable sums in defraying the cost of construction before it received reimbursement. As a consequence, BarChris was in constant need of cash to finance its operations—a need that grew more pressing as operations expanded. By early 1961, BarChris needed additional working capital. The proceeds of the sale of the debentures involved in this action were to be devoted, in part at least, to filling that need.

Although BarChris continued to build alleys in 1961 and 1962, it became increasingly apparent that the industry was overbuilt. Operators of alleys, often inadequately financed, began to fail. Precisely when the tide turned is a matter of dispute, but at any rate, its ebbing was painfully apparent in 1962. In October 1962, BarChris came to the end of the road. On October 29, 1962, it filed in this court a petition for an arrangement under Chapter 11 of the Bankruptcy Act. BarChris defaulted in the payment of the interest due on November 1, 1962, on the debentures.

The registration statement, filed before the sale of debentures, contained a prospectus as well as other information. The prospectus contained, among other things, a description of BarChris's business, a description of its real property, some material pertaining to certain of its subsidiaries, and remarks about various other aspects of its affairs. It also contained financial information. It included a consolidated balance sheet as of December 31, 1960, with elaborate explanatory notes. These figures had been audited by Peat, Marwick.

Plaintiffs challenge the accuracy of a number of these figures. They also charge that the text of the prospectus, apart from the figures, was false in a number of respects, and that material information was omitted. Each of these contentions, after eliminating duplications, will be separately considered.

The various falsities and omissions are as follows:

1. 1960 Earnings

   (a) Sales

As per prospectus	$9,165,320
Correct figure	8,511,420
Overstatement	$653,900

   (b) Net Operating Income

As per prospectus	$1,742,801
Correct figure	1,496,196
Overstatement	$246,605

   (c) Earnings per Share

As per prospectus	$.75
Correct figure	.65
Overstatement	$.10

2. 1960 Balance Sheet

   Current Assets

As per prospectus	$4,524,021
Correct figure	3,914,332
Overstatement	$609,689

3. Contingent liabilities as of December 31, 1960, on alternative method of financing

As per prospectus	$750,000
Correct figure	1,125,795
Understatement	$375,795
Capitol Lanes should have been shown as a direct liability	$325,000

4. Contingent liabilities as of April 30, 1961

As per prospectus	$825,000
Correct figure	1,443,853
Understatement	$618,853
Capitol Lanes should have been shown as a direct liability	$314,166

5. Earnings figures for quarter ending March 31, 1961

   (a) Sales

As per prospectus	$2,138,455
Correct figure	1,618,645
Overstatement	$519,810

   (b) Gross Profit

As per prospectus	$483,121
Correct figure	252,366
Overstatement	$230,755

6. Backlog as of March 31, 1961

As per prospectus	$6,905,000
Correct figure	2,415,000
Overstatement	$4,490,000

7. Failure to disclose officers' loans outstanding and unpaid on May 16, 1961 — $386,615

8. Failure to disclose use of proceeds in manner not revealed in prospectus	
Approximately	$1,160,000
9. Failure to disclose customers' delinquencies in May 1961 and BarChris's potential liability with respect thereto	Over $1,350,000
10. Failure to disclose the fact that BarChris was already engaged, and was about to be more heavily engaged, in the operation of bowling alleys	

McLean, District Judge

It is a prerequisite to liability under Section 11 of the Act that the fact which is falsely stated in a registration statement, or the fact that is omitted when it should have been stated to avoid misleading, be "material."

The average prudent investor is not concerned with minor inaccuracies or with errors as to matters which are of no interest to him. The facts which tend to deter him from purchasing a security are facts which have an important bearing upon the nature of condition of the issuing corporation or its business.

Judged by this test, there is no doubt that many of the misstatements and omissions in this prospectus were material. This is true of all of them which relate to the state of affairs in 1961.

The misstatements and omissions pertaining to BarChris's status as of December 31, 1960, however, present a much closer question. These debentures were rated "B" by the investment rating services. They were thus characterized as speculative, as any prudent investor must have realized. It would seem that anyone interested in buying these convertible debentures would have been attracted primarily by the conversion feature, by the growth potential of the stock. The growth which the company enjoyed in 1960 over prior years was striking, even on the correct figures. It is hard to see how a prospective purchaser of this type of investment would have been deterred from buying if he had been advised of these comparatively minor errors in reporting 1960 sales and earnings.

Since no one knows what moves or does not move the mythical "average prudent investor," it comes down to a question of judgment. It is my best judgment that the average prudent investor would not have cared about these errors in the 1960 sales and earnings figures, regrettable though they may be. I therefore find that they were not material within the meaning of Section 11. The same is true of the understatement of contingent liabilities by approximately $375,000.

This leaves for consideration the errors in the 1960 balance sheet figures. Would it have made any difference if a prospective purchaser of these debentures had been advised of these facts? There must be some point at which errors in disclosing a company's balance sheet position became material, even to a growth-oriented investor. On all the evidence I find that these balance sheet errors were material within the meaning of Section 11.

Since there was an abundance of material misstatements pertaining to 1961 affairs, whether or not the errors in the 1960 figures were material does not affect the outcome of this case except to the extent that it bears upon the liability of Peat, Marwick. That subject will be discussed hereinafter.

The "Due Diligence" Defenses   Every defendant, except BarChris itself, to whom, as the issuer, these defenses are not available, has pleaded this affirmative defense. Each claims that (1) as to the part of the registration statement purporting to be made on the authority of an expert (which, for convenience, I shall refer to as the "expertised portion"), he had no reasonable ground to believe and did not believe that there were any untrue statements or material omissions, and (2) as to the other part of the registration statement, he made a reasonable investigation, as a result of which he had reasonable ground to believe and did believe that the registration statement was true and that no material fact was omitted. As to each defendant, the question is whether he has sustained the burden of proving these defenses.

The only expert, in the statutory sense, was Peat, Marwick, and the only parts of the registration statement which purported to be made upon the authority of an expert were the portions which purported to be made on Peat, Marwick's authority.

The registration statement contains a report of Peat, Marwick as independent public accountants dated February 23, 1961. This relates only to the consolidated balance sheet of BarChris and consolidated subsidiaries as of December 31, 1960, and the related statement of earnings and retained earnings for the five years then ended. This is all that Peat, Marwick purported to certify. It is perfectly clear that it did not purport to certify the 1961 figures, some of which are expressly stated in the prospectus to have been unaudited.

I turn now to the question of whether defendants have proved their due diligence defenses. The position of each defendant will be separately considered.

Auslander Auslander was an "outside" director, i.e., one who was not an officer of BarChris. He was chairman of the board of Valley Stream National Bank in Valley Stream, Long Island. In February 1961 Vitolo, the president and a founder of BarChris, asked him to become a director. Vitolo gave him an enthusiastic account of BarChris's progress and prospects. As an inducement, Vitolo said that when BarChris received the proceeds of a forthcoming issue of securities, it would deposit $1,000,000 in Auslander's bank.

In February and early March 1961, before accepting Vitolo's invitation, Auslander made some investigations of BarChris. He obtained Dun & Bradstreet reports which contained sales and earnings figures for periods earlier than December 31, 1960. He caused inquiry to be made of certain of BarChris's banks and was advised that they regarded BarChris favorably.

On March 3, 1961, Auslander indicated his willingness to accept a place on the board. Shortly thereafter, on March 14, Kircher sent him a copy of BarChris's annual report for 1960. Auslander observed that BarChris's auditors were Peat, Marwick. They were also the auditors for the Valley Stream National Bank. He thought well of them.

Auslander was elected a director on April 17, 1961. The registration statement in its original form had already been filed, of course without his signature. On May 10, 1961, he signed a signature page for the first amendment to the registration statement, which was filed on May 11, 1961. This was a separate sheet without any document attached. Auslander did not know that it was a signature page for a registration statement. He vaguely understood that it was something "for the SEC."

Auslander attended a meeting of BarChris's directors on May 15, 1961. At that meeting he, along with the other directors, signed the signature sheet for the second amendment, which constituted the registration statement in its final form. Again, this was only a separate sheet without any document attached. Auslander never saw a copy of the registration statement in its final form.

At the May 15 directors' meeting, however, Auslander did realize that what he was signing was a signature sheet to a registration statement. This was the first time that he had appreciated that fact. A copy of the registration statement in its earlier form as amended on May 11, 1961 was passed around at the meeting. Auslander glanced at it briefly. He did not read it thoroughly.

At the May 15 meeting, the officers stated that everything was in order and that the prospectus was correct. Auslander believed this statement.

In considering Auslander's due diligence defenses, a distinction is to be drawn between the expertised and non-expertised portions of the prospectus. As to the former, Auslander knew that Peat, Marwick had audited the 1960 figures. He believed them to be correct because he had confidence in Peat, Marwick. He had no reasonable ground to believe otherwise.

As to the non-expertised portions, however, Auslander is in a different position. He seems to have been under the impression that Peat, Marwick was responsible for all the figures. This impression was not correct, as he would have realized if he had read the prospectus carefully. Auslander made no investigation of the accuracy of the prospectus. He relied on the assurance of the officers, and upon the information he had received in answer to his inquiries back in February and early March. These inquiries were general ones, in the nature of a credit check. The information which he received in answer to them was also general, without specific reference to the statements in the prospectus, which was not prepared until some time thereafter.

It is true that Auslander became a director on the eve of the financing. He had little opportunity to familiarize himself with the company's affairs. The question is whether, under such circumstances, Auslander did enough to establish his due diligence defense with respect to the nonexpertised portions of the prospectus.

Section 11 imposes liability in the first instance upon a director, no matter how new he is. He is presumed to know his responsibility when he becomes a director. He can escape liability only by using the reasonable care to investigate the facts which a prudent man would employ in the management of his own property. In my opinion, a prudent man would not act in an important matter without any knowledge of the relevant facts, in sole reliance upon representations of persons who are comparative strangers and upon general information which does not purport to cover the particular case. To say that such minimal conduct measures up to the statutory standard would, to all intents and purposes, absolve new directors from responsibility merely because they are new. This not a sensible construction of Section 11, when one bears in mind its fundamental purpose of requiring full and truthful disclosure for the protection of investors.

I find and conclude that Auslander has not established this due diligence defense with respect to the misstatements and omissions in those portions of the prospectus other than the audited 1960 figures.

Peat, Marwick   The part of the registration statement purporting to be made upon the authority of Peat, Marwick as an expert was, as we have seen, the 1960 figures. But because the statute requires the court to determine Peat, Marwick's belief, and the grounds thereof, "at the time such part of the registration statement became effective," for the purposes of this affirmative defense, the matter must be viewed as of May 16, 1961, and the question is whether at that time Peat, Marwick, after reasonable investigation, had reasonable ground to believe and did believe that the 1960 figures were true and that no material fact had been omitted from the registration statement which should have been included in order to make the 1960 figures not misleading. In deciding this issue, the court must consider not only what Peat, Marwick did in its 1960 audit, but also what it did in its subsequent "S-1 review." The proper scope of that review must also be determined.

Most of the actual work was performed by a senior accountant, Berardi, who was then about thirty years old. He was not yet a C.P.A. He had had no previous experience with the bowling industry. This was his first job as a senior accountant. He could hardly have been given a more difficult assignment.

The purpose of reviewing events subsequent to the date of a certified balance sheet (referred to as an S-1 review when made with reference to a registration statement) is to ascertain whether any material change has occurred in the company's financial position which should be disclosed in order to prevent the balance sheet figures from being misleading. The scope of such a review, under generally accepted auditing standards, is limited. It does not amount to a complete audit.

Peat, Marwick prepared a written program for such a review. I find that this program conformed to generally accepted auditing standards. Among other things, it required the following:

Review minutes of stockholders, directors and committee meetings.
Review latest interim financial statements and compare with corresponding statements of preceding year. Inquire regarding significant variations and changes.
Review the more important financial records and inquire regarding material transactions not in the ordinary course of business and any other significant items.
Inquire as to changes in material contracts.
Inquire as to any significant bad debts or accounts in dispute for which provision has not been made.
Inquire as to newly discovered liabilities, direct or contingent.

Berardi made the S-1 review in May 1961. He devoted a little over two days to it, a total of 20½ hours. He did not discover any of the errors or omissions pertaining to the state of affairs in 1961 which I have previously discussed at length, all of which were material. The question is whether, despite his failure to find out anything, his investigation was reasonable within the meaning of the statute.

What Berardi did was to look at a consolidating trial balance as of March 31, 1961, which had been prepared by BarChris, compare it with the audited December 31, 1960, figures, discuss with Trilling certain unfavorable developments which the comparison disclosed, and read certain minutes. He did not examine any "important financial records" other than the trial balance. As to minutes, he read only what minutes he was given, which consisted only of the board of directors' minutes of BarChris.

In substance, what Berardi did was he asked questions, he got answers which he considered satisfactory, and he did nothing to verify them.

Berardi had no conception of how tight the cash position was. Since he never read the prospectus, he was not even aware that there had ever been any problem about loans from officers.

During the 1960 audit Berardi had obtained some information from factors, not sufficiently detailed even then, as to delinquent notes. He made no inquiry of factors about this in his S-1 review. He was content with Trilling's assurance that no liability theretofore contingent had become direct.

There had been a material change for the worse in BarChris's financial position. That change was sufficiently serious so that the failure to disclose it made the 1960 figures misleading. Berardi did not discover it. As far as results were concerned, his S-1 review was useless.

Accountants should not be held to a standard higher than that recognized in their profession. I do not do so here. Berardi's review did not come up to that standard. He did not take some of the steps which Peat, Marwick's written program prescribed. He did not spend an adequate amount of time on a task of this magnitude. Most important of all, he was too easily satisfied with glib answers to his inquiries.

This is not to say that he should have made a complete audit. But there were enough danger signals in the materials which he did examine to require some further investigation on his part. Generally accepted accounting standards required such further investigation under these circumstances. It is not always sufficient merely to ask questions.

Here again, the burden of proof is on Peat, Marwick. I find that that burden had not been satisfied. I conclude that Peat, Marwick has not established its due diligence defense.

Acquiring capital from the general public raises securities law questions. Therefore, before doing so, JTS, Inc., must be willing to comply with the regulations and risk the legal liability that they impose. (Note that other provisions in the securities laws exist that, under some circumstances, modify the basic registration statement filing, previously discussed. Their discussion, however, is beyond the scope of this survey.)

A major factor in making JTS, Inc., securities attractive is their liquidity—the ease with which a holder may sell the securities to someone else. If finding a potential buyer would be time-consuming or difficult, then a securities holder would be less likely to invest in JTS, Inc., in the first place. Furthermore, a belief in the fairness of market transactions is fundamental. The alternative is to create self-protective devices or simply not to participate. Neither alternative encourages investors to buy JTS, Inc., securities. In fact, they discourage it.

Both active and ethical securities markets are vital for capital acquisition. If the markets do not exist, or their unfairness undermines public faith in them, then public sources of capital will be far harder to come by. Consequently, securities markets are specially regulated by law. Securities markets are different than markets found for furniture, automobiles, or tomatoes. None of these markets are vital to capital acquisition activities in a market economy.

TRADING IN SECURITIES: ETHICAL BUYING AND SELLING PRACTICES

A discussion of insider trading will be used to illustrate how the law imposes ethical standards on those who buy or sell securities. Insider trading describes a transaction in which one party has important confidential information about the securities: information that he is duty-bound not to use, but does so, anyway, by trading the securities himself or providing the information to someone else who does. Evaluate insider trading using the ethical model from Chapter 7. The *insider* clearly ignores legitimate interests of others, such as the company whose information he appropriates for personal gain, and the person from whom he buys or to whom he sells the securities.

Note the following two elements of insider trading under the securities laws:

1. *Information Access:* Inside traders have important information about securities that is not publicly available. For example, Charles Smith is on JTS, Inc.'s board of directors. During today's meeting, the board decided to reduce dividend payments by fifty percent. One would anticipate that when this information is disclosed, investors may not be willing to pay as much for JTS, Inc., shares as they may have paid before. Then, the market price will decline, and a holding of one thousand JTS, Inc., shares that were valued at $40 each ($40,000) yesterday, may fetch only $37,500 today.

2. *Duty Not to Use the Information:* Ordinarily, a person may use whatever information that he possesses. However, limitations arise from certain legal relationships. One example of a limitation is in a contract. A person may contractually agree to keep information confidential that could otherwise be used *at will.* For example, an auditing firm may promise to keep what it learns while working for a client confidential.

Another common example involves fiduciaries. Members of a board of directors owe fiduciary duties that limit their use of corporate information. As a JTS, Inc., board member, Charles Smith owes a fiduciary duty. Until JTS, Inc., discloses its dividend reduction plan, Smith is required to keep the information confidential. If he publicizes it ahead of time (or otherwise uses it contrary to JTS, Inc.'s interests), his fiduciary duty will be breached.

When both elements (access to confidential information that one is duty-bound not to use) converge and securities are traded, insider trading occurs. The *insider* then faces two legal problems—first, breach of contract (or fiduciary duty); and second, violation of securities laws. Assume that Charles Smith sold his JTS, Inc., securities before the dividend reduction decision was made public. He not only breached his fiduciary duty, but he also engaged in insider trading.

The Thought Problem, "Insider Trading or Not?", provides a further illustration of insider trading. Note, however, that unlike Charles Smith, Ray Dirks did not violate insider trading laws. Do you know why?

thought problem

Insider Trading or Not? Ray Dirks was an

officer of a New York broker-dealer firm who specialized in providing investment analysis of insurance company securities to institutional investors. On March 6, Dirks received information from Ronald Secrist, a former officer of Equity Funding of America. Secrist alleged that the assets of Equity Funding were vastly overstated as the result of fraudulent corporate practices. He urged Dirks to verify the fraud and disclose it publicly.

Dirks decided to investigate the allegations. He visited Equity Funding of America's headquarters in Los Angeles and interviewed several officers and employees of the corporation. The senior management denied any wrongdoing, but certain corporation employees corroborated the charges of fraud. Neither Dirks nor his firm owned or traded any Equity Funding stock, but throughout his investigation, he openly discussed the information he had obtained with a number of clients and investors. These people included five investment advisors who liquidated holdings of more than $16 million of Equity Funding securities.

During the two-week period in which Dirks pursued his investigation and spread word of Secrist's charges, the price of Equity Funding stock fell from $26 per share to less than $15 per share. This led the New York Stock Exchange to halt trading on March 27. Shortly thereafter, California insurance authorities impounded Equity Funding's records and uncovered evidence of the fraud.

Consider whether or not Dirks violated the insider trading prohibition of the securities laws. Did Ray Dirks have access to important confidential information about Equity Funding of America? Did he have a contractual or fiduciary duty not to use that information?

Source: Dirks v. Securities and Exchange Commission, *103 S.Ct. 3255 (United States Supreme Court 1983).*

The United States is not the only country that prohibits insider trading of securities. The importance of assuring the general public that securities markets are fair has led other members of the *Group of*

■ **FIGURE 13.5** Regulation of
Insider Trading in G-7 Countries

Source: R. Biegen, L. Pashkoff, P. Roche, "Countries Strengthen Insider Trading laws," *National
Law Journal,* November 13, 1995, page C19.

France

France was the only G-7 nation other than the United States to comprehensively regulate insider trading before 1980. Both administrative regulation and criminal
statutes may be applied to those who improperly trade in securities.

Germany

Insider trading became illegal for the first time in 1994 with the enactment of the
Second Financial Markets Promotion Act. A federal government office, the *Bundesauf-
sichsamt fur den Wertpapierhandel,* was charged with enforcing this law.

Italy

Italy first regulated insider trading in 1991. An administrative agency, *Consob,* has
been charged with enforcing the prohibition.

Japan

Although Japan has prohibited insider trading since 1948, enforcement has been virtually nonexistent. The first case was not brought until 1982. Japan strengthened its
laws in 1988, but enforcement and exposure of insider trading activities have
remained questionable.

Seven (G-7) to adopt similar regulations. The Group of Seven consists
of the following major industrial nations—Canada, France, Germany,
Italy, Japan, the United States, and the United Kingdom. Figure 13.5
provides a sample of their insider trading laws.

Summary

The law provides structures through which a business may raise capital. The fundamental legal principle is the contract. A company may
promise to repay a loan, and both the debtor and the creditor may
define their relationships through their agreement. Materials in
Chapters 8 and 9 should be reviewed to understand the basics of contract law.

However, capital acquisition raises additional legal issues. One
issue is that property law works together with contracts to provide a
hedge for the creditor if the debtor fails to repay as agreed. Two
important ideas about the legal concept of property should also be
emphasized. First, the law categorizes property (real and personal
property, tangible and intangible personal property). Depending on
the category, different laws apply to facilitate the parties accomplish-
ing the same goal. Second, is the idea that property is a bundle of
legal rights. As such, more than one person may hold rights to the
same piece of property. These general property law concepts were
used in this chapter to explain how the law enables parties to secure
loans.

The final legal issue discussed in this chapter was securities regulation. Companies may acquire capital from the general public by offering promises to repay parts of a loan (bonds) or by selling pieces of
the business (shares of stock). Federal securities regulation has two
objectives—first, the disclosure of important information; and second, to encourage ethical buying and selling practices. Therefore, the
law imposes costs on firms who seek capital by creating regulatory
standards.

Review Questions

1. Define the following terms:
   a. Unsecured loan
   b. Secured loan
   c. Real property
   d. Intellectual property
   e. Registration statement
   f. Insider trading

2. How does the law distinguish real property from personal property?

3. Would the law classify a brick in the same way if that brick was one of a stack of fifty at a construction site or if it was part of a wall of a three-story building? If so, why? If not, why not?

4. Why does the law provide property rights status to ideas?

5. ABC, Inc., raised $100,000 in capital by taking out an unsecured loan with XYZ Lenders. Describe how the law facilitates this process. What risks exist for XYZ Lenders, and how may they alleviate them?

6. Your firm needs $250,000 in order to install a new line in your manufacturing process. Your firm owns the land where its factory is located and the machinery that is in it. However, Credit Company is unwilling to lend you the money even though you promise to pay it back at an interest rate that is higher than usual. Can you make any suggestions that may make Credit Company reconsider?

7. Why would a bank want to secure a loan that it makes to a local corporation? What bodies of law facilitate this decision?

8. ABC Corporation plans to issue a new series of bonds to be offered to the general public throughout the United States. The bonds are valued at $50 million. What must the corporation do to avoid problems with the securities laws? Limit your discussion to materials contained in this chapter.

9. You are a member of the board of directors of XYZ Corporation. At the annual meeting of the board held in January, you are given a lengthy document and are told that it is a registration statement to be filed with the SEC in the morning. Since the document was distributed about fifteen minutes before the meeting was to adjourn, you do not have an opportunity to read it. What concerns should you have about signing this document?

10. XYZ Corporation filed a registration statement with the SEC regarding a new issuance of securities. The statement fails to note that most of the proceeds from the sale of these securities will be paid to executives as a year-end bonus. The language of the document states: "The funds will be used to enhance corporate productivity." In addition, the document significantly understates corporate liabilities and overvalues corporate assets. Finally, the document fails to indicate that most of the accounts receivable are actually bad debts. Does this pose a legal risk, and if so, to whom? Explain your answer.

11. Your spouse is the administrative assistant to the president of Oil Co., Inc., a major petroleum organization. On August 1, your spouse tells you about a major petroleum discovery made by the corporation. This discovery, it is believed, will be the largest one ever

recorded. The corporation decided to withhold announcement of the find until it may purchase the land rights to cover all of the drilling sites. The next day, you and your spouse use all joint savings to purchase Oil Co., Inc., stock. In October, the find is announced, and the stock price jumps. Are there any potential problems for you and your spouse under the securities regulations? Discuss your answer.

12. You, a student, are having dinner in a nice restaurant in the financial district of a city you are visiting. At the table next to you is a group that is discussing a decision to decrease the dividend being paid on ABC Corporation stock. The corporation has never before cut its dividends. You suddenly realize that the group is the board of directors of that company. Furthermore, you enjoy investing in stock and have studied the fortunes of ABC Corporation. You are very surprised to hear about the dividend decision. If you sell your ABC Corporation stock before the corporation announces its dividend cut, could you expect problems to arise under federal securities law? Explain your answer.

Note

[1]A. Menen, *Rama Retold* (London: Chatto and Windus, 1954), p. 231. Menen's book is a prose version of Valmiki's epic poem from the Indian Enlightenment, *The Ramayana*.

6

Part

REGULATION OF BUSINESS

Chapter 14

PRODUCTS LIABILITY

In Chapter 10, Assessing External Costs of Doing Business: Tort Liability, three theories of tort liability were discussed—intentional torts, negligence, and strict liability in tort. Injured parties rely on these theories of recovery when they have sustained an injury as a result of the actions of another party.

Products liability law arises partly from torts law and partly from contracts law; however, it is a distinct body of law. Products liability law pertains to the question of who should pay for the injuries that arise from defective products. A troublesome fact is that even when the seller has exercised the highest level of care concerning the design and production of its products, such products sometimes seriously injure or kill people. Courts then face the difficult situation of assigning loss to one of two innocent people—the business that introduced the product to the marketplace, or the injured party.

The law has evolved over time in this area. As discussed in the first part of this chapter, the courts initially refused to place the loss on sellers in the absence of some evidence of wrongdoing on the seller's part. Since the 1960s, however, American law has changed so that sellers are sometimes forced to pay for losses, even in the absence of wrongdoing by the seller.

Products Liability and History

Historically, the law permitted only the person who purchased a product to sue, and it permitted that person to sue only his or her immediate seller. Before the Industrial Revolution, this policy probably created very few problems because of the small number of rather simple products purchased by the average person. The farmer who purchased a plow to pull behind his ox probably bought it directly from a village blacksmith. Any disputes could be resolved directly between the blacksmith and the farmer.

Because people purchased only a few simple products in the course of their lives, the courts tended to believe that purchasers could easily determine for themselves the quality of products. For centuries, the courts followed the doctrine of caveat emptor. In other words, the courts placed the risk of loss for dangerous products on the injured party. Such courts assumed that the injury occurred because of the failure of the injured party to carefully examine a product before purchasing and using it. Such decisions mirrored the prevailing American desire for everyone to look out for himself or herself—that is, to be self-reliant. The public and the courts believed that the injured parties, not society, should take care of themselves.

The doctrine of caveat emptor furthered the development of American industry by making the production of products less expensive. Injured parties, rather than manufacturers, absorbed the losses associated with product injuries. During the Industrial Revolution, however, the courts slowly began to alter their approach to this problem. The public began to question whether or not an individual, as opposed to business, should bear the costs of being injured by a product. As products and the manufacturing process became more complex, avoiding injuries became more difficult—even for highly self-reliant people.

The thinking in America shifted from an acceptance of the proposition that self-reliant individuals should protect themselves to a belief that society and business should bear the cost of the inevitable injuries some people sustained.

PRIVITY OF CONTRACT

During most of the nineteenth century, the courts permitted injured parties to recover solely on the basis of a contractual theory of recovery. However, in 1852, the New York Court of Appeals accepted the argument that a seller could be held liable in tort. Even so, many injured people found it difficult, if not impossible, to recover any compensation for their injuries. The major doctrine that prevented people from recovering was the requirement that the plaintiff in a personal injury suit be in **privity of contract** with the defendant—that is, there must have been a direct contractual relationship between the injured party and the defendant. In many cases, the injured person had purchased the goods from a retailer. Thus, the buyer was in privity of contract only with the retailer and not with anyone else in the distributive chain. As a practical matter, plaintiffs generally prefer to institute suit against well-heeled defendants, especially if the plaintiffs have sustained very serious injuries. It is pointless to receive a large judgment against a defendant who has little money. For this reason, the average plaintiff would prefer filing suit against a manufacturer as opposed to a retailer or, worse yet, against a private individual. Today, this is possible.

Suppose that Tom purchased a new automobile manufactured by Acme Corporation. Acme Corporation, in turn, purchased component parts from various suppliers. One of Acme's suppliers delivered a defective wheel, which Acme used on the vehicle sold to Tom. Tom, of course, purchased the vehicle from an automobile dealer in his hometown, not directly from Acme Corporation. While Tom was driving the car, the wheel collapsed. At one time, the only person Tom could bring suit against was the retail dealer from whom he purchased the automobile. A major departure occurred in 1916 in the case *MacPherson v. Buick Motor Company*, when the New York Court of Appeals abandoned the requirement of privity of contract in negligence suits. The Managerial Perspective, "Driver Injured by Vehicle," is based on this case.

As time passed, other courts followed the lead set by the New York court. Today, privity of contract is not a bar to negligence suits. Thus, in the previous example, Tom could bring suit against the manufacturer, the distributor, or the retailer.

Following the decision in the MacPherson case, courts across the United States gradually moved in the direction of holding manufacturers liable for the injuries caused by their products. The fact that the injured party did not purchase the product directly from the defendant no longer prevented the injured party from bringing suit against the defendant based on negligence as a theory of recovery.

managerial perspective

Driver Injured by Vehicle
Buick Motor Company, a manufacturer of automobiles, sold an automobile to a retail dealer who, in turn, resold the car to MacPherson. While operating the car, the wheel suddenly collapsed, throwing MacPherson out of the car and injuring him. One of the wheels had been made out of defective wood, and its spokes had crumbled into fragments. Buick Motor Company had not made the wheels, but it had bought them from another manufacturer. Evidence showed that the defects in the wheel could have been discovered by reasonable inspection, and the inspection had been omitted. The court ruled that MacPherson could sue Buick Motor Company directly for its negligence in the manufacture of this vehicle even though MacPherson was not in privity of contract with Buick Motor Company.

Source: MacPherson v. Buick Motor Company, *111 N.E. 1050*
(Court of Appeals of New York 1916).

Negligence

Chapter 10 discussed the topic of negligence, and that torts of negligence arise from careless or heedless actions. Courts apply negligence in the same manner to the products liability field as in torts cases.

Consider the MacPherson case. Is a manufacturer that purchases a wheel acting in a careless manner when it puts the wheel on a car it is producing without first inspecting that wheel? Judge Cardozo, the judge in *MacPherson v. Buick Motor Company*, thought the manufacturer was careless.

The four elements in a tort of negligence are:

1. *Duty.* Everyone has a duty to act as a reasonable person. Suppose that Acme Ladders manufactures ladders. When it designs, tests, and manufactures its ladders, it will be held to this duty.

2. *Breach of Duty.* Behavior that fails to meet the reasonable person standard is said to breach the duty. If Acme Ladders uses rotten wood in manufacturing the steps on its ladders, it will have breached its duty because a reasonable manufacturer would not have used rotten wood in constructing a ladder.

3. *Causation.* The breach of duty must cause an injury. Suppose that Tom, a painter, climbs up his Acme Ladder, and the top step breaks because it was rotten. Therefore, Tom's injury would have been caused by Acme Ladder's decision to use rotten wood in manufacturing the ladder. Thus, the causation element would have been met.

4. *Injury.* Some person or property must be damaged. In this situation, if Tom fell and broke his leg as a result of stepping on the ladder, Tom would have been injured. Therefore, the fourth element necessary in establishing a case based on negligence would have been met.

Sellers have a number of duties regarding the products that they sell. For example, a manufacturer of a product has a duty *not* to adopt a design that makes the product dangerous for the uses for which it is manufactured. This means that a manufacturer must exercise due care in the design of all of its products. Putting a product on the market that later is determined to be unsafe for normal use may result in liability for physical injuries caused to people by the product.

A manufacturer also has a duty to conduct reasonable tests and exercise reasonable care while inspecting its product to discover latent defects before putting the product on the market. Think about the MacPherson case presented earlier in this chapter. Judge Cardozo ruled that the Buick Motor Company—in failing to inspect a wheel before installing it on MacPherson's car—had breached its obligation to make a reasonable inspection of parts incorporated by Buick Motor Company onto the final assembled vehicle.

Sellers also have a duty to warn the public of the dangerous propensities associated with their products if the public would be unable to recognize the dangers posed by the products. For example, suppose that Acme Cleavers manufactured a kitchen knife. Would it be necessary for Acme Cleavers to warn the public of the dangers associated with using a sharp knife? No. Such dangers are obvious and not latent. Virtually every person who picks up a knife knows that it may cause severe injuries to the user or other people if the knife is not handled carefully. What if Karl, a temperamental, high-strung chef at the Uptown Restaurant, threw one of his knives at his assistant, Debra, because she prematurely opened the oven causing Karl's soufflé to fall. If the knife struck Debra and injured her, could she sue the manufacturer of the knife because Acme Cleavers failed to warn Karl that throwing the knife at Debra could injure her? No.

Other products, however, may not be quite as obvious in the dangers they pose. Suppose that Karl, frustrated at the collapse of his soufflé, takes out his butane lighter and lights a cigarette in order to calm his shattered nerves. When he ignites the lighter, it explodes and burns Karl's face, neck, and chest. Does a lighter—which potentially could explode—pose a latent hazard to users such as Karl? Should he have been warned of the explosion hazard associated with the butane lighter? As of 1987, the Consumer Product Safety Commission reported that more than two hundred people a year died of lighter injuries and twenty-five of them were children. You will note that today's lighters have a warning on them.

Even if a manufacturer places a warning on its products, other questions concerning the warning adopted by a seller may arise. For example, was the warning adequate? Was the warning clear and intelligible? Was it written in a language that people coming into contact with the product could read?

Another example of the dangers of products is detailed in the *First Commer. Trust Co. v. Lorcin Eng., Inc.*, case. Does Lorcin Engineering, Inc., have any duty to Stephanie M. Jungkind, the person killed by a product manufactured by Lorcin, for its negligence in the marketing of its handgun?

First Commer. Trust Co. v. Lorcin Eng., Inc.

Supreme Court of Arkansas
321 Ark. 210, 900 S.W.2d 202, *1995 Ark. LEXIS 383 (1995)*

Stephanie M. Jungkind was shot and killed by Michael Catlett. Garry's Pawn Shop sold Catlett the .380 pistol, manufactured by Lorcin Engineering, Inc., which was used by Catlett to murder Jungkind. In this case Jungkind's estate, represented by

First Commercial Trust Co., brought suit against Lorcin Engineering, Inc. First Commercial Trust Co. alleged that Lorcin Engineering, Inc., was negligent in marketing this weapon to the public in light of the fact that it should have known certain people may purchase the gun with the intent to injure or kill others. It also contended that Lorcin Engineering, Inc., failed to provide Garry's Pawn Shop with a description of prospective purchasers who were likely to misuse the gun. It also negligently failed to warn Garry's Pawn Shop so as to enhance Gary's ability to identify probable misusers of Lorcin's .380 pistol. This negligence on Lorcin Engineering, Inc.'s part was alleged to be a contributing proximate cause of Jungkind's death.

Lorcin Engineering, Inc., argued that it owed no duty to Jungkind and was not liable to her estate based on negligence as a theory of recovery. The trial court granted a motion for summary judgment in favor of Lorcin Engineering, Inc. The Supreme Court of Arkansas affirmed.

Tom Glaze, Associate Justice

First Commercial primarily relies upon *Franco, Adm'x v. Bunyard,* 261 Ark. 144, 547 S.W.2d 91 (1977), and *Cullum & Boren v. Peacock,* 267 Ark. 479, 592 S.W.2d 442 (1980), in arguing that liability based upon common law negligence should be imposed upon Lorcin as the manufacturer and supplier of its .380 handguns ultimately sold to customers. In sum, it theorizes that, because common law liability can be imposed upon a retailer selling firearms to customers, manufacturers like Lorcin should also bear similar responsibility, especially when the manufacturer withholds information that bears upon public safety decisions in selling such firearms.

Neither the Bunyard nor Peacock case supports First Commercial's contentions. First Commercial concedes, as it must, that both of those cases bear upon a retailer's common law negligence liability in selling a gun to a customer. Those cases in no way suggest such liability applies to the manufacturer or supplier of guns.

The "special relationship" requirement utilized in Arkansas cases in imposing a legal duty in tort liability situations resulting from the criminal acts of third parties is also enunciated in *Delahanty v. Hinckley,* 564 A.2d 758 (D.C. 1989). There, Thomas Delahanty sustained injuries from a "Saturday Night Special" handgun employed by John Hinckley when Hinckley attempted to assassinate President Ronald Reagan. The court rejected Delahanty's negligence argument in his attempt to impose tort liability upon the manufacturer of the handgun, stating as follows:

"In general no liability exists in tort for harm resulting from the criminal acts of third parties, although liability for such harm sometimes may be imposed on the basis of some special relationship between the parties" *Hall v. Ford Enterprises, Ltd.,* 445 A.2d 610, 611 (D.C. 1982). Appellants have alleged no special relationship with the gun manufacturer and have suggested no reasonable way that gun manufacturers could screen the purchasers of their guns to prevent criminal misuse.

In the present case, no special relationship exists between Lorcin, Garry's or the ultimate purchaser of its handgun. First Commercial agrees Lorcin had no control over its retailers or dealers, nor does a federal or state law otherwise impose a duty upon Lorcin as a manufacturer of a firearm sold to the purchaser.

Courts in other jurisdictions have also rejected contentions similar to First Commercial's. For example, in *Riordan v. International Armament Corp.,* the court held that no common law duty exists upon the manufacturer of a nondefective handgun to control the distribution of that product to the general public, as distribution was intended for the general public "who presumably can recognize the dangerous consequences in the use of handguns and can assume responsibility for their actions." In addition, the court in Hinckley acknowledged and then rejected the plaintiff's argument that, while no malfunction or defect of the handgun caused his injury, the manufacturer still had a duty to warn of the dangers of criminal misuse of the gun. The Hinckley court held, in addressing whether manufacturers had a duty to warn of the criminal misuse of a gun, that there is no duty to warn when the danger, or potentiality of danger, is generally known and recognized. The court further concluded that, because hazards of firearms are obvious, the manufacturer had no duty to warn.

In view of the foregoing authority which overwhelmingly rejects placing a duty upon a firearm manufacturer in like circumstances as those described here, we uphold the trial court's dismissal of First Commercial's complaint against Lorcin.

■ **FIGURE 14.1** Duties of Manufacturers

> 1. Manufacturers must exercise reasonable care in the design of their products.
>
> 2. Manufacturers have a duty to conduct reasonable tests and to exercise reasonable care in inspecting their products in order to discover latent defects.
>
> 3. Manufacturers have a duty to warn the public of any latent dangers posed by the use of their products.

Figure 14.1 summarizes some of the obligations imposed on product manufacturers under negligence as a theory of recovery.

The 1960s and 1970s

From the time of the Civil War to 1916, a person who purchased a product that injured him or her had been able to sue the seller for the injuries caused by defective products. In the MacPherson case, Judge Cardozo opened the legal floodgates—to a considerable degree—with his decision. The MacPherson case, and other state court decisions adopting the same rationale as the MacPherson decision, made it possible for any injured party to sue anyone in the distributive chain—including the manufacturer—based on negligence as a theory of recovery.

REASONABLE CARE

By the 1960s, attorneys were very familiar with trying cases based on negligence as a theory of recovery in either tort or products liability cases. However, some injured parties fought for a new theory of recovery—one that would permit them to recover even in instances where the defendant had exercised reasonable care. Consider the following situation. Suppose that Stanton and Melissa Voll visited downtown Kansas City. While there, they decided to go to the top of the Cyrus Building to catch the breathtaking view. After taking in the scenic vista from the top of the Cyrus Building, the Volls entered an Odis Elevator. Immediately after the doors closed, the elevator fell to the ground floor—a twenty-story drop. Miraculously, they both survived the fall, but it broke every bone in their bodies. If the Volls sued Odis, based on negligence as a theory of recovery, they would be unable to recover if Odis established at trial that it had exercised reasonable care. Injured parties in situations like this argued that the law should permit them to collect even in the absence of evidence that the defendant failed to exercise reasonable care. After all, even if Odis had exercised reasonable care, the Volls still sustained injuries—injuries they would not have sustained if they had not used an Odis Elevator to descend from the Cyrus Building.

QUALITY—OR THE ABSENCE OF QUALITY

Another factor undoubtedly served as the impetus for the courts and legislatures to reach out for a new products liability theory of recovery is the virtual collapse in the quality of many products in the American marketplace. While some companies operating in the 1960s and 1970s certainly made excellent products, such as Boeing's airplanes and I.B.M.'s computers, it was pretty obvious to nearly everyone in America that the phrase *American quality* had become an oxymoron. Innumerable articles filled magazines and newspapers in America decrying the collapse of quality manufacturing. A study by the American Society for Quality Control, involving a survey of seven thousand households, revealed that people thought that the quality of products had declined.[1]

The average consumer suspected that businesses were focused on making short-term profits rather than high-quality products. According to an article in *The Wall Street Journal*, "Many of the staples of modern homes or office environment—copying machines, television sets, automobiles—share a tendency to go on the blink. We are forever summoning the repairman."[2]

Of course, manufacturers recognized the widespread discontent with the shoddy merchandise reaching the public, and manufacturers tried to take action in doing something about it. At the same time, American business publications launched an attack on the government for attempting to promote higher quality products. For example, in an article in *Fortune* magazine, Walter Guzzardi placed the blame for product injuries on the users of products. In challenging the need for air bags in automobiles he wrote: "Like so many other losses of freedom, this loss will hurt more people than it helps. The beneficiaries will be those who are reckless, for we shall be guaranteeing them compensation for the injuries they sustain, the cost of which they ought to bear themselves."[3]

In the early 1980s, many companies launched a major effort in trying to enhance the quality of their products. In the 1980s, General Motors introduced the X body line of cars. Alex Mair, head of GM's technical staff stated: "We made a giant step with the X cars and by the middle of the decade the process will have a noticeable effect on all our products."[4]

This giant step must have constituted only a couple of inches because it was soon manifestly apparent that the X body cars were riddled with defects. In a 1983 article in *The Wall Street Journal*, the author noted that X body cars had undergone fifteen recalls for various defects between 1979 and March 1983. They had developed, quite understandably, a reputation for shoddy workmanship, unreliability, and safety defects.[5]

Joyce Hall, the founder of one of America's great companies, Hallmark Cards, stated:

> It troubles me that there's a great compromise with quality in America today. This has affected us adversely in all walks of life.
>
> Is it any wonder that the consumerism movement has become a great force in this country? It may be too critical at times, but more often it's right. Its success has clearly demonstrated a need. And manufacturers and

right. Its success has clearly demonstrated a need. And manufacturers and retailers should take it seriously and apply it constructively.[6]

At least one business leader of the times, Joyce Hall, acknowledged what every consumer in America could plainly see for himself or herself that product quality had dropped precipitously.

Another voice urging that American manufacturers wake up and move in the direction of improving the products being made was W. Edwards Deming. Deming's theories gave rise to the Total Quality movement in America. Deming had a number of theories about how to improve the quality of the products being made in America. His theories were developed based on his work with Japanese manufacturers following World War II. Japan had to build its industries from the ground up following the war, and Deming helped advise many of these companies. By the late 1970s, it was apparent to the average automobile purchaser that a huge quality gap existed between American automobiles and Japanese automobiles. Clearly, the Japanese manufacturers had listened to consumers and worked hard at making reliable, quality products. Detroit was in the unpleasant position of having to try and play catchup with Japanese automakers—something that Detroit struggles with to this very day.

How does this topic tie in with products liability law? When products are designed and assembled so poorly that they must be repeatedly recalled, it is not surprising that some of these products cause injuries and death to people.

By the early 1970s the innumerable instances of dangerous, shoddy, unreliable products irresponsibly released to the marketplace without adequate testing had upset the general public so much that state legislatures and the courts turned en masse to a new theory of recovery—strict liability in tort.

Courts and legislatures became receptive to this new theory partly because they were concerned about how to get the message across to corporate America that the public wanted better and safer products. Members of organizations, such as the American Trial Lawyers Association, argued that consumer resistance to purchasing American products was not sufficient in forcing manufacturers to produce high-quality, safe products. Manufacturers needed some incentive, and that incentive would be provided through a revision of the products liability law.

Carole Wilkins, Executive Director of the Quality Resource Center, made the following comment regarding the issue of quality: "The real interest in quality probably came about because of liability suits. If no one is going to sue these firms, and if no one is going to demand quality, the company can give purchasers what they want but the laws have forced the manufacturer to re-evaluate his quality problems."[7]

Strict Liability

As the years passed, plaintiffs became weary of the difficult problems of proof associated with negligence and the various defenses to warranty cases. In many cases, people who sustained injuries as a result of a defective product found themselves unable to recover, not because they were not injured, but because of some technical rule of law. As more and more people sustained injuries, the mood in the courts and the legislatures gradually began to shift from protecting business to protecting consumers. People began to argue that the manufacturer is in the best position to shoulder any loss caused by its products. A manufacturer has the power to produce better and safer products. The public is powerless to control the quality of products on the marketplace. Attorneys argued that by placing more responsibility on corporations to produce safe products, corporations would be encouraged to take more care in the design, manufacture, testing, and inspection of products.

In some instances, neither the manufacturer nor the consumer really is at fault. Sometimes a bad product reaches the marketplace even though the manufacturer takes every step possible to keep this from occurring. When this happens, who ought to bear the loss—the injured party or the manufacturer? Attorneys increasingly began to accept the idea that a manufacturer is in the best position to insure against any possible loss caused by its products. If one of two innocent people must bear the loss caused by a defective product, let the manufacturer purchase insurance and bear the loss.

This idea of **strict liability** gained popularity following Judge Traynor's famous comments in *Escola v. Coca-Cola Bottling Co. of Fresno*. A waitress in a restaurant was injured when a glass bottle of Coca-Cola exploded in her hand. Neither she nor anyone else was able to explain why this accident occurred. In ruling in her favor, Judge Traynor wrote:

> I believe the manufacturer's negligence should no longer be singled out as the basis of a plaintiff's right to recover in cases like the present one. In my opinion it should now be recognized that a manufacturer incurs an absolute liability when an article he has placed on the market, knowing that it is to be used without inspection, proves to have a defect that causes injury to human being. . . . Even if there is no negligence, however, public policy demands that responsibility be fixed wherever it will most effectively reduce the hazards to life and health inherent in defective products that reach the market.

FROM FAULT TO NO FAULT

A breakthrough came in 1963 in *Greenman v. Yuba Power Products* when the California Supreme Court accepted the concept of strict liability in tort. After the acceptance of this theory of recovery by the California Supreme Court, other courts and legislatures throughout the country slowly began to adopt this rule. By the late 1970s, most states across the United States permitted parties to sue under strict liability in tort.

Prior to the adoption of strict liability in tort, the law permitted a person to recover under negligence only if he or she could prove that the seller failed to act reasonably and prudently. The law therefore limited recovery to cases in which the injured party was able to demonstrate that the defendant acted in some manner that the law regarded as improper.

A seller who acted with reasonable care would prevail in a negligence suit. However, if the plaintiff sued on the basis of strict liability in tort, the plaintiff may prevail even if "the seller has exercised all possible care in the preparation and sale of his product"—in other words, even though the seller acted with reasonable care. Thus, strict liability in tort shifts some of the risk associated with products from the buyer to the seller. The courts assume that sellers may protect themselves from the costs of suits by purchasing insurance.

SECTION 402A

The *Restatement (Second) of Torts* adopted the concept of strict liability in tort, which now appears in Section 402A. It reads as follows:

1. One who sells any products in a defective condition unreasonably dangerous to the user or consumer or to his property, is subject to liability for physical harm thereby caused to the ultimate user or consumer, or to his property, if

    a. the seller is engaged in the business of selling such a product, and

    b. it is expected to and does reach the consumer or user without substantial change in the condition in which it is sold.

2. The rule stated in subsection (1) applies although

    a. the seller has exercised all possible care in the preparation and sale of his product, and

    b. the user or consumer has not bought the product from or entered into any contractual relation with the seller.

The *Restatement* adopts a rule that is almost one of absolute liability on the part of the seller. It makes the seller liable even if it exercised "all possible care in the preparation and sale" of the product. In a negligence case, evidence of this type would absolve the defendant of any liability. Under strict liability in tort, it is irrelevant whether or not the seller acted negligently. As long as the plaintiff is able to establish the other elements, he or she recovers even if no evidence of negligence exists on the part of the defendant.

Consider the following situation. Lee Iacocco, a Ford Motor Company Vice President, originated the idea of building a car that weighed less than two thousand pounds and would sell for less than $2,000. Styling considerations took precedence over engineering considerations in the soon-to-be-notorious Ford Pinto. In order to fit the gas tank into the Pinto design, Ford engineers placed the fuel tank behind the rear axle with only nine or ten inches of crush space. This left the Pinto highly vulnerable to rear-end collisions. For added costs of about $8 per vehicle, the engineering department calculated that the risks associated with this design could have been substantially reduced. Ford Motor Company instead chose to engage in a cost benefit analysis and decided that millions of dollars could be saved during the 1974–1975 period by delaying implementation of the engineering department's recommendations.

Could a person collect damages from Ford Motor Company if he or she was injured while driving a Ford Pinto based on negligence as a theory of recovery? All Ford Motor Company would need to argue is that it exercised reasonable care in the design on this car. On the other hand, if the injured party proceeded with his or her case on the

The Ford Pinto

Mrs. Gray purchased a Ford Pinto in 1972. She had owned it only six months, and the car had three thousand miles on it at the time of the incident in question. While pulling onto the San Bernardino Freeway, Gray's car stalled and coasted to a halt. The driver of a Ford Galaxie travelling directly behind her was unable to stop in time to avoid a collision with Gray's Pinto. The Ford Galaxie collided with Gray's car at approximately twenty-eight to thirty-seven miles per hour. The impact of the Galaxie pushed the Pinto's gas tank forward and caused a puncture from either the flange or one of the bolts on the differential housing. Fuel sprayed from the punctured tank into the passenger compartment. The Pinto was engulfed in flames on impact. Gray died in the fire, and Richard Grimshaw, a passenger in the car, suffered severe and permanently disfiguring burns on his entire body.

Memos from Ford Motor Company's own tests revealed that the Pinto failed rear-end crash tests. Every test made at more than twenty-five miles per hour resulted in a ruptured fuel tank. Through the results of the crash test, Ford Motor Company knew that the Pinto's fuel tank and rear structure would expose users to serious injury or death in a twenty- to thirty-mile-per-hour collision.

Ford Motor Company could have corrected this defect for only $11 per car. The company engaged in a cost benefit analysis—arriving at the decision to reject the advice of its own engineers to adopt a safer design. Their analysis projected that it would save $121 million by delaying implementation of the design change. Therefore, Ford Motor Company chose to delay implementation of the design change—knowing its failure to do so would result in the deaths and injuries of many people.

What do you think? Was the action of Ford Motor Company in delaying the design change ethical?

Source: Grimshaw v. Ford Motor Company, *174 Cal.Rptr. 348 (Court of Appeals, Fourth District 1981).*

basis of strict liability in tort, whether Ford Motor Company exercised reasonable care or not would be irrelevant. The principle issues that must be established are that: (1) Ford adopted a defective design for the Pinto; and (2) the defective design made the vehicle unreasonably dangerous to users; and (3) the product injured someone. An individual could certainly argue that the gas tank design was defective, and that the gas tank design made Pintos unreasonably dangerous. Therefore, it is much more likely that one could recover based on strict liability in tort as a theory of recovery than one based on negligence.

The Ethical Perspective, "The Ford Pinto," deals with a famous case involving a Ford Pinto.

The *Restatement* also eliminates the need to establish a direct contractual relationship between the plaintiff and the defendant—that is, it eliminates the absence of privity of contract as a defense in a strict liability case. This permits an injured party to sue anyone in the distributive chain: manufacturers, distributors, or retail sellers. Any user or consumer is permitted to bring suit. Furthermore, many states permit bystanders to bring suit. Suppose a person on a skateboard lost control because a roller came off of the skateboard. If the person on the skateboard crashed into John, John would be an innocent bystander injured by the failure of the skateboard. Many states permit a person in John's position to bring suit against the manufacturer of the skateboard, the distributor, or the retail seller.

Plaintiffs must establish that the product in question was expected to, and in fact did, reach the consumer without substantial change in the condition in which it was sold. In the case of packaged goods, such a requirement creates few difficulties for the plaintiff. Suppose Mrs. Jones purchases some hair dye to change the color of her hair. If the formula of the dye causes users to lose their hair, and Mrs. Jones's hair falls out, she may sue the seller for damages. As the dye comes in a package, she will have no problems proving the product was in the same condition as when it was sold. But suppose Mrs. Jones was injured, instead, in her two-year-old car when the brakes failed. If she brings suit against the manufacturer, will she be able to prove that the brakes were in the same condition as when the vehicle was sold to her? Obviously, this creates a substantial burden of proof. Many people may have touched the brakes. These people may have somehow tampered with the brakes and caused them to fail; in this case, the manufacturer would not be liable.

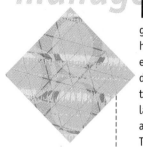

managerial perspective

Failure to Warn

Jay Outlaw pumped air into his tire. The gauge registered between thirty-five and forty-five pounds per square inch. When he began to release air from the tire, the tire exploded, injuring his right eye and ear. The explosion was caused when heat, produced by continuous contact of the deflated tire with the surface of the highway, created a temperature hot enough to melt the sidewall. Firestone, the manufacturer of the tire, knew of this risk. Outlaw contended that Firestone failed to give an adequate warning that a tire operated at low pressure for an extended period of time would melt down and explode. The Eleventh Circuit Court of Appeals ruled that a seller must warn of any nonobvious risk of serious injury when the product is used in its intended manner. The jury could therefore have concluded that Firestone should have warned Outlaw of this risk.

Source: Outlaw v. Firestone Tire and Rubber, *770 F.2d 1012 (1985).*

Section 402A applies only to people regularly engaged in selling a particular product. If a person purchases an automobile from a local automobile dealer, clearly the dealer is in the business of selling automobiles. The dealer could be liable. But suppose the buyer purchased the automobile from a next-door neighbor. The neighbor, as he or she is not regularly engaged in selling automobiles, would have no liability.

Courts treat a product as defective if it lacks a necessary warning for alerting people to the dangers associated with its use. Manufacturers do not need to warn users of obvious dangers—only those dangers not apparent to an ordinary person using the product. The Managerial Perspective, "Failure to Warn," deals with a danger many people do not appreciate—the potential of a hot tire exploding.

Some products pose obvious risks. Anyone who ever drank a six-pack of beer in a couple of hours realizes that the consumption of excessive quantities of alcohol in a short duration of time makes certain activities risky—such as coming home in dad's car after drinking the six-pack, climbing up the stairs of the bar, or trying to walk a straight line. Anyone who consumes a few drinks may experience the effects of alcohol for himself or herself.

Excessive consumption of alcohol creates a host of problems in the United States and throughout the world. It touches the lives of virtually everyone. In America, as in the rest of the world, excessive drinking causes many tragedies. Every year drunk drivers kill more than 20,000 people and permanently injure thousands of others. The influence of alcohol plays a part in many criminal acts. Excessive consumption of alcohol contributes to innumerable cases of spouse and child abuse. Businesses lose billions of dollars because of loss of work, on-the-job injuries, and medical problems caused by the long-term abuse of alcohol. Obviously, most people realize the typical dangers associated with the abuse of alcohol. The law requires no warning for these dangers.

At the same time, alcohol poses certain risks that may not be obvious even to a regular drinker. These dangers are not necessarily obvious merely because a person drank a lot of alcohol in one evening.

Refer to the Thought Problem, "Student Dies from Drinking Tequila," as an example of this situation.

Student Dies from Drinking Tequila

Marie Brinkmeyer was eighteen years old and in her first semester at Texas A&I University. On November 14, 1983, Brinkmeyer went to the University Liquor Store and purchased a bottle of Pepe Lopez Tequila. She drank straight shots of tequila with her friends that evening. Around 10:00 P.M. her friends escorted her to her room. They found her dead the next morning, allegedly as a direct result of acute alcohol intoxication. Prior to the time of her death, Brinkmeyer had little exposure to the use of alcohol. Brinkmeyer's mother had warned her of the dangers of impaired physical capacity that may result from the consumption of alcohol, but her mother had not warned her that alcohol could be lethal because her mother was unaware of this fact. The liquor store owner who sold Brinkmeyer the tequila stated that he knew a person could die from an alcohol overdose, but he admitted that he had acquired his knowledge through college chemistry courses. No evidence showed that Brinkmeyer was aware of the fact that if a person consumes too much alcohol, he or she could die.

What do you think? Does the absence of a warning on the tequila bottle stating that drinking too much tequila could kill a person render the product defective and unreasonably dangerous for users or consumers? Why may the dangers associated with excessive alcohol consumption be obvious, and therefore no warning would be required?

Source: Brune v. Brown Forman Corporation, *758 S.W.2d 827 (Court of Appeals of Texas, Corpus Christi 1988).*

It should be noted that as of November 1989, the Alcoholic Beverage Labeling Act requires beverage containers to bear the following warning:

> GOVERNMENT WARNING: (1) According to the Surgeon General women should not drink alcoholic beverages during pregnancy because of the risk of birth defects. (2) Consumption of alcoholic beverages impairs your ability to drive a car or operate machinery, and may cause health problems.

This Act specifically states that no other statement relating to health may be required by any state.

UNREASONABLY DANGEROUS

The requirement that gives the courts the greatest problem is the requirement that the product be in a "defective condition unreasonably dangerous to the user or consumer or to his property." The states have adopted various positions regarding the terminology "defective condition unreasonably dangerous." Some states have greatly modified these concepts.

For example, some courts have found that the marketing of handguns is an unreasonably dangerous activity. Courts that are willing to hold sellers of handguns liable are attempting to stretch strict liability law to its limits. The *Fraust v. Swift and Company* case also represents a willingness by a court to give a very broad interpretation to the term **unreasonably dangerous.**

Fraust v. Swift and Company

United States District Court, W.D. Pennsylvania
610 F. Supp. 711 (1985)

A products liability action was brought against Swift and Company, a peanut butter manufacturer, by Judith Fraust, the mother of Isaac Fraust, a sixteen month old child who choked while eating peanut butter spread on bread. The child subsequently died of severe brain damage. Swift claimed that as a matter of law its product should be declared to be not unreasonably dangerous.

The plaintiff's theory is that the peanut butter supplied by the defendant was unsafe for its intended use because it lacked a warning that it should not be fed to children under four years of age. Fraust contends that peanut butter is dangerous to children under four years of age because of its texture and consistency and the immature eating and swallowing abilities of children that age.

Teitelbaum, Chief Judge

Liability cannot be imposed on the seller for failure to warn of a danger associated with its product if the danger was or should have been known to the user. The issue of necessity of warnings must also be considered in light of any contradictory promotional activities on the part of the seller. The Court cannot say as a matter of law that Isaac's mother knew or should have known of the danger associated with feeding a peanut butter sandwich to him.

As its second argument, defendant contends that because plaintiffs do not allege that the peanut butter was not in the condition expected by the ordinary consumer it was not unreasonably dangerous as a matter of law. Although at first this argument appears different from defendant's first argument, it is really a variant of the same argument.

Comment (i) to section 402A of the *Restatement (2nd) of Torts* differentiates those products which are by their very nature unsafe but not defective from those which can truly be called defective. Comment (i) states:

> Good whiskey is not unreasonably dangerous merely because it will make some people drunk, and is especially dangerous to alcoholics; but bad whiskey, containing a dangerous amount of fuel oil, is unreasonably dangerous. Good tobacco is not unreasonably dangerous merely because the effects of smoking may be harmful; but tobacco containing something like marijuana may be unreasonably dangerous. Good butter is not unreasonably dangerous merely because, if such be the case, it deposits cholesterol in the arteries and leads to heart attacks; but bad butter, contaminated with poisonous fish oil, is unreasonably dangerous.

Defendant argues that similarly good peanut butter is not unreasonably dangerous because a young child may choke on it. Defendant then prematurely ends its analysis. However, comment (j) goes on to explain why good whiskey and good butter; and by inference, good tobacco; although "unsafe" are not defective, even without a warning of their dangers.

> . . . a seller is not required to warn with respect to products, or ingredients in them, which are only dangerous, or potentially so, when consumed in excessive quantity, or over a long period of time, when the danger, or potentiality of danger, is generally known and recognized. Again the dangers of alcoholic beverages are an example, as are also those of foods containing such substances as saturated fats, which may over a period of time have a deleterious effect upon the human heart.

That is, because these "unsafe" products present known dangers no warning is required. Therefore, although "unsafe," they are not defective.

Again the Court cannot say as a matter of law that the danger of a sixteen month old choking on a peanut butter sandwich is generally known and recognized so that admittedly good peanut butter, without warning of such a danger, is not unreasonably dangerous.

EMOTIONAL INJURIES

The courts in America generally have not been willing to permit people who suffered from mental injuries to collect in the absence of some evidence of an accompanying physical injury. The Managerial Perspective, "Perfected Pets and a Rabid Skunk," represents the traditional view regarding this question.

Figure 14.2 summarizes the requirements that must be met in order to recover under strict liability in tort.

DEVELOPMENTS IN PRODUCTS LIABILITY LAW

As indicated earlier, the courts assumed when they adopted strict liability in tort as a theory of recovery that businesses would be able to protect themselves from suits by purchasing liability insurance. However, because the insurance industry lacked information on its risk exposure under this theory of recovery, insurance companies responded to the adoption of strict liability in tort in the late 1970s by drastically raising their insurance rates, limiting coverage, and in some cases refusing to sell insurance to certain businesses. The response created a products liability crisis as many manufacturers found themselves paying astronomical increases in premiums. This trend continued as courts awarded large judgments to people in America on the basis of strict liability in tort. Throughout the 1970s and 1980s, many courts expanded the ability of people to sue by accepting new arguments posed by injured parties. The Managerial Perspective, "Market Share Liability," illustrates one such innovative argument.

Some companies, particularly small ones, found themselves unable to purchase an adequate amount of insurance to protect themselves from potential suits. Many of these businesses closed their doors.

Other companies closed their doors because the large number of strict-liability-in-tort suits filed against them overwhelmed the businesses. Many companies that sold highly dangerous products, such as asbestos, found refuge in the federal bankruptcy laws. In 1982, the Johns Manville Corporation, a seller of asbestos, filed a bankruptcy petition to reorganize the company. So many people filed personal injury suits against The Johns Manville Corporation that it needed to resort to the protection of the bankruptcy laws to stay in business. When a company produces a product that injures a large number of people, it may be faced with a situation in which the claims of all of the plaintiffs exceed the total assets of the company. In such a case, the courts need a system to divide up the available assets of the company in an orderly manner. Bankruptcy laws allow a company to set aside a pool of money to be divided up among all of those injured by a company's products.

Perfected Pets and a Rabid Skunk

On June 21, 1979, Janice Sease bought a pet skunk from defendant, Perfected Pets, Inc., a pet shop in Portland, Oregon. The pet shop had purchased the skunk from defendant Taylor's Pets, Inc. Nine or ten days after Sease bought the skunk, it began to attack and bite people, lose fur, and develop sores on its body. The skunk did not bite Brad Hill, but he came into contact with its saliva when he had open cuts and scratches on his arms.

The skunk died, and Sease took it to a veterinarian for an autopsy. The veterinarian told her the skunk was rabid. A doctor from the Oregon State Health Division ordered rabies treatments for other people the skunk had bitten. Hill's physician concluded that because of his history and allergies, the rabies injections could cause anaphylactic shock and death, and the doctor advised Hill against them. Hill did not take the injections, nor did he contract rabies.

The defendants argued that Hill did not suffer any physical harm because he did not take the injections and did not suffer illness or death from contact with the skunk's saliva. They contended that he only suffered anxiety because he knew that he could develop rabies.

The court agreed and ruled that Hill could not recover because he had not suffered any physical harm.

Source: Sease v. Taylor's Pets, Inc., *700 P.2d 1054 (Court of Appeals of Oregon 1985).*

■ **FIGURE 14.2** Requirements for Recovery under Strict Liability in Tort

The injured party must establish that all of the following criteria pertained to the product and/or the defendant.

1. Defendant sold a product in a defective condition.
2. The product was unreasonably dangerous to users or consumers.
3. The injured party sustained a physical injury.
4. The seller was engaged in the business of selling such a product.
5. The product was substantially in the same condition at the time it injured the plaintiff as when it was sold by the defendant.

The vast number of suits filed by plaintiffs generated a lot of activity by business. For years, manufacturers lobbied Congress to adopt a federal law of products liability that would preempt all state laws—thus making products liability law uniform throughout the United States. Such lobbying efforts failed because the bills proposed by industry sought to eliminate strict liability in tort as a theory of recovery. Manufacturers tried to get Congress to return the law in the United States to a negligence theory of recovery. The effect generated widespread opposition by consumer groups and plaintiff's lawyers.

Business groups also attempted to attack the contingency fee system of paying plaintiff's lawyers. Plaintiffs' attorneys share in the award or settlement obtained by the injured parties. Sometimes, the attorneys receive as much as the injured party receives—or more! Industry argues that the contingency fee system encourages litigation. Businesses argue that allowing only billing on an hourly basis for

managerial perspective

Market Share Liability

Many years ago, Abbott Laboratories, as well as a number of other drug companies, manufactured the synthetic drug, DES. DES was administered to mothers who were pregnant for the purposes of preventing miscarriages. At the time of the administration of the drug, it was unknown—but was later discovered—that the drug may cause cancerous vaginal and cervical growths in the daughters exposed to it before birth. In recent years, a number of women have, in fact, developed cancer. These women want to recover but are unable to prove which company manufactured the drug that injured them.

In the seminal case, *Sindell v. Abbott Laboratories,* 607 P.2d 924 (California Supreme Court 1980), the court decided that each manufacturer's liability would approximate its responsibility for the injuries caused by its own products. This has since been referred to as market share liability. A number of courts, but not *all* courts, have adopted this as a theory of recovery when the plaintiff is unable to identify which company manufactured the product that injured him or her. In the states that have adopted this theory of recovery, it is much easier for an injured party to establish a case, and thus the possibility of recovering for injuries is much higher than in states that have not adopted this theory of recovery.

services may reduce the number of suits that attorneys file. Needless to say, the bar rejects the abolition of the contingency fee system.

On other fronts, industry prevailed over the bar. Some states adopted legislation that makes it more difficult for injured people to recover. For example, some states prohibited suits arising from the failure of products that are more than ten years old. Other states placed limits on the amount of punitive damages a plaintiff may recover.

Industry also responded to the flood of suits by ceasing production of certain products—or by reducing the number of changes in existing products. Does a decline in innovations in products serve the best interests of the country? At one time, many sellers manufactured football helmets. Because of the number and size of the verdicts, the law whittled down the number of football helmet manufacturers to just a handful, while at the same time the price of helmets soared. At one time, many drug companies manufactured whooping cough vaccine. Today, only one firm manufactures this product.

Many firms follow a better and more successful approach to dealing with the onslaught of suits. Suits arise because sellers fail to properly design, manufacture, assemble, test, or inspect their products. Astute companies today work to correct these problems by getting everyone involved in producing high-quality products. This involves eliminating design errors, selecting better raw materials, reducing assembly line errors, increasing the testing of products, and improving warnings. When bad products reach the market, their manufacturers act faster to correct the defects in the products. They try to get everyone involved who may reduce the risk of producing bad products. To some extent, therefore, products liability law has forced industry in a very positive direction. It has forced companies to

INTERNATIONAL
PERSPECTIVE

Products Liability
in the European Union

The European Union issued a directive that makes producers of products strictly liable for the goods they place
on the market. An injured person needs only to establish
that the product was defective, that the defective product resulted in the plaintiff's injury, and the extent of
damages sustained by the plaintiff. The directive requires
member countries of the European Union to actually
adopt specific legislation implementing this directive.
Both Germany and Great Britain, among others, have
adopted this directive.

Source: Laurie Mathewson, "Har-
monization of Product Liability
Laws in the European Community: A Comparative Analysis
of the Approaches of the Federal Republic of Germany and
the United Kingdom," *Law and
Policy in International Business,*
Summer 1993.

produce better products. The International Perspective, "Products Liability in the European
Union," presents an example of the worldwide
adoption of this concept.

By the late 1980s, the courts began to respond
to the widespread outcry over higher insurance
rates, failures of companies, withdrawals of products from the market, and a slowdown in product
innovations. Some courts have become more
receptive to defenses asserted by the seller.

When a manufacturer does a good job designing and assembling products and warning users,
many courts and legislatures are willing to accept
the manufacturer's argument that it should not be
liable to the plaintiff for his or her injuries. Even
so, in light of the tremendous number of settlements and verdicts against companies, the best
long-term strategy for a company is to continue to
make every possible effort to ensure that it produces the highest quality, best designed products.
These products need to be accompanied by clearly
written, easily understood instructions that warn
people coming into contact with the products
about how to use them.

Summary

Over the last hundred years or so, the courts and the legislatures have
expanded the theories of liability in the products liability field. They
have gradually made it easier for an injured person to recover for any
injuries he or she has sustained as a result of coming into contact with
a product. At one time, it was virtually impossible for a person
injured by a product to sue at all unless he or she actually purchased
the product in question. Furthermore, the injured person could sue
only the business that actually sold the product. As a result, it was
extremely difficult to sue anyone other than retail sellers. Today, it is
possible to sue virtually anyone in the distributive chain. Furthermore, a person does not have to be the purchaser of a product in
order to sue.

For many years plaintiffs had to establish their cases by relying on
negligence as a theory of recovery. This was not a totally satisfactory
theory of recovery from the injured party's standpoint because the
injured party needed to establish that the defendant had failed to
exercise reasonable care. Beginning in the late 1960s, courts and state
legislatures began to permit injured parties to sue under the new theory of strict liability in tort. A business that sells a product in a defective condition unreasonably dangerous to people may be sued for any
personal injuries caused by the defective product. This is true even if
the seller exercised all possible care in the preparation and sale of the
product. Suits by consumers have encouraged sellers to take more
care in making certain that their products are safe.

Review Questions

1. Define the following terms:
   a. Negligence
   b. Privity of contract
   c. Strict liability in tort

2. List and explain the theories under which a manufacturer or seller of a product may have liability to a person injured by a product.

3. Acme Automobiles produced the Wing automobile. Dan Lowell purchased a Wing from a retailer, Hometown Dealer. Acme Automobiles had purchased the battery for the car from International Batteries. Due to a defect in the battery installed in Lowell's car, the battery exploded in his face. Lowell wants to sue Acme Automobiles directly. Will the doctrine of privity of contract prevent him from suing Acme Automobiles in light of the fact that he did not purchase the car directly from Acme Automobiles?

4. Acme Automobiles produced the Saber automobile. Rachel Schwartz purchased a Saber. The model she purchased had a bench seat with a floor shifter in the middle of the seat. The Saber was clearly designed to hold three passengers in the front seat. While riding in the middle of the bench seat, Mark Reynolds was thrust forward and impaled on the gear shifter when Schwartz was forced to stop suddenly. Would Acme Automobiles be liable under a negligence as a theory of recovery?

5. A suit by decedent's (that is, the deceased's) family alleged that the manufacturer of a bulldozer was liable in negligence and strict liability in tort for the defective design of the machine. When decedent was struck, the bulldozer was in the process of reversing to position itself to move forward to spread and tamp down fill; decedent was behind the bulldozer directing dump trucks in depositing fill that was to be spread and tamped by the bulldozer at a later time. Before backing up, the operator of the bulldozer, who had not observed decedent for about five minutes, looked to the rear to ascertain if it was clear, but he did not see decedent, who was standing thirty to forty feet behind the vehicle. The operator testified that there was a substantial blind spot to the rear of the bulldozer because of its design. The bulldozer had no rearview mirrors and no audible or visible backup warning signal. Is the manufacturer liable for its failure to include these design features?

6. Martin applied Ben-Gay to his chest because he was suffering from a cold. When he attempted to light a cigarette, the match head fell off and struck his chest. This caused the Ben-Gay to catch on fire. Martin was severely burned. Nowhere on the package did the company warn that Ben-Gay was flammable. Is the company liable to Martin for his injuries?

7. When Ford Motor Company produced the 1966 Ford Fairlane, it used a flange-mounted gasoline tank rather than a strap-mounted tank. The top of the flange-mounted tank served as the floor of the trunk. The only shield separating the trunk compartment from the passenger compartment was a fiberboard panel and the rear seat padding. Neither of these materials significantly limits the passage of

fire. The cost of placing a shield between the passenger compartment and the fuel-containing system would only be $1 plus a half hour of labor time. Buehler was involved in a rear-end collision in which he was seriously injured. Had such a shield been in place, it would have substantially reduced the risk of injury to Buehler by having provided him additional time to escape from the accident. Should Ford Motor Company be held liable to Buehler under the strict liability in tort theory of recovery?

8. Lamb was eating an oven-roasted chicken that her daughter had prepared. She accidentally swallowed the pop-up thermometer inserted in the chicken by the supplier which indicated when the chicken was properly cooked. Lamb brought suit on the theory that the thermometer was dangerous because it could be inadvertently ingested, that the arrowlike points at its ends made it prone to being caught in the intestine if swallowed, and that the defendant had neither tested the thermometer for safety nor issued warnings concerning the danger of ingestion. Will the plaintiff prevail?

9. Woodworth was copiloting a Learjet. He was killed when a loon flew through the jet's windshield. Woodworth's family alleged that the windshield should have been designed to resist bird impact. Learjet argued that windshields should not have to withstand the impact of the eleven and a half pound loon. Who should win?

10. Maybelline is the manufacturer of cosmetic products. Walker was applying Maybelline mascara and accidentally scratched the cornea of her left eye with the applicator brush. Walker eventually became blind in that eye as a result of an infection from the defendant's mascara.

Maybelline knew that scratching of the eye surface with a mascara brush posed a danger of infection by the bacteria present in the mascara. Maybelline placed the following warning on the back side of the card that went with the mascara: "Note: In case of eye irritations or infections or scratches, do not use this or any eye cosmetic. Consult a physician at once." Does this constitute an adequate warning by Maybelline?

11. Cox brought a products liability suit. He alleged that he developed asbestosis as a result of exposure to Eagle-Picher's asbestos products. At trial, Cox was permitted to show that having asbestosis increased his risk of contracting lung cancer. He sought damages for present emotional distress caused by his fear of developing cancer and damages for the risk of developing cancer in the future. Will he be able to recover on either of these theories?

Notes

[1] Louise Cook, "Product Quality: For Better or Worse?", *The Kansas City Star*, April 26, 1981, page 6F.

[2] "Out of Order," *The Wall Street Journal*, January 5, 1981, page 1.

[3] Walter Guzzardi, Jr., "The Mindless Pursuit of Safety," *Fortune*, April 9, 1979, page 64.

[4] Jeremy Main, "The Battle for Quality Begins," *Fortune*, December 29, 1980, page 31.

[5] Douglas Sease, "X-Cars, Once GM's Pride, Getting a Shoddy Reputation with Owners," *The Wall Street Journal*, March 3, 1983, page 23.

[6] "More Need, More Opportunity," *The Kansas City Times*, November 1, 1982, page A14.

[7] Carole Carmichael, " 'Quality' Industry Is Gaining in Importance," *The Kansas City Star*, May 20, 1981, page 17A.

Chapter
15

CONSUMER AND
ENVIRONMENTAL LAW

An examination of American history reveals periods of relative inactivity by the average person, and intervals in which the American populace became galvanized by one or more issues. As observed elsewhere in this textbook, following the Civil War, the law tended to favor the industrialization of America. By the end of the nineteenth century, workers and farmers began to express their frustration with America's increasing interest in multinational industrial enterprises. This led to attempts at breaking up huge businesses, such as the Standard Oil Trust and the United States Steel Corporation. Once mobilized, employees progressed from the idea of breaking up big companies into smaller units to the notion of improving working conditions of the average plant employee.

Throughout the early part of the twentieth century, workers joined together in labor unions. The workers of that time attempted to act as a group, as opposed to working individually to improve their working environment. The actions of labor unions demonstrated to other people in society how they, too, could profit from engaging in concerted activities. One group, in particular, took a lesson from the unions—those people seeking civil rights. From the 1930s and later, civil rights organizations brought people together as an attempt to achieve, through concerted behavior, what could not be achieved through individual action—the equality of treatment.

In subsequent chapters, the examination of antitrust laws, labor laws, and employment laws is discussed, all of which grew out of the actions of people working together to obtain changes both in the law and in society. In this chapter, two areas of the law are discussed that sprung to life as a result of people committed to transforming life in America—consumer law and environmental law. In the late 1960s and early 1970s, profound changes occurred in America in both of these areas of law.

Consumer Law

During the 1960s, activists mobilized members of the public in an attempt to reconstruct American society. Students challenged the actions of the United States government during the Vietnam War, civil rights leaders led sit-ins at lunch counters and marches in the streets, hippies engaged in a form of protest referred to as *dropping out* of society, and publishers railed against the sexual repression so manifest in America in the 1950s and 1960s. At the same time, consumer activists increased the awareness of Congress and the state legislatures about the shabby manner in which some businesses treated people in our society.

One could date the start of the consumer law movement as the year of 1962. In that year, President Kennedy ushered in the most recent wave of consumer legislation when he announced his *consumer bill of rights*, which declared that consumers had a right to better protection. A very prominent member of the consumer movement of the 1960s and 1970s, Ralph Nader, spurred the growth of the new laws. His book on the Chevrolet Corvair, entitled *Unsafe at Any Speed*, castigated General Motors for its indifference toward consumer safety in designing and manufacturing the Corvair. General Motors placed the engine in the rear of the Corvair, an innovative design for its time. Regrettably, the engine placement made the Corvair very unstable in certain driving conditions. For example, a driver attempting to make a sharp turn found it difficult to maintain control of the car. The Corvair design posed a significant hazard to the public that most people did not recognize until the release of Nader's book. The Ethical Perspective, "Consumer Activist Exposes Product Defects," further illustrates this point.

The consumer movement of the 1960s and 1970s eventually led to the adoption of much stricter laws dealing with defective products—a topic discussed in Chapter 14. But many other profound changes flowed out of the consumer movement. It resulted in the passage of a host of federal and state laws that greatly increased the complexity of engaging in business in America today.

As an illustration of the changes that took place in the lending industry, consider a typical lender. Suppose that International Lenders wants to loan out money to customers at the highest possible rate of interest. International also wishes to make certain its borrowers repay their loans in a timely fashion; thus, it wants to lend to reliable borrowers. To further protect itself, International Lenders wants to secure repayment of its loans with property owned by the borrowers. To the extent market conditions force it to lend to less creditworthy borrowers, the firm probably will attempt to charge more for its loans. Prior to the enactment of the laws discussed in this chapter, a company such as International Lenders exercised considerable discretion in structuring its actions.

Some lenders abused this discretion by making it difficult for creditworthy people to obtain credit. These lenders denied credit to certain people whom they believed posed a higher risk to them. However, widely held views in society influenced the perceptions of lenders concerning risk. This illustrates the interrelationship of widely held beliefs in society and business behavior.

For example, lenders tended to stereotype women. Most lenders assumed that typical women wanted to stay at home rather than continue to work throughout their lives. Thus, lenders viewed women as only temporarily in the workforce until they got married or had babies. Because many lenders operated on this assumption, they refused to consider the income of working women in deciding whether or not to make loans.

Industry beliefs failed to track the pervasive changes taking place in American society during the early 1970s. Many women entered the

ETHICAL PERSPECTIVE

Consumer Activist Exposes Product Defects

Suppose that the Acme Automobile Corporation created a radically new vehicle in an attempt to produce a car that met the motoring needs of youthful drivers. The cost of designing and manufacturing this car—the Tiger—ran into the hundreds of millions of dollars, so the company embarked on a major marketing campaign to convince the public of the desirability of purchasing this new car. The public rewarded Acme Automobile Corporation with brisk sales of the car. Soon after the automobile reached the market, Acme Automobile Corporation learned of Mike Wilson's attempts to discredit the vehicle. Wilson felt that the tiger posed a significant safety hazard to drivers and passengers.

As an executive at Acme Automobile Corporation, what do you think the appropriate response should be to Wilson's activities—ignore Wilson's actions, or work with Wilson to learn how to improve the car, or spy on Wilson in an attempt to gain information that could be used to destroy his credibility? Explain *why* you have answered in the way you did.

General Motors took the latter approach in dealing with Ralph Nader. Nader sued General Motors and collected hundreds of thousands of dollars from the company. Nader used this money to hire a large staff of bright, young attorneys. His organization brought suit against other companies that Nader thought were acting contrary to the best interest of society. Nader and his associates have been extremely energetic in pushing Congress and the courts to adopt a more consumer-focused orientation.

workforce in the early 1970s with the intention of remaining permanently employed. Such stereotypical beliefs on the part of lenders probably never coincided with the actual behavior of the majority of women. Throughout the history of this nation, millions of women have worked their entire lives. Even so, lenders continued to refuse to recognize this fact. They treated women stereotypically and refused to recognize their incomes in deciding whether or not to grant loans.

Congress responded with the Equal Credit Opportunity Act, discussed later in this chapter. This act, along with much of the other legislation discussed in this chapter, was passed because industry failed to adopt practices consistent with the needs and wants of the general public.

In this chapter, the focus is on one particular aspect of consumer law—the laws passed by Congress that deal with the consumer as a borrower. In the 1990s, practically everyone borrows money for one purpose or another—to purchase a home, a car, clothing, gasoline, and innumerable other items.

Anyone who needs additional cash has a variety of sources from which to acquire credit. A borrower may go to a bank or a credit union to finance the purchase of an automobile. A person who lacks an established credit record may choose to borrow money from a finance company. Many stores provide financing for the purchase of products; in fact, many department stores make more money on their financing operations than on the actual sales of their products. For higher priced purchases, the retailer may sell the instrument signed by the debtor to a finance company or bank. Alternatively, the buyer may use a credit card in order to pay for the goods or services that he or she purchases.

TRUTH IN LENDING ACT

Suppose that Amy wishes to purchase a new Chevrolet. She knows that her bank, the First National Bank, offers automobile loans. The General Motors Acceptance Corporation also finances consumers. If either lender would be willing to lend money to her, Amy probably cares only about one thing—who will lend the money to her for the least amount of money? After all, a dollar from G.M.A.C. is no different than a dollar from the First National Bank. The dollars that she may receive from G.M.A.C. are not in any way superior to those that could be provided by the First National Bank. Of course, this point has never been lost on lenders either. They realize that well informed borrowers have few reasons to do business with anyone but the least expensive lender.

How may Amy determine the best place to borrow the money for financing her automobile purchase? She must ask each lender what it charges for a loan. This sounds relatively simple, but in reality, finding out this information was anything but simple prior to the passage in 1969 of the Consumer Credit Protection Act. One section of this Act is commonly referred to as the Truth in Lending Act. The purpose of it was to enable consumers to make meaningful comparisons among the rates charged by different lenders. Before this time, lenders expressed the amount charged for the use of money in different ways. This made a comparison of rates by unsophisticated consumers virtually impossible.

Suppose that Amy lived in 1960 rather than today. The General Motors Acceptance Corporation may inform her that it charges only eight percent interest, whereas the bank may tell her that it assesses a ten percent fee for automobile loans. This sounds somewhat straightforward—unfortunately, it is not. In fact, the bank loan may have been the cheaper deal because of the manner in which the bank and G.M.A.C. calculated their interest rates. The average person with a high school education did not stand a chance of being able to figure out which lender offered the best deal.

To remedy situations like this, Congress passed the Truth in Lending Act in order to force lenders to make certain disclosures to consumer borrowers. The principle feature of the Truth in Lending Act pertains to the obligation it imposes on consumer lenders to make a full disclosure of the information necessary for the average consumer for assessing a meaningful comparison of the cost of borrowing from one lender as opposed to another. The proponents of this act reasoned that arming borrowers with more information would force lenders to compete on terms and conditions of the consumer loans.

■ *Finance Charge*

Borrowers need to know the total dollar amount they will pay for the use of credit—referred to in the Truth in Lending Act as the *finance charge*. The finance charge provided by a lender to a potential borrower must include not only the interest costs the borrower will pay, but also such other costs as service charges and appraisal fees.

Consider this example. Suppose that Kaisy and Greg Hill intend to purchase a new home, and they want to borrow $100,000. They visit two lenders—First Savings Association, and Federal Savings Association. Assume that all other charges are identical, but First Savings Association charges a one percent origination fee (one percent of the total amount borrowed). On the other hand, Federal Savings Association assesses no such fee. This means that the finance charge provided to the Hills by First Savings Association will be $1,000 higher than the finance charge imposed by Federal Savings Association for making the same loan. Since it is assumed that all other terms and conditions of the two loans are identical, it would be cheaper for the Hills to take out a loan at Federal Savings Association.

■ *Annual Percentage Rate*

A second item that the average borrower needs to understand before taking out a loan is the percentage cost of credit on a yearly basis—referred to in the Truth in Lending Act as the *annual percentage rate (A.P.R.)*.

Using the example with the Hills, suppose that First Savings Association informs the Hills that its A.P.R. on housing loans is ten percent, but Federal Savings Association indicates that it will make the identical loan on the same terms for 9.5 percent. What does this mean on a $100,000 loan? In the first year, it means that the Hills would pay approximately $9,500 in interest to Federal Savings Association, but they would end up paying roughly $10,000 to First Savings Association for borrowing the same $100,000. Once again, this suggests that their best option would be to take out a loan at Federal Savings Association.

■ *Right to Cancel Contract*

A very important right given to consumers under truth in lending is the right to cancel contracts involving loans on their homes. The act permits a consumer to rescind a transaction for three business days after entering into a contract, if the consumer uses his or her home as security for the loan. (This act permits a contract to be canceled *only* if the borrower uses his or her home as security for the loan.) If a person elects to rescind the loan, the security interest is voided and the consumer is not liable for any finance charge.

It should be noted that the three-day period during which a person has the right to cancel a contract does not start to run until the proper truth in lending disclosures are provided to the consumer. This means that even several years after a person enters into a transaction the loan still may be canceled, as the three-day period has not yet run. Suppose on January 1, 1997, Mary hires Acme Home Improvement Company to remodel her bathroom. She agrees to pay Acme $5,000 to perform this work. One of the papers she signs gives Acme a mortgage on her home. If the proper disclosures have been provided to Mary, she has three business days from January 1 to cancel the transaction. Suppose instead that Acme carelessly fails to provide her with certain information required by the Truth in Lending Act. The contractor performs the work. Mary starts paying on her note on February 1, 1997. Later in that year, she falls behind on the note, and Acme starts a legal action to foreclose its mortgage. At this point, Mary may exercise her right to cancel the transaction because the three-day period has not yet begun to run. Acme, therefore, may not take her home in payment of this debt. Mary is not liable for any finance charges on this loan. Of course, she still must pay the contractor for the work it performed on her home.

The Managerial Perspective, "Borrowers Cancel Loan," illustrates how a borrower may validly cancel a loan on his or her home even years after the origination of the loan on the home—if the lender failed to comply with the provisions of the Truth in Lending Act.

■ *Lost or Stolen Credit Cards*

People have only a limited liability in the event that unauthorized charges appear on their credit cards. The most an individual may be liable for as a result of unauthorized credit card use is $50 on each card. This applies only to charges made before the loss or theft of the card is reported to the credit card company. *Oclander v. First National Bank of Louisville* illustrates the issue of determining when the use of a credit card is unauthorized.

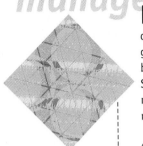

managerial perspective

Borrowers Cancel Loan

Mr. and Mrs. Hughes took out a loan from the Guaranty State Bank of St. Paul in the early 1980s. The Hughes gave the bank a mortgage on their home. The proceeds of the mortgage were to be used to remodel the family residence. In 1984, the Hughes sent the Guaranty State Bank of St. Paul a letter in which they stated that the bank had failed to make some disclosures required by the Truth in Lending Act. They exercised their right to rescind and cancel the loan on their home.

The court ruled that even though a significant period of time had passed since the Hughes took out the loan, as they never received the proper disclosures as mandated by the Truth in Lending Act, the Hughes were free at this point to cancel the loan on their home.

Source: FDIC v. Hughes Development Co., Inc., *684 F. Supp. 616 (United States District Court, District of Minnesota 1988).*

Oclander v. First National Bank of Louisville

Court of Appeals of Kentucky
700 S.W.2d 804 (1985)

Monica Oclander and Bonifacio Aparicio opened a MasterCard account on October 20, 1981. In July 1982, Oclander notified the bank that she was separated from Aparicio. The bank *blocked* the account from additional charges. It informed Oclander how to restore her credit. She returned the forms sent to her by the bank. Oclander informed the bank that she had destroyed the credit card issued to Aparicio, and she had retained the other card. On the basis of this representation, the bank unblocked her account. Aparicio, who in fact still held a credit card, thereafter charged $11,319.43 to the account while traveling in Spain. Oclander argued that she was not responsible for the charges because they were unauthorized. The court disagreed and ruled for the bank.

Dunn, Judge

Congress recognized some time ago that the area of credit card liability needed to be dealt with in a uniform manner. Accordingly, 15 U.S.C.A. § 643 provides protection for a card holder against "unauthorized" charges made on an account. Obviously, this was to protect the card holder in cases where the card had been stolen or lost and was being used to make "unauthorized charges." § 1643 limits the liability of a card holder where there has been "unauthorized use." Title 15 U.S.C.A. § 1602(o) defines the term "unauthorized use" to mean "a use of a credit card by a person other than the card holder who does not have actual, implied, or apparent authority for such use and from which the card holder receives no benefit." If the person using the card has either actual, implied, or apparent authority then the charges are authorized and the limitations imposed by § 1643 do not apply and Ms. Oclander would be liable for all charges made on the account as set out under the "Terms of Agreement." Thus, the issue of liability turns on whether the charges made by Bonifacio Aparicio were authorized.

> Apparent authority exists where a person has created such an appearance of things that it causes a third person to reasonably and prudently believe that a second party has the power to act on behalf of the first person (*Walker Bank & Trust Company v. Jones*).

Bonifacio Aparicio did in fact have a card in his possession with his name on it as a joint card holder and presented the card to merchants who had no reason to question his authority to use it. Mr. Aparicio was in possession of a card which was a representation to merchants (third parties) to whom they were presented that he (second-parties/card bearers) was authorized to make the charges. This is not a case where charges were made on an expired card, or the card was obtained through fraud or other wrongdoing. Mr. Aparicio was actually in possession of one of the cards and at all times was ostensibly authorized to make charges on the account. If Ms. Oclander had accurately explained the situation to the Bank and told them that Mr. Aparicio was in possession of one of the cards, or at the very least, that she did not have possession of both cards, then the Bank would have maintained the "block" it had originally placed on the account in July, and none of the charges made during Mr. Aparicio's buying spree would have been chargeable to the Bank.

The Bank did not even require that the cards be surrendered but only that they be accounted for by Ms. Oclander. Ms. Oclander failed to do so, and as a result the Bank has suffered damages for which she should be held accountable.

FAIR CREDIT REPORTING ACT

Consider the example mentioned earlier involving the purchase of a home by Kaisy and Greg Hill. Based on the low annual percentage rate and finance charge that Federal Savings Association would assess them for borrowing $100,000, the Hills decide to go through the formal process of applying for a loan. The fact that the Hills apply for a loan does not mean that they automatically will receive the money.

In the Hills case, Federal Savings Association will undoubtedly require the Hills to pay for a credit report that Federal Savings Association will obtain from a credit bureau. Such a report provides a history of the borrowing activities of a person. Most significantly, it sometimes indicates that a person is thirty, sixty, or ninety days late in repaying certain debts. Suppose that the Hills' credit report provided to Federal Savings Association by the Local Credit Bureau reveals that, within the last six months, they were more than ninety days late in making their car payment. This suggests that the Hills either are over their heads in debt and are unable to pay the debts they currently owe, or they are quite irresponsible regarding paying back their debts. In either case, if the credit report contains such erroneous information, it is very likely that Federal Savings Association will not loan the Hills the money to purchase a home.

Even the best run businesses make mistakes now and then. For example, the individual entering the data in the computer system may incorrectly list the Hills as being late on a car payment, when in fact this information should have gone into the Hulls' credit report. When the loan officer at Federal Savings Association looks at the report on the Hills, he or she would, in fact, draw the wrong conclusion because the report provided by the Local Credit Bureau contained false information regarding the Hills. The Hills will then be denied credit because of misinformation in their credit report.

Years ago, many people in situations like the Hills often found themselves unable to obtain the information on which the lender based its decision to deny credit. Even if people learned who provided the report in question, consumers often found it virtually impossible to get the credit bureau to take any action in correcting the misleading information in their credit report.

The Fair Credit Reporting Act changed all of this by giving a consumer who has been denied credit because of an adverse credit rating the following rights: (1) the right to receive the name and address of the agency that keeps the consumer's report; (2) the right to review at least a summary of the information held by the credit bureau; (3) the right to demand that any important error be investigated and corrected if the bureau finds an error in the report; and (4) if the person disagrees with the findings of the bureau, the right to prepare a short statement, which must be included in the record in the future.

How the Fair Credit Reporting Act effects someone in a situation like that of the Hills will be further examined. When the Federal Savings Association denies the Hills a loan based on a credit report supplied by the Local Credit Bureau, Federal Savings Association must give the Hills the name and address of the Local Credit Bureau. The Hills then may write to the Local Credit Bureau in order to obtain a copy of the report provided to the Federal Savings Association. When the Hills review their credit report, they will see the late car payment that was erroneously attributed to them rather than to the Hulls. Most likely, when they draw the credit bureau's attention to this erroneous information in their file, the information will be removed from their credit report and the Hills will be able to obtain a loan to purchase a home.

The Thought Problem, "Credit Bureau Investigates Error," deals with the duty of a credit bureau to investigate an alleged error in a credit report.

thought problem

Credit Bureau Investigates Error

Thomas K. Pinner worked at a Sherwin-Williams store managed by James E. Schmidt. Pinner maintained a personal charge account at the store. A considerable tension developed between Pinner and Schmidt. During this time period, Pinner alleged that several fictitious charges had been added to his account at the Sherwin-Williams store. The store reported Pinner's account as delinquent to Chilton, a credit reporting agency. Thereafter, Pinner attempted to purchase some tires on credit. The tire store refused to grant Pinner credit because of the erroneous information in the credit report provided by Chilton to the tire store. After obtaining a copy of his credit report, Pinner disputed the charges with Sherwin-Williams and asked Chilton to investigate the matter. Chilton then contacted Schmidt, who verified that the account was delinquent. After another store denied Pinner credit, he requested a copy of his credit report. The report listed the Sherwin-Williams debt as an undisputed delinquent account. Chilton had not amended to Pinner's credit file the fact that the amount was in dispute.

Did Chilton do everything that it was required to do under the Fair Credit Reporting Act?

Source: Pinner v. Schmidt, *805 F.2d 1258 (United States Court of Appeals, Fifth Circuit 1986).*

EQUAL CREDIT OPPORTUNITY ACT

The Equal Credit Opportunity Act (ECOA) makes it illegal for creditors to discourage applicants from applying for a loan, refuse a loan to a qualified person, or lend money on terms different from those granted to similar people because of the applicant's sex, race, marital status, national origin, religion, or age, or because the applicant receives public assistance income. The act initially was aimed at sex and marital status discrimination. Studies in the early 1970s indicated that women had a far more difficult time securing credit than did men. For example, single women were less likely to obtain credit than single men. Those who did receive credit, on marriage would need to reapply for credit in the husband's name. Newly married men were not required to reapply. Furthermore, creditors were often unwilling to count a wife's income when a married couple sought credit.

Thus, the ECOA attempted to remove barriers to the credit markets that existed for certain people for reasons unrelated to financial status. Since credit is an important aspect of society, Congress acted to make it available on a nondiscriminatory basis to anyone who is creditworthy.

FAIR DEBT COLLECTION PRACTICES ACT

The final consumer protection act in this section deals with the manner in which a business may go about collecting a debt. Suppose that Margaret worked at an oil company, but due to a recent downsizing, Margaret lost both her job and her health insurance. Before she was able to obtain some health insurance, an uninsured motorist hit her daughter, Melinda, necessitating a two-week hospital stay. The hospital sent Margaret a bill for $35,500 for Melinda's time in the hospital. Margaret explained to the hospital collections department that she had no money with which to pay this bill. Thereafter, the hospital sent the bill to a debt collection service. Would it be proper for the debt collector to threaten beating Margaret or to prosecute her if she failed to pay the entire debt within the next twenty-four hours?

Unfortunately, unethical debt collectors sometimes engaged in this type of behavior prior to the passage of the Fair Debt Collection Practices Act. This act places significant restraints on the actions of someone who is attempting to collect a debt for another person. For example, false or misleading representations used to collect a debt have been prohibited by this act. In addition, the act makes it unlawful to threaten to file criminal charges because a person fails to pay a debt. Thus, in the prior example, the debt collector's threat to have Margaret imprisoned would violate this act. The act makes it illegal to use threats of physical violence in attempting to collect a debt. It would be improper for the debt collector to threaten to beat Margaret up if she failed to pay the debt in the next twenty-four hours.

The Fair Debt Collection Practices Act deals only with the activities of debt collectors. The act defines the term *debt collector* so as to cover the activities of all third party debt collectors—that is, anyone, other than the original creditor, who regularly collects debts for others. In the prior example, if the hospital attempted to collect the debt from Margaret, it would be acting as Margaret's creditor, not as a debt collector. The hospital would not be subject to the provisions of the act. On the other hand, when the hospital refers the hospital bill to a collection agency, the agency will be treated as a debt collector for purposes of the act, and it is subject to the provisions of the Fair Debt Collection Practices Act.

Consider whether or not George Heintz is subject to the provisions of the Fair Debt Collection Practices Act in the next example. Darlene Jenkins borrowed money from the Gainer Bank in order to purchase a car. Jenkins failed to pay the loan, so the bank brought suit against her. In an attempt to settle the suit, the bank's attorney, George Heintz, wrote Jenkins a letter claiming that she owed the bank $4,173 for insurance. The bank claimed that it was forced to purchase such insurance because Jenkins had not kept the car insured as she had promised in the loan documents she signed.

Jenkins claimed that Heintz had violated the Fair Debt Collection Practices Act by making a false representation of the amount of a debt. Heintz claimed that the act did not apply to his actions because he was an attorney engaged in litigation. The United States Supreme Court ruled that the act applies to an attorney engaged in litigation because the attorney is a *debt collector*, as is defined under the act. The Court returned the case to the trial court to determine if Heintz had violated the act by making a false representation.[1]

Unfortunately, even after the passage of the Fair Debt Collection Practices Act, some consumers still find themselves subjected to abusive collection practices. For example, in 1991 and 1992, an employee of the Allied Adjustment Bureau made profanity-laced phone calls to Albert and Marianne Driscol, threatened to take out a contract on their lives if they failed to pay up, called Marianne Driscol's place of work with a bomb threat, and called her office thirty-six times in an hour. The attorney representing the Driscols in the subsequent suit against Allied Adjustment Bureau stated that more than two hundred and fifty people called him seeking help with similar situations.[2]

Environmental Law

During the 1960s, some Americans questioned certain commonly accepted ways of doing business. Activists seized on the obviously deteriorating quality of the American environment. Factories in Gary, Indiana, spewed out smoke so thick that it cast a pall of pollutants over the town. In Los Angeles, a yellow haze of fumes from the omnipresent automobile made it difficult for some people to breathe. It looked like deadly factory wastes such as mercury would soon leave Lake Erie dead. Pollution so overwhelmed one river in Ohio—the Cuyahoga—that the river actually caught fire. The liberal use of chemicals by farmers resulted in a torrent of chemicals flowing into the rivers from which people downstream drew their drinking water. Towns, in turn, dumped raw sewage into rivers, thus further damaging the water. Even people in the privacy of their own backyards saw evidence of the desecration of the environment. Deadly DDT sprayed by home gardeners resulted in the deaths of birds throughout America. We were poisoning not only ourselves, but our pets and the wildlife as well.

Some people trace the origins of the environmental movement in America to Rachael Carson's book, *Silent Spring*. This book chronicled the harmful effects that pesticides had on the environment. Prior to this time, hardly anyone gave any consideration to the damage done to the country by the activities of manufacturers, sewage systems, trash dumps, farmers, and even homeowners. *Silent Spring* helped raise the consciousness of everyone regarding the dangers posed to the environment by unchecked pollution. At that time, people believed that actions could go unchecked without damaging living conditions. Carson's book alerted people to the fact that things could not go on as they had in the past.

WHAT IS POLLUTION?

Pollution is more extensive than emitting particles into the air or dumping waste into a river. *Pollution* may be defined as the human-caused diminished capacity of the environment to perform its functions. This may involve dumping noxious chemicals into a ground-water supply, thereby making the water unsafe to drink. It may involve harvesting trees or planting crops in such a manner as to deplete the soil or encourage erosion. It may involve a mine that leaves a scar on the Earth where rolling hills once existed. All of these activities adversely affect living conditions. All may be considered pollution, and all are monitored by environmental laws.

■ Causes of Pollution

Although pollution is not new, its extent and its consequences became very serious in the 1960s because of the convergence of four factors. One was high population densities. An old saying has it that a river cleans itself every ten miles. This aphorism may have been true decades ago. A community of five thousand people may have been able to dispose of its untreated sewage in a passing river without environmental harm. But as the community grew to thirty-five thousand people, the dumping of the untreated sewage began to pollute. The river could no longer handle the increased waste. Large numbers of people concentrated in smaller areas strained the capacity of the environment.

Not only did the community increase in population, but its members used more resources than their predecessors, a second factor in the ecological crisis. Modern appliances created a greater demand for electricity. Families that may have had one automobile began to acquire two or more. As personal income increased, people were able to afford more products and luxuries. Pollution occurs at each stage of the production cycle. It occurs in the making of the product, during its distribution, and in its consumption. As demand for products increased, so did the demands on the environment to supply the resources.

Business practices made up another major factor of the pollution problem. Factories that were built to meet increased demand spewed added particles into the air and dumped more waste into the water. New types of products and manufacturing processes created more deadly forms of pollutants. Disposable products (beverage containers, cigarette lighters, and pens, for example) replaced reusable or returnable products. Nonbiodegradable plastic containers began to replace paper products.

Antipollution Technology in Japan

More than twenty years ago, Japan adopted tough air
and water pollution control standards as well as antipollution incentives for its industry.

Japan developed highly efficient, nonpolluting technology. This technology is at least ten years ahead of
what is available in other countries. The Japanese Ministry of International Trade and Industry (MITI) foresees
a large international market for this technology. As
worldwide interest in the environment rises, Japanese
firms are positioned to supply the basic equipment to
meet the need. In fact, Japanese international diplomatic
policy promotes such an end. In 1990, MITI proposed a
plan for international consideration, called New Earth 21,
that would restore the environment to its pre-Industrial
Revolution condition over the next hundred years. Note
which country has the technology to begin meeting this
goal. As one writer commented:

"[A] world community that
decides to save itself by saving the global environment
will be promoting many
large Japanese interests."

Source: From J. Newhouse,
"The Diplomatic Round: Earth
Summit," *The New Yorker,* June 1,
1992, pages 64, 69.

A final factor in the ecological crisis was that the
legal and economic systems did not discourage
the use of the environment as a dumping ground.
The firm that refused to use a river as a sewer would
need to make additional expenditures in order to
purify its wastes. Competitors who continued to
pollute would have those funds available for alternative productive uses. Since the legal system did
not prevent such dumping, the economic system, in
a sense, rewarded those who chose the *free* method
of waste disposal.

None of these factors was a lone culprit, but
coming together they caused a crisis in the ability
of the environment to fulfill its important functions. During the late 1960s and early 1970s, concern for the environment led the different levels of
government to seek legal solutions to the problems of pollution.

A concern with environmental quality is not
uniquely American. The International Perspective,
"Antipollution Technology in Japan," discusses
Japan's approach to environmental issues.

COMMON LAW REMEDIES

Even prior to the passage of the federal environmental laws, ways of dealing with activities that
damaged the environment existed. At one time,
people who objected to the activities of a polluter
resorted to bringing a suit in court based on some
violation of the common law. But the remedies that were available in
a case by case property rights dispute proved ineffective for controlling pollution. The *Boomer v. Atlantic Cement Company* case illustrates
the shortcomings associated with relying on the common law to stop
the pollution of the environment.

Boomer v. Atlantic Cement Company

Court of Appeals of New York
257 N.E.2d 870 (1970)

Atlantic Cement Company operated a large cement plant in the vicinity of Albany,
New York. Homeowners in the surrounding area objected to the dirt, smoke, and
vibration generated by the activities at the cement plant. They asked the court to
enjoin the operation of the plant based on the argument that the plant constituted a
nuisance—an act that annoys or disturbs the enjoyment of property by its owner. The
court declined to enjoin the operation of the plant.

Bergan, Judge

It seems apparent that the amelioration of air pollution will depend on technical
research in great depth; on a carefully balanced consideration of the economic
impact of close regulation; and of the actual effect on public health. It is likely to

require massive public expenditure and to demand more than any local community can accomplish and to depend on regional and interstate controls.

A court should not try to do this on its own as a by-product of private litigation and it seems manifest that the judicial establishment is neither equipped in the limited nature of any judgment it can pronounce nor prepared to lay down and implement an effective policy for the elimination of air pollution. This is an area beyond the circumference of one private lawsuit. It is a direct responsibility for government and should not thus be undertaken as an incident to solving a dispute between property owners and a single cement plant—one of many—in the Hudson River valley.

The rule in New York has been that a nuisance will be enjoined although marked disparity be shown in economic consequence between the effect of the injunction and the effect of the nuisance.

But to follow the rule literally would be to close down the plant at once. This court is fully agreed to avoid that immediately drastic remedy; the difference in view is how best to avoid it.

To grant the injunction unless defendant pays plaintiffs permanent damages as may be fixed by the court seems to do justice between the contending parties. All of the attributions of economic loss to the properties on which plaintiffs' complaints are based will have been redressed.

The nuisance complained of by these plaintiffs may have other public or private consequences, but these particular parties are the only ones who have sought remedies and the judgment proposed will fully redress them.

It seems fair to both sides to grant permanent damages to plaintiffs which will terminate this private litigation. The theory of damage is the "servitude on land" of plaintiffs imposed by defendant's nuisance.

The judgment, by allowance of permanent damages imposing a servitude on land, which is the basis of the actions, would preclude future recovery by plaintiffs or their grantees.

Jasen, Judge (dissenting)

It has long been the rule in this State that a nuisance which results in substantial continuing damages to neighbors must be enjoined. To now change the rule to permit the cement company to continue polluting the air indefinitely upon the payment of permanent damages is, in my opinion, compounding the magnitude of a very serious problem in our State and Nation today.

I see grave dangers in overruling our long-established rule of granting an injunction where a nuisance results in substantial continuing damage. In permitting the injunction to become inoperative upon payment of permanent damages, the majority is, in effect, licensing a continuing wrong. It is the same as saying to the cement company, you may continue to do harm to your neighbors so long as you pay a fee for it. Furthermore, once such permanent damages are assessed and paid, the incentive to alleviate the wrong would be eliminated, thereby continuing air pollution of an area without abatement.

In a day when there is a growing concern for clean air, highly developed industry should not expect acquiescence by the courts, but should, instead, plan its operations to eliminate contamination of our air and damage to its neighbors.

Consider the Thought Problem, "Is Odorous Feedlot a Nuisance?" In light of the fact that a nuisance is an act that annoys or disturbs the enjoyment of property by the owner, ask yourself if the Spur Industries Operation qualifies as a nuisance, and if so, to what sort of remedy should Del Webb be entitled?

Is Odorous Feedlot a Nuisance?

In 1956, a feedlot was developed by Marion Welborn in a rural area near Phoenix, Arizona. By 1959, twenty-five cattle feeding pens operated in a seven mile radius of Welborn's feedlot. At this time, Welborn was feeding around 8,500 head of cattle on thirty-five acres. In 1960, Spur Industries, Inc., took over the operations from Welborn.

In 1959, Del E. Webb Development Company began to develop a retirement community called Sun City. It purchased twenty-thousand acres of farmland. By May 1960, more than five hundred homes had been completed approximately two and a half miles north of the Spur Industries Operation. By 1967, Del Webb's development company had expanded to where more than 1,300 of its lots were so close to Spur Industries's operations that they were unfit for development because of the feedlot operation.

Del E. Webb Development Company brought suit alleging that the feedlot was a public nuisance because of the flies and the odor that were interfering with the Sun City homes. At this point, Spur Industries, Inc., was feeding between twenty thousand and thirty thousand head of cattle. There was no doubt that some of the citizens of Sun City were unable to enjoy their property due to the operation of the feedlot.

Did the actions of Spur Industries, Inc., constitute a nuisance?

Source: Spur Industries, Inc. v. Del E. Webb Development Co., *494 P.2d 700 (1972).*

FEDERAL REGULATION OF THE ENVIRONMENT

Federal environmental law may be divided into two categories—one is a full disclosure of the environmental effects of major federal government activity; and the second category consists of a number of statutes (and accompanying administrative regulations) aimed at limiting pollution. Together these approaches have resulted in more than hundreds of billions of dollars being spent on compliance by business since the laws enactment. It has also resulted in tremendous strides being made in reducing the amount of environmental damage.

■ *NEPA*

The National Environmental Policy Act of 1969 (**NEPA**) was enacted as a full-disclosure statute. It recognized that federal activity had major environmental consequences. The purposes of the act were stated by Congress in Section 2:

> To declare a national policy which will encourage productive and enjoyable harmony between man and his environment; to promote efforts which will prevent or eliminate damage to the environment and biosphere and stimulate the health and welfare of man; to enrich the understanding of the ecological systems and national resources important to the Nation; and to establish a Council on Environmental Quality.

NEPA requires an environmentally related decision-making technique. If federal activity has a major effect on the environment, then a detailed report, called an **environmental impact statement,** must be prepared. This report analyzes the effect of the project on the human environment. If the activity *may* have an effect on the environment, then the environment is to be considered along with the other factors involved in the planning.

The act is significant in that it clearly recognizes federal government responsibility for the quality of the environment. However, it is not a means for eliminating causes or sources of pollution. Nor does it provide a legal right to a clean and unpolluted environment. The *Breckinridge v. Rumsfeld* case is an example of the application of NEPA. Note that if the federal activity is challenged in court because no environmental impact statement (or an inadequate statement) has been prepared, a court may order the project stopped until a statement has been properly prepared. NEPA does not require an analysis of all effects on federal activities. It is aimed at the protection of the environment.

Breckinridge v. Rumsfeld

United States Court of Appeals, Sixth Circuit
537 F.2d 864 (1976)

On November 22, 1974, the secretary of defense announced 111 actions involving realignment of units and the closing of particular military bases. One of the actions affected the Lexington-Bluegrass Army Depot (LBAD) to the extent that eighteen military and 2,630 civilian jobs would be eliminated in the Lexington area. The army prepared an environmental assessment, which concluded that because there was to be no significant effect on the human environment, a formal environmental impact statement was not required. Additionally, a nongovernment research institution, Batelle Columbus Laboratories, studied the possible socioeconomic impact of the action and concluded that the Lexington area would suffer only minimal short-term unemployment as a result of the partial closing.

The question presented on this appeal involves the breadth to be given to the term *human environment* as used in the National Environmental Policy Act (NEPA). Specifically, does action by the United States Army that reduces jobs and transfers personnel from the Lexington-Bluegrass Army Depot to depots in California and Pennsylvania constitute "a major Federal action significantly affecting the quality of the human environment"?

Phillips, Chief Judge

In the present case there is no long term impact, no permanent commitment of a national resource and no degradation of a traditional environmental asset, but rather short term personal inconveniences and short term economic disruptions. We conclude that such a situation does not fall within the purview of the act.

The contention that NEPA goes beyond what might be stated to be the "physical environment" is not in dispute. Environmental impact statements have been mandated in such diverse instances as construction of a federal jail in the back of the United States Court House in Manhattan.

Although factors other than the physical environment have been considered, this has been done only when there existed a primary impact on the physical environment.

In discussion of NEPA on the floor of the Senate, Senator Jackson provided insight into the breadth of the statute:

What is involved is a congressional declaration that we do not intend, as a government or as a people, to initiate actions which endanger the continued existence or the health of mankind: That we will not intentionally initiate actions which will do irreparable damage to the air, land, and water which support life on earth.

An environmental policy is a policy for people. Its primary concern is with man and his future. The basic principle of the policy is that we must strive in all that we do, to achieve a standard of excellence in man's relationships to his physical surroundings.

To extend the meaning of NEPA to apply to the factual situation involved in this case would distort the congressional intent.

NEPA is not a national employment act. Environmental goals and policies were never intended to reach social problems such as those presented here.

DIRECT STATUTORY CONTROL OF POLLUTION

In addition to NEPA, Congress passed a large number of statutes specifically addressed to deal with certain environmental issues, such as air pollution, water pollution, toxic waste disposal, the use of insecticides and pesticides, and strip mining.

These direct controls of pollution involve efforts by Congress, which enacted the statutes, and a federal administrative agency—generally the Environmental Protection Agency—which promulgates regulations to carry out the policies established by Congress in the statutes.

WATER QUALITY—FISHABLE AND SWIMMABLE

One of the most important areas of government regulation of the environment concerns the water in America. In passing the Federal Water Pollution Control Act, Congress hoped to achieve two goals: (1) to make our waters fishable and swimmable, and (2) to eliminate the discharge of pollutants into navigable waters. The Federal Water Pollution Control Act limits the amount of pollutants that may be discharged by any source.

One should realize that chemicals may come back to haunt us. Suppose that Acme Insect Control uses the chemical chlordane in order to rid a home of termites. Chlordane may leach into the soil and from the soil into a river. The chlordane falls to the bottom of the river where a catfish absorbs the chemical by filtering sediment through its gills. Chlordane builds up in the fat of the fish. When a person catches and fries the catfish, cooking does not destroy chlordane. Thus, the chemical works its way into the bodies of the people who eat the catfish. Since pest control companies used chlordane as a means of killing termites, it is obvious to see how dangerous the application of chlordane may be to everyone in the community.

WATER QUALITY—DRINKABLE

The second important act passed by Congress in order to protect our waters is the Safe Drinking Water Act. This act is designed to protect the drinking water supplied to the public by a public water supply system. The basic idea behind the Safe Drinking Water Act is to ensure that the water people drink will not be injurious because of some dangerous substance in the water.

Figure 15.1 graphically illustrates how otherwise pristine water becomes undrinkable. Factories may release dangerous chemicals into rivers. Farmers may spray their crops with pesticides. Sewage from cities may seep into the ground and down to the water table. Dangerous substances located in landfills may ooze into the water supply as well. These are the types of substances the Safe Drinking Water Act is designed to guard against.

■ **FIGURE 15.1** Sources of Drinking Water Contamination

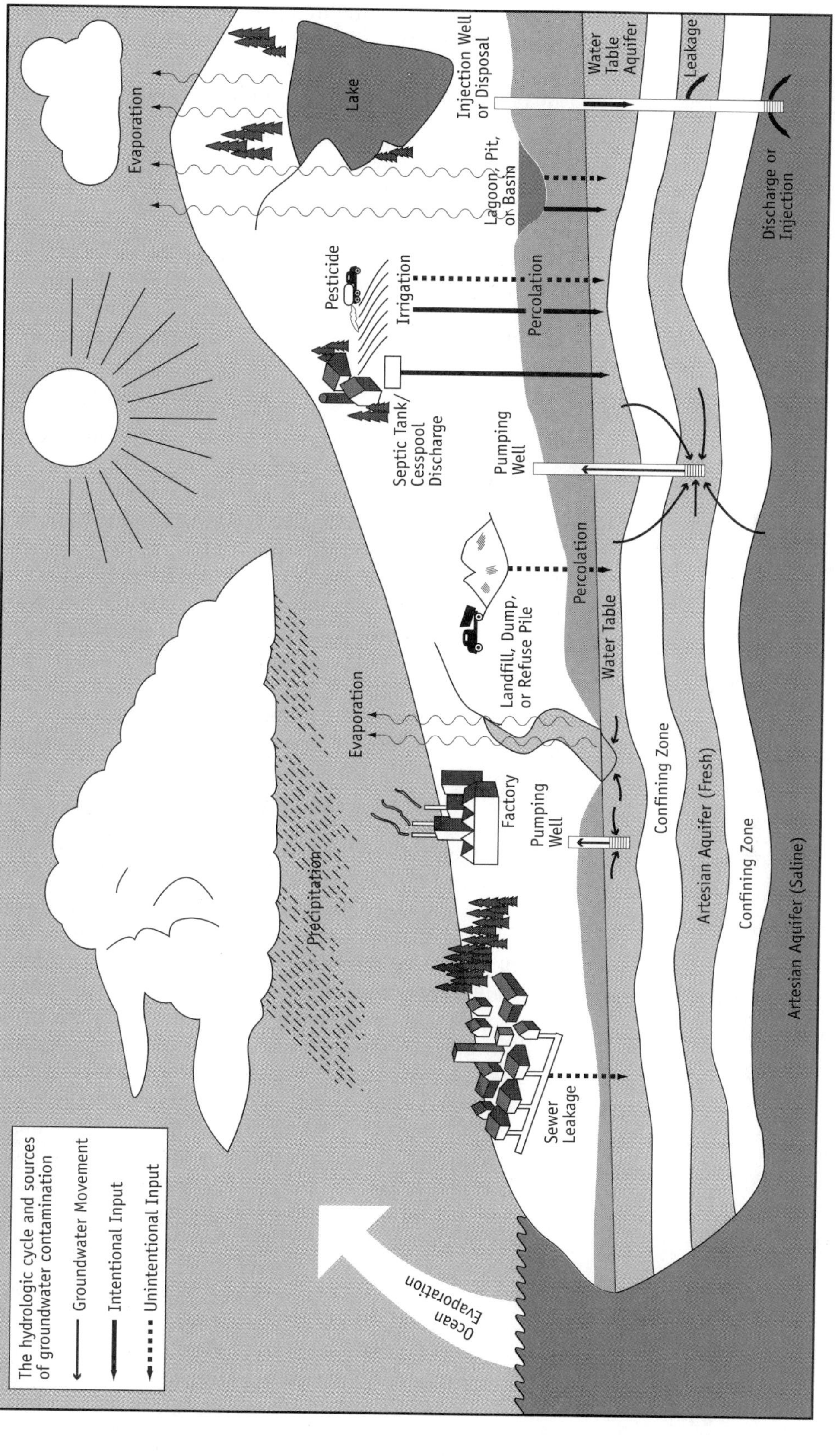

The hydrologic cycle and sources of groundwater contamination

— → Groundwater Movement
▬▶ Intentional Input
▪▪▶ Unintentional Input

As with other antipollution legislation, a great debate exists over exactly how pure the drinking water should be. Should the water be as pure as glacier water? Rudyard Kipling, an English author, wrote the poem *Gunga Din* about a soldier in India dying of thirst.

> An' he guv 'arf-a-pint 'o water green:
> It was crawlin' and it stunk,
> But of all the drinks I've drunk,
> I'm gratefullest to one from Gunga Din.

While a soldier who is dying of thirst probably would be thankful for the dirty, stinking water provided to him by Gunga Din, hopefully we can do better than dirty, stinking water in the United States today. But just how much better is a matter subject to considerable controversy.

AIR QUALITY

Congress passed the Clean Air Act in order to make certain that the air we breathe will not harm us or the environment. For example, the act limits the amount of carbon monoxide in the air. In a very automobile-oriented city like Los Angeles, each automobile spews carbon monoxide into the atmosphere. If totally uncontrolled, then carbon monoxide in the air in Los Angeles may make the entire area uninhabitable. In fact, this is rapidly becoming a reality in many major cities around the world. Mexico City, which is located on a plateau one mile above sea level, is one the world's most populous cities. The air hangs above Mexico City allowing the pollutants generated by automobiles and factories to envelop the city. The carbon monoxide generated by automobiles has made the air quality in Mexico City among the worst in the world.

The Clean Air Act requires states that had failed to achieve the national air quality standards established by the Environmental Protection Agency to establish a permit program regulating new sources of air pollution. A permit may not be issued for a new source of air pollution unless certain conditions have been met. The EPA adopted a regulation that allows states to adopt a plantwide definition of air pollution. Under this definition, an existing plant that contains several pollution-emitting devices may install or modify one piece of equipment without meeting the permit conditions if the alteration will not increase the total emissions from the plant. Thus the EPA's decision allows states to treat all of the pollution-emitting devices in a plant as though they were encased in a single *bubble*.

In examining the question of whether or not The Bubble Concept adopted by the EPA was consistent with the Clean Air Act, the United States Supreme Court upheld the use of The Bubble Concept because it is an attempt to accommodate progress in reducing air pollution with economic growth.[3]

Over the last two decades, we have learned a great deal about the environment. We now know for example, that chlorofluorocarbons pose a serious threat to human survival.

One popular use of chlorofluorocarbons (CFCs) was as a refrigerant in older automobile air conditioners (freon). Manufacturers also widely used CFCs in aerosol cans.

In 1987, governments around the world signed a landmark international agreement. This agreement outlaws the manufacture of chlorofluorocarbons in the United States and most developed countries. Scientific research revealed that CFCs destroy the Earth's protective ozone layer. While at first it seemed like this would create a significant problem for manufacturers, alternatives are now available on the market that do not damage the environment. The cost of abandoning CFCs, however, will run into the billions of dollars worldwide.

OTHER ENVIRONMENTAL LAWS

Due to the host of other federal environmental laws, just two of these acts will be noted now. Toxic substances may ruin the environment. The Resource Conservation and Recovery Act regulates the treatment, storage, and disposal of hazardous waste. Hazardous wastes must be disposed of in such a manner as to not damage the environment. For example, at one time, it may have been possible to transfer certain hazardous wastes to the city dump. The problem with this approach, as illustrated in Figure 15.1, is that in certain landfills, these wastes may percolate down to the water table and eventually destroy water supply sources.

A very controversial law—the Comprehensive Environmental Response Compensation and Liability Act (CERCLA)—imposes liability on present and past owners and operators of a facility where hazardous materials were deposited or stored. The contentious issue here concerns who will bear the cost of cleaning up sites with hazardous materials in them.

Some money has been recovered from polluters. A notorious toxic dumping site, Love Canal, involved residents in an area in New York who were sold homes constructed over a toxic dumping site. Many of the residents became ill. The government became involved and spent more than $100 million to clean up the Love Canal area. It brought a suit against the polluters. The suit lasted more than sixteen years, finally coming to a conclusion in 1996 when the government recovered $129 million from the Occidental Chemical Corporation.

The government, through taxes, has created a fund to clean up contaminated waste sites. While hundreds of sites like the Love Canal area have been restored, more than a thousand more serious sites remain to be cleaned up.

Pollution is a worldwide problem, as illustrated in the Thought Problem, "Bulgarian Pollution."

Bulgarian Pollution
Bulgaria, located on the Black Sea southeast of Russia, was controlled by Todor Zhivkov, the secretary general of the Bulgarian Communist Party, from 1954 until the collapse of the communist regime in November 1989. Like the Soviets, the Bulgarians favored giant enterprises.

The environment in Bulgaria gradually collapsed because the former communist leaders placed such a low priority on the environment as opposed to the development of heavy industry in Bulgaria.

Bulgarian citizens now suffer from high lead levels, respiratory diseases, cancer, birth defects, mental retardation, and other serious health problems that are all likely attributable to the sad state of the environment.

Regrettably, at the same time—when the Soviet Union collapsed—Bulgaria's economy also collapsed. Industrial production has dropped significantly in addition to its volume of exports. Bulgaria is also straddled with significant debt. It needs to clean up its environment, but it is desperately struggling to survive.

In light of the difficulties that Bulgaria is experiencing in the transition to a free market economy, what do you think should or *can* be done about the tragic state of Bulgaria's environment?

Source: Brent Yarnal, "Bulgaria at a Crossroads," *Environment,* December 1995, pages 7–33.

TRADEOFFS BETWEEN EFFICIENCY AND THE ENVIRONMENT

The interests of business and society conflict when it comes to the issue of cleaning up the environment. First of all, it costs money to clean up existing sources of pollution. Who should pay for these costs? Many businesses have resisted the idea of absorbing the cost of cleaning up the environment. The additional cost associated with this task may add so much to the cost of their services or products that the companies become uncompetitive. For this reason, these businesses would prefer that someone else pay for the cost of cleaning up the environment. The same argument also applies to making the environment safe in the future. If a business must use a less efficient process in order to avoid further damaging the environment, then this may make the business uncompetitive. Consequently, many businesses are reluctant to adopt more environmentally friendly processes.

In the *Boomer v. Atlantic Cement Company* case, that appeared earlier in this chapter, Judge Bergan overtly referred to the serious economic consequences associated with the stringent application of the law to the Atlantic Cement Company. Judge Bergan recognized the tradeoffs that may be made between improving the environment and keeping the cement plant in business. This is a recurring theme that is continuously heard in battles between environmentalists and the business community. Congress and the courts must delicately balance the need to protect the environment with the need to maintain efficient, competitive businesses.

ENDANGERED SPECIES ACT OF 1973

No where has the battle between those advocating economic efficiency and those favoring strong laws protecting the environment been more aggressively fought than in the arena of the Endangered Species Act of 1973. Interestingly, former President Richard Nixon, a conservative Republican, supported the passage of the Endangered Species Act of 1973. Nixon observed in signing the act into law: "Nothing is more priceless . . . than this rich array of animal life with which our country has been blessed."

The aggressive pursuit of certain *cute* animals such as whales, elephants, and tigers has resulted in the virtual annihilation of these species. Quite possibly, in the next twenty years, tigers may entirely disappear from the face of this planet joining the list of today's extinct animals such as the dodo. While an erect polar bear may look handsome in an individual's library, along with a tiger skin rug on the floor and the mounted head of an eland hanging on the wall, if everyone decorated their homes in this fashion, these animals would definitely be extinct. Former President Kennedy's wife, Jacqueline Onassis, proudly wore a leopard skin coat and carried an alligator bag while living in the White House. Can every American woman adopt such attire without decimating these animals? Poachers shoot elephants and leave their carcasses to rot just so they may sell the elephant's ivory tusks for use in chess sets. Some people in Asia purchase rhinoceros horns because they believe the horns are an aphrodisiac. If you reflect on the decimation of the world's wild animals, one cannot help but think that many of the world's most dangerous animals need help, because the world's most dangerous animal—man—is on the verge of eradicating all of them.

In the world at this moment, at least 5.7 *billion* people exist. Men and women need space for homes, schools, and offices. Land must be cultivated in order to grow food for these people to eat. The mere expansion of the world's human population is annihilating other species of animals.

The people who lobbied for the passage of the Endangered Species Act wanted to protect our planet not only for humans, but its other inhabitants as well. This act protects any animal in danger of extinction—these animals are classified as *endangered*. Species that are likely to become endangered are classified as *threatened*. The act designated the Fish and Wildlife Service and the National Marine Fisheries Service to create and enforce plans for the recovery of endangered and threatened species. The act prohibits the taking of listed species whether by killing them or by destroying their habitat. The issue of the destruction of an animal's habitat most closely brings the goals of this act directly into conflict with the interests of private property owners and workers.

One of the more famous instances of such a conflict concerns the attempt to protect the habitat of the northern spotted owl in the Pacific Northwest. In order to protect the owl's habitat, the government has restricted lumber companies from cutting trees in a large area. These restrictions directly affect people in the lumber industry and have cost thousands of workers their jobs. This instance is a classic conflict between the needs of industry and the needs of endangered species. Should an entire industry be damaged in order to protect the spotted owl? Owners and workers in the timber industry think it is unreasonable to restrict logging in the Pacific Northwest in light of the significant economic impact on the economy.

Environmental law involves a tradeoff to some extent. Private property rights are extremely important and deserve serious consideration when making or implementing any governmental policy. Wildlife is also extremely important. The Endangered Species Act, in the eyes of many workers, landowners, and business executives, strikes a balance weighted way too far in the direction of protecting wildlife. It does not give sufficient weight to the economic needs of these people. Environmentalists, on the other hand, view the law's effect as minor when weighed against the almost certain eradication of certain animals from the planet. Once they are gone, no one can bring them back.

Sensational cases stir discussion and tend to make the news. The Thought Problem, "The Tipton Kangaroo Rat," discusses one of the most sensational prosecutions pursuant to the Endangered Species Act.

thought problem

The Tipton Kangaroo Rat The Tipton

kangaroo rat is critically endangered. Ming-Tang Lin, a California farmer, lived on land that was listed as a natural habitat for the Tipton kangaroo rat. Lin was told, on at least four separate occasions, that he could not plow his land without first obtaining a permit. In spite of receiving these warnings, Lin went ahead, without getting the necessary permits, and plowed part of his land—destroying 330 acres of the Tipton kangaroo rat's habitat. In order to stop this destruction of habitat, in February 1994, five armed federal agents, as well as three state game wardens and fourteen biologists, swooped down on Lin's Kern County property. Agents arrested Lin and seized his tractor.

Farmers were upset that the Fish and Wildlife Service was seemingly driving them out of business in order to save a rat. The Fish and Wildlife Service naturally took the position that it was merely enforcing the act.

Which is more important—the private property rights of the farmer or the survival of the Tipton kangaroo rat? Did the government go too far in this case? Do rats have a right to live?

Source: Ted Williams, "Defense of the Realm," *Sierra,* January/February 1996, pages 39, 131–132. See also, T. H. Watkins, "What's Wrong with the Endangered Species Act? Not Much—and Here's Why," *Audubon,* January/February 1996.

We see the tradeoff between the environmental needs of the country and private property rights in many other contexts. For example, in 1983, the federal government launched the Rails to Trails program to convert seven thousand miles of former railroad track bed into public trails. These trails allow hikers or bikers a place to go. The property owners argue that the hikers and bikers are interfering with their privacy. They fear the Rails to Trails program will bring crime to their doorsteps and will result in a decline in the value of their property.[4]

Summary

Throughout the 1960s and 1970s, people in America began to request more protection from business practices than in the past. Previously, the public simply accepted things as part of the way in which businesses operated.

Consumers were particularly upset over the manner in which the business system treated them when they went to borrow money. Women, solely on the basis of sex, were denied credit. Lenders expressed the costs of credit in such a confusing manner that only the most intelligent people could understand the true cost of credit. When people were denied credit, it frequently was impossible to get credit reporting agencies to provide accurate statements of their credit history. Finally, some debt collectors engaged in abusive practices in the course of attempting to collect a debt. Congress passed laws dealing with all of these practices. Today, it is much easier to get credit and to understand the cost of credit, and it is much less likely that a person will be unfairly treated if he or she fails to pay a debt.

During the same time frame, Congress changed the law relating to the pollution of the environment from one that essentially relied on the common law to one based on statute. It required businesses to stop polluting the air and water, and it also required those businesses that created existing environmental problems to pay for the cost of cleaning up the damage they did to the environment. Today, the environment in America is much less polluted than it was only a few decades ago. Even so, people need to recognize that some sort of tradeoff must be made between our desire for a clean environment and our need for a vibrant economy. Where this tradeoff should be made is the source of considerable controversy.

Review Questions

1. Define the following terms:
   a. Environmental impact statement
   b. N.E.P.A.
   c. Nuisance
   d. Pollution
   e. Truth in Lending

2. Sally Jenkins purchased an automobile for her private use from Joe's Used Cars. She agreed to pay Joe in equal installments for the car over the next two years. Although Joe told Jenkins that the installment payments included an interest charge, the amount of interest to be paid was never disclosed. Furthermore, the interest rate was also not disclosed. May Joe's Used Cars expect to have problems with this loan transaction? Explain your answer.

3. Kirt and Alysa Grant obtained a mortgage to purchase a home from Federal Savings Association in January 1997. At the time of making the loan, Federal Savings Association failed to make certain disclosures required by the Truth in Lending Act. In February 1998, Alysa got laid off from her job due to a major corporate downsizing. As a result of the loss of her income, the Grants failed to make their mortgage payments and Federal Savings Association is now attempting to foreclose. Is there anything that the Grants may do to keep their home?

4. When Jill Student enrolled in the university, her parents gave her a credit card. They arranged with the Charge-it Credit Card Company for a card to be issued in her name on their account. After Jill began to receive low grades, her parents decided to take away her credit card. She refused to relinquish it. They telephoned Charge-it Credit Card Company to cancel their credit account. Charge-it informed them to

send in all of the outstanding cards on their account. This procedure for cancellation was provided in the credit card contract. No cards were submitted to the company for three months. In the meantime, Jill charged $2,000 worth of merchandise. Her parents have been sued for that amount by Charge-it. They contend that they should, at most, be liable for $50. Discuss your answer.

5. Mary Jones and Tom Smith were accountants, employed by the same firm. Their positions and salaries were identical. Both were unmarried, with approximately the same monthly expenses. They also had a similar credit history. On July 5, Jones and Smith visit on separate occasions, the Loan Company to borrow $5,000. Smith is given a one-page information sheet to fill out. Jones must prepare a ten-page questionnaire as well as provide three personal references. On completion of the documents, Smith is immediately granted the loan. Jones must meet with officers of Loan Company for a personal interview. Note that the financial information on both Jones and Smith's information sheets was virtually the same. Jones was granted the loan, but was to pay interest at three percent higher than market rates. When Jones learned about Smith's different experience with the same company, she became angry. Does Jones have a claim against Loan Company? Discuss your answer.

6. Fire Fighter's Fund hired O'Hanlon Reports to conduct a personal investigation of James Millstone. When he was denied credit, he asked to see his credit report. The agency failed to provide the entire report to him until he had gone to great effort to obtain it. The report contained a number of false statements, such as the allegation that Millstone used drugs and gave wild parties. The agent who filed the report talked to only one person in obtaining this information. Did O'Hanlon violate the Fair Credit Reporting Act?

7. Crystal Bagley worked as a waitress at the Top Hat Tavern. The Top Hat Tavern did not provide her with health insurance, and she lacked enough income to purchase it on her own. A drunk driver struck her car, and she took the car to Joe's Garage for repairs. Joe charged $850 for his work. When Bagley failed to pay Joe, he sent the bill to the Deadbeat Collection Agency. Deadbeat Collection Agency threatened to kill her if she failed to pay the bill. Is there anything Bagley may do about the collection agency's techniques?

8. Discuss *The Bubble Concept* used by the Environmental Protection Agency in addressing pollution by a single plant—noting, in particular, its effect on corporate decision making.

9. The Army Corps of Engineers is planning to dam a river in order to create a large reservoir. The reservoir will replace farmland and woodland that currently surrounds the dam site. Discuss how this project is regulated by the federal environmental laws.

10. Jack owned a farm. A stream of pure water flowed through it. One of the main reasons Jack purchased the farm was to enjoy the benefits the stream provided. Jack diverted water from the stream to use in his house. Soon after purchasing the farm, XYZ, Inc., began dumping wastes into the stream. The corporation's plant was located upstream from Jack's farm. The stream became polluted, and Jack could no

longer use the stream's water for household purposes. In addition, the pollution discolored the water and caused it to smell. Discuss any common law claims Jack may have against XYZ, Inc. Why are Jack's common law remedies not as good as those provided by federal law today?

11. You are the project manager for ABC Corporation. Your job involves coordinating all aspects of new factory construction that the corporation undertakes. A new plant under construction in Arizona will be bleaching paper and, as a byproduct, will produce dioxin, a highly toxic chemical that will be discharged into the air. Why should you be concerned, as the project manager, about the effect of this new undertaking on the environment?

12. The government wants to release an endangered species of wolves in a federal park near your ranch. You raise sheep. You think the actions of the government interfere with your property rights. On what basis could the government justify its actions?

Notes

[1]*Heintz v. Jenkins*, 115 S.Ct. 1489 (United States Supreme Court 1995).
[2]"Abusive Collectors to Pay," *The National Law Journal*, September 5, 1995, page A27.
[3]*Chevron v. Natural Resources Defense Council, Inc.*, 104 S.Ct. 2778 (1984).
[4]Rae Tyson, "Public Trails, Property Rights Cross Paths," *USA Today*, November 30, 1995, page 9A.

Chapter

16

EMPLOYEE RIGHTS IN THE WORKPLACE: DISCRIMINATION AND WRONGFUL DISCHARGE

hat were once considered employer prerogatives are now regulated by law. Employment discrimination and wrongful discharge are legal doctrines that limit an employer's power. Job-related decisions that are based on certain factors (e.g., race, sex) may no longer be made. Furthermore, firing an employee for an arbitrary reason not related to job performance may lead to a tort suit. Consequently, the personnel practices of business had to change as the law redefined the relationship between employer and employee.

Employment Discrimination

Discriminate means to choose or differentiate. At one time, saying that someone was *discriminating* complimented a high-quality taste (for example, having discriminating taste in music meant a person had quality taste). Discriminating people listened to Toscanini, while the hoi polloi enjoyed Spike Jones (this use of the term *was* a long time ago). Today, the word *discriminate* conjures an unsavory image. In the workplace, it describes an employer making decisions based on employees' innate characteristics rather than on their skills. The employees are not treated as human beings with intrinsic worth, but rather as symbols (e.g., black or white, male or female).

However, the *law* of employment discrimination is far more complex than this notion. First of all, it does not prohibit all irrational employer discriminations—it prohibits only those actions based on certain factors. For example, an employer may refuse to promote left-handed people even though such a characteristic has nothing to do with job skills. It is an arbitrary characteristic. In the absence of regulation or a contractual provision, the employer retains the power to have a solely right-handed workforce if he or she so chooses. The Ethical Perspective, "Discrimination, but Not Illegal," provides another example.

In addition, what the law defines as *discrimination* is far more complex than choosing, say, caucasian workers instead of hispanic ones, or males instead of females. An employer also risks legal sanction if an indirect discriminatory effect arises from a practice that was thought to be nondiscriminatory. As an example, consider an employee evaluation system that tried to be fair, yet resulted in a disproportionate number of Hispanic-Americans being rejected for promotions.

The statute having the greatest effect on employment practices is Title VII of the Civil Rights Act of 1964. However, many other laws exist that also have had an effect, most of which are beyond this chapter's scope. Federal statutes such as the Equal Pay Act and the Age Discrimination in Employment Act are examples. Additionally, state law and local ordinances may also play a role. So many changing factors come into play that these laws could be the focus of another course.

TITLE VII: CIVIL RIGHTS ACT OF 1964

The Civil Rights Act of 1964 was the culmination of a long struggle by African-Americans for equal treatment under the law. One of its provisions, Title VII, pertains to employment. Title VII prohibits discrimination based on race, color, national origin, religion, or sex.

As initially proposed, this legislation did not prohibit sex discrimination. In the early 1960s, the idea that women could be police officers, construction workers, or business executives was considered too far-reaching. Nonetheless, the statute—when finally enacted—did list *sex* as one of the prohibited categories of job discrimination. Ironically, during the statute's debate in the House of Representatives, the sex discrimination amendment was offered by an opponent as a tactic for defeating the bill. The gambit misfired and sex discrimination became part of the law.

An administrative agency, the Equal Employment Opportunity Commission (EEOC) was created to oversee Title VII. The EEOC has the power to investigate allegations of employment discrimination and may file charges against businesses, unions, or employment agencies. Additionally, the EEOC—in its fact-finding role—may hear evidence from the employee and employer and attempt to reach a resolution of the complaint. Finally, the agency promulgates regulations that provide guidance about certain employment practices to businesses concerned with the agency's perspective.

In mid-1995, more than 100,000 employment discrimination claims were pending with the EEOC. Thirty-five percent of the claims concerned racial discrimination; twenty-eight percent pertained to sex discrimination (including sexual harassment); and twenty-one percent regarded disability discrimination (a topic discussed later in this chapter). During 1994, it took nearly eleven months for the EEOC to process a claim, and seventy-five percent more cases were pending that year than just three years earlier.

Title VII has the following two goals:

1. To limit social conflict by providing the opportunity for all workers to compete without regard to certain personal characteristics

2. To provide a means of entry of the formerly excluded into the economic mainstream through the removal of discriminatory barriers

Discrimination artificially distorts labor markets. People who are excluded from certain jobs tend to cluster in other types of jobs that remain open to them, thereby misallocating individual's skills. Furthermore, basing pay on discriminatory policies relegates people to lower economic straits which is irrespective of their talent or potential contribution to the economy. Prohibiting employment discrimination is a way the law

ETHICAL
PERSPECTIVE

Discrimination, but Not Illegal

Kenneth Ulane had been a licensed pilot since 1964. From 1964–1968, he was in the army and flew a number of combat missions in Vietnam for which he was decorated. In 1968, he was hired as a pilot by Eastern Airlines.

Ulane was a transsexual. Although he was male, he felt like a female from early childhood onward. While in the military, Ulane sought medical assistance and later began taking female hormones. In 1980, Ulane underwent sex-change surgery. Thereafter, a revised birth certificate was issued that listed Ulane as a female. Further, her Federal Aviation Association flight status was changed to show that she was a female pilot. However, Ulane's surgery did not make her a biological female. She was unable to bear children, and her chromosomes remained male.

Eastern Airlines did not know about Ulane's surgery. It knew her only as *Kenneth Ulane*—one of the organization's male pilots. Once the company discovered that Ulane was a transsexual, Eastern Airlines fired her. Ulane filed a sex discrimination complaint.

The court held that Title VII's prohibited sex discrimination clause only applied to discrimination against men or women. The prohibition did not include transsexuals or any other sexual identity disorder. Thus, by the terms of the statute, Eastern Airlines did not discriminate against Ulane.

Evaluate the airline's decision to fire Ulane based on the ethics materials in Chapter 7. Recall that legal and ethical analysis do not necessarily yield the same conclusions.

Source: Ulane v. Eastern Airlines, Inc., *742 F.2d 1081 (United States Court of Appeals, Seventh Circuit 1984).*

may facilitate the smooth functioning of labor markets. The International Perspective, "Worldwide Pay Inequality," is an example of wage discrepancies in different countries around the world.

Reaching the goals of Title VII proved far more complex than the enactment of a single statute could provide. Difficult questions about employment practices that had long-embraced discriminatory customs found their way into court. Note how the law required business managers to reconsider long-established employment policies.

INTERNATIONAL
PERSPECTIVE
Worldwide Pay Inequality

The United Nations has developed a means of comparing inequality between the sexes. The five countries with the least inequality include:

1. Sweden
2. Finland
3. Norway
4. Denmark
5. United States

The pay differential between women and men has also been studied. The worldwide mean shows that women earn 74.9 percent of the total that men earn. The following statistics include some specific country figures:

China: Women earn 59.4 percent of what men earn.
Canada: Women earn 63 percent of what men earn.
United States: Women earn 75 percent of what men earn.

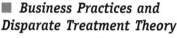

Turkey: Women earn 84.5 percent of what men earn.
Australia: Women earn 90.8 percent of what men earn.

Source: "Conference Mondiale sur les Femmes" (special section), *Le Monde,* August 31, 1995, page iv.

■ *Business Practices and Disparate Treatment Theory*

Using any part of Title VII's prohibited factors as a means of distinguishing between workers is called *disparate treatment.* Thus, setting pay scales based on employees' race, color, or national origin would violate the act. In addition, making job interview decisions based on the sex or religion of the applicant would also be a violation. The first task for a business manager, therefore, is to review personnel practices to make sure none of them use Title VII factors as a means of distinguishing between interviewees or employees.

However, disparate treatment may occur in less obvious ways. Stereotypical attitudes may affect judgments to such an extent that Title VII violations may arise. For example, assume that ABC, Inc., has shorn any hint of discrimination from its procedures to promote candidates. All employees are evaluated based on how well they fit into the team concept that ABC, Inc., values in its workforce. However, some of the executives who make promotion decisions believe that devout Catholics do not have sufficient team spirit. Therefore, they review the promotion files of all Catholic employees with more rigor than they do for employees of other religious faiths. This practice is disparate treatment under Title VII. In this hypothetical situation, Catholics—because of their religion—are treated differently than other employees being considered for promotion.

Price Waterhouse v. Hopkins provides another example. It was unquestionable that Ann Hopkins had an abrasive personality and lacked interpersonal skills. These shortcomings alone could have been sufficient to squelch her hopes of partnership in Price Waterhouse. However, Hopkins—being female—made those shortcomings more negative in the evaluation process than they would have been for a male candidate. Stereotypical attitudes about the proper decorum for women influenced the Price Waterhouse evaluation process. In fact, after Hopkins' first attempt for partnership was rejected, one of her male supporters suggested that she act more *female* in the future by walking differently, wearing makeup and jewelry, and having her hair styled.

After the decision by the United States Supreme Court was rendered, the case was heard again in the federal district court. This court found that Price Waterhouse had discriminated against Hopkins, and it ordered that she be made a partner. What suggestions could you make to Price Waterhouse to ensure that another Hopkins-type employment discrimination issue would not arise in the future?

Price Waterhouse v. Hopkins

United States Supreme Court
109 S.Ct. 1775 (1989)

Ann Hopkins had worked at Price Waterhouse's Office of Government Services in Washington, D.C., for five years when the partners in that office proposed her as a candidate for partnership. Thirteen of the thirty-two partners who had submitted comments on Hopkins supported her. Three partners recommended that her candidacy be placed on hold; eight stated that they did not have an informed opinion about her; and eight recommended that she be denied partnership. Consequently, Hopkins was neither offered nor denied admission to the partnership; instead, her candidacy was held for reconsideration the following year.

During the evaluation, the partners in Hopkins's office praised her character as well as her accomplishments, describing her in their joint statements as "an outstanding professional" who had a "deft touch," and "strong character, independence, and integrity." Clients appear to have agreed with these assessments.

On too many occasions, however, Hopkins's aggressiveness apparently spilled over into abrasiveness. Staff members seem to have borne the brunt of Hopkins's brusqueness. Long before her bid for partnership, partners evaluating her work had counseled her to improve her relations with staff members. Although later evaluations indicated an improvement, Hopkins's perceived shortcomings in this important area eventually doomed her bid for partnership. Virtually all of the partners' negative remarks about Hopkins—even those of partners supporting her—had to do with her *interpersonal skills*.

There were clear signs, though, that some of the partners reacted negatively to Hopkins's personality because she was a woman. One partner described her as "macho"; another suggested that she "overcompensated for being a woman"; a third advised her to take "a course at charm school." Several partners criticized her use of profanity; in response, one partner suggested that those partners objected to her swearing only "because it's a lady using foul language."

In previous years, other female candidates for partnership also had been evaluated in sex-based terms. As a general matter, candidates were viewed favorably if partners believed that they maintained their femininity while becoming effective professional managers; in this environment, to be identified as a "women's libber" was regarded as a negative comment. In previous years, one partner repeatedly commented that he could not consider any woman seriously as a partnership candidate and believed that women were not even capable of functioning as senior managers—yet the firm took no action to discourage his comments and recorded his vote in the overall summary of the evaluations.

When the partners in Hopkins's office refused to repropose her for partnership, she sued Price Waterhouse under Title VII, charging that the firm had discriminated against her on the basis of sex in its decisions regarding partnership.

Justice Brennan

According to Price Waterhouse, an employer violates Title VII only if it gives decisive consideration to an employee's gender, race, national origin, or religion in making a decision that affects that employee. On Price Waterhouse's theory, even if a plaintiff shows that her gender played a part in an employment decision, it is still her burden to show that the decision would have been different if the employer had not discriminated.

In passing Title VII, Congress made the simple but momentous announcement that sex, race, religion, and national origin are not relevant to the selection, evaluation, or compensation of employees. Congress' intent to forbid employers to take gender into account in making employment decisions appears on the face of the statute. We take these words to mean that gender must be irrelevant to employment decisions. To construe the words "because of" as colloquial shorthand for "but-for causation," as does Price Waterhouse, is to misunderstand them. When, therefore, an employer considers both gender and legitimate factors at the time of making a decision, that decision was "because of" sex and other, legitimate considerations—even if we may say later, in the context of litigation, that the decision would have been the same if gender had not been taken into account.

To say that an employer may not take gender into account is not, however, the end of the matter, for that describes only one aspect of Title VII. The other important aspect of the statute is its preservation of an employer's remaining freedom of choice. We conclude that the preservation of this freedom means that an employer shall not be liable if it can prove that, even if it had not taken gender into account, it would have come to the same decision regarding a particular person.

In saying that gender played a motivating part in an employment decision, we mean that, if we asked the employer at the moment of the decision what its reasons were and if we received a truthful response, one of those reasons would be that the applicant or employee was a woman. In the specific context of sex stereotyping, an employer who acts on the basis of a belief that a woman cannot be aggressive, or that she must not be, had acted on the basis of gender. As for the legal relevance of sex stereotyping, we are beyond the day when an employer could evaluate employees by assuming or insisting that they matched the stereotype associated with their group, for in forbidding employers to discriminate against individuals because of their sex, Congress intended to strike at the entire spectrum of disparate treatment of men and women resulting from sex stereotypes.

An employer who objects to aggressiveness in women but whose positions require this trait places women in an intolerable and impermissible Catch-22: out of a job if they behave aggressively and out of a job if they don't. Title VII lifts women out of this bind.

The stereotyping in this case did not simply consist of stray remarks. On the contrary, Hopkins proved that Price Waterhouse invited partners to submit comments; that some of the comments stemmed from sex stereotypes; that an important part of the Policy Board's decision on Hopkins was an assessment of the submitted comments; and that Price Waterhouse in no way disclaimed reliance on the sex-linked evaluations. This is not, as Price Waterhouse suggests, "discrimination in the air"; rather, it is, as Hopkins put it, "discrimination brought to ground and visited upon" an employee.

■ *Business Practices and Disparate Impact Theory*

Disparate impact arises when an otherwise neutral practice or policy is actually discriminatory. For example, assume that ABC, Inc., decided to give raises only to its tall employees (defined as those people who are more than six feet in height). At first glance—although this requirement seems irrational—it does not appear on Title VII's proscribed list of factors: race, color, national origin, religion, or sex. However, on further reflection, this *neutral* standard would most likely have a discriminatory effect against women. Far fewer females than males would be able to meet the six-foot requirement to qualify for the pay raises. Thus, it has a disparate impact based on sex.

Note that ABC, Inc., had no intention of excluding women from pay raise eligibility. A disparate impact may arise innocently—from a *neutral* factor. The problem is that the seemingly neutral factor serves as a substitute for direct discrimination. After all, since few women would be tall enough to qualify for the raise, it makes little difference to them whether the exclusion was based on their sex or their height.

However, merely because a *neutral* factor has a disparate impact does not mean that employment discrimination occurs. Factors that are job related are acceptable. ABC, Inc.'s policy of connecting pay raises to employee height could not be justified as job related. Even professional basketball teams do not follow this practice. Thus, ABC, Inc.'s policy violated Title VII.

As the United States Supreme Court stated in *Griggs v. Duke Power Co.* (1971):

> Nothing in the Act [Title VII] precludes the use of testing or measuring procedures; obviously they are useful. What Congress has forbidden is giving these devices and mechanisms controlling force unless they are demonstrably a reasonable measure of job performance. Congress has not commanded that the less qualified be preferred over the better qualified simply because of minority origins. Far from disparaging job qualifications as such, Congress has made such qualifications the controlling factor, so that race, religion, nationality, and sex become irrelevant. What Congress has commanded is that any tests used must measure the person for the job and not the person in the abstract.

Assume that ABC, Inc., modified its pay raise policy to give raises to any employee who exceeds company-wide sales targets for six consecutive months. Assume further in this example, that women as a group do not exceed sales targets as often as men. Thus, like the height requirement cited above, ABC, Inc.'s new policy would have a disparate impact on women. However, this new policy would not constitute employment discrimination. The policy may be justified for business reasons. Only better-performing employees of either sex receive pay raises as incentives.

Business managers need to assess all aspects of their personnel practices with the Title VII theory of *neutral* factors in mind. Chevron Corporation, for example, provided its executives with expertly crafted job selection guidelines by which applicants were to be evaluated. In doing so, the corporation sought to strengthen its argument that *job relatedness* was at the heart of its procedures, in the event women or minorities were underrepresented in a certain job group and an employment discrimination claim was filed.

The *Bradley v. Pizzaco of Nebraska, Inc. d/b/a Domino's Pizza* case provides another example of a *neutral* factor that was found to have a disparate impact. Why was this so? Assume that you are an executive with Domino's Pizza, Inc. How could you accommodate the company's desire that its employees be clean-shaven without risking that a no-beard policy be considered employment discrimination?

Bradley v. Pizzaco of Nebraska, Inc. d/b/a Domino's Pizza

United States Court of Appeals, Eighth Circuit *939 F.2d 610 (1991)*

Domino's grooming policy prohibits company employees from wearing beards. Pizzaco, a Domino's franchisee, hired Langston Bradley to deliver pizzas, but fired him within two weeks because he would not remove his beard. Bradley is a black man who suffers from pseudofolliculitis barbae (PFB), a skin disorder affecting almost half of all black males. The symptoms of PFB—skin irritation and scarring—are brought on by shaving, and in severe cases PFB sufferers must abstain from shaving altogether. Domino's policy, however, provides for no exceptions. As Pizzaco's owner explained, "You must be clean-shaven to work for Domino's."

Bradley brought a disparate impact case against Domino's Pizza, Inc. and Pizzaco of Nebraska, Inc. (collectively Domino's), claiming his discharge for failure to comply with Domino's no-beard policy violates Title VII because the policy discriminates against black males.

Fagg, Circuit Judge

This case is about a facially neutral employment policy that discriminates against black males when applied. Title VII forbids employment policies with a disparate impact unless the policy is justified by legitimate employment goals. To make a prima facie case of disparate impact, the EEOC must identify a specific employment practice that has a significantly disparate impact on black males. Through expert medical testimony and studies, the EEOC demonstrated Domino's policy necessarily excludes black males from the company's workforce at a substantially higher rate than white males. In so doing, the EEOC has shown Domino's facially neutral grooming requirement operates as a "built-in headwind" for black males.

The record shows PFB almost exclusively affects black males, and white males rarely suffer from PFB or comparable skin disorders that may prevent a man from appearing clean-shaven. Nevertheless, Domino's contends that the EEOC failed to show black males with PFB who could not shave were turned away or were fired for failing to comply with Domino's no-beard policy. We disagree. There is no requirement that disparate impact claims must always include evidence that actual job applicants were turned down for employment because of the challenged discriminatory policy. The reason is self-evident: a discriminatory work policy might distort the job applicant pool by discouraging otherwise qualified workers from applying.

The EEOC's evidence makes clear that Domino's strictly enforced no-beard policy has a discriminatory impact on black males. PFB prevents a sizable segment of the black male population from appearing clean-shaven, but does not similarly affect white males. Domino's policy—which makes no exceptions for black males who medically are unable to shave because of a skin disorder peculiar to their race—effectively operates to exclude these black males from employment with Domino's. Thus, having concluded the EEOC has shown Domino's grooming policy falls more harshly on blacks than it does on whites, we must reverse the district court's holding that the EEOC failed to make a prima facie showing of disparate impact.

The Thought Problem, "Evaluating Employment Qualifications," provides another opportunity to consider Title VII principles.

thought problem

Evaluating Employment Qualifications
You are a manager with XYZ, Inc. Your company intends to hire some typists, and it has prepared a list of qualifications for these jobs. Review the following qualifications—in light of the employment discrimination matters previously discussed.

1. All applicants must have read the Bible and believe its contents are the word of God.

2. All applicants must be able to trace at least one parent's ancestry to a European nation.

3. All applicants must be able to lift at least a hundred pounds.

4. All applicants must be able to type at least forty words per minute.

Assume for this illustration that statistics show that all people within a fifty-mile radius of XYZ, Inc.'s facility would be qualified under the first two qualifications. However, only forty percent of the women meet the third standard, and only a third of the men meet the fourth.

DEVELOPMENTS UNDER TITLE VII

■ Affirmative Action

Although Title VII prohibits employers from using race and sex as factors in decision making, times come up when they may do so within the law. This usage is called *affirmative action.* Employers may make race- and sex-conscious decisions, provided they are consistent with the goals and context of discrimination laws. This means such decisions will favor people who have attributes like those who were previously affected by discriminatory practices.

Recall the context in which employment discrimination laws arose. African-Americans and women were being deprived of job opportunities based on their race or sex. The antidiscrimination statutes were enacted to remedy this. No need existed for legislation to prohibit discrimination against white males. Any nasty and unfair treatment they experienced at work resulted from reasons other than race or sex. Employment discrimination laws were not meant to be an employee's bill of rights.

The remedial goals of Title VII were not only to remove discrimination, but also to integrate potential discrimination targets into the economic mainstream. Affirmative action was considered a practical means of quickly achieving the following goals:

■ *Remove Discrimination:* Review the Price Waterhouse v. Hopkins case. Stereotypical attitudes caused and led to the finding of sex discrimination problems. Consider what may have occurred if the Price Waterhouse promotion policy had been reviewed by a fair number of women partners. It is unlikely that the firm's job advancement procedures would have remained unchanged. A goal of affirmative action was to integrate the workplace quickly so that job decisions would not be based on stereotypes.

■ *Economic Mainstream:* Review the International Perspective, "World-wide Pay Inequality," which compares salary levels between men and women. Affirmative action was a means to place qualified minorities into higher-paying jobs from which they had previously been excluded, so that the wage gap originally caused by discrimination could be adjusted quickly.

In 1979, the United States Supreme Court upheld a union-management voluntary affirmative action plan that was aimed at ending racial imbalance in Kaiser Aluminum Corporation's craft workforce. Racial segregation had definitely played a role in hiring for these higher-paying jobs prior to the enactment of Title VII.

The Managerial Perspective, "Affirmative Action in Operation," provides another example of affirmative action. Note that Diane Joyce was qualified for the job that she was chosen for under the plan. A few years after this, Joyce sought another promotion, this time to road foreman. She scored highest on both the oral and written tests required of applicants, but she did not get the job. A man, who ranked fifth, was promoted to road foreman, instead.

However, consider Paul Johnson's position. Other jobs would come up, according to the Court, and he was still employed. But, the same could have been said about Diane Joyce, if Paul Johnson had been hired as road dispatcher.

Johnson's concern was the *reason* that Joyce was given the job—because of her sex. Had the tables been turned and he had been chosen because he was male, a clear violation of Title VII would have existed. Affirmative action made the difference.

Thus, affirmative action has been controversial. Recently, some political leaders have called for its end. Others have suggested that it be changed to favor only lower economic groups. *Reverse discrimination* claims like the one filed by Paul Johnson have also increased. In 1988, six percent of the race discrimination complaints were reverse discrimination charges. In 1994, the number had increased to more than eight percent. The courts have also increased their scrutiny of affirmative action plans by requiring more precise showings before one could have a potential complaint.

Furthermore, some potential beneficiaries of affirmative action plans are concerned that they may have been given preferential treatment. These people fear that their talents and accomplishments will be overlooked once they are labeled *affirmative action* hires. Consequently, with this changing environment, the future of affirmative action is uncertain.

■ *Sexual Harassment*

Sexual harassment is considered sex discrimination and in violation of Title VII of the Civil Rights Act of 1964. It constitutes an abuse of power. Often, sexual harassment occurs when a male supervisor exploits his authority by preying on female employees. The victim must choose between tolerating the conduct or risking unfavorable job-related consequences. The following two types of conduct may be classified as sexual harassment:

■ *Sex as a Condition of Work:* Submitting to harassment is a condition of the victim's continued employment or decisions made about one's job.

managerial perspective
Affirmative Action in Operation

An affirmative action plan was adopted by the Santa Clara County Transportation Agency based on a study that showed the number of women in its workforce was far less than the proportion of women in the county's labor force. The affirmative action plan set aside no specific number of positions for women but authorized the consideration of sex as a factor when evaluating qualified candidates for jobs in which members of such groups were poorly represented.

Diane Joyce applied for a road dispatcher job and was among nine finalists, all of whom were deemed qualified. After an interview, Paul Johnson was rated second and Joyce was ranked third. Prior to the second round of interviews, Joyce contacted the county's affirmative action office because she feared she would not receive a fair interview. She had had disagreements with two of the three members of the panel. The county's affirmative action officer knew that the county had no women in road dispatcher positions and, thus, it was recommended that Joyce be given the job.

Paul Johnson claimed that he was discriminated against on the basis of sex in violation of Title VII. The agency's affirmative action plan was upheld.

The Court stated, "We therefore hold that the Agency appropriately took into account as one factor the sex of Diane Joyce in determining that she should be promoted to the road dispatcher position. The decision to do so was made pursuant to an affirmative action plan that represents a moderate, flexible, case-by-case approach to effecting a gradual improvement in the representation of women in the Agency's workforce. Such a plan is fully consistent with Title VII, for it embodies the contribution that voluntary employer action can make in eliminating the vestiges of discrimination in the workplace."

As for Paul Johnson's interests, the Court noted, "Seven of the applicants were classified as qualified and eligible, and the Agency Director was authorized to promote any of the seven. Thus, denial of the promotion unsettled no legitimate firmly rooted expectation on the part of the petitioner Paul Johnson. Furthermore, while the petitioner in this case was denied a promotion, he retained his employment with the Agency, at the same salary and with the same seniority, and remained eligible for other promotions."

Source: Johnson v. Transportation Agency, Santa Clara County, *55 U.S.L.W. 4379 (United States Supreme Court 1987).*

For example, assume that Jack Smith is Mary Jenkins's boss. She is being considered for promotion. He tells her that unless she submits to his sexual demands, she will be removed from the promotion list. Note the abuse of power. There would be nothing voluntary or willing about the relationship. It could not even be considered a seduction. Smith is using his job-related position to try and extort sexual favors from Jenkins.

■ *Hostile Workplace Environment:* The job becomes intolerable because of a sex-charged atmosphere in the workplace.

Dirty jokes, vulgar slurs, crude comments, and leers may create an unbearable atmosphere that interferes with an employee's performance and makes his or her job unbearable. This behavior does not need to be condoned by a supervisor. Fellow employees or customers may also create a hostile workplace environment.

At some point, the occasional *inappropriate* story or *four-letter* expletive goes beyond being the exception in an otherwise serious work environment and becomes the norm. It is then that a hostile workplace environment may arise. Crude gestures, graffiti, and explicit drawings or photographs have also been found to be sexually harassing when festooning the workplace.

Review the ethics materials in Chapter 7. The ethics standard in Chapter 7 states that all people have intrinsic value and, therefore, are not merely a means to another's ends. Apply this standard to what exists in a hostile workplace environment. Have the victim's interests been considered, or have only the interests of the perpetrators been contemplated?

Although most sexual harassment cases have a woman victim, the principles also apply to men. In Wisconsin, a jury awarded damages to a male employee who was demoted because he rejected a female supervisor's sexual advances. In another case, sexual harassment was found to exist when two male employees had to choose between having sex with their boss's secretary or losing their jobs.

A business organization's interest in preventing sexual harassment was heightened after the *Meritor Savings Bank v. Vinson* (1986) case. Not only will the transgressive supervisor face Title VII sanctions in this case but so will his employer. Cases involving sexual harassment often name the company as a defendant. This takes on added significance because the law permits the award of compensatory and punitive damages in sexual discrimination cases.

Meritor Savings Bank v. Vinson

United States Supreme Court *54 U.S.L.W. 4703 (1986)*

Mechelle Vinson filed sexual harassment charges against Meritor Savings Bank and Sidney Taylor, her supervisor. Taylor denied her allegations as did the bank. The bank further asserted that any harassment by Taylor was unknown and committed without the bank's consent. Even though the lower court held that Vinson had not proved her sexual harassment allegation, it addressed the standard of liability for employers. It is this liability issue that concerned the Supreme Court.

Justice Rehnquist

Although the District Court concluded that respondent had not proved a violation of Title VII, it nevertheless went on to consider the question of the bank's liability. Finding that "the bank was without notice" of Taylor's alleged conduct, and that notice to Taylor was not the equivalent of notice to the bank, the court concluded that the bank therefore could not be held liable for Taylor's alleged actions. The Court of Appeals took the opposite view, holding that an employer is strictly liable for a hostile environment created by a supervisor's sexual advances, even though the employer neither knew nor reasonably could have known of the alleged misconduct. The court held that a supervisor, whether or not he possesses the authority to hire, fire, or promote, is necessarily an "agent" of his employer for all Title VII purposes, since "even the appearance" of such authority may enable him to impose himself on his subordinates.

The EEOC, in its brief as amicus curiae, contends that courts formulating employer liability rules should draw from traditional agency principles. Examination of those principles has led the EEOC to the view that where a supervisor exercises the authority actually delegated to him by his employer, by making or threatening to make decisions affecting the employment status of his subordinates, such actions are properly imputed to the employer whose delegation of authority empowered the supervisor to undertake them. Thus, the courts have consistently held employers liable for the discriminatory discharges of employees by supervisory personnel, whether or not the employer knew, should have known, or approved of the supervisor's actions.

This debate over the appropriate standard for employer liability has a rather abstract quality about it given the state of the record in this case. We do not know at this stage, whether Taylor made any sexual advances toward respondent at all, let alone whether those advances were unwelcome, whether they were sufficiently pervasive to constitute a condition of employment, or whether they were "so pervasive and so long continuing . . . that the employer must have become conscious of [them]."

We therefore decline the parties' invitation to issue a definitive rule on employer liability, but we do agree with the EEOC that Congress wanted courts to look to agency principles for guidance in this area. While such common-law principles may not be transferable in all their particulars to Title VII, Congress' decision to define "employer" to include any "agent" of an employer, surely evinces an intent to place some limits on the acts of employees for which employers under Title VII are to be held responsible. For this reason, we hold that the Court of Appeals erred in concluding that employers are always automatically liable for sexual harassment by their supervisors. For the same reason, absence of notice to an employer does not necessarily insulate that employer from liability.

Finally, we reject petitioner's view that the mere existence of a grievance procedure and a policy against discrimination, coupled with respondent's failure to invoke that procedure, must insulate petitioner from liability. While those facts are plainly relevant, the situation before us demonstrates why they are not necessarily dispositive. Petitioner's general nondiscrimination policy did not address sexual harassment in particular, and thus did not alert employees to their employer's interest in correcting that form of discrimination. Moreover, the bank's grievance procedure apparently required an employee to complain first to her supervisor, in this case Taylor. Since Taylor was the alleged perpetrator, it is not altogether surprising that respondent failed to invoke the procedure and report her grievance to him. Petitioner's contention that respondent's failure should insulate it from liability might be substantially stronger if its procedures were better calculated to encourage victims of harassment to come forward.

Accordingly, the judgment of the Court of Appeals reversing the judgment of the District Court is affirmed.

After the *Meritor Savings Bank v. Vinson* (1986) decision, business executives faced the risk of higher *costs* being assessed against their firms if they did not confront the issue of sexual harassment in the workplace. In fact, major corporations have been doing just that. For example, Honeywell prepared a detailed handbook that clearly indicates prohibited conduct in the workplace (e.g., wolf whistles, leers). Du Pont instituted a sexual harassment prevention program that has been attended by nearly seventy-five percent of its employees. As a result, sexual harassment complaints decreased.

DISCRIMINATION AGAINST THE DISABLED

Title VII of the Civil Rights Act of 1964 did not apply to discrimination based on a physical or mental disability. Consequently, denying jobs to qualified wheelchair users, for example, *because* of that fact was not illegal. The first attempt to remedy this situation occurred in 1973 with the passage of the Rehabilitation Act. The Rehabilitation Act prohibited discrimination based on a disability but was limited to employers having ties to the federal government (e.g., government contractors or recipients of federal funds). Thus, most private employment practices were not affected. Furthermore, the Rehabilitation Act did not explicitly authorize federal administrative agencies to create enforcing regulations. Not until 1980, after an executive order, was the regulatory rule-making process begun and not until 1985 did some administrative rules become final.

Consequently, the disabled had few remedies when faced with discriminatory treatment. Hearings before Congress provided evidence that confirmed this supposition: the disabled were denied jobs, prevented from eating in restaurants, required to sit in the back of theaters, and unable to use public transportation. In one shameful incident, children with Down's syndrome were prohibited entry to a zoo because the keeper thought they would upset the chimpanzees.

■ *The Americans with Disabilities Act of 1990*

In 1990, the Americans with Disabilities Act (ADA) was enacted. It is a broad-ranging statute that seeks to integrate the disabled into the economic and social mainstream of the country. Not only does it cover employment situations (the focus of this section), but it also addresses other areas of American life where the disabled have faced barriers—public services, private transportation, accommodations and services provided by private companies, and telecommunications. Thus, virtually no business is untouched by ADA: restaurants may need to print menus in braille or provide a reader for customers with visual impairments; professional offices (e.g., legal and accounting firms) may need to remove or modify architectural barriers that impede access of the wheelchair-bound; or telecommunications companies may need to provide equipment so that the hearing-impaired may use their services.

Under ADA, a person is considered disabled if a physical or mental impairment substantially limits one or more of that person's major life activities. Businesses may not discriminate against such individuals and, furthermore, are required to reasonably accommodate them. Consequently, the Americans with Disabilities Act does not merely forbid the making of arbitrary distinctions. It also mandates that affirmative steps be taken by business to facilitate full participation by the disabled, provided that doing so would not be an undue hardship.

But what *exactly* does this mean? When does accommodation stop being *reasonable* and begin to become undue hardship? What steps must a business take to minimize the risk of liability exposure under ADA? These questions have no precise answers. The act is vague here, anticipating communications between businesses and the affected disabled.

By the end of September 1995, more than 54,000 disability discrimination complaints had been filed with the EEOC. About forty percent of these complaints were filed by workers with back injuries, mental illnesses, or neurological illnesses. Since the statute does not contain a list of covered disabilities, nor does it provide a precise definition of what constitutes a disability, the EEOC and the courts have been left with the task of doing so.

For example, a paraplegic superior court judge was denied the opportunity to coach at third base for his son's Little League team. The national Little League office had a policy that prohibited wheelchairs from the playing field because of concern over player injuries. The judge sued under ADA, and a federal district court overturned the Little League policy on two grounds. First, the policy did not provide that the condition of the disabled wheelchair user be individually assessed in relation to the safety concern. Second, the policy failed to provide for any means of **reasonable accommodation**.[1]

Another example concerned the Becker CPA Review Course. The Department of Justice sued on behalf of a hearing-impaired individual who was not provided a sign language interpreter when taking the review course. A movie theater complex was sued because it failed to provide wheelchair-accessible seating throughout the theater. The issue in both of these cases is the meaning of the reasonable accommodation provision of the act.

Even though the uncertainty over the ADA's scope leads to complaints, many are dismissed at the outset. For example, approximately forty percent of the complaints filed with the EEOC are dismissed because they have no reasonable cause. Nonetheless, businesses are required to take the initiative under the act; in order to do so, a manager may consider applying the ethics standard from Chapter 7 to situations involving disabled workers—that is, all human beings have intrinsic worth and are not merely a means to another's ends. The Ethical Perspective, "Sears and the Disabled: An Ethical Approach," illustrates a company that has taken an ethical approach to situations dealing with disabled employees.

■ *Employment and ADA*

The Americans with Disabilities Act prohibits discrimination in any aspect of employment if a disabled person with (or without) reasonable accommodation by the employer may perform the essential functions of the job. This standard contains two complex ideas. First, one must be able to separate the essential features of a particular job from those that are merely tangential, convenient, or customary. It is only the essential features that are

---

Sears and the Disabled: An Ethical Approach

A recent in-depth study of Sears, Roebuck & Co. documented its efforts to accommodate disabled workers. The study was done at a surprisingly low cost, and most disputes were resolved without litigation. As Hamilton Davis, assistant general counsel for Sears, stated: "The bulk of our accommodations are common sense and any company should be able to provide them."

Sears has more than 300,000 employees and the average cost of accommodating the disabled was $45 each. Nearly three-fourths of the accommodations cost nothing and consisted of scheduling changes and modified job duties. Sales employees who had foot surgery were permitted to wear tennis shoes to ease the pain. A female employee with a skin allergy was granted her request not to wear hosiery.

However, other accommodations did require expenditures. For example, the company spent $500 to install restroom handrails to accommodate an employee using a wheelchair. The company spent $400 on a special fire alarm system for Sears' hearing-impaired employees. The study found that only 141 disability discrimination complaints were filed with the EEOC against Sears between 1990 and August 1995—a low number for a company of its size. Only three of these claims are currently in litigation.

Source: F. Schwadel, "Sears Sets Model for Employing Disabled," *The Wall Street Journal,* March 4, 1996, page B6.

germane to determining whether or not a disabled person is qualified for the job.

For example, assume that ABC, Inc., requires that its retail salesclerks stand near the merchandise when dealing with customers. On its face, it would seem that a wheelchair-bound applicant could readily be rejected because of an inability to meet the *standing* requirement. However, under ADA one must inquire about the essential features of the salesclerk position. Such a job, at its core, involves marketing goods on a one-to-one basis with the customer. Whether this occurs while standing or sitting seems incidental. Consequently, ABC, Inc.'s rejection of a wheelchair-bound applicant because of an inability to meet its *standing* requirement would most likely raise a liability risk under ADA.

Once the essential functions of the job are identified, an individual may not be rejected for that job because of a disability if through reasonable accommodation that individual could successfully perform those functions. In short, the employer must make an effort to modify normal business practices that impede the disabled. The statute, however, does not provide the business executive with a comprehensive list cross-referencing disabilities with required accommodations. Instead, the act is open-ended, contemplating that the employer and the individual may jointly determine what steps would be necessary to minimize the effects of the disability. Some typical responses would include making the workplace accessible and usable, restructuring the job requirements, and acquiring special equipment.

For example, assume that XYZ, Inc., needed to hire a typist to transcribe audiotapes. Since an essential function of the job is the ability to hear the tapes, a hearing-impaired applicant would be at a decided disadvantage. However, that alone would not be a sufficient reason to reject the applicant. Special amplification equipment may be acquired that would enable the disabled applicant to do the job. Consequently, typing skills of the applicant should be the key factor, independent of the hearing impairment. If the disabled applicant was the better typist, XYZ, Inc., would need to acquire the equipment in order to meet the reasonable accommodation standard.

However, the employer is not required to undergo unreasonable hardship in making such an accommodation. Cost, resources of the business, and the effect on the operation of the business are all factors that may transform an accommodation into a hardship. Thus, if the amplification equipment in the previous example was extraordinarily expensive, XYZ, Inc., does not need to acquire it. However, if other, less expensive means exist to ameliorate the effects of the applicant's hearing impairment, XYZ, Inc., must consider them.

As noted earlier, the Americans with Disabilities Act is not limited to the job application. All aspects of employment are covered—job testing, selection procedures, promotions, and so on. The Thought Problem, "AIDS Health Insurance Benefits and the ADA," illustrates the wide-ranging effect of the statute on business practices.

thought problem

AIDS Health Insurance Benefits
and the ADA
John Collimore was a dispatcher with the Connecticut Refining Company. On October 27, 1991, he was diagnosed as HIV-positive. In December, Connecticut Refining Company reduced its employee health coverage for AIDS-related treatments. This coverage was scheduled to begin, retroactively, on November 1, 1991. Thus, the $1 million health policy became a $10,000 policy for employees afflicted with AIDS.

Collimore discovered this change in his coverage in February 1992. He filed an Americans with Disability Act complaint with the EEOC, which ruled in June 1993 that there was cause to believe the statute had been violated. The case was settled in March 1994, under the following terms:

■ Connecticut Refining Company and its health plan administrator agreed to pay Collimore $35,000 for the emotional anguish he suffered by the loss of nearly all of his health insurance benefits.

■ Collimore's $1 million health policy was restored as long as he remained employed by Connecticut Refining Company.

■ Connecticut Refining Company agreed to pay for the training of all its employees in AIDS awareness and their rights under the ADA.

■ No retaliatory action was to be taken against Collimore and any disciplinary action against him was to be reported to the EEOC.

What effect do you think that this result might have on other employees?

Source: T. Scheffey, "Uncapping AIDS Health Benefits," *Connecticut Law Tribune,* March 21, 1994, page 1.

WRONGFUL DISCHARGE

Traditionally, the law provided one limitation on a business's power to fire an employee—contract law. For example, assume that Jack Smith had a three-year employment contract with ABC, Inc. As long as Smith did not breach his part of the contract, ABC, Inc., could not discharge him during the contract's three-year term without risking a lawsuit. However, few employees work under such *term* contracts. For the most part, no time period is a part of their contracts with employers. This arrangement is said to be *at-will employment.*

Under the *at-will employment doctrine,* an employee may be fired for no cause or for any cause whatsoever without a legal wrong being found to have been committed by an employer. Under this doctrine, none of the following scenarios would create employer liability:

■ An employee is chronically absent from work and is therefore fired by the employer.

■ An employee laughs inappropriately and is fired by the employer.

■ An employer discovers that an employee does not root for the Kansas City Chiefs football team. This employee is fired.

■ An employer, in a surly mood, fires the first employee he sees one morning.

Similarly, the employee may also quit for any reason or no reason. Thus, under *at-will employment*, the employer–employee relationship exists only as long as both parties want it to last. If one of them decides to end it, the law will not stand in the way.

Although conventional wisdom points to the late nineteenth century as the time when the at-will employment doctrine originated, more careful scholarship suggests that it has always been a part of the American legal landscape.[2] In theory, even though either the employer or the employee could sever the *at-will* relationship without legal consequences, the doctrine worked most often against the interests of the employee. It reinforced the power that an employer had over its workforce.

Today, the at-will employment doctrine has changed. At first, modifications were made through legislation. The Wagner Act, discussed in Chapter 17, made it unlawful for employers to fire workers who engaged in union activities. Furthermore, the employment discrimination statutes—some of which were previously discussed—also limited the employer's discretion under the at-will employment doctrine. Therefore, discharging a worker because of race, sex, or disability could raise legal claims.

Changes in the doctrine have also occurred through judicial decision. Employers have been found liable under tort law for *wrongful discharge*. For example, in May 1992, a Texas jury found that an executive was wrongfully discharged for refusing to file a false financial report. The executive was awarded $124 million. As of Spring 1995, twenty-five thousand such suits were pending throughout the United States. The employees win most of these suits (more than sixty-seven percent) and damages average $640,000. In forty percent of the cases, punitive damages are also awarded to the employee.

No other industrialized country has had a similar increase in wrongful discharge litigation and costly verdicts against businesses. However, the United States is also the only major industrial power without a *just cause statute* that limits employers' discretion in firing employees.

The risk of a wrongful discharge claim arises if an employee is fired for reasons that violate public policy. Refusing to file false reports with the government is an example, as is resisting participation in an illegal scheme. These *public policy* reasons may be tied to statutory or constitutional provisions that provide guidance to the norms the employer has violated. However, not all cases may be so readily classified. A precise definition of *public policy violation* does not exist, as the *Wagenseller v. Scottsdale Memorial Hospital* case suggests. Can you evaluate the issue in *Wagenseller v. Scottsdale Memorial Hospital* based on the ethics model provided in Chapter 7? Would you suggest that ethically suspect reasons for terminating an employee invite close scrutiny for finding a *wrongful discharge*?

Wagenseller v. Scottsdale Memorial Hospital

Supreme Court of Arizona
710 P.2d 1025 (1985)

Catherine Wagenseller began her employment at Scottsdale Memorial Hospital as a staff nurse in March 1975, having been personally recruited by the manager of the emergency department, Kay Smith. Wagenseller was an at-will employee—one hired without a specific contractual term.

Most of the events surrounding Wagenseller's work at the hospital and her subsequent termination are not disputed. For more than four years, Smith and Wagenseller maintained a friendly, professional working relationship. In May 1979, they joined a group consisting largely of personnel from other hospitals for an eight-day camping and rafting trip down the Colorado River. According to Wagenseller, *an uncomfortable feeling* developed between her and Smith as the trip progressed— a feeling that Wagenseller ascribed to "the behavior that Kay Smith was displaying." Wagenseller states that this included public urination, defecation, and bathing; heavy drinking; and "grouping up" with other rafters. Wagenseller did not participate in any of these activities. She also refused to join in the group's staging of a parody of the song *Moon River,* which allegedly concluded with members of the group mooning the audience. Smith and others allegedly performed the *Moon River* skit twice at the hospital following the group's return from the river, but Wagenseller declined to participate there as well.

Wagenseller contends that her refusal to engage in these activities caused her relationship with Smith to deteriorate and caused her termination. She claims that after the river trip, Smith began harassing her, using abusive language, and embarrassing her in the company of other staff. Other emergency department staff reported a similar marked change in Smith's behavior toward Wagenseller after the trip, although Smith denied it. On November 1, 1979, Wagenseller was terminated.

Up to the time of the river trip, Wagenseller had received consistently favorable job performance evaluations. Two months before the trip, Smith completed an annual evaluation report in which she rated Wagenseller's performance as "exceed[ing] results expected," the second highest of five possible ratings.

Feldman, Justice

In recent years there has been apparent dissatisfaction with the absolutist formulation of the common law at-will rule. With the rise of large corporations conducting specialized operations and employing relatively immobile workers who often have no other place to market their skills, recognition that the employer and employee do not stand on equal footing is realistic. In addition, unchecked employer power, like unchecked employee power, has been seen to present a distinct threat to the public policy carefully considered and adopted by society as a whole. As a result, it is now recognized that a proper balance must be maintained among the employer's interest in operating a business efficiently and profitably, the employee's interest in earning a livelihood, and society's interest in seeing its public policies carried out. Today, courts in three-fifths of the states have recognized some form of a cause of action for wrongful discharge.

The most widely accepted approach is the "public policy" exception, which permits recovery upon a finding that the employer's conduct undermined some important public policy. There is no precise definition of the term, "public policy." In general, it can be said that public policy concerns what is right and just and what affects the citizens of the state collectively. It is to be found in the state's constitution and statutes and, when they are silent, in its judicial decisions. Although there is no precise line of demarcation dividing matters that are the subject of public policies from matters purely personal, a survey of cases in other states involving retaliatory discharges shows that a matter must strike at the heart of a citizen's social rights, duties, and responsibilities before the tort will be allowed.

It may be argued, of course, that our economic system functions best if employers are given wide latitude in dealing with employees. We assume that it is in the public interest that employers continue to have that freedom. We also believe, however, that the interests of the economic system will be fully served if employers may fire for good cause or without cause. However, the interests of society as a whole will be promoted if employers are forbidden to fire for cause which is "morally wrong." We hold that an employer may fire for good cause or for no cause. He may not fire for bad cause—that which violates public policy.

In the case before us, Wagenseller refused to participate in activities which arguably would have violated our indecent exposure statute. While this statute may not embody a policy which "strikes at the heart of a citizen's social rights, duties and responsibilities," we believe that it was enacted to preserve and protect the commonly recognized sense of public privacy and decency. The statute does, therefore, recognize bodily privacy as a "citizen's social right." The nature of the act, and not its magnitude, is the issue. The legislature has already concluded that acts fitting the statutory description contravene the public policy of this state. The relevant inquiry here is not whether the alleged "mooning" incidents were either felonies or misdemeanors or constituted purely technical violations of the statute, but whether they contravened the important public policy interests embodied in the law. The law enacted by the legislature establishes a clear policy that public exposure of one's anus is contrary to public standards of morality. We are compelled to conclude that termination of employment for refusal to participate in public exposure of one's buttocks is a termination contrary to the policy of this state, even if, for instance, the employer might have grounds to believe that all of the onlookers were voyeurs and would not be offended. In this situation, there might be no crime, but there would be a violation of public policy to compel the employee to do an act ordinarily proscribed by the law.

We have little expertise in the techniques of mooning. We cannot say as a matter of law, therefore, whether mooning would always violate the statute. We deem such an inquiry unseemly and unnecessary in a civil case. Compelled exposure of the bare buttocks, on pain of termination of employment, is a sufficient violation of the policy embodied in the statute to support the action, even if there would have been no technical violation of the statute.

Summary

The laws of employment discrimination and wrongful discharge affect the relationship between employers and employees. Title VII of the Civil Rights Act of 1964 prohibited employment discrimination on the basis of race, color, sex, religion, or national origin. A violation would arise if an employer used any of these factors in making job-related decisions or if otherwise *neutral* factors had the same effect.

Business managers, in response to employment discrimination laws, modified their personnel policies. Job qualifications were carefully assessed to ensure that they reflected the skills necessary for the work to be done. Further, affirmative action plans were often adopted as a means of integrating the workforce. These business policies were designed to limit company exposure to employment discrimination claims.

However, complex Title VII issues remain. Note the Hopkins case and how a procedure for selecting partners from employee candidates could lead to discrimination problems. In addition, affirmative action continues to raise complex questions about the twin goals of the Civil Rights Act—equal opportunity and integrating members of one-time disfavored groups into the economic mainstream. Finally, given the increasing presence of women in the workplace, the issues of sex discrimination and sexual harassment have taken on added importance. Business managers should note that a Title VII violation will occur if the workplace is deemed to create a hostile environment.

Of course, other statutes also seek to provide equal employment opportunities. One of the most important statutes is the American with Disabilities Act. Like Title VII, it prohibits discrimination; however, the difference between the two is that the ADA focuses on disabilities. The ADA also requires employers to reasonably accommodate their disabled workers.

In addition, judicial decisions have also affected employment relationships. One example is the emergence of the *wrongful discharge theory*. Traditionally, most employer–employee contracts were *at-will*—either party could end the relationship at any time without legal liability to the other. However, wrongful discharge cases have placed limits on the employer's right to do so. The precise contours of such a tort remain to be decided.

Review Questions

1. Define the following terms:
   a. Equal Employment Opportunity Commission (EEOC)
   b. Disparate treatment
   c. Disparate impact
   d. Hostile workplace sexual harassment
   e. Wrongful discharge

2. The Acme Company refused to hire Ann Jones as a telegrapher. The company argued that because of the arduous nature of the work, women were physically unsuited for the job. At times, the job requires work in excess of ten hours a day and eighty hours a week. It requires heavy physical effort, such as lifting objects weighing more than twenty-five pounds. May the company refuse to hire Jones for this position?

3. Jane Smith applied for a job as a prison guard. She was rejected because she failed to meet the 125-pound minimum weight and the 5'2" minimum height requirements. Statistics show that these requirements would exclude more than thirty-three percent of all females while excluding only 1.2 percent of all males from such a position. Is there a risk that a Title VII violation may be found?

4. ABC, Inc., sells canned tomatoes. It requires that all of its employees enjoy eating tomatoes. Jack Smith, an African-American, was fired by ABC, Inc., when the company discovered that tomatoes were his least-favorite food. Note that tomatoes are disliked equally among all groups. Assess Smith's claim that his discharge violates Title VII.

5. Discuss affirmative action under Title VII. What are the arguments in favor and against it?

6. You have been appointed vice president of sales for ABC, Inc. Thirty top sales representatives report to you. They are divided into five teams according to the areas of the world in which they work.

Three of the teams are fully integrated—men and women representing a number of races. The other two teams are homogeneous—white men only. ABC, Inc.'s policy of not sending sales representatives to locations in which they may face hardship on the basis of race or sex is the reason for two nonintegrated teams. Do you detect any problems with this policy? What if the last three promotions from the groups of sales representatives went to people who had been assigned, at one time, to the nonintegrated teams?

7. Jim Kozolowski worked for XYZ, Inc., a large company that specialized in holiday events. He applied for a promotion in the company to head its St. Patrick's Day division. However, he was rejected because management was looking for someone of Irish ancestry who was also Catholic. Kozolowski's grandparents emigrated from Poland. He is Jewish. Does XYZ, Inc., face a risk of Title VII liability?

8. Assume that you are a consultant for XYZ, Inc., in the situation in problem #7. Would you make any suggestions regarding how the company may modify their standards for selecting the head of the St. Patrick's Day division?

9. You are the director of nursing services in a major private hospital. Virtually every nurse in the hospital is a woman. A new hospital policy provides that in each department, all hires, promotions, and transfers should aim for a goal of creating an employee profile to match that of qualified workers in the surrounding community. Note that fifty-one percent of the members of your community are women. Should you follow the directive? If so, explain the program you may establish to do so. If you decide *not* to follow the directive, explain why.

10. Bill Jones, a recent college graduate, was hired for an entry-level management position at ABC, Inc., a large corporation. His immediate supervisor is Mary Smith who is two years older than him. They knew each other in college and dated occasionally when Jones was a sophomore. Smith believes that Jones has matured quite a bit in the last three years. She would like to date him. Would she risk a claim of sexual harassment if she asks Jones out? What if she compliments Jones on his tie? What if they had never dated in the past?

11. You are the manager of a department in ABC, Inc., a major corporation. Six employees—all in their late twenties; of the same sex, race, religion, and national origin; and having no disabilities—work under your supervision. The atmosphere of your department is festive in an odd sort of way. Any person in the news who is "different" (in the areas previously noted) is the subject of jokes, wall posters, lunchtime skits, and the like. You believe that, although crude, this behavior creates workplace cohesion that is necessary for the department's success. If a candidate for a new position in your department is different (in the areas previously noted) from the current six employees, would you decide not to hire that person? If so, do any risks exist? If not, and the person is hired, do any risks exist?

12. Jack Johnson applied for a sales representative position with ABC, Inc. The job involves extensive travel and requires an ability to create lasting business relationships with customers. Johnson has

excellent credentials. However, during his interview, ABC, Inc., noticed that Johnson had only one eye. The other had been removed after a childhood accident. Because of this, ABC, Inc., decided not to hire Johnson. Does the company face any employment discrimination risk?

13. XYZ, Inc., needs to hire an accountant. Mary Jones applied for the job. She had difficulty getting to the interview because she uses a wheelchair, and XYZ, Inc.'s accounting office in on the second floor of a building that has no elevator. Other XYZ, Inc., offices are on the ground floor. Assuming that Jones is the best applicant, may XYZ, Inc., choose another applicant because Jones cannot easily get to the accounting office? Would XYZ, Inc., have an obligation to *reasonably accommodate* Jones's disability? If so, how?

14. Bill Smith was an executive with ABC, Inc. His supervisors told him to *fix* prices that ABC, Inc., would charge with their competitors. This violates antitrust law, but the supervisors ordered Smith to do it anyway. Smith refused and, therefore, was fired. Does Smith have a claim against ABC, Inc.?

Notes

[1]The ADA illustrations are described in R. Samborn, "A Quiet Birthday," *National Law Journal*, March 1, 1993, pages 1, 42.

[2]If you are interested in legal history, read this article: D. Ballam, "The Traditional View on the Origins of the Employment-at-Will Doctrine: Myth or Reality?" 33 *American Business Law Journal*, 1 (1995).

Chapter 17

PROTECTION
OF THE EMPLOYEE
AND LABOR RELATIONS

A century ago, most people in the United States lived on farms or in small villages. People knew each other. The employer who treated his employees unfairly risked the condemnation of his church and the community. Business owners valued their reputation. As time passed and the Industrial Revolution took hold in the United States following the Civil War, mass production and the development of a national railroad system caused both businesses and cities to grow. Business owners began to operate companies with thousands of employees and plants located throughout the United States or even around the world. In such an environment, a person did not need to worry as much about what his neighbors or employees thought of him. In the latter half of the nineteenth century, employers were virtually unrestrained by reputation or by law.

The government, in accordance with laissez faire economics, passed few laws protecting workers from exploitation. When the government did pass such statutes, the courts tended to strike down these acts as an interference with the liberty of employees to freely contract as guaranteed to them by the Due Process Clause of the United States Constitution. Recall the Lockner case discussed in Chapter 8 which detailed the high water mark of the unwillingness of the United States Supreme Court to uphold legislation protecting employees. Such a legal environment left employees to fend for themselves. The Industrial Revolution created an imbalance in the bargaining power between employees and employers with the deck clearly stacked in favor of companies.

Workers realized that in order to protect their lives and families in this kind of environment, they needed to engage in joint action to achieve their goals. They also needed to lobby Congress and the state legislatures to pass laws protecting them. This chapter considers some of the workers' most important legislative achievements of the early part of the twentieth century—workers compensation laws, child labor law, minimum wage, unemployment compensation, and the crowning achievement of the labor movement: laws protecting the right of employees to engage in joint action.

Workers' Compensation Laws

During the Industrial Revolution many farmers moved from rural areas to cities where jobs were located in America's fast-growing industries. As the machine age unfolded, an increased number of machine-related injuries began to occur. The people injured by these new machines turned to the courts for compensation. The law they encountered greatly favored employers.

While the law did permit an employee to sue his or her employer for an on-the-job injury, the law required the injured party to establish that his or her employer had somehow been negligent. Furthermore, the courts favored the interests of industry, and they adopted three major doctrines that employers used as a defense in negligence cases—contributory negligence, assumption of the risk, and the fellow servant doctrine. These legal rules favored the developing industrial base of the country by limiting its exposure to liability claims. As a result, the legal environment fostered the values of economic growth by placing the risk of loss on those who were injured.

CONTRIBUTORY NEGLIGENCE

As discussed in Chapter 10, "Assessing External Costs of Doing Business: Tort Liability," the doctrine of contributory negligence provided that if the injured party and the defendant were both negligent—resulting in the plaintiff's injury—then the plaintiff would not be permitted to recover for his or her injuries. In order to recover, the injured party needed to establish that the defendant was solely at fault. Even the slightest degree of negligence by the injured party was enough to deny recovery to the plaintiff.

For example, suppose that Jack worked in a slaughterhouse in Chicago. He carved up carcasses of beef with a large knife. One day, while whacking away at a carcass, Jack placed his hand in the way of his knife and sliced off his thumb. One could certainly argue that Jack caused his own injury and, therefore, the slaughterhouse should not have to compensate Jack for his injury.

ASSUMPTION OF THE RISK

Assumption of the risk provided that if a person was voluntarily in a position where risk of injury existed, and injury occurred, then the employer had no responsibility for the injury. Suppose that Jack worked in a foundry instead. Red hot steel flowed everywhere. If some of the steel came into contact with Jack's leg, the employer may have successfully argued in the nineteenth century that by taking the job, Jack voluntarily put himself in a position where a risk of injury from contact with molten steel existed.

FELLOW SERVANT DOCTRINE

Another rule that limited the ability of workers to collect damages was called the fellow servant rule. This doctrine prohibited workers from suing their employers for job-related injuries caused by another employee. Since few employers were actually on the shop floor, in the mine, or in the railroad yard, this doctrine also limited the ability of the worker to recover for injuries.

The *Farwell v. Boston and Worcester Railroad* case illustrates the application of the doctrines of assumption of the risk and fellow servant rule to workplace injuries.

Farwell v. Boston and Worcester Railroad

Supreme Court of Massachusetts
45 Mass. 49 (1842)

The plaintiff was employed by the defendant as an engineer. His duties included the management and care of the engines and cars running on the railroad between Boston and Worcester. He alleged that on October 30, 1837, another employee, Whitecomb, negligently operated the switching apparatus, causing the engine and cars on which the plaintiff was working to be thrown from the tracks. In the process, the plaintiff was thrown to the ground, and his hand was crushed and destroyed when a wheel from one of the cars passed over it.

Shaw, Chief Justice

The question is, whether, for damages sustained by Farwell by means of the carelessness and negligence of Whitecomb, the party injured has a remedy against their common employer.

The general rule, resulting from considerations of justice as well as of policy, is, that he who engages in the employment of another for the performance of specified duties and services, for compensation, takes upon himself the natural and ordinary risks and perils incident to the performance of such services, and in legal presumption, the compensation is adjusted accordingly. And we are not aware of any principle which should except the perils arising from the carelessness and negligence of those who are in the same employment. These are perils which the servant is as likely to know, and against which he can as effectually guard, as the master. They are perils incident to the service, and which can be as distinctly foreseen and provided for in the rate of compensation as any others.

We are of opinion that where several persons are employed in the conduct of one common enterprise or undertaking, and the safety of each depends much on the care and skill with which each other shall perform his appropriate duty, each is an observer of the conduct of the others, can give notice of any misconduct, incapacity or neglect of duty, and leave the service, if the common employer will not take such precautions, and employ such agents as the safety of the whole party may require. By these means, the safety of each will be much more effectually secured, than could be done by a resort to the common employer for indemnity in case of loss by the negligence of each other. Regarding it in this light, it is the ordinary case of one sustaining an injury in the course of his own employment, in which he must bear the loss himself, or seek his remedy, if he have any, against the actual wrong-doer.

In applying these principles to the present case, it appears that the plaintiff was employed by the defendants as an engineer, at the rate of wages usually paid in that employment, being a higher rate than the plaintiff had before received as a machinist. It was a voluntary undertaking on his part, with a full knowledge of the risks incident to the employment; and the loss was sustained by means of an ordinary casualty, caused by the negligence of another servant of the company. Under these circumstances, the loss must be deemed to be the result of a pure accident, like those to which all men, in all employments, and at all times, are more or less exposed; and like similar losses from accidental causes, it must rest where it first fell, unless the plaintiff has a remedy against the person actually in default; of which we give no opinion.

The legal doctrines of contributory negligence, assumption of the risk, and the fellow servant doctrine made it much easier for employers to win on-the-job personal injury cases in the nineteenth century. Nonetheless, scholars at the time criticized these and other similar doctrines for their harsh treatment of the injured. As the nineteenth century moved towards a close, political pressure arose for reforms in this area; and by the early part of the twentieth century, many states passed laws modifying these doctrines. Even so, an injured employee still needed to establish negligence on the part of the employer, which was not an easy thing to accomplish.

COMPENSATION OF INJURED WORKERS

In response to the effect of the nineteenth-century application of contributory negligence, assumption of the risk, and the fellow servant doctrine to the workplace, states began to examine what could be done to better protect workers. In 1911, Wisconsin passed the first workers' compensation act that survived judicial scrutiny. By 1920, forty-three states had adopted laws to protect workers who were injured on the job. Today, all states have a workers' compensation law.

Workers' compensation is a system of no fault social insurance—that is, employees receive money whether the employer, a fellow employee, or the employee himself or herself was at fault for the accident, as long as the employee can establish the following two criteria:

1. the injury was accidental
2. the injury arose out of and in the course of employment

Suppose that Sandra worked for McDonald's in 1997. While at work, Sandra rushed to the counter with a cup of coffee in her hand. She carelessly spilled hot coffee on herself when she accidentally bumped into another employee, resulting in a severe burn on her leg. The fact that a fellow employee and her own negligence partially contributed to her injury will not bar Sandra from collecting damages. Sandra could collect for any medical expenses she incurred as a result of this accident and, if she must take time off the job, she could also collect money for her loss of income. In order to collect, Sandra does *not* need to establish that McDonald's was somehow at fault for her injuries.

Suppose, instead, that Sandra felt frustrated from working long hours at McDonald's for low pay. In order to escape from work that day, she picked up the coffee pot and intentionally poured its contents on her leg. Her injury in this case would not be accidental, and she could not recover damages. Alternatively, suppose that Sandra purchased a cup of coffee as she was leaving work to go home. When she arrived at home, she dropped the coffee on herself. Insofar as workers' compensation laws are concerned, such an injury did not arise out of and in the course of employment, and it is therefore not compensable.

Money to pay for injuries that employees sustain on the job comes from their employers. Employers generally purchase workers' compensation insurance to cover such losses. Companies must pass the cost of this insurance on to purchasers of their products and services—in the final analysis, the public pays for workers' injuries.

In the 1970s, states greatly expanded the number of employees covered by workers' compensation acts so that virtually every employee today falls within the scope of these acts. The federal government provides workers' compensation coverage for its employees. State governments also insure their workers.

Why would employers favor a system of laws that bars them from asserting the defenses mentioned earlier and holds them responsible for an employee's on-the-job injuries regardless of fault? When states set up these laws, both sides gained something. Workers' compensation laws removed on-the-job accidents and injuries from the tort law system meaning that an employee injured on the job *cannot* file a negligence suit in court against his or her employer. The employee forfeits this right.

If an employee sustains an on-the-job injury, the injured worker files a claim with his or her employer. Most of the time, the company simply pays the claim. If for some reason the employer or the employer's insurance carrier declines to pay, then the employee files a claim with the state administrative agency that handles such disputes—as opposed to filing suit in a court. The state workers' compensation agency proposes a settlement figure to the parties. If one of the parties disagrees with the agency's proposed settlement, then that party files an appeal of the proposed settlement with an appellate board working for the agency. After that, either party generally may file an appeal of the agency's final decision and receive a court review of the agency's handling of the case.

Workers' compensation laws provide a number of advantages. Employers no longer are subject to court cases brought by employees injured on the job. Employers know what payments will be made, and they are able to plan for them like any other regular cost of doing business. Employees are assured of reasonably prompt payment for work-related injuries. The doctrines that made it extremely difficult to collect for injuries from an employer are no longer in effect. The new system eliminates much litigation which, in the past, caused a great deal of delay in the injured worker's receiving monetary compensation. The costs and attorney's fees associated with such suits have been substantially decreased.

One of the problems with workers' compensation statutes—from the standpoint of employees—is that pursuant to these laws the benefits received tend to be far less than what an employee could receive in litigation against the employer. Consequently, plaintiff's attorneys sometimes try to skirt the prohibition against filing suits in court. For example, an attorney representing an injured party may argue that his or her client's injury was the result of an intentional act by the employer. While the law prohibits employees from filing suits in court based on some negligent act by their employer, workers' compensation laws do not prohibit court cases based on injuries that arise out of the intentional acts of an employer.

The Thought Problem, "Employees Exposed to Fumes," deals with the issue of an alleged intentional act by an employer.

Employees Exposed to Fumes

On February 22, 1979, eight employees of Cincinnati Milacron Chemicals filed suit against their employer. They alleged that they had been exposed to the fumes and noxious characteristics of certain chemicals within the scope of their employment. The employees asserted that Cincinnati Milacron Chemicals knew such conditions existed, but it failed to correct the conditions and failed to warn the employees of the existing dangers. The employees alleged that the failure was intentional, malicious, and in willful and wanton disregard of the health of the employees, and as a direct result of the company's actions, they were injured.

What do you think? Should the employees be able to bring suit in court for the injuries they sustained as a result of Cincinnati Milacron Chemicals's actions?

Source: Blankenship v. Cincinnati Milacron Chemicals *(Supreme Court of Ohio, 433 N.E.2d 572 1982.)*

The workers' compensation system is now nearly a century old. In the last few decades, states have raised benefit payments and broadened the definition of job-related injuries covered by the acts. Sadly, some employees have taken advantage of these newly expanded acts. Recent reports indicate that rampant fraud exists in the worker's compensation system. In some cases, attorneys and doctors have induced workers to lie about their health or sources of injuries in order to file false claims. For example, a disabled construction worker in Colorado was collecting full disability benefits while, at the same time, working at other construction sites. He was videotaped participating in a jet skier competition (William Tucker, *Insight on the News*, January 3, 1994). Fraud of this nature raises the cost of employers workers' compensation premiums. In states where insurance costs have risen dramatically, some employers have chosen to leave the state. It is in everyone's best interest to attempt preventing such fraudulent behavior.

Child Labor Law People who were active in the labor movement in the late nineteenth century objected to the hiring of young children to work in the nation's factories. Prolabor forces reasoned that children belonged in school—not on the factory floor. They feared that such labor may damage childrens' health and stunt their intellectual and emotional growth. If a parent forces a child to drop out of school at an early age in order to work, then that person's lack of education will significantly decrease future opportunities for that child. One could certainly argue that forcing children to work at an early age—rather than go to school—perpetuates poverty.

Early in the twentieth century, states began to pass laws protecting children by prohibiting children from working before a certain age. During President Franklin Roosevelt's term, Congress passed the Fair Labor Standards Act that, among other things, laid down some nationwide rules regarding the issue of child labor. Perhaps the most significant feature of this act is that it prohibits children from working, for the most part, prior to reaching age fourteen. The Fair Labor Standards Act also limits the number of hours that may be worked by children who are fourteen or fifteen years of age and prohibits them from working in hazardous jobs. People who are sixteen or seventeen years of age are not limited in the number of hours they may work, but the law prohibits them from working at any job classified as hazardous. By age eighteen, men and women are free to work as they please.

The Ethical Perspective, "Child Labor around the World," deals with the issue of labor by children throughout the world.

Minimum Wage Another section of the Fair Labor Standards Act, passed in 1938, introduced the minimum wage to United States workers. The act originally set the minimum wage at twenty-five cents per hour. Congress raised the minimum wage to $4.75 per hour in 1996, and on September 1, 1997, it will rise to $5.15 per hour. Assuming that a person works forty hours per week, a hypothetical minimum wage earner would make $206 per week or $10,712 per year. People attempting to support a family on $10,712 per year obviously are not living in a grand manner. Two thirds of the people making minimum wage are adults, and one third of them are the sole support for their families.

The minimum wage law generates a great deal of controversy. Many people argue that raising the minimum wage destroys jobs. In addition, they claim that employers—when confronted with a rising minimum wage—reduce the number of jobs at their place of employment. These jobs tend to be entry type work that gives industrious employees the opportunity to advance to higher-paying occupations. On the other hand, other writers assert that people with more money may purchase more goods. More money in the economy generates more demand which in turn generates more jobs.

Unemployment Compensation

The labor movement achieved another victory in the late 1930s with the passage of laws regarding unemployment compensation. Unemployment compensation provides wage replacement to employees who have lost their jobs. This, in turn, helps stabilize the overall economy. Employees who have money to spend—even though they are not currently employed—inject money into the economy and help counter any economic downturn. Much of Roosevelt's "New Deal" legislation contributes to a smoother economy than that which existed in the United States before the 1930s. Before the election of President Roosevelt, the economy periodically experienced a number of wild panics and depressions. Acts such as the unemployment compensation laws and the Social Security Act helped stabilize the economy thus resulting in much less volatile conditions since the 1930s.

The Social Security Act of 1935 provided for unemployment compensation benefits. Today, the unemployment compensation laws involve participation by both federal and state governments. All states have adopted federally approved plans, and most employees today are covered by these laws. If an employee loses his or her job, state unemployment laws provide temporary income. Workers who quit their jobs or who are fired for cause are generally not qualified to receive benefits.

Most state-administered plans provide approximately twenty-six weeks of benefits to qualified employees. When unemployment levels are unusually high in a state, an additional thirteen weeks of benefits are available to people who have used up their regular unemployment compensation benefits.

ETHICAL PERSPECTIVE

Child Labor around the World

Millions of children throughout the world, due to the poverty of their parents, find themselves working on farms or in businesses. While some types of work may be harmless, the fact remains that a child working in a factory cannot, at the same time, be going to school. Without education, such a person faces limited opportunities in life.

Many of the children working throughout the world come from oppressed ethnic groups and castes already marginalized in their countries. As an illustration of how bad things may get, consider the case of Iqbal Masih, a Pakistani, who was chained to a carpet loom from the age of four until the age of ten, when he escaped and thereafter was murdered.

What do you think? Do Americans have a right—an obligation—to see that Western values are observed by companies working in foreign lands? If the United States attempts to ban the importation of products produced by children, then are we merely trying to impose our standards in countries where our values will not work? Does anyone have a right to assign a higher value to one group of people than to another group of people?

Sources: Pharis J. Harvey, "Where Children Work: Child Servitude in the Globe," *The Christian Century,* April 5, 1995; Nomi Morris, "Kid's at Work: Child Labor Is on the Rise as Countries Rush into the Global Economy," *Maclean's,* December 11, 1995.

Federal and state taxes on employers finance the operation and benefits of unemployment compensation plans. To some extent, the amount any given employer must contribute varies according to the level of past unemployment compensation claims that have been made by the employer's former employees. Employer costs and employee benefits vary from state to state.

As noted earlier, the overall thrust of New Deal legislation was to stabilize the economy. Following World War II, economic conditions in the United States have tended to be rather tranquil, with the exception of a few severe recessions during the early 1970s and early 1980s.

The final section of this textbook addresses the most significant accomplishment of the labor movement in the United States— the passage of laws recognizing the right of employees to bargain collectively.

Labor Management Relations

HISTORICAL BACKGROUND

The recognition of Unions as agents to bargain on behalf of employees did not take place peacefully in the United States. Unions fought companies in the streets and in the halls of Congress and the state legislatures throughout the early part of the twentieth century.

The first early union success came with the passage of the Railway Labor Act in the 1920s. The Railway Labor Act regulated labor relations in the railroad industry and heralded the beginning of public acceptance of unions. Congress moved even closer to accepting unions when it passed the Norris-LaGuardia Act in 1932 which drastically limited the power of the federal courts to issue injunctions against strikes, picketing, and boycotts.

The crowning achievement of the labor movement came with the passage of the National Labor Relations Act (Wagner Act) in 1935. This law guaranteed employees the right to join together to form unions for bargaining on behalf of the employees. The National Labor Relations Act created the National Labor Relations Board. The two primary functions of the board are to conduct representation elections and to determine whether or not management or unions have engaged in activities prohibited by the law.

Before considering in greater detail the various unfair labor practices by employers, first look at the conduct of representation elections by the National Labor Relations Board.

CONDUCT OF REPRESENTATION ELECTIONS

A regional office of the National Labor Relations Board determines the composition of bargaining units and conducts representation elections. The goal of the board is to provide conditions in which the workers may exercise a free, uncoerced choice in any election.

■ **FIGURE 17.1** Ways a Union May Become the Representative of the Employees in a Bargaining Unit

1. The union wins a representation election.
2. The employer voluntarily recognizes the union.
3. The employer commits a serious unfair labor practice prior to a representation election.

Figure 17.1 lists the three ways in which a union may become the designated bargaining representative of the employees.

First consider the election process. In order to convince the board to hold a representation election, a union needs to obtain evidence of workers' support for the union in the designated bargaining unit. The union typically asks the workers to sign cards authorizing the National Labor Relations Board to conduct a representation election. Once the union has thirty percent of the workers' support, the board will set a date for an election to take place. During the time *after* the filing of the petition for an election but *before* the actual election, both the employer and the union must be careful not to do anything threatening or coercing toward the employees. In order to prevail if an election takes place, a majority of the employees who actually vote in the representation election must vote in favor of the union.

The second manner in which a union becomes the bargaining representative of the employees is when the employer voluntarily recognizes the union. If the union is able to demonstrate to the employer that a majority of the employees favor the union, then the employer may simply agree to accept the union as the bargaining representative of the employees. This does not happen often since most employers tend to resist unionization.

The final manner in which a union may become the bargaining representative of the employees is when the employer commits a serious unfair labor practice prior to a representation election. This is somewhat of an unusual situation. An example is discussed in the *NLRB v. Gissel Packing Co.* case.

NLRB v. Gissel Packing Co.

United States Supreme Court *395 U.S. 575 (1969)*

The union obtained authorization cards from a majority of the employees in the designated bargaining unit, and it demanded recognition by the employer. The employer refused to bargain on the grounds that the authorization cards were inherently unreliable. The employer also carried out a vigorous antiunion campaign.

The National Labor Relations Board ordered the employer to recognize the union based solely on the authorization cards without first conducting an election. The Court of Appeals reversed the NLRB, and the United States Supreme Court ruled for the union.

Chief Justice Warren

The first issue facing us is whether a union can establish a bargaining obligation by means other than a Board election. A union is not limited to a Board election.

It was early recognized that an employer had a duty to bargain whenever the union representative presented "convincing evidence of majority support." It was recognized that a union did not have to be certified as a winner of a Board election to invoke a bargaining obligation; it could establish majority status by other means under the unfair labor practice provisions of Section 8 (a) (5)—by showing convincing support, for instance, by a union called strike or strike vote, or, as here, by possession of cards signed by a majority of the employees authorizing the union to represent them for collective bargaining purposes.

An employer can insist on a secret ballot election, unless, in the words of the Board, he engages "in contemporaneous unfair labor practices likely to destroy the union's majority and seriously impede the election."

In short, we hold that the 1947 amendments did not restrict an employer's duty to bargain under Section 8 (a) (5) solely to those unions whose representation status is certified after a Board election.

Remaining before us is the propriety of a bargaining order as a remedy for a Section 8 (a) (5) refusal to bargain where an employer has committed independent unfair labor practices which have made the holding of a fair election unlikely or which have in fact undermined a union's majority and caused an election to be set aside. We see no reason now to withdraw this authority from the Board. If the board could enter only a cease-and-desist order and direct an election or a rerun, it would in effect be rewarding the employer and allowing him to profit from his own wrongful refusal to bargain, while at the same time severely curtailing the employees' right freely to determine whether they desire a representative. The employer could continue to delay or disrupt the election processes and put off indefinitely his obligation to bargain; and any election held under these circumstances would not be likely to demonstrate the employees' true, undistorted desires.

The Thought Problem, "Must an Election Be Held?", deals with the question of whether or not the National Labor Relations Board must hold a representation election before recognizing a union.

thought problem

Must an Election Be Held?

A union that wished to represent the employees of the Linden Lumber Company obtained authorization cards from a majority of Linden's employees. It demanded that the company recognize it as the bargaining representative of these employees. Linden Lumber Company asserted that it doubted the union's claim that a majority of the employees supported the union. Linden Lumber Company refused to bargain with the union until the union asked for a representation election and won that election.

What do you think? Must Linden Lumber Company recognize the union in light of the fact that the union has authorization cards signed by a majority of Linden's employees?

Source: Linden Lumber Company v. NLRB *(United States Supreme Court, 95 S.Ct. 429 1974.)*

Figure 17.2 illustrates the steps that take place in order for a union to become the bargaining representative of the employees.

The Wagner Act makes a number of practices by management unfair labor practices. A summary of these categories appears in Figure 17.3.

■ **FIGURE 17.2** Steps in Becoming a Bargaining Representative of the Employees

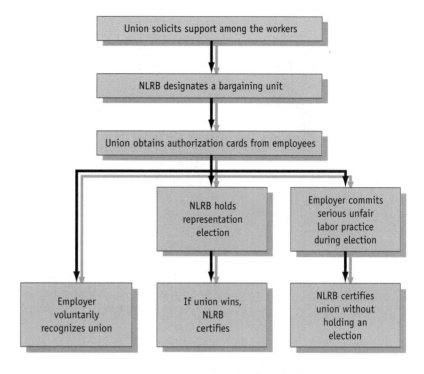

■ **FIGURE 17.3** Unfair Labor Practices by Management

1. Interference, restraint, or coercion of employees in their efforts to form, join, or assist labor organizations
2. Domination or support of a labor organization
3. Discrimination in order to encourage or discourage membership in any labor organization
4. Discrimination against any employee for filing charges or giving testimony
5. Refusal to bargain collectively with the representatives of the employees

EMPLOYER INTERFERENCE WITH EMPLOYEE RIGHTS

The National Labor Relations Act makes it illegal for an employer to interfere, restrain, or coerce employees in their efforts to form, join, or assist labor organizations. This situation comes up when assessing who has access to the company property. Obviously, it is difficult to organize workers if the company may refuse to let union organizers on company property. On the other hand, what right should people have to come on private property against the wishes of the owner of that property?

If this situation arises, then the law must resolve a conflict between the property rights of the employer and the rights of other people—in this case, unions. A union wants to come into the plant to speak with workers in order to get its message across to them. An employer often wishes to limit this contact, hoping that the employees will not gain an interest in unionizing. Regarding the organizational activities on an employer's premises, the property rights of the company must be weighed against the union's need for access to convey its message to the employees.

In *NLRB v. Babcock & Wilcox Co.*, the Court examined Babcock's nondistribution of literature rule. The rule prohibited nonemployees from distributing literature in the company parking lot. The union argued that contact with employees was practically impossible except on company property. Ninety percent of the workers drove to the plant. This argument failed to persuade the Court which ruled that Babcock & Wilcox Co. had no obligation to permit distribution of union literature by nonemployees. It did suggest that if no other means of communicating with the employees existed, then the Board may be justified in ordering a company to permit contacts on company property. In the *NLRB v. Babcock & Wilcox Co.* case, the Court found it was possible to reach the employees without entering company property.

The *Lechmere, Inc. v. NLRB* case deals with the same question as the *NLRB v. Babcock & Wilcox Co.*—whether or not an employer may prohibit nonemployees from distributing literature in a company parking lot.

Lechmere, Inc. v. NLRB

United States Supreme Court *112 S.Ct. 841 (1992)*

The United Food and Commercial Workers Union wanted to organize the employees at a retail store owned by Lechmere, Inc. The store is located in the Lechmere Shopping Plaza. A parking lot, partly owned by Lechmere, Inc., adjoins the shopping plaza. Nonemployee union organizers entered Lechmere, Inc.'s parking lot and placed handbills on cars in an area used mainly by employees. Lechmere, Inc.'s manager informed them that Lechmere, Inc., prohibited solicitation or handbilling of any kind on its property.

The union alleged that Lechmere, Inc., had violated the National Labor Relations Act by barring nonemployee organizers from its parking lot. The United States Supreme Court disagreed and ruled for Lechmere, Inc.

Justice Thomas

This case requires us to clarify the relationship between the rights of employees under § 7 of the National Labor Relations Act, 49 Stat. 452, as amended, 29 U.S.C. § 157, and the property rights of their employers.

Section 7 of the NLRA provides in relevant part that "[e]mployees shall have the right to self-organization, to form, join, or assist labor organizations." Section 8(a)(1) of the Act, in turn, makes it an unfair labor practice for an employer "to interfere with, restrain, or coerce employees in the exercise of rights guaranteed in [§ 7]." By its plain terms, thus, the NLRA confers rights only on *employees,* not on unions or their nonemployee organizers. In *NLRB v. Babcock & Wilcox Co.,* however, we recognized that insofar as the employees' "right of self-organization depends in some measure on [their] ability . . . to learn the advantages of self-organization from others," § 7 of the NLRA may, in certain limited circumstances, restrict an employer's right to exclude nonemployee union organizers from his property. It is the nature of those circumstances that we explore today.

While no restriction may be placed on the employees' right to discuss self-organization *among themselves,* unless the employer can demonstrate that a restriction is necessary to maintain production or discipline, no such obligation is owed nonemployee organizers. As a rule, then, an employer cannot be compelled to allow distribution of union literature by nonemployee organizers on this property. As with many other rules, however, we recognized an exception. Where the location of a plant and the living quarters of the employees place the employees beyond the reach of reasonable union efforts to communicate with them, employers' property rights may be required to yield to the extent needed to permit communication of information on the right to organize.

The threshold inquiry in this case, then, is whether the facts here justify application of *Babcock's* inaccessibility exception.

As we have explained, the exception to *Babcock's* rule is a narrow one. It does not apply wherever nontrespassory access to employees may be cumbersome or less-than-ideally effective, but only where the *location of a plant and the living quarters of the employees* place the employees *beyond the reach* of reasonable union efforts to communicate with them. Classic examples include logging camps and mountain resort hotels.

Babcock's exception was crafted precisely to protect the § 7 rights of those employees who, by virtue of their employment, are isolated from the ordinary flow of information that characterizes our society. The union's burden of establishing such isolation is, as we have explained, "a heavy one," and one not satisfied by mere conjecture or the expression of doubts concerning the effectiveness of nontrespassory means of communication.

Because the union in this case failed to establish the existence of any "unique obstacles" that frustrated access to Lechmere's employees, the Board erred in concluding that Lechmere committed an unfair labor practice by barring the nonemployee organizers from its property.

The judgment of the First Circuit is therefore reversed, and enforcement of the Board's order denied.

The Managerial Perspective, "Distribution of Literature," deals with employee distribution of literature.

■ *Threats and Benefits*

Because the NLRB wishes to conduct an election in an atmosphere conducive to the free exercise of an employee's beliefs, coercive tactics by an employer violate that act.

But threats of reprisal are not the only form of coercion. An employee's right to exercise his or her free will may be influenced by promises of benefits. In these cases, the board examines (1) the timing and impact of the benefits, (2) whether or not the employer places conditions on the granting of benefits, and (3) whether or not any valid reasons exist for the conferring of benefits other than the election. Conferring benefits puts the employer in an awkward position when he or she grants them before an election. Custom is crucial in these cases. An employer who regularly grants increases each year around October 1 probably may grant one at that time even if an election is scheduled.

The *NLRB v. Exchange Parts Co.* case discusses the issue of granting benefits.

Distribution of Literature

The United Food and Commercial Workers Local 72 began an organizational campaign of Pizza Crust. Pizza Crust prohibited off-duty employees from using the parking lot for the distribution of union literature.

The court ruled that it is a settled matter that an employer may not prohibit its employees from distributing union literature in nonworking areas during nonworking times, absent a showing that a ban is necessary to maintain plant discipline or production. It held that the Pizza Crust rule interfered with the employees' rights to organize.

Source: National Labor Relations Board v. Pizza Crust of Pennsylvania, Inc. *(United States Court of Appeals, Third Circuit, 862 F.2d 49 1988.)*

NLRB v. Exchange Parts Co.

United States Supreme Court *375 U.S. 405 (1964)*

A representation election to unionize Exchange Parts Co.'s employees was to be held. Shortly before the election, respondent, Exchange Parts Co., sent its employees a letter denouncing the union and listing all previous benefits granted by the company to the employees. The list also announced new benefits for the employees, including a birthday holiday, longer vacations, and increased wages for holiday work. The union lost the election. The NLRB held that the letter violated Section 8(a)(1) of the National Labor Relations Act. The Court of Appeals would not enforce the NLRB's order and the NLRB appealed. The Supreme Court ruled in favor of the NLRB.

Justice Harlan

This case presents a question concerning the limitations which Section 8(a)(1) of the National Labor Relations Act places on the right of an employer to confer economic benefits on his employees shortly before a representation election. The precise issue is whether that section prohibits the conferral of such benefits, without more, where the employer's purpose is to affect the outcome of the election. For reasons given in this opinion, we conclude that the judgment below must be reversed.

Section 8(a)(1) makes it an unfair labor practice for an employer "to interfere with, restrain, or coerce employees in the exercise of the rights guaranteed in Section 7." We think the Court of Appeals was mistaken in concluding that the conferral of employee benefits while a representation election is pending, for the purpose of inducing employees to vote against the union, does not "interfere with" the protected right to organize.

The broad purpose of Section 8(a)(1) is to establish "the right of employees to organize for mutual aid without employer interference." We have no doubt that it prohibits not only intrusive threats and promises but also conduct immediately favorable to employees which is undertaken with the express purpose of impinging upon their freedom of choice for or against unionization and is reasonably calculated to have that effect. The danger inherent in well-timed increases in benefits is the suggestion of a fist inside the velvet glove. Employees are not likely to miss the inference that the source of benefits now conferred is also the source from which future benefits must flow and which may dry up if it is not obliged. The danger may be diminished if, as in this case, the benefits are conferred permanently and unconditionally. But the absence of conditions or threats pertaining to the particular benefits conferred would be of controlling significance only if it could be presumed that no question of additional benefits or renegotiation of existing benefits would arise in the future; and, of course, no such presumption is tenable.

DOMINATION OR SUPPORT OF A UNION

The National Labor Relations Act also prohibits employer domination or support of a union. This provision was aimed at the employer who, in order to subvert the employee's efforts to unionize, organizes its own union. In this manner, a company could be assured of a weak union, favorably disposed to the goals of the company and easier to deal with than a powerful independent union.

DISCRIMINATION TO ENCOURAGE OR DISCOURAGE UNION MEMBERSHIP

It is an unfair labor practice for an employer to discriminate when it pertains to hiring or any term or condition of employment in order to encourage or discourage union membership. Suppose that an employee who is active in the union comes into work five minutes late one day. Would it be unlawful to fire such an employee? As indicated, an employer must not discriminate in the employment of workers on the basis of union membership. If the employer treats a person who is active in the union more harshly for an offense than it treats other employees, the company runs the risk of violating the act. In the case of the late worker, if the company took no action in the past against other employees who came in late, but it fired the employee who was active in the union, most likely the NLRB would find that the company violated the law.

The Managerial Perspective, "Mexican Nationals," deals with an attempt by an employer to punish its employees for engaging in union activities.

DISCRIMINATION AGAINST EMPLOYEES WHO FILE CHARGES OR GIVE TESTIMONY

The National Labor Relations Act makes it an unfair labor practice for an employer to discharge or discriminate against an employee because the employee filed charges or gave testimony related to enforcement of this act. Many employees may refuse to cooperate with the National Labor Relations Board if they believed their employers could fire them. This provision restricts employers from taking vindictive actions against their employees.

REFUSAL TO BARGAIN COLLECTIVELY WITH THE REPRESENTATIVE OF THE EMPLOYEES

The National Labor Relations Act makes it an unfair labor practice for an employer to refuse to bargain collectively with the representatives of the employees. It requires the parties to meet and confer with each other; however, it does not require the parties to arrive at an agreement or to make concessions.

managerial perspective

Mexican Nationals

The employees of Sure Tan voted to unionize the company. Thereafter, Surak, the president of Sure Tan, sent a letter to the Immigration and Naturalization Service (INS) asking that the INS check the status of a number of its employees. The president knew these employees were Mexican nationals who were present illegally in the United States, without visas or immigration papers authorizing them to work. The INS agents discovered five illegal aliens. These people soon left the country. The National Labor Relations Board accused Sure Tan of taking this action in order to discourage union membership. The United States Supreme Court examined this case and ruled that Sure Tan, Inc., had violated the act because it took this action in order to discourage union membership.

Source: Sure Tan, Inc. v. NLRB *(United States Supreme Court, 104 S.Ct. 2803 1984.)*

Certain matters must be discussed by the parties. These are mandatory topics of negotiation. Examples of mandatory subjects of bargaining on which the parties must bargain are wages, merit increases, pensions, disciplinary rules, seniority, nonstrike provisions, and contracting out work to nonemployees.

When a company is bargaining with a union it may not make unilateral changes on a mandatory subject of bargaining. For example, if an employer changed its sick-leave policy during the negotiation sessions without first offering this to the union, then the company is not bargaining in good faith. On the other hand, if an employer offers something to a union at the bargaining table and the parties thereafter reach an impasse in their negotiations, the employer may then unilaterally grant its employees the benefit that the union rejected.

■ *Bargaining in Good Faith*

Much of the negotiation process between the company and the union takes place on a give-and-take basis. Presumably, the company devises a range of wages and benefits it will offer, and the union sets up a scale of wages and benefits it hopes to receive. If the parties fail to agree, a strike may occur. What if, rather than secretly holding back the best offer, a company puts the best offer on the table at the beginning of the bargaining session and then communicates the information to the employees? The *NLRB v. General Electric Co.* case discusses this strategy.

NLRB v. General Electric Co.

United States Court of Appeals, Second Circuit
418 F.2d 736 2nd Cir. (1969), Cert. Den. 397 U.S. 965 (1970)

After a crippling strike in 1946, General Electric Co. changed its bargaining tactics. It made its best offer to the union at the beginning of negotiations, and then it heavily publicized the offer to employees. The NLRB found three specific unfair labor practices and an overall failure to bargain in good faith—a violation of Section 8(a) of the National Labor Relations Act. The court of appeals was petitioned to enforce the NLRB's order against General Electric Co.

Kaufman, Judge

In addition to the three specific unfair labor practices, GE is also charged with an overall failure to bargain in good faith.

The Board chose to find an overall failure of good faith bargaining in GE's conduct. Specifically, the Board found that GE's bargaining stance and conduct, considered as a whole, were designed to derogate the Union in the eyes of its members and the public at large. This plan had two major facets: first, a take-it-or-leave-it approach ("firm, fair offer") to negotiations in general which emphasized both the powerlessness and uselessness of the Union to its members; and second, a communications program that pictured the Company as the true defender of the employees' interests, further denigrating the Union, and sharply curbing the Company's ability to change its own position.

Given the effects of take-it-or-leave-it proposals on the Union, the Board could appropriately infer the presence of anti-Union animus, and in conjunction with other similar conduct could reasonably discern a pattern of illegal activity designed primarily to subvert the Union.

GE argues forcefully that it made so many concessions in the course of negotiations—concessions which, under Section 8(d), it was not obliged to make—that its good faith and the absence of a take-it-or-leave-it attitude were conclusively proven, despite any contrary indicia on which the Trial Examiner and the Board rely.

The company's stand, however, would be utterly inexplicable without the background of its publicity program. Only when viewed in that context does it become meaningful. We have already indicated that one of the central tenets of "the Boulware approach" is that the "product" or "firm, fair offer" must be marketed vigorously to the "consumers" or employees, to convince them that the Company, and not the Union, is their true representative. GE, the Trial Examiner found, chose to rely "entirely" on its communications program to the virtual exclusion of genuine negotiations, which it sought to evade by any means possible. Bypassing the national negotiators in favor of direct settlement dealings with employees and local officials forms another consistent thread in this pattern. The aim, in a word, was to deal with the Union through the employees, rather than with the employees through the Union.

The Company's refusal to withhold publicizing its offer until the Union had had an opportunity to propose suggested modifications is indicative of this attitude. The command of the Boulware approach was clear: employees and the general public must be barraged with communications that emphasized the generosity of the offer, and restated the firmness of GE's position.

In order to avoid any misunderstanding of our holding, some additional discussion is in order. We do not today hold that an employer may not communicate with his employees during negotiations. Nor are we deciding that the "best offer first" bargaining technique is forbidden. Moreover, we do not require an employer to engage in "auction bargaining," or compel him to make concessions, "minor" or otherwise.

We hold that an employer may not so combine "take-it-or-leave-it" bargaining methods with a widely publicized stance of unbending firmness that he is himself unable to alter a position once taken. Such conduct, we find, constitutes a refusal to bargain "in fact." It also constitutes, as the facts of this action demonstrate, an absence of subjective good faith, for it implies that the Company can deliberately bargain and communicate as though the Union did not exist, in clear derogation of the Union's status as exclusive representative of its members under Section 9(a).

The petition for review is denied, and the petition for enforcement of the Board's order is granted.

EMPLOYER'S FREE SPEECH

In light of the fact that the First Amendment of the Constitution of the United States clearly guarantees everyone living in the United

managerial perspective

Free Speech Prior to a representation election, President Saeki stated that the plant had lost $36 million in the last seven years, and that the parent company refused to subsidize the plant any further so that more losses would lead to plant closure. Saeki stated that his goal was for the plant to break even. The plant manager, Hanson, predicted that Kawasaki would find it difficult to operate under a United Auto Workers contract with restrictive job classifications.

The court reviewing these statements held that an employer may express opinions or predictions—reasonably based on fact—about the possible effects of unionization on its company. Such statements must be carefully phrased on the basis of objective facts to convey consequences beyond management's control or to convey a management choice already decided. The court ruled that these statements were permissible.

Source: United Automobile, Aerospace and Agricultural Implement Workers of America v. National Labor Relations Board *(United States Court of Appeals, Ninth Circuit, 834 F.2d 816 1987.)*

States the right of free speech, one would not think that employers would run into trouble when they exercised this right. After the passage of the Wagner Act, the National Labor Relations Board construed many employer statements as unfair labor practices. In response to the NLRB decisions, Congress passed a law explicitly protecting the right of employer's to speak. The law states that an employer's written or oral speech will not be regarded as evidence of an unfair labor practice if such expression contains no threat of reprisal or force or promise of benefit. An employer thus may communicate its general views as to unionization so long as the employer does not make any threats or promises. Employers are free to state only what they think will be the economic consequences of unionization that are out of their control and do not constitute reprisals.

Suppose that the president of Acme Corporation—after the NLRB sets a date for a representation election—states that if the employees vote for a union, he will fire all of them. Such a statement contains a threat, and thus violates the law. It interferes with the employees freedom to vote *for* or *against* a union. Alternatively, suppose that the president states that if the employees unionize, then company costs will go up, thus making it more difficult for the company to compete in the marketplace. Such a remark is protected as it states the economic consequences of unionization out of the control of Acme Corporation.

The Managerial Perspective, "Free Speech," discusses statements made by a manager prior to a representation election.

COLLECTIVE BARGAINING PROBLEMS

Years ago, prior to the adoption of the National Labor Relations Act, businesses operated free of constraints imposed by either labor or government. When labor began to impinge on management's prerogative to act as it pleased, many businessowners voiced their anger over the intrusion of labor on their decision-making powers. One may easily understand the frustration of businesspeople. Businesses operate in a competitive environment, both nationally and internationally. The aims of labor often conflict with the long-term competitive survival of a company. Higher wages, more fringe benefits, shorter working hours, and safe working conditions all impinge on the ability of a company to put out its product at the lowest possible price. Companies that deny their workers such benefits may choose to lower their prices in order to obtain a larger share of the market. Alternatively, they may elect to pay higher dividends in order to attract more capital for expansion over the long run. The company with the lowest labor costs may end up driving competitors who pay better wages out of business.

Things may, of course, get out of hand as the International Perspective, "High Wages in Germany," illustrates.

The demands of labor place managers in an awkward position. They may want to improve the salaries of their workers, but paying those wages may eventually bankrupt their companies. Because the success or failure of a business depends on the business acumen of its managers, management argued for years that labor should not have any voice in the operation of companies. Businessowners perceived labor's demand for higher wages as an unwarranted intrusion on their decision-making powers. Even so, today management shares its power to guide the destiny of a company with labor, government, and society. Businesses must work with these groups.

What does labor want from management today? The foremost goal of the union movement for the last century has been an improvement in the standard of living for its members. In this respect, unions have been quite successful. This success contributed to union growth early in this century. In 1956, unions represented 33.4 percent of nonagricultural employees. By 1968, this figure had fallen to 27.8 percent. By 1977, it had dropped further to 26.2 percent. By 1989, unions represented less than seventeen percent of all nonagricultural workers. Today, unions represent probably around fourteen percent of all workers. As the number of people in unions drops, it should not be surprising to see the support for the goals of unions to decline as well.

Today, the labor force consists of a greater percentage of white-collar workers than ever before in history. Service industries employ more people than in the past. The government employs more workers. Unions find it difficult to organize white-collar workers. At the same time, blue-collar workers—a group in which unions have

INTERNATIONAL PERSPECTIVE

High Wages in Germany

Following World War II, the Federal Republic of Germany began to guarantee workers in Germany increasingly better benefits. Partly because of the extensive benefits given to the workers, Germany is experiencing levels of unemployment in the mid-teens and general political discontent. The average German is entitled to twenty-five to thirty-two days of paid vacation plus ten to thirteen days off due to state and religious holidays. The government guarantees its citizens health care and a generous pension. If unemployed, former workers receive sixty-seven percent of their net wages for up to fifteen months, and fifty-seven percent of their wages in welfare assistance thereafter. Taxes, generally, are quite high.

Germany now has the highest total manufacturing costs in the world—$30.32 per hour—as opposed to $19.29 in the United States, $15.21 in Britain, or $6.32 in Portugal. Obviously, if a country wants to sell its products to other countries, such a high labor cost creates serious problems. Many German firms, therefore, have established plants in countries outside of Germany where benefits are lower.

Sources: Amity Shlaes, "When Benefits Are Problems: Germany's Social Contract Woes," *Current,* January 1995; Mary Williams Walsh, "Global Economy Catches Up with Workers in Germany," *The Los Angeles Times,* February 25, 1996.

historically been quite popular—have been displaced by technological advances. More jobs on the assembly line have fallen victim to automation. Furthermore, many companies deal more effectively with worker demands than in the past.

In the 1980s, another problem became manifestly apparent—companies around the world began to flood the American market with their goods. Quite often, these products cost less and are of higher quality than comparable American-made goods. Americans began to flock to foreign products that they perceived as being a better value for their money.

How may companies give workers good benefits and better working conditions yet still remain competitive in the worldwide marketplace? This will certainly be the major challenge for management in the twenty-first century.

Summary

In the late nineteenth century, workers found themselves confronted with a radically different environment. Most of them previously worked on a farm or for a small company. The Industrial Revolution and the development of the nation's railroads changed all of this. Now many employees worked for giant national or even international organizations. They possessed very little bargaining power. Employees eventually concluded that they needed to work together to protect themselves.

Among the many legislative achievements of the labor movement early in the twentieth century were workers' compensation laws, the minimum wage, laws prohibiting child labor, and unemployment compensation laws. States adopted workers' compensation laws which permit an injured employee to recover for accidental injuries that occur on the job even if the employee cannot demonstrate that the employer was somehow negligent. In return for getting this right, employees gave up their right to file a suit in court.

The Fair Labor Standards Act created the minimum wage—originally set at twenty-five cents per hour. Today, the law requires employers to pay no less than $5.15 per hour to covered employees. In addition, the Fair Labor Standards Act also prohibited child labor. For the most part, it restricts children under the age of fourteen from working, and it sets limitations on the work performed by people between the ages of fourteen to eighteen. At age eighteen, workers are free to engage in all types of work. Unemployment compensation laws have two goals—to stabilize the economy and to provide income for out-of-work employees. Employees may receive up to twenty-six weeks of unemployment benefits and, in some cases, as high as thirty-nine weeks of benefits.

The greatest achievement of the labor movement was the passage of the National Labor Relations Act. This act created the National Labor Relations Board which conducts representation elections and handles labor disputes.

Much of the NLRB's time is devoted to conducting representation elections. An employer may voluntarily recognize a union that represents a majority of its employees, but elections generally must be held before a union may become the designated bargaining representative for a group of employees.

The labor laws place a number of obligations on management. Certain types of activities are treated as unfair labor practices. An employer may not discriminate against workers to encourage or discourage union membership. In addition, an employer may not discriminate against workers who file charges or give testimony under the labor act. Once the board recognizes a union as the bargaining representative for the employees, it is an unfair labor practice for an employer to refuse to bargain in good faith with the union. The union and the employer must meet and confer with each other. They are not required to arrive at an agreement or make concessions; however, certain subjects must be considered at the bargaining table. The National Labor Relations Act protects employer speech as long as it does not contain a threat or a promise of benefits.

Review Questions

1. Define the following terms:
   a. Mandatory subjects of bargaining
   b. Minimum wage
   c. Unemployment compensation
   d. Workers' compensation

2. Discuss the defenses to on-the-job personal injury claims that arose during the nineteenth century and that limited an injured person's right to recover damages.

3. Adamson worked at the International Freight Corporation. He sorted boxes being unloaded from airplanes. One day, his sleeve got caught in the conveyor belt, and his arm was pulled into the belt. In order to collect under workers' compensation, what does Adamson need to establish?

4. Jenkins worked for the ABC Chemical Corporation which produced a certain chemical that emitted dangerous fumes during the production process. Exposure to these fumes over a period of time could cause permanent injury. ABC Chemical Corporation knew about the dangers in the production process and knew that its safety procedures were below standards. The only time the corporation met required safety procedures was when a government inspector toured the factory. At other times, procedures were set that allowed fumes to be emitted. One day, Jenkins was exposed to a dangerous level of fumes and was injured. Could Jenkins recover under the workers' compensation law?

5. Steel Corporation learns from the NLRB that a union has filed a petition to conduct a representation election. One week before the election, Steel Corporation grants two extra paid vacation days to employees and agrees to increase everyone's salary by twenty-five cents per hour if the employees vote against the union. Does this violate the labor law?

6. A union obtained thirteen signed authorization cards from a plant with thirty employees and demanded recognition as the bargaining agent for the company's production and maintenance

employees. The employer refused to recognize the union, and the union filed unfair labor practice charges with the NLRB. How should the NLRB rule on the charge? Has the union done enough to obtain recognition?

7. During contract negotiations, an employer unilaterally implemented a new system of automatic wage increases, changes in sick-leave benefits, and merit increases, even though these matters were subjects of pending contract negotiations. Was this new implementation a violation of the duty to bargain collectively?

8. Acme Corporation required its employees to wear company-provided uniforms. Acme Corporation charged employees for these uniforms. The union requested that Acme bargain over the price charged for the uniforms. Must Acme Corporation bargain over this issue?

9. The NLRB scheduled a representation election. Prior to the election, the employer told the employees that if they voted in favor of a union, the plant would be closed. Is it lawful to make such a statement with a representation election pending?

10. The National Labor Relations Board scheduled a representation election to cover the workers at the Acme plant. During this time, Acme engaged in unfair labor practices that made the holding of a fair election impossible. Under these circumstances, must the union win a representation election to become the bargaining agent for the employees?

Chapter 18

ANTITRUST LAW

W hen the colonists separated from Britain, ninety percent of the residents of the United States derived their income from agriculture. One of America's presidents at the time, Thomas Jefferson, envisioned an America made up of independent farmers. Jefferson failed to anticipate the arrival of the Industrial Revolution in Europe which spread to the United States after the Civil War. By the end of the nineteenth century, many people—rather than living the self-reliant lives that Jefferson imagined—planned their incomes would come from working for others in large industrial enterprises.

The populace began questioning the manner in which big businesses conducted themselves. Journalists uncovered innumerable unfair business practices; for example, the Standard Oil Company employed corporate spies to learn about the activities of its competitors. Some railroads charged more money for hauling freight shorter distances than for longer distances. Populist presidential candidates such as William Jennings Bryan campaigned against big business. Populists, in particular, argued that big business practices hurt small businesses, farmers, and the working man. They concluded that the average person would be better off if big businesses were forced to compete with each other. The antitrust laws discussed in this chapter constitute a code of fair competition.

What Is the Meaning of Antitrust?

TRUSTS

Many people are familiar with trusts. As commonly used, the term **trust** refers to a property right held by one person (the trustee) for the benefit of another person (the beneficiary). The trustee controls and manages property for the benefit of the beneficiary of the trust. Many people today utilize trusts to lower their estate taxes, designate that their funds be used in a particular manner, or protect their spouses and children. The trustee invests the money and distributes the interest to the beneficiaries. Trusts of this nature are perfectly legal and quite common.

ANTITRUST

The antitrust laws are directed not at this type of trust, but at unlawful restraints of trade and monopolies. The term *antitrust* in this sense applies to the trusts created by men like John D. Rockefeller, who founded the Standard Oil Trust, the trustees of which managed the business affairs of a number of independent oil companies. Many industries developed large trusts that, in effect, constituted single businesses run by a board of trustees.

Forces That Produced the Antitrust Laws

Figure 18.1 lists the forces that caused Congress to pass the antitrust laws.

■ **FIGURE 18.1** Forces That
Produced the Antitrust Laws

The Desire for Equal Opportunity for All People
The Increasing Concentration of Wealth in the Hands of a Small Number of People
Individualism
Mass Production
The Populist and Farmers

EQUAL OPPORTUNITY

As people moved off of farms and into cities, they took their work ethic with them. At the heart of the movement for the passage of the antitrust laws lies the American Dream of equal opportunity for those people who were willing and able to work—the right of people to advance due to their own efforts—in contrast to Europe where great estates and titles passed from father to son whether the son worked hard or not.

Horatio Alger wrote a series of books that reflected this American outlook on life. Alger's books typically featured a central character who rose to a position of wealth and prominence solely through his hard work and honesty. The public probably read Alger's works because the books reinforced their conviction that one needed only to be honest and hard working to succeed in America. Writing more eloquently than Horatio Alger—but reflecting the same philosophy—Ralph Waldo Emerson penned the phrase, "A man should let his reach exceed his grasp."

In a sense, the writings of Alger and Emerson implied that people in America—unlike the serfs on European estates—were the masters of their fate. Nineteenth-century farmers understood the importance of diligently tilling the soil. A hard-working American farmer could literally see the fruits of his labor.

People working for subsistence wages in the dangerous, big-city factories of the late nineteenth century in America began to wonder whether or not Alger's and Emerson's views correctly reflected reality. They wondered if their hard work would reward them or their employer? If so, why did more of America's exploding wealth not trickle down to them? Blue-collar workers—like farmers and small businessmen—worried that big businesses interfered with their opportunity to advance through their own efforts.

CONCENTRATION OF WEALTH

Andrew Carnegie, a nineteenth-century immigrant from Scotland, seemed to personify the American Dream. He came to America with nothing; but over the course of his life, Carnegie amassed hundreds of millions of dollars through the operation of his multinational company—the Carnegie Steel Corporation (later called United States Steel). By no means was Carnegie the only person getting fabulously rich in America at that time. As business enterprises like steel, oil, and railroads grew larger, their owners became extremely wealthy.

As the rich looked at America, they sought explanations for why they lived like European princes, while at the same time the average worker in the United States toiled away for pennies a day. Social Darwinism provided them with an answer—the inequality in the distribution of wealth resulted from their unique attributes. In other words, Social Darwinism reinforced the conviction of the affluent that they *deserved* to be wealthy—much like the ancient Egyptian Pharaohs actually believed themselves to be gods living on earth. While Social Darwinism may have been comforting to the privileged few, it angered the general population that embarked on its own search for an explanation for the growing disparity in incomes. They suspected that the concentration of wealth in the hands of a few monopolists—people or groups of people who exclusively control a particular field of business—resulted from a suppression of competition by big business.

INDIVIDUALISM

The American frontier contributed to the growth of a belief in individualism—the right to live life in the manner a person thinks is best. The men and women who settled the West wished to live free of governmental restraints. These self-reliant individuals believed people could advance through individual enterprise. Once the farmland was all settled, it seemed to many that only small business remained as a means to self-betterment. But in the late nineteenth century, many people also saw wealth gradually falling into the hands of the elite; indeed, with businesses growing larger and larger, some people foresaw the day when a few people would control all businesses.

MASS PRODUCTION

Mass production contributed heavily to the growth of large national and international enterprises. For example, where a rifle had been created formerly by a craftsperson step by step, industrialists learned to assemble rifles by assigning particular steps to various workers on a line. With each person performing a single repetitive task, a manufacturer could produce many more rifles. Industrialists applied this same process to the manufacture of shoes, the slaughter and dressing of beef, the weaving of materials, and the sewing of clothes. Every manufacturing enterprise produced more products faster by using the techniques of mass production. Over time, the neighborhood tailor or cobbler gave way to large, national manufacturers.

Businesses learned how to produce goods cheaply and in quantity. However, they needed a market for the large quantity of goods being produced. Cobblers who sold shoes only to people in their towns did not have any problems disposing of their goods. But a company that manufactured enough goods for hundreds of towns needed new methods of getting the goods into the customers' hands.

This increasingly became a possibility in the 1870s and 1880s, with the rapid expansion of the American railway system which became one of the finest and most extensive systems in the world. The railway system created a means for the mass producer to get its goods to a larger market. Large companies began to compete in many sections of the country virtually overnight. These big businesses became formidable competitors for local manufacturers. The sudden competition created a sort of "shock of the new," and a consequent distaste, among many people for big business.

The growth of mass production and the expansion of the railway system, the indigenous American quest for individualism, the growing inequality of the distribution of wealth, and the desire to maximize opportunity for all willing workers all contributed to the legal environment in the late nineteenth century.

THE POPULISTS AND FARMERS

One interest group that worried over the changing structure of America—the move away from small farms and small businesses—was the populists. The populists objected to the growth of large oil, packing, and steel companies. They favored small, local, individually owned businesses, which they claimed were more accountable and less corrupt than the large national enterprises springing up across America.

Another group particularly upset by higher prices was farmers. While the large meat-packing companies and grain elevators kept prices for farm products low, farmers paid high prices for farm equipment. Farmers argued that big business kept farm prices artificially low, and at the same time sold them products at artificially inflated prices.

Populists, farmers, and small businessowners saw competition as the method by which markets could be kept open. They viewed competition as the means to ensure that individual enterprise would be rewarded. The obstructions to competition created by the industrialists appeared to be unfairly eroding the rewards for hard work by the siphoning off of large profits to big business. These groups favored competition as the means for keeping prices to consumers as low as possible.

The widespread belief in the virtues of free, unfettered competition led ultimately to the election of Congresspeople committed to passing antitrust legislation. These elected representatives passed the Sherman Act of 1890.

Objectives of the Antitrust Laws

Figure 18.2 lists the goals promoted by the passage of the antitrust laws.

The Sherman Act reflected the wishes of a diverse set of interest groups—farmers, populists, small businessowners, frontierspeople, and others—who wished to put an end to unfair business practices. Congress responded to their complaints by passing the Sherman Act.

In the style of the times, Congress used vague language in drafting this act. When Congress uses vague language, this vests in the courts

■ **FIGURE 18.2** **Goals Promoted by the Passage of the Antitrust Laws**

1. Competition
2. Economic Efficiency
3. Limitation on Size of Businesses
4. Distribution of Wealth
5. Promotion of Business Opportunities

more power to determine the meaning of the act than would have been the case had the people writing the law used more specific language. Neither the legislative history of the Sherman Act nor the language of the act itself gave the courts clear-cut direction as to what Congress wanted to accomplish and how Congress intended to enforce the act. Consequently, the courts have created a body of law in this field on a case-by-case basis.

Some commentators view the original act as a lukewarm attempt to appease various groups without clearly adopting their aims. Indeed, in the first antitrust case to reach the Supreme Court, *United States v. E. C. Knight Co.* (1895), the Court narrowly interpreted the power of the government to act pursuant to the Sherman Act. The Knight case held that manufacturing was not commerce, and therefore a monopoly of the sugar manufacturing industry was not covered by the Sherman Act. Subsequent decisions avoided this doctrine, but the case illustrates the point that the Supreme Court initially construed the act quite narrowly, thus hampering antitrust enforcement, and certainly the Court did not offer the broad interpretation the people who worked for its passage probably hoped for.

Whether or not Congress intentionally watered down the language of the act so as to make vigorous enforcement impossible, the vague language of the act did give the Court great latitude in deciding which business actions Congress intended to prohibit. But it was clear that Congress chose market competition—not government regulation—as the method best suited for achieving its goals.

Before examining the specific objectives of the act, consider this situation. Jose Gomez came to the United States from Mexico. After years of hard work, he saved enough money to open an office supply store in the Los Angeles suburb of Riverside. As time passed, businesses in the area became familiar with his operation, and his office supply store gradually sold more and more material and furniture.

First examine Gomez's store from his own perspective. Would Gomez welcome it if another office supply store moved in down the block from his location? After years of struggling, he may be concerned that the new store would draw customers away from his business and thus financially injure him.

How may customers in the Riverside area regard this new entrant into the market? More than likely, consumers would favor the added competition because it would work as a check on Gomez's prices. If Gomez charges too much, people would go to the new store down the block. In order to lure them back, Gomez would need to lower his prices. This means less money for Gomez—but customers would benefit, because they would be getting more goods for their dollars.

The first goal furthered by the antitrust laws—enhanced competition—works to the benefit of consumers by keeping prices at a competitive level.

COMPETITION

Over the years, the courts have identified the furtherance of competition as one of the foremost goals of the antitrust laws. Almost without exception, the courts have favored the promotion of competition over any other social goal that may be accomplished through the enforcement of the antitrust laws. Many people argue that vigorous competition lowers the price of goods and promotes the efficient allocation of resources. Competition also limits business power; in a competitive market, individuals cannot take advantage of the people with whom they deal. If a seller charges too high of a price for wares, buyers are able to purchase them from someone else. Many people regard this alternative as producing fairer results than would decisions by private people or the government as to what and how much to produce. Arguably competition also helps to keep businesses small and opportunity open for everyone, and to distribute money throughout society rather than to a few powerful people.

While competition between businesses promotes the interests of consumers, it does not automatically mean that businesses want more competition. In fact, because competition makes survival more difficult, businesses often try to stifle it. Consider the Ethical Perspective, "Eliminating the Competition," regarding this point.

Competition is undoubtedly the bane of businesses which is why they try to avoid or destroy it, as the General Motors example illustrates. How would competition affect a business such as Gomez's office supply store? How would competition advance the interests of consumers in the Riverside area? Most likely, if confronted with more competition, Gomez will be forced to keep his prices low enough to prevent his customers from patronizing the new office supply store.

ECONOMIC EFFICIENCY

Another aim of the antitrust laws is to improve the economic performance of individual firms and the economy as a whole. Through vigorous enforcement of the antitrust laws, the government hopes to ensure that those companies that need resources the most, and are willing to pay the most for them, will receive a proper allocation of society's funds. By this means, it is hoped, output will be increased, new techniques of production will be utilized, and new and better products will be developed.

Picture what may happen if we had no competition—for example, if the government regulated all production. Suppose the government had ordered the production of buggy whips. This action would have consumed some of our resources. When someone came along who wished to make automobiles, extra resources may not be available to develop this new mode of transportation. The automobile may never

---

ETHICAL
PERSPECTIVE

Eliminating the Competition

If only a good mass transit system existed in every city. The sad fact is, at one time, every city did have this.

In the 1930s, the Pacific Electric Utility Company operated an electric train system in Los Angeles. From downtown Los Angeles, it branched as far east as San Bernardino, Santa Ana, Pasadena, Burbank, and Glendale. Where is the electric train system that Los Angeles desperately needs today? It seems that the nation's oil, tire, and automobile companies realized that the electric railway system threatened their industries. In 1932, General Motors created the United Cities Motor Transit Company. The sole reason for its creation was to buy up electric streetcar companies.

In order to raise more money to buy more electric railway systems, General Motors combined with Firestone Tire and Rubber Company, Standard Oil of California, Mack Truck, Greyhound Bus Company, and other companies in creating the National City Lines, Inc. By 1949, General Motors had been involved in the replacement of more than a hundred city electric railway systems.

What do you think? Did these companies act ethically in buying and destroying many of America's well developed streetcar lines and replacing them with buses and automobiles?

Source: Russell Mokhiber, *Corporate Crime and Violence: Big Business Power and the Abuse of Public Trust,* Sierra Club Books, 1988.

have been developed if the government had misallocated the available resources to the buggy whip manufacturer.

It is noteworthy that Americans tend to accept the idea of minimal intervention by the government in matters that concern business. This theory was advocated by the English economist Adam Smith. The antitrust laws reflect the belief that competition between firms is the touchstone of economic development. However, this view is not shared by all, as the International Perspective, "Japanese Control of the Economy," illustrates.

In general, the courts apply the antitrust law to encourage efficiency. In this way, the courts help those enterprises that may most efficiently utilize our valuable resources and that are best able to devise cheaper methods of production and improved products. These firms will be permitted to prosper. The less efficient and more poorly run businesses will fall by the wayside. In the final analysis, society will prosper because it will be getting the biggest return on its investment of resources.

The Managerial Perspective, "The Standard Oil Trust," deals with the economic efficiencies created by the formation of the Standard Oil Trust.

More efficient businesses such as the Standard Oil Trust serve the interests of consumers because consumers get more for their money. What impact would a more efficient competitor have on a business such as Gomez's office supply store? Suppose that a national office supply store such as Office Max—as opposed to another individual store owner—moved in down the block from Gomez's office supply store. Just as the Standard Oil Trust operated so much more efficiently that it could underprice other oil companies, a national office supply store may also be in a position to underprice Gomez and gradually drive him out of business. This appeals to consumers because they get more for their money. From Gomez's standpoint, however, the arrival of a national chain may spell the end of the American Dream for him.

Japanese Control of the Economy

In the United States, many people think the government should not take a part in directing the decisions of businesses. However, not every country accepts such a minimal role for the government in the economy. Japan is an excellent example of a prosperous nation in which the government controls large-scale economic decisions. Japan's Ministry of International Trade and Industry has guided the economic development of Japan since the 1940s. The government has pushed businesses in particular directions and supported their efforts to exploit specific markets such as automobiles and consumer electronics.

The Japanese government's intervention in private business decisions is in stark contrast to that advocated by Adam Smith in his book, *The Wealth of Nations*. Smith supported a minimal role for government. The United States, Great Britain, Australia, and many other countries tend to accept this idea as the proper role of government. They believe that firms will prosper if the government just lets them compete with each other. Japan, on the other hand, follows the philosophies of Hegel and Friedrich List. Japan manages its economy and in the process has produced one of the world's most prosperous economies.

Source: Chalmers Johnson, "Looking at the Sun: The Rise of the New East Asian Economic and Political System," *The Atlantic Monthly,* January 1995.

LIMITATION ON SIZE

Populists viewed big businesses as bad businesses. Even today, people castigate *big business*. One could argue that the antitrust laws serve to limit the size of big business—or to protect small, independent businesses. People who espouse the anti-big business viewpoint fear placing too much power in the hands of a single business. History shows that unchecked power may be abused by the wrong people.

How may the arrival of a big office supply store negatively affect Gomez's operation? Suppose that a national office supply firm

managerial perspective

The Standard Oil Trust

John D. Rockefeller lured or forced many previously independent oil companies to join with him in the creation of the gigantic, multinational Standard Oil Trust. By 1882, an alliance of forty companies acting together produced more than ninety percent of the kerosene made in the United States—then the key product refined from crude oil. Over time, the Standard Oil Trust built three enormous refineries. It cost an oil refinery that produced a mere two thousand barrels per day 2.5 cents to produce each gallon of kerosene. A six thousand-gallon-per-day refinery, on the other hand, could reduce its cost of production to a mere half a penny per gallon of kerosene. The Standard Oil Trust was such an efficient organization that it could ship kerosene to Europe and still undercut the price charged for Russian kerosene.

As time passed, the Standard Oil Trust simply became increasingly more efficient as it acquired the best employees, the latest technology, and the most advanced plants. Other oil companies faded out of existence because Standard could sell its kerosene for less money than it cost its competitors to refine oil—and, the Standard Oil Trust could still make a profit.

Source: Shlomo Maital, "Tales of Scale and Scope," *Barron's,* February 13, 1995, page 54.

gradually grew so efficient and competitive that it drove all other competitors out of business—including Gomez's store. Once this firm becomes the only seller in the market—a monopolist—what keeps it from raising its prices far above those that Gomez previously charged? One way to prevent this problem from arising in the first place is to encourage competition, which will in turn limit the size of business firms.

Note that some of the antitrust laws *not* discussed in this textbook favor the preservation of small businesses. These laws reflect the idea that the United States needs small businesses even if they are less efficient. Today, it appears that increasingly less emphasis is being given by the Department of Justice and the Federal Trade Commission to those statutes that favor small businesses. The government has tended not to enforce these laws because they interfere with the efficient operation of firms.

OTHER POSSIBLE GOALS

The other goals of fairness and the populist goals of distribution of wealth and promotion of business opportunities really have not been given great emphasis by the courts in the enforcement of the antitrust laws. Some commentators assert that these populist goals should not be given *any* weight in formulating rules in the antitrust field, and that the courts should focus on a procompetitive policy that promotes economic efficiencies. They contend that to promote these other populist goals over economic efficiency would make the antitrust laws costly, futile, and impossible to administer. Not every scholar in the antitrust field shares this view. Some argue that noneconomic goals—such as the distribution of economic power, the increase in opportunity for more people to enter business, and the preference for small businesses—are laudable goals that should be promoted through antitrust enforcement. Nonetheless, the cases over the years and more recent cases, in particular, do seem to favor the goals of economic efficiency and competition. The populist goals seem to have been ignored over the decades as the courts have chosen not to emphasize them at the expense of economic efficiency.

THE ROLE OF TECHNOLOGY

While competition and economic efficiency certainly contribute to the overall prosperity of any given country, another important factor unquestionably contributes to economic prosperity—the development of technology. People debating about the pros and cons of the antitrust laws really did not give much consideration to the role of technology. Consider for a moment, however, the opportunities created by advances in technology. In the 1940s, Underwood Typewriter Company and Royal McBee Typewriter dominated the typewriter market in the United States. Both were multimillion-dollar corporations. In the 1950s, IBM swept the standard typewriter out of the offices of the world. As Underwood Typewriter Company and Royal McBee Typewriter failed to keep up with the advances in technology, they lost their control of the market. In the mid-1970s, word processors came into existence. By the mid-1980s, personal computers with word-processing software virtually wiped out all other existing forms of typing.

In many ways, one may regard the entire business system as a form of creative destruction. IBM—through creativity—destroyed Underwood Typewriter Company and Royal McBee Typewriter; then the personal computer took over virtually all of the market that IBM had created with its electric typewriter in the 1950s. This process happens repeatedly.

At one time, people in the United States communicated by mail. It took weeks or months for communications to go from one coast to the other. In the mid 1800s, investors created the Pony Express which rushed letters across the country. Not long after the Pony Express, Western Union developed its telegraph lines across the United States, thus wiping out the Pony Express. Around the turn of the twentieth century, Alexander Graham Bell invented the telephone which decreased people's reliance on the telegraph. In the 1970s, Federal Express came along to deliver packages with shorter delivery times. With the invention of the personal computer, people today may communicate instantaneously by fax and e-mail.

At times, it seems that the real rule of business is to innovate or die. Businesses must constantly change or evolve. Changing technology has altered the world—and it sometimes catches us totally off guard.

Who could have seen the changes wrought by Thomas Edison's invention of the moving picture?

One of the biggest motion picture companies in the United States was founded by "Uncle" Carl Laemmle, Sr., the founder of Universal Pictures. Laemmle decided to move his dry goods operation to

Chicago from Wisconsin. Laemmle finally picked a particular location because in dry goods, "Merchants needed long counters." Around 1902, a man came into his store, looked around, and offered Laemmle $10 to rent the store for the evening to show some moving pictures. Laemmle asked the man why he wanted to rent *his* place. The man replied, "Because for best results, you have to have a long store." By 1906, Laemmle had founded a company called The Nickelodeons. He kept renting more pictures, and then Laemmle decided to make his own films which eventually led to the Universal Film Manufacturing Company. Laemmle once remarked, "Sometime, when I think back on the whole thing, I wonder what would have happened to my life, and to so many other lives, if I hadn't happened to rent that long store. I mean to say, what if I'd rented a different store?"[1]

Overview of the Federal Antitrust Laws

Among other acts, Congress passed the Sherman Act in 1890 which outlaws monopolies and restraints of trade. All of the candidates in the 1912 presidential election vowed to further strengthen the laws to combat the trusts. In 1914, Congress fortified the antitrust laws by passing the Clayton Act and the Federal Trade Commission Act. The Federal Trade Commission Act created the Federal Trade Commission. The Clayton Act and the FTC Act were passed in response to the misuse of economic power by the trusts.

Enforcement of the Antitrust Laws

The Department of Justice represents the federal government in the courts. Figure 18.3 illustrates the structure of the Department of Justice. The antitrust division of the Department of Justice has the power to bring either criminal or civil suits pursuant to the Sherman Act or the Clayton Act. While the Department of Justice has the exclusive right to bring criminal suits, it shares some of the responsibility for enforcing the antitrust laws with the Federal Trade Commission. It should be noted that private parties and state attorneys general may also bring civil suits to enforce these acts.

Two topics of great importance in the antitrust field will now be examined—monopolies and restraints of trade.

Monopolies

The Sherman Act outlaws both monopolies and attempts to monopolize. Section 2 of this act makes it illegal to monopolize or conspire with others to monopolize any part of the nation's commerce. Most challenges to monopolistic behavior are brought under Section 2 of the Sherman Act.

WHAT IS A MONOPOLY?

When the courts speak of a **monopoly,** they are referring to a firm that deliberately engages in conduct to obtain or maintain the power

■ **FIGURE 18.3** **Structure of the Department of Justice**

Source: *The United States Government Manual 1991–92,* Washington, DC: U.S. Government Printing Office, 1991.

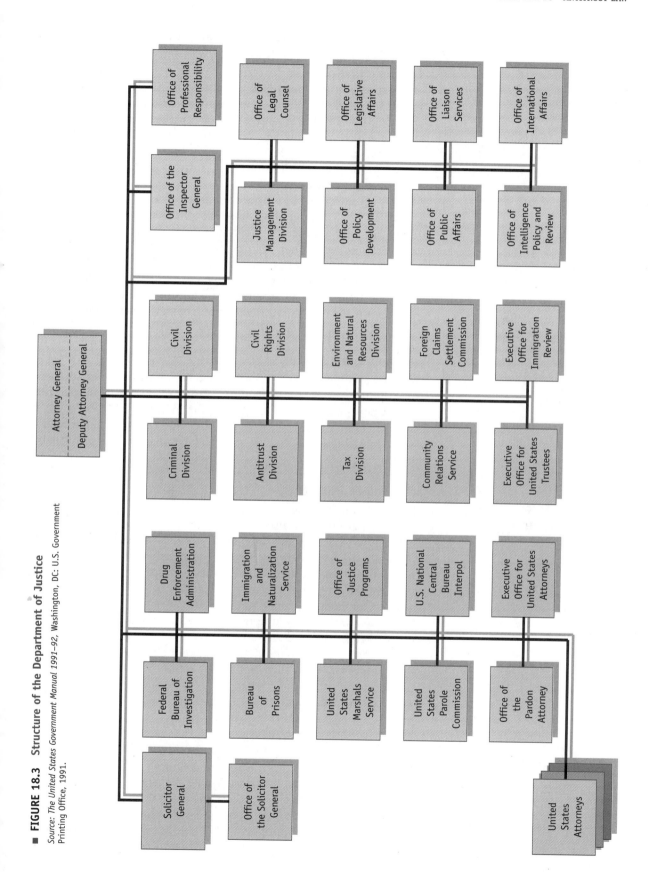

to control prices or exclude competition in some part of trade or commerce. The courts do not require a firm to be the sole business operating in a particular market—other firms may be operating in the market but they must lack the power to influence prices or output in the market. Contrast a monopolistic industry with an industry composed of several large firms each possessing a major part of the trade in a given market. The courts refer to these firms as **oligopolies.** In a *competitive system*, many firms each producing the same product exist, with none of the firms possessing the power to control prices or output.

A good example of a monopoly occurred in 1993 with home video games. In 1993, Nintendo of America controlled eighty-five percent of the United States market for home video games. With an eighty-five percent market share, Nintendo of America definitely had the power to control prices or exclude competition in this market. How would a court analyze a business such as Nintendo of America for monopoly purposes? In labeling Nintendo of America as a monopoly, certain factors must be examined before designating it as an unlawful monopoly.

■ Geographic Market

In order to arrive at the conclusion that a given business constitutes a monopoly, the relevant geographic market must first be determined for purposes of analysis. The geographic market could be a town, a state, a region, or the nation. In the Nintendo of America example, it was assumed that the relevant geographic market is the entire United States.

■ Product Market

In addition to making a determination as to the relevant geographic market, a court must also define the relevant product market in a monopoly case. In the Nintendo of America example, the relevant product market was defined as home video games. However, the product market does not need to be defined so narrowly. Instead, a court may choose to define the relevant product market as all forms of games—for example, board games, cards, sporting activities, and so forth—that people play at home. If a court narrowly defines the product market as home video games, Nintendo of America had eighty-five percent of this market in 1993. On the other hand, if a court defined the product market as all games played at home, Nintendo of America possessed a much smaller share of that product market and would therefore probably not be found to possess a monopoly.

■ Anticompetitive Effects

For the most part, courts go through the same analysis in monopoly cases. The court first determines the geographic market in which a business operates; then the court decides the relevant product market. After making these determinations, the court then examines whether any anticompetitive effects associated with this monopoly exist. If none exist, then the monopoly will be ruled lawful. The law prohibits only *unreasonable* monopolies. Consequently, it is possible—under certain circumstances—to possess a monopoly but still not be in violation of the antitrust laws.

ARE ALL MONOPOLIES ILLEGAL?

Not every monopoly violates the antitrust laws. Some businesses, such as utilities, are natural monopolies. The states give these businesses the exclusive right to operate in a certain territory. Other businesses fall within an exemption to the antitrust laws. Article I, Section 8, of the United States Constitution gives monopolies to authors in the form of copyrights and gives patents to inventors. The framers of the U.S. Constitution reasoned that such protection for authors and inventors encourages work in these areas. One object of marketing certainly is to give a product a unique identification in the minds of consumers. If consumers perceive a company's product as different from any other product on the market, they may pay a higher price for its product. There is nothing illegal about a company trying to project a unique, favorable image of its products in the minds of the public. To the extent that such a campaign succeeds, the company has obtained a kind of monopoly.

Absent one of these situations, a company that becomes a monopoly in a given geographic and product market may violate the Sherman Act.

THE CURRENT TEST APPLIED IN MONOPOLY CASES

The United States Supreme Court announced a two-part test for monopolization in *United States v. Grinnell Corp.*, 384 U.S. 563 (1966). In order to have unlawfully monopolized a market, the defendant must (1) possess monopoly power in the relevant market; and (2) have willfully acquired or maintained that power as distinguished from growth or development as a consequence of a superior product, business acumen, or historical accident.

Consider how a court may apply this rule. Suppose that Steel Corporation sold rolled steel in the United States. It eventually acquired ninety percent of the U.S. market for rolled steel. The product market most likely would be defined as rolled steel. The geographic market most likely would be defined as the United States. Since Steel Corporation has ninety percent of this market, a statement could be made that it has monopoly power in the relevant market—that is, the power to control prices or to exclude competition from this market.

The second part of the Grinnell test gives this type of business a defense. If Steel Corporation's growth was attributable to a superior product, business acumen, or historical accident—even if it possesses monopoly power in the relevant market—the monopoly is lawful. Suppose that all of its major competitors went bankrupt. In this situation, Steel Corporation could argue that its growth was attributable to a historical accident. On the other hand, if Steel Corporation arrived at a ninety percent market share by willfully acquiring it, or if Steel Corporation willfully maintained that power in light of its ninety percent market share, it has violated the Sherman Act. What the cases seem to emphasize is that if a company seizes every opportunity as it arises with the intent of becoming a monopolist, then it has willfully acquired its monopoly position and has violated the Sherman Act.

Consider the Thought Problem, "Is Ticketmaster a Monopoly?" What criteria would need to be established in order to make a determination that Ticketmaster is an unlawful monopolist?

thought problem

Is Ticketmaster a Monopoly?

Ticketmaster sells tickets for concerts. Ticketmaster—a very efficient operator—places its outlets in shopping malls, music stores, and other locations that are convenient to the concert-going members of the public. In many markets, Ticketmaster is the only seller of concert tickets. It charges $3 to $6 per ticket for its services which, of course, increases the price of tickets. Ticketmaster, in turn, pays a fee to promoters for every ticket sold in exchange for exclusive contracts with the promoters. Ticketmaster sometimes loans money to promoters in order for them to meet the guarantees of stadium acts. Making these loans helps ensure that concerts actually will take place.

What criteria must be established in order to make a determination that Ticketmaster is an unlawful monopolist?

Source: Charles Bilodeau, "Pearl Jam's War on Reality: Is Ticketmaster a Monopoly?", *Consumer's Research Magazine,* June 1995.

Restraints of Trade

Section 1 of the Sherman Act outlaws restraints of trade. The act prohibits contracts, combinations, or conspiracies in restraints of trade.

ELEMENTS OF A CASE

The criteria that must be established before a corporation or person may be deemed in violation of Section 1 include (1) a contract, combination, or conspiracy; and (2) a restraint of trade. Early in the history of this act, in the *Standard Oil Co. v. United States* (1911) landmark case, the Supreme Court ruled that the act outlaws only *unreasonable* restraints of trade. In the Standard Oil case, the Court created the *Rule of Reason*—that is, unreasonable restraints of trade are unlawful, but the Sherman Act permits reasonable restraints of trade. The courts determine whether or not a restraint is reasonable. In following the Rule of Reason, a court must examine whether an agreement hinders or promotes the purposes of the Sherman Act.

Consider the following example. Suppose that Acme Filing Cabinets controls fifty-five percent of the U.S. market for filing cabinets; International controls twenty-two percent of the market; and Standard controls fifteen percent of the market. The presidents of the three companies met with each other in Palm Beach, Florida. At that meeting, they enter into an agreement that each company will charge the same prices for their filing cabinets. By entering into an agreement, the presidents fulfilled the first element necessary for establishing a case. When they agreed to charge the same prices, this unreasonably restrains trade in the filing cabinet market. Such an agreement violates Section 1 of the Sherman Act.

PER SE RULE

Some types of restraints of trade unquestionably contravene the spirit of the Sherman Act. For these types of activities, the courts have adopted a rule stating that if a business engages in the forbidden act, it will be held to have violated the Sherman Act. This is referred to as the *Per Se Rule,* as opposed to the Rule of Reason. A court reviewing the case will not engage in the same extended analysis of the effect of the conduct on the business system that a court would engage in if the activity were analyzed under the Rule of Reason. When a situation presents a clear-cut violation of the Sherman Act, the courts apply the Per Se Rule and find a violation of the act without the necessity of engaging in an extended consideration of the economic effects of a defendant's conduct.

■ Horizontal Market Divisions

Consider this example. Topco operated as a purchasing agent of twenty-five different grocery chains and provided products to them under the Topco name. Topco geographically divided the market among its members. The United States Supreme Court looked at this arrangement and concluded that this was a classic example of a per se violation of Section 1 of the Sherman Act. If competitors at the same level of the market structure enter into an agreement to allocate territories in order to minimize competition, it is not necessary to engage in an economic analysis of their actions. The sole proof of their agreement to divide territories will be sufficient for establishing a violation of the act. Horizontal territorial limitations serve no purpose other than limiting competition. The Court thus found Topco's territorial restrictions to be illegal per se.[2]

The Topco case establishes a rule stating that competitors at the same level of market structure—as opposed to combinations of people at different levels of the market structure (for example, combinations of manufacturers and distributors, which are termed *vertical* restraints)—may not allocate territories in order to minimize competition. These horizontal market divisions are illegal per se.

The *Palmer v. BRG of Georgia, Inc.* case deals with a division of territories between two companies.

Palmer v. BRG of Georgia, Inc.

United States Supreme Court
111 S.Ct. 401 (1990)

Harcourt Brace Jovanovich Legal and Professional Publications (HBJ) is the nation's largest provider of bar review materials and lecture services. Both BRG and HBJ offered Georgia bar review courses in the 1970s. In early 1980, they entered into an agreement that gave BRG an exclusive license to market HBJ's material in Georgia and to use its trade name "Bar/Bri." The parties agreed that HBJ would not compete with BRG in Georgia and that BRG would not compete with HBJ outside of Georgia.

Palmer contends that the price of BRG's course was enhanced by reason of this agreement and that the agreement violated Section 1 of the Sherman Act. The United States Court of Appeals for the Eleventh Circuit held that to prove a per se violation under a geographic market allocation theory, the plaintiff had to show that the defendants had subdivided some relevant market in which they had previously competed.

Per Curiam

The District Court and the Court of Appeals erred when they assumed that an allocation of markets or submarkets by competitors is not unlawful unless the markets in which the two previously competed is divided between them.

In *United States v. Topco Associates, Inc.* we held that agreements between competitors to allocate territories to minimize competition are illegal. One of the classic examples of a *per se* violation of Section 1 is an agreement between competitors at the same level of the market structure to allocate territories in order to minimize competition. This Court has reiterated time and time again that horizontal territorial limitations are naked restraints of trade with no purpose except stifling of competition. Such limitations are *per se* violations of the Sherman Act.

The defendants in Topco had never competed in the same market, but had simply agreed to allocate markets. Here, HBJ and BRG had previously competed in the Georgia market; under their allocation agreement, BRG received that market, while HBJ received the remainder of the United States. Each agreed not to compete in the other's territories. Such agreements are anticompetitive regardless of whether the parties split a market within which both do business or whether they merely reserve one market for one and another for the other. Thus, the 1980 agreement between HBJ and BRG was unlawful on its face.

PRICE FIXING

This brings up the issue of price fixing. Price fixing is one of those areas of conduct treated by the courts as a per se violation of Section 1 of the Sherman Act. No extended analysis of the effect of the defendant's activities is necessary. The proof that a defendant entered into a contract, combination, or conspiracy to fix prices is sufficient to find it in violation of the Sherman Act.

In *United States v. Trenton Potteries* (1927), the Supreme Court explained why it regarded price-fixing agreements as so offensive to the purposes of the Sherman Act. Trenton Potteries manufactured vitreous pottery. It fixed prices and limited the sale of its pottery to specific companies. Justice Stone, speaking for the majority, wrote the following concerning price-fixing agreements:

> The aim and result of every price-fixing agreement, if effective, is the elimination of one form of competition. . . . The reasonable price fixed today may through economic or business changes become the unreasonable price of tomorrow. Once established, it may be maintained unchanged because of the absence of competition secured by the agreement. . . . Agreements which create such potential power may well be held to be in themselves unreasonable unlawful restraints, without necessity of minute inquiry whether a particular price is reasonable or unreasonable.

Trenton Potteries argued that it fixed only *reasonable* prices. The Court rejected the reasonable price defense in this case. This means that even if a company that sets a price for its product at the same level that competition would have produced violates Section 1, if it enters into a contract, combination, or conspiracy with any other firm or person to fix prices at this level. The contracts in this case were between Trenton Potteries and the people to whom Trenton sold its products.

The question remained, however, whether price fixing was illegal per se if the people or companies that set the prices *lacked the market power* actually to fix prices. The Supreme Court answered this question definitively in the *United States v. Socony-Vacuum Oil Co.* case.

United States v. Socony-Vacuum Oil Co.

United States Supreme Court
310 U.S. 150 (1940)

At the time of this suit, the major oil refiners were able to respond to changes in demand by increasing or decreasing their inventories, production, or price. The major refiners thought they were being hurt by the fact that independent refiners lacked storage capacity for their gasoline. Because of this, the independents were forced to offer their gasoline on the spot market for immediate delivery to dealers. This caused the price of gasoline to vary greatly.

To eliminate the price fluctuations, the major producers entered into a program of bidding for and buying gas on the spot market that they were capable of storing. The major producers entered into the arrangement in order to stabilize the price of gasoline. There was no actual formal contractual commitment to purchase the gasoline, either between the majors or between the majors and the independent refiners. It was more of a gentlemen's agreement or understanding. The prices did rise and stabilize in the markets in which the parties were operating during 1935 and 1936. The government charged that the major oil companies had violated Section 1 of the Sherman Act. The Supreme Court agreed.

Justice Douglas

There was abundant evidence that the combination had the purpose to raise prices. And likewise, there was ample evidence that the buying programs at least contributed to the price rise and the stability of the spot markets, and to increases in the price of gasoline sold in the Mid-Western area during the indictment period. That other factors also may have contributed to that rise and stability of the markets is immaterial. Proof that there was a conspiracy, that its purpose was to raise prices, and that it caused or contributed to a price rise is proof of the actual consummation or execution of a conspiracy under Section 1 of the Sherman Act.

The fact that sales on the spot markets were still governed by some competition is of no consequence. For it is indisputable that that competition was restricted through the removal by respondents of a part of the supply which but for the buying programs would have been a factor in determining the going prices on those markets.

Any combination which tampers with price structures is engaged in an unlawful activity. Even though the members of the price-fixing group were in no position to control the market, to the extent that they raised, lowered, or stabilized prices they would be directly interfering with the free play of market forces. The Act places all such schemes beyond the pale and protects that vital part of our economy against any degree of interference. Congress has not left with us the determination of whether or not particular price-fixing schemes are wise or unwise, healthy or destructive. It has not permitted the age-old cry of ruinous competition and competitive evils to be a defense to price-fixing conspiracies. It has no more allowed genuine or fancied competitive abuses as a legal justification for such schemes than it has the good intentions of the members of the combination.

Under the Sherman Act a combination formed for the purpose and with the effect of raising, depressing, fixing, pegging, or stabilizing the price of a commodity in interstate or foreign commerce is illegal per se. Where the machinery for price-fixing is an agreement on the prices to be charged or paid for the commodity in the interstate or foreign channels of trade, the power to fix prices exists if the combination has control of a substantial part of the commerce in that commodity. Where the means for price fixing are purchases or sales of the commodity in a market operation or, as here, purchases of a part of the supply of the commodity for the purpose of keeping it from having a depressive effect on the markets, such power may be found to exist though the combination does not control a substantial part of the commodity. In such a case that power may be established if as a result of market conditions, the resources available to the combinations, the timing and the strategic placement of orders and the like, effective means are at hand to accomplish the desired objective. But there may be effective influence over the market though the group in question does not control it. Price-fixing agreements may have utility to members of the group though the power possessed or exerted falls far short of domination and control. Monopoly power is not the only power which the Act strikes down, as we have said. Proof that a combination was formed for the purpose of fixing prices and that it caused them to be fixed or contributed to that result is proof of the completion of a price-fixing conspiracy under Section 1 of the Act. The indictment in this case charged that this combination had that purpose and effect. And there was abundant evidence to support it. Hence the existence of power on the part of members of the combination to fix prices was but a conclusion from the finding that the buying programs caused or contributed to the rise and stability of prices.

Accordingly we conclude that the Circuit Court of Appeals erred in reversing the judgments on this ground. A fortiori the position taken by respondents in their cross petition that they were untitled to direct verdicts of acquittal is untenable.

■ *Socony-Vacuum Oil Case*

The Socony case illustrates several points. Whether the price established through a contract, combination, or conspiracy is reasonable is irrelevant. The Court also rejected the argument that the manufacturers needed to set prices in order to avoid the ruinous competition created by sellers on the spot market. Ruinous competition is *not* a defense to a price-setting scheme. The Court stated, "Under the Sherman Act a combination formed for the purpose and with the effect of raising, depressing, fixing, pegging, or stabilizing the price of a commodity in interstate commerce is illegal per se." The Court also implied that even if the defendants lacked the power to influence prices—that is, even if they lacked market power to influence the price of oil—they violated the Sherman Act simply by entering into such an agreement to fix prices.

Why was the Court so hard on price fixers? After all, if the price that is fixed is the price that would have prevailed in a fully competitive market, how is the public interest prejudiced? The Court answered this in the Trenton Potteries example. The reasonable price fixed today could become an unreasonable price tomorrow. It would place an unreasonable burden on the courts to recognize the reasonable price defense. The government would be forced to monitor prices and relitigate a case if it appeared that the price fixers changed their price from a reasonable price to an unreasonable price. A Per Se

Rule minimizes the time the courts must spend on a price-fixing scheme. Furthermore, it provides a clear-cut rule for people in business to follow. Anyone who fixes the price of his or her product does so at the risk of being prosecuted for a violation of the antitrust laws.

■ *Maximum Prices*

What if, rather than agreeing on a given price, several manufacturers enter into an arrangement in which they agree to charge buyers no more than a certain price—a maximum price. Setting a maximum price, as well as any other tampering with the price system of the free market, violates the antitrust laws.

Rather than agreeing to require their purchasers to resell a commodity at a maximum price, manufacturers may agree simply to charge their customers a minimum price. Agreements among manufacturers to charge all customers no less than a stated price also violates the Sherman Act.

We now know that setting a minimum or a maximum price, stabilizing prices, and fixing prices in any way all violate the Sherman Act.

ANALYSIS OF SECTION 1 CASES

When faced with a Section 1 case, a given court first asks if the parties entered into an agreement. If so, should the agreement be covered by a Per Se Rule? Activities that clearly violate Section 1, such as price fixing, fall under a per se form of analysis. The government, in a price-fixing case, need only prove an agreement to fix prices between two or more parties. It does not need to prove any harmful effects.

If a court analyzes a case under the Rule of Reason, it looks for harmful effects. It then examines the legitimate beneficial effects of the agreement—that is, those which are procompetitive. The *purpose* of the defendants are often looked to as a guide to interpreting effects. This is often a very critical move by the court in its application of the Rule of Reason approach. (The court does not examine broader social policy arguments other than the furtherance of competition and efficiency.) Finally, the court examines whether or not *less restrictive alternatives* exist for achieving the goals the defendants wish to achieve. If they are able to achieve the same results in another way, one that does not injure competition, the court likely will rule against the defendants.

Consider the International Perspective, "Keiretsu," and ask if such an arrangement would be permissible in America.

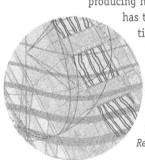

Summary

Many forces contributed to the passage of the Sherman Act—the growth of mass production, the expansion of the railway system, American individualism, a desire to redistribute wealth, and a desire to maximize opportunity for workers. Populists, farmers, and small businessowners in 1890 succeeded in convincing Congress that the best way to achieve these goals was through an act that promoted competition and economic efficiency.

The law vests the Department of Justice and the Federal Trade Commission with the primary responsibility for enforcing these acts. Private businesses and individuals may also enforce the antitrust laws.

Section 2 of the Sherman Act outlaws unreasonable monopolies. When a court is confronted with the charge that a firm allegedly has violated the act, the court must make two important decisions—it must first decide the relevant geographic market, and it then must identify the product market. Both of these criteria must be decided for the purposes of the suit before deciding whether or not the monopoly in question is unlawful. The court then examines any anticompetitive effects created by this monopoly.

The Sherman Act also outlaws unreasonable restraints of trade. The Court has created two rules in this area. Certain types of activities are illegal per se, while other conduct is analyzed under the Rule of Reason. Price fixing is a good example of an activity that is always in violation of the Sherman Act. Any attempt to fix prices with another firm violates the law.

Review Questions

1. Define the following terms:
    a. Monopoly
    b. Per Se Rule
    c. Restraints of trade
    d. Rule of Reason

2. What forces produced the antitrust laws?

3. What objectives do the courts regard as furthered by the antitrust laws?

4. What is the two-part Grinnell test for monopolization?

5. Explain the difference(s) between the Rule of Reason and the Per Se Rule as applied to restraints of trade.

6. Aluminum Corporation sells eighty percent of all aluminum produced in the United States. It has been a very aggressive competitor. Does the fact that it controls such a large percentage of all steel sold in the United States mean that it is an unlawful monopoly?

7. International Grocery Stores entered into an agreement with Acme Grocery Stores. International agreed to open stores only in the eastern half of the United States in return for Acme agreeing to open stores only in the western half of the United States. Is such an agreement lawful?

8. National Oil Company entered into an agreement with United States Oil Company. The companies agreed to purchase gasoline on

the spot market in order to stabilize the price of gasoline. They did not intend to suppress competition. Is such an agreement lawful?

9. Aspen is a ski resort. Ski Company operated three ski facilities for downhill skiing. Since 1962, an all-Aspen, six-day ticket had been sold that permitted skiers to use all of the facilities in the Aspen area. The operator of Highlands—the other mountain—participated in this all-Aspen ski ticket. In 1978, Ski Company discontinued selling the all-Aspen ticket. It refused to participate in an all-Aspen ticket and took action that made it difficult for Highlands to market an all-Aspen ticket. If Highlands asserts that Ski Company is engaged in an unlawful monopoly, how should the court define the product market and the geographic market for purposes of its analysis?

10. Three producers of steel entered into an agreement to set the price of steel at a certain minimum price. Is such an agreement lawful? Would such an agreement be lawful if they agreed to set a maximum price?

Notes [1]Garson Kanin, *Hollywood,* New York: The Viking Press, 1974, p. 73–74.
[2]*United States v. Topco Associates, Inc.*, 405 U.S. 596 (1972).

7

Part

INTERNATIONAL REGULATION OF BUSINESS ACTIVITY

Chapter
19

INTERNATIONAL LAW

A casual examination of the news reveals widespread wars, terrorism, disagreements, and conflict. Many of these disputes may be traced back centuries or even millennia; for example, many nations trace territorial claims back to ancient times. Countries grasp power and territory for awhile, and then they lose control to some other country.

In no small part, many of these battles boil down to trying to maintain or improve the economic condition of the citizens of a country. Wealthy countries want to remain affluent and emerging countries hope to fulfill the rising expectations of their populace. Many laws get passed in order to further the interests of a particular country or region. To a great extent, governments act as if international business is a zero sum game—that is, if your country gains a dollar, then my country loses a dollar. In fact, mutually advantageous transactions may result in improving the lot of all people on the planet.

International business took place thousands of years ago. In ancient Greece, the Athenians grew and prospered by trading with other nearby countries. During the twelfth century, Marco Polo travelled to the Far East and brought back spices and silks to Europe which set off a demand for items from faraway lands. By the seventeenth century, the English, Dutch, Spanish, and French all engaged in businesses around the globe—particularly in the trade of agricultural products.

The Industrial Revolution and mass production allowed businesses to trade goods on an even greater global scale. In the 1870s, the Standard Oil Trust became probably the first global, multinational corporation. Since the 1870s, dramatic advances in technology and communications now permit people to conduct business around the world with ease. We live in a global community in which goods, services, information, and money pass easily from one place to another. Consequently, businesspeople need an awareness of the basic laws associated with international business transactions.

American multinational businesses must deal with three sets of laws—international law, United States law, and the domestic law of the foreign country in which the firm operates. In this chapter, the focus is on international commercial law and U.S. law. While the domestic legal codes of countries around the world are important, they are too many and too diverse to be considered in this chapter.

International Commercial Law

What is international commercial law? International commercial law is the product of the consensus among trading nations that culminated in various unilateral, bilateral, and multilateral government accords and voluntary nongovernment agreements.

Enforcing International Law

Bear in mind that nations pass laws. If a business residing in a nation fails to comply with that country's law, a whole system exists to *force* the company to comply with the law. If a person violates a government's criminal law, the police and other law enforcement agencies may arrest him or her, and the prosecutor will bring charges in court. A court may impose a jail term and/or a fine to punish the guilty party. The government, or private individuals, may bring a civil suit to compel a person to act in compliance with the law.

But without some form of enforcement mechanism, how may anyone force governments and businesses to abide by international accords? Nations may enter into agreements whereby they consent to be governed by some international rule, but even this does not assure that people will abide by it. A good example of this issue concerns the General Agreement on Tariffs and Trade (GATT)—a treaty discussed later in this chapter. After the United States government ratified this agreement in 1994, President Clinton—rather than resolving a dispute over automobiles with Japan in accordance with the provisions of GATT—chose instead to privately negotiate a settlement with the Japanese government. This suggests that nations may agree to abide by international agreements, but they may or may not comply with them in the final analysis if the agreements do not serve the needs of their countries. History is littered with broken promises. Even the United States broke many treaties with Native Americans in order to accommodate the wishes of the tidal wave of European immigrants who came to America in search of inexpensive land.

In spite of such lapses, nations do enter into treaties with other nations, and most often they comply with the provisions of these accords.

The Sources of International Commercial Law

Where may people find the sources of international law? The most important source of international law may be found in treaties signed between nations. A *treaty* is an agreement between two or more nations that is binding on the nations and must be performed by them in good faith. In the case of the United States, Article II, Section 2, of the United States Constitution permits the President to negotiate a treaty, which then becomes the supreme law of the United States if two-thirds of the members of the United States Senate ratify the treaty.

The Managerial Perspective, "U.S. Kidnaps Mexican Citizen," discusses the interpretation of a treaty entered into between the United States and Mexico.

GENERAL AGREEMENT ON TARIFFS AND TRADE

One of the most important treaties signed by the United States in this century is the General Agreement on Tariffs and Trade (GATT). One of its most important features is the reduction of tariffs imposed by countries on imported goods.

■ Tariffs

When a country wishes to restrict the flow of goods from other nations, it imposes a tax—called a *tariff*—on these imported goods

managerial perspective

U.S. Kidnaps Mexican Citizen
Humberto Alvarez-Machain is a citizen and a resident of Mexico. He was indicted for the kidnapping and murder of a U.S. Drug Enforcement Administration (DEA) special agent. On April 2, 1980, Alvarez-Machain was forcibly kidnapped from his medical office in Guadalajara, Mexico, and flown by private plane to El Paso, Texas, where he was arrested by DEA officials. The DEA was responsible for his abduction.

The United States and Mexico had previously signed an extradition treaty. This treaty provided that neither country was obligated to deliver its own nationals to the other party, but one country's executive authority may extradite a person at the request of the other country. The United States Supreme Court read the treaty as not specifying the only way in which one country may gain custody of a person in another country for the purposes of prosecution. The language of the treaty does not support the argument that the treaty prohibits abductions outside of its terms. The Court therefore held the abduction of Alvarez-Machain from Mexico to be lawful under the terms of the treaty with Mexico.

Source: United States v. Alvarez-Machain *(United States Supreme Court, 112 S.Ct. 2188 1992).*

but not on domestic goods of the same nature. Tariffs raise the price of imported products, and thus discourage consumption of imports. Importers frequently question the manner in which the government classifies an item being imported. Products may be classified in various ways. Importers are likely to argue that the goods in question should be classified in the manner that will result in the lowest possible tax. Consider the Thought Problem, "Are Rakes Horticultural Tools?", regarding this issue.

thought problem

Are Rakes Horticultural Tools?
James S. Baker Imports argued that two importations of lawn rakes manufactured in Japan should not be classified as *rakes, other* under the United States Tariff Schedules. This classification was subject to an assessment of duty at the rate of fifteen percent. Baker argued that the rakes in question should instead be classified as *agricultural or horticultural tools*, and thus subject to a duty at the rate of only 7.5 percent. The United States argued that the term *horticultural* does not embrace those tools used on the lawn, since the caring for and growing of a lawn is not a horticultural pursuit. The dictionary definition of horticulture is the cultivation of a garden, orchard, or nursery; the cultivation of flowers, fruits, vegetables, or ornamental plants. Should the court rule that the rakes in question were subject to the lower tax?

Source: James S. Baker (Imports) v. United States, *292 F. Supp. 1014 (United States Customs Court, Second Division, November 19, 1968).*

■ *General Agreement on Tariffs and Trade (GATT)*
The first real progress toward global agreement on tariffs came at the end of World War II. In 1947, the United States and twenty-two other nations completed negotiations on the GATT. Today, more than a

hundred nations are members of this organization. The ultimate goal of the GATT is to reduce tariffs and nontariff trade barriers. The GATT has evolved into a complex framework for regulating trade since it monitors the flow of thousands of products.

In every country, vested interests try to protect domestic businesses or industries from foreign competition. People fear that more efficient producers abroad may succeed in either lowering their profit margins or actually driving them out of business. Recall from Chapter 18 on the antitrust laws that the Standard Oil Trust was such an efficient operator that it could produce kerosene in the United States, ship it to Europe, and still make a profit.

Calls to protect domestic producers sometimes get out of hand, as was the case with the passage of the Tariff Act of 1930—otherwise known as the Smoot-Hawley Tariff. This law raised the taxes on goods imported to the United States to the highest level in history in an attempt to protect domestic producers. The Smoot-Hawley Tariff made it extremely difficult for businesses in other countries to profitably ship goods to the United States for sale. Countries that could not sell goods to the United States found it difficult to repay the debts they owed to Americans.

Other nations, unsurprisingly, responded in kind by passing restrictive tariffs that made it difficult for U.S. businesses to export their goods. The total effect of these protectionist laws was to dramatically reduce global trading, thus arguably increasing the length and severity of the Great Depression of the 1930s.

■ World Trade Organization (WTO)

In order to even further reduce trade barriers between nations, particularly pertaining to services and intellectual property such as patents and copyrights, more than a hundred nations entered into further negotiations in the 1980s to revise GATT, and they came up with a new agreement in 1994. Effective in 1995, the World Trade Organization replaced the organization that previously issued rulings on the GATT. The WTO has greater powers to resolve disputes. Nations now bring trade disputes before the World Trade Organization. If the WTO fails to resolve the disagreement within sixty days, the dispute goes to a panel of trade experts. GATT permits the parties to appeal the decision of the trade experts to an appellate body whose decision is final and binding.

NONTARIFF TRADE BARRIERS

While a nation may attempt to protect industries within its borders by imposing stiff tariffs on imported goods, it may use other means to accomplish the same goal.

■ Quotas

Countries often use *quotas* to limit the flow of imported goods. A quota stipulates that only a certain amount of a good will be allowed to enter the country during a given period of time. Sometimes, by paying a special tax, an importer may be able to import an additional amount of goods in question above that specified by the quota. For example, the United States—in order to protect the domestic automobile industry—could adopt a quota of one million foreign automobiles each year. If this happens, domestic automakers may be tempted to lift the price of their goods.

■ Domestic Content Laws

Frequently used by countries, *domestic content laws* require that a certain percentage of a good's value be produced in the domestic economy. If a country passes such a law, a foreign firm may be forced to build a plant in that nation as opposed to importing goods made elsewhere.

■ Voluntary Restraint Agreements

Voluntary restraint agreements are informal, nonbinding constraints on the foreign producer. For example, Japan has agreed to limit its car exports to the United States.

■ Domestic Investment Restrictions

Domestic investment restrictions often require that a certain portion of a business be domestically owned. Certain industries may be totally closed to foreigners.

Nontariff restraints and tariffs arguably hurt consumers in the country with such restraints. For example, Japan protects its farmers who grow rice in Japan. Many Japanese consumers eat rice, but they must pay an artificially high price for it because Japan insulates the rice producers from foreign competition. One may argue that if a foreign company may produce an item more efficiently than domestic producers, the domestic producers should get out of that business. Generally, few inefficient companies accept this argument, and they prefer to resort to some form of protection from competition such as the tariff.

Legal Disputes with Foreign Governments

In order to maintain good relationships among nations, a number of legal rules have been developed. These rules are premised on the assumption that a nation ought to be able to control activities *within its borders,* and that other nations should honor these decisions.

SOVEREIGN IMMUNITY DOCTRINE

Should the decision of a foreign nation be honored by United States courts? At one time, the sovereign immunity doctrine offered foreign governments complete immunity from lawsuits. Today, the Foreign Sovereign Immunities Act distinguishes between governmental acts and private commercial acts. The act immunizes foreign governments from suit when they act in a governmental capacity. For example, if the government of Brazil chooses to send a particular diplomat to the United States to represent Brazil, U.S. courts cannot review the wisdom of this decision.

On the other hand, a foreign government that engages in commercial activity in the United States, or whose commercial activities have a direct effect in the United States, must submit to the jurisdiction of U.S. courts. Suppose that the Brazilian government decided to produce and sell cars to people living in the United States. Brazil would be acting in a commercial, rather than a governmental manner. Since Brazil would be engaging in commercial activities in the United States, its actions could be reviewed by U.S. courts.

The *Martin v. Republic of South Africa* case deals with the Foreign Sovereign Immunities Act. The court dismissed a suit filed in the United States against the Republic of South Africa.

Martin v. Republic of South Africa

United States Court of Appeals, Second Circuit
836 F.2d 91 (1987)

Barry J. Martin is a U.S. citizen. While travelling with a dance group in South Africa, he was a passenger in a car involved in an accident. After the accident, an ambulance from the Transvaal Department of Hospital Services (a service owned and operated by the Republic of South Africa) arrived at the scene of the accident and transported the driver of the car to the Paul Kruger Hospital run by the South African government, where he was treated.

Martin was left at the scene of the accident, allegedly because he was black. Eventually Martin was transported by private automobile to the Paul Kruger Hospital and allegedly was forced to walk into the hospital, where he waited several hours expecting to receive medical care. Martin never received medical treatment at the Paul Kruger Hospital, but instead was transported to the H. F. Verwoerd Hospital (also run by the South African government), sixty-five miles away. Upon arriving at the hospital, he was diagnosed as quadriplegic. After more than twenty-four hours at this hospital, he received medical treatment for the first time, but only after being granted "honorary White status."

Upon his return to the United States, Martin sued the Republic of South Africa and the hospitals in question for his injuries sustained in South Africa. The critical issue was whether or not South Africa's conduct caused "a direct effect in the United States" with the meaning of the Foreign Sovereign Immunities Act. The district court and the court of appeals ruled for the government of South Africa.

Timbers, Circuit Judge

For there to be original jurisdiction, the claim against the foreign state must fall within an exception to the basic premise, set forth in 28 U.S.C. § 1604 (1982), that foreign states generally are immune from the jurisdiction of federal and state courts.

The specific exception involved on this appeal is 28 U.S.C. § 1605(a)(2) (1982), which provides in relevant part:

(a) A foreign state shall not be immune from the jurisdiction of courts of the United States or of the States in any case—

(2) in which an action is based . . . upon an act outside the territory of the United States in connection with a commercial activity of the foreign state elsewhere and that act causes a direct effect in the United States[.]

The focus of our inquiry is to determine whether the appellees' acts caused a "direct effect in the United States" within the meaning of § 1605(a)(2), i.e., whether the effect was sufficiently "direct" and sufficiently "in the United States" to support the claim of the foreign state to sovereign immunity.

Appellant here asserts that, where South Africa's activities have caused a citizen to return to the United States permanently disabled, the foreign state has caused a "direct effect in the United States." We disagree.

Our holding on the issue raised on this appeal conforms with the holdings of all courts that have considered a claim for *personal injuries* sustained in a foreign state when the plaintiff asserted that the "direct effect in the United States" was the continued physical suffering and consequential damages that persisted once the plaintiff returned.

We hold that South Africa's acts did not have a "direct effect in the United States" within the meaning of § 1605 (a)(2) of the FSIA, and that the district court therefore correctly dismissed the complaint for lack of subject matter jurisdiction.

The Thought Problem, "Can Engineer Sue Saudi Arabia?", concerns the activities of the Kingdom of Saudi Arabia.

thought problem

Can Engineer Sue Saudi Arabia?

The Kingdom of Saudi Arabia owns and operates a hospital in Riyadh, as well as Royspec Purchasing Services—the hospital's purchasing agent in the United States. The Hospital Corporation of America recruited Nelson for a position as a monitoring systems engineer at the hospital. Nelson signed an employment agreement and attended an orientation session in the United States. In December 1983, he went to Saudi Arabia to work in the hospital. In March 1984, he discovered safety defects in the hospital's oxygen and nitrous oxide lines that posed fire hazards. He reported these defects. Hospital officials instructed Nelson to ignore the problems.

Nelson alleged that in September 1984, agents of the Saudi Arabian government arrested him. He further alleged that government agents transported him to jail where he was shackled, tortured, beaten, and deprived of food for four days. After thirty-nine days in jail, a United States Senator obtained his release from jail, and he was permitted to leave the country.

Is it possible for Nelson to file an action in the United States for the personal injuries he sustained while in custody in Saudi Arabia?

Source: Saudi Arabia v. Nelson (United States Supreme Court, 113 S.Ct. 1471 1993).

ACT OF STATE DOCTRINE

The Act of State Doctrine requires nations to respect the independence of foreign governments. Courts in one country are not to hear cases that deal with the acts of a government *within its own territory.* This doctrine strikes a balance between the three branches of U.S. government. It reflects the thinking that the executive branch of government ought to be in control of foreign policy matters. If the courts in one nation were to intervene in such disputes, then their actions could interfere with the attempts of the executive branch of government to resolve these matters.

The Act of State Doctrine no longer grants blanket immunity to foreign governments. This doctrine provides a defense to a nation engaging in an act to promote the public interest. For example, if a country nationalizes foreign firms in the oil industry, and it was in the public interest to do so, U.S. courts do not have the power to review the action of the foreign country *within its own territory.*

As with the Sovereign Immunity Doctrine, the law recognizes a commercial exception to the Act of State Doctrine. In *Alfred Dunhill of London, Inc. v. Republic of Cuba* (1976), the Court ruled that the concept of the Act of State Doctrine should not be extended to include the repudiation of a purely commercial obligation by a foreign sovereign. For example, if the German government sold bonds in the United States and subsequently defaulted on the bonds, it could not avail itself of the Act of State Doctrine to prevent lawsuits.

The International Perspective, "OPEC Price Fixing," deals with the actions of the Organization of Petroleum Exporting Countries (OPEC).

The Act of State Doctrine often arises in cases dealing with the expropriation of property. *Expropriation* may be broken into two separate issues— the right to take property and the right to compensation. While the right to take property is anchored in both domestic and international law, no international agreement exists as to what constitutes adequate compensation or when it should be paid. When a foreign government seizes the property owned by American citizens in a foreign country, the Act of State Doctrine may prevent them from suing in the United States.

INTERNATIONAL PERSPECTIVE

OPEC Price Fixing

OPEC is an organization of petroleum-producing and exporting nations. It was formed in 1960 by Iran, Iraq, Kuwait, Saudi Arabia, and Venezuela. Prior to the formation of OPEC, these countries were plagued with fluctuating oil prices. The absence of coordination among them resulted in an oversupply of oil on the world market and low oil prices. After the formation of OPEC, the price of crude oil increased more than tenfold. The International Association of Machinists (IAM) filed suit in the United States against the Organization of Petroleum Exporting Countries. IAM argued that the actions of OPEC constituted price fixing in violation of the U.S. antitrust laws.

The United States Supreme Court noted that the Act of State Doctrine prevents U.S. courts from getting involved in politically sensitive disputes that would require them to judge the legality of the act of a foreign state. Because the United States needs to operate consistent with a deliberate foreign policy developed in consideration of competing economic and political considerations, the courts should not get involved in such cases.

Because the IAM suit would interfere with the efforts of the political branches of government, the Court held that the courts should not become involved in this case.

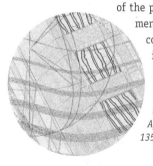

Source: International Association of Machinists v. OPEC *(United States Court of Appeals, Ninth Circuit, 649 F.2d 1354 1981).*

SETTLEMENT OF DISPUTES

Treaties do not always exist to guide nations in the resolution of a dispute, therefore a commercial enterprise may choose to file suit in a U.S. court against a foreign country. Because such a case involves a foreign nation, it may entail political, as well as financial, considerations. Such suits may create tension with foreign countries. For this reason, the law gives the President the power to settle the claims of U.S. citizens and a foreign government in order to minimize the tension between the U.S. and the foreign government.

Consider the International Perspective, "Iran Takes Americans Hostage," which deals with this issue.

Activities by American Companies Overseas

CONTRACTUAL PROBLEMS

■ Choice of Law Clause

Often in international contracts, the parties insert a **choice of law clause.** By inserting such a clause, the parties determine the governing law of the contract. For example, the agreement may stipulate English law or the law of the state of New York. New York State law rather than American law is specified because the laws of the fifty states differ.

Common law countries, such as the United States and Great Britain, will usually respect the right of the parties to choose the governing law of the contract. If the clause stipulates English law, American courts will normally apply English law and vice versa. Civil law countries, such as Germany and France, show less respect for the parties' right to contract and may uphold a choice of law clause only if the contract or the parties bear some connection to the chosen law. Certain Latin American nations—also civil law countries—ignore choice of law clauses completely and apply their own laws to contracts that are performed in their countries.

■ Choice of Forum Clause

A **choice of forum clause** determines the location of the court or arbitration proceeding. An agreement that stipulates arbitration in London or New York implicitly means that English or New York courts will have jurisdiction in proceedings to compel arbitration or enforce arbitral awards. The United States Supreme Court ruled in *The Bremen v. Zapata* (1972) that "the forum clause should control absent a strong showing that it should be set aside. . . ." Thus, the more reasonable a choice of forum clause is, the more likely it is that the courts will uphold the clause in the United States.

ARBITRATION

A clause in a contract may specify that all disputes concerning the contract will be settled by means of arbitration. Usually, arbitration is preferred to litigation because it circumvents several problems associated with litigation—for example, a tremendous backlog of cases may be before the court, causing long delays.

Iran Takes Americans Hostage

Iran took American citizens hostage. On January 19, 1981, Iran released the hostages in accordance with an agreement negotiated by former President Carter. The agreement provided that all litigation brought by American citizens against Iran would be terminated, and their claims would be resolved through binding arbitration.

Charles T. Main International, an engineering firm, brought an action to recover payment for services rendered in connection with Iranian electrification projects. It argued that the President exceeded his constitutionally granted powers in negotiating this agreement with Iran.

The court examining this case noted that international agreements settling claims by nationals of one country against the government of another country are an established international practice. It is generally accepted that the President possesses the power, in times of crisis, to settle such claims. The President needs the flexibility to diffuse an international crisis in order to prevent a crisis from escalating into war.

The court found that the President acted to resolve what was indisputably a major crisis in the relations of the United States. His settlement of this and other claims was necessary to resolve a dispute between the United States and Iran. Therefore, the court dismissed the suit brought by Charles T. Main International.

Source: Charles T. Main International v. Khuzestan Water and Power Authority *(United States Court of Appeals, First Circuit, 651 F.2d 800 1981).*

Ideally, an arbitration clause includes exclusive remedies for all issues so that litigation is completely avoided. In addition, all parties should relinquish the right to pursue the matter in the courts. A single arbitrator is generally best. If one party is domiciled in a common law country and the other in a civil law country, the right to engage in discovery should be included, since civil law codes do not always allow for discovery. The location of the proceeding is extremely important, since local law may determine the applicable procedure and substantive law. An arbitral body, such as the American Arbitration Association, United Nations Committee on International Trade Law, or International Chamber of Commerce, should be stipulated. "Ad hoc" arbitration is also a possibility. In this case, the arbitration is administered according to the exact specifications of the parties without regard to any institutional framework.

The International Chamber of Commerce is the oldest international arbitral institution and has established rules and procedures for the arbitration process.

Courts worldwide will usually enforce the orders of arbitrators and judgment awards, even though the arbitration agreement prevents the courts from judging the merits. For the parties to obtain the maximum benefit from arbitration, they must construct an arbitration agreement in advance and with great attention to detail, since this will reduce conflicts and expedite the arbitration process.

Mitsubishi Motors Corporation v. Soler Chrysler-Plymouth, Inc., is a United States Supreme Court case dealing with the enforceability of agreements to arbitrate.

Mitsubishi Motors Corporation v. Soler Chrysler-Plymouth, Inc.

United States Supreme Court
105 S.Ct. 3346 (1985)

Mitsubishi entered into a contract with Soler Chrysler-Plymouth, Inc. The contract required arbitration by the Japan Commercial Arbitration Association of all disputes arising with respect to the contract. A dispute arose between the parties, and Mitsubishi brought suit in federal court under the federal Arbitration Act and the Convention on the Recognition and Enforcement of Foreign Arbitral Awards seeking an order to compel arbitration. Soler Chrysler-Plymouth, Inc., counterclaimed that Mitsubishi had violated the Sherman Act. The court of appeals ruled that Soler Chrysler-Plymouth, Inc., could not be forced to arbitrate its antitrust claim. The United States Supreme Court reversed.

Justice Blackmun

As in *Scherk v. Alberto-Culver Co.*, we conclude that concerns of international comity, respect for the capacities of foreign and transnational tribunals, and sensitivity to the need of the international commercial system for predictability in the resolution of disputes require that we enforce the parties' agreement, even assuming that a contrary result would be forthcoming in a domestic context.

Even before Scherk, this Court had recognized the utility of forum-selection clauses in international transactions. Scherk establishes a strong presumption in favor of enforcement of freely negotiated contractual choice-of-forum provisions. Here, as in Scherk, that presumption is reinforced by the emphatic federal policy in favor of arbitral dispute resolution. And at least since this Nation's accession in

1970 to the Convention, and the implementation of the Convention in the same year by amendment of the federal Arbitration Act, that federal policy applies with special force in the field of international commerce.

There is no reason to assume at the outset of the dispute that international arbitration will not provide an adequate mechanism. To be sure, the international arbitral tribunal owes no prior allegiance to the legal norms of particular states; hence, it has no direct obligation to vindicate their statutory dictates. The tribunal, however, is bound to effectuate the intentions of the parties. Where the parties have agreed that the arbitral body is to decide a defined set of claims which includes, as in these cases, those arising from the application of American antitrust law, the tribunal therefore should be bound to decide that dispute in accord with the national law giving rise to the claim.

Having permitted the arbitration to go forward, the national courts of the United States will have the opportunity at the award enforcement stage to ensure that the legitimate interest in the enforcement of the antitrust laws has been addressed. The Convention reserves to each signatory country the right to refuse enforcement of an award where the recognition or enforcement of the award would be contrary to the public policy of that country. While the efficacy of the arbitral process requires that substantive review at the award-enforcement stage remain minimal, it would not require intrusive inquiry to ascertain that the tribunal took cognizance of the antitrust claims and actually decided them.

Accordingly, we require this representative of the American business community to honor its bargain, by holding this agreement to arbitrate enforceable . . . in accord with the explicit provisions of the Arbitration Act.

FOREIGN CORRUPT PRACTICES ACT

When buying or selling goods or services abroad, a businessperson may encounter someone who insists on a bribe as a condition to engaging in a business transaction. Should an American company give such a bribe? The following material suggests that giving a bribe likely is unlawful.

The law in this area came about when former President Nixon became ensnared in the Watergate coverup and found himself forced to leave office in disgrace. In the course of investigating the activities of the President, it became clear that many companies, when operating abroad, engaged in the practice of bribing foreign officials. Many people in the United States thought that companies should not be corrupting foreign officials. In response to public opinion Congress, in 1977, passed the Foreign Corrupt Practices Act in an attempt to curb questionable payments made by businesses to foreign officials. In passing this act, congresspeople and senators voiced their concern over the fact that information being supplied to the Securities and Exchange Commission and to corporate shareholders contained false information. Corporations were not disclosing information relating to payoffs made in foreign countries; therefore, the financial information supplied to the public by these corporations was not totally accurate. Members of Congress also worried that bribery of foreigners by U.S. corporations may adversely affect our relationship with other countries.

This act makes it unlawful for a business or individual to offer to pay a foreign official anything of value for the purpose of obtaining or retaining business. The principle issue is whether or not the payment was made with the intent of causing a foreign official to misuse his or her official position in order to obtain business.

Furthermore, it is improper to pay an intermediary *while knowing* that any portion of the payment will be used as a bribe. This latter provision actually decreased the severity of the prior law. Businesses expressed concern that the prior law made them liable even if they had reason to know that a payment may be used as a bribe. Now, it must be established that the business, in fact, knew that the payment would be used as a bribe.

The act contains several exceptions. Grease payments may be made to ministerial or clerical workers to get them to perform their jobs. For example, if a clerk is required to give a business a permit, but is rather slow at doing this, a business may make a payment to encourage the clerk to do the job. In such an instance, a business is not getting anything that it is not entitled to anyway. Another exception deals with payments that are lawful under the written laws of the foreign country.

Consider the Ethical Perspective, "Bribery to Obtain Business," which deals with the issue of bribery.

ETHICAL PERSPECTIVE

Bribery to Obtain Business

Bribery has taken place in many countries for centuries. In Mexico, it is called the *mordida;* in Egypt, it is referred to as the *baksheesh.* The fact is—in order to conduct business in many places around the world, some form of payment must be made in order to get business. The Foreign Corrupt Practices Act puts American firms at a competitive disadvantage, because their counterparts around the world are not similarly restrained by such a statute.

Suppose that your firm, an American company, is bidding on a construction project in Russia. A government official informs you that he intends to give the bid to the business that provides him with the largest bribe. You learn that members of a German firm have, in fact, offered a bribe to the official. In light of the fact that the Foreign Corrupt Practices Act prohibits such an activity, could you ethically give him a kickback in order to get the contract?

EXTRATERRITORIAL APPLICATION OF U.S. LAWS

From time to time, Congress has attempted to extend the reach of U.S. law beyond the borders of the United States. For example, the Civil Rights Act of 1991 extended the protection of Title VII of the 1964 Civil Rights Act and the Americans with Disabilities Act to American citizens employed in foreign countries by U.S. employers. When a U.S. company operates in a foreign country, it should be alert to the possibility that it may be required to abide by U.S. law even though it is on foreign soil.

Summary

People have traded goods and services since ancient times. Dramatic advances in technology and communications now permit businesses to operate throughout the world. People in business need an awareness of international commercial law. International commercial law is the product of the consensus among trading nations that culminated in various government accords and voluntary nongovernment agreements.

Since World War II, governments around the world have been gradually eliminating barriers to free trade. One of the biggest barriers to the free flow of goods are tariffs. Tariffs are taxes placed on imported goods but not on domestic goods. To help achieve the goal of reducing tariffs, a number of nations have entered into an agreement called the General Agreement on Tariffs and Trade (GATT). The World Trade Organization (WTO) now operates pursuant to this agreement to resolve disputes between nations.

When a business tries to sue a foreign government, it frequently finds that U.S. courts lack jurisdiction over the case because of the Sovereign Immunity Doctrine and the Act of State Doctrine. Sometimes courts will hear a dispute involving a foreign government if the government was involved in commercial—as opposed to governmental—activities. The President of the United States, in certain cases, may enter into an agreement with a foreign nation settling suits of U.S. citizens against a foreign government.

American companies operating abroad need to protect themselves in the event of a dispute. To protect their interests, businesses generally use certain clauses in their contracts, such as choice of law and choice of forum clauses. One clause that appears in most international contracts is an arbitration clause. Companies often prefer arbitration over litigation.

Businesses in America find themselves in an unusual situation if they attempt to engage in business abroad. Officials in many countries around the world expect a bribe as a condition of engaging in transactions with foreigners or even people living within the borders of their countries. The Foreign Corrupt Practices Act prohibits businesses from giving bribes to foreign officials in order to get business. This puts American businesses at a disadvantage because other countries do not have an act that is comparable to the Foreign Corrupt Practices Act.

The United States has been severely criticized by other countries for attempting to enforce certain laws, such as the U.S. antitrust laws, beyond the physical borders of our country. Foreign countries regard this as an infringement of their sovereignty.

Review Questions

1. Define the following terms:
   a. Choice of forum clause
   b. Choice of law clause
2. Why may arbitration be preferred to litigation?
3. What is the difference between the Act of State Doctrine and the Foreign Sovereign Immunities Act?
4. How does the doctrine of separation of powers relate to the Act of State Doctrine?
5. What possible alternatives are open to a business firm that wishes to make money in foreign countries?
6. Nigeria contracted to purchase huge quantities of Portland cement. It overbought and was unable to accept delivery of the cement because its harbors became clogged with ships waiting to unload. It repudiated its contracts. When sued in the United States, it asserted the Sovereign Immunity Doctrine as defense. Will Nigeria prevail on this defense?

7. Allied Bank made loans to three Costa Rican banks. The Costa Rican banks executed promissory notes for the amounts in question to Allied Bank. Several years later, the Costa Rican government issued a law preventing any institution in Costa Rica from paying any external debt. Allied Bank brought suit in the United States against these Costa Rican banks. The banks raised as defenses the Sovereign Immunity Doctrine and the Act of State Doctrine. Will the Costa Rican banks prevail on any of these arguments?

8. An agency of the Mexican government, Pemex, was conducting mineral exploration in the Bay of Campeche. Zernicek, an employee of an American company hired by Pemex to perform certain work, was exposed to excessive doses of radiation as a result of the negligence of Pemex. After returning to the United States, Zernicek became ill. He filed suit in the United States against Pemex. Pemex alleges that it cannot be sued because of the Foreign Sovereign Immunities Act. Zernicek alleged that his injury constituted a "direct effect in the United States" such that it came within the commercial activities exception to the Foreign Sovereign Immunities Act. Is Zernicek correct?

9. The U.S. government wishes to punish Mendez for activities he engaged in while living in his own country—Spain. An extradition treaty exists between Spain and the United States. May U.S. officials kidnap Mendez from Spain and try him in the United States?

10. ABC Corporation wants to import some fabrics into Russia. A clerk performing essentially ministerial functions insists on receiving $100 before permitting ABC Corporation's fabrics to enter the country. May ABC Corporation lawfully pay the clerk a bribe? What if, instead, a high-ranking governmental official insisted on receiving $1,000 as a bribe in return for the Russian government's purchase of ABC Corporation's fabrics? Could ABC Corporation lawfully pay this official the money?

Appendix A
Where to Find the Law

It takes a considerable amount of time to become highly proficient in legal research. The first time you try to locate something generally takes the most time, but the whole process becomes easier with practice.

In order to locate material, one generally needs to know how it is categorized. You may get a very good feel for many of the categories of law by examining the Table of Contents of this text. For example, suppose a person received a serious injury while riding in a defective vehicle. Such a case concerns an issue related to the law of products liability.

In the course of performing their jobs, many nonlawyers find it necessary to keep abreast of some area of law. Jobs often require employees to keep learning about the law even after graduating from school. For example, an engineer may need to know about developments in environmental law in order to make certain the work performed by the engineer complies with the requirements of the law. People in bank trust departments, human resource departments, tax accountants, and a host of other people regularly consult legal publications. Some of these people develop a genuine expertise in an area of law due to their daily contact with certain types of business problems.

Many nonlegal sources provide valuable information about changes in the law. The daily newspaper in your city likely discusses major United States Supreme Court cases, state supreme court cases, and new federal and state laws. *The Wall Street Journal, Business Week, The New York Times, Newsweek,* and *Time* all provide updates on the law. Most companies receive trade publications from their trade associations. These publications contain information on legal developments of interest to people in that line of business. Many businesspeople receive newsletters written expressly for their industry. One may even consult scholarly publications, such as *The Harvard Business Review.* All of these sources help keep the business community informed about the law.

Attorneys also rely on other publications, such as *The American Bar Association Journal, The National Law Journal,* or *U.S. Law Week.* Attorneys receive updates from other sources such as newsletters that keep them posted on changes in the law.

The sources listed next all may be located in the typical university law school law library. One may also often find some of them in the main public library in your city. Large law firms, major corporations, and the state legislatures all have extensive legal libraries as do many county bar associations. It may be possible to use these sources simply by asking for permission.

CONSTITUTIONAL LAW

All laws in America must conform to the provisions of the United States Constitution (except treaties negotiated by the President and ratified by the Senate). The text of the Constitution of the United States of America appears in Appendix B. One could also find the Constitution, as well as cases that have interpreted the Constitution, by looking at the *United States Code Annotated* or the *United States Code Service*—both of which are discussed in the following material.

All state laws must comply with the provisions of the United States Constitution as well as the state's constitution. For example, a law passed by the California legislature must comply with both the provisions of the U.S. Constitution and the California Constitution. One may locate a state constitution in the same books in which one finds the state statutes.

FEDERAL STATUTORY LAW

One of the most important areas of law today is statutory law—laws enacted by the United States Congress and by state legislatures. Cities and towns also possess the power to pass statutory laws, which are called ordinances. Laws passed by Congress occupy a very important place in American law.

A member of Congress initially proposes a bill. If both houses of Congress adopt this bill and the President of the United States signs the bill (which is generally required), it then becomes law. This law is published in several places. All of the laws passed at the end of a session of Congress are published in chronological order in the *United States Statutes at Law.*

Generally, practicing attorneys try to locate the text of a law in a more user-friendly publication, the *United States Code,* published by the U.S. government. The *United States Code* is arranged by title, and each title has been given a number. For example, the Sherman Antitrust Act is found in Title 15—"Commerce and Trade." Titles in turn are subdivided into sections. Attorneys refer to a federal statute by title and section number: 15 U.S.C. 1 thus refers to a statute that may be found in Title 15 in subsection 1. Attorneys generally do not own the *United States Code* but instead own an unofficial version of it such as the *United States Code Annotated* (published by West Publishing Company) or the *United States Code Service, Lawyers' Edition* (published by Lawyers Co-Operative Publishing Company). Both of these unofficial sources contain additional useful information such as references to cases that have involved the particular federal statute one is examining and other relevant publications by the same publisher.

FEDERAL ADMINISTRATIVE REGULATIONS

Students sometimes confuse the difference between laws passed by Congress—called statutes—and rules passed by federal agencies—called government regulations. Agencies cannot simply create law. All federal agencies must act pursuant to a grant of authority to these agencies contained in a federal statute. Federal agencies only have the power to create regulations governing a certain area of the law designated by Congress.

Federal administrative regulations must first be published in the *Federal Register* to be effective. In order to locate such an administrative regulation, it is easiest to consult the *Code of Federal Regulations*. Just as the *United States Code* is organized by title and section number, the *Code of Federal Regulations* is organized into fifty titles and rules within each title are given section numbers. For example, a reference to the rules relating to the apprehension of aliens may be found in 8 C.F.R. 242.2 *et seq.* The Immigration and Naturalization Service's rule thus may be found in Section 242.2 of Title 8. Title 8 deals with aliens and nationality. *Et seq.* refers to all of the sections that relate to the cited section and which follow the section number in sequence. All of the regulations issued by an agency may be found in the *Code of Federal Regulations*.

STATE STATUTES

Much of the law in America appears in the form of state statutes. Just as at the federal level of government, a member of a state legislature must propose a bill. If both houses pass the bill and the governor signs the bill (the governor generally must sign a bill), the bill becomes law. State laws passed each session of the legislature generally are published in books called *session laws* which are published in chronological order like the federal *Statutes at Large*.

These statutes have been rearranged in more user-friendly publications often referred to as *codes* or *revised statutes* or the like. These are published by state governments or by private publishers. State codes frequently are annotated—that is, they contain additional information such as references to cases that have involved the respective statutory provisions. One needs to consult the particular publication to see how the material is arranged and supplemented.

FEDERAL CASES

Three important federal courts exist—the federal trial courts (district courts), the federal courts of appeals, and the United States Supreme Court.

One may locate the decisions of the federal district courts in West Publishing Company's *Federal Supplement* (F. Supp.). In referring to (citing) a case lawyers generally state the name of the case, a volume number of the publication in which the case appears, the name of the publication in which it appears, the first page in the volume in which the case appears, and the date of the case. You could find the Powell case—*Powell v. National Football League*, 678 F. Supp. 777 (1988)—by looking in volume 678 of the *Federal Supplement*. The first page of the case will appear on page 777 of that volume. The case was decided in 1988.

If the parties appeal a case to a federal court of appeals, the citation to the case is very similar. All federal court of appeals cases appear in West Publishing Company's *Federal Reporter* (F. or F.2d). For example, the appeal of the Powell case appears in *Powell v. National Football League*, 888 F.2d 559 (1991). You could find the Powell case by looking in volume 888 of the *Federal Reporter*. The first page of the case will appear on page 559. The case was decided in 1991.

Note Figure A.1 which shows the thirteen federal judicial circuits, each of which has a court of appeals in it. It is not possible to appeal the decision of a federal trial court to any one of the thirteen courts of appeals listed in this figure that one desires. Decisions of federal trial courts located in a given state *must* be appealed to the court of appeals for the federal circuit indicated in this figure. For example, appeals relating to matters that arise in the District of Columbia go to the District of Columbia Circuit. The Court of Appeals for the Federal Circuit hears such appeals as those relating to patents and copyrights and other specialized matters. Decisions of the federal trial courts in Illinois must be appealed to the court of appeals for the seventh circuit, whereas decisions of the federal trial courts in California must be appealed to the court of appeals for the ninth circuit.

Sometimes the Supreme Court examines a case. Supreme Court cases appear in three different publications—the *United States Reports* (U.S.) published by the federal government, West Publishing Company's *Supreme Court Reporter* (S.Ct.), and the Lawyers' Co-Operative publication *Lawyers' Edition of the Supreme Court Reports* (L.Ed. or L.Ed.2d). Most attorneys generally use one of the latter two publications. Many of the cases in this text are decisions of the Supreme Court. One cites them in a similar fashion to that discussed earlier. The Socony-Vacuum Oil case appears in Chapter 18 of this textbook. Its citation is as follows: *United States v. Socony-Vacuum Oil Co.*, 310 U.S. 150 (1940). You could find this case by looking in volume 310 of the *United States Reports*. The

■ **FIGURE A.1** The Thirteen Federal Judicial Circuits

First Circuit *(Boston, Mass.)* Maine, Massachusetts, New Hampshire, Puerto Rico, Rhode Island

Second Circuit *(New York, N.Y.)* Connecticut, New York, Vermont

Third Circuit *(Philadelphia, Pa.)* Delaware, New Jersey, Pennsylvania, Virgin Islands

Fourth Circuit *(Richmond, Va.)* Maryland, North Carolina, South Carolina, Virginia, West Virginia

Fifth Circuit *(New Orleans, La.)* Louisiana, Mississippi, Texas

Sixth Circuit *(Cincinnati, Ohio)* Kentucky, Michigan, Ohio, Tennessee

Seventh Circuit *(Chicago, Ill.)* Illinois, Indiana, Wisconsin

Eighth Circuit *(St. Louis, Mo.)* Arkansas, Iowa, Minnesota, Missouri, Nebraska, North Dakota, South Dakota

Ninth Circuit *(San Francisco, Calif.)* Alaska, Arizona, California, Guam, Hawaii, Idaho, Montana, Nevada, Northern Mariana Islands, Oregon, Washington

Tenth Circuit *(Denver, Colo.)* Colorado, Kansas, New Mexico, Oklahoma, Utah, Wyoming

Eleventh Circuit *(Atlanta, Ga.)* Alabama, Florida, Georgia

District of Columbia Circuit *(Washington, D.C.)*

Federal Circuit *(Washington, D.C.)*

first page of the case will appear on page 150. The case was decided in 1940. Quite often a citation to a Supreme Court decision lists all three of these sources.

STATE CASES

State cases are an important source of the law. Most state trial court decisions have not been published. It is generally possible to find the decisions of state appellate courts. Many states publish their own cases. Some states do not.

Whether or not a state publishes its own appellate court decisions, a person looking for a state court decision may find that decision in one of the regional units of the *National Reporter System* (West Publishing Company). The *National Reporter System* publishes the state decisions as shown in Table A.1. For example, if one

wanted to locate a decision of the Kansas Supreme Court, one could find that in the *Pacific Reporter*. If one wanted to find a decision of the Missouri Supreme Court, it could be located in the *Southwestern Reporter*.

State court decisions are cited in much the same manner as federal court decisions. Consider the case *Parker v. Twentieth-Century Fox Film Corporation*. The citation on this case is: 474 P.2d 689 (1970). You may find the original version of this case in volume 474 of the *Pacific Reporter, Second*. (Older cases appear in the *Pacific Reporter*. More recent cases appear in the *Pacific Reporter, Second* series.)

FINDING THE LAW

A wide variety of approaches may be employed in finding the applicable law. Quite often a person wants more

■ **TABLE A.1** Regional Units of West Publishing Company's National Reporter System

ATLANTIC REPORTER

Connecticut	New Jersey
Delaware	Pennsylvania
Maine	Rhode Island
Maryland	Vermont
New Hampshire	

NORTHEASTERN REPORTER

Illinois	(New York)*
Indiana	Ohio
Massachusetts	

NORTHWESTERN REPORTER

Iowa	North Dakota
Michigan	South Dakota
Minnesota	Wisconsin
Nebraska	

PACIFIC REPORTER

Alaska	Nevada
Arizona	New Mexico
(California)*	Oklahoma
Colorado	Oregon
Hawaii	Utah
Idaho	Washington
Kansas	Wyoming
Montana	

SOUTHEASTERN REPORTER

Georgia	Virginia
North Carolina	West Virginia
South Carolina	

SOUTHERN REPORTER

Alabama	Louisiana
Florida	Mississippi

SOUTHWESTERN REPORTER

Arkansas	Tennessee
Kentucky	Texas
Missouri	

*Note: California and New York each have their own Reporter System.

than just the official publication. It is useful to look at some commentary on the law as well. Indeed this may lead to a better understanding of the law.

One source that a person with little familiarity with the law may want to examine is a legal encyclopedia. Legal encyclopedias cover all of the law of the United States. Consequently they have many volumes. The Lawyers Co-Operative Publishing Company publishes one such encyclopedia—*American Jurisprudence 2d (Am Jur.2d)*. By using the index or table of contents one may find a discussion of the law that governs the topic one wants to research. *Am Jur* also contains references to other useful sources such as the *American Law Reports*. ALR contains in-depth memoranda on the topics it covers.

A very useful source often utilized today by practicing attorneys is the treatise. Treatises are in-depth examinations of a particular area of law by experts in that field of law. In a treatise one will find references to all of the law—constitution, statutory, administrative, or case law—that relates to the topic dealt with by the treatise. For example, one of the authors of this textbook, John Gergacz, has written a treatise, *Attorney Corporate Client Privilege*, 2nd edition, which is published by Clark Boardman Callaghan.

For example, suppose that you wish to research a question relating to the law of the sale of goods. One may turn to the *Uniform Commercial Code Reporting Service*. This multivolume publication deals with all of the laws concerning the Uniform Commercial Code. The UCC deals with, among other topics, the law relating to the sale of goods. By examining the index or the table of contents it is possible to locate the information desired.

If a person has a particular topic in mind and wants a very high-quality discussion of that area of law, he or she may consider reading a law journal article. There are literally hundreds of law journals in America. Journals published by law schools are called *law reviews*. The authors of this text have written many law review articles. You may find law journal articles by examining the *Index to Legal Periodicals*. Suppose that you wanted to find an article dealing with whether or not a misrepresentation in an advertisement may be the basis of a products liability suit. By looking under the term "products liability" in the *Index to Legal Periodicals* one may find all of the law review articles relating to products liability. In your search you may come across an article written by one of the authors of this textbook: Douglas Whitman, *Reliance as an Element in Product Misrepresentation Suits: A Reconsideration*, 35 Southwestern Law Review 741–773 (1981). This citation means that you may find this article in volume 35 of the Southwestern Law Review (published by the Southern Methodist University School of Law). The articles appear on pages 741 to 773. It was published in 1981.

One final note should be made. Because the law changes, it is necessary to keep publications current. Soon after a hard-bound volume comes out, new cases, statutes, and regulations may make the information in the bound volume out of date. Rather than republishing a new hard-bound volume, publishers often issue a *pocket part* (an update on the law) on a quarterly or annual basis. In many of the sources you examine, you will find some material that supplements each hardbound volume. Sometimes this information is put at the back of a bound book—which is where the phrase *pocket parts* originated. In other cases publishers simply release a paperback supplement to each bound book. When you research the law, look for material that supplements the hardbound book. By examining this additional information your legal search will be more up to date.

COMPUTERIZED LEGAL RESEARCH

At one time it was necessary to be located near a large law library in order to have access to all of the materials useful to a person who wants to do legal research. While law schools still have certain publications that cannot be found elsewhere, the great bulk of the law today may be located simply by having access to either WESTLAW, operated by West Publishing Company, or LEXIS, owned by Thompson Publishing. Both of these provide comprehensive, online information service. All of the material discussed in the preceding material may be located in the databases for these services.

Many people searching for the law today use a computerized form of legal research because one may find the most current state of the law in these databases. LEXIS and WESTLAW put statutes, cases, and administrative regulations on their databases immediately after they are issued.

Both of these legal search systems require users to search only a portion of the entire database. A user must provide instructions to LEXIS and WESTLAW as to which of the many databases the user wants the computer to examine. Limiting the search in this manner makes it faster for the computer to find the desired information than if the computer had to search through the entire database.

Once a person has designated a particular database to be searched, the next step is to specify a search request. There are many ways to create a search request. A common method is to ask the computer to search for certain designated words. For example, if a person wants to see information on employment discrimination concerning women, one could ask the computer to search for documents in a designated database that contains the words "employment discrimination" and "women."

Once the computer locates a set of documents, the user may look at the citations retrieved, look at portions of the documents retrieved, or look at the entire text of each document located. If a person finds useful information, he or she may read the material while online or have the information printed for examination at a later date.

Hopefully, this information will be useful to you in your study of the law.

Appendix B
The Constitution of the United States of America

We the People of the United States, in Order to form a more perfect Union, establish Justice, insure domestic Tranquility, provide for the common defense, promote the general Welfare, and secure the Blessings of Liberty to ourselves and our Posterity, do ordain and establish this Constitution for the United States of America.

ARTICLE I

Section 1
All legislative Powers herein granted shall be vested in a Congress of the United States, which shall consist of a Senate and House of Representatives.

Section 2
The House of Representatives shall be composed of Members chosen every second Year by the People of the several States, and the Electors in each State shall have the Qualifications requisite for Electors of the most numerous Branch of the State Legislature.

No Person shall be a Representative who shall not have attained to the Age of twenty five Years, and been seven Years a Citizen of the United States, and who shall not, when elected, be an Inhabitant of that State in which he shall be chosen.

Representatives and direct Taxes shall be apportioned among the several States which may be included within this Union, according to their respective Numbers, which shall be determined by adding to the whole Number of free Persons, including those bound to Service for a Term of Years, and excluding Indians not taxed, three fifths of all other Persons. The actual Enumeration shall be made within three Years after the first Meeting of the Congress of the United States, and within every subsequent Term of ten Years, in such Manner as they shall by Law direct. The number of Representatives shall not exceed one for every thirty Thousand, but each State shall have at Least one Representative; and until such enumeration shall be made, the State of New Hampshire shall be entitled to chuse three, Massachusetts eight, Rhode Island and Providence Plantations one, Connecticut five, New-York six, New Jersey four, Pennsylvania eight, Delaware one, Maryland six, Virginia ten, North Carolina five, South Carolina five, and Georgia three.

When vacancies happen in the Representation from any State, the Executive Authority thereof shall issue Writs of Election to fill such vacancies.

The House of Representatives shall chuse their Speaker and other Officers; and shall have the sole Power of Impeachment.

Section 3
The Senate of the United States shall be composed of two Senators from each State, chosen by the Legislature thereof, for six Years; and each Senator shall have one Vote.

Immediately after they shall be assembled in Consequence of the first Election, they shall be divided as equally as may be into three Classes. The Seats of the Senators of the first Class shall be vacated at the Expiration of the second Year, of the second Class at the Expiration of the fourth Year, and of the third Class at the Expiration of the sixth Year, so that one third may be chosen every second Year; and if Vacancies happen by Resignation or otherwise, during the Recess of the Legislature of any State, the Executive thereof may make temporary Appointments until the next Meeting of the Legislature, which shall then fill such Vacancies.

No Person shall be a Senator who shall not have attained to the Age of thirty Years, and been nine Years a Citizen of the United States, and who shall not, when elected, be an Inhabitant of that State for which he shall be chosen.

The Vice President of the United States shall be President of the Senate, but shall have no Vote, unless they be equally divided.

The Senate shall chuse their other Officers, and also a President pro tempore, in the Absence of the Vice President, or when he shall exercise the Office of President of the United States.

The Senate shall have the sole power to try all Impeachments. When sitting for that Purpose, they shall be an Oath or Affirmation. When the President of the United States is tried, the Chief Justice shall preside: And no Person shall be convicted without the Concurrence of two thirds of the Members present.

Judgment in Cases of Impeachment shall not extend further than to removal from Office, and disqualification to hold and enjoy any Office of honor, Trust or Profit under the United States: but the Party convicted shall nevertheless be liable and subject to Indictment, Trial, Judgment and Punishment, according to Law.

Section 4

The Times, Places and Manner of holding Elections for Senators and Representatives, shall be prescribed in each State by the Legislature thereof: but the Congress may at any time by Law make or alter such Regulations, except as to the Places of chusing Senators.

The Congress shall assemble at least once in every Year, and such Meeting shall be on the first Monday in December, unless they shall by Law appoint a different Day.

Section 5

Each House shall be the Judge of the Elections, Returns and Qualifications of its own Members, and a Majority of each shall constitute a Quorum to do Business; but a smaller Number may adjourn from day to day, and may be authorized to compel the Attendance of absent Members, in such Manner, and under such Penalties as each House may provide.

Each House may determine the Rules of its Proceedings, punish its Members for disorderly Behaviour, and, with the Concurrence of two thirds, expel a Member.

Each House shall keep a Journal of its Proceedings, and from time to time publish the same, excepting such Parts as may in their Judgment require Secrecy; and the Yeas and Nays of the Members of either House on any question shall, at the Desire of one fifth of those Present, be entered on the Journal.

Neither House, during the Session of Congress, shall, without the Consent of the other, adjourn for more than three days, nor to any other Place than that in which the two Houses shall be sitting.

Section 6

The Senators and Representatives shall receive a Compensation for their Services, to be ascertained by Law, and paid out of the Treasury of the United States. They shall in all Cases, except Treason, Felony and Breach of the Peace, be privileged from Arrest during their Attendance at the Session of their respective Houses, and in going to and returning from the same; and for any Speech or Debate in either House, they shall not be questioned in any other Place.

No Senator or Representative shall, during the Time for which he was elected, be appointed to any civil Office under the Authority of the United States, which shall have been created, or the Emoluments whereof shall have been encreased during such time; and no Person holding any Office under the United States, shall be a Member of either House during his Continuance in Office.

Section 7

All Bills for raising Revenue shall originate in the House of Representatives; but the Senate may propose or concur with Amendments as on other Bills.

Every Bill which shall have passed the House of Representatives and the Senate, shall, before it become a Law, be presented to the President of the United States; if he approve he shall sign it, but if not he shall return it, with his Objections to that House in which it shall have originated, who shall enter the Objections at large on their Journal, and proceed to reconsider it. If after such Reconsideration two thirds of that House shall agree to pass the Bill, it shall be sent, together with the Objections, to the other House, by which it shall likewise be reconsidered, and if approved by two thirds of that House, it shall become a Law. But in all such Cases the Votes of both Houses shall be determined by Yeas and Nays, and the Names of the Persons voting for and against the Bill shall be entered on the Journal of each House respectively. If any Bill shall not be returned by the President within ten Days (Sundays excepted) after it shall have been presented to him, the Same shall be a Law, in like Manner as if he had signed it, unless the Congress by their Adjournment prevent its Return, in which Case it shall not be a Law.

Every Order, Resolution, or Vote to which the Concurrence of the Senate and House of Representatives may be necessary (except on a question of Adjournment) shall be presented to the President of the United States; and before the Same shall take Effect, shall be approved by him, or being disapproved by him, shall be repassed by two thirds of the Senate and House of Representatives, according to the Rules and Limitations prescribed in the Case of a Bill.

Section 8

The Congress shall have Power to lay and collect Taxes, Duties, Imposts and Excises, to pay the Debts and provide for the common Defence and general Welfare of the United States; but all Duties, Imposts and Excises shall be uniform throughout the United States;

To borrow Money on the credit of the United States;

To regulate Commerce with foreign Nations, and among the several States, and with the Indian Tribes;

To establish an uniform Rule of Naturalization, and uniform Laws on the subject of Bankruptcies throughout the United States;

To coin Money, regulate the Value thereof, and of foreign Coin, and fix the Standard of Weights and Measures;

To provide for the Punishment of counterfeiting the Securities and current Coin of the United States;

To establish Post Offices and post Roads;

To promote the Progress of Science and useful Arts, by securing for limited Times to Authors and Inventors the exclusive Right to their respective Writings and Discoveries;

To constitute Tribunals inferior to the supreme Court;

To define and punish Piracies and Felonies committed on the high Seas, and Offenses against the Law of Nations;

To declare War, grant Letters of Marque and Reprisal, and make Rules concerning Captures on Land and Water;

To raise and support Armies, but no Appropriation of Money to that Use shall be for a longer Term than two Years;

To provide and maintain a Navy;

To make Rules for the Government and Regulation of the land and naval Forces;

To provide for calling forth the Militia to execute the Laws of the Union, suppress Insurrections and repel Invasions;

To provide for organizing, arming, and disciplining, the Militia, and for governing such Part of them as may be employed in the Service of the United States, reserving to the States respectively, the Appointment of the Officers, and the Authority of training the Militia according to the discipline described b Congress;

To exercise exclusive Legislation in all Cases whatsoever, over such District (not exceeding ten Miles square) as may, by Cession of particular States, and the Acceptance of Congress, become the Seat of the Government of the United States, and to exercise like Authority over all Places purchased by the Consent of the Legislature of the State in which the Same shall be, for the Erection of Forts, Magazines, Arsenals, dock Yards, and other needful Buildings;—And

To make all Laws which shall be necessary and proper for carrying into Execution the foregoing Powers, and all other Powers vested by this Constitution in the Government of the United States, or in any Department or Officer thereof.

Section 9

The Migration or Importation of such Persons as any of the States now existing shall think proper to admit, shall not be prohibited by the Congress prior to the Year one thousand eight hundred and eight, but a Tax or Duty may be imposed on such Importation, not exceeding ten dollars for each Person.

The Privilege of the Writ of Habeas Corpus shall not be suspended, unless when in Cases of Rebellion or Invasion the public Safety may require it.

No Bill of Attainder or ex post facto Law shall be passed.

No Capitation, or other direct, Tax shall be laid, unless in Proportion to the Census or Enumeration herein before directed to be taken.

No Tax or Duty shall be laid on Articles exported from any State.

No Preference shall be given by any Regulation of Commerce or Revenue to the Ports of one State over those of another; nor shall Vessels bound to, or from, one State, be obliged to enter, clear, or pay Duties in another.

No Money shall be drawn from the Treasury, but in Consequence of Appropriations made by Laws; and a regular Statement and Account of the Receipts and Expenditures of all public Money shall be published from time to time.

No Title of Nobility shall be granted by the United States: And no Person holding any Office of Profit or Trust under them, shall, without the Consent of the Congress, accept of any present, Emolument, Office, or Title, of any kind whatever, from any King, Prince, or foreign State.

Section 10

No State shall enter into any Treaty, Alliance, or Confederation; grant Letters of Marque and Reprisal; coin Money; emit Bills of Credit; make any Thing but gold and silver Coin a Tender in Payment of Debts; pass any Bill of Attainder, ex post facto Law, or Law impairing the Obligation of Contracts, or grant any Title of Nobility.

No State shall, without the Consent of the Congress, lay any Imposts or Duties on Imports or Exports, except what may be absolutely necessary for executing its inspection Laws: and the net Produce of all Duties and Imposts, laid by any State on Imports or Exports, shall be for the Use of the Treasury of the United States; and all such Laws shall be subject to the Revision and Controul of the Congress.

No State shall, without the Consent of Congress, lay any Duty of Tonnage, keep Troops, or Ships of War in time of Peace, enter into any Agreement or Compact with another State, or with a foreign Power, or engage in War, unless actually invaded, or in such imminent Danger as will not admit of delay.

ARTICLE II

Section 1

The executive Power shall be vested in a President of the United States of America. He shall hold his Office during the Term of four Years, and, together with the Vice President, chosen for the same Term, be elected, as follows:

Each State shall appoint, in such Manner as the Legislature thereof may direct, a Number of Electors, equal to the whole Number of Senators and Representatives to which the State may be entitled in the Congress: but no Senator or Representative, or Person holding an Office of Trust or Profit under the United States, shall be appointed an Elector.

The Electors shall meet in their respective States, and vote by Ballot for two Persons, of whom one at least shall not be an Inhabitant of the same State with themselves. And they shall make a list of all the Persons voted for, and of the Number of Votes for each; which List they shall sign and certify, and transmit sealed to the Seat of the Government of the United States, directed to the President of the Senate. The President of the Senate shall, in the presence of the Senate and House of Representatives, open all the Certificates, and the Votes shall be counted. The Person having the greatest Number of Votes shall be the President, if such Number be a Majority of the whole Number of Electors appointed; and if there be more than one who have such Majority, and have an equal Number of Votes, then the House of Representatives shall immediately chuse by Ballot one of them for President; and if no Person have a Majority, then from the five highest on the List the said House shall in like Manner chuse the President. But in chusing the President, the Votes shall be taken by States, the Representation from each State having one Vote; A quorum for this Purpose shall consist of a Member or Members from two thirds of the States, and a Majority of all the States shall be necessary to a Choice. In every Case, after the Choice of the President, the Person having the greatest Number of Votes of the Electors shall be the Vice President. But if there should remain two or more who have equal Votes, the Senate shall chuse from them by Ballot the Vice President.

The Congress may determine the Time of Chusing the Electors, and the Day on which they shall give their Votes; which Day shall be the same throughout the United States.

No Person except a natural born Citizen, or a Citizen of the United States, at the time of the Adoption of this Constitution, shall be eligible to the Office of President; neither shall any Person be eligible to that Office who shall not have attained to the Age of thirty five Years, and been fourteen Years a Resident within the United States.

In Case of the Removal of the President from Office, or of his Death, Resignation, or Inability to discharge the Powers and Duties of the said Office, the Same shall devolve on the Vice President, and the Congress may by Law provide for the Case of Removal, Death, Resignation or Inability, both of the President and Vice President, declaring what Officer shall then act as President, and such Officer shall act accordingly, until the Disability be removed, or a President shall be elected.

The President shall, at stated Times, receive for his Services, a Compensation, which shall neither be encreased nor diminished during the Period for which he shall have been elected, and he shall not receive within that Period any other Emolument from the United States, or any of them.

Before he enter on the Execution of his Office, he shall take the following Oath or Affirmation:—"I do solemnly swear (or affirm) that I will faithfully execute the Office of President of the United States, and will to the best of my Ability, preserve, protect and defend the Constitution of the United States."

Section 2

The President shall be Commander in Chief of the Army and Navy of the United States, and of the Militia of the several States, when called into the actual Service of the United States; he may require the Opinion, in writing, of the principal Officer in each of the executive Departments, upon any Subject relating to the Duties of their respective Offices, and he shall have Power to grant Reprieves and Pardons for Offences against the United States, except in Cases of Impeachment.

He shall have Power, by and with the Advice and Consent of the Senate, to make Treaties, providing two thirds of the Senators present concur; and he shall nominate, and by and with the Advice and Consent of the Senate, shall appoint Ambassadors, other public Ministers and Consuls, Judges of the supreme Court, and all other Officers of the United States, whose Appointments are not herein otherwise provided for, and which shall be established by Law: but the Congress may by Law vest the Appointment of such inferior Officers, as they think proper, in the President alone, in the Courts of Law, or in the Heads of Departments.

The President shall have Power to fill up all Vacancies that may happen during the Recess of the Senate, by granting Commissions which shall expire at the End of their next Session.

Section 3

He shall from time to time give to the Congress Information of the State of the Union, and recommend to their Consideration such Measures as he shall judge necessary and expedient; he may, on extraordinary Occasions, convene both Houses, or either of them, and in Case of Disagreement between them, with Respect to the Time of Adjournment, he may adjourn them to such Time as he shall think proper, he shall receive Ambassadors and other public Ministers; he shall take Care that the Laws be faithfully executed, and shall Commission all the Offices of the United States.

Section 4

The President, Vice President and all civil Officers of the United States, shall be removed from Office on Impeachment for, and Conviction of, Treason, Bribery, or other high Crimes and Misdemeanors.

ARTICLE III

Section 1

The judicial Power of the United States, shall be vested in one supreme Court, and in such inferior Courts as the Congress may from time to time ordain and establish. The Judges, both of the supreme and inferior Courts, shall hold their Offices during good Behaviour, and shall, at Times, receive for their Services, a Compensation, which shall not be diminished during their Continuance in Office.

Section 2

The judicial Power shall extend to all Cases, in Law and Equity, arising under this Constitution, the Laws of the United States, and Treaties made, or which shall be made, under their Authority;—to all Cases affecting Ambassadors, other public Ministers and Consuls;—to all Cases of admiralty and maritime Jurisdiction;—to Controversies to which the United States shall be a Party;—to controversies between two or more States;—between a State and Citizens of another State;—between Citizens of different States,—between Citizens of the same State claiming Lands under Grants of different States; and between a State, or the Citizens thereof, and foreign States, Citizens or Subjects.

In all Cases affecting Ambassadors, other public Ministers and Consuls, and those in which a State shall be Party, the Supreme Court shall have original Jurisdiction. In all the other Cases before mentioned, the supreme Court shall have appellate Jurisdiction, both as to Law and Fact, with such Exceptions, and under such Regulations as the Congress shall make.

The Trial of all Crimes, except in Cases of Impeachment, shall be by Jury; and such Trial shall be held in the State where the said Crimes shall have been committed; but when not committed within any State, the Trial shall be at such Place or Places as the Congress may by Law have directed.

Section 3

Treason against the United States, shall consist only in levying War against them, or in adhering to their Enemies, giving them Aid and Comfort. No Person shall be convicted of Treason unless on the Testimony of two Witnesses to the same overt Act, or on Confession in open Court.

The Congress shall have Power to declare the Punishment of Treason, but no Attainder of Treason shall work Corruption of Blood, or Forfeiture except during the Life of the Person attained.

ARTICLE IV

Section 1

Full Faith and Credit shall be given in each State to the public Acts, Records, and judicial Proceedings of every other State. And the Congress may by general Laws prescribe the Manner in which such Acts, Records, and Proceedings shall be proved, and the Effect thereof.

Section 2

The Citizens of each State shall be entitled to all Privileges and Immunities of Citizens in the several States.

A Person charged in any State with Treason, Felony, or other Crime, who shall flee from Justice, and be found in another State, shall on Demand of the executive Authority of the State from which he fled, be delivered up, to be removed to the State having Jurisdiction of the Crime.

No Person held to Service or Labour in one State, under the Laws thereof, escaping into another, shall, in Consequence of any Law or Regulation therein, be discharged from such Service or Labour, but shall be delivered up on Claim of the Party to whom such Service or Labour may be due.

Section 3

New States may be admitted by the Congress into this Union; but no new State shall be formed or erected within the Jurisdiction of any other State; nor any State be formed by the Junction of two or more States, or Parts of States, without the Consent of the Legislatures of the States concerned as well as the Congress.

The Congress shall have Power to dispose of and make all needful Rules and Regulations respecting the Territory or other Property belonging to the United States; and nothing in this Constitution shall be so construed as to Prejudice any Claims of the United States, or of any particular State.

Section 4

The United States shall guarantee to every State in this Union a Republican Form of Government, and shall protect each of them against Invasion; and on Application of the Legislature, or of the Executive (when the Legislature cannot be convened) against domestic Violence.

ARTICLE V

The Congress, whenever two thirds of both Houses shall deem it necessary, shall propose Amendments to this Constitution, or, on the Application of the Legislatures of two thirds of the several States, shall call a Convention for proposing Amendments, which, in either Case, shall be valid to all Intents and Purposes, as Part of this Constitution, when ratified by the Legislatures of three fourths of the several States, or by Conventions in three fourths thereof, as the one or the other Mode of Ratification may be proposed by the Congress; Provided that no Amendment which may be made prior to the Year One thousand eight hundred and eight shall in any Manner affect the first and fourth Clauses in the Ninth Section of the first Article; and that no State, without its Consent, shall be deprived of its equal Suffrage in the Senate.

ARTICLE VI

All Debts contracted and Engagements entered into, before the Adoption of this Constitution, shall be as valid against the United States under this Constitution, as under the Confederation.

This Constitution, and the Laws of the United States which shall be made in Pursuance thereof; and all Treaties made, or which shall be made, under the Authority of the United States, shall be the supreme Law of the Land; and the Judges in every State shall be bound thereby, any Thing in the Constitution or Laws of any State to the Contrary notwithstanding.

The Senators and Representatives before mentioned, and the Members of the several State Legislatures, and all executive and judicial Officers, both of the United States and of the Several States, shall be bound by Oath or Affirmation, to support this Constitution; but no religious Test shall ever be required as a Qualification to any Office or public Trust under the United States.

ARTICLE VII

The Ratification of the Conventions of nine States, shall be sufficient for the Establishment of this Constitution between the States so ratifying the Same.

AMENDMENT I [1791]

Congress shall make no law respecting an establishment of religion, or prohibiting the free exercise thereof; or abridging the freedom of speech, or the press; or the right of the people peaceably to assemble, and to petition the Government for a redress of grievances.

AMENDMENT II [1791]

A well regulated Militia, being necessary to the security for a free State, the right of the people to keep and bear Arms, shall not be infringed.

AMENDMENT III [1791]

No Soldier shall, in time of peace be quartered in any house, without the consent of the Owner, nor in time of war, but in a manner to be prescribed by law.

AMENDMENT IV [1791]

The right of the people to be secure in their persons, houses, papers, and effects, against unreasonable searches and seizures, shall not be violated, and no Warrants shall issue, but upon probable cause, supported by Oath or Affirmation, and particularly describing the place to be searched, and the persons or things to be seized.

AMENDMENT V [1791]

No person shall be held to answer for a capital, or otherwise infamous crime, unless on a presentment or indictment of a Grand Jury, except in cases arising in the land or naval forces, or in the Militia, when in actual service in time of War or public danger; nor shall any person be subject for the same offense to be twice put in jeopardy of life or limb; nor shall be compelled in any criminal case to be a witness against himself, nor be deprived of life, liberty, or property, without due process of law; nor shall private property be taken for public use, without just compensation.

AMENDMENT VI [1791]

In all criminal prosecutions, the accused shall enjoy the right to a speedy and public trial, by an impartial jury of the State and district wherein the crime shall have been committed, which district shall have been previously ascertained by law, and to be informed of the nature and cause of the accusation; to be confronted with the Witnesses against him; to have compulsory process for obtaining witnesses in his favor, and to have the Assistance of counsel for his defence.

AMENDMENT VII [1791]

In suits at common law, where the value in controversy shall exceed twenty dollars, the right of trial by jury shall be preserved, and no fact tried by a jury, shall be otherwise re-examined in any Court of the United States, than according to the rules of the common law.

AMENDMENT VIII [1791]

Excessive bail shall not be required, no excessive fines imposed, nor cruel and unusual punishments inflicted.

AMENDMENT IX [1791]

The enumeration in the Constitution, of certain rights, shall not be construed to deny or disparage others retained by the people.

AMENDMENT X [1791]

The powers not delegated to the United States by the Constitution, nor prohibited by it to the States, are reserved to the States respectively, or to the people.

AMENDMENT XI [1798]

The judicial power of the United States shall not be construed to extend to any suit in law or equity, commenced or prosecuted against one of the United States by Citizens of another State, or by Citizens or Subjects of any Foreign State.

AMENDMENT XII [1804]

The Electors shall meet in their respective states and vote by ballot for President and Vice-President, one of whom, at least, shall not be an inhabitant of the same state with themselves; they shall name in their ballots the person voted for as President, and in distinct ballots the person voted for as Vice-President, and they shall make distinct lists of all persons voted for as President, and of all persons voted for as Vice-President, and of the number of votes for each, which lists they shall sign and certify, and transmit sealed to the seat of the government of the United States, directed to the President of the Senate;—The President of the Senate shall, in the presence of the Senate and House of Representatives, open all the certificates and the votes shall then be counted;—The person having the greatest number of votes for President, shall be the President, if such number be a majority of the whole number of Electors appointed; and if no person have such majority, then from the persons having the highest numbers not exceeding three on the list of those voted for as President, the House of Representatives shall choose immediately, by ballot, the President. But in choosing the President, the votes shall be taken by states, the representation from each state having one vote; a quorum for this purpose shall consist of a member or members from two-thirds of the states, and a majority of all the states shall be necessary to a choice. And if the House of Representatives shall not choose a President whenever the right of choice shall devolve upon them, before the fourth day of March next following, then the Vice-President shall act as President, as in the case of the death or other constitutional disability of the President. The person having the greatest number of votes as Vice-President, shall be the Vice-President, if such number be a majority of the whole number of Electors appointed, and if no person have a majority, then from the two highest numbers on the list, the Senate shall choose the Vice-President; a quorum for the purpose shall consist of two-thirds of the whole number of Senators, and a majority of the whole number shall be necessary to a choice. But no person constitutionally ineligible to the office of President shall be eligible to that of the Vice-President of the United States.

AMENDMENT XIII [1865]

Section 1

Neither slavery nor involuntary servitude, except as a punishment for crime whereof the party shall have been duly convicted, shall exist within the United States, or any place subject to their jurisdiction.

Section 2

Congress shall have power to enforce this article by appropriate legislation.

AMENDMENT XIV [1868]

Section 1

All persons born or naturalized in the United States, and subject to the jurisdiction thereof, are citizens of the United States and of the State wherein they reside. No State shall make or enforce any law which shall abridge the privileges or immunities of citizens of the United States; nor shall any State deprive any person of life, liberty, or property, without due process of law; nor deny to any person within its jurisdiction the equal protection of the laws.

Section 2

Representatives shall be appointed among the several States according to their respective numbers, counting the whole number of persons in each State, excluding Indians not taxed. But when the right to vote at any election for the choice of electors for President and Vice President of the United States, Representatives in Congress, the Executive and Judicial officers of a State, or the members of the Legislature thereof, is denied to any of the male inhabitants of such State, being twenty-one years of age, and citizens of the United States, or in any way abridged, except for participation in rebellion, or other crime, the basis of representation therein shall be reduced in the proportion which the number of such male citizens shall bear the whole number of male citizens twenty-one years of age in such State.

Section 3

No person shall be a Senator or Representative in Congress, or elector of President and Vice President, or hold any office, civil or military, under the United States, or under any State, who, having previously taken an oath, as a member of Congress, or as an officer of the United States, or as a member of any State legislature, or as an executive or judicial officer of any State, to support the Constitution of the United States, shall have engaged in insurrection or rebellion against the same, or given aid or comfort to the enemies thereof. But Congress may by a vote of two-thirds of each House, remove such disability.

Section 4

The validity of the public debt of the United States, authorized by law, including debts incurred for payment of pensions and bounties for services in suppressing insurrection or rebellion, shall not be questioned. But neither the United States nor any State shall assume or pay any debt or obligation incurred in aid of insurrection of rebellion against the United States or any claim for the loss or emancipation of any slave; but all such debts, obligations and claims shall be held illegal and void.

Section 5

The Congress shall have power to enforce, by appropriate legislation, the provisions of this article.

AMENDMENT XV [1870]

Section 1

The right of citizens of the United States to vote shall not be denied or abridged by the United States or by any

State on account of race, color, or previous condition of servitude.

Section 2
The Congress shall have power to enforce this article by appropriate legislation.

AMENDMENT XVI [1913]
The Congress shall have power to lay and collect taxes on incomes, from whatever source derived, without apportionment among the several States, and without regard to any census or enumeration.

AMENDMENT XVII [1913]
The Senate of the United States shall be composed of two Senators from each State, elected by the people thereof, for six years; and each Senator shall have one vote. The electors in each State shall have the qualifications requisite for electors of the most numerous branch of the State legislatures.

When vacancies happen in the representation of any State in the Senate, the executive authority of each State shall issue writs of election to fill such vacancies; *Provided*, That the legislature of any State may empower the executive thereof to make temporary appointments until the people fill the vacancies by election as the legislature may direct.

This amendment shall not be construed as to affect the election or term of any Senator chosen before it becomes valid as part of the Constitution.

AMENDMENT XVIII [1919]

Section 1
After one year from the ratification of this article the manufacture, sale, or transportation of intoxicating liquors within, the importation thereof into, or the exportation thereof from the United States and all territory subject to the jurisdiction thereof for beverage purposes is hereby prohibited.

Section 2
The Congress and the several States shall have concurrent power to enforce this article by appropriate legislation.

Section 3
This article shall be inoperative unless it shall have been ratified as an amendment to the Constitution by the legislatures of the several States, as provided in the Constitution, within seven years from the date of the submission hereof to the States by the Congress.

AMENDMENT XIX [1920]
The right of citizens of the United States to vote shall not be denied or abridged by the United States or by any State on account of sex.

Congress shall have power to enforce this article by appropriate legislation.

AMENDMENT XX [1933]

Section 1
The terms of the President and Vice President shall end at noon on the 20th day of January, and the terms of Senators and Representatives at noon on the 3d day of January, of the years in which such terms would have ended if this article had not been ratified; and the terms of their successors shall then begin.

Section 2
The Congress shall assemble at least once in every year, and such meeting shall begin at noon on the 3d day of January, unless they shall by law appoint a different day.

Section 3
If, at the time fixed for the beginning of the term of the President, the President elect shall have died, the Vice President elect shall become President. If a President shall not have been chosen before the time fixed for the beginning of his term, or if the President elect shall have failed to qualify, then the Vice President elect shall act as President until a President shall have qualified; and the Congress may by law provide for the case wherein neither a President elect nor a Vice President elect shall have qualified, declaring who shall then act as President, or the manner in which one who is to act shall be selected, and such person shall act accordingly until a President or Vice President shall have qualified.

Section 4
The Congress may by law provide for the case of the death of any of the persons from whom the House of Representatives may choose a President whenever the right of choice shall have devolved upon them, and for the case of the death of any of the persons from whom the Senate may choose a Vice President whenever the right of choice shall have devolved upon them.

Section 5
Sections 1 and 2 shall take effect on the 15th day of October following the ratification of this article.

Section 6
This article shall be inoperative unless it shall have been ratified as an amendment to the Constitution by the legislatures of three-fourths of the several States within

legislatures of three-fourths of the several States within seven years from the date of its submission.

AMENDMENT XXI [1933]

Section 1
The eighteenth article of amendment to the Constitution of the United States is hereby repealed.

Section 2
The transportation or importation into any State, Territory, or possession of the United States for delivery or use therein of intoxicating liquors, in violation of the laws thereof, is hereby prohibited.

Section 3
This article shall be inoperative unless it shall have been ratified as an amendment to the Constitution by conventions in the several States, as provided in the Constitution, within seven years from the date of the submission hereof to the States by the Congress.

AMENDMENT XXII [1951]

Section 1
No person shall be elected to the office of the President more than twice, and no person who has held the office of President, or acted as President, for more than two years of a term to which some other person was elected President shall be elected to the office of the President more than once. But this Article shall not apply to any person holding the office of President when this Article was proposed by the Congress, and shall not prevent any person who may be holding the office of President, or acting as President, during the term within which this Article becomes operative from holding the office of President, or acting as President during the remainder of such term.

Section 2
This article shall be inoperative unless it shall have been ratified as an amendment to the Constitution by the legislatures of three-fourths of the several States within seven years from the date of its submission to the States by the Congress.

AMENDMENT XXIII [1961]

Section 1
The District constituting the seat of Government of the United States shall appoint in such manner as the Congress may direct:

A number of electors of President and Vice President equal to the whole number of Senators and Representatives in Congress to which the District would be entitled if it were a State, but in no event more than the least populous State; they shall be in addition to those appointed by the States, but they shall be considered, for the purposes of the election of President and Vice President, to be electors appointed by a State; and they shall meet in the District and perform such duties as provided by the twelfth article of amendment.

Section 2
The Congress shall have power to enforce this article by appropriate legislation.

AMENDMENT XXIV [1964]

Section 1
The right of citizens of the United States to vote in any primary or other election for President or Vice President, for electors for President or Vice President, or for Senator or Representative in Congress, shall not be denied or abridged by the United States or any State by reason of failure to pay any poll tax or other tax.

Section 2
The Congress shall have power to enforce this article by appropriate legislation.

AMENDMENT XXV [1967]

Section 1
In case of the removal of the President from office or of his death or resignation, the Vice President shall become President.

Section 2
Whenever there is a vacancy in the office of the Vice President, the President shall nominate a Vice President who shall take office upon confirmation by a majority vote of both Houses of Congress.

Section 3
Whenever the President transmits to the President pro tempore of the Senate and the Speaker of the House of Representatives his written declaration that he is unable to discharge the powers and duties of his office, and until he transmits to them a written declaration to the contrary, such powers and duties shall be discharged by the Vice President as Acting President.

Section 4
Whenever the Vice President and a majority of either the principal officers of the executive departments or of such other body as Congress may by law provide, transmit to

the President pro tempore of the Senate and the Speaker of the House of Representatives their written declaration that the President is unable to discharge the powers and duties of his office, the Vice President shall immediately assume the powers and duties of the office as Acting President.

Thereafter, when the President transmits to the President pro tempore of the Senate and the Speaker of the House of Representatives his written declaration that no inability exists, he shall resume the powers and duties of his office unless the Vice President and a majority of either the principal officers of the executive department or of such other body as Congress may by law provide, transmit within four days to the President pro tempore of the Senate and the Speaker of the House of Representatives their written declaration that the President is unable to discharge the powers and duties of his office. Thereupon Congress shall decide the issue, assembling within forty-eight hours for that purpose if not in session. If the Congress, within twenty-one days after receipt of the latter written declaration, or, if Congress is not in session, within twenty-one days after Congress is required to assemble, determines by two-thirds vote of both Houses that the President shall continue to discharge the same as Acting President; otherwise, the President shall resume the powers and duties of his office.

AMENDMENT XXVI [1971]

Section 1
The right of citizens of the United States, who are eighteen years of age or older, to vote shall not be denied or abridged by the United States or by any State on account of age.

Section 2
The Congress shall have power to enforce this article by appropriate legislation.

Glossary

A

Act of State Doctrine The doctrine that states that a court in one country will not sit in judgment on the acts of another government done within its own territory.

Actual Authority Authority for an agent to act that is granted either expressly or by implication by the principal.

Administrative Rule Making Administrative agency function to promulgate rules and regulations having the same force and effect as laws passed by a legislature.

Adversary System Theory that all of the facts will be uncovered and the truth will come out if each side in a dispute presents its case in the best possible light.

Advisory Opinion Advice given by the courts to other branches of government concerning the law or the constitutionality of a proposed law.

Affirmative Action Plans Plans designed to ensure that all people have an opportunity to work at a given company.

Agency Adjudication The function of an administrative agency to hear complaints, similar to a judicial function.

Agency Shop A contract with a union that does not require employees to join the union but does require them to pay union dues and initiation fees.

Agent A person who has the power to act on behalf of a principal.

Ally Doctrine The doctrine that permits unions to picket secondary employers doing the work of a primary employer.

Amicus Curiae Brief A brief filed in a case by someone who is not a party to that case. Amicus curiae means "a friend of the court."

Answer The response filed in court by the defendant to the plaintiff's petition. It states the defendant's response to each of the plaintiff's allegations.

Apparent Authority A doctrine covering agents and contracts with third parties by which authority exists in the absence of actual authority.

Appellant Party in a case who petitions a court of appeals to review the decision of a lower court.

Appellate Court A court that reviews the rulings of a trial court when the losing party in a trial case is dissatisfied with the verdict.

Appellee The party in a case against whom an appeal is filed.

Assignee The person to whom an assignment of right is made.

Assignment The process of transferring rights from one person to another.

Assignor A person who makes an assignment of a right.

Attorney–Client Privilege A privilege by which a client's confidential discussions with an attorney remain confidential.

B

Bankruptcy Estate All of the debtor's legal and equitable interests in property owned as of the date of the filing of the bankruptcy petition, except for exempt property, and interests in certain property that the debtor becomes entitled to within 180 days after the filing of the bankruptcy petition.

Bench Trial A trial that is heard only by a judge and not by a jury.

Bill of Rights The first ten amendments to the U.S. Constitution.

Blind Trust A legal and business relationship in which one person holds in trust and invests the property of another. The person whose property is being held is precluded from knowing the assets in the trust or the investments made on his behalf.

Blue Sky Laws State laws attempting to regulate the securities industry.

Bona Fide Occupational Qualification (BFOQ) A job qualification that arises when religion, sex, or national origin is a requirement that is reasonably necessary to operate the business.

Boycott A concerted effort by someone or some group to encourage people to stop doing business with someone.

Brandeis Brief A brief making use of social science studies to supplement more traditional legal arguments. First used by Louis D. Brandeis.

Brief Written argument to the court concerning points the parties want the court to consider.

Burden of Proof The duty of a party to substantiate an allegation or issue to avoid dismissal of that issue early in the trial or in order to convince the trier of facts as to the truth of the claim and therefore win at trial.

C

Cause of Action A legal claim or complaint for which a party may seek redress in a court.

Caveat Emptor Literally, let the buyer beware. A doctrine in which the buyer of a product assumed any risk associated with the purchase or use of the product.

Certiorari A procedure of appellate practice whereby a higher court is given the opportunity to review a decision by a lower court.

Challenge for Cause The right of an attorney to ask that a person be disqualified from serving on a jury because of the person's bias or prejudice.

Choice of Forum Clause A contractual provision that specifies where a dispute arising under a contract will be tried.

Choice of Law Clause A contractual provision that specifies the law of the country or state that will be applied in the event of a contract dispute.

Civil Case Case in which the plaintiff institutes suit against the defendant for some civil wrong.

Civil Litigation All of the trial work of our judicial system that does not involve the violation of a criminal statute.

Civil War Amendments The Thirteenth, Fourteenth, and Fifteenth Amendments to the U.S. Constitution.

Class Action A lawsuit or legal action brought on behalf of a large number of people with similar claims.

Close Corporation A type of corporate organization in which there are few shareholders. Corporate shares are not sold on an organized market. Often, close corporate shareholders are related to one another. Frequently, close corporations are small businesses.

Closed-End Circuit A credit plan in which a person borrows a fixed amount that is to be repaid over a designated period of time.

Closed Shop An agreement, now illegal, by an employer to hire only members of a union.

Closing Argument The point during a trial, after the conclusion of the presentation of evidence, with the attorneys present their final arguments to the judge or jury concerning a case.

Codification A process whereby case law is transformed into a statute. Its goal is to clear up confusion that may exist with conflicting case precedents, thus enhancing predictability in the law.

Colgate **Doctrine** A doctrine by which a manufacturer may unilaterally announce that it will not deal with customers who fail to abide by the price it sets for a product.

Commerce Clause A provision in the U.S. Constitution created to protect interstate commerce from discriminatory state action.

Commercial Speech Doctrine The doctrine that states commercial speech is protected by the U.S. Constitution.

Common Law The body of law formulated and created by judicial decision.

Common Law Copyright The property right in a written item as recognized by common law.

Common Situs A location where employees from several employers work at the same place.

Comparable Worth The concept that employers should pay workers the same wage rate if their jobs are of comparable worth, or equal value, to the employer.

Comparative Negligence A doctrine in the law of torts. The relative negligence of the plaintiff and defendant are considered, and the damages ultimately awarded are reduced by the proportion of the plaintiff's negligence.

Compensatory Damages Those damages necessary to place the aggrieved party in the same position he or she would have occupied had the contract not been breached in the first place.

Concurring Opinion An opinion, written by an appellate court justice, that agrees with the appellate court's decision but disagrees with the reasoning of the court.

Conglomerate Merger A business combination or merger in which there are no economic relationships between the acquiring and the acquired firm.

Consent Decree An agreement between parties that they will be bound by a certain stipulated set of facts.

Consequential Damages Special damages that could have been foreseen at the time of the breach of contract but which do not directly flow from the breach of contract.

Consumer A person who buys or borrows for personal, family, or household use.

Contract An agreement, obligation, or legal tie whereby a party binds himself or herself, expressly or impliedly, to pay a sum of money or to perform or omit to do a certain act or thing.

Contract of Adhesion A contract heavily weighted to favor the party that possesses significantly more bargaining power.

Conversion A doctrine in the law of torts. Conversion arises when someone wrongfully uses (or takes) another's property.

Copyright Legal protection provided by statute for original works of authorship or composition. It includes books, music, and computer software.

Corporation A business organizational form that is considered to be a legal being. It may have perpetual life, and it insulates its owners (shareholders) from personal liability.

Counterclaim A claim presented by a defendant against the plaintiff. Answers often contain counterclaims against the plaintiff.

Counter-offer An offer made by the offeree to the offeror that would materially alter the original offer and thus require acceptance by the offeror.

Countervailing Duties Special duties used to offset a foreign subsidy.

Creditor Beneficiary A person who is not a party to a contract. If the contract is performed, one of the parties to the contract will be discharged from a duty or debt he or she owes to this person.

Criminal Case Case in which a prosecutor representing the state or federal government brings suit against the defendant for an alleged violation of law.

Criminal Law Branch or division of law that defines crimes, treats their nature, and provides for their punishment.

Cross Examination The point when an attorney for the opposing party asks questions of a witness who is testifying.

Custom A nation's present habits and an important aspect of its system of laws.

D

Debt A financial obligation owed by one person or business to another.

Debt Collector A person or business that tries to collect from people or businesses who fail to pay a debt.

Defendant The party in a case against whom criminal charges have been filed (in criminal law) or against whom a legal claim has been filed (in a civil suit).

Deposition The process of questioning under oath, prior to trial, the witnesses and parties to a lawsuit.

Dicta Portions of a judge's opinion that are not the ruling in the case.

Dilatory Tactics The practice of delaying a case simply for the purpose of delay.

Direct Examination The point when an attorney calls a witness to testify and asks the witness questions.

Discovery A process before a trial begins through which opposing counsel may learn the case to be presented by the other side.

Disparate Impact A theory of employment discrimination law in which an otherwise neutral job requirement has the effect of unlawfully discriminating against a protected group.

Disparate Treatment A theory of employment discrimination law in which a prohibited means of distinguishing between individuals is used (e.g., race, sex).

Dissenting Opinion An opinion, written by an appellate court justice, that disagrees with the outcome of the case being decided.

Diversity of Citizenship A situation when all of the plaintiffs are from states other than the state of residence of any of the defendants.

Documentary Credit An instrument in which a bank agrees to pay another party if certain conditions in the instrument have been complied with by the presenting party.

Domestic Content Law A law that requires a certain percentage of a good's value be produced in the nation that passed the law.

Donee Beneficiary A person who is not a party to a contract that was made for that person's benefit.

Double Jeopardy Clause The provision in the U.S. Constitution that prohibits the government from bringing a criminal action against a person twice for the same offense.

Due Diligence Defense A doctrine arising under the 1933 Act in which those liable (other than the issuer) for material omissions or misstatements in the registration statement may be exonerated.

Due Process Clause A constitutional principle which requires that government actions not be arbitrary or capricious. Its concern is with establishing fundamental procedural fairness in our system of government.

Dumping Selling products or services in a foreign market at less than their fair value.

E

Economic Strike A strike solely to force an employer to grant the employees better wages or working conditions.

Ejusdem Generis Doctrine A method of interpretation in which a general phase is inserted after a series of specific words in a statute. The general phrase shall be interpreted to include words of the same kind as those used in the preceding series.

Eminent Domain The right of the government to take property from a private owner for public use. Just compensation must be paid to those private owners.

Enabling Act A congressional statute that calls into existence a federal administrative agency.

Environment Impact Statement An analysis of the effect of major federal activity on the environment as required by the National Environmental Policy Act.

Equal Employment Opportunity Commission (EEOC) Federal administrative agency charged with the enforcement of Title VII of the Civil Rights Act of 1964.

Equal Protection Clause The clause in the U.S. Constitution that requires equal treatment of people.

Equity A separate body of law developed independently from the common law, based on rules of fairness and justice.

Escape Clause A provision in GATT that permits countries to raise tariffs if there is a serious threat to domestic industry as a consequence of earlier trade reductions.

Executive Order An order issued by the President of the United States or the governor of a state.

Executive Privilege Doctrine under which the President is able to keep certain communications from being disclosed in court.

Ex Parte An application by one party to a case made to a judge without first giving notice of the application to the other party.

Expert Fact Finding An alternative dispute resolution proceeding in which a neutral third party makes a decision based on a set of facts.

Express Warranty A statement of fact, description or sample or model that is part of the basis of the bargain between the parties.

Expropriation The seizure of foreign-owned property by a government.

F

Featherbedding A union requirement, now illegal, that an employer pay for work not performed.

Federal Mediation and Conciliation Service An agency created by the Taft-Hartley Act to assist parties to labor disputes in industries affecting commerce to settle such disputes through conciliation and mediation.

Federal Register The official public notice organ of the federal administrative agencies.

Felony Generic term to distinguish certain crimes such as murder, robbery, and larceny from minor offenses known as misdemeanors. The distinction lies in the extent of punishment provided.

Fiduciary Duty The duty of a person who is vested with power over another's property to act with good faith, diligence, and loyalty with regard to that property.

Fixture Personal property that is so attached to or used with real property that it is considered to be a part of real property.

Formal Settlement An agreement to resolve a case entered into after a complaint is filed against a party.

Fraud A deliberate misrepresentation or nondisclosure of a material fact made with the intent that the other party will rely on it, and in fact the party to whom the statement is made does rely on it to his or her detriment.

Full Warranty The Magnuson-Moss Act requires certain consumer products to be labeled has having either a full or limited warranty. Products with a full warranty must meet certain requirements specified in the act.

G

GATT General Agreement on Tariffs and Trade. A trade agreement between many of the world's countries.

General Verdict A decision for one of the parties to a case without any special findings of fact.

Grand Jury A proceeding to determine whether there exists probable cause to initiate a criminal proceeding.

H

Habeus Corpus (Writ of) A common law writ that brings a prisoner before a court. Prisoners use such writs to obtain a court review as to whether or not a person was imprisoned in accordance with the requirements of the law.

Hearsay Evidence of a statement that is made other than by a witness while testifying at trial that is offered to prove the truth of the matter stated.

History A nation's past and an important aspect of its system of law.

Holder in Due Course A person who is in possession of a negotiable instrument who has taken it in good faith, for value, and without notice of any claim or defense that exists against the instrument.

Horizontal Merger The acquisition of one company by another company producing the same product or similar product and selling it in the same geographic market.

Hostile Workplace Sexual Harassment Circumstances that make a job intolerable because of a sex-charged atmosphere that has been created at work.

Hot Cargo A clause, now illegal, stating that workers are not required to handle nonunion material.

Hung Jury When a jury is unable to arrive at a verdict.

I

Illusory Promise A promise in which the obligation to perform is entirely optional on the part of one of the parties.

Implied Agency Rule In contract law, if the offer does not state that the acceptance will not be effective until it is received, the moment an acceptance is sent by an authorized means a contract is effective.

Implied Warranty of Merchantability The guarantee that arises automatically by operation of law that goods sold by a seller will be fit for the purposes for which such goods are normally sold and will pass without objection in the trade.

Incidental Beneficiary A person who is not a party to a contract who obtains a benefit that was not intended by the parties to the contract.

Indictment A finding by a grand jury that reasonable grounds exist to believe that a crime has been committed. It is not a final determination or conviction.

Informal Settlement An agreement to resolve a case entered into before a complaint has been filed against a party.

Informational Picketing Picketing designed to advise the public that an employer does not have a union contract with its employers.

Injunction An order by a court that prohibits or restrains a party from doing a particular act.

Innocent Misrepresentation Unintended misrepresentation of a product that causes injury to a person.

In Personam Jurisdiction The power of a court to make a decision that affects the legal rights of a specific person.

Insider Trading Trading in securities by someone who has information on those securities not available to the general investing public and who has a duty not to use the information for personal

benefit. Under the 1934 Act, certain people who buy or sell securities having secret material information are liable both civilly and criminally.

Intellectual Property Original ideas that are considered intangible personal property, such as patents, copyrights, trademarks, and trade secrets.

Intended Beneficiary The person who the parties to a contract wanted to benefit through the performance of the contract.

Intentional Tort A tort in which the aim of a certain act is to cause injury.

Interrogatories Written questions submitted to a person concerning a case that must be answered under oath.

Investigative Consumer Report A report gathered by a company about a person's credit history. The Fair Credit Reporting Act calls this an investigative consumer report.

Investment Contracts Type of security that includes a large number of unusual schemes.

J

Judgment on the Pleadings A motion at the close of the pleading state made by any party to a suit that alleges the other party is not entitled to prevail at trial.

Judicial Immunity The inability of a dissatisfied litigant to sue the judge.

Judicial Review The power of a court to review a statute and declare it void if it violates various constitutional guarantees.

Jurisdiction The power or authority of a court to hear a particular legal dispute.

Jurisdictional Dispute A dispute between unions as to which union is entitled to perform certain work.

Justiciable A dispute that may properly be decided by a court.

L

Legal Lawful.

Legal Benefit Receiving something that one had no prior legal obligation to receive.

Legal Detriment The requirement that a party does or promises to do something which there was no prior legal duty to do or refraining from doing something that there was no prior legal duty to refrain from doing.

Legislative History A body of documentation created at the time a statute was drafted. A judge will consult the documents, consisting of reports, studies, speeches, etc., to determine the legislature's purpose in enacting the statute.

Limited Liability The characteristic of a corporation by which no individual member of the corporation is liable for claims made against it.

Limited Liability Company A new form of business organization that is rapidly being embraced by the states. It provides limited liability for its owners who may manage the business and who have a right to share in its profits.

Limited Partnership Business organization with characteristics of both a corporation and a partnership; often used for a tax shelter.

Limited Warranty The Magnuson-Moss Act requires certain consumer products to be labeled as having either a full or limited warranty. Limited warranties are those that do not comply with the act's requirement for a full warranty.

Liquidated Damages (Clause) A clause in a contract that specifies the amount of damages a party must pay if it breaches the contract.

Lobbying Activity to influence a bill that is being considered by a legislature.

Lockout   An employer's refusal to allow employees to work.

Long-Arm Statutes   Statutes that permit a plaintiff to obtain service of a summons and petition beyond the physical borders of a state.

M

Mandatory Subjects of Bargaining   Those topics which an employer must discuss with the designated bargaining representative of the employees.

Material Breach   A substantial failure of one of the parties to a contract to perform his or her obligations pursuant to the contract.

Mediation   A proceeding used to try to resolve disputes. The mediator tries to help the parties to a dispute work out their differences.

Minimum Wage   The minimum pay that an employer who is subject to the Fair Labor Standards Act must pay an employee.

Minitrial   An informal procedure used by parties in which a simplified version of the case is presented to a neutral party for a decision. The decision in the minitrial is not binding on the parties.

Mirror Offer Rule   The common law rule of contracts that requires an acceptance to be in exactly the same terms as the original offer.

Misdemeanor   Misconduct or offense inferior to a felony.

Missouri Plan   A method of appointing judges whereby a panel recommends suitable candidates for the judiciary and voters are periodically questioned in the voting booth whether to retain the judge or not.

Mitigation of Damages   The obligation of the injured party in a breach of contract to keep losses or damages as small as possible.

Monopoly   The power to fix prices or exclude competition, coupled with policies designed to use or preserve that power.

Motion   A request to the court for an order or rule in favor of the party making the motion.

Motion for a Directed Verdict   A motion by which the moving party states that the other side has failed to prove all of the facts necessary to establish a case.

Motion for a Judgment Notwithstanding the Verdict   Motion in which, at the conclusion of a trial, after the verdict is announced, the defeated party asks the judge to set the verdict aside because it was not supported by evidence or the law.

Motion for Summary Judgment   A motion which states that there is no genuine issue of material fact remaining to be decided in the case, therefore the judge should grant the motion and decide who should prevail in the case.

Motion to Dismiss   A motion made by the defendant which alleges that even if everything in the plaintiff's petition is assumed to be true, the plaintiff still is not entitled to a remedy, and therefore the plaintiff's petition should be dismissed.

N

Natural Law   An overriding sense of justice or fairness that is fundamental to the law.

Negligence   A lapse in an acceptable pattern of conduct that creates an unreasonable risk of injury.

NEPA   The National Environmental Policy Act of 1969, the purposes of which are to encourage harmony between humans and the environment and to eliminate environmental damage.

NLRB (The National Labor Relations Board)   A national public agency created by statute to enforce the provisions of the National Labor Relations Act—not a tribunal for the enforcement of private rights through administrative remedies. An agency of the United States, an entity apart from its members, having legal capacity to sue in the federal courts to carry out its statutory functions.

Nolo Contendere   An admission of every essential element of the offense stated in the charge. It is tantamount to an admission of guilt for the purpose of the case, but it is only a confession and does not dispute the case or constitute a conviction or determination of guilt.

Nominal Damages   A token sum awarded to a party in light of a breach of contract that did not produce any financial loss to the aggrieved party.

Nuisance   An act that annoys or disturbs the enjoyment of property by its owner.

O

Offer   A manifestation by a person of a desire to enter into a contract.

Offeree   The person to whom an offer is made.

Offeror   The person who makes an offer.

Oligopoly   An industry composed of several large firms, each possessing a major part of trade in a given market.

Open-End Credit   A credit plan that permits a person to keep charging on an account until he or she reaches a certain amount. The account may be paid off in full or in installments.

Opening Statement   The statement made by the attorney in a case prior to the actual presentation of evidence. It generally provides an overview of what evidence will be presented and what the attorneys have to prove.

Option Contract   A special contract which provides that a certain offer will remain open to a certain offeree upon the offeree providing some consideration.

Organization Picketing   Picketing designed to convince employees to sign up with the union.

P

Parens Patriae   Suit brought by the attorney general of a state on behalf of people living in that state.

Parent-Subsidiary Corporation   A business enterprise in which one corporation (the parent) owns controlling shares in other corporations (subsidiaries).

Parol Evidence Rule   A rule of evidence that prevents the introduction of oral testimony in a court proceeding which adds to, alters, or varies the terms of a written agreement.

Partnership   A type of business organization. It consists of two or more people co-owning a business that is a profit-seeking enterprise. These co-owners (called partners) are legally indistinguishable from their partnership business.

Per Curiam Opinion   A latin phrase meaning "by the court." When used in a judicial opinion, it means that the opinion is joined by all of the judges of that court.

Peremptory Challenge   The right of an attorney to strike certain prospective jurors from the jury panel. This is exercised by the attorneys after the conclusion of the voir dire.

Per Se   The rule that a court need not inquire into the reasonableness of a case before determining that it is a violation of the antitrust laws, if an anticompetitive business

activity is blatant in its intent and pernicious in its effect.

Petition   A document filed with a court by the plaintiff asking the court to grant the plaintiff some type of relief. The petition states paragraph by paragraph the nature of the claims the plaintiff has against the defendant and the relief requested of the court.

Petit Jury   A jury that hears evidence presented by witnesses at trial, and based on instructions given to them by the judge, renders a decision in a case.

Piercing the Corporate Veil   Doctrine in corporate law under which a court will ignore the limited liability protection of the corporate form and hold those members behind it personally liable.

Plain Meaning Doctrine   A method of statutory interpretation in which the court looks solely at the ordinary and usual meaning of the words of the statute to determine what the statute says.

Plaintiff   The party in a civil suit who commences the action.

Pleadings   The documents filed by the respective parties to a lawsuit that state their contentions. The first pleading is the petition, filed by the plaintiff, to which the defendant is required to file an answer.

Pollution   The human-caused diminished capacity of the environment to perform its function.

Precedent   A previously decided case that serves as authority for a court's decision in a current dispute.

Predictability in the Law   The principle that application of a law must be able to be envisioned at the time conduct is undertaken. In absence of predictability in the law, no activity would be legally safe to do.

Preemption   The doctrine that deprives a state of the power to

pass legislation dealing with the same matters as covered in federal legislation.

Preponderance of the Evidence   The standard of proof required in civil cases. A party has met this burden of proof when its evidence is more convincing to the trier of fact than the opposing evidence.

Prescription   Doctrine that confers a property right on a person who uses another's land without permission and without interruption for twenty years (usually).

Pretrial Conference   A conference held by a judge prior to trial concerning an upcoming trial. The purpose is to try to narrow the issues of the case and to attempt to encourage a settlement of the case.

Preventive Law   An attorney's advice to a client on a variety of legal matters in order to minimize the possibility of future legal problems for the client.

Primary Employer   The employer for whom employees engaged in collective activity work.

Primary Line Competitive Injury   Price discrimination by which a national firm attempts to put a local competitive firm out of business by lowering its prices only in the region where the local firms sell their products.

Primary Pressure   Direct pressure put on an employer by its own employees.

Principal   In agency law, the employer or person for whom an agent acts.

Private Judging   An alternative dispute resolution proceeding in which the parties select a person who acts just like a judge would in a case.

Private Panels   An alternative dispute resolution proceeding set up by the parties to a dispute to handle disagreements.

Privity of Contract   A direct relationship between the parties to a contract.

Probate   Process in law by which a will is proven and its terms given effect.

Promise   Voluntary commitment by a person to another person to perform in some manner or refrain from some action in the future.

Promisee   The person to whom a promise is made.

Promisor   The person who makes a promise.

Promissory Estoppel   The doctrine that makes certain contracts binding although they are not supported by consideration.

Property   A relationship between the holder of rights and all others recognized and enforced by government.

Prospectus   A summary of the information contained in a registration statement. It is provided to all offerees of the initial issuance of the securities.

Proximate Cause   A term of art in tort law that refers to a policy that limits to scope of a tortfeasor's liability. The act that is the dominant cause or is in a close relation to an injury is said to be the proximate cause of that injury.

Publicly Traded Corporation   A type of corporate organization in which the shares of stock are traded on an organized market such as the New York Stock Exchange.

Public Use   The only reason that entitles government to exercise its right of eminent domain.

Public Policy   Generally accepted standards of conduct in the community.

Punitive Damage   Damage that is awarded by a court in order to punish a party that has violated the law.

Q

Quota   A limit on the importation of a certain type of good imposed by a country.

R

Ratification   The acceptance by the principal of the benefits of a contract entered into by an agent in absence of an authority. The principal is thereafter bound by that contract.

Real Property   Land and fixtures that are things firmly attached to land (e.g., trees, office towers).

Reasonable Accommodation   A term that is used in both Title VII of the Civil Rights Act of 1964 and in the Americans with Disabilities Act. It provides that a business must consider reasonable changes in its operations or procedures to adjust to either the religious practices or disabilities of its employees (or applicants for jobs).

Reasonable Application of the Law   The principle that the law must be known or publicly available to consult. It is a concept contained in the Due Process Clause of the U.S. Constitution and is meant to prevent secret laws from being applied.

Reasonable Person   Used in tort law as a test for actionable conduct. A reasonable person acts with ordinary care and prudence.

Recognition Picketing   Picketing used to convince the employer to recognize the union.

Recusal   A situation in which a judge declines to hear a case because of fear that a personal bias may affect its outcome.

Registration Statement   Under the 1933 Act, a company issuing new nonexempt securities must file a full disclosure statement with the SEC. This statement is called a registration statement.

Res Ipsa Loquitur   A doctrine in the law of torts which presumes that the defendant was the negligent cause of an accident. Rather than requiring the plaintiff to prove that the defendant was negligent, the doctrine shifts the burden to the defendant to prove that he or she was not negligent.

Restatement of Contracts   An analysis of contract law based on existing judicial decisions.

Restatement (Second) of Torts   A scholarly work that discusses the law of torts as it exists across the United States. It also includes suggestions for changes the scholars think ought to be adopted by the states with respect to the law of torts.

Restraint of Trade   In antitrust law, business combinations or practices that seek to stifle competition and obstruct the market from its natural operation.

Restrictive Covenant   In a contract, an agreement by one of the parties to the contract not to engage in certain behavior in a designated area for a designated period of time at the conclusion of the contractual relationship.

Retail Price Maintenance   Scheme in which a single manufacturer and a retail seller or distributor agree to set the price at which a commodity may be sold.

RICO   The Racketeer Influenced Corrupt Organization Act.

Rights   Powers of free action that a person has and that are recognized by law.

Rule Making   A process by which administrative agencies promulgate regulations.

Rule of Reason   Court decision stating that only unreasonable restraints of trade and unreasonable attempts to monopolize violate the Sherman Act.

S

Search Warrant   Written order by a court that gives the police the right to search certain premises or property for items that may be used, if found, as evidence in a criminal trial.

Secondary Line Competitive Injury   A price discrimination that causes injury to certain buyers.

Secondary Pressure   A boycott of an employer other than the employer with whom the employees have a dispute.

Secondary Pressure Action   Action taken against a customer or supplier of an employer in order to pressure the employer to settle a labor dispute in favor of the employees.

Secured Loan   A contract in which one party advances money to another in return for a promise to have it repaid and for the receipt of a right in some property owned by the borrower. This property right gives the creditor the power to foreclose on that property if the borrower breaches the contract.

Securities   Stocks, bonds, and other investment contracts.

Securities and Exchange Commission (SEC)   Federal commission responsible for administering federal securities laws.

Separate but Equal   The constitutional doctrine put forth in *Plessy v. Ferguson* (1896) that the equal protection clause was not violated if segregated facilities were equivalent.

Separation of Powers   The principle by which each of the three branches of government—executive, legislative, and judicial—

has different functions so that no one of them becomes too powerful.

Settlement Conference   A conference held by a judge prior to a trial which may be used by the judge to encourage the parties to settle their case.

Sexual Harassment   Unwelcome sexual advances, requests for sexual favors, and other verbal or physical conduct of a sexual nature.

Small Claims Court   Special courts set up in every state in order to handle relatively minor civil claims.

Sole Proprietorship   A means by which a business may be owned. It is not a formal type of business organization. Its primary characteristic is that it has one owner, and this owner and the sole proprietorship business are legally indistinguishable.

Sovereign Immunity Doctrine   The doctrine under which governments are immune from suit when engaging in governmental acts.

Special Verdict   A verdict in a case where a jury makes specific findings concerning the facts presented at trial.

Specific Performance (Doctrine of)   An order compelling a party to perform his or her obligations under a contract.

Stare Decisis   A doctrine of judicial decision making that governs the application of precedent to a current dispute. The doctrine provides for stability in the legal system by having current disputes controlled by decisions in past cases.

Statute of Frauds   The statute which requires that certain types of contracts be in writing to be enforceable.

Statute of Limitations   A statute which specifies that a certain type

of case must be filed in a certain designated period of time after the cause of action arises.

Strict Liability   The standard of culpability to which a seller will be held for breach of an implied warranty that is imposed as a matter of public policy on a product he sells. Such liability is *strict liability* because it attaches even though the seller has exercised all possible care in the preparation and sale of his or her product.

Strict Liability in Tort   The products liability doctrine which holds the seller of a product responsible for physical injuries caused by that product if the product was in a defective condition unreasonably dangerous to users or consumers.

Substantial Performance   The performance of contractual obligations with only minor deviations from the specifications in the contract.

Summary Judgment   A decision by a court in a case without holding a trial. It occurs on motion of a party that since the facts of the case are not in dispute, the court should make a ruling based on the law.

Summary Trial   A trial in which a summary of the case is presented to a judge or jury. Decisions in such cases may not be binding on the parties depending on the agreement between the parties.

Summons   A document issued by a court which is served on the defendant, notifies him that suit has been instituted by the plaintiff, and requires the defendant to answer the plaintiff's petition in a certain designated period of time.

Surface Bargaining   A situation in which the employer goes through the outward motions of bargaining but is really not willing to negotiate.

T

Technological Infeasibility The inability of industry to comply with environmental regulations because existing technology is inadequate.

Third Party Beneficiary A person who is not a party to a contract but who will benefit from the performance of the contract.

Tort A body of law covering civil wrongs other than breaches of contract.

Treaty An agreement between two or more nations that is binding on the nations and must be performed in good faith.

Trespass The unauthorized, intentional entry upon the land of another.

Trial Court The first step in resolving disputes in the judicial system. Evidence is given, and a verdict is rendered.

True Bill A grand jury's endorsement of an indictment that it finds supported by the evidence presented to them.

Trust An obligation arising out of confidence reposed in a person, for the benefit of another, to apply property faithfully and according to such confidence.

Trustee in Bankruptcy A person who holds title to the bankrupt's property at the direction of a court. The trustee collects all of the property from the bankrupt, liquidates it, and distributes the money to the creditors of the bankrupt.

Truth in Lending Act Act passed by Congress in 1969 in order to make meaningful comparisons between the rates charged by different lenders.

U

Ultra Vires Limitation of agency power by which no act outside the power granted may be performed. Such acts would be voidable.

Unconscionability A lack of meaningful choice in a contractual relationship coupled with a contract term that is so one-sided as to be oppressive.

Unemployment Compensation Wage replacement to employees who have lost their jobs.

Unfair Labor Practice Strike A strike in response to an unfair labor practice committed by an employer.

Uniform Commercial Code A model code that deals with sale of goods, commercial paper, secured transactions, and other commercial activities.

Union Shop An agreement that employees must join a union within a certain period after they begin to work for an employer.

Unreasonably Dangerous More dangerous than would be contemplated by an ordinary consumer.

Unsecured Loan A contract in which one party promises to repay money advanced by another party.

V

Venue The place in which the suit is tried.

Vertical Merger A merger between or joining of two firms that have a buyer-seller relationship—that is, one produces a product that is then sold to the other.

Vicarious Liability A doctrine in the law of agency. It provides that the principal will be liable to those injured by an agent's tort if that tort occurred within the course and scope of the principal's business. The key is whether or not the agent's actions that led to the tort may be described as being primarily business-related.

Voir Dire The period in a trial when the attorneys question prospective jurors concerning their qualifications to sit as jurors in the case.

W

Workers' Compensation State system of insurance whereby employees injured on the job would receive damages from a fund made up of employers' premiums.

Work Preservation Clause An agreement designed to preserve work for certain employees.

Writ A written court order requiring the party to whom it is addressed to do whatever is required by the writ.

Wrongful Discharge A tort law theory that arises when an employee is fired for a reason that violates public policy.

Z

Zoning Local government ordinances regarding use of land.

Index